AN ANGLER'S DICTIONARY

Merry Christmas
to Grandpa
Love from
Ty + Cole
1985

fishing

AN ANGLER'S DICTIONARY

BY HENRY BEARD
& ROY McKIE

WORKMAN PUBLISHING
NEW YORK

Library of Congress Cataloging in Publication Data

Beard, Henry.
   Fishing: an angler's dictionary.
1. Fishing—Dictionaries—Anecdotes, facetiae, satire, etc.
I. McKie, Roy. II. Title.
SH411.B43 1983   799.1'0207   82-40498
ISBN 0-89480-357-3
ISBN 0-89480-355-7 (pbk.)

Produced by Edward T. Riley

Cover and book design: Paul Hanson

Workman Publishing Company
1 West 39 Street
New York, New York 10018

Manufactured in the United States of America

First printing May 1983

10   9   8   7

To all those who have heard the call of the fish.

Aquarium

A

Advice	Two or more pieces of contradictory angling information contained in a single phrase or sentence.
Angling	The art of fishing, as practiced by those who seek to catch fish not for profit or for food, but rather for the sport involved. The commonly accepted source of the term "angling" is an ancient Indo-European word, *anka*, meaning "hook" or "to fish with a hook," but several other words are also likely candidates, including *enka* ("unwise expenditure" or "useless task"); *unglo* ("one who is tormented by insects"); *onku* ("loud or frequent lamentation"); *angi* ("to deceive"); *inkla* ("to repeat a foolish act"); *onklo* ("possession by demons"); and *angla* ("love of pointless suffering").
Aquarium	Glass-walled enclosure for the display of fish. Although some fishermen do keep fish as pets, this hobby is not recommended for anyone even faintly interested in angling, as the urge to match wits with a finny quarry, however tame, is eventually bound to overcome other considerations. Aquariums with bulletproof glass and locked lids, such as the bulky but impenetrable "Fish Fort" or the armored "Patton Fish Tank" are available, but, frankly, fishermen will spare themselves much trouble if they simply select some other avocation equally well suited to their temperaments but less fraught with disturbing temptation, such as roller-skating, collecting string, or raising bees.
Artificial	Type of synthetic bait rejected by a finicky fish because it is too large or too small, or because it has the wrong shape, bears the wrong coloration, or makes the wrong motions in the water. *See* NATURAL.

Bait Casting

Atlantic	Ocean that separates a large segment of the English-speaking fishing population into two distinct subgroups: the gregarious, flashy American fisherman and the drab, solitary British angler. Both are characterized by elaborate tales, shifty eyes, and generally unreliable scales.

B

Backing Down	*1.* Maneuver in which the captain of a charter boat moves his craft in reverse toward a hooked fish to help the fisherman to take in line without stress and bring his prize aboard. *2.* Maneuver in which the fisherman retracts comments made to the captain following conversion of his fish into chowder by the boat's propellers.
Baffling	*1. n.* Compartmentalized interior construction of a down-filled sleeping bag. *2. adj.* Perplexing or puzzling, as in a baffling problem involving a sleeping bag, such as how to put a mass of bedding the size of a small pony into a receptacle designed to hold shaving articles.
Bait Casting	Angling method developed in the 19th century whose basic component is a revolving reel that must be carefully controlled by hand. Because of the danger of the line outrunning the reel and becoming tangled, bait-casting outfits are tricky to use. Nevertheless, many anglers find in that deficiency a desirable feature, since the sight of a reel festooned with loops of knotted fishing line renders their gear virtually theftproof, eliminates any interest fellow anglers might have had in borrowing it, and magically discourages requests for fishing information or assistance.

Bamboo	Eye-pleasing, but extremely expensive and difficult-to-maintain type of rod, used primarily by anglers who fish for compliments.
Bamboozle	To convince an angler to purchase a bamboo fishing rod.
Barnacle	The only marine species whose successful accumulation in large numbers on a deep-sea fishing boat can be accepted on the basis of an unverified oral report.
Barracuda	Jocular term for operator of a boat-charter company.
Bass	A large number of different fish are colloquially called bass, but the enormously popular largemouth and smallmouth bass are generally being referred to when the term is used. These two desirable fish are very similar looking, and given that fact, and the overuse of the word "bass," there is often some confusion in the mind of the novice as to exactly what it is he has caught. A simple process of elimination is the best way to proceed. Examine the specimen. If it lacks laces and a telltale leather "tongue," and if it is not a large, black, doughnut-shaped rubbery object with deep "treading" on its circumference, it is probably a fish. Does it have fins? Case closed. Now, since you have caught it, it is almost certainly not a trout, a salmon, or a muskellunge. All right, let's narrow down the field a bit more. Show your catch to a fellow fisherman. If he smirks, it is a perch or crappie. If he giggles, it is a carp or sunfish. If he laughs out loud, it's a pike. On the other hand, if he frowns, shakes his head slowly back and forth, and mutters under his breath, it is definitely a bass. The final question is, is it a smallmouth bass or a largemouth bass? Well, smallmouth bass are canny and moody and take considerable skill to catch, and since they don't grow quite as large as their cousins, a smallish

Barracuda

Bluefish

fish is a quite respectable prize. The heavier largemouth bass are gluttonous dopes that can be caught by a dunce. The only way most people can tell the two apart is by taking a close look at the head. Since you are going to have to remove the head before cooking this delicious fish, you might as well do so right away. Discard it. Congratulations on catching a smallmouth bass!

Bedrock

1. Type of stream bottom consisting of bare rock. *2.* Bothersome stony object found under sleeping bags.

Billfish

An informal term for any of the large salt-water game fishes, such as the sailfish and swordfish, whose upper jaws extend into sharp spears. They are called billfish because, following a day's outing in search of one of these magnificent creatures, the captain of a sport-fishing boat traditionally presents the angler who chartered her with an enormous bill in a short, but emotional dockside ceremony.

Blackfish

1. Common name for the tripletail and the tautog, two unrelated salt-water fishes caught in coastal areas of the eastern U.S. *2.* Common name for any fish caught in waters frequented by oil tankers.

Bluefish

Rapacious, carnivorous fish that, during feeding periods, will strike at almost anything, including other bluefish. Their insatiable appetites have made them an object of some disdain to those fishermen who prefer to test their skill against wilier and more elusive species. For these anglers, the challenge in bluefishing lies in finding something the fish will *not* bite. Snowflake paperweights, bicycle pumps, Yo-Yos, and anvils have all been tried with varying degrees of nonsuccess, but it takes a special blend of inappropriate tackle and awkward movements of the rod to overcome a bluefish's hunger. It's a rare angler indeed who doesn't come away from a stint in the surf or on a pier or on a party boat "full-handed" and frustrated, loaded down with "freezer ballast" and grumbling about the ones that didn't get away as he disgustedly discards the old faucet, broken toilet tank mechanism, or other "sure misfire" anti-lure he had placed so much trust in.

Bluegill	*1.* Tasty panfish often sought by ice fishermen. *2.* Slang term for common condition suffered by ice fishermen.
Blue Marlin	Highly prized and difficult-to-catch salt-water game fish.
Blue Moon	Period during which blue marlin may be caught.
Bonefish	Skittish, much-sought-after game fish found in shallow-water "flats" in Florida, the Bahamas, and the Caribbean. Bonefishing can be a grueling and nerve-wracking sport for the fisherman, but it is exciting and enjoyable to watch, and spectators often pause to take in the action as the angler goes through an amazing series of unpredictable movements, ranging from tooth-jarring slaps as a sandfly finds its target on a sunburned neck to breathtaking leaps as a piece of sharp coral pierces a shoe. And once in a while, onlookers may be lucky enough to witness a sensational run when a small ground shark or poisonous ray sends the spooked bonefisherman into a flurry of rapid strides and jerky hops, and he churns the water white in a mad dash for dry land, filling the tropical air with a burst of language of unforgettable richness and color.
Brook Trout	Breed of native trout that was common in American rivers before the hordes of European brown trout were introduced in the 1880's, but which are now usually only found in the headwaters of the better private streams. They are ag-

Bluegill "Common Condition Suffered by Ice Fishermen."

gravatingly choosy fish, and are easily put off by loud, flashy lures tied with synthetic substances such as polyester or tinsel, and about the only chance of taking one is with a lightly gin-soaked "very dry fly" tied in a conservative plaid or tattersall pattern.

Bucket	Clumsy form of metallic footgear found on fishing boats.
Bug	*1.* Large surface lure. *2.* Individual who is crazy about fishing. *3.* Insect that is crazy about *2.*

C

California Yellowtail	Valued sport fish found off the southern Pacific coast of the U.S. The best lures for catching yellowtail are bean sprouts, leather or silk lures with a clearly legible designer label, or spinners made from body jewelry, foreign car keys, or small silver spoons.
Camera	Small, but quite heavy object used by anglers to store small amounts of water and a canister of spoiled film.
Camp	As used by fishermen, a term denoting the place where the outboard motor broke. *See* CHUB.
Can	The only place where salmon are sure to be found with any degree of certainty.
Cane Pole	The simplest fishing rig, consisting of a long stick with a length of line permanently attached to its tip. It is a common bit of fishing lore among the uninitiated that a barefoot boy equipped with such a pole and using a bent pin for a hook and worms for bait will invariably go home with more fish than an expensively outfitted angler. This is

Bugs

Char

arrant nonsense. There is simply no substitute for the subtlety of mind and singleness of purpose of the dedicated bait caster or fly fisherman. Perhaps he flashes a bogus, but convincing, game warden badge and confiscates the little rascal's lucky catch; maybe he places a fatherly hand lightly on the lad's shoulder and speaks firmly, yet kindly, of the horrors of the reform school that await truants apprehended by a concerned citizen and delivered to the proper authorities; or it could be that he simply offers a tantalizing "dough ball" of wadded dollar bills to the dimwitted adolescent, suggesting in an offhand manner some of the cavity-producing delicacies that might take the place of a tiresome meal of bass or trout. But whatever his methods, the experienced angler will always get the fish, for a youth's crude skill is no match for his cunning.

Canoe	Long, narrow, sharp-ended boat in which the typical lake fisherman passes through the most dramatic portion of the metamorphosis that began with his emergence from his cocoonlike sleeping bag at dawn. At first huddling in the unfamiliar craft as he adjusts to his new environment, he rises unsteadily to his feet, extends his fishing rod, and then goes into a brief flying phase, followed by a long aquatic or swimming stage.
Catch-and-release	*1.* Term for stretch of public stream where fish caught must be released alive. *2.* Term for stretch of private stream where trespassers caught are released after a lecture, a series of threats, and a brief introduction to a large dog.
Char	*1.* Group of fishes, including the lake and brook trout, which are related both to salmon and to other trout. *2.* Common method of cooking *1* over a campfire.

Club

Cheese	Surprisingly effective bait the use of which is frowned upon by dedicated anglers who find it most unsporting, and who prefer the time-honored technique of using artificial lures that imitate the natural insect food consumed by fish. Many anglers compromise and combine efficiency with tradition by strictly confining themselves to native American cheeses, which they fashion into fanciful shapes that mimic flies and bugs—Royal Velveeta, Lunchwagon, Cheddar Midge, and Edam's Fancy are just a few of the popular patterns. Another much-favored approach is to employ a hybrid lure consisting of a conventional dry or wet fly and a surreptitiously applied gob of cheese. This method is particularly effective when hypercritical fly fishermen are angling in the immediate vicinity, for it takes a sharp eye to spot the dairy product in a Krafty Devil, Swiss Knight, Yellow Fox, or Wisconsin Special.
Chicken	Tuna of the land.
Chub	*1.* Informal name for the fallfish and various small carp. *2.* Sound made by malfunctioning outboard motor during repeated attempts to start it. *See* KAPOK.
Chum	*1.* Fish heads or innards, raw clams, smelly garbage, and the like, which are chopped up and thrown over the side of a salt-water fishing vessel to attract game fish. *2.* Friendly fellow angler who will chop up fish heads and innards, raw clams, smelly garbage and the like and throw them over the side for you while you concentrate on keeping a recently eaten meal in its proper location.
Club	*1.* Long bar of wood used to render fish senseless. *2.* Place with a long bar of wood where fishermen go to render themselves senseless.

Creep

Cod	Game fish usually taken from party boats in ocean waters during winter months. The most critical part of cod fishing occurs long before the fishing grounds are reached. This is the all-important "rise," which takes place in the dark at about 5 A.M. when the dramatic "strike" of the alarm clock turns the motionless, quiescent angler into a thrashing, seething mass of elbows and bedclothes and sends him into a heart-stopping "leap." If at this point the clock is thrown sharply across the room with an abrupt, powerful arm stroke, then chances are that the angler is about to enter a prolonged dormant phase, and there is little hope that cod will be taken that day.
Corrosion Resistant	Term found on articles of fishing equipment indicating that they are capable of withstanding the harmful effects of salt-water exposure for 91, 181, or 366 days, depending on the nature of the guarantee.
Creel	Lightweight, easily carried wickerwork basket in which the day's catch is placed.
Creep	Angler who insists on examining the contents of another fisherman's creel.
Croaker, Grouper, Snapper	1. Informal names for three groups of salt-water game fish. 2. Informal names for the three basic types of anglers: the noisy croakers, who cough and clear their throats when absolute silence is essential; the overly convivial groupers, who borrow your lures, sample your lunch, and help you lose fish during netting; and the mean-spirited snappers, who respond to an angler's casual remark about the weather with a pointed request that he go smoke a fish.
Custom-made	Bilked to order.

D

Dam

Installation for the production of hydroelectoral power. Dams with a capacity for generating 100,000 votes or more are not uncommon, particularly in western states.

Darters

Small members of the perch family. The fight to save a darter species—the Tennessee snail darter—from extinction postponed completion of a major dam for several years and focused attention on these tiny, fast-moving fish. But for the small group of fanatic anglers who pursue this little minnow throughout the U.S., the darters have always had a value far out of proportion to their diminutive size. Armed with ultralight "pencil" rods, a few yards of 2-ounce line on a thimble reel, microscopic plankton lures, and a thumb net, they stalk shallow headwaters and creeks, waiting for the almost inaudible "pipple" of a bull darter breaking the surface and snatching the proferred bait in its minuscule jaws. Then, forefingers tensed to absorb the knuckle-wrenching shock of the sudden 2- or 3-foot darting maneuvers that give this plucky bantam its name, they play the colorful tab-tail for 10 or 20 seconds—it often seems more like a minute or two—until beached and quickly dispatched with a sharp flick of the fingernail, it joins the rest of the day's catch in the distinctive lapel creel that is the trademark of the darter enthusiast. A "keeper" in most states is ⅞-inch; 1½ inches or more is a very good fish; and anything over 3 inches is a trophy suitable for mounting on a key chain or tie clip.

Dolphin

Aggressive tropical game fish that is a true fish, and is in no way related to the playful, intelligent, and often helpful

Dry Flies (Basic Patterns)

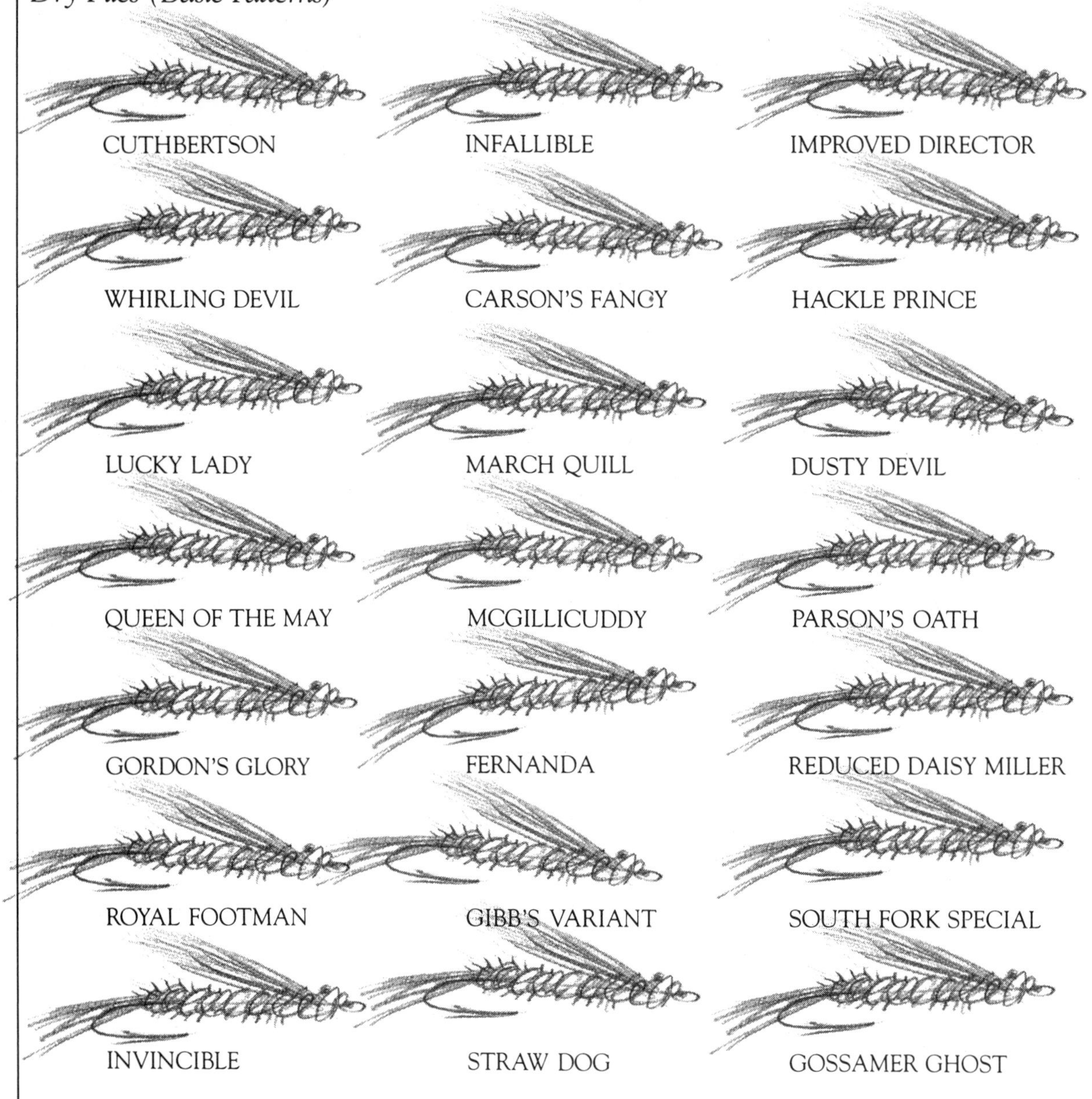

CUTHBERTSON

INFALLIBLE

IMPROVED DIRECTOR

WHIRLING DEVIL

CARSON'S FANCY

HACKLE PRINCE

LUCKY LADY

MARCH QUILL

DUSTY DEVIL

QUEEN OF THE MAY

MCGILLICUDDY

PARSON'S OATH

GORDON'S GLORY

FERNANDA

REDUCED DAISY MILLER

ROYAL FOOTMAN

GIBB'S VARIANT

SOUTH FORK SPECIAL

INVINCIBLE

STRAW DOG

GOSSAMER GHOST

aquatic mammal, the porpoise. The confusion between the two names is based on a superficial similarity in the shape of their snouts and not on any shared beneficial behavioral traits, as shipwrecked sailors learn to their dismay when the dull-witted, but malevolent dolphins push them off their rafts, eat their life preservers, and nudge them out to sea.

Dope	*1.* Any fluid applied to a dry fly to make it float. *2.* Any individual who applies this substance to a wet fly.
Dry Flies	Fly-fishing lure designed to float on the surface of the water. There are hundreds of different kinds, and they are hard to tell apart, but they all fit into one of six basic categories: Mashed, Bent, Slimy, Hairless, Hookless, and Hopeless.
Dun	*1.* The second stage in the development on rivers of the mayfly. *2.* The second stage in the purchase on credit of fishing gear.
Dusk	Brief twilight period that separates the time when fish don't bite because they can see the line from the time when fish don't bite because they can't see the lure.

E

Earthworm	There are probably as many different lures as there are fishermen, but none is more universally effective in catching fresh-water fish than that old stand-by, the earthworm. Worms can be bought from bait shops in most fishing areas, but many anglers prefer to raise their own to assure themselves of a plentiful and virtually cost-free supply. This is not difficult to do. Worms are easily collected from a garden after a heavy rain, and may be stored for long periods in a cool, dark place in a box filled with damp

shredded newspaper, moistened leaves, wet moss, or some similar bedding material, with a little corn meal or powdered milk thrown in for food. But a word of warning: anglers are by nature sweet-tempered and sensitive, and they often go overboard, constructing elaborate houses with individual beds for their night crawlers and naming favorite worms. This is not a good idea, for when the time comes to pop Maria, Constance, and Esmeralda into a bait can or slip a hook through Reginald, the tearful fisherman may find that he simply lacks the heart to bid farewell to his wriggling friends.

Exaggeration

Formal term for a collection of fishermen, i.e., an *exaggeration* of anglers.

F

False Cast

1. Technique used by fly fishermen after an unsatisfactory cast to straighten a kinked line and increase its velocity. *2.* Strap-on plaster device worn to work by sly fishermen after an unexplained absence to strengthen a weak line and improve its credibility.

Fathom

1. n. Measurement of ocean depth, often made on fishing boats with an electronic sounding device called a fathometer. *2. v.* To comprehend, as in, "I cannot fathom why I paid six hundred dollars for a malfunctioning electronic device that does nothing but smoke and squeak."

Fighting Chair

Elaborate, swivel-mounted seat in the stern of a seagoing charter boat in which a salt-water fisherman struggles with his overpowering urge to order the captain to turn around and return to port.

Filleting   Dangerous and messy form of mumbledypeg played on a kitchen counter with a dull knife and a large fish.

Fish   The only living creature in any given stretch of stream, river, lake, or bay that doesn't have a hook in it and isn't smoking a pipe.

Fish Story   The use of nonstandard terms for the estimated size of a fish that eluded capture has tended to unnecessarily undermine the veracity of well-meaning anglers. Adherence to the internationally recognized Rules for Reporting Lost Fish will not only eliminate possible confusion or misinterpretation, but will also go far toward improving the overall credibility of anglers everywhere:

FLASH OF SCALES UNDER WATER: Lunker
SLIGHT RIPPLE: Bruiser
AUDIBLE SPLASH: Whopper
PERCEPTIBLE NIBBLE: Giant
HARD TUG ON LINE: Monster
MISSING LURE OR SNAPPED LEADER: Leviathan
BROKEN LINE: Behemoth
LOST ROD: Fishzilla.

Fishing Trip   Journey undertaken by one or more anglers to a place where no one can remember when it has rained so much.

Flatfish   1. Any of a number of species of salt-water bottom fish characterized by a horizontal swimming posture. 2. Any fish left in the path of a beach buggy.

Fluke   1. Summer flounder. 2. Catching a summer flounder.

Fly Box   1. Plastic or metal container for storing flies. 2. To exchange blows in a sparring contest with any of the two-winged insects of the order Diptera. Fishermen are generally not belligerent individuals, but it's common to see them en-

Fish Story (Presentation of the Evidence)

gaged in a furious bout with a huge fly, bobbing and weaving and making quick jabs and thrusts at what seems to be thin air. Shrewd onlookers invariably put their money on the insect, favoring its agility, speed, and staying power over the angler's size, weight, and ability to absorb punishment, much of it self-inflicted, and these aerial featherweights seldom disappoint their backers.

Fly Casting

This is the most elegant, but also the most demanding form of fresh-water fishing, because unlike other casting methods, in fly fishing it is the line itself rather than the lure at the end of it that is cast toward the target, and 30 or more feet of casting line must be stripped of the reel and set into controlled motion overhead with precise, whiplike movements of the rod. Accurate fly casting is very difficult to master, but it appeals to fishermen who prefer finesse to force and measure their success as much in the quality of the cast as in the quantity of the catch. Such a fisherman, standing in a crystal mountain stream, is the very epitome of the sportsman, as he carefully gauges the wind and water and instinctively makes a hundred minor but crucial calculations. He moves the supple rod back and forth in an easy rhythm, and the faintly whispering line describes subtle parabolas in the air, the infinitesimal fly dancing at its tip, the hook sparkling in the sun. At last, with a final graceful overhead stroke, he shoots the delicate loops through the air. Time stands still. And then a weird, almost animal cry shatters the silence as a well-honed barb bites into the posterior of an angler just downstream. Now comes the elemental test of a fly fisherman's mettle. Without a moment's hesitation, he cuts his line, nimbly makes his way to the stream bank, scoops up his gear, and deposits it in his car with a practiced flick of the wrist. Then, with deft

hand motions perfected by long practice, he turns on the ignition, spins the wheel, and speeds away. Is he disappointed? No, for he'll soon fish again—in another county—and he has the satisfaction of knowing that, in a fellow angler's fish story, he's the one that got away.

Flying Fish   *1.* Remarkable tropical fish capable of skimming over the waves for 100 feet or more on tiny winglike fins. *2.* Any undesirable fresh-water or salt-water fish, such as carp or scup, which, after being caught by an angler seeking more valuable fish, is propelled violently through the air with a brisk arm movement.

Fork   The point at which an unproductive river divides into two unpromising streams.

G

Gadget   Bright, alluring object with an inconspicuous price tag placed in a prominent position in a bait and tackle shop or moved slowly under the nose of a browsing angler.

Game Fish   Any fish that puts up as much of a fight when being caught as the angler's spouse did prior to his departure.

Gravel Bar   *1.* Mound or bank of pebbles found in streams and rivers. *2.* Candy product that has melted and resolidified in the bottom of a pack or duffel bag.

Grayling   Beautiful and very shy game fish, once quite common in the U.S. but now only found in Canada and Alaska. It's hard to generalize about this fish, but very broadly speaking, the best time to fish for grayling is an hour or two before you arrive at a stream or shortly after you leave. As far as lures go, almost any fly not in your fly book or vest is

Flying Fish

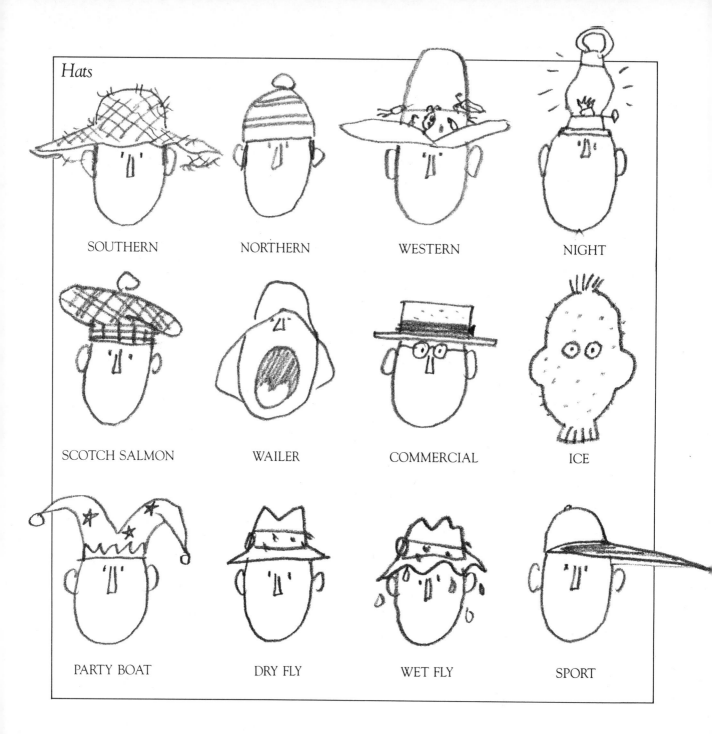

Hats

SOUTHERN

NORTHERN

WESTERN

NIGHT

SCOTCH SALMON

WAILER

COMMERCIAL

ICE

PARTY BOAT

DRY FLY

WET FLY

SPORT

a pretty good bet, though you might have had some luck with the one that got hooked in your pocket. There's a good deal of debate about casting methods, but whether you let the fly drift by the fish so gently that it doesn't notice it or tweak it so it spooks it, the results are about equal. As for the likeliest places to find grayling, the best spot to be is on the other side of the river, 10 miles upstream, or back at that pool you passed 3 hours ago.

Guide

1. One of a series of ring-shaped metal loops through which the line passes on a fishing rod. Typically, there is one just above the butt, several along the midsection, and one at the tip. *2.* Professional fishing assistant. Fishermen should be aware that guides planning the loading of the boat, the number and type of meals to be served, and the degree of service to be provided, divide the angler into three basic sections: the butt, the midsection, and the tip.

H

Habitat

Place where a particular species of fish was last week.

Haddock

Very important commercial fish, related to cod, found in ocean waters off New England. It has long been a favorite of preparers of institutional food since its somewhat gluey flesh can be easily formed into sticks, cakes, lumps, slabs, nuggets, and balls, and will generally not disintegrate when cooked if coated with a protective batter made of equal parts plaster of Paris and blackboard chalk and fried for no longer than 3 hours at 1,100° F.

Hat

Anything on the head of a fisherman that does not bite or fly away when struck sharply with the hand.

Ice Fishing

Hatch	Simultaneous appearance on a single stretch of stream of a large number of insects of the same species which causes fish to rise and feed voraciously and makes them somewhat susceptible to capture. It is impossible to predict exactly when a hatch will take place, but generally speaking, they occur on Mondays, during unusually heavy rains, or on the Wednesday immediately preceding or immediately following a long holiday weekend.
Hook	Irritating but highly reliable device used to quickly locate the position of one's thumb at the bottom of a tackle box.
Hot Spot	*1.* Place on any given stream or lake, usually known only to locals, where fish can be found. *2.* Place in the center of the palm of the right hand of locals where money may be placed to help find *1.*

I

Ice Fishing	Winter fishing method in which anglers use a variety of specialized equipment to catch colds.
Inchworm	Tiny moth larva favored as food by trout and as bait by trout fishermen, who, from force of deep-rooted habits, invariably refer to them as foot-and-a-halfworms.
Indoor Casting	The angler anxious to improve his casting skills can profitably practice indoors. This is an ideal exercise, since it does away with the major inconveniences of fishing, such as cold water, bugs, tedious and costly trips to remote places, and the troublesome fish itself, while preserving the display of delicate skill that is the essence of fine fishing technique.

Indoor Casting

Seated by the pool with a cool drink or reclining on a comfortable "casting couch" in his own living room, the home fisherman can, depending on his level of experience, use simple tackle and subtle casts to change television channels, turn on a light, snatch a detective novel off a distant shelf, procure a snack from the kitchen, or restrain an unruly child. And for those who miss the realism of stalking a quarry, the appropriate gear may be used to have a little sport with the Avon lady, walk a pet in bad weather without leaving the house, or obtain produce from a neighbor's garden.

| **In-flight Testing** | As a free service to anglers embarking on fishing trips, all major airlines subject fishing rods, tackle boxes, and other gear to an exhaustive series of rigorous trials intended to spot any flaws in design or packaging. There is no need to make special arrangements for this procedure—just hand your angling paraphernalia to the attendant at the check-in counter. It will be immediately placed on a high-speed conveyor belt to begin its carefully planned ordeal. The exact testing process is a closely guarded industry secret, but based on an examination of samples of fishing outfits that have undergone this thorough shakedown, it involves the application of every form of compression, concussion, corrosion, vibration, and perforation known to modern science, and if your rig emerges in usable condition, you can take justifiable pride in the knowledge that you are the owner of rugged, reliable, and absolutely indestructible fishing equipment. |

| **Insect Repellent** | One of a number of "gag" items available in bait and tackle shops. |

Knot (Basic Procedure)

STEP I

STEP II

STEP III

STEP IV

J

Jackknife   Indispensable cutting tool generally found in the pocket of a different jacket, beneath the front seat of the car, or under the roll of screening on the table in the garage.

Jig   Crude but effective artificial lure made up of a metal head and some form of dressing designed not to imitate a particular food favored by fish, but to attract their attention through its motions in the water. Jigs are the simplest and most ancient of fishing lures, and in fact, the oldest known evidence of angling is a carved elk horn jig mounted on a bone hook found deeply embedded in a petrified log near the remains of a remarkably well-preserved, 14,000-year-old Swiss lake village. Interestingly enough, next to it were the sharply broken remains of a rough-hewn oak pole and a small woven reed basket containing the bones of three tiny, long-extinct minnows.

K

Kapok   *1.* Silky fibers used as stuffing in boat cushions. *2.* Promising backfiring sound made by outboard motor after 30 pulls of the starting cord. *See* MUMMICHOG.

Kit   Prepackaged, partly finished, unassembled object, such as a fishing rod, which comes in a box containing all but three of the required parts; a list of 220-volt power tools essential for its completion; and pages 1-12 and 24-32 of the Dutch language instructions.

Knot   A tangle with a name.

Lake (The Fishing Cycle Explained)

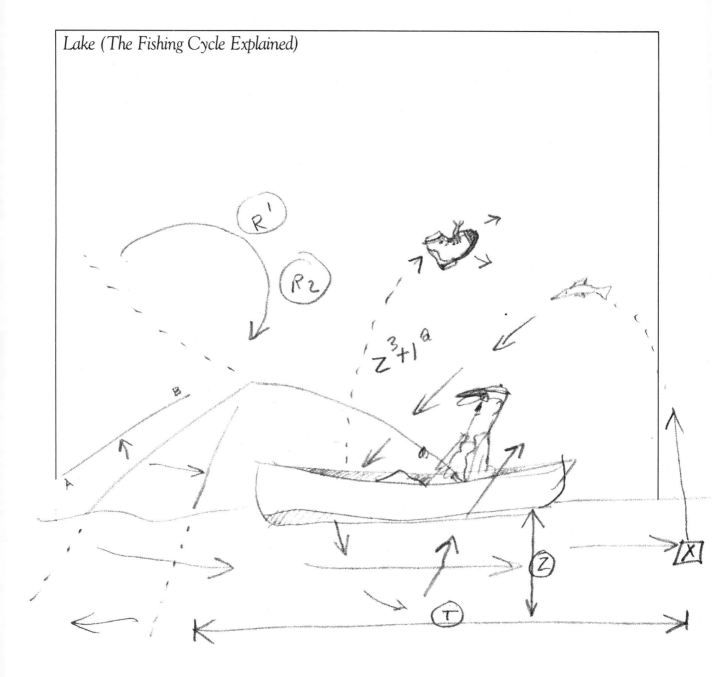

Kokanee	Landlocked dwarf salmon of a type known as sockeye, a term that is thought to be derived from an angler's typical response to disparaging comments made by fellow fishermen on the small size of the specimen he caught.

L

Lake	Ecologists classify lakes as being oligotrophic (low in nourishment) or eutrophic (high in nourishment), and while terms such as these are of some interest to anglers eager to learn about the life cycles of various fish species, most fishermen prefer to know whether a given lake is autocatastrophic (approachable only by deeply rutted dirt roads); peptobismolic (unfit to drink); psychomotorphobic (frequented by maniacs in overpowered speedboats); or photosoporific (characterized by natural scenic beauty that leads fellow anglers to take hundreds of boring pictures of it for slide shows and home movies).
Leader	Short length of nylon or wire that connects a snagged lure to a tangled line.
Leadhead	*1.* Slang term for a particular type of metal jig. *2.* Unpleasant cranial condition suffered in the morning hours by dedicated anglers who, in the interests of better understanding their quarry, spent the previous evening attempting to imitate fishes' widely noted ability to process large amounts of liquid.
Leech	*1.* Blood-sucking parasitic worm that attaches itself with a pair of suckers to the legs of wading fishermen. The bite is not really all that serious, and since the leech introduces a small amount of an irritating anticoagulant into the

wound, the most sensible thing to do is to leave the leech in place until it drops off of its own accord, at which point it will have withdrawn the itch-producing substance. 2. Aaaaaaaaaaaaaaaaaaaaaaaaaaaaaaaaaaaaaaaaaaaaaagh.

License
Permit issued upon payment of a modest fee that allows fishermen to lose lures in a specified area.

Lie
1. A place in a stream, river, or lake where fish lurk. 2. Any simple declarative statement made by an angler about the location of such a place; or the number, size, and type of fish observed there; or the circumstances under which one or more of them escaped capture.

Limit
Maximum number of a particular fish that an angler can take in a day. This number varies from place to place and species to species, but like the speed of light, it is a largely theoretical restriction with little practical application.

Line
Length of filament stretched between two fishing rods and joined at its midpoint by a pair of linked hooks.

Lodge
Overnight accommodation in fishing area. The term is sometimes used rather loosely, but in most areas, to be classified as a lodge rather than a motel, an establishment must meet certain criteria: it must possess 90 percent of the *National Geographics* published between 1955 and 1970; it must have a black-and-white television set manufactured prior to 1965; it must have no more than six items on its menu at any one time—and one of them must be corned beef hash; it must have a sign reading We Aim To Please, You Aim Too, Please prominently posted in the downstairs men's room and a copy of "The Angler's Prayer" displayed in the main hallway; there must be at least six blue spruces,

forty whitewashed boulders, and one large deaf dog on the grounds; the operation of any plumbing fixture in any portion of the building must be clearly audible to every occupant of the building; and the proprietor or proprietress must be able to expound at length, without notes, on all the major theories of climatological change, including the greenhouse effect, the sunspot cycle, the melting of the ice caps, and the effect of rocket-launchings on rain.

Logjam

1. Obstruction in a stream or river caused by an accumulation of tangled tree trunks. *2.* Unpleasant sticky substance found on tree trunks used as seats at campsite breakfasts.

Luck

One of the most frustrating circumstances in fishing occurs when two anglers in the same boat experience dramatically different results: one catches fish methodically, the other gets nary a nibble. Obviously, the "unlucky" angler is doing something wrong, and if this happens to you, you should take a moment to critique your technique. First, examine your posture. When your companion casts, are you reaching forward to nudge him with your elbow or inconspicuously shifting your weight back and forth to impart a disorienting rocking motion to the boat? Second, are you paying enough attention to the lure? Have you surreptitiously daubed your fellow angler's fly or plug with motor oil or insect repellent or some smelly rod glue? And what about the retrieve? Have you slipped a small amount of honey into the moving parts of his reel mechanism and imparted kinks and twists in any line he has stripped off onto the bottom of the boat? And when you assist your colleague in netting fish, do you use the backhand flub and the underwater hook snap? Well, we could go on, but remember, in angling, skill always wins out over luck.

Lure

Anything used to attract fish. There are basically two kinds: those fishermen swear by, and those they swear at.

M

Maintenance

It only takes a few moments at the end of each fishing season to ensure that your gear will be in proper condition for use the following year. Of course, each individual fisherman will have his own maintenance program, but we recommend the basic procedures listed here, which have been perfected over many years by countless anglers:

(a) Put reels in the pockets of an old army jacket or overcoat—do not remove line.

(b) Disassemble fishing rod, slip into a partly opened umbrella, and lean in a dark corner.

(c) Place an open can of lubricating oil in tackle boxes and store them upside down on the floor or a high shelf.

(d) Roll waders, vest, and other pieces of clothing into a tight ball and throw into the back of the closet.

(e) Drop any loose hooks and lures into your landing net and store under the kitchen sink.

(f) Toss tools, gadgets, and leftover fly dope into creel and wedge behind couch.

Map

Handy, schematic representation of all the various roads in a given area that you are not currently on.

Matching the Hatch

1. The art of creating, out of bits of feather and hair, convincing replicas of insects being eaten by fish for use as bait. 2. The far more demanding practice of trussing up and immobilizing the actual insect itself with tiny hand-

cuffs, shackles, and leg irons prior to attaching it to a hook. This exacting craft, which may entail, before each cast, two hours or more of patient labor to turn, say, a single millipede into a little chain gang, is favored by ultratraditional anglers, but has been opposed for years by the Society for the Prevention of Cruelty to Insects. However, due to that organization's very small membership—34 at last count—and the fact that all but six of them are currently incarcerated in institutions for the disturbed, its protests have had little practical effect.

Measurement of Fish	There are a number of different methods of determining the overall length in inches of fresh-water fish, and anglers are free to choose the one that suits them best. The most common are: the distance from the center of the tail of the fish, while still hooked, to the tip of the fishing rod; the distance from the tip of the snout to the end of the handle of the landing net; the distance from the front of the gill of a fish held in the hand to the inside edge of the holder's elbow; four times the angler's shoe size or five times his hat size; and the temperature in degrees Fahrenheit, divided by 2 (summer) or multiplied by 2 (winter).
Minnow	1. Informal term for any very small fish. 2. Embryonic stage of a large fib.
Mummichog	1. Coastal fish useful as bait and as a predator of mosquito larva. 2. Disappointing sound made by outboard motor on the thirty-first through the five hundredth try.
Myth	Technical term for a basic piece of factual angling information contained in one fishing book when referred to by the author of another fishing book.

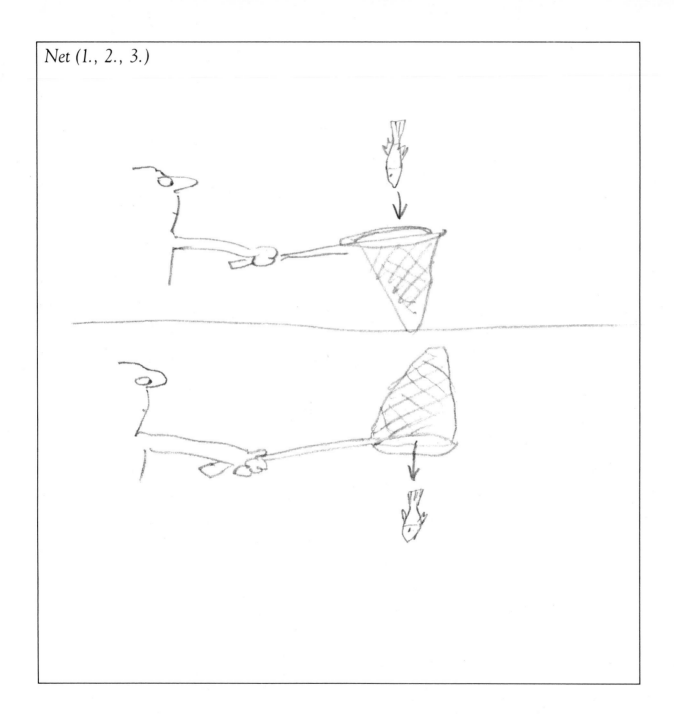

Net (1., 2., 3.)

N

Natural
Type of organic bait rejected by a finicky fish because it is too large or too small, or because it has the wrong shape, bears the wrong coloration, or makes the wrong motions in the water. *See* ARTIFICIAL.

Net
1. n. Woven mesh bag attached to a circular wood or metal frame on which a handle is mounted used to remove hooked fish from the water. *2. v.* To land or capture a fish, as in, "I netted 15 one-pound trout." *3. adj.* The final or actual amount or weight following adjustments for loss and reductions due to overstatement, as in, "Well, if we're talking net here, maybe it was one 15-ounce trout."

Nymph
1. The underwater stage of certain insects eaten by fish or any fly designed to imitate it. *2.* The words "Net!", "Now!", "No!", "Nuts!", and "Ninny!" as spoken to a companion by a fly fisherman holding loops of fly line in his mouth.

O

Oar
Clumsy wooden implement used to moisten boat occupants.

Ob
Siberian river familiar to anglers who have spent a rainy week in a cabin with a 47-card poker deck, the March, 1957, issue of *Colliers*, and 20 crossword puzzle books.

Opening Day
The first day of the angling season in some parts of the country is April first, which is often referred to by the name April Fisherman's Day or a similar term honoring the sport, and even nonfishermen get into the spirit of this

Party Boat

popular national pastime by practicing harmless deceptions on one another.

P

Panfish

Anything removed from the water that will fit into a frying pan and does not melt, smolder, or give off sparks when cooked.

Party Boat

Large salt-water fishing craft that carries a sizable number of fishermen, each of whom is charged a fixed fee for the outing, which usually includes bait and sometimes the use of fishing tackle as well. Party boats are almost always crowded, and since the individual who catches the largest fish generally wins a pool made up of contributions by all on board, tempers can quickly flare in close quarters when lines become tangled—as they inevitably do—or when a nearby angler's clumsiness causes a fish to be lost. For this reason, adherence to a few simple forms of shipboard etiquette is very important. For example, an individual should always be tapped lightly from behind on the right shoulder before being struck on the nose or chin; if bait has been handled recently, hands should be thoroughly washed before being placed around the neck of a fellow fisherman whom one wishes to throttle; an angler who fails to respond to a slow 10-count is presumed to have given up his fishing position along the rail; and under no circumstances should an individual be knocked overboard while the fish are biting.

Plastic Lures

Pattern

Characteristic size, shape, color, and texture of an artificial fly. Anglers achieve a specific look by tying various kinds of bird feathers and animal hair onto the shank of a hook. Although there are dozens of patterns, most anglers create and carry two basic kinds of designs: "dummies"—or "foolers"—which are carefully crafted out of substances and colors with a proven ability to alarm and annoy fish, are prominently displayed on a hat brim or vest pocket, and are generously lent to fellow anglers for copying or immediate use; and "actuals," highly effective stream-tested designs that are hidden in a small box or tucked away in an inside pocket.

Perch

1. Popular panfish found in a number of aquatic habitats. *2.* Standing place, such as a slippery bank, wet rock, or rickety dock, from which an angler was fishing for perch shortly before he unexpectedly entered the perch's habitat.

Plastic Lures

Lifelike and effective plastic imitations of worms, frogs, squid, and other favorite fish foods are widely used, but many anglers are unaware of other equally convincing and useful stream-side accouterments, including the unbelievably realistic 12-foot Vinylmouth, a snake which—when placed in a highly visible spot—can reliably clear a mile or two of stream of competing anglers in less than a minute, and the radio-controlled Mesmerizers, a pair of totally believable rubber decoys (either the 19-inch rainbow trout or the 22-inch largemouth bass) that are capable of executing up to 40 different preprogrammed teasing maneuvers designed to keep dozens of potentially bothersome fellow fishermen glued to a worthless downstream pool or a barren stretch of lake shore for hours on end.

Playing	1. Series of rod, reel, and line motions used by the angler to tire a hooked fish and eventually drive it—in a state of exhaustion—into a net. 2. Series of tantalizing nibbles, tail flips, and short jumps used by fish to madden a hooked angler and eventually drive him into a state of mind that will result in someone coming after him with a net.
Plug	Plastic or wooden lure designed to imitate various species of bait fish. Typically, they produce a popping noise or a provocative motion as they are pulled through the water that is intended either to attract the attention of fish or to annoy them into striking. In the latter category of effects, the most elaborate plug is the costly, but lethal Raspberry, which uses a small waterproof cassette recorder and an underwater loudspeaker to make a variety of hisses, boos, hoots, and catcalls, interspersed with prerecorded gibes like, "Hey, minnow-breath, are you going to bite me or just sit there like a pile of silt and make bubbles?" and, "You know why fish live in the water? Because they're all wet! Har, har, har."
Poaching	1. Stealing fish. 2. Method of disposing of the evidence by boiling it into an unrecognizable sludge.
Pocket Water	1. Stream surface condition characterized by pools of water which form downstream from large rocks. 2. Small impoundment of water often encountered by anglers when fishing for keys, change, folding money, or matches.
Poncho	Portable sweat hut.
Pond	Large volume of water surrounding a snapping turtle.
Portage	The shortest distance between two hernias.

Prize Fish	Any fish that weighs more than the gear used to catch it.
Put-and-take	Form of fishing offered by commercial operators who stock ponds with tame, easily caught hatchery trout or panfish and charge a fee for anglers to catch them. Most of these enterprises are aboveboard and offer harmless—if dull—sport, but *caveat piscator*: there are a number of shady, fish-by-night operations around that provide exciting, but thoroughly rigged diversions such as "three-pond monte," "crappie shooting," and "the old shellfish game," and unwary anglers can end up going home with both empty pockets and empty creels.
Put Down	To spook a fish. Although fish see things somewhat differently from the way humans do, most have quite good vision, and unexpected or unfamiliar shapes can quickly scare them off. Anglers eager to improve their chances of getting close to particularly skittish species, like wild trout, have gone so far as to invest in modern dance lessons to be able to imitate saplings or shrubbery, but a far simpler method is to acquire one of the new, amazingly realistic rubber fish suits with lifelike scales and fin-shaped waders. Another excellent choice, if cost is no object, is the Motor Maggot, a natural-looking 14-foot mechanical caterpillar, which provides comfortable fishing positions for two anglers whose rods project through apertures in the "head," closely mimicking an insect's antennae. It is available in a choice of colorations to blend with local flora, and thanks to a unique muffling system which makes exhaust noises sound like the cry of a whippoorwill (albeit an unusually deep-voiced specimen), it can approach right to the stream edge without scaring a nervy trout.

Prize Fish

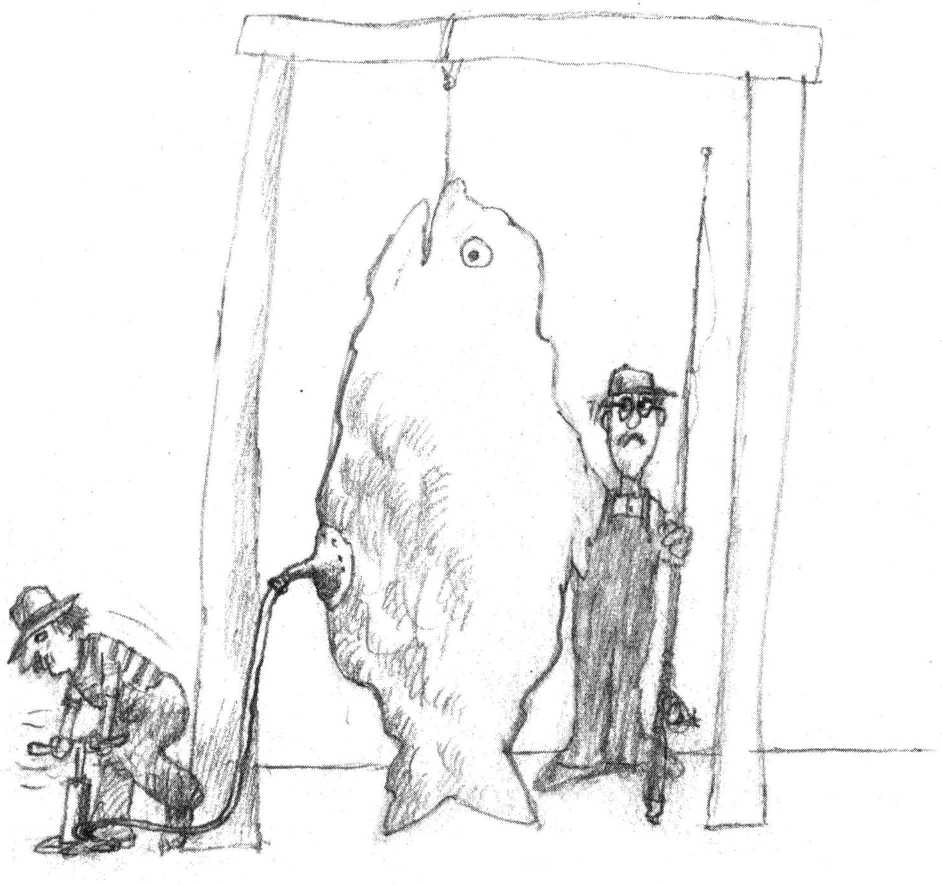

Q

Quill
Type of feather material attached to a hook shank to imitate the look of an insect's segmented body. How it is that, say, a trout, which has extremely acute eyesight, can mistake a crude clump of duck feathers and deer fur for some insect it sees every day is a complete mystery, but it certainly undermines the concept of fish as "brain food."

R

Records
The names of current holders of records for game fish are widely published in fishing journals, but individuals who have set new marks in other categories of angling often go unsung. This seems a bit unfair, and it is hoped that this short list will go a long way toward rectifying the more serious omissions:

TIRE: 1965, Lake Ontario, 51½ pounds, 35 inches in diameter, Mr. Edward T. Rutherford.

BOOT: 1971, Boston Harbor, 7¼ pounds, size 11, Mr. Vincent Castelli.

OBSTRUCTION: 1958, Santee Reservoir, cypress stump, 36 pounds, 22 inches, Mr. Billy Conners.

JETSAM, FRESH-WATER: 1976, Colorado River, G.E. Toaster, 11 pounds, 28 inches (to tip of electric cord), Mrs. Alice Leighton.

JETSAM, SALT-WATER: 1960, Pebble Beach, golf club bag with clubs, 38¼ pounds, 44 inches, Mr. Thomas P. Landsdowne.

River

Reel

Cylindrical device attached near the end of a fishing rod for winding up or letting out line. There are several different types and sizes designed for a wide range of fishing situations, but they all offer the angler the option of two basic settings: "wheeeeee," in which at the slightest pull, the line is paid out in a series of erratic loops at very high speed; and "fonk," in which the reel spontaneously stops revolving with a sharp metallic sound, instantly dividing the line into two sections of unequal length.

Regionalisms

A source of both charm and confusion in the world of angling is the prevalence of local terms. For example, the ubiquitous water-skier found throughout the U.S. in summer months is known to fishermen variously as the bay dunce, lake lout, water turkey, harbor dolt, pond boob, surf oaf, or river clod, and an angler fishing close by is referred to in different parts of the country as a blockhead, fathead, meathead, lunkhead, blunderhead, dunderpate, numbskull, knucklehead, lamebrain or nitwit. It can all be a little bewildering, but it does add color to the sport!

Reservoir

A flood named after a congressman.

River

Any stretch of moving water large enough to be crossed by a bridge from which fishing is prohibited.

Rod

Flexible, tapered stick that is the basic tool of angling. Many fishermen find rods of even average length to be awkward to carry, but they can easily be shortened to a more convenient size by removing the top few inches with an ordinary car door, station wagon tailgate, or trunk lid.

Rod Belt

1. A belt with a cup where the butt of a surf rod may be rested. *2.* Brief drink of a stimulating beverage.

Rules of Thumb ("Don't Let Anyone Hold Your Fish.")

Rod Casting
The discouraged angler who has decided to bid farewell to his hobby should do so with the same style and attention to form that he displayed while he practiced it. Stand on a stream bank, lake shore, pier, or beach, with feet placed comfortably apart, and grasp the fishing rod by the cork handle. Select a sinker large enough to overcome the natural buoyancy of the rod, attach it securely to the line, then slip the hook over the lowest guide, tightening and locking the reel so that the rod has a slight bend. Hold the rod straight out in front of you, then smoothly raise your arm over your head until the rod is almost parallel with the ground behind you. Make any brief remarks you wish, then with a fast, overhead whipping motion of the arm and elbow, propel the rod forward and slightly up. Just before release, give a quick snap of the wrist, and as the rod strikes the water, "dust" your hands with a few brisk sliding motions of one palm across the other.

Rowboat
Small craft that is so named because its occupation by more than one angler immediately causes a row.

Rules of Thumb
Given the enormous number of different fishing techniques, very few maxims have universal application, but the handful that do are worth committing to memory:
(a) Never drink beer in waders.
(b) Never fish with a notary public.
(c) Don't tell jokes in canoes.
(d) On ocean-going party boats, always fish to windward.
(e) On camping trips, always bring cheap books with large, soft pages.
(f) Never ask a game warden where he got his hat.
(g) Don't take advice from people with missing fingers.

S

Salmon

During those rare times when these magnificent fish are biting, they provide some of the most sensational sport in angling, and even during the many long days when they aren't, they still offer some diversion to occupy patient anglers in fishing camps, since they are an incredibly rich source of obscure Scrabble words, including kype, redd, parr, vomer, milt, smolt, grilse, and kelt.

Saskatchewan

Explosive nasal sound produced by anglers in northern climes during winter months.

Scads

1. Members of the Carangidae family of fishes. 2. Lots and lots of scads, as for example at a Carangidae family reunion.

Scales

1. Annoying things on fish. 2. Annoying things on docks.

Scotland

Peculiar land that is the birthplace of golf and sport salmon fishing, a fact which may explain why it is also the birthplace of whiskey.

Scrod

1. *n.* Commercial name for young cod or haddock fillets. 2. *v.* Having been unfairly dealt with in a business transaction at a bait-and-tackle shop.

Sea Food

Anglers who live near the shore can be assured of a ready supply of delicious and healthful fish products with a minimum of trouble and expense if they keep their eyes open and use a little common sense. There's no need for costly rods and reels or budget-busting boat charters, because the telephone company in most areas has listed the likeliest spots where fish can be "taken" in a handy guide printed on yellow paper. You'll be in luck any time from about nine in the morning until five in the evening (except Sunday), and the only "lure" you'll need is the old reliable greenback or spondulix, though if you insist on a little sport, you can always try a rubber check or a plastic credit card first.

Seaweed Form of marine life sought after by vegetarian sportsmen. With the exception of the giant kelp, most species of algae don't put up much of a fight, but for the angler on an ocean-going "scumboat," the deceptively offhand remark from a crewman that "it looks like there's some algae up ahead," the sodden gurgle as the large hooks bite into the shimmering green mass, and the arm-numbing struggle to boat the bubbling glob of treacherous goo are the stuff of oft-told tales whenever two or three "weed-eaters" gather for a bowl of sea lettuce and some clam juice and swap stories of man against mush and "the ton that got away."

Shad The only fish more difficult to eat than to catch.

Sinker Lead weight attached to the end of a length of fishing line to facilitate the speedy disposal of unwanted lures.

Slip *1.* Mooring system in which a boat is tied alongside one of a series of floating piers projecting at right angles from a dock. *2.* The most common method of entering such a boat.

Smelt *1. n.* Small, oily fish that occurs in large schools in both fresh and salt water. *2. v.* Discovered or located through the use of the olfactory sense. The best method of finding misplaced fish.

Sneck, Garrison (1857-1909) Noted angler and author of *The Superiority of Gray-Winged Fly Patterns in Trout Streams.*

Slip

Spearfishing

Snell, Francis — (1849-1909) Noted angler and author of *An Exhaustive Comparison of Wet Streamers with Unsatisfactory Alternatives, Particularly the Gray- and Buff-Winged Flies.*

Snood, Herman — (1853-1909) Noted angler and author of *The Outstanding Qualities of the Buff-Winged Fly Conclusively Demonstrated Over Wet Streamers and All Gray-Winged Patterns.*

Snook, Gideon — (1855-1934) Noted angler and author of *An Absolute Refutation of Previous Misguided Theories on Flies and Streamers Propounded by Witless Amateurs.* It was Snook who arranged the ill-fated fishing party of April, 1909, for the purpose, as he wrote to a friend in the celebrated letter that played so large a part at his trial, "of finally resolving this question of which lure is preferred by the trout—I suppose I can endure the company of these three button-brains for one day if it means settling this matter once and for all". His later books include *Fly-Tying with Wrists Restrained, Practice-Casting in Confined Spaces,* and *Some Reflections on the Hudson River at Ossining, New York.*

Solitude — The state of being closer to nature than to the nearest flush toilet.

Spanish Mackerel — Medium-sized, Atlantic game fish found as far south as Brazil. They are typically caught by sport fishermen using a hook tied with a strip of bright cloth and baited with a dab of pommade, and by commercial fishermen employing castanets.

Spearfishing — Unique underwater angling method that combines the sports of diving, fishing, and hunting, and, when sharks are sighted, Olympic swimming.

Spin Casting

Angling method employing a fishing rod whose reel is completely enclosed in a cone-shaped housing. Release of the line during the cast is accomplished with a handy push-button operated by the thumb. The relatively trouble-free operation of this simple, automatic rig often makes it an object of vocal disparagement by anglers using more traditional gear, but aficionados of spin-casting outfits take such chaffing and light-hearted abuse in stride and patiently bide their time, for they find that its almost foolproof operation leaves their minds free to concentrate on formulating complex, elegant insults, such as, "Sir, if it is your intention to cover this stream with a web, might I suggest that you hire spiders?" to which the preoccupied fly caster or bait caster, his hands fumbling with five feet of knotted fishing line, is usually only capable of replying, "Oh, yeah? Your mother."

Spinner

Fishing lure consisting of a metal blade with a hole in it which spins freely on a swivel or shaft. The most common spinner shapes are the Willowleaf, the Indiana, the Colorado, and the Idaho, but some new ones have been introduced recently, including the Texas, which is a solid silver disk the size of a hubcap; the New Jersey, which is made of a durable alloy that will not dissolve in waters with a high chemical content; the Canada, or Mapleleaf, which is actually just an Indiana with the words *spinner/spinneur* engraved on it; and the New York, which is basically a flat slab of lead designed to stun fish on the cast.

Spool

Smooth, hard container from which—during daylight hours when fish are biting—there periodically hatches the full-blown snarl or tangle.

Spoon	Type of metal fishing lure popular on backwoods fishing trips since if it is unsuccessful in attracting fish, it may be used to consume the contents of a can of Dinty Moore beef stew.
Squid	*1.* Any of a variety of marine cephalopods often used as bait for salt-water fish. *2.* The sound made when one inadvertently steps on a marine cephalopod left on deck.
Still Fishing	Fishing technique usually characterized by a long stretch of time spent by the angler lying quietly, followed by a shorter period during which he lies noisily.
Strike	The moment when, with a quick rolling or lunging motion, an unseen quarry suddenly takes the hook of an angler fishing the spot you left 10 minutes ago.
Suckers	*1.* Type of bait fish favored by anglers fishing for muskellunge. *2.* Anglers fishing for muskellunge.
Sudden Jerk	Recent purchaser of a beach buggy.
Surf Fishing	Angling for shore-feeding fish, usually from a beach. Although this is generally done in early morning and early evening hours, surf fishermen must be alert to the presence of swimmers—large, semiaquatic creatures who are normally quite playful, but can become extremely ill-tempered when hooked.

T

Tackle	Any fishing gear which, when left on the ground or the bottom of a boat, is capable of suddenly halting an angler's forward progress toward a desired goal.

Tarpon (Trophy Size)

Tag

Identifying label affixed to a member of a given species as an aid in determining its migratory patterns and any significant changes in size, form, and habits. A greater knowledge of the mysterious world of fishing has been gained from a study of individuals marked in this manner, whose sometimes incredible wanderings have been documented with the assistance of a world-wide network of cooperative amateurs. Just to cite one example of their work, a mature stockbroker labeled in 1981 in Rye, New York, with an unobtrusive aluminum badge clipped to his favorite hat was found to have traveled in a single year to Quebec, New Brunswick, Wyoming, Montana, Oregon, Ireland, Austria, and Norway. When finally reencountered in a bar in Tampa, Florida, it turned out that he had not caught a single fish during this entire period. Still, although he had lost 27 pounds, and had a seriously depleted bank account, his eyes were bright, his pulse was strong, and he was about to embark on a fishing expedition to Costa Rica. Perhaps one day through a study of cases like these we will have some clue to the extraordinary impulse that triggers these truly heroic journeys!

Tarpon

In the opinion of many salt-water anglers, this primitive Atlantic species is the ideal game fish. It is only found in places that cost a good deal of money to get to. It is often accompanied by sharks. It is nearly impossible to hook, and once hooked, equally difficult to boat. When boated, it often has enough fight left to injure the fisherman or damage the boat. It has hundreds of large sharp scales, and its flesh is bony and inedible. All it lacks are a foul odor, poisonous spines, and the teeth of a piranha, but presumably crossbreeding will one day rectify these omissions.

Test

Teddy Fish — Notoriously unsuccessful child's plush toy introduced in the Christmas season of 1957 by the ill-starred FarKo company, manufacturers of the Tango Hoop, the Busbee Flying Derby, and the Spittle Ball.

Tent — Cumbersome device composed of fabric and tubing used by fishermen camping in the woods to collect specimens of local insects.

Test — Fishing line is clearly marked with its test—that is, the amount of linear force, in pounds, that can be exerted on it before it breaks. But an angler has enough to do playing the wily adversary at the end of his line without trying to mentally estimate linear stresses, so here is a brief table of the strains exerted by the most commonly hooked casting targets:

HAT: 1 lb.	CAR AERIAL: 15 lbs.
PICNIC LUNCH: 3 lbs.	VINE OR BUSH: 30 lbs.
SHOE (loose): 4 lbs.	SAPLING: 40 lbs.
TWIG: 10 lbs.	SHOE (on foot): 55 lbs.
BOX OF LURES: 12 lbs.	BACK OF JACKET: 175 lbs.

Thumb — Fingerlike appendages of limited mobility found at the ends of the hands. Interestingly, most anglers and fly-tyers have ten of them.

Tippling — Method of night fishing in which each cast is followed by a short pull or tug on a bottle held in the free hand. This can lead to erratic casting, but it has the advantage that after a fairly brief period, fish are caught two at a time.

Traditional — Any fishing technique that was conclusively proven to be impractical, ineffective, unnecessarily costly, or impossibly time-consuming prior to the year 1900. See UNSPORTING.

Trash Fish

Commercial fishermen's slang term for undesirable fish species that were once discarded, but are now actively sought owing to the increase in the demand for seafood and the decline of stocks of more favored fish. In some cases, this wider harvest has necessitated judicious reclassification, and that, in turn, has led to confusion among anglers seeking to identify their catches. Here are a few of the former names, followed by the common designations under which they now appear in fish markets:

GRUNDGE: Sea steak   SEA SCAB: Surf veal
SWINEFISH: Sweetfish   GRUBBER: Brown sole
GUMHEAD: Black snapper   SKULKIN: Gray trout
SLUDGEON: Bay bass   STINKER: Sugar cod
RATFIN: Breadfish

Troll

1. v. To trail a bait behind a moving boat. *2. n.* Legendary creature thought to dwell in secluded spots in rivers from which it lures people to their doom.

Trout

1. Greatly valued food and game fish belonging to the Salmonidae family. *2.* Legendary creature thought to dwell in secluded spots in rivers from which it lures people to their doom.

Tuna

There are a number of varieties of this tasty game fish, but from the sport fisherman's viewpoint, the most important is the giant bluefin, examples of which have been known to exceed 1,000 pounds. It's hard to imagine a fish of that size, but perhaps a few comparisons will help: a half-ton bluefin would be equal to 2,345 sandwiches, 880 gallons of tuna-noodle casserole (standard recipe), or a bowl of tuna fish dip 28 feet in diameter and 7 feet deep!

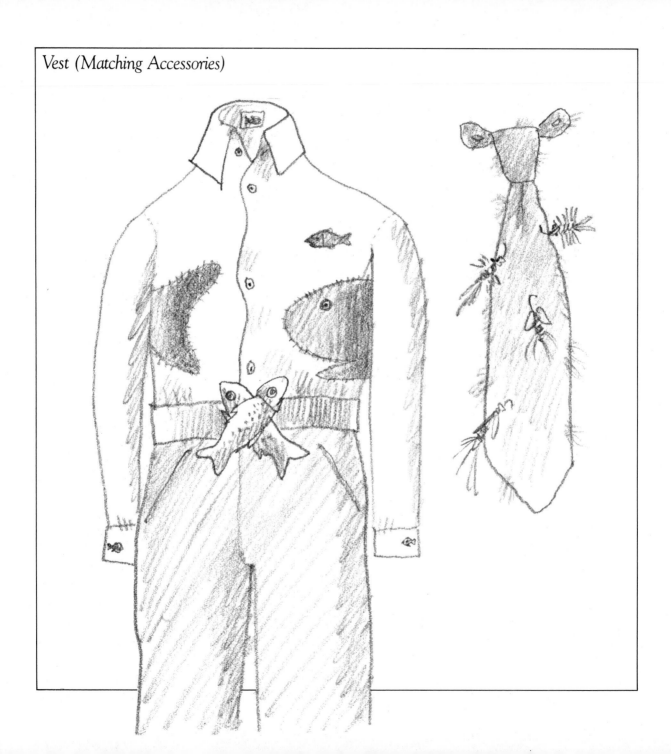

Vest (Matching Accessories)

U

Unsporting
Any fishing technique that has as its chief object the capture of fish rather than the accumulation of fishing equipment.

Utility Boat
All-purpose runabout used by many fishermen. Simple, but more specialized, fishing boats like the johnboat, the surf dory, and the Adirondack guide boat have been around for over a century, but the appearance in the last two decades of highly refined fishing craft—most notably, luxurious bass boats crammed with electronic gear and battery powered accessories and elaborate salt-water fishing boats that are little more than machines for catching fish—has begun to trouble many anglers. It's a matter of personal taste where the line between angling and fish murder lies, but certainly the recently introduced LCT (Landing Craft, Trout) with its insect radar and hydraulic dry- and wet-fly catapults is awfully close to it, and the new and deadly sonar-equipped salmon submarines are well over it.

V

Vest
Ideal fresh-water fishing garment. In its pockets, or pinned or clipped to its fabric, anglers carry a large number of tools, accessories, and gadgets which, while perhaps not absolutely essential, definitely make for more enjoyable angling. There are hundreds of doodads to choose from, but certainly no fly fisherman should be without: a ⅛ normal size matchbook to place next to fish prior to taking a picture; a pocket blowtorch or one of those little battery

powered chain saws for cutting through tough tangles; a set of false-nose-and-eyebrow glasses for a quick disguise during embarrassing mishaps on one's home grounds; a vest-pocket dictionary of epithets, either the classic *Blue Streak Handbook* or *Corwin's 1,001 Streamside Imprecations*; a couple of brush grenades to get your line loose from undergrowth on the opposite bank; a floating, glow-in-the-dark martini shaker; a box of irresistible, but highly laxative Trout Whammies or Bass Blasters to drop in the water by the handful to punish uncooperative fish; a tube of fast-acting but easily removable Warden Baffler wicker glue to cement shut an incriminating creel; and one of the patented "just one more hour" stopwatches that sounds a soothing chime after 21 minutes.

W

Wading The most common means through which a dry-fly fisherman is transformed into a wet-fly fisherman.

Wading Staff Although there are specially designed collapsible metal poles to help anglers keep their balance as they pick their way along slippery rocks in freezing, fast-moving streams, many fishermen prefer to use an old golf club, ski pole, or the handle of a hoe, which not only serve as cheap and reliable substitutes, but also provide a comforting reminder of the constant availability of alternative pastimes.

Wahoo *1.* Salt-water game fish in the mackerel family. *2.* Remark made by an angler who inadvertently sits on a treble-hooked salt-water fishing lure.

Walton (Carrying on the Great Tradition)

Walleye

1. Large member of the perch family with great sport value that is almost always fished for after sundown. *2.* Discoloration of the skin around the eye suffered by walleye fishermen returning home in the dark.

Walton, Isaak

Although it was really his younger asssociate, Charles Cotton, who provided the most enduring practical fishing advice, Walton has had by far the more lasting influence on the art of angling because of the lyrical quality of the prose he used to communicate his passion for fishing. One short example of his poetic discourse will suffice to illustrate the charming style that has earned for *The Compleat Angler* so reliable an audience from generation to generation:

"And when you prepare to spin out a tale, see that your hands do not tremble, nor your eyes dart to and fro, and do not permit your hands to wander hither and thither, but hold the one carelessly over your heart, as if proclaiming an oath, and the other open in front of you, as if to say, 'See, I conceal nothing.' And when you commence to speak, take a great care to do so in a voice neither excessively loud, nor over-much meek, for just as you would not choose to drive a small nail with a sledge, or a bolt with a muffin, so too must you suit the tone to the purpose. And as to the contents of your little story, be guided thus: expand, but do not entirely invent. It is blasphemy and pure folly to usurp the role of the Creator and cause to appear upon the waters some imaginary monster which, perchance, snatched away your pole, made mincemeat of your leggings, mouthed a pony, and bore away your luggage on its back. But if you gently take one of His trout, and in a spirit of generous indulgence cause it to gain a foot or two of extra measure in the course of the telling, you will have the favor of your listeners, for truly the most mammoth specimen of a fish with which men are acquainted is far easier to swallow, as it were, than the tiniest exemplar of one yet unseen."

Water Release

The periodic release of impounded water into downstream areas by the managers of irrigation dams is announced by a series of siren signals. Anglers should be alert for these warnings and leave the stream immediately on hearing

Yard

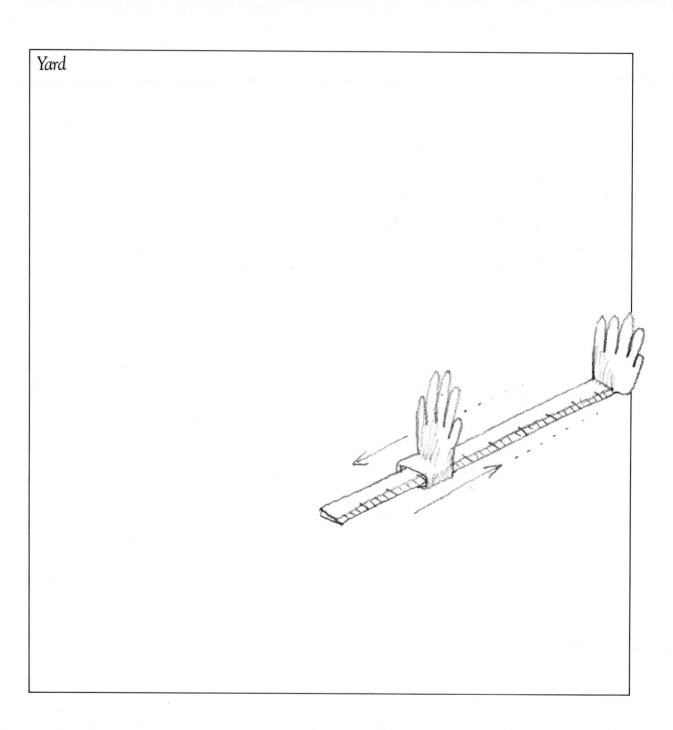

them. Incidentally, devices which mimic the sounds of these sirens are available "under the counter" at tackle shops. Ask for a Hoot 'n' Scoot or a De-Krowder.

Wrist   In an angler, the ache that connects the cuts and sores to the pulls and strains.

X

X.   Symbol for hybrid. A great deal of work has been done crossbreeding fish, notably trout, salmon, and char, to produce new strains and improved fishing. There have been a few successes, like the splake and the tiger trout, but most of the hybrids are short-lived, infertile, or genetically unstable. Somewhat more promising have been the occasional dramatic improvements in fishermen that have appeared due to accidental crosses. In England, for example, the common incidence of intermarriage between Episcopal bishops and female anglers have produced a number of good-natured and totally honest Bishermen. In Florida, there have been reports of a few CompTrollers, the patient, meticulous, and rather dull result of a match between a deep-sea fishing enthusiast and a certified public accountant. And in the Northeast, trained observers have spotted the unmistakable progeny of unions between dedicated anglers and woman attorneys—the methodical, dextrous, and unbelievably devious Anglawyer.

Y

Yard   Unit of measurement. In angling, 17 inches.

Z

Zen Angling

It should come as no surprise that Zen, the noted Japanese Buddhist sect devoted to patient meditation and total concentration, produced not only students devoted to the practice of archery, but also adherents of the equally demanding art of angling. The father of Zen fishing was the monk Takesushi (1514?-1588?), who perfected the use of the bunku, a fishing apparatus of such subtlety that it would put even the greatest contemporary purist to shame. It consisted solely of a rare variety of silkworm specially bred to eat bamboo leaves. In his greatest catch, Takesushi reported having set one of his prize specimens loose on a likely looking bamboo plant along a trout stream outside Kyoto in the spring of 1555. The voracious worm stripped the sapling bare, ending at its top, where in early fall it began to form a cocoon for the winter. The October wind blew the now dead bamboo stalk forward and wedged it in a picturesque rock whose aesthetic qualities and fortuitous position the sharp-eyed sage had spotted months earlier. The wind also knocked the silkworm loose and left it dangling over a quiet pool. Trying to spin its way to freedom, it lengthened the delicate silk filament on which it hung until it came to the surface of the water, whereupon it was seized by a 92-dyami (44-pound) trout, which Takesushi, who had timed his arrival to the minute, pulled from the stream with a delicate motion of the long bamboo pole.

Zen Lying

Spiritual discipline founded by the Zen monk Takesushi.

Zzzzzzz

1. Sound made by patient angler waiting for a bite. *2.* Sound made by insect about to deliver one.

Zzzzzzzzz

BENJAMIN SPOCK, M.D., practiced pediatrics in New York City from 1933 to 1947. Then he became a medical teacher and researcher at the Mayo Clinic, the University of Pittsburgh, and Case Western Reserve University in Cleveland. The author of eleven books, he was a political activist for causes that vitally affect children: disarmament, day care, schooling, housing, and medical care for all. He had two sons, a stepdaughter, and four grandchildren, and was married to Mary Morgan. Dr. Spock died March 15, 1998, at age 94, shortly after completing work on this seventh edition.

Dr. Spock's Baby and Child Care has been translated into thirty-nine languages and has sold fifty million copies worldwide since its first publication in 1946.

STEVEN J. PARKER, M.D., is a pediatrician with special training and interest in the behavioral and developmental issues of children. He is an associate professor of pediatrics at the Boston University School of Medicine and director of the Division of Behavioral and Developmental Pediatrics at Boston Medical Center. He runs a holistic pediatric program for children with special needs and a behavioral-developmental assessment clinic at Boston Medical Center.

Dr. Parker has written more than thirty professional articles and is the author of a book for professionals entitled *Behavioral and Developmental Pediatrics: A Handbook for Primary Care.*

Books by Dr. Benjamin Spock

Baby and Child Care
   (and Steven J. Parker, M.D.)
Feeding Your Baby and Child
   (with Dr. Miriam E. Lowenberg)
Raising Children in a Difficult Time
A Teen-ager's Guide to Life and Love

Published by POCKET BOOKS

DR. SPOCK'S
BABY AND CHILD CARE

7TH EDITION

BENJAMIN SPOCK, M.D., AND STEVEN J. PARKER, M.D.

Illustrations by Sharon Scotland

POCKET BOOKS

New York London Toronto Sydney Tokyo Singapore

POCKET BOOKS, a division of Simon & Schuster Inc.
1230 Avenue of the Americas, New York, NY 10020

Copyright 1945, 1946, © 1957, 1968, 1976, 1985, 1992 by Benjamin Spock, M.D. Copyright renewed © 1973, 1974, 1985, 1996 by Benjamin Spock, M.D. Revised and updated material copyright © 1998 by The Benjamin Spock Trust

ISBN: 0-671-53763-6

First Pocket Books trade paperback printing of this revised edition
June 1998

10   9   8   7   6   5   4   3   2

POCKET and colophon are registered trademarks of
Simon & Schuster Inc.

Illustrations on pages 81, 88, 138, 139, 204, 205, 260, 263, 266, 270, 294, 298, 309, 389, 402, 408, 421, 481, 483, 523, 720, 725, 726, 758, 759, 760, 761, 762, 763, 764 by Sharon Scotland, based on the work of Dorothea Fox, the original illustrator.

Front cover photos: top left, © 1995 Don Mason/The Stock Market; top right, Jade Albert/FPG International LLC; bottom left, © Terry Vine/Tony Stone Images; bottom right, Kozlowski Productions/FPG International LLC. Back cover photos: left, Jade Albert/FPG International LLC; right, © 1995 Don Mason/The Stock Market.

Printed in the U.S.A.

To Mary Morgan

She has done an enormous amount of work in the preparation of this seventh edition of *Baby and Child Care*. She has shown initiative and judgment in visualizing, in tracking down, and in keeping in close touch with the consultants we have needed. She has organized and reorganized the thousands of pages of manuscript that have kept getting out of control. Sometimes, in an editorial emergency, she has pitched in herself to put in the computer a bunch of pages that were crucial to the context at the moment. She is a fast learner and can do anything she sets her mind to.

Meanwhile, she has fed me life-preserving but delicious meals, never failed to remind me to take my many medicines.

She has delighted our constantly enlarging circle of friends with her Arkansas accent and wit as we've moved every six months from San Diego to Maine to Miami to Maine and back to San Diego again.

She drives our RV like a suave truck driver. She has learned from each breakdown in engine, electrical system, or heating system how to make repairs.

I couldn't write or live without her. I am fortunate that she is also my wife.

CONTENTS

BEFORE THE CHILD IS BORN

CARE OF YOUR NEWBORN

BREAST- AND BOTTLE-FEEDING

FEEDING IN THE FIRST YEAR

CARE DURING THE FIRST YEAR

ONE-YEAR-OLDS

TWO-YEAR-OLDS

THREE- TO SIX-YEAR-OLDS

SIX- TO ELEVEN-YEAR-OLDS

ADOLESCENCE

RAISING PHYSICALLY HEALTHY CHILDREN

RAISING MENTALLY HEALTHY CHILDREN

COMMON BEHAVIOR PROBLEMS

COMMON DEVELOPMENTAL CHALLENGES

DEVELOPMENTAL DISABILITIES

SCHOOL AND LEARNING PROBLEMS

DAY CARE, BABY-SITTERS, AND OUT-OF-HOME ISSUES

NEW ISSUES: PREPARING FOR THE TWENTY-FIRST CENTURY

DIFFERENT FAMILY CONSTELLATIONS

FAMILY STRESSES AND CRISES

MEDICAL ISSUES

ACKNOWLEDGMENTS

From Dr. Spock:

My special thanks goes to Nancy Sturdee, my assistant, in Camden, Maine, who kept this book together in her head as well as in the computer. She organized the whole manuscript and coordinated sending material to various people, including the publisher. She even got various family members to pitch in over the holidays in order to meet the deadline. Her commitment and dedication are unmatched except by her devotion and love for me. Thank you, Nancy.

Our San Diego pediatrician and child analysis friends gave us more than just work on the book. Their care for me during our move to La Jolla was one of tender compassion. Cal Calarusso, Bob and Phyllis Tyson, Dick Buchta, and Marty Stein all came to work on the book, gave their ideas, and encouraged and inspired me. I now call La Jolla my home with these friends whom I love and who have made me feel at home in California.

I want to thank my editor Jane Cavolina, at Pocket Books, who has given so much attention to the seventh edition of *Baby and Child Care.* I won her in a raffle, and I've always been grateful.

My thanks for all our legal work go to Andy Boose and Paul Herman, who did our contracts and agreements with love and support.

My thanks go to Bob Lescher, my agent, who has seen me through many of the seven editions of *Baby and Child Care.* Bob has been a tremendous supporter of all my work.

Extra thanks go to those contributors and consultants who gave much of their time to see that this seventh edition was more fully expanded. Charles Attwood worked on diet along with Neal Barnard. Ted Croll, our pediatric dentist friend, shared with us his ideas for dental hygiene care for children. Ellen Freedman worked on preventing injuries,

Bob Schwebel gave us a very exciting new look at alcohol and other drugs. Bob Vinci supplied us with material on first aid. Carol Kaplan and Harriet Leve gave a broader and more understanding look at gay and lesbian parents. Laura Levy Jana, an up-and-coming new pediatrician from Cleveland, gave us her firsthand experience with her new baby, Bethany. She found time for both revising *Baby and Child Care* and parenting Bethany. Henry Heimlich gave us great contributions on our first aid section. Suzanne Havala contributed to the diet section, Alisha Hardee helped with a list of clothing and supplies, Martin Greenberg contributed work on fathering, and Linda Grant consulted on adolescence. We are very grateful to Mary Caffery for her contribution to the AIDS-HIV section.

We were very fortunate to have Norma Nero back working with us after years apart. And also Miyun Park who was always so gracious and generous with her time. We thank Joanna Sturdee for her extra time in our office, and Lynda Long who came from Saint Thomas to take care of me.

Also my thanks to John Kennell, my friend and colleague, for his many contributions to the care and feeding chapters; Reed Mangels for contributions on diet; Dale Martin, my dermatologist; Meredith McCarty for her input on diet; Janice Nero and Laura Nottie for clothing and equipment suggestions; Steve Seligman for emotional development issues; Sam Spector for illness and medical issues; and I have special envy and thanks for our computer expert, Ellen Levy, who took the disks and did miracles with them to make them readable and workable.

Our thanks go to the staff at Pocket Books for over fifty years of continuous support—Jane Cavolina, our editor; Jill Parsons, our copyeditor; Gina Centrello, president and publisher; Donna O'Neill, executive managing editor; Liz Hartman, director of publicity, and Theresa Zazycki, our publicist; Stephen Llano, production editor; and Brett Freese and Cindy Ratzlaff. Much thanks to our longtime illustrator Dorothea Fox and also to our new illustrator, Sharon Scotland, whose work was so similar that we knew it came from the same spirit. Our photographer and friend Mark Wallack gave us his love as well as his work. For this, Mark, I thank you and love you.

Special Acknowledgment to Martin Stein, M.D.

I have a special acknowledgment for Marty Stein, a pediatrician from San Diego, because of his help with the completion of this seventh edition of *Baby and Child Care.* Marty has been practicing and teaching pediatrics at the University of California at San Diego School of Medicine since 1975. His experience in caring for both well and sick children has been very valuable.

When I first entered Marty's office, I found an examining table much like the one I had built when I was first in practice in the 1930s in New York City. I built steps leading up to a trapdoor for the child to open and emerge on top of the examining table. I knew Marty and I were the same kind of baby doctor once I saw this same kind of examining table in his office.

His careful contribution and advice gave this edition its finishing touches. He reread all of the work, edited, and made meaningful suggestions and contributions. We worked together with ease and enjoyment. I have the deepest respect, appreciation, and admiration for him.

From Dr. Parker:

I'd like to express my gratitude to some of the many people who have supported and encouraged me throughout this challenging enterprise. First, I owe so much to my wife Karen Kemper Parker, whose happy combination of love and uncanny psychological insight always sustained, informed, and supported me during this project when I needed it most. To my parents, Hyman and Ann Parker, for their wonderful parenting and love throughout my life. They taught me from the earliest years that there was no more worthwhile way to spend a life than by caring for children. To my brother, Philip Parker, who is simply the nicest person I know, and the rest of his family—Fran, Bekah, and Daniel. To T. Berry Brazelton with whom I studied as a fellow and who remains a trusted friend and cherished mentor, for his brilliant insights, his thoughtfulness and his infectious joie de vivre. To Barry Zuckerman, boss and friend for over a decade, who has taught me how to creatively and effectively advocate for the needs of disadvantaged children and has given my career a boost at various critical junctures. To the inspiring staff in the Division of Behavioral and Developmental Pediatrics at Boston Medical Center, valued colleagues on whom I rely for new insights into children, for advice on where the revisions should be made, and who collectively make my work environment such a joy: Margot Kaplan Sanoff, Betsy Groves, Marilyn Augustyn, Tracy Magee, Maria Trozzi, Josh Greenberg, Amy Bamforth, Jean Zotter, Remetrious Pena, Sue O'Brien, Naomi Honigsberg, Adrienne Nunley, Magarita Pagan, Genevieve Theodat, and Cheri Craft. To Linda Grant, Bob Vinci (the goombah), and Ellen Friedman, who made major contributions to the revisions of the sections concerning the adolescent, emergency care, and injury prevention, respectively, and whose friendship and talent are much appreciated and much admired. To Jill Nellis, Donna Davenport, Jeanne McCarthy, and Margaret Lavoye, who provided invaluable and timely administrative help. To Bill Harris, whose unstinting and tenacious advocacy for children is a model of a life well spent and who graciously provided me with a wonderful environment in which to work on the book during my sabbatical. A more congenial, supportive environment never existed for a writer, and I'm grateful to the rest of the Trowbridge crew— Robie Harris, a marvelous author of children's books; Boardy Lloyd; Marie Baratta; and Dee Dee Sheedy—for the grace, generosity, and good humor with which they welcomed me into their space. To Libby Keller, John Bowers, and Bob Stacks, with whom I was in private practice for five years and who served as superb role models of how to be a good primary care doc. To Richard Ronder and the rest of Team Columbus for giving me the opportunity to appreciate the needs of children with developmental disabilities. To Bob Lescher, our agent, who offered sage counsel when I needed it most and for whose integrity and talent I have the utmost respect. To Michael Rothenberg, who could not have been nicer or more supportive and helpful to me throughout this process. Most of all, thanks to all of the children and families I've had the privilege of caring for during my career. It is an honor to be a part of your lives. Finally, thank you, Ben Spock, for having the confidence and faith to allow me the privilege of helping you revise your masterpiece.

A LETTER TO THE READER

Most of you have a doctor or nurse practitioner you can consult. They know your child, and therefore they are in the best position to advise you wisely. By glancing at a rash or asking a couple of questions over the telephone, the doctor or nurse practitioner may find a solution to a problem that may not be found by consulting a book. This book is not meant to be used for diagnosis or treatment; it's only meant to give you a general understanding of children, their troubles, and their needs. It is true that certain sections of the book offer emergency advice for those parents who are out of reach of a doctor or nurse practitioner, because it is better for these parents to have general advice than no advice at all. However, the advice of a doctor or nurse practitioner should always be preferred if available.

The most important thing I have to say is that you should not take too literally what is said in this book. Every child is different, every parent is different, every illness or behavior problem is somewhat different from every other. All I can do is describe the most common developments and problems in the most general terms. Remember that you are more familiar with your child's temperament and patterns than I could ever be.

Warning: Salesmen of children's encyclopedias, sets of books on child care, nursery furniture, children's clothing, and equipment may claim that Dr. Spock is intimately connected with their enterprises in some way, or at least endorses their products. All such claims are fraudulent and should be disregarded. I have no connection with any such enterprises and never endorse a commercial product or service. I write a regular column for *Parenting* magazine, and I have authored or co-authored several separate books, but they are sold only through regular bookstores and paperback outlets, never door-to-door.

ABOUT THIS SEVENTH EDITION OF
DR. SPOCK'S BABY AND CHILD CARE

New Material and Emphases

An entire chapter has been given to the ever-increasing problems of divorce, single-parent families, and the difficulties of the stepparent relationship. There are expanded sections on breast-feeding, the working mother, injury prevention, and for the first time, pediatric dental health. To encourage healthier diets, new information on nutrition in infants and children has been added. The section on first aid and adolescents has been updated. New sections, such as the ones on HIV-AIDS, open adoption, gay and lesbian families, alcohol and other drugs, computer literacy, and the Internet, focus on current critical concerns among parents. Some diseases have been de-emphasized because they are no longer prevalent, and a few others have been added. (There has never been room for more than the most common of the hundreds of diseases that exist.) All factual material in the book has been updated. A glossary of medical terms has been added to assist parents in the health care of their children.

Raising Children in a Troubled Society

American society in the 1990s is extraordinarily stressful. Normal family tensions are heightened in many ways: Our society is excessively competitive and materialistic; many working parents find less satisfaction and pleasure at their jobs while the good day care they depend on becomes harder to find; there is less spiritual and moral direction compared to the past; the traditional supports of the extended family and community are breaking up; and a growing number of people are concerned about the deterioration of the environment and international relations. These and other problems are discussed more fully in the Afterword: A Better World for Our Children.

I believe that there are two changes needed to relieve these tensions and move toward a more stable society. The first is to raise our children with different, more positive ideals. Children raised with strong values beyond their own needs—cooperation, kindness, honesty, tolerance of diversity—will grow up to help others, strengthen human relations, and bring about world security. Living by these values will bring far greater pride and fulfillment than the superficial success of a high-paying position or a new luxury car.

The second change is for us to reclaim our government from the influence of giant corporate interests that care little for human individuals, the environment, or world peace, and whose only aim is maximal profit. We must become much more politically active, so that our government will serve the needs of all citizens.

To find out more about the local, state, and national groups who are working on the problems that concern you the most, you can write to The Children's Defense Fund, 25 E Street NW, Washington, DC 20001, and mark your envelope "Attention: Field Division." They have worked with Congress for over twenty years on the programs most needed by children and families.

The Question of Permissiveness

Though I've been accused of permissiveness, I don't consider myself permissive at all, and **all** the people who've used this book and spoken to me about it feel the same way. The people who call me permissive all admit that they haven't read the book and wouldn't use it.

The accusation came for the first time in 1968—twenty-two years after the book came out—from a prominent clergyman who objected strongly to my opposition to the war in Vietnam. He said that my advice to parents to give "instant gratification" to their babies and children was what

ABOUT THIS SEVENTH EDITION

made these babies grow up to be irresponsible, undisciplined, unpatriotic young adults who opposed their country's war in Vietnam.

There is no instant gratification in this book. I've always advised parents to respect their children but to remember to ask for respect for themselves, to give firm, clear leadership, and to ask for cooperation and politeness.

DR. SPOCK'S

BABY AND CHILD CARE

THE PARENTS' PART

Trust Yourself

1. You know more than you think you do. Soon you're going to have a baby. Maybe you have one already. You're happy and excited, but if you haven't had much experience, you wonder whether you are going to know how to do a good job. Lately you have been listening more carefully to your friends and relatives when they talk about bringing up a child. You've begun to read articles by "experts" in the magazines and newspapers. After the baby is born, the doctors and nurses will begin to give you instructions too. Sometimes it sounds like a very complicated business. You find out all the vitamins a baby needs and all the immunizations. One mother tells you she couldn't live without disposable diapers; another swears by cloth diapers. You hear that a baby is easily spoiled by being picked up too much, but also that a baby should be held as much as possible. Some say that fairy tales make children nervous, others that fairy tales are a wholesome outlet for children's fears.

Don't take too seriously all that the neighbors say. Don't be overawed by what the experts say. Don't be afraid to trust your own common sense. Bringing up your child won't be a complicated job if you take it easy, trust your own instincts, and share concerns with your friends, family, and doctor or nurse practitioner. We know for a fact that the natural loving care that kindly parents give their children is a hundred times more important than their knowing how to

1

make a diaper fit tight or just when to introduce solid foods. Every time you pick your baby up—even if you do it a little awkwardly at first—every time you change her, bathe her, feed her, smile at her, she's getting the feeling that she belongs to you and that you belong to her. Nobody else in the world, no matter how skillful, can give that to her.

It may surprise you to hear that the more people have studied different methods of bringing up children, the more they have come to the conclusion that what good mothers and fathers instinctively feel like doing for their babies is usually best after all. All parents do their best job when they have a natural, easy confidence in themselves. Better to make a few mistakes from being natural than to try to do everything letter-perfect out of a feeling of worry.

2. How you learn to be a parent. Fathers and mothers don't really find out how to care for and manage children from books and lectures, though these may have value in answering specific questions and doubts. They learned the basics from the way they themselves were brought up while they were children. That's what they were always practicing when they "played house" and cared for their dolls. If a child is raised in an easygoing way, then he is likely to be the same kind of parent. Likewise, a child who is raised by strict parents is likely to become a relatively strict parent himself. We all end up at least somewhat like our parents, especially in the way we deal with our children, though most of us will want to change some aspects of how we were brought up. To some of you this is a happy prospect; others may find it an alarming thought. In any event, *every* parent has had the experience—and you will too, if you haven't yet—of, when talking to their child, hearing the voice coming from their lips to be that of their mother or father, with exactly the same tone and exactly the same words!

As you embark upon parenthood, you might think about just how your parents raised you and, with the perspective of an adult, what you now see as positive and constructive. You might also consider the ways they raised you that you absolutely don't want to repeat with your child. Having a child offers you the wonderful opportunity to think about what made you the kind of person you are today and what kind of parent you would like to be. It is just that kind of insight that will help you to understand and trust your own instincts and become a more confident parent.

You'll find that you will learn about how to be a parent gradually, through the experience of caring for your children. It's taking care of your baby, finding out that you can feed, change, bathe, and burp successfully, and that your baby responds contentedly to your ministrations that will give you confidence and feelings of familiarity and love. These are then the foundation of a solid, trusting relationship with your child. But don't expect to feel that way right off the bat.

All parents expect to influence their children, but many are surprised to find that it's a two-way street and that they learn an enormous amount about themselves and about the world from their parenting and from their children. You may find, as many others have, that being a parent becomes the most important step in your own growth and maturation as a person.

Parents Are Human

3. Parents have needs too. Books about child care, including this one, put so much emphasis on the *child's* needs—for love, for understanding, for patience, for consistency, for firmness, for protection, for comradeship—that parents sometimes feel physically and emotionally exhausted just from *reading* about what is expected of them. They get the impression that they are meant to have no needs or life of their own apart from their children. And they can't help feeling that any book that seems to be standing up for children all the time is going to be critical of parents when anything goes wrong.

To really be fair, this book should have an equal number of pages about the genuine needs of parents: their frustrations (both inside and outside the home), how tired they get, the human need to hear, at least once in a while, that they are doing a good job. There is an enormous amount of hard work that goes along with child care: preparing the proper diet, washing clothes, changing diapers, cleaning up messes, stopping fights and drying tears, listening to stories that are hard to understand, joining in games and reading books that aren't very exciting to an adult, trudging around zoos and museums, responding to pleas for help with homework, being slowed down in housework and yard work by eager helpers, going to parent-teacher association meetings on evenings when you are tired, and so on.

Additionally, children's needs always seem to come before the parents'. They account for a good part of the family budget, from the high rent or mortgage on a large enough house to the shoes that wear out or are outgrown in no time at all. Children keep parents from parties, trips, theaters, meetings, games, friends. Spontaneity is a long-lost friend and the fact that you still prefer having children, wouldn't trade places with a childless couple for anything, doesn't alter the fact that you miss your freedom.

The fact is that child rearing is a long, hard job, the rewards are not always immediately obvious, the work is often undervalued, and parents are just as human and almost as vulnerable as their children.

Of course, parents don't have children because they want to be martyrs. They have them because they love children and want to raise their very own, especially when they remember being loved so much by their own parents when they were little. Taking care of their children, seeing them grow and develop into fine people, gives most parents—despite the hard work—their greatest satisfaction in life. It is a creative and generative act on every level. Pride in other worldly accomplishments usually pales in comparison.

4. Needless self-sacrifice and excessive preoccupation. Many conscientious young people facing the new responsibility of parenthood feel that they are being called on to give up all their freedom and all their former pleasures, not as a matter of practicality, but almost as a matter of principle. Others just get obsessed. They forget their hobbies and interests. Even if they do occasionally sneak off, they feel too guilty to get full enjoyment. They come to bore their friends and each other. In the long run, they chafe at the imprisonment and can't help unconsciously resenting the baby.

I think that the temptation to become totally absorbed in

the baby should be resisted and particular attention paid to sustaining a loving intimate relationship with your partner. After you have made all the necessary sacrifices of time and effort to your children, carve out some quality time with your partner. Remember to look at each other, smile at each other, and express the love you feel. Make an effort to find enough privacy—and energy—to continue your sexual relationship. Remember that a close, loving relationship between parents is the most powerful way children learn about how to be intimate with another person, a lesson that your child is likely to carry into his or her adult relationships. So one of the best things you can do for your child, as well as for yourself, is to work to let your children deepen, not inhibit, your relationship with your partner.

What Are Your Aims in Raising a Child?

5. Raising children is more and more puzzling for many parents because we've lost a lot of our old-fashioned convictions about what kind of morals, ambitions, and character we want them to have. We are uncertain and worried about what kind of world awaits them as adults. The pace of social change is almost overwhelming. We can barely keep up with the latest dangers and opportunities for our children's well-being: drugs, violence, the information superhighway . . . the list seems endless.

In an uncertain world, with more uncertainty to come, we do well to ask ourselves just what our goals are in raising our children. Is doing well in school our most important objective for them? Is the ability to sustain intimate human relationships more important? Do we want them to be individualistic with a competitive edge so they can succeed in a dog-eat-dog society? Or do we want them to learn to cooperate and sometimes to renounce their own desires for the good of others? If the ultimate goal of raising children is the fashioning of a fully formed adult, then just what kind of person do we want that adult to be in order to be a happy and productive member of society?

These questions cut to the heart of much of raising children. Parenting is about choices. In order to decide what's best for your child, you will always be well served to

5

step back and think about these tough questions before making a decision. So many parents get totally caught up in the difficult day-to-day issues of *how* they are parenting that they lose perspective about *why* they are parenting in the first place. I hope that raising your children will help you to understand your own ideas about what's *really* important to you in life and that this insight will guide the choices you make about raising your child.

6. Other times and other countries. Parents' aspirations for their children have always been influenced by the culture and times in which they live. In the past it was almost universally assumed that humanity's main function in the world—aside from survival—was to serve God by carrying out His purposes, as revealed by religion. Much the same was true in America during the Colonial period. Parents back then did not have the relatively modern notion that a goal of life might be fulfillment or happiness, and children were constantly exhorted to overcome their base natures in order to grow up to be pleasing in God's eyes.

In certain countries, such as China and Israel, it has been believed that serving the country is most important. With this idea in mind, parents, religious leaders, and teachers in those countries usually agree about what virtues are to be encouraged in children: lawfulness, cooperativeness, studiousness, dedication to the specific principles of the nation. In other parts of the world, it has been assumed that children are born and raised to serve the aims of the extended family or clan, and should prepare themselves for jobs important to the family. Children must revere and defer to their elders. They may even be forced to marry a stranger chosen by their parents for the purpose of advancing the family's welfare. In a way, this simplifies child rearing for the parents because they all agree with what child rearing means. This is in contrast to America where each family has to decide for itself what its aims are, whether they are primarily materialistic or spiritual, whether religion is to play an important role or whether a certain psychological theory is the determinant.

When parents have a kind of moral certainty about the goals of raising children, they usually don't have to keep wondering and worrying about whether they are doing the right thing. It all follows from the expectations of the culture. Everybody agrees with those expectations and adheres to the same child-rearing practices. It's all crystal clear. Young parents learn about the aims and methods for rearing their children from ancient traditions and from having the extended family nearby to advise and help.

But this security is often lacking in the present day. In the United States, for example, very few children are raised to believe that their principal destiny is to serve their family, their country, or their God. Generally children are given the feeling that they can set their own aims and occupations in life, according to their inclinations. We are raising them to be rugged individualists, with success often measured in material terms. An English anthropologist said that whereas in most countries children are taught to look up to their parents as rather distinguished superior people, in the United States parents will say to their child, "If you don't do better than I've done, you're a failure."

The support from a close extended family is likewise often absent. Our ancestors left their homelands because they were impatient with old ways and had the courage to face the unknown. Ever since, their descendants have been restlessly moving from place to place in search of opportunity, often raising their children hundreds or thousands of miles away from any relatives.

For this reason, many parents have turned to professional advisers, books like this one, and psychological theories to get the help they need. The problem is that psychological concepts and advice about child rearing don't help much unless they are backed up by a sense of what's right and proper—in other words by a firm foundation of core values.

7. We are disillusioned. In my sixty years as a pediatrician, I have witnessed marvelous changes in our society. Modern medicine can perform wonders, and children have never been healthier. Technology has provided all of us with comforts that, only a few decades ago, even the very rich couldn't have dreamed of. We are much more aware of what is happening around the world—the global village has become a reality. And there is the promise of much more to come.

At the same time I have witnessed an increasing tendency in

literature, plays, and movies to belittle the kindly and spiritual aspects of humanity and to focus on its cruder side. Manners in social life have been coarsened and long-held religious beliefs eroded. The mass media cater to children's lowest tastes. And the gap between rich and poor—between the haves and the have-nots—in our society has widened.

In many ways we have lost our faith in the meaning of life and our confidence to understand our world and our society. My point here is that you are raising your children in the context of very confusing and rapidly changing times at the end of the twentieth and beginning of the twenty-first century. Your goals and aspirations for your child are going to be greatly influenced by these times and the prevailing ideals and beliefs. A central core of values and beliefs—ones that remain unshaken by tumultuous social changes—will serve as your best compass as you chart a course for your family. I hope that, at least once in a while, after yet another hectic day, you will sit back and reflect on where you are going and whether your day-to-day interactions with your children reflect your true values and dreams for their future.

Why Feelings Are Different for Different Children

8. Everybody knows that children are born with quite different temperaments. Some by nature seem active and outgoing, others are quiet and shy. Some are easy to raise and others just plain difficult. Like it or not, you can't order the kind of child you want, you have to take what you get.

What happens if the child you've got differs from the kind of child you thought you wanted? In my experience, this can be a major source of heartache between parent and child if you aren't aware of it. Of course, parents have well-formed personalities, too, which they can't change overnight. One gentle couple might be ideally suited to raise a boy with a sensitive nature but may not be nearly so ready for an energetic, assertive boy whom they find baffling and challenging, no matter how much they love him. Another couple may handle a spunky son with ease and joy but be quite disappointed with a quiet, thoughtful one.

It doesn't really matter that the parents are intelligent

people who well know that they can't order the kind of child they wanted most. Being human, they have irrational expectations and can't help feeling let down.

Additionally, as children become a little older they may remind us, consciously or unconsciously, of a brother, sister, father, or mother who made life hard for us at times. A daughter may have traits like her mother's younger sister, who used to be always in her hair, and yet the mother may have no conscious realization that this is the cause of a lot of her irritation. A father may be excessively bothered by timidity in his young son and never connect it with the fact that he himself had a terrible time overcoming his shyness as a child.

Some people call this *goodness of fit*—that is, how well your expectations, goals, hopes, dreams, and aspirations for your children fit with the talents and temperament they were born with. It is this fit that will play a significant role in determining how well things go for you and your children as you go about the business of raising them.

In my experience it is goodness-of-fit issues that seem to cause the most discipline and other problems for parents. If, for example, you are chronically disappointed that your child is not a math whiz or well coordinated, and if you spend a significant amount of time trying to make him what he is not (and does not have the inborn talent to be), then I can guarantee trouble is brewing—both for you and your child. If, on the other hand, you can learn to accept and love your child for who he really is (and not what you would like him to be) then your life together is likely to be a lot smoother.

Are Parents Meant to Love All Their Children Equally?

9. This question worries a lot of conscientious parents because they suspect that in some ways they don't. They reproach themselves because they have different feelings about each of their children. I think they are expecting the impossible of themselves.

Good parents love their children equally in the sense that they are devoted to each one, want the best for all of them, and will make any necessary sacrifices to achieve this. But since all children are quite different, no parent can feel just the same about any two of them. It's human and normal and inevitable that we should feel quite differently about each of our children, that we should be impatient with certain characteristics in some of them and proud of others.

I think that it is the acceptance and understanding of these different feelings, rather than feeling guilty about them, that will allow you to treat all of your children with the love and special attention each one needs.

The Father as Parent

10. A father's capability and responsibility. Men, especially the husbands of women with outside jobs, have been participating increasingly in all aspects of home and child care. There is no reason why fathers shouldn't be able to do these jobs as well as mothers, and contribute equally to the children's security and development. But the benefit may be lost if this work is done as a favor to the wife, since that implies that raising the child is not really the father's work but that he's merely being extraordinarily generous.

There are increasing numbers of fathers married to women with full-time out-of-home jobs, and these men assume the major share of care for the children and home while their children are small. At its best, parenting occurs in the spirit of equal partnership.

I think that a father with a full-time job, even if the mother is staying at home, will do best by his children, his wife, and himself if he takes on half or more of the management of the children (and also participates in the housework) when he is home from work and on weekends. The mother's leadership and patience will probably have worn thin by the end of the day—as would the father's if he were alone with the children all day! On the other hand, some mothers find it difficult to allow fathers to assume control, perhaps because they are worried that if they are not the "official" family nurturer, then what exactly is their role in life? Children will profit from experiencing a variety of styles of leadership and control by both parents—styles that neither exclude nor demean, but enrich and complement the other.

In child care, fathers can certainly give bottles, feed solid foods, change diapers (for too long fathers have gotten away with the clever ruse that they lacked the intelligence, manual dexterity, and visual-motor skills to be capable of changing a smelly diaper), select clothes, wipe away tears, blow noses, bathe, put to bed, read stories, fix toys, break up quarrels, help with questions about homework, explain rules, and assign duties. Fathers can participate in the whole gamut of domestic work: shopping, food preparation, cooking and serving, dishwashing, bed making, housecleaning, and laundry. My mother taught me these jobs beginning when I was around age seven.

When a father does his share of the work at home as a matter of course, he does much more than simply lighten his wife's work load and give her companionship. It shows that he believes this work is crucial to the welfare of the family, that it calls for judgment and skill, and that it's his responsibility as much as hers when he is at home. This is what sons and daughters need to see in action if they are to grow up with equal respect for the abilities and roles of men and women.

Pay and prestige have traditionally been men's prime values in twentieth-century America. From my point of view, this emphasis has played a major role in misleading many men into excessive competitiveness, excessive materialism, frequent neglect of relationships with wives and children, neglect of friendships, neglect of community relationships and of cultural interests, and stress-related health problems. I don't mean to deny that a sufficient income is absolutely essential—for the two-parent family and even more important for the single-parent family. What I am concerned about is that our obsession with getting ahead at work often puts an intolerable strain on family life and makes many women as well as men view the outside job as their central responsibility in life.

I believe that both boys and girls should be raised with a deep conviction that the family is the richest and most enduring source of satisfaction in life. Then women could feel less pressure to accept men's traditional values, and men, freed from their narrow obsession with work and status, could begin to practice women's many skills and try to adopt their values. It will be a great day when fathers and mothers consider the care of their children as important to them as their jobs and careers, and when all career decisions are balanced with careful consideration of their effect on family life.

You know, I've talked to a lot of parents. As their children became adults and moved out of the home, not one mother or father has ever said to me that they regretted spending too much time with their families. But I can't tell you how many have regretted that they didn't carve out more time to spend with their families when they had the chance.

Quality Time

11. When both parents, or single parents, have outside jobs, they usually try to arrange work schedules that will give them maximum time with their young children. In two-parent families, the attention of one parent at a time can be quite satisfying to children. Preschool children can be regularly allowed to stay up late in the evenings if it is possible for them to regularly sleep late in the mornings or have a nap at day care. The exact number of hours of companionship is less important than the quality or spirit of the time spent together, and this is what's behind the expression "quality time."

From a practical point of view, "quality time" implies interactions that are close, nurturing, and lovingly responsive. Quality time can occur during driving time, mealtimes, any and all routine times together. Trips to the supermarket or department store can always be enhanced with time for talking and listening and teaching. So quality time does not imply doing anything out of the ordinary. It is the accumulated day-to-day interactions, not dramatic trips to the circus, that have the most profound effect on the child's development.

The idea of quality time in itself is fine. But I'm concerned that a few conscientious, hardworking parents take it as an obligation to be talking, playing, reading with their children, long after patience and enjoyment have run out. Parents who regularly ignore their own needs and wishes in order to provide quality time for their children may come to resent the sacrifice, and then the spirit of friendliness and responsiveness dissipates. And a child who senses that he can make

12

his parent give him more time than the parent feels like giving is encouraged to become pesky and demanding.

I have another concern about the expression "quality time." Some parents misinterpret the phrase to mean that it really doesn't matter how much time they spend with their children, as long as the time they do spend is jam-packed with "quality." But *quantity* of time is also important—time spent together in unexciting tasks with mundane interactions. Children need to simply be around their parents, watching them in action, learning from their day-to-day example, and knowing they are an important part of their lives. The trick is to find the right balance: to spend as much time as possible with your children, but not at the expense of fulfilling some of your own personal needs.

Special Time

12. I like the concept of "special time" as a way to make sure there is at least some quality time every day. Special time is a brief period—five to fifteen minutes is usually sufficient—that you set aside every day to spend with each child individually. What's "special" about special time is not what you actually do with your child—you can do a puzzle, take a trip to the store, or just talk together. What's special is that it is your personal, exclusive time together, when your child gets your undivided attention. Special time shouldn't be taken away as a punishment; it's earned simply by virtue of being your child and being loved. It acknowledges the specialness of that child to you, even if you can't always spend time together in the daily hustle and bustle.

The Temptation to Spoil

13. Working parents may find that because they are starved for their child's company, and perhaps because they feel guilty about seeing her so little, they are inclined to shower her with presents and treats, bow to all her wishes regardless of their own, and generally let her get away with murder. When a child finds that her parents are appeasers, it doesn't satisfy her—it's apt to make her greedy.

It's fine for working parents to show their child as much

agreeableness and affection as comes naturally, but they should also feel free to stop when they're tired, to consider their own desires, avoid giving presents daily, spend only what money is sensible, expect reasonable politeness and consideration from their children—in other words, act like self-confident, all-day parents. The child will not only turn out better but will enjoy their company more.

Parental Sexual Relations After Delivery

14. The process of pregnancy, labor, and delivery may interfere (for a time) with many parents' sexual relations. Near the end of pregnancy, intercourse may become uncomfortable or at least physically challenging. Following delivery there is a normal period of time of discomfort, readjustment of the body to its pre-pregnancy state, hormonal shifts, and the hard work, sleep deprivation, and fatigue of caring for a newborn. Sex may be crowded out for days, weeks, even months.

This can also be a difficult time for a man's libido. He may be tired. For some men the shift in perspective of their partner from lover to mother is difficult to reconcile with sexual feelings. All manner of deep emotional contradictions may arise. Some men, for example, have been raised with the "Madonna or whore complex." It's hard for them to reconcile that a woman could be both a mother and a lover; the feelings may seem mutually incompatible (just as some of us can't even begin to picture our parents as sexual beings, even though we are the proof incarnate of that sexuality).

If you recognize that sexual intercourse may be slow in returning, you won't be so alarmed at its temporary absence. And a cessation of sexual intercourse should not mean that you cease all sexual relations. Take time for cuddling, hugging, kissing, a romantic word, an appreciative glance, an unexpected gift of flowers.

Balancing parenthood with the other aspects of your life is one of the skills of successful parenting and successful marriage. Almost all parents get sexually back on track after a while. What makes the biggest difference is that, in the tumult of caring for a new baby, they don't lose sight of how much they love and care for each other, and that they make a conscious effort to express that love by word and by touch. Suggested activities could be reading poetry aloud to each other, going for a walk together (without the baby), exchanging warm oil massages, meditating together, having a quiet meal together, and sharing lots of hugs and kisses.

Parents as Companions

15. Children need friendly, accepting parents. Boys and girls need chances to be around their parents, to be enjoyed by them, and to do things with them. Unfortunately, working parents are apt to come home wanting most of all to relax after a long day. If they understand how valuable their friendliness is, they will feel more like making a reasonable effort to at least greet the children, answer questions, and show an interest in anything they want to share. I say **reasonable** because I don't think the conscientious father or mother should force himself or herself beyond his or her endurance. Better to chat for fifteen minutes enjoyably and then say, "Now I'm going to read my paper," than to spend an hour grumpily playing.

The child with only one parent, temporarily or permanently, is discussed in Sections 959–965.

The parents' part in discipline is discussed in Sections 644–662.

There's more on the parents' relations with son and daughter in Sections 426–432.

16. A boy needs a friendly father. Sometimes a father is so eager to have his son turn out perfect that it gets in the way of their having a good time together. The man who is eager for his son to become an athlete may take him out at an early age to play catch. Naturally, every throw, every catch, has its faults. If the father is constantly criticizing, even in a friendly tone, the boy becomes uncomfortable inside. It isn't any fun. Also, it gives him the feeling of being no good, in his father's eyes and in his own. A boy comes around to an interest in sports in good time if he's naturally self-confident and outgoing. Feeling approved of by his father and mother helps him more than being coached by him. A game of catch is fine if it's the son's idea and if it's for fun.

A boy doesn't grow spiritually to be a man just because he's born with a male body. The thing that makes him feel and act like a man is being able to pattern himself after men and older boys with whom he feels friendly. He can't pattern himself after a person unless he feels that this person likes him and approves of him. If a father is always impatient or irritated with him, the boy is likely to feel uncomfortable not only when he's around his father but when he's around other men.

So a father who wants to help his son grow up comfortable about being a man shouldn't jump on him when he cries, scorn him when he's playing games with girls, or force him to practice athletics. He should enjoy him when he's around, give him the feeling he's a chip off the old block, share a secret with him, take him alone on excursions sometimes.

17. A girl needs a friendly father, too. A friendly father plays a different but equally important part in the development of a girl. She only patterns herself after him to a limited degree, but she gains confidence in herself as a girl and a woman from feeling his approval. In order not to feel inferior to boys, she should believe that her father would welcome her in backyard sports, on fishing and camping trips, in attendance at ball games, whether or not she wants to accept the invitation. She gains confidence in herself from feeling his interest in her activities, achievements, opinions, and aspirations.

By learning to enjoy the qualities in her father that are particularly masculine, a girl is getting ready for her adult life in a world that is half made up of men. The way she makes friendships with boys and men later, the kind of man she eventually falls in love with, the kind of married life she makes, are all influenced strongly by the kind of relationship she has had with her father throughout her childhood and by the relationship her parents enjoy with one another.

18. Mothers as companions. Boys and girls need their mother's companionship in more ways than just the time they spend together in their daily routines. They need opportunities for special activities with her, the same way they need them with their father. These could be trips to museums, movies or sporting events, or going hiking or bicycle-riding. The point is that it shouldn't be an obligation for the mother, but something both she and the children really enjoy.

19. What about single parents? I have stressed the importance of children's relationships with both their mother and father. But what if, as is commonly the case, there is only one parent at home or, less commonly, the parents are of the same sex? Must the child's psychological well-being inevitably suffer?

The answer to this question is a resounding no. While it is true that children need both male and female role models, those role models need not live in the same house. What children need most of all is nurturing and love, a consistent presence in their lives who provides emotional support and teaches them the ways of the world. A child growing up with a single parent who can provide these necessities will be far better off than a child whose mother and father neglect his needs because of their own unhappiness. Most children from single-parent families find role models outside the home—a special uncle or aunt, perhaps, or a close friend of the family.

We have learned that children are resilient: give them what they need and they will blossom. It is the necessities of love, consistency, and care that come first in a child's life. With those in hand, a child can do well in all sorts of different family constellations (see Sections 959–997).

THE CHILD'S PART

The Development of Children

A Fascinating Process

20. They're repeating the whole history of the human race.
There's nothing in the world more fascinating than watching a child grow and develop. At first you think of it as just a matter of growing bigger. Then, as the infant begins to do things, you may think of it as "learning tricks." But it's really more complicated and full of meaning than that.

In some ways, the development of each child retraces the whole history of the human race, physically and spiritually, step by step. Babies start off in the womb as a single tiny cell, just the way the first living thing appeared in the ocean. Weeks later, as they lie in the warm amniotic fluid, they have gills like fish and tails like amphibians. Toward the end of the first year of life, when they learn to clamber to their feet, they're celebrating that period millions of years ago when our ancestors got up off all fours and learned to use their fingers with skill and delicacy.

21. How does this single cell turn into a baby and how does that baby learn to walk and to talk and to think? This is a question that has intrigued mankind almost since the beginning of time because it addresses the big questions: Who are we? What are we here for? Where are we going?

Developmental psychology has used painstaking scientific research to study how children develop, and we have learned much. But there is a lot more that is still mysterious.

In some ways human development appears to be a simple, obvious process with laws that are understandable through simple common sense. At the same time, it is the most complex, mysterious process on earth. In this section I want to discuss some of what science has taught us about a child's development, to increase your interest and fascination with the process of development in your child, a process that is at once the most ordinary and extraordinary on earth, and one to which you will both bear witness and play a large role in its outcome.

The Development of the Brain

22. Of all the discoveries about child development made in the late twentieth century, perhaps none is so fascinating as how a young child's experience changes the development of the cells in his brain. For decades, scientists believed that the human brain was shaped solely in accordance with the child's genetic blueprint. Biology was destiny. However your genes told your brain to grow, that was exactly how it was formed.

The real picture is far more interesting and far more complex. First, the human brain contains about 100 billion nerve cells (neurons) and each connects to about 10,000 other neurons. Each cell can send up to 100 messages a second to its neighbors. You can see that the possible number of interconnections between the nerve cells of the brain is beyond measure.

It turns out that these interconnections of nerve cells in the brain—scientists call it the architecture of the brain— are, to a significant degree, determined by the infant and young child's experiences in the world. This is extraordinary news: a young child's environment actually helps to determine the structure of her brain.

Now we understand that early experiences—especially those in the first years of life when the brain is growing and interconnections between the nerve cells occur at a very fast rate—actually change the structure of the brain. Then, when the brain stops growing and stops making new connections (sometime during middle childhood), the job is done and the die is cast. That doesn't mean that the process of development stops, but it does mean that the complexity and richness of the brain itself is pretty much set. In computer terms, the hard drive is completed and awaits programming. Then we all have to make the best of what we've got; the critical period of brain development is over.

Rich, emotionally positive experiences tend to promote certain complex brain connections. Negative experiences also reinforce certain connections in the brain, although perhaps not the ones we would like to see, such as connecting a feeling of fear to a certain sound or smell. A lack of stimulation causes there to be fewer connections and a less complex network of neurons in the brain all together. Babies growing up in a home filled with anxiety and tension seem to have fewer tools with which to cope with their feelings. They are also easily overwhelmed by their feelings.

This, in part, explains why children from nurturing, attentive homes seem to do better in all aspects of life, compared to children who have been relatively neglected. That is why scientists believe that early experiences play a significant role in the long-term process of development, and that is why, right from the start, the business of child rearing is so vitally important, not only to the child and to the family, but to our society as a whole.

23. Superbabies? This new information does not mean that we can (or should) try to create superbabies by relentless stimulation and education, starting right after birth. The best experiences for an infant appear to be those she inherently enjoys—those that are rich with love and caring and security, and those that make sense to her. (How can you tell if something makes sense to an infant? Easy: they smile, they laugh, they coo.) The best learning occurs when an infant is happy, relaxed, attentive, and actively involved, not when she is being oppressed with cold, unwanted, and unnatural stimulation.

So our brains are affected by experience, but they still have limits set by our genetic endowment. Very few of us can be Mozart or Michael Jordan, no matter how much our parents played music to us or how early they placed a large orange ball in our crib. The lesson of the new scientific knowledge about the brain development of young children is to think of ways to encourage their potential, whatever it might be, not to try to artificially surpass that potential.

The What of Development

24. When psychologists think about a child's development, they usually start by dividing it into mental development and motor development. Mental development includes cognitive development (how we learn to understand and make sense of the world), emotional development, and language development. Motor development is often divided into gross motor development (like learning to sit up, walk, and climb) and fine motor development (like picking up a small object or holding a crayon).

These aspects of a child's development are the *what* of development—that is, what does a child do and when does she do it. The what of development has led to research on thousands of children in an attempt to learn, for example, when the average child first walks and talks. There are developmental timetables you can consult to see if your child is doing exactly what she is "supposed" to be doing and when she is supposed to be doing it.

For fifty years I have resisted putting such developmental timetables in this book. First off, every baby and child's pattern of development is different from every other child's. One may be very advanced in her general body strength and coordination—a sort of infant athlete. And yet she may be slow in doing skillful things with her fingers or in talking. Children who turn out later to be smart in schoolwork may have been very slow to talk in the beginning. Likewise, children of average talent may have shown advanced early development.

I think it's a big mistake to obsessively note exactly when every developmental milestone is achieved compared to the "average" baby. What is most important is that the child's general pattern is a progressively forward one. Besides, development tends to go in forward spurts and backward slides. There is often a backward slide just before a forward move. Parents should not become alarmed when there are regressions, any more than they should try to speed up those developmental attainments. There is no evidence that making a concerted effort to teach a child to walk or talk or read early has any real long-term benefit, and it could cause some problems as well as frustrate parents. Children need an environment that allows for the next developmental achievement but doesn't push the child into it.

25. Like all parents, you watch your child grow and develop with a mixture of intense feelings. When she is coming along speedily, you are proud of her and proud of yourself for having produced her. As she shows her delight in her new accomplishments and in discovering the amazing world around her, you live over again the most pleasant part of your own childhood.

But you may find that you are quick to worry if there are any signs that she is failing to keep up with her previous progress or to keep up with other children you know about. You feel not only anxious but vaguely guilty, as if you are not doing enough. That's the way good parents are made. Anything the slightest bit out of line makes them wonder whether they are caring for their child properly, whether they have given her a worthy inheritance, whether something they were made to feel guilty about in their own past is affecting her.

Remember that your child's early pattern of development is unique and usually due more to the child's nature than to her nurture (assuming, of course, a reasonably nurturing and stimulating environment). She is just growing and developing at her own normal pace. So look at developmental timetables to your heart's content, but be sure to take them with a large grain of salt. And by all means discuss any delays that you are concerned about with your doctor or nurse practitioner.

26. Enjoy your child's development. I hope you enjoy each stage of your baby's development, whether it's a little "early" or a little "late." The odds are on your side that your baby's development is perfectly normal. It's a shame to worry about insignificant developmental variations when you could be celebrating them instead.

The How and Why of Development

Temperament: The How of Development

27. The how of development refers to your child's temperament; the *why* refers to her motivation for doing what she does. In the long run, these aspects of development are probably as important as your child's specific abilities. For example, the child who is not motivated to excel may not do well in school no matter how bright she may be. The child whose temperament makes him fun to be around may achieve more success than a child who has greater talent but has a less winning personality.

28. Someone once said that the concept of temperament was created by the first parent who had a second child. Most parents and professionals believe that babies are born with very different personalities right from the start. Some are relaxed and easy going, others appear more intense and dramatic. These inborn differences in how a child responds to the world are called temperament.

As children get older, temperamental differences become more apparent. There are many aspects of temperament in children: their activity level, how distractible they are; how intensely they express their emotions; if they generally have a positive or negative mood; if they are especially sensitive to sound, touch, taste, light, or temperature; if they are shy and inhibited around strangers; if they can easily adapt to a new, unexpected situation; if they persist in whatever task is at hand. Put these all together and you have a description of a child's temperament.

I think that understanding your child's temperament is extremely important. Some parents are locked in struggles with their children because they blame their child for a temperamental trait he was born with. Some children are simply more difficult to raise because they have a difficult temperament.

29. But mostly temperament is important because it affects the fit between you and your child. When Stella Chess and Alexander Thomas followed children with very difficult temperaments from birth to middle age, they were surprised at what they found. They expected to find that children with difficult temperaments would fare worse in later life. Instead they found that it was not so much what kind of temperament the child was born with as the goodness of fit between the child's temperament and the parents' caretaking style. For example, take a very active, inquisitive child. One set of parents might find the activity level annoying and dangerous. They might constantly exhort their child to "Sit still!" and "Behave!" They may be angry at her mischievous nature. That child will then grow up feeling that "I'm a bad girl because I'm always getting into trouble." This is an example of a poor fit.

Another set of parents with the same child might view the child's inquisitiveness with great pride. They marvel at her energy level and provide lots of opportunities for her to run it off. With pride, they call her a spark plug and enjoy her sense of adventure. This child will grow up with a positive sense of herself, because of the good fit with her parents' expectations and caretaking style.

Parents who provide a good fit with their child's temperament often have certain traits in common. First, they understand their child's temperament and accept it. They do not try to force the child to be something other than what he is. Because of this understanding, they use sensitive strategies to deal with behavior problems when they arise. They use their strong parental leadership skills to gently steer the energy of their very active child, but not at the expense of his self-esteem. For example, an active three-year-old will have a hard time sitting still during a long lunch at a restaurant. If one of her parents could take her out and let her run, both will enjoy the outing more.

Language Development

30. It is almost unimaginable to think of what our lives would be like without language, so enmeshed are we in the spoken and written word. Language scientists believe that each one of us is programmed to learn language, that communicating via language is such an important part of what made human beings successful that it can't be left to chance for a baby to learn it. Rather, the tracks in our brains leave no choice. Nothing is left to chance except the specific language that we learn. One child learns English and another Swahili, which have different superficial structures. But it is the same process that drives both, and the same universal deep structure underlies all languages. When it comes to language, we are all truly one mankind, brothers and sisters under the skin.

Watching an infant come to learn to speak is thrilling. Let me give you a whirlwind tour through the process. Initially, infants are born with no capacity for speaking language. We do know that they pay attention to language more than other sounds, especially the language of their mother (which they have been hearing in the womb for some months). However, what comes out of their mouths is pretty random.

As with all development, the infant begins to assert control over what once occurred by accident. She begins to realize that she is making the sounds she hears. Sometimes there is even a big response in the environment to those sounds (as the adults exclaim: "Did you just hear her say 'Mama'? Hey, say 'Mama' again."). She begins to make the sounds of her own accord. At first the sounds are the most natural for her to make, such as "ba-ba-ba" or "da-da-da." This marks the beginning of babbling, which usually begins at around four months of age. The infant takes increasing pleasure in making more and more noise. But these sounds have no intrinsic meaning. They do not signify an object or a desire. Hence, they are not language.

Over the next few months the infant begins to play with the tone and musical qualities of the sounds. At this time babies who are hearing primarily English will babble with an English rhythm, while Chinese babies, for example, will begin to show the tones of the Chinese language. At around nine months of age the infant will begin to put these sounds together creatively—"ba-da-goo-la"—and vary the musicality of those sounds. This is called jargoning, and, for all the world sounds like a language of its own. These speech sounds still are not language, though, because they don't really mean anything.

31. Somewhere around the first birthday, the infant has a brilliant idea: "That sound I hear actually represents that object which I care about so much" (e.g., bottle, mother, or father). It is a startling idea, and the baby soon goes to work to confirm his discovery. As in all language development, understanding comes before the ability to speak the words, just like adults learning a second language who can understand far more than they can speak.

A short time after this breakthrough, the one-word stage begins. The infant uses his long-practiced ability to make sounds to now make meaningful sounds or words. At first the words refers to beloved objects ("bottle," "Dada," "Mama"). Next words move on to actions ("go," "eat"), adjectives ("cold"), and social niceties ("bye-bye"). The one-word stage is a mysterious one because the infant tries to communicate more than one idea through only a single word. Sometimes the meaning is easy to decipher: "bottle" translates to "Bring me my bottle." Other times, the utterance is far more enigmatic, leading to frustration sometimes of both parent and infant.

It takes about six months, when the child is a year and a half old, before the infant comes up with another good idea: two words can be put together to convey meaning. Scientists studying the two-word phrase have noted that it is the same in all languages—for example a noun and a verb ("doctor gone") or an adjective and a noun ("my cookie"). The two-word phrase conveys much more meaning. Perhaps it is this success in communication that escalates the child's acquisition of new words. At two years of age a child increases their vocabulary at a rate of about one new word every two hours, a pace that continues through adolescence.

32. There is no three-word phase. Once the child has the hang of it, she begins to put words together at an astonishing clip and with surprising grammatical accuracy. As in most developmental spurts, the child scientist constructs hypotheses about how to make new words or put them together. She always starts with a general hypothesis and then refines it over time.

33. For example, making plurals. The child soon decides that adding an *s* to the end of any word makes it mean more than one. It's a pretty good hypothesis, and it gets the job done, except when there are irregular plurals. It doesn't help to correct a child at this stage; the rules just don't fit with the way she sees the world. For example if you persist in telling the child that the word is "mice" and not "mouses," the best you can hope for is a look of comprehension and the response "I saw lots of mices." These general rules of language get refined through experience and through the generation of more sophisticated hypotheses—for example, that not all plurals require an *s* at the end.

And so the process inexorably rolls on. By the time she is four or five years old the child has basically mastered most of the rules of her language and has a vocabulary of upwards of 8,000 words.

Cognitive Development: Piaget's Theory

34. How do children learn to make sense of the world? This is the question asked by scientists looking at **cognitive development.** The most influential thinker in this area has been a Swiss psychologist named Jean Piaget (Pee-ah-*jhay*). Piaget initially derived his theories of cognitive development simply by making careful observations of his three young children. He then spent the rest of his life trying to prove these theories through careful scientific study, but it was watching the day-to-day development of his children that informed all of his ideas. You can do the same with your children.

Piaget believed that human development proceeds in stages that are the same for everybody. Through a careful description of these stages, he explained how an infant with little ability to think abstractly comes to be able to reason logically, create hypotheses about how things work, and invent new ideas and behaviors that he has never seen or heard before.

Piaget viewed infants and children as "little scientists."

He believed we are born with a drive to make sense of the world and that we do so by constantly conducting experiments. Take, for example, a four-month-old who keeps dropping food off the high chair and then looking for it. He is experimenting with the idea of **object permanence** and asking himself the question: "If I drop this food and I can't see or touch it anymore, does it still exist?"

Until the child engages in this experiment, *out of sight is out of mind.* Nothing really exists for the infant except what he is seeing and hearing and touching at that time. Think about it: It does require a leap of faith to understand that even when you can't see something, it still exists. Infants begin to learn this concept in the first months and they do so by trial and error. At three months, the infant drops the pacifier or bottle by accident and is surprised to see it on the floor a few seconds later. This happens again, and then again. Slowly it begins to dawn on him that the object on the floor is the same as was just in his hand.

The little scientist goes into action. He begins to purposely drop things on the floor. He then looks down and sees them. He repeats the experiment. Success! He continues to drop things on the floor, over and over and over. Infants love to play "peekaboo" for the same reason: The face is there and then it's not and then it is. The infant's capacity to continue this game is boundless because it is exactly one of the questions he is working on at that stage of his development. Once he is satisfied that faces continue to exist even if he can't see them, peekaboo falls by the wayside and a new game, one that is appropriate to his current developmental questions, arises.

Finally, when his research on dropping things is completed to his satisfaction, he has the idea that if he just saw something and now it's gone, it must be on the floor. If it's not on the floor, then it probably no longer exists. It is not until the next stage, at about eight months, that the infant's ideas about object permanence become more sophisticated and he begins to search elsewhere for missing objects.

35. Piaget called the first two years of life the sensorimotor period. By this he meant that infants and toddlers learn by doing, by exercising their senses and motor abilities. Their ability to make sense of the world is based on what happens in the physical world and their ability to comprehend abstraction remains quite limited. By the end of the second year, however, they have a much better ability to use ideas and abstract theories to understand the world. At this time, for example, the infant knows that objects continue to exist whether or not you can actually see or touch them.

After moving on from the sensorimotor period, children go through three more stages: pre-operational, concrete operations, and formal operations. Piaget does not believe that a child can skip any stage; one stage grows out of the last in a continuous fashion. Each new ability to make sense of the world grows out of his understanding of the previous stage and is changed by new experiences and better theories to make sense of those experiences. Each stage implies the child is better able to live in the world of ideas, to be able to put ideas together and to come up with new ideas.

An understanding of cognitive development leads to an important point: children are not just little adults. Rather, they understand the world in a fundamentally different way than do most adults. Depending on their cognitive stage, they are usually more egocentric—that is, they see the world as revolving around them. While this can be exasperating for parents, it is a perfectly normal way for preschool children to view the world. At this age, children's understanding of cause and effect is more magical: things don't always have to happen for a logical reason. I think this is why magic shows are so appealing to adults. They put us in touch with how we saw the world when we were children, when everything was magic.

In my experience, parents sometimes have problems with their children because they don't really appreciate how fundamentally differently they and their children see the world. Consequently they think their child is capable of more understanding than he really is. This is why they sometimes offer a long intellectual explanation to a two-year-old of why she should share. Although sharing is not part of any child's way of seeing the world at that stage, that doesn't mean that it won't be later on. This same misunderstanding causes some adults to tell teenagers not to smoke because they might get lung cancer and die in forty years.

Much better to speak to teens about immediate consequences, like bad breath, decreased endurance, and looking
stupid. That's what really counts in their world.

Emotional Development

36. Children's emotional needs. It's in the first two to three
years of life that children's personalities are being most
actively molded—by the attitudes of the parents or of the
others who provide most of their care. In earlier times the
babies who lived in understaffed orphanages or who spent
their days lying neglected in their cribs in day nurseries used
to wither in body, in intellect, and in emotions, never fully
to recover. Whereas a baby who's cared for mainly by
loving, enthusiastic parents, perhaps with the help of others, surges ahead. Some of the things the parents give her are
their visible love, their pride and joy in her tiny accomplishments, thoughtful playthings, answers to her questions, and
a willingness to let her play freely as long as she does no
damage. They read to her and show her pictures. These are
the attitudes and activities that foster emotional depth and
keen intelligence.

Whether children will grow up to be lifelong optimists or
pessimists, whether warmly loving or cool, whether trustful
or suspicious, will depend to a considerable extent on the
attitudes of the individuals who have taken responsibility
for a major portion of their care in their first two years.
Therefore, the personalities of parents and caregivers are of
great importance.

One person acts toward children as if they are basically
bad, always doubting them, always scolding them. Such
children may grow up doubting themselves, full of guilt. A
person with more than average hostility finds a dozen
excuses every hour for venting it on a child, and the child
acquires a corresponding hostility. Other people have the
itch to dominate children, and unfortunately they can
succeed.

In the first year, a baby has to depend mainly on the
attentiveness, intuition, and helpfulness of adults to get her
the things that she needs and craves. If the adults are too

insensitive or indifferent to her, she may become somewhat apathetic or depressed.

37. A very particular need of young children is continuity in their caregivers. From the age of a few months babies come to love, and count on, and get their security from the one or two people who take the major part of their care. Even at six months babies will become seriously depressed, losing their smile, their appetite, their interest in things and people, if the parent who has cared for them disappears. There will be a depression, lesser in degree, if a person who assists the parent on a regular basis leaves. Small children who have been moved from one foster home to another, several times, will lose some of their capacity to love or trust deeply, as if it's too painful to be disappointed again and again.

So it's important that the parent or other person who has taken the major part of a child's care not give it up during the first two or three years, or at least give it up only after a substitute has very gradually taken over. It's important to be as sure as possible that a substitute plans to stick with the job. It's important, in the group care of young children, that if there are two or more staff people assigned to one group of children, each child be assigned to one person so that there will be a relationship more like that of child and parent.

38. Emotional needs after three years. Now I want to discuss the more general emotional needs of children of all ages, especially after three years.

Children know that they are inexperienced and dependent. They count on their parents for leadership, love, and security. They are always watching their parents, instinctively, and patterning themselves after them. This is how they get their own personalities, their strength of character, their assurance, their ability to cope. They are learning, in childhood, how to be adult citizens, workers, spouses, and parents, by identifying with their parents (see Section 427).

The greatest gift from parents is love, which they express in countless ways: a fond facial expression, spontaneous demonstrations of physical affection, pleasure in their children's accomplishments, comforting them when they are hurt or frightened, controlling them to keep them safe and to help them become responsible people, giving them high ideals.

It's the parents' (or caregivers') love that creates an answering love in children. It's from this lovingness toward parents that children go on to form all their positive relations in life—with friends, teachers, spouses, offspring, neighbors, and fellow workers.

Children gain trust in themselves from being respected—as human beings—by their parents (or caregivers). This self-assurance helps them to be comfortable with themselves and with all kinds of people, for the rest of their lives. Respect from parents is what teaches children to give respect to their parents in turn.

39. Boys and girls, by three years, focus on their parents' roles. A boy, by the age of three years, senses that his destiny is to be a man, so he watches his father particularly—his interests, manner, speech, pleasures, his attitude toward work, his relationships with his wife and with his sons and daughters, how he gets along with and copes with other men.

A girl's need of a father is not as obvious on the surface but is just as great underneath. Half her relationships throughout life will be with males. She gets her ideas about what males are supposed to be primarily from watching her father. The kind of man she eventually falls in love with and marries will probably reflect in one way or another the personality and attitudes of her father—for example, whether he's dominating or gentle, loyal or straying, pompous or humorous.

A mother's personality will be copied in many respects by her admiring daughter. How the mother feels about being a woman, a wife, a mother, a worker, will make a strong impression on her daughter. How she gets along specifically with her husband will influence her daughter's future relationship with her husband.

A mother is her son's first great love. In obvious or subtle ways this will set his romantic ideal. It will influence not only his eventual choice of a wife but how he gets along with her.

40. Two parents are preferable. I feel, from pediatric and psychiatric experience, that, if possible, it is preferable for children to live with two parents (one may be a stepparent), if the parents love and respect each other. Then children will know both sexes realistically as well as idealistically, and will have a pattern of marital relations to guide them when they are adults. The two parents will be able to support each other emotionally. They will be able to balance or counteract each other's unjustified worries and obsessions about the children.

This is not to say that children can't grow up to be healthy without two parents; many do. If they lack a father, they create one—in their imagination—out of what they remember, what their mother has told them, and the appealing characteristics of friendly men they see from time to time. This synthetic father supplies fairly well the masculine image they need to grow on. Similarly a child without a mother creates one from memory, family stories, and relationships with other women. Certainly it would be a great mistake for a parent to make a hasty, unsuitable marriage just to provide a child with a second parent.

Motivation Theory:
The Why of Development

41. Perhaps the most influential theorist about child development in the twentieth century has been Sigmund Freud. After becoming a pediatrician, I received training in psychiatry and Freudian psychoanalysis. What I learned about human nature and child development from that training has greatly influenced my understanding of children, parents, and families. It is the underlying psychology of this book.

Freud also believed that all children pass through the same distinct stages. Instead of describing children's way of thinking (like Piaget), Freud focused on how our biological instincts—for sex, for food, for immediate satisfaction but also for security—collide with the child's social experiences, especially within the family. Freud studied how these biological drives become channeled into following the rules of civilized society rather than into the pursuit of their satisfaction.

Freud believed that if a child got stuck in one of the early stages of development, all subsequent stages would be affected.

For Freud, emotional maturity was the ultimate goal of childhood whereas Piaget looked for a high degree of abstract reasoning. One of Freud's main purposes in exploring his patients' unconscious minds with them was to relieve them of their phobias (fears), obsessions, and hysterical (anxiety-driven) symptoms so that they could function more effectively and happily in their daily lives. My purpose in borrowing some of Freud's findings has been to understand the stages of healthy emotional development so that I could help parents understand the normal as well as the problem behavior of their children.

Nature or Nurture?

42. There are many ways to make sense of the mysterious process of human development. Theories abound. Some believe that the process of development is all due to heredity. We are born with certain talents and personalities, and these are the biggest determinant of who we are and what we become. These scientists use as evidence the fascinating studies of identical twins who were reared in different families but who nonetheless bear striking, sometimes uncanny, similarities to each other in their personalities.

Others contend that we are all pretty much totally the product of our environments. That which the environment rewards is that which we learn to do and that which the environment punishes is that which we learn not to do. This theory—called behaviorist theory—contends that all human learning can be understood by focusing simply on rewards and punishments. This school of thought lies behind many time-honored discipline strategies, such as time-out, sticker charts, and taking away privileges.

Probably a kernel of truth lies within every theory of child development. Certainly no one would deny that children are born with different temperaments and developmental timetables. On the other hand, there is no question that just how a child is raised has a lot to do with the kind of adult she becomes. In extreme cases the environment can be so damaging that the child's innate talents never blossom. But how we turned out had a lot to do with the way our parents raised us and with our childhood experiences.

A Transactional Model of Child Development

43. The transactional model of child development helps to resolve this split between nature and nurture. A person is neither the product of just her environment nor just her genetic makeup. Rather, it is the complex interaction between the two that is key.

Let me give an example. A child is born with a talent for music. In one family this talent for music is expressed early on by the child constantly singing and listening to music. Sensing their child's interest in music, sensitive parents play even more music and give him a toy xylophone to play at age two. The child's growing interest and skill with music spurs the parents to offer even more musical experiences, which in turn fuels the child's talent and desire to play.

The transactional analyst would say that both the child's talent and his environment affected his development. The child was born with a talent for music, yes. But that talent changed the environment by inducing his parents to provide more musical experiences at home. Those experiences in the environment, in turn, fueled the child's talent and motivation, which in turn motivated his parents to provide even more musical enrichment. In this way the child's inborn talent and temperament changed the environment, which in turn changed the child's motivation and behavior, which in turn changed the environment in new ways, which in turn . . .

The transactional model explains why brothers and sisters always grow up in a "different" family. By that I mean that the environment of family life is always changing to accommodate the personalities and number of its members.

A firstborn child grows up with very different experiences than a middle or youngest child. A child who is temperamentally difficult to raise has a very different experience with her parents than does her easygoing brother. The child changes the environment which in turn changes the child. The child's development is a complex dance in which nature and nurture both lead and are led.

I like the transactional model as a way to think about child-rearing questions. Let's say you're having a difficult time with your argumentative two-year-old. The transactional model would tell you first to think about what your child is bringing to the interaction. Is it a difficult temperamental trait that's bothering you? Is she stubborn by nature? Does she have an intense response to everything? Does she resist change in her usual routine? And how does her developmental stage play into the situation? Because of her age, is she unable to delay gratification for any period of time? Does she lack the ability to talk to you about what's bothering her, and is that why she's more likely to have tantrums? The child represents one piece of the puzzle.

The next questions to ask yourself are these: What is my role in all of this? Am I somehow rewarding the very behaviors I am trying to stop by paying too much attention to them? Am I making unreasonable demands by expecting a two-year-old to be a model citizen? Am I unconsciously irritated by the child because she reminds me of my sister with whom I don't get along?

Finally, you need to put the two together to achieve a full picture of what is going on and to determine what you might do to stop it. How are my child's temperament and developmental stage contributing to this problem behavior? And just how is my behavior affecting my child? More importantly, what do I need to change to break this self-perpetuating cycle of trouble? How can I better understand the forces behind my child's behavior so as to improve my response to it?

This may sound highly theoretical to some of you, but it's exactly such questions many parents are always asking themselves, even if they are not aware of it. I think that by understanding this model of child development, you'll be better equipped to understand the transactional forces behind your child's behavior and development, and this will help you figure out what role you can play to facilitate that development and improve the child's behavior.

Gender Differences

44. People are apt to show admiration for the accomplishments of little boys and for the cuteness of little girls. Girlish clothes are designed to make an adult say, "How pretty you look!" This is complimentary in one sense, but it also gives girls a sense that they are primarily appreciated for their appearance rather than their achievements. Often children's books show boys building things or going on adventures while girls watch the boys or play with dolls. Girls are commonly warned not to climb trees or onto garage roofs because they are not strong enough or will get hurt more easily. Boys are given toy cars, construction sets, sporting equipment, and doctor kits. Girls are given dolls, sewing sets, nurse kits, and articles of adornment. There's nothing wrong with any of these gifts in themselves, especially if the child asks for them. The harm comes when adults consistently impose these distinctions, implying that females (or males) are good only at a limited number of occupations (see Section 957).

Boys are assigned chores in the garage, in the basement, or on the lawn; girls work inside the house. Of course housework is important to the welfare of the whole family, so it should be accorded dignity, but when it is done only by females, in a society that gives so much prestige to males, it will be considered menial by both sexes.

Boys often cover up their own feelings of inadequacy or inferiority by taunting girls, saying that they are not able to run fast or throw a ball and so can't be on the team. Some parents and teachers tell girls that, by their nature, they won't be able to study advanced mathematics or physics or function as engineers. By adolescence many girls have become convinced that they will be inferior to men in such capabilities as abstract reasoning, complex planning skills, and emotional control. The acceptance of these aspersions in itself destroys self-confidence and may bring about the very impairment of abilities that are alleged (by many men and some women) to be inborn in females.

45. Worries about homosexuality. When parents think that their little boy is effeminate or their little girls too masculine, they may wonder whether the child will grow up to be homosexual. Because of prevailing prejudices against homosexuality, this can create worry and anxiety in parents. However, the fact that a girl or boy might want to play with children of the opposite sex, and might enjoy their activities and toys, doesn't tell us anything about his or her future sexual orientation. A small percentage of children, regardless of their gender behavior in their early years, grow up to be gay, and a majority grow up heterosexual (see page 322).

If a boy exclusively wanted dresses and dolls, preferred to play only with girls, and said he wanted to be a girl, I would consider the possibility that something had gotten mixed up in his identification as a result of misunderstandings or anxieties. Because this can be a great source of unhappiness for the child, who may be rejected by his peers, his behavior should be looked into by a professional. If a girl wants to play a lot with boys, and occasionally wishes she were a boy, she's most likely reacting to taunts about girls not being good or strong or clever enough, and testing her own limits, or she may be showing a positive identification with her father or brother. However, if she wants to play *only* with boys and is always unhappy about being a girl, I'd suggest taking her for a consultation with a professional.

46. What is homosexuality? In our society, between 5 percent and 10 percent of adult men and women are gay or lesbian. Experts have had difficulty calculating exact percentages because there is still considerable stigma attached to being gay or lesbian.

Although gays and lesbians are now more visible in our popular culture—in films, magazines, and television—and public figures like musicians, fashion designers, athletes, and even politicians are increasingly willing to declare that they are gay or lesbian, many people still have an unreasonable fear of homosexuality. This fear is called homophobia.

In its most common form, it is the fear heterosexuals have that they could be gay, and the view that gays and lesbians are abnormal. These fears may lead to treating homosexuals as scapegoats, saying they brought the AIDS plague on themselves, or that parents should avoid allowing their children close contact with gay and lesbian adults. In its most violent form, homophobia leads to hate crimes (gay bashing) and to laws that limit the freedoms of gays and lesbians.

Some parents think that if their children have contact with gay or lesbian adults, that they may "become gay." But there is absolutely no evidence the sexual orientation of either gay or heterosexual children can be changed or influenced through example. Mental health professionals, scientists, and other experts are actively debating whether people are born predisposed to a heterosexual or homosexual orientation, or whether it is psychological and emotional experiences that make the determination. But experts agree that a person's basic or primary sexual orientation is set by the very earliest years of development. Whatever lifestyles a child is exposed to or protected from will have no bearing on his or her primary adult sexual orientation.

If your child asks about gays and lesbians, or if you're talking generally to a child of six or older about sex, I think you can explain quite simply that some men and women fall in love with and live with people of the same sex.

47. Is it necessary to reinforce sex roles? The main thing that gives a boy a strong sense of male identity is not the toy cars or cowboy suits he's given but his positive relationship with his father in early childhood. This relationship makes him want to grow up to be the same kind of person.

If a father anxiously turns down his son's request for a doll or otherwise shows his worry that the boy has "girlish" tastes, the child's masculinity is not reinforced. In fact, the boy may sense that his own and his father's masculinity are doubtful or inadequate. If the father is confident in his own masculinity he can help his son develop the "mothering" side of fatherhood by supporting the doll play.

In the same way, a girl looks to her mother for an image of herself. A mother who encourages her daughter to explore many activities and to break through the limits, and does this herself, will raise a confident, strong daughter. But a mother who is overly anxious about her own femininity and sexual attractiveness to men may put too much emphasis on her daughter's feminine development. If she only gives her dolls and cooking sets to play with, and always dresses her in cute, frilly clothes, she is sending a distorted message about female identity.

It's also important for girls to forge a positive relationship with their fathers. If fathers neglect or ignore daughters, or refuse to play ball games with them or to include them in activities like camping and fishing, they might instill in them a sense of inferiority and reinforce role stereotypes.

I think it is normal for little boys to want to play with dolls and for little girls to want to play with toy cars, and it's quite all right to let them have them. A boy's desire to play with dolls is parental rather than effeminate, and it should help him to be a good father. There is no harm in boys and girls wearing unisex clothes—jeans and T-shirts, for example—if that's what they want—or for girls to have dresses, if that's their preference.

As for chores, I believe that it's sound for boys and girls to be given basically the same tasks, just as I think it's wise for men and women to share in the same occupations, at home and outside. Boys can do as much bed making, room cleaning, and dishwashing as their sisters. And girls can take part in yard work and car washing, as I hope their mothers will. I don't mean that boys and girls can't swap certain chores or that it all has to come out exactly even, only that there should not be obvious discrimination or differentiation. The example of the two parents will have a strong influence.

In thinking about children's identification with parents it is important to remember that the boy's identification is largely with his father, but also usually with his mother to a lesser degree or, more accurately, in a certain respect. I'm sure I became a pediatrician because I identified with my mother's intense love of babies. She had five more after me, and I remember my great pleasure in giving bottles and in soothing a fretful sister by pushing her up and down the porch in her white wicker carriage.

I think of girl patients who identified with a father who

was a bird-watcher or an immunologist (the mother had no such interests). So identification is a matter of degree or interest or attitude rather than 100 percent male or female. In this sense everyone identifies in some respect or degree with the opposite sex. This gives them understanding of the opposite sex as they grow up, and a richer, more flexible personality. It also benefits the society as a whole by allowing a mixture of attitudes in any occupation.

Since there is no such thing as a 100 percent identification with one's own sex, it's best to let children grow up with whatever mixture of identifications, attitudes, and interests that has developed in them, as long as they can accept comfortably what they are. This is better than making them feel ashamed and anxious because of parental disapproval.

How Human Beings Get Their Aspirations

48. In the three- to six-year-old period children mature by means of an intense adoration of their parents—not the parents as the neighbors see them, but glorified. They overestimate their parents' wisdom, power, and attractiveness. The boy yearns to be like his idealized father and spends all day practicing, in activities and manner. At the same time he develops a strong romantic attachment to his mother and idolizes her as his feminine ideal. As such she will strongly influence his choice of a wife when he grows up.

For the girl it's the other way around. She yearns to be like her mother—in occupation and in having babies of her own. She forms a possessive romantic attachment to her father.

Because children are so very aware at this dependent age of how much their parents' love means to them, they are now inspired with a similar capacity to love generously their parents and other people. Out of this will eventually grow their devotion to their own children and their altruism toward humanity.

In this same three- to six-year-old period several other significant emotional developments take place. Both girls and boys become fascinated with marriage and having babies. It is hard to convince boys that they can't grow babies inside themselves. Their frustrated rivalry with girls about this is believed to be one of the sources of creativity in the arts, inventions, and machines.

In nature's scheme of things the intense attachment to the two parents, having served their purpose of setting the children's ideals and advancing their maturity, must then be greatly diminished, so that they can begin the next big step—between six and twelve years—of becoming emotionally more independent of parents and oriented instead toward the outside community and its ways of doing things. This is brought about by a dramatic shift in feelings toward each parent.

Children's romantic attachment to the parent of the opposite sex gradually arouses increasingly uncomfortable feelings of rivalry with the parent of the same sex. This as well as a continued sense of defeat and recognition of generational differences, forces them eventually, by about the age of six or seven, to suppress guiltily their possessiveness toward the parent of the opposite sex and, along with it, fascination with marriage, with having babies, and with sex differences. They are able to sublimate (transform) these interests into impersonal, abstract interests such as the three R's, science, and nature study. They turn away impatiently from both parents as idols. Instead they revere God, government authorities, laws, and the heroes of history, fiction, TV, and the comics.

It is fascinating to realize that what distinguishes human beings so sharply from other creatures are these attitudes developed soon after the age of five: inhibition and sublimation of sexuality; interest in symbols, abstractions, systems, and rules; capacity for being inspired by heroes, God, and spiritual ideals. These very human characteristics are brought out first by the special loves for each parent and then by having to give up the romantic attachment to one because of fear of rivalry with the other and acceptance of the differences in generations.

The hormonal pressures of adolescence break up this impersonal middle-childhood adjustment. The child's sexual and romantic drive now insists on some form of expression, and it gradually breaks through the old inhibitions. Nevertheless, part of it will still be held in reserve and invested in idealistic aspirations—to the degree that the parents have these. The boy's romantic adoration of his mother, suppressed for years, veiled, disembodied, now lends mystery, chivalry, and spirituality to his awakening love for a girl. He will want to protect, please, idolize her. Similarly, the girl's adoration of her father now can be seen as she invests her awakening love in a boy with the same qualities.

Human beings' idealization of the opposite sex also combines with their drive to create and this is a major inspiration for their creativity in architecture, engineering, technical inventiveness, scientific discovery, literature, drama, music, and painting. A classic example is Dante's *Divine Comedy* which was inspired by and dedicated to Beatrice, a woman the poet had only seen, never known. To tie together this spiritual sequence: human beings can build a magnificent reality in adulthood out of what was only an illusion in early childhood—their loving, joyous, trusting, ingenuous, unrealistic overidealization of their two parents.

These capacities in people are developed highly in a few individuals, moderately in many, hardly at all in others. The capacity—for idealism, creativity, spirituality—is latent in all children. Whether they will realize them all will depend partly on their parents. At three and four years they will over-idealize their parents anyway. If parents have aspirations, if they have a respect for themselves, for each other, and for their children, then their offspring will continue to be inspired by their pattern, even after they appear to turn away from their parents in later childhood.

BEFORE THE CHILD
IS BORN

Pregnancy and Delivery

49. Mixed feelings about pregnancy. We have an ideal about motherhood which says that every woman is overjoyed when she finds that she is going to have a baby. She spends the pregnancy dreaming happy thoughts about the baby. When it arrives, she slips into the maternal role with ease and delight. Love is instantaneous, bonding like glue.

This is all true to a degree—more in one case, less in another. But it is also, of course, only one side of the picture. We now know what wise women have known all along—that there are normal negative feelings connected with a pregnancy, too, especially the first one.

To some degree, the first pregnancy spells the end of carefree irresponsible youth. The maidenly figure goes gradually into eclipse and, with it, sprightly grace. Both effects are temporary but very real. A woman realizes that after the baby comes there will be distinct limitations on her social life and other outside pleasures. No more hopping into the car on the spur of the moment to see a movie. No more coming home at any odd hour. The family budget has to be spread thinner, and her husband's attention (and her own) will soon be directed to another very demanding suitor indeed.

50. Feelings are different in every pregnancy. The changes to be expected because of the arrival of one more child do not look so drastic after you have had one or two, but a mother's spirit may rebel at times during any pregnancy. There may be obvious reasons why one pregnancy is more strained: perhaps it came unexpectedly soon, or one of the parents is having tensions at work, or there is serious illness on either side of the family, or there is disharmony between mother and father. Other times, there may be no apparent explanation.

An obstetrician I know says he sometimes senses an inner crisis with the second or third pregnancy in parents who had been happily looking forward to a family of that size. A mother who really wants more than one child may still be disturbed during the next pregnancy with sudden doubts about whether she will have the time, the physical energy, or the unlimited reserves of love that she imagines will be called for in taking care of another child. Or the inner doubts may start with the father, who feels somewhat neglected as his wife becomes more and more preoccupied with the children. In either case, one spouse's disquiet soon has the other one feeling dispirited also. Each parent may have less to give the other as the pregnancy progresses and concerns persist.

I don't want to make these reactions sound inevitable. I only want to reassure you that they do occur in the very best of parents, that usually they are part of the normal mixed feelings during pregnancy, and that in the great majority of cases they are temporary. Often the child's arrival proves to be less of a challenge in some ways than for parents who had no negative feelings at all as the parents have had time to think about and work through their natural ambivalence and worry. That can be a more difficult task once the baby is born and all reserves are used in the care of the baby.

51. The father during pregnancy. A man may react to his wife's pregnancy with various feelings: protectiveness of the wife, increased pride in the marriage, pride in his virility (that's one thing men always worry about to some degree), anticipatory enjoyment of the child. But there can also be, way underneath, a feeling of being left out (just as small children may feel rejected when they find their mother is pregnant), which may be expressed as crankiness toward his wife, wanting to spend more evenings with his men friends, or flirtatiousness with other women. These reactions are no help to his partner, who craves extra support at the start of this unfamiliar stage of her life.

52. The supportive father in pregnancy and delivery. There was a time, not so long ago, when a father wouldn't have *dreamed* of reading a book like this on child care, but the formerly clear-cut boundaries of "women's work" and "men's work" are now blurred. It's not even all that unusual for a father to stay home and care for the children while the mother goes off to work. I can't tell you what a refreshing change this is, compared to how rigidly we used to define what a mother was allowed to do and what was acceptable for a father to do.

Many fathers are now an integral and essential part of the pregnancy and labor. A father may go to prenatal doctor visits and attend childbirth classes with his wife. He may be an active participant in the labor and in some hospitals may "catch" the infant as it is born, cut the cord, or carry the child to the nursery and watch over him while the mother is being cared for in the delivery room. If the mother is unwell or if the baby has special problems, the father may be the parent most actively involved with the baby in the early hours after the baby's birth. He no longer has to be the lonely, disgruntled onlooker.

53. Love for the baby comes gradually. Many parents who are pleased and proud to be pregnant find it hard to feel a personal love for a baby they've never seen or felt. Love is elusive and means different things to different people. When the baby begins to move some parents begin to accept that it's a real person after all, and affection begins to grow. Others begin to feel affection when they watch the first ultrasound that shows a beating heart. For others, it's not really until they are well into the care of their baby. Again, there is no "normal" time to fall in love with your baby; it will come in its time. You shouldn't feel guilty if your feelings of love and attachment aren't as strong as you think they should be. There is no real right or wrong. Love may come early. It may come late. But 999 times out of a 1,000, it comes when it needs to.

Even when feelings during pregnancy are primarily positive and the anticipation is all that could be desired, there may be a letdown, especially for first-time parents, when the baby actually arrives. They expect to recognize the baby immediately as their own flesh and blood, to respond to the infant with an overwhelming rush of maternal and paternal feelings, and to bond like epoxy, never to feel anything but love again. But in many cases this doesn't happen on the first day or even the first week. Instead it's a gradual process that isn't complete until they have been home together for a little while and the physical energy depletion of labor and delivery and the emotional energy depletion of the whole process dissipates.

Most of us have been taught that it's not fair to hope that the baby will be a girl or a boy, in case it turns out to be the opposite. I wouldn't take this too seriously. We can't really begin to imagine and love a future baby without picturing it as being one sex or the other. That's one of the early steps of the prenatal attachment process. I think that all expectant parents have a preference for a girl or a boy during each pregnancy, even though most of them will be quite ready to love a baby who turns out to be the opposite. So enjoy your imaginary baby and don't feel guilty if you soon learn on a prenatal ultrasound that the baby is not the sex you had imagined. You'll have plenty of time to reconfigure your fantasies.

54. What kind of delivery do you want? Parenting is about choices and one of the first you will be asked to make is the kind of childbirth you'd prefer. When I started as a pediatrician there wasn't a lot of choice. Spinals and epidurals were both used. Then you might get to see your baby for a few minutes when you awoke. Breast-feeding was out of the question for any self-respecting mother. And because we were so worried about the transmission of infection to the baby—an infection which we could not treat because we had no antibiotics—the baby would spend the next week in the nursery, carefully ministered to by well-scrubbed nurses in antiseptic white gowns and hats, while the mother lay flat on her back and "recovered."

We've come a long way since those days, and now the choices are many. "Natural" childbirth or with local analgesia, such as an epidural? Continuous labor support by a doula, partner, or other children in the delivery room? Lying down or squatting? Birthing room or delivery room? Home or hospital? Doctor or midwife? Rooming in or a little more rest? Home right away or in one day or two days? Visiting nurse?

As a pediatrician, I've attended enough deliveries to know that no one method suits every woman. Every woman responds differently to the stresses of labor and delivery. Some take great pride in receiving no medications at all. A good friend of mine, upon entering the hospital to have her third child introduced herself to the anesthesiologist and, in no uncertain terms, explained where, when and how the epidural was to be administered. For some women, labor is a painful experience to be simply endured; others consider it a profound, moving experience. Some show immediate love and affection for their infant; others, after hearing the infant is just fine, simply want to sleep for a little while. Some will push with each contraction for endless hours; others want help in the process and scream for a cesarean section. And I've seen some exhausted woman scream at their well-meaning husbands to get out of the delivery room and leave them and the baby alone for the rest of their lives. And all turn out to be wonderful, loving parents.

I mention this only because I've seen parents berate themselves for not having the labor and delivery they had expected. They worry that the cesarean section will affect their ability to bond with their infant. They fear that the use of forceps implies some sort of failure on their part. They see the anesthesia that was finally given as a sign that they were weak and not worthy of parenthood.

Parenthood is an ideal guilt-generating business, and labor often delivers the first volley. I think this situation has come about in part because of misconceptions about the bonding process (see Section 117) and in part because of the fantasy that everything has to be perfect for the child to do well. Of course nothing could be further from the truth. First off, the "perfect" parent has yet to see the light of day. Secondly, there is no need to be "perfect" or to follow any one script. The process of human development is powerful.

There is plenty of room for variation and even for making mistakes. Infants are incredibly resilient. As long as the infant is healthy, the type of childbirth is unlikely to have long-term consequences, unless there is so much guilt attached to the memory that it has a negative effect on parental self-confidence or starts the process with a strong but misguided sense of guilt.

So my advice is to have your baby however seems right for you and your family. Then don't worry if what happens doesn't follow the script. Being a parent is tough enough without creating problems where there really aren't any.

55. Choosing the baby's doctor or nurse practitioner. While you are pregnant, you will be thinking of finding a physician or nurse practitioner for your baby, if you don't already have one. Who should it be and how can you tell if the person will work out? In some cases the family physician who has delivered the baby will go on seeing her afterward. A family doctor who is used to taking care of babies can do just as good a job as the specialist, unless some unusual problem comes up. But most of you will deliver your baby with the help of an obstetrician, and you'll need to find a doctor or nurse practitioner for your baby.

As you go about finding one, you should think about the qualities you'd like him or her to have. Some parents get along best with a doctor who is casual and not too fussy about details. Others parents want to be given directions down to the last detail. You might have more confidence in an older, more seasoned professional or you might prefer one who is younger and more recently trained. If you have definite feelings about what kind of doctor you want, discuss the matter with your obstetrician and with friends who know the available pediatric practices.

56. Prenatal visit. If this is your first baby or if you are moving to a new area, I'd strongly recommend a prenatal visit to several doctors or nurse practitioners. There is nothing like actually meeting someone to know if they have the type of personality that will make you feel trusting and comfortable enough to talk about whatever is on your mind.

Here are some questions you can ask during your visit: Do you practice alone or with partners? How are phone calls handled? What happens if my baby becomes ill after office hours? What if we have an emergency during the day? What kinds of health insurance do you accept? What are your fees? Which hospital do you use? How much time is allotted for well-child checkups? If you are considering a nurse practitioner, you might ask when he or she would typically consult a physician.

Choose a couple of other issues to discuss that are important to you, such as her views on breast-feeding, on allowing you to be present if your child needs to have a painful procedure, and on how she handles issues that are not strictly "medical," such as behavior problems or developmental concerns. You will emerge from the visits with a better feel for what you want in a doctor or nurse practitioner. (Personally, on top of everything else, I'd look for warmth and a good sense of humor.)

You can then consider your impression of the office staff and the office itself. Are there things for children to do in the waiting room? Does the space appear child-friendly? You can also decide the type of practice that best suits you: a private office, a hospital-based clinic, or a community health center. In my experience, each of these sites usually provides excellent care; choosing one or the other is simply a matter of where you would feel most comfortable.

57. A doctor or a nurse practitioner? More and more pediatric care is being delivered by nurse practitioners—and, in some communities, by physician's assistants. A nurse practitioner is a registered nurse who has received additional training, and usually a masters' degree, so that he or she can function like a doctor in many ways—by performing well-baby and well-child checkups and in treating the usual childhood illnesses. Some nurse practitioners specialize further and become experts in subspecialty care, such as the care of premature infants in the neonatal intensive care unit.

Nurse practitioners always work with a doctor to whom they go if they have questions. In many states nurse practitioners can write prescriptions for routine problems without a physician's signature; in others the doctor must co-sign everything. In my experience, nurse practitioners can provide excellent care. I wouldn't hesitate to use one if he or she comes highly recommended and/or you have had a prenatal visit and hit it off.

Planning the Homecoming

58. Callers and visitors. The birth of a baby is an occasion that brings relatives and friends flocking to congratulate the parents and to see the baby. This is gratifying to the parents and fills them with pride. However, too much of it may be exhausting to the mother. How much is too much? It's very different in different cases. Most mothers tire easily the first few weeks at home. They have just felt the effects of some intense hormonal changes. Their usual sleep pattern has been disrupted. Perhaps more important still are the emotional shifts that are called for, especially with the first baby.

Visitors are pure pleasure to some people—relaxing, distracting, rejuvenating. To most of us, however, only a few old friends have such a good effect. Other visitors, to a greater or lesser degree, make us somewhat tense, even when we enjoy seeing them, and leave us somewhat fatigued, especially if we aren't feeling well. When a new mother becomes tired out, she can get off on the wrong foot at the time of the most important transition in her life, and this is too bad for everybody. I think a new mother should set strict limits for visitors right from the start, see how it goes, and then increase the number very gradually if she finds she has plenty of strength left over.

59. Visitors playing with the baby. Most visitors get all excited when they see babies. They want to hold them, joggle them, tickle them, jounce them, waggle their heads at them, and keep up a blue streak of baby talk. Some babies can take a lot, some can't take any, and most are in between. A parent has to use her or his judgment about how much is wise and then be very firm. This is hard to carry out, though, because it's one of the great pleasures of parenthood to have people enjoy the baby. Most babies are easily tired, too, by strange places and strange happenings, as visits to the doctor's office prove.

60. Arranging for extra help in the beginning. If you can figure out a way to get someone to help you the first few weeks you are taking care of the baby, by all means do so. Trying to do everything yourself can exhaust and depress you, and this can start you and the baby off on the wrong foot.

Your mother may be the ideal helper, if you get along with her easily. If you feel she is bossy and still treats you like a child, this is not the time to have her. You will want to feel that the baby is your own and that you are doing a good job. It will help to have a person who has taken care of babies before, but it's most important of all to have someone whom you enjoy having around.

If you can afford to hire a housekeeper or **doula** for a few weeks, you will have the advantage of being free to let her go if she doesn't work out right. In one way, a housekeeper is best—the mother can have the satisfaction of taking complete care of her baby from the start—but a housekeeper is hard to find and expensive.

"Doula" is a Greek word that means "woman's helper." It refers to an experienced woman who guides and assists a new mother in her infant-care tasks. Over the past few years this term has been used to refer to the continuous support a female companion provides during labor and birth. Although she may be professionally trained, a doula performs no medical tasks. Her role is to provide emotional, physical, and informational support to the laboring woman and her family.

Promising results from several studies have demonstrated that doula-supported women need fewer cesarean sections. Additionally, providing a labor companion resulted in fewer obstetric interventions, shorter labors, and fewer perinatal problems. The long-term effects of support during labor on mother-infant attachment, maternal self-esteem, and postpartum depression are currently being investigated by researchers at Case Western Reserve University School of Medicine.

61. How long should you engage a helper for? It will depend, of course, on your finances, on your desire to take over, and on your strength. Each day as your strength increases, take over a little more of the work. If, near the end of the second week, you find that you still get tired easily, then by all means keep the helper if you can.

Most expectant parents feel a little scared at the prospect of taking sole charge of a helpless baby for the first time. If you have this feeling, it doesn't mean that you won't be able to do a good job or that you have to have a nurse to show you how. But if you feel really panicky, you will probably learn more comfortably with an agreeable relative, if this can be arranged.

If you can't have regular help, you may be able to afford and find a person to come in once or twice a week to do the cleaning, help you catch up on the housework, and watch the baby for a few hours while you go out.

Equipment and Clothing

62. Getting things ahead of time. Some parents don't feel like buying anything until they have their baby. The only reason I know for this hesitation is superstition or the cultural belief that buying things ahead of time might cause the pregnancy to come to a bad end. The advantage of getting and arranging everything ahead of time is that it lightens the parents' burden later. A certain number of mothers feel tired and easily discouraged when they begin taking care of the baby themselves. A little job like buying half a dozen nipples looms as an ordeal. Mothers who have gotten depressed have said to me afterward, "The next time, I'm going to buy everything I need way ahead. Every piece of clothing is going to be in its place."

What do you really need, in the way of equipment, to take care of a new baby? There are no exact rules, but here are some suggestions. When trying to decide which brand to purchase, however, you are on your own. I'd suggest you check the most recent copies of journals such as *Consumer Reports* for the latest information on safety, durability and practicality.

Outside the Home

63. Car seat. No baby should leave the nursery without a crash-worthy car seat. There are three types of car seats. The first type is designed just for newborns. They are called **car seat carriers.** They are designed for rear-facing positions in cars and recommended for infants up to 20 pounds and/or 27 inches. The big advantage to this car seat is that it has handles and is removable from the base. These car seats usually have a hood that shades the baby's eyes from the sun. This car seat also has latches on the back that will attach to most shopping carts. Some manufacturers have also designed a stroller that the car seat attaches to after being removed from the car. The fabric is machine washable.

The second type is called a **convertible car seat.** It is designed for a newborn or a toddler and is recommended for children up to 40 pounds and/or 42 inches. This car seat both reclines and sits in an upright position. The material is machine washable. This car seat is designed for either a forward- or reverse-facing position.

The third type is called a **booster car seat.** They are recommended for children 30 to 60 pounds and/or up to 55 inches. This car seat allows older children to see out of the windows of a car. It is very similar to the booster seats used in restaurants.

I try to discourage parents from attaching toys to the bar on the car seat. The first thing that a child's face will hit in a car accident is that toy. You also need to be warned about putting children in the front seat if a car is equipped with a passenger-side airbag. The child should be placed in the back seat. In fact, all children are generally safer in the back seat.

Consumer Reports frequently updates its ratings of car seats. I'd also suggest you send for "The Family Shopping Guide to Car Seats" from the American Academy of Pediatrics (see Resource Section for address) and call the Auto Safety Hot Line (800-424-9393) for information on car seat safety notices.

64. Water supply. If you are using well water, it's important to have it tested for bacteria and nitrates before the baby arrives. Nitrate salts in well water can cause blueness of the baby's lips and skin. Write or call your county or state health department. Also discuss fluoride supplements with your doctor.

Nursery Equipment

65. A place to sleep. You may want to get a beautiful expensive bassinet, lined with silk. But the baby doesn't care. All she needs is sides to keep her from rolling out, and something soft but firm in the bottom for a mattress. (I prefer firm surfaces and would avoid very soft mattresses. Some scientists believe that babies can more easily suffocate if they lie face down on a very soft mattress.) A simple bassinet on wheels is convenient at first. Sometimes there's a cradle that's been in the family for many years, or the parents want to make a cradle, especially for their first child. Most parents, however, start with a crib with a bumper pad to go all around the inside. Cribs should have slats less than $2\frac{3}{8}$ inches apart, a snug-fitting mattress, childproof side locking mechanisms, no sharp edges or lead paint, and at least 26 inches from the top of the rail to the mattress set at its lowest level.

Most mattresses are now constructed of foam-wrapped, coiled innersprings with a waterproof covering or high-density foam with a moisture-repellent covering. You can make a mattress by obtaining the proper size foam and covering it with a waterproof enclosure. The sides of a small bassinet will probably have to be lined to protect your baby from injury. Bumper pads for the sides of the crib are helpful in keeping the heat from escaping through the infant's head. Your baby doesn't need a pillow for her head, and you should not use one.

66. Something to change and dress her on. You can change and dress the baby on a low table or bathroom counter, where water is handy, or on the top of a bureau that is at a comfortable height. Changing tables with a waterproof pad, safety straps, and storage shelves are convenient, though expensive, and may not be adaptable for other uses later. Some types fold; some have an attached bath.

Other Equipment

67. A diaper bag is very useful when you leave the house with your baby. It should have compartments for diapers, wipes, ointment, a folding plastic changing pad, and nursing bottle.

68. A covered diaper pail should hold three gallons. If you are going to wash your own cloth diapers, rinse the soiled ones in the toilet right away (hold tight as you flush) and then let them soak in the pail with a cup of borax per gallon of water. If you're going to use a diaper service, they will provide a container.

69. An inclined plastic seat in which the baby can be strapped, carried short distances, set down almost anywhere, and from which she can watch the world go by, is a most useful accessory. (Some infant car seats can be used for this purpose too.) The base should be larger than the seat; otherwise it will tip over when the baby gets active. There are also cloth seats that move with the infant's movement. Be careful about placing babies in any kind of seat on countertops and tables, as the baby's movements could inch the seat off the edge.

Inclined plastic seats are now called bouncer seats. The material is machine washable. Some of the seats vibrate, some rock, some bounce, and some have handles for carrying. This is a nice extra, but not necessary, since you can use a car seat around the house to seat or rock a child.

The seat tends, however, to be overused in the sense that the baby is apt to be always in it and so is deprived of bodily contact with people. A baby should be held for feedings, comforting and at other times.

70. A rectal thermometer is necessary to take rectal or axillary (armpit) temperature, or you may want to use an ear thermometer, but they are more expensive. (See Section 1047.)

71. A child's nose syringe with bulb suction is helpful to remove mucus during colds, if the mucus is interfering with feeding.

72. Intercoms can be inexpensive and may be plugged into any wall outlet or operate on batteries. These are especially useful if the baby will be sleeping in a room out of range of the parents' hearing.

73. Play yards (playpens) (manufacturers no longer use the word "playpen") are controversial. Some parents and psychologists disapprove of the imprisonment of a baby in a pen, fearing that it may cramp the child's spirit and desire to explore. I see what they mean. But I've known many babies who spent several hours a day in pens and who still ended up demon explorers with high spirits. But neither of these opinions proves anything definite.

This item is very useful to have around the house for times when your baby can't be watched carefully. As a practical matter it's hard for me to see how a parent can cook a meal, or do much else, after a baby has learned to crawl around, unless the baby is in a pen part of the time. It can also be used for naps. Some pens are designed with an add-on bassinet, which sits at a higher level than the base of the play yard, eliminating the need for a separate bassinet, and can be used as a crib. This is especially useful in the play yards designed to fold into compact travel-size cases that can be used as portable cribs/play yards. They are recommended for children up to 30 pounds or up to 34 inches tall.

If you are going to use a play yard, you should start putting the baby in it each day from about three months. Babies differ—some tolerate play yards well—some poorly. If you wait until a baby starts to crawl (six to eight months), the play yard will surely seem like a prison and will be met with persistent howls.

74. Infant walkers are a major cause of injury. Aside from providing temporary amusement, their benefits are nonexistent and their dangers clearly proven. They should not be used. Manufacturers now make stationary walkers that bounce, swivel, or rock. They come with toys attached for entertainment and are much safer for children.

75. Rocking and bouncing swings can be useful for infants, as can stationary seats that look like walkers without wheels. They work either by battery power or by a wind-up mechanism. The back in the swing reclines or sits in an upright position. Some of the swings come with toys attached. The padding is removable for washing. These swings are recommended for children up to 25 pounds and are especially useful for a baby with colic or one who likes continual movement.

76. Scales. If a baby is doing well and is seen by the doctor regularly, there is no real need to have scales at home. I think that scales generally are a waste of money and space and tend to cause worry rather than prevent it.

Bedding

77. Blankets are usually made of acrylic or a polyester-cotton combination. These are easy to wash and non-allergenic. Even if you use a sleep bag or sleeper as the baby's principal bed covering, you will probably need a couple of blankets for extra covering when it's cold. A knitted shawl is a particularly convenient form of blanket for babies because it wraps around them so easily when they are up, and stays tucked in when it is over them in bed. Make sure there are no long threads for the baby to wrap around fingers or toes! Also avoid knit blankets with large holes that a baby could get caught in. Acrylic blankets and shawls are both warm and washable. Blankets should be large enough to tuck well under a crib mattress. Cotton receiving blankets, which have little warmth, are useful for wrapping around the baby who would otherwise kick off the bed coverings or for tightly swaddling the young baby who is comfortable and secure and can sleep only when held immobile.

78. Waterproof sheeting of plastic or rubber. Most popular is sheeting that has a flannelette backing on both surfaces. I've had mothers tell me this sheeting is wonderful. It stays in place, and the sheet does not slip on it. It is more comfortable in case the baby happens to get in contact with it. Since it allows some circulation of air under the baby, there is usually no need to cover it with a quilted pad, and this makes a saving in laundry. However, in hot weather you may still need a pad, too. The sheeting should be washed (it will go in the machine) each day if it gets wet with urine, so you will need two.

The waterproof sheeting should preferably be large enough to tuck in around the mattress. Otherwise the edges of the mattress may get wet at times. Incidentally, the plastic cover that comes on most new mattresses is not sufficient by itself. Sooner or later urine gets into the air holes and makes it smell.

Additional small squares of flannel-backed sheeting will save more laundry. Place one under the baby's hips. It will keep the bedsheet dry if the baby stays in one place. You can also use one as a lap protector.

A thin plastic bag such as that used to cover clothes from the dry cleaner should never be used in a crib because of the danger of suffocation if the baby's head gets tangled in it.

79. Pads. If you are using plain waterproof sheeting (without flannel backing), you will need to cover it with a quilted pad. This is to absorb moisture and allow some circulation of air under the baby's body; otherwise the skin stays too hot and wet. The number of pads you will need will depend on how often the laundry is done, how much the baby wets or spits up. You will need three anyway, and six are more convenient.

80. Sheets. You will need three to six sheets. If you are using a small bassinet at first, you can use diapers for sheets. For anything larger, the best sheets are made of cotton stockinette. They are easy to wash, quick to dry, spread smoothly without ironing, and do not feel clammy when wet. Fitted sheets can be bought to cover the crib mattress.

Clothing

81. All sleepwear from infant through size 14 is required by Federal Law to be flame-resistant. Read the washing instructions for each garment about how to retain its flame-retardant properties. Don't use any soap—bar, liquid, or powder—or any liquid bleach or liquid softener, all of which remove the fire-retardant protection. Currently, manufacturers recommend low-sudsing detergent. Look on the box, to be sure that the laundry product is safe for fabric that's been treated with a fire retardant. Check underclothes and outer clothes for labels.

Remember that your baby will be growing very rapidly during the first year, so be sure you buy her clothing to fit loosely. Except for diaper covers, it's generally better to begin with three- to six-month-size clothes instead of new-born or "layette-sized" clothing.

A baby or child doesn't need more in the way of clothing or covering than an adult; if anything, less. For example, nightgowns are entirely practical and can be worn night and day. The mittens on the ends of the sleeves, which are to keep babies from scratching themselves, can be worn open or closed. The long gowns make it harder for babies to kick off their coverings; the short ones may be preferable for hot weather. Buy three or four anyway. It would be convenient to have two or three more, especially if you don't have a washer and dryer.

82. Sleep bags and sleepers. By six months, when babies can move about in their cribs, most parents find it more practical to put them to bed in sleep bags or sleepers than to try to keep blankets over them. (They simply crawl out from under their covers.) The bags are shaped like long nighties, which cover the feet and have sleeves. Many of them can be let out in the length and shoulders as the child grows. The sleepers are shaped like coveralls or snowsuits, enclosing each leg separately, including the foot. (The sole of the foot may be of tough, non-skid material.) It is most convenient when the zipper on a sleeper goes from neck to foot. Check the insides of the feet regularly. They can collect hair, which can wind around the baby's toes and be painful.

If a baby or child is going to sleep in a room warm enough so that you would be comfortable wearing a cotton shirt or sleeping under a cotton blanket, the baby's bag or sleeper shouldn't be warmer than cotton blanketing. If the room is cold enough so that an adult would require a good wool or acrylic blanket for covering, the baby will need a heavier bag or sleeper and a blanket.

83. Shirts. There are three styles of undershirt: pullover, side-snap closing, and a one-piece type that slips over the head and snaps around the diaper. The type with side snaps is slightly easier to put on a small, limp baby. Medium weight and short sleeves should be sufficient unless a baby will live in an unusually cold house. Some brands have tabs to pin cloth diapers to, which will help an inexperienced parent keep the diapers from falling down. However, if you are concerned about keeping the stomach covered, you may want a one-piece shirt with snaps at the bottom (called a onesie). Take labels and care tags out so they don't irritate the baby's neck. The most comfortable fabric for children is 100% cotton. Half tee shirts work well with one-piece outer outfits like rompers. Onesies or snap tee shirts work well with all outfits so the baby's stomach is not exposed. Start with the one-year-old size or, if you are fussy about fit, the six-month size. Buy at least three or four. It would be convenient to have two or three more, especially if you don't have a washer and dryer.

84. Stretch suits are increasingly popular for daytime wear for babies, but can be used for sleeping. They snap or zip from the neck down one or both legs. Zippers have to be carefully zipped to avoid pinching the skin. Check the insides of the feet regularly. They can collect hair, which can wind around the baby's toes and be painful.

85. Sacks and kimonos are short jackets and long gowns, front opening, usually of flowered cotton flannelette, to be worn over shirt or nightie for a dressier appearance; not essential, often a shower present.

86. Sweaters are useful to add extra warmth over or under the other clothes when the baby is up, under other coverings when in bed. Be sure that the neck opening has sufficient give or that there are shoulder snaps, well-secured buttons, or zippers up the back.

87. A bunting is a zippered bag in which the baby is encased up to the shoulders, usually with an attached hood. Make sure it has an opening in the center for the car seat buckle.

A snowsuit or pram suit has a coverall shape and also encloses the feet. It may come in one or two pieces, and often has a hood. It should zip or snap from neck to foot.

88. Other clothes. To cover the baby's ears **knitted acrylic or cotton caps** are all right for going outdoors in the kind of weather that makes grown-ups put on caps, or for sleeping in an equally cold room. Avoid using caps that are too large at night because they could cover the baby's face as she moves around while sleeping. For milder weather, caps are unnecessary; most babies don't like them anyway. You don't need **booties and stockings,** at least until your baby is sitting up and playing around in a cold house. **Dresses** make a baby look pretty, but are otherwise unnecessary, and bothersome to the baby and the parent. A **sun hat,** with a chin strap to keep it on, is useful for the baby who will tolerate it. See Section 332 about **shoes.**

Some parents find good used clothes or hand-me-downs as a good choice for rapidly growing children. Watch for scratchy lace on clothes, close to the face and arms. It can make even an adult irritable. Headbands are cute but if they're too tight or itchy (or if a ponytail is too tight), they can cause the head to hurt.

Diapers

There are three choices: cloth diapers that you buy and wash yourself (the least expensive method); a diaper service that provides cloth diapers and launders them; and disposable diapers (the most expensive).

89. Cloth diapers come unfolded or pre-folded. The unfolded are much more versatile; you can use them for sheets in a bassinet, for towels, etc. The most popular materials for diapers are gauze, cotton flannel, and bird's-eye. The gauze diapers are quicker drying but do not hold as much of the urine when the baby is larger. Two dozen will cover your needs if you wash them every day and don't use too many for sheets, towels, etc. Six dozen will cover all possible needs. Get the large size. If you buy about one-third of your total prefolded and two-thirds unfolded, you'll have the advantages of both.

90. Disposable diapers, because of their convenience, are very popular in the United States, but they have created an ecological nightmare. First, they take up an enormous amount of landfill space. Second, they're not biodegradable. (If you read the fine print in some manufacturers' claims for biodegradability, you discover that the plastic "degrades" into fine bits of plastic after many years' exposure to sunlight.) Third, the feces go into the garbage as untreated waste, which pollutes the groundwater, creating a public health hazard. Even if you decide to use disposable diapers, it's helpful to have a pack of cloth diapers, for burping pads, lap pads, changing table covers, etc. You must change disposable diapers as often as you would cloth diapers. They can *seem* dry because they absorb moisture well, but they still need changing. If disposable diapers begin to leak, it's time to graduate to the next larger size (see Sections 122–125).

91. Diaper pins. They should be rustproof, stainless steel with a lock head for safety. You'll need four to start with.

92. Diaper wipes. You can use a washcloth with soap and water, but if you want the convenience of diaper wipes use the ones without chemicals and perfume. The wipes that contain alcohol and other chemicals, and perfumes, may cause rashes.

93. Diaper covers are used over cloth diapers. There are many different natural fiber or synthetic covers, which vary in price and absorbency. Covers come in pull-on, snap-on, and self-fastening styles. The elastic at the edges is less irritating when enclosed in a soft binding.

As long as your baby's skin is clear in the diaper region, you can use diaper covers as much as is convenient. When there is diaper rash, leave them off. Wash them each day. Make sure the fit is not confining or tight around your baby's legs.

Bathing

94. Someplace to bathe her. The baby can be bathed in the kitchen sink, especially if it has a spraying faucet which works like a mini shower—great for rinsing the baby's hair and for keeping him warm and happy—a plastic tub (get one with a wide edge to rest your arm on), a dishpan, or a washstand. You can sit on a high stool at the sink. Molded plastic bathing tubs and contoured liners of sponge material to fit the baby's body are available and generally inexpensive. If you use a sponge liner, it should be dried thoroughly in a clothes dryer after each use, to prevent the growth of harmful bacteria.

A **bath thermometer** is not necessary, but can be a comfort to the inexperienced parent. Always test the water temperature with your hand anyway. Water should never be hot, always lukewarm. Also, never run warm water into the tub or sink while the baby is in it unless you are sure that the temperature is constant. The temperature setting on water heaters should be set at a maximum of 120°F to prevent scalding.

Toiletries

95. Cotton balls are useful at bath time, for wiping the baby's eyes. However, cotton pads are less likely to shred over the eyes.

Any **mild soap** is satisfactory. Avoid liquid baby soaps and deodorant soaps; they may cause rashes. There are tearproof shampoos and separate shampoos for body bath for the child who has sensitive skin.

Baby lotion is not really necessary unless the child's skin is dry, though parents enjoy applying it. Many parents now prefer to use creams and lotions which don't have scent or color added and which most often cost less than the usual baby products.

Baby oils, most of which are made of mineral oil, have

been used extensively for dry or normal skin or for diaper rash. But tests have shown that mineral oil itself may cause a very mild rash in some babies. So it is sensible not to use it routinely unless you find by testing that it has more advantage than disadvantage in your baby's case.

Use of baby **talcum powder** should be avoided. Talcum powder is especially irritating to the lungs and can cause significant problems if inhaled.

An ointment containing lanolin and petrolatum, in tube or jar, protects the skin when there is diaper rash.

Infant **nail scissors** have blunted ends, though many parents find **infant nail clippers** easier to use and less likely to cut the baby.

See Section 1092 for other items to keep in your medicine cabinet.

Feeding Equipment

96. Breast pumps. If you're planning to nurse and express your milk regularly—many working mothers do it for weeks or months—you'll probably find a breast pump helpful. See Section 203 on Breast-Feeding.

97. Nursing bottles. Even if you expect to breast-feed, buy at least three, for occasional bottle feedings, water, and juice. If you know ahead of time that your baby is not going to breast-feed, buy at least nine of the 8-ounce bottles. You will use six to eight a day in the beginning for the formula. Plastic bottles don't break when adults or babies drop them. You'll need to have a bottle brush, too.

Water and juice can be given just as well from 8-ounce bottles, even though they are unnecessarily large. But some parents prefer 4-ounce bottles for this purpose. Two or three of these will be enough.

There are also **disposable bottles** consisting of thin, flexible, sterilized plastic liners that are ready to be used with a rigid plastic holder.

98. Nipples. A dozen if the baby will be bottle-fed, a half-dozen if breast-fed. You should have a few extra in case you are having trouble making the nipple holes the right size.

You'll also need a nipple brush. Nipples made with silicone are more expensive but don't deteriorate from boiling and milk fat. There are all kinds of specially shaped nipples, but no scientific proof for the claims made by their manufacturers. Nipples are sold with different size holes to vary the flow rate according to age. Also, some withstand boiling and wear and tear better than others. Be sure to follow instructions as to when to replace old nipples.

99. Pacifiers. If you decide to use them, three or four will do (see Sections 808–811).

100. Bibs. Small round bibs are useful for keeping drool off the clothes. For the mess that babies or children always make with their solid food they need a large bib of plastic, nylon, or terry (or a combination), preferably with a pocket along the lower edge to catch the food that comes running down. Plastic is easily rinsed, but just looks uncomfortable to the adult. Be sure there is a cloth binding around the neck. A terry bib can also be used for wiping the face if you can find a dry corner. Bibs make wonderful gift items.

101. For mixing formula, it's convenient to use a quart measure marked in ounces. But you can use any measuring cup marked in ounces and then mix in any saucepan, pitcher, or jar that holds a quart.

It's also helpful to have a long-handled spoon for stirring, a set of measuring spoons if you are going to make evaporated milk formula, a punch-type can opener, and an eggbeater or whisk to mix commercial powdered formula. Always mix formula exactly as described on the label. Premixed formula is available in jars, but it is the most expensive type. The powder jars are the least expensive. The concentrates are in between in price.

102. For sterilizing bottles, you'll need a pail, kettle, or roaster with lid, preferably 8 inches high and 9 inches in diameter so that it will hold eight bottles vertically in a wire bottle rack. There are stove-top sterilizers, and also electric sterilizers that turn themselves off. Tongs that are plastic- or rubber-coated in the part that grips the bottle are good for handling hot bottles. (Most parents won't need to sterilize, so this equipment won't be necessary.) Dishwashers are usually hot enough to provide sufficient sterilization.

103. Bottle warmer. It isn't considered necessary any longer to warm a baby's bottle. It can of course be warmed in any kind of container. An electric warmer is very handy when the hot water supply is undependable. There is a special warmer that plugs into an automobile cigarette lighter. *Never warm a baby's bottle in a microwave oven.* The milk can be scalding when the bottle feels cool. Test the milk temperature on the underside of your wrist.

104. A food grinder or blender will puree cooked vegetables, fruits, and meats so that the baby can eat what the family eats. Organic fruits and vegetables without chemicals or pesticides are great choices. Making your own baby food helps you avoid the expense of baby food in jars, many of which are diluted with starches and water. Some hand-operated grinders can be put in the dishwasher.

Outings

105. Carriers to carry a baby on the parent's chest, back, or side are useful for shopping, walks, visits, housework, and fretful periods. They provide physical and emotional closeness. The **chest carrier** may look awkward, but it is favored by more parents for young babies because it is easy to get the baby in and out, you can see and check on her, and the physical and emotional contact is the closest. Parents will want to carry a very young baby in front in order to keep an eye on her. Chest carriers need to be used early and regularly or neither the parent nor infant may be able to tolerate them. People who do use them regularly soon find them indispensable. The side carrier has almost the same advantages. *Caution: Do not drive a car with your baby in a chest carrier or in anything except a car seat.*

106. Framed backpacks are satisfactory, and are easy to carry on long walks, for older babies who can sit straight.

The top rim needs to be padded for when a sleeping baby's face rests on it. You cannot sit comfortably—on a bus, for example—while wearing a backpack. Some types can be propped up as infant seats. The soft chest carrier can usually be converted for use on the back.

A front carrier made of soft material is an effective and soothing way to carry an infant.

Babies and parents enjoy the closeness of a back carrier.

107. Government-approved, dynamically tested automobile restraints—a carrier for a baby, a seat for a child—are essential pieces of equipment for all children who ever ride in a car—and what child doesn't? See Section 63.

A baby should be able to ride reclining backward, strapped into a carrier, in the back seat of the car. The older infant may face forward in a reclining position. A child between 20 and 45 pounds should be strapped into a special seat that protects her from side crashes as well as head-on crashes. If you are using a car seat that requires a top anchor, never use it without that anchor. (Be sure the anchor is installed according to the directions.)

In buying, borrowing, or renting a car carrier or seat,

don't take one unless it conforms to a Federal Motor Vehicle Safety Standard of 1981 or later, and is labeled as "dynamically (crash) tested." It's a good idea to take your car seat along when you are traveling to visit friends or relatives. Use it during the trip, on the plane or bus, and then you'll have it with you for riding in the car when you reach your destination.

I think the best way to teach children good safety habits in the car is to have a rule that the car doesn't get started up until the children are in their car seats and the older children (over 45 pounds) and grown-ups have their seat belts on. If you absolutely have to take a child in a car without a car seat, the best place for the child is in the back seat, not in the arms of a passenger in the front seat or loose on the rear deck of a station wagon or truck bed. *Do not use one seat belt for two children together, or for an adult holding a small child in a chest carrier or on her lap.*

There are now many free or low-cost loan, rental, or purchase programs for carriers and car seats. You can find out about them from the nursery of the hospital where you deliver your baby, or from your doctor or local public health nurse, or check your HMO or insurance to see about coverage.

For up-to-date information on car seats, you can write to the Office of Public Education, American Academy of Pediatrics, 141 Northwest Point Boulevard, Elk Grove Village, IL 60009; or call them at 800-433-9016 or 708-228-5005.

108. A carriage (pram) is used primarily by parents in cities in the northeastern part of the United States to take their babies on daily outings or to give them naps in, on the porch. They get a lot of satisfaction and use out of it. But in most parts of this country parents don't think about carriages—or outings.

109. A stroller is a handy way to take a young child shopping and on other errands, especially for those in cities who don't have a car at their disposal. A folding "umbrella" stroller can be easily carried on a bus or in a car, but be sure it's a sturdy one. Children should always be strapped into their strollers. There are convenient strollers available where the car seat snaps on and off of the stroller frame and allows for easy transferring from car to stroller without having to wake up a sleeping infant.

110. Carryall bassinet. This is a combination of a carrying bassinet and diaper bag in which the baby can sleep while you are visiting friends. It folds up for storage.

The following is a generous list of items to take along on outings, but some are not necessary:

—Bassinet
—Changing table
—Crib
—Baby monitor
—Dresser
—Lamp
—Mobile
—Bumper, comforter and sheet
—4 crib sheets
—3 crib mattress pads
—2–5 blankets
—Pacifier
—First-aid kit
—Breast pump
—Night light
—Swing
—Jumper
—Crib toys
—Active toys
—Toy box
—High chair
—Booster seat
—Play yard
—2–8 bottles
—Bottle warmer
—Bottle sterilizer
—Disposable nurser

—Car seat
—Stroller
—Baby carriage
—Diaper bag
—Portable playpen or crib
—Head support pad for infants in car seat
—Baby bath tub
—6 washcloths
—4 hooded bath towels
—Nail scissors
—Brush and comb
—Soap, shampoo, lotion, oil, cotton swabs, baby wipes, diaper ointment, bath toys
—6 onesies
—3–6 hats and booties
—3–6 receiving blankets
—4–6 sleep and play outfits
—4–6 bibs
—3–8 gowns/sleepers
—4 dozen cloth diapers per month or 10 disposable diapers per day

___Feeder for strained foods

___Dishes and utensils

___Safety gates, latches

___Outlet covers

___8 safety pins

___1 take-me-home outfit

___1 snowsuit or bunting

___1-3 sweaters

CARE OF YOUR NEWBORN

Enjoy Your Baby

111. Don't be afraid of your baby. From what some people—including some doctors—say about babies demanding attention, you'd think that they come into the world determined to get their parents under their thumbs by hook or by crook. This isn't true. Your baby is born to be a reasonable, friendly—though occasionally demanding—human being.

Don't be afraid to feed her when you think she's really hungry. If you are mistaken, she'll merely refuse to take much. Don't be afraid to love her and enjoy her. Every baby needs to be smiled at, talked to, played with, fondled—gently and lovingly—just as much as she needs vitamins and calories. That's what will make her a person who loves people and enjoys life. The baby who doesn't get any loving will grow up cold and unresponsive.

Don't be afraid to respond to other desires of hers as long as they seem sensible to you and as long as you don't become a slave to her. When she cries in the early weeks, it's because she's uncomfortable for some reason or other—maybe it's hunger or indigestion, or fatigue, or tension. The uneasy feeling you have when you hear her cry, the feeling that you want to comfort her, is meant to be part of your nature, too. Being held, rocked, or walked may be what she needs.

Spoiling doesn't come from being good to a baby in a sensible way, and it doesn't come all of a sudden. Spoiling comes on gradually when parents are too afraid to use their common sense or when they really want to be slaves and encourage their babies to become slave drivers.

Everyone wants the child to turn out to be healthy in her habits and easy to live with. But each child herself wants to eat at sensible hours and later to learn good table manners. Her bowels (as long as the movements don't become too hard) will move according to their own healthy pattern, which may or may not be regular; and when she's a lot older and wiser, you can show her where to sit to move them. She will develop her own pattern of sleep according to her own needs. In all these habits she will sooner or later want to fit into the family's way of doing things, with only a minimum of guidance from you.

112. Enjoy children as they are—that's how they'll grow up best. Every baby's face is different from every other's. In the same way, every baby's pattern of development is different. One may be very advanced in her general bodily strength and coordination—an early sitter, stander, walker—a sort of infant athlete. And yet she may be slow in doing careful, skillful things with her fingers, or in talking. Even babies who are athletes in rolling over, standing, and creeping may turn out to be slow to learn to walk. Babies who are advanced in their physical activities may be very slow in teething, and vice versa. Children who turn out later to be smart in schoolwork may have been so slow in beginning to talk that their parents were afraid for a while that they were slow; and children who have just an ordinary amount of intelligence are sometimes very early talkers.

I am purposely picking out examples of children with mixed rates of development to give you an idea of what a jumble of different qualities and patterns of growth each individual person is composed.

One baby is born to be big-boned and square and chunky, while another will always be small boned and delicate. Some individuals really seem to be born to be fat. If they lose weight during an illness, they gain it back promptly afterward. The troubles that they have in the world never take away their appetites. The opposite kind of individuals stay on the thin side, even when they have the most nourishing food to eat, even though life is running smoothly for them.

Love and enjoy your children for what they are, for what they look like, for what they do and forget about the qualities that they don't have. I don't give you this advice just for sentimental reasons. There's a very important practical point here. The children who are appreciated for what they are, even if they are homely, or clumsy, or slow, will grow up with confidence in themselves and happy. They will have a spirit that will make the best of all the capacities that they do have, and of all the opportunities that come their way.

But the children who have never been quite accepted by their parents, who have always felt that they were not quite right, will grow up lacking confidence. They'll never be able to make full use of what brains, what skills, what physical attractiveness they have. If they start life with a handicap, physical or mental, it will be multiplied tenfold by the time they are grown up.

113. Babies aren't frail. "I'm so afraid I'll hurt her if I don't handle her just right," a parent may say about her first baby. You don't have to worry; you have a pretty tough baby. There are many ways to hold her. If her head drops backward by mistake, it won't hurt her. The open spot on her skull (the fontanel) is covered by a tough membrane— tough as canvas—that isn't easily injured. The system to control body temperature is working quite well in most babies if she's covered halfway sensibly. She has good resistance to most germs. During a family cold epidemic, she's apt to have it the mildest of all. If she gets her head tangled in anything, she has a strong instinct to struggle and yell. If she's not getting enough to eat, she will probably cry for more. If the light is too strong for her eyes, she'll blink and fuss. She knows how much sleep she needs, and takes it. She can care for herself pretty well for a person who can't say a word and knows nothing about the world.

Early Feelings

114. The blue feeling. It's possible that you will find yourself feeling discouraged for a while when you first begin taking care of your baby. It's a fairly common feeling, especially with the first. You may not be able to put your finger on anything that is definitely wrong. You just weep easily. Or you may feel bad about certain things. One woman whose baby cries quite a bit feels sure that he has a real disease, another that her husband has become strange and distant, another that she has lost all her looks.

A feeling of depression may come on a few days after the baby is born or not until several weeks later. The commonest time is when a mother comes home from the hospital. It isn't just the work that gets her down. She may even have someone to do all the work, for the time being. It's the feeling of being responsible for the whole household again, plus the entirely new responsibility of the baby's care and safety. Then there are all the physical and hormonal changes at the time of birth, which probably alter the mother's mood to some degree.

The majority of mothers don't get discouraged enough in this period to ever call it depression. The reason I mention it is that several mothers have told me afterward, "I'm sure I wouldn't have been so depressed or discouraged if I had known how common this feeling is. Why, I thought that my whole outlook on life had changed once and for all." You can face a thing much better if you know that a lot of other people have gone through it, too, and if you know that it's just temporary.

If you begin to feel blue or discouraged, try to get some relief from the constant care of the baby in the first month or two, especially if the child cries a great deal. Go to a movie, or to the mall. Buy yourself a much-wanted dress. Work on some new or unfinished project—writing, painting, sewing, building—something creative and satisfying. Visit a good friend occasionally. Take the baby along if you can't find anyone to baby-sit. Or get your friends to come and see you. All of these are tonics. If you are depressed, you may not feel like doing these things. But if you make yourself do them, you will feel better. And that's important for the baby and your husband as well as yourself.

If the depression does not lift in a few days or if it is

becoming worse, you may be suffering from what is referred to as postpartum depression, and you should promptly get in touch with your doctor, who might refer you to a mental health professional. A psychiatrist or analyst can be of great assistance and comfort at such a time.

When a mother feels blue and thinks that her husband seems indifferent, there are two sides to consider. On the one hand, anyone who is depressed feels that other people are less friendly and affectionate. But on the other hand, it's natural for a father, being human, to feel left out when his wife and the rest of the household are completely wrapped up in the baby. So it's a sort of vicious circle. The mother (as if she didn't have enough to do already!) has to remember to pay some attention to her husband. And she should encourage him to share in the care of the baby.

115. The father's opportunity in the early weeks at home. A father shouldn't be surprised if he finds that he has mixed feelings at times toward his wife and toward his baby— during the pregnancy, during all the commotion of the labor and delivery stage, and after they are all home again. He can remind himself that his feelings are probably not nearly so churned up as his wife's, especially after the homecoming. She has been through an intense hormonal change. If it's her first baby, she can't help feeling anxious. Any baby will make great demands on her strength and spirits at first.

What all this adds up to is that most women need a great deal of support and comfort from their partners at this time. To be able to give a lot to the baby, they must receive more than usual. Partly it's the need of the father's full participation in the care of the baby, and in the housework. Even more it's emotional support: patience, understanding, appreciation, affection. The father's job may be complicated by the fact that if his wife is tired and upset she won't have the spirit to be appreciative of his efforts. In fact, she may be complaining. But if he realizes how much she needs his help and love, it will encourage him to give it anyway.

116. The first few weeks at home, most new parents find that they are more anxious than usual and just plain exhausted. They worry about the baby's crying and fretful spells, suspecting that something is seriously wrong. They worry about every sneeze and every spot of rash. They tiptoe into the baby's room to see whether she is still breathing. It's probably instinctive for parents to be overly protective at this period. I suppose it's nature's way of being sure that the millions of new parents throughout the world, some of whom may be immature, take their new responsibility seriously. A little concern might be a good thing. Fortunately it wears off.

Bodily Contact and Other Bonds

117. We've put distance between mothers and babies. Before birth, babies are not only enveloped and warmed and nourished by their mothers, they participate in every bodily movement their mothers make.

After birth, in many of the more natural, nonindustrial parts of the world, most babies are held against their mothers all day long by cloth carriers of one kind or another, and they sleep with her at night. They continue to share in all their mothers' movements as their mothers go about their regular jobs whatever they may be—food gathering and preparing, tilling, weaving, house care. The babies are breast-fed the instant they whimper. They not only hear but feel the vibrations of their mothers' words and songs.

In many societies, as babies get a little older, they are carried about most of the day on the hips or backs of their slightly older sisters.

Our society has thought up a dozen ingenious ways to put distance between mothers and their babies.

We have invented anesthetized childbirth, so a mother misses the dramatic evidence of having carried and borne her baby herself. Babies are whisked away to a nursery where other people care for them, leaving parents with the impression they are not very competent. Babies are fed commercial formulas from bottles, so mothers and babies lose the opportunity for the most intimate bond in child rearing.

We've thought up the idea of propping bottles on babies'

chests so that parents can be tending to other chores during the relatively short periods when young babies are awake and feeding.

To us it seems natural to put our babies on flat firm mattresses, in immobile cribs, preferably in quiet rooms.

We have infant seats in which babies can be strapped so that they don't have to be held when they're awake or restless or being moved about.

We put babies in pens where they can be kept out of trouble without having to be picked up, moved, or carried. This is in contrast to the most successful treatment for the hurts, the slights, the sadness of infants, children and adults—a good hug.

Two doctor friends of mine, John Kennell and Marshall Klaus, who have spent months observing natural baby care in an Indian village in Guatemala, point out that there appears to be no spitting, no crying, no fretfulness, no colic there. Yet mothers have never heard of burping.

Drs. Kennell and Klaus have also watched what mothers in America naturally do when allowed to have their babies with them soon after birth. They don't just look at them. They spend a lot of time touching their limbs and bodies and faces with their fingers. Months later these mothers have easier relations with their babies and their babies are more responsive than those whose mothers don't have these opportunities to touch soon after birth.

But if, for any reason, you didn't have this earliest contact with your baby, don't worry. This attachment and bonding process, as it's called, will happen—with mother, father, and siblings—as soon as physical contact with the baby begins. For example, it can occur with a baby who's in an incubator when you reach in through the portholes and stroke him.

I think that parents in our society can get a better perspective on our methods by comparing them with what comes naturally in simpler societies.

118. How to be natural. I'd draw the following conclusions:

Natural childbirth and rooming-in should be available for all who want them. (If the parents who would like them will all make a point of asking for them, all hospitals, doctors, and nurses will eventually get the message.)

Mothers and fathers should have their baby to hold and fondle for an hour after the baby is born, especially if rooming-in is not available.

Breast-feeding should be encouraged, especially by nurses and doctors, and relatives.

Bottle-propping should be avoided except when there's no choice—as when a mother of twins has no help and has to prop for one baby, at least, at each feeding.

Mothers and fathers should try to use a cloth carrier more than the infant seat for going places with the young baby and for comforting the baby when fussy or colicky. The carrier is even more valuable when used to carry the baby on the chest rather than on the back.

Caring for Your Baby

119. Being companionable with your baby. Be quietly friendly with your baby whenever you are with him. He's getting a sense of how much you mean to each other all the time you're feeding him, burping him, bathing him, dressing him, changing his diapers, holding him, or just sitting in the room with him. When you hug him or make noises at him, when you show him that you think he's the most wonderful baby in the world, it makes his spirit grow, just the way milk makes his bones grow. That must be why we grown-ups instinctively talk baby talk and waggle our heads when we greet a baby, even grown-ups who are otherwise dignified or unsociable.

One trouble with being an inexperienced parent is that part of the time you take the job so seriously that you forget to enjoy it. Then you and the baby are both missing something. Naturally I don't mean that you should be talking a blue streak at him all the time he's awake, or constantly joggling him or tickling him. That would tire him out, and in the long run might make him tense and spoiled. You can be quiet much of the time you are with him. It's the gentle, easygoing kind of companionship that's good for him and good for you. It's the comfortable feeling that goes into your arms when you hold him, the fond, peaceful expression on your face when you look at him, and the gentle tone in your voice.

120. Companionship without spoiling. It's good for a baby during his play periods to be somewhere near his parents (and brothers and sisters, if any) so that he can see them, make noises at them, hear them speak to him, have them show him a way to play with something occasionally. But it isn't necessary or sensible for him to be in a parent's lap or arms or to have his mother or father amusing him for the majority of the time. He can be enjoying their company, profiting from it, and still be learning how to occupy himself. When new parents are so delighted with their baby that they are holding him or making games for him most of his waking hours, he may become quite dependent on these attentions and demand more and more of them.

121. Things to watch and things to play with. Young babies begin waking earlier and earlier, especially at the end of the afternoon. At such times they want something to do and they want some companionship. At two, three, and four months, they enjoy looking at bright-colored things and things that move, but mostly they enjoy looking at people and their faces. Outdoors, they are delighted to watch leaves and shadows. Indoors, they study their hands, pictures on the wall. There are bright-colored plastic shapes on strings ("mobiles") that you can suspend between the top rails of the crib. Place them just within arm's reach—not right on top of babies' noses—for the time when they begin reaching. You can make mobiles yourself—cardboard shapes covered with colored paper that hang from the ceiling or from a lighting fixture and rotate in slight drafts (they aren't strong enough for playing with or healthful for chewing)—or you can hang suitable household objects within reach—spoons, plastic cups, for instance. All of these toys are nice, but never forget it is human companionship, above all else, that babies love and that particularly fosters their development.

Diapers

See Sections 89–93 about diapers, diaper wipes, and diaper covers.

122. Diapering. Many parents prefer pre-folded cloth diapers which close with Velcro. If you prefer the old-fashioned way, the only important things in putting it on are to have the most cloth where there is the most urine and not to have so much diaper bunched between the legs that they are kept widely separated. With a full-size newborn baby and the usual large square or rectangular diapers, you can fold as in the pictures. First fold lengthwise so that there are three thicknesses. Then fold about one-third of the end over. As a result, half of the folded diaper has six layers, the other half has three layers. A boy needs the double thickness in front. A girl needs the thickness in front if she lies on her abdomen, in back if she lies on her back. When you put in the pin, slip two fingers of the other hand between the baby and the diaper to prevent sticking the child. The pins work better if you keep them stuck into a bar of soap. Or you can run the open pins through your hair just before pinning the diaper.

One Way to Fold a Cloth Diaper

Fold lengthwise to make three thicknesses. Then fold one-third of the end over. When putting on the pin, protect the baby with two fingers between the diaper and the baby's skin.

Most parents change the diapers when they pick the baby up for feeding and again before they put the child back to bed. Parents who are very busy have found they can save time and laundry by changing only once at each feeding—usually after it, because babies frequently have a bowel movement while eating. Most babies are not bothered by being wet. But a few are extra sensitive and have to be changed more often. If children have sufficient covers over them, the wet diaper does not feel cold. It is when wet clothing is exposed to the air that evaporation makes it cold.

If a baby drenches the diaper and the bed, it may be worthwhile using two diapers at a time or a plastic cover. The second diaper may be too bulky if put on the same way as the first. You can pin it around the waist like an apron. Or it can be folded to make a thick but narrower panel down the middle of the first diaper.

123. In cleaning the baby after a bowel movement, you can use plain water on cotton balls or a washcloth, or baby lotion and tissues, or diaper wipes. For girls, always wipe them from front to back. It isn't necessary to wash the baby when changing a wet diaper. When you're changing a baby boy, put a spare diaper loosely over his penis, until you're ready to fasten the diaper. This will keep you from getting sprayed if he happens to urinate before you're done. *Wash your hands with soap and water after changing the diaper.* This prevents the spread of harmful germs.

124. Disposable diapers come in a variety of types and sizes. Many parents today choose to use disposable paper diapers. They are readily available, convenient and easy to use. Adhesive tape at the sides of the paper diaper substitutes for the pins used with cloth diapers. Change disposable diapers as often as you would a cloth diaper. They can *seem* dry because they absorb moisture well, but still need changing. The costs of cloth and disposable diapers are similar when a diaper service is used. Cloth diapers washed at home bring a savings to the family. Some families choose to use cloth diapers as an environmental statement—less paper, fewer lost trees.

125. Washing the diapers. You want a covered pail partially filled with water to put used diapers into as soon as they are removed. If it contains a one-half cup of borax or bleach per gallon of water, this helps in removing stains. When you remove a soiled diaper, scrape the movement off into the toilet with a knife, or rinse it by holding it in the toilet while you flush it (hold tight). Clean the diaper pail each time you do a diaper wash.

Wash the diapers with mild soap or mild detergent in a washing machine or washtub (dissolve the soap well first), and rinse two or three times. The number of rinsings depends on how soon the water gets clear and on how delicate the baby's skin is. If your baby's skin isn't sensitive, two rinsings may be enough.

If your baby has a tendency to develop diaper rash, you may need to take additional precautions—at least at the times the rash appears, and perhaps regularly (see Sections 347–351).

If the diapers (and other clothes) are becoming hard, unabsorbent, and gray with soap deposit (the same as the ring in the bathtub) you can soften them and clean them by using a water conditioner. Don't use a fabric softener— these leave a coating which decreases the absorbency of diapers.

Bowel Movements

126. The gastrocolic reflex. The bowels are apt to move soon after a meal in most individuals because the filling of the stomach tends to stimulate the intestinal tract all the way down. This hookup is called the gastrocolic reflex *(gastro* = stomach, *colic* = intestines). The movement is more apt to occur after breakfast because of the resumption of stomach and intestinal activity after the long night's quiet.

Sometimes this reflex works very actively in the early months of life, especially in a breast-fed baby, who may have a movement after every nursing. More inconvenient still is the pattern of the occasional babies who begin to strain soon after the start of each feeding, produce nothing, but keep straining so hard, as long as the nipple is in their mouths, that they can't nurse. You have to let their intestines quiet down for fifteen minutes and try again.

127. Meconium. For the first day or so after birth, the baby's movements are composed of material called meconium, which is greenish-black in color and of a smooth, sticky consistency. Then they change to brown and to yellow. If a baby hasn't had a movement by the end of the second day, the doctor should be notified.

128. The breast-fed baby may have many or few movements daily. Most have several movements a day in the early weeks. Some have a movement after every nursing. The movements are usually of a light-yellow color and may be watery, pasty, or seedy, or they may have the consistency of thick cream soup. They are practically never too hard.

Many breast-fed babies change from frequent to infrequent movements by the time they are one, two, or three months old. (This occurs because breast milk is so well digested, there is little residue to make up bulk in the movements.) Some then have one movement a day, others a movement only every other day or even less often. This is apt to alarm a parent who has been brought up to believe that everyone should have a movement every day. But there is nothing to worry about so long as the baby is comfortable. The breast-fed baby's movement stays just as soft when it is passed every two or three days or even less frequently.

Some of these breast-fed babies who have infrequent movements begin to push and strain a lot when two or three days have gone by. Yet the movement is soft when it does come out. The only explanation I can offer for this is that the movement is so liquid that it doesn't put the right kind of pressure on the inside of the anus, where the movement comes out. Adding 2 to 4 teaspoons of pureed and strained prunes to the daily diet usually helps, even though the baby doesn't otherwise need solid food yet. There is no call for cathartics in this kind of difficulty. I think it is better not to use suppositories or enemas, for fear the baby's intestines will come to depend on them. Try to solve the problem with prunes or prune juice.

129. The bottle-fed baby's movements. The baby who is fed commercially prepared formula usually has between one and four movements a day at first, though an occasional baby has as many as six. As he grows older, the number tends to decrease to one or two a day. The number is unimportant if the consistency of the movement is good and if the baby is doing well.

Movements in babies fed formula are most often pasty and of a pale-yellow or tan color. However, some young babies always have stools that are more like soft scrambled eggs (curdy lumps with looser material in between). This is not important if the baby is comfortable and gaining well.

The commonest disturbance of the bowel movements in the baby on cow's milk is a tendency to hardness. This is discussed in Sections 342–344 on constipation.

A very few bottle-fed babies have a tendency to loose, green, curdy movements in the early months. If the movements are always just a little loose, this can be ignored, provided the baby is comfortable, gaining well, and the doctor or nurse practitioner finds nothing wrong.

130. Changes in the movements. You can see that it doesn't matter if one baby's movements are always a little different from another baby's movements, as long as each is doing well. It's more apt to mean something, and should be discussed with the doctor or nurse practitioner, when the movements undergo a real change. For example, green movements can occur with both breast-fed and bottle-fed babies. If the movements are always green, and the baby is doing fine, there is nothing to be concerned about. If they were previously pasty and then turn lumpy, slightly looser, slightly more frequent, it may be a spell of indigestion or a mild intestinal infection. If they become definitely loose, frequent, greenish, and the smell changes, this is almost certainly due to an intestinal infection, whether it is mild or severe. Generally speaking, changes in the number and consistency of the movements are more important than changes in color. A bowel movement exposed to the air may turn brown or it may turn green. This is of no importance.

Mucus in the bowel movements is common when a baby has diarrhea, and it is just another sign that the intestines are irritated. Similarly, it may occur in indigestion. It can also come from higher up—from the throat and bronchial tubes of a baby with a cold, or of a healthy newborn baby— some babies form a great deal of mucus in the early weeks.

When a **new vegetable** is added to the diet (less frequently in the case of other foods), part of it may come through looking just the same as it went in. If it also causes signs of irritation, such as looseness and mucus, give much less the next time. If there is no irritation, you can keep on with the same amount or increase slowly until the baby's intestines learn to digest it better. Beets can turn the whole movement red.

Small streaks of blood on the outside of a bowel movement usually come from a crack, or "fissure," in the anus, caused by hard bowel movements. The bleeding is not serious in itself, but the doctor should be notified so that the constipation can be treated promptly. This is important for psychological as well as physical reasons (see Section 753).

Larger amounts of blood in the movement are rare and may come from malformations of the intestines, from severe diarrhea, or from intussusception (see Sections 1135–1136). The doctor should be called or the child taken to a hospital promptly.

The Bath

Most babies, after a few weeks' experience, have a wonderful time in the bath, so don't rush it. Enjoy it with your baby.

131. Before any feeding. It's usually most convenient in the early months to give the bath before the midmorning feeding, but before any feeding is all right—not after a feeding, because you want the child to go to sleep then. By the time your baby is on three meals a day, you may want to change to before lunch or before supper. As the child gets older still and stays up for a while after supper, it may work out better to give the bath after supper, especially if she needs her supper early. Bathe her in a reasonably warm room—the kitchen, if necessary.

132. A sponge bath if you prefer. Though it's the custom in the United States to give a complete tub or sponge bath every day, it certainly isn't necessary more than once or twice a week, so long as the baby is kept clean in the diaper area and around the mouth. On the days when you don't give him a full bath, give a sponge bath in the diaper area. The tub bath is apt to be frightening at first to the inexperienced parent—the baby seems so helpless, limp, and slippery, especially after having been soaped. Babies may feel uneasy in the tub at first, because they can't be well supported there. You can give a sponge bath for a few weeks until you and your baby feel more secure, or even for months, until she can sit up, if you prefer. It is usually advised that a tub bath not be given until the navel is healed. Check with your doctor or nurse practitioner.

You can give a sponge bath on a table or in your lap. You'll want a piece of waterproof material under the baby. If you are using a hard surface like a table, there should be some padding over it (large pillow or folded blanket or quilt) so that the baby won't roll too easily. (Rolling frightens young babies.) Wash the face and scalp with a washcloth and clear warm water. (The scalp can be soaped once or twice a week.) Lightly soap the rest of the body when and where needed with the washcloth or your hand. Then wipe the soap off by going over the whole body at least twice with the rinsed washcloth, paying attention to creases.

133. The tub bath. Before starting the bath, be sure you have everything you need close at hand. If you forget the towel, you'll have to go after it holding a dripping baby in your arms.
Take off your wristwatch. An apron protects your clothes. Have at hand:

- soap
- washcloth
- towel

- absorbent cotton for nose and ears if necessary
- lotion
- shirt, diaper, pins, nightie

The bath can be given in a washbowl, dishpan, kitchen sink, or enamelware tub. Some newer tubs have sponge cutouts to support and position the baby properly. The regular bathtub is hard on a parent's back and legs. For your own comfort, you can put a dishpan or enamelware tub on a table, at which you sit, or on something higher like a dresser, at which you stand. You can sit on a stool at the kitchen sink. The water should be about body temperature (90–100°F). A bath thermometer is a comfort to the inexperienced parent but is not necessary. Always test the temperature with your elbow or wrist. It should feel comfortably warm but not hot. Use only a small amount of water at first, an inch or two deep, until you get the knack of holding the baby securely. A tub is less slippery if you line it with a towel or diaper each time.

A Tub Bath

Your hand under the arm, your wrist supporting the head.

Hold the baby so that her head is supported on your wrist, and the fingers of that hand hold her securely in the armpit. Wash the face first, with a soft washcloth, without soap, then the scalp. The scalp needs to be soaped only once or twice a week. Wipe the soap suds off the scalp with a damp washcloth, going over it twice. If the washcloth is too wet, the soapy water may get into the eyes and sting. (There are shampoos for babies that do not sting the eyes as much as ordinary shampoos.) Then you can use the washcloth or your hand to wash the rest of the body, arms, and legs. Wash lightly between the outer lips of the vagina. (See Section 141 about washing the circumcised or uncircumcised penis.) When you use soap, it's easier to soap your hand than a washcloth when your other hand is occupied. If the skin gets dry, try omitting soap except for once or twice a week.

If you feel nervous at first for fear you'll drop the baby in the water, you can soap her while she is on your lap or on a table. Then rinse her off in the tub, holding her securely with both hands. Use a soft bath towel for drying, and blot rather than rub. If you begin giving the tub bath before the navel is completely healed, dry it thoroughly after the bath with cotton balls.

134. Ears, eyes, nose, mouth, nails. You need to wash only the outer ear and the entrance to the canal, not inside. Use only a washcloth, not a cotton swab (which just pushes the wax further in). Wax is formed in the canal to protect and clean it.

The eyes are bathed constantly by the steady flow of the tears (not just when the baby is crying). This is why it is unnecessary to put any drops in the eyes while they are healthy.

The mouth ordinarily needs no extra care.

The nails can be cut easily while the baby sleeps. Clippers may be easier than nail scissors. There are manicure scissors with ball points.

The nose has a beautiful system for keeping itself clear. Tiny invisible hairs in the cells lining the nose keep moving the mucus and dust down toward the front of the nose, where it collects on the large hairs near the opening. This tickles the nose and makes the baby sneeze or rub the collection out. When you are drying the baby after the bath, you can first moisten and then gently wipe out any ball of dried mucus with the corner of the washcloth. Don't fuss at this too long if it makes the baby angry.

Sometimes, especially when the house is heated, enough **dried mucus** collects in the noses of small infants to partially obstruct the breathing. Then each time they breathe in, the lower edges of the chest are pulled inward, or "retracted." The lips may even become slightly blue. An older child or adult would breathe through the mouth, but most babies can't leave their mouths open. If your baby's nose becomes obstructed at any time of day, you can first moisten and then remove the mucus as in the previous paragraph.

135. Lotion. It's fun to apply lotion to a baby after a bath, and the baby likes it, too, but is really not necessary in most cases. (If it were, nature would provide it.) Baby powder should be avoided. Occasionally, the small powder particles are inhaled into the baby's lungs. This can cause an irritation of the lining of the airways and lungs. A baby lotion may be helpful when the skin is dry or there is a mild diaper rash. Baby oils (which are different from lotions) and mineral oil have been less often used since it has been shown that they sometimes cause a mild rash. Sesame oil may be used.

The Fontanel

136. The soft spot on the top of a baby's head is where the four pieces of bone that make up the top of the skull have not yet grown together. The size of the fontanel at birth is different in different babies. A large one is nothing to worry about, and it's bound to be slower to close than a small one. Some fontanels close as early as nine months and slow ones not till two years. The average is at twelve to eighteen months.

If the light is right, you can see that the fontanel pulsates at a rate between the breathing rate and the beat of the heart.

Parents worry unnecessarily about the danger of touching the soft spot. Actually, it is covered by a membrane as tough as canvas, and there is no risk of hurting a baby there with ordinary handling.

The Navel

137. The healing of the navel. When still in the mother's womb, the baby is nourished through the blood vessels of the umbilical cord. Just after birth, the doctor ties the cord and cuts it off close to the baby's body. The stump that's left withers like a raisin and eventually drops off, usually in about two or three weeks, though it may take several weeks. When the cord falls off, it leaves a raw spot, which takes a number of days, occasionally a number of weeks, to heal over. The raw spot should merely be kept clean and dry, so that it won't get infected. If it is kept dry, a scab covers it until it is healed. It doesn't need a dressing and will stay drier without one. Once the cord falls off, the baby can have tub baths. Just dry the navel afterward with a corner of the towel, or cotton balls if you like, until it is all healed. There may be a little bleeding or drainage a few days before the cord falls off and until the healing is complete.

It is wise to keep the diaper below the level of the unhealed navel, so that it doesn't keep it wet. If the unhealed navel becomes moist and produces a discharge, it should be protected more carefully from constant wetting by the diaper, and cleaned each day with a cotton swab dampened with alcohol, used in the skin fold around the cord. If healing is slow, the raw spot may become lumpy with what's called granulation tissue, but this is of no importance. The doctor may apply a chemical that will hasten drying and healing.

If the navel and the surrounding skin become red and/or there is a smelly discharge, infection may be present. You should get in touch with your doctor or nurse practitioner right away. Until you can reach the doctor, you should apply warm, wet dressings.

If the scab on the unhealed navel gets pulled by the clothing, there may be a drop or two of blood. This amount is of no importance.

The Penis

138. The foreskin is the sleeve of skin that covers the head (glans) of the penis when the baby is born. The open end of the foreskin is already large enough to let the baby's urine out, but small enough to protect the opening (meatus) of the penis from diaper rash. (See Section 1145 about sores on the end of the penis.) As the baby grows, the foreskin normally begins to separate from the glans, and starts to become retractable. It usually takes about three years for this separation and retractability to become complete. It may take longer for some boys, even until adolescence, to have a fully retractable foreskin, but this is no cause for concern. Routine washing, even without retracting the foreskin, will keep the penis clean and healthy.

At the end of the baby's foreskin you may see a white, waxy material (smegma). This is perfectly normal. Smegma is secreted by the cells on the inside of the foreskin, as a natural lubricant between the foreskin and the glans. (It also lubricates the head of the penis during intercourse.)

139. Circumcision means the cutting off of the foreskin, which leaves the head of the penis exposed. It is usually done within the first week of the baby's life. The exact origins of circumcision are unknown, but it has been practiced for at least 4000 years, in many parts of the world and for many reasons. For Jewish and Muslim people, it has religious significance. In some cultures, it's a puberty rite, marking a boy's passage to adulthood.

In the United States, in the twentieth century, circumcision has commonly been performed for other reasons. Some parents worry that it will upset their uncircumcised son to look different from his circumcised father or older brothers or friends at school. Many doctors believe that the normal accumulation of smegma under the foreskin may cause occasional mild inflammation or infection, although routine washing seems to be just as effective in preventing these problems as circumcision. Scientists used to think that the wives of uncircumcised men were more likely to get cervical cancer, but modern research has disproved this. Studies in the late 1980s suggested that uncircumcised boys tend to get more urinary tract infections during childhood, but circumcised boys also get urinary tract infections.

Between 1980 and 1990, the number of babies being circumcised in the United States decreased from 90 percent to about 60 percent. If you are considering circumcision, you should know that it's a relatively safe operation. There are some risks from the procedure, such as bleeding or infection, which usually can be treated easily. Circumcision is clearly painful for the baby, although some doctors are now using local anesthesia that appears to help. In general, babies recover from the stress of the operation in about twenty-four hours. If your baby seems to be uncomfortable for longer than this, or if there is persistent oozing of blood or swelling of his penis, report it to your doctor promptly. A spot of blood or several spots on successive diaper changes merely means that a small scab has been pulled off.

I feel that there's no solid medical evidence at this time to support routine circumcision. The choice is best left up to the parents. Some opt circumcision for religious, family, or cultural reasons. In other cases, I recommend leaving the foreskin the way nature meant it to be.

140. Circumcision after infancy. The question of circumcision is sometimes raised later in childhood because of irritation or masturbation—not good reasons in my opinion. On the rare occasion when it may be considered medically necessary to circumcise an older boy, discuss it with him beforehand. Show him the sleeve of skin that will be removed and be sure he understands that he will still have a complete and uninjured penis. Let him know that his penis will be sore at first, but it will heal quickly. Give him plenty of time to think about it and ask questions. Be patient, because he may need to ask the same question several times, or in several different ways. Be sure he understands that the operation is not a punishment for masturbation.

141. Care of the penis. Good genital hygiene is important from birth on, whether the penis is circumcised or not. It's part of children learning general habits of personal cleanliness.

If the baby isn't circumcised, the penis should be washed whenever the baby is given a bath. You don't have to do anything special to the foreskin; just a gentle washing around the outside of it will remove any excess accumulation of smegma. Some parents may want to be extra sure that the foreskin and glans are as clean as possible. In this case, you can clean beneath the foreskin by pushing it back very gently, just until you meet resistance. Wash away the smegma, and rinse well. *Never forcibly retract the foreskin.* This could cause infections or other complications. The foreskin will become more retractable by itself over time.

If the baby is circumcised, change his diaper often while the wound is healing. This will lessen the chance of irritation or infection from his urine and bowel movements. During this healing time, about a week, follow your doctor's advice on taking care of the baby's penis: what to do about the bandage, bathing and drying, and using an ointment or lotion. After the wound has healed, you can wash the penis just as you do the rest of the baby, during the bath.

It is common for boy babies to have erections of the penis, especially when the bladder is full or during urination. This has no importance.

Clothing, Fresh Air, and Sunshine

142. Room temperature. There is no pat answer to the question of how much covering to put on a baby. Only rough guidelines can be offered. Babies under 5 pounds don't have a very good system for keeping the body at the right temperature. Between 5 and 8 pounds, however, they don't usually need to be heated from the outside; they can take care of themselves in a comfortable room, say 65°F to 68°F. By the time they weigh 8 pounds, their heat regulator is working well and they are getting a layer of fat that helps them stay warm. Now their room for sleeping can be allowed to go as low as 60°F in cool or cold weather.

Babies and children should not be put to sleep directly in front of an air conditioner because that could lower their body temperatures to dangerous levels. The same applies to heat vents, radiators, or space heaters, which can raise their temperatures too high.

A room temperature of 65°F to 68°F for eating and playing is right for babies weighing over 5 pounds, just as it is for older children and adults.

In cold weather the air contains much less moisture. When this air is heated in a house it becomes relatively drier still, especially when the temperature rises above 70°F. Dry, hot air dries and hardens the mucus in the nose and parches the air passages generally. This makes the baby uncomfortable and may lower the ability to resist infections.

The problem of providing cool enough air for a baby is further complicated by the inexperienced parents' natural anxiety and protectiveness. They tend to keep their baby in a too hot room and too well covered, besides. Under these conditions some babies even develop heat rash in winter.

Most people accustomed to heated houses let the temperature gradually get hotter all winter, without noticing it, and come to demand excessive heat. One way to counteract this in a private house is with a thermostat, which turns the furnace down when the desired temperature (65°–68°F) is reached. In an apartment or private house without a thermostat, the parents should hang a house thermometer in a prominent place and glance at it several times a day until they become so attuned to a range of 65°F to 68°F that they notice a higher temperature without looking.

I think there's a general tendency to overdress babies, even among experienced parents. A normal baby has as good an internal thermostat as an adult, as long as he isn't put into so many layers of clothing and covering that his thermostat isn't allowed to work properly.

143. Clothing. Babies and children who are reasonably plump need less covering than an adult. More babies are overdressed than underdressed. This isn't good for them. If a person is always too warmly dressed, the body loses its ability to adjust to changes, and is more likely to become chilled. So, in general, put on too little rather than too much and then watch the baby. Don't try to put on enough to keep the hands warm, because most babies' hands stay cool when they are comfortably dressed. Feel the legs or arms or neck. Best guide of all is the color of the face. Babies who are getting cold lose the color from their cheeks, and they may begin to fuss, too.

When putting on sweaters and shirts with small openings, remember that a baby's head is more egg-shaped than ball-shaped. Gather the sweater into a loop, slip it first over the back of the baby's head, then forward, stretching it forward as you bring it down past the forehead and nose. Then put the baby's arms into the sleeves. When taking it off, pull the baby's arms out of the sleeves first. Gather the sweater into a loop as it lies around the neck. Raise the front part of the loop up past the nose and forehead while the back of the loop is still at the back of the neck, then slip it off toward the back of the head.

In cold weather a warm cap is essential because babies lose lots of their body heat from their heads. A cap in which to sleep in very cold weather should be of knitted acrylic, so that if it slips over the face the baby can breathe through it.

144. Practical coverings. It is better to use all-acrylic blankets or bags when a baby is sleeping in a cool room (60°F–65°F). They have the best combination of warmth and washability. Knitted shawls tuck and wrap more easily than woven blankets, especially when the baby is up, and because they are thinner you can adjust the amount of covering to the temperature more exactly than with thick blankets. Avoid coverings that are heavy, such as solid-feeling quilts.

Sleep bags can't be kicked off, as blankets can; sleepers are sensible by the time a baby can stand.

In a warm room (over 72°F) or in warm weather, a baby really only needs cotton covering. There are now cotton thermal blankets said to be adaptable to cold or warm temperatures.

All blankets, quilts, and sheets should be large enough to tuck securely under the mattress, so that they will not work loose. Waterproof sheets and pads should either be large enough to tuck in securely or should be pinned or tied down at all corners so that they will not come loose. Alternatively, you can sew Velcro on the mattress corners, railing, and the corners of the sheets to secure them.

The **mattress** should be firm and flat enough so that the baby will not lie in a depression. A crib or carriage mattress should fit well, so that there is no space around the edges in which the baby might get wedged. Use no pillow in crib or carriage.

145. Taking the baby outdoors for fresh air. Changes of air temperature are beneficial in toning up the body's system for adapting to cold or heat. A bank clerk is much more likely to become chilled staying outdoors in winter than a lumberjack, who is used to such weather. A baby living continuously in a warm room usually has a pasty complexion and may have a sluggish appetite.

It's good for a baby (like anyone else) to get outdoors for two or three hours a day, particularly during the season when the house is heated. I grew up and practiced pediatrics in the northeastern part of the United States, where most conscientious parents took it for granted that babies and children should be outdoors two or three hours a day. Children love to be outdoors and it gives them pink cheeks and good appetites. So I can't help but believe in the tradition.

An 8-pounder can certainly go out when it's 60°F or above. The temperature of the air is not the only factor. Moist, cold air is more chilling than dry air of the same temperature, and wind is the greatest chiller. Even when the temperature is cooler, a 12-pound baby can be comfortable in a sunny, sheltered spot if dressed appropriately.

If you live in a city and have no yard to park the baby in, you can push the child in a carriage. If you get in the habit of carrying the baby in a carrier on your chest or back, you will be wonderfully conditioned as the baby gets bigger. The baby will love riding in close contact with you, and be able to look around or sleep. If you enjoy being out and can afford the time, the more the better.

146. Sunshine and sunbaths. Direct sunshine contains ultraviolet rays, which create vitamin D right in the skin. In the days before all babies automatically got all the vitamin D they needed from their formula or vitamin drops, and before the harmful effects of ultraviolet rays were fully understood, I recommended sunbaths for babies. Now that a connection has been proven between excessive exposure to ultraviolet rays early in life and the development of skin cancer in later life, I strongly advise against sunbathing at any age.

Dermatologists (skin specialists) now recommend that the skin be protected by a cream or lotion with a sunblock factor of at least 15 when a baby or child (or adult) is going to be exposed to direct sunlight or to the reflected rays of the sun at the beach or in a boat. This means covering all exposed skin surfaces with cream or lotion. Most babies and children will be protected from the sun with a 15 cream or lotion. Those with more sun-sensitive skin may require a higher sun blocker. Babies at the beach should have a hat and be kept under a beach umbrella (see Sections 635–639 on Sun Protection).

If you have a fair-skinned child and live in a sunny climate, putting on sunblock cream or lotion should be part of his daily routine before leaving the house in the morning. And a second application should be done before he goes out to play after school.

There are five effective chemicals in sunblocks or sun-screens: PABA esters, cinnamates, benzophenones, titani-um dioxide (or zinc oxide), and parsol. Be sure that one or more of these are listed on the container. In a country like the United States, where sunbathing is such a habit and a tan is considered "healthy," beautiful, and sexually attrac-tive, taking a firm stand against sunbathing is hard. But the prevention of skin cancer is certainly worth it.

Sleep

147. Mixing up day and night. The first sleep problem many new parents face is a baby who has mixed up day and night. He seems to like to sleep more during the day; his wakeful hours tend to be at night. This shouldn't be too surprising. After all, he could care less if it's night or day, so long as he's fed, cuddled, and kept warm and dry. In the womb, it was pretty dark anyway, and he never had the chance to accommodate to the day-night cycle.

For this reason, I give all parents the same advice. Play with your baby a lot during the daytime. Wake him up to feed him if the usual amount of time has elapsed since the last feeding. If you're going to play with him, do it when it's light outside. Nighttime is a different story. When you feed him after dark, do it efficiently and without as much fanfare. *Never* wake him to feed him when it's dark out, unless there is a medical reason to do so. Let him learn very early on that daytime is fun time and nighttime is kind of low-key and boring. He'll soon learn to adjust his rhythm to be more awake during the day and to sleep for longer periods at night.

148. How much should a baby sleep? Parents often ask this question. Of course, the baby is the only one who can answer it. One baby seems to need a lot, and another surprisingly little. As long as babies are satisfied with their feedings, comfortable, get plenty of fresh air, and sleep in a cool place, you can leave it to them to take the amount of sleep they need.

Most babies in the early months sleep from feeding to feeding if they are getting enough to eat and not having indigestion. There are a few babies, though, who are unusually wakeful right from the beginning, and not because anything is wrong. If you have this kind of baby, there's nothing you need to do about it.

As babies get older, they gradually sleep less and less. You're apt to notice it first in the late afternoon. In time they become wakeful at other periods during the day. Each baby develops a personal pattern of wakefulness and tends to be awake at the same time every day. Toward the end of the first year, most babies are down to two naps a day; and between one year and a year and a half, they will probably give up one of these. It is only during infancy that you can leave the amount of sleep entirely up to the baby. A child by the age of two is a much more complicated being. Excitement, worries, fear of bad dreams, competition with a sister or brother may keep children from getting the sleep they need.

149. Going to bed. Many babies easily get used to the idea that they always go to bed and to sleep right after a meal. Many other babies are very sociable after meals. You can choose which routine fits best with the schedule of the whole family. It is good for babies to get used to falling asleep in their own beds, without company, at least by the time any three-month colic is over. This is one way to prevent later sleep problems. A baby who expects to be held and rocked before she goes to sleep may want such comfort for months or even years. Then, when she awakens in the night, she may want these pleasures again. For parents who want to hold and rock their baby, this is fine. But for those who will eventually resent it, it's best not to get started.

Many adults also have bedtime rituals or comforters. We like our pillow just right and the covers to fit a certain way. Some people can sleep well only in their own beds because they are uncomfortable without all familiar things and sounds around them. Babies are just the same. If they learn to sleep only while being held, that can become the only way for them to get to sleep. If, on the other hand, they learn to put themselves to sleep, then they can also do so in the middle of the night and save their parents a lot of sleepless nights (see Section 773 on Sleep).

So I recommend that, once the baby is three or four months old, that you try to put her to bed while she's awake and let her learn to get herself to sleep, let her go to sleep alone. You'll be glad when she begins to awaken at night and has the habit of getting herself back to sleep.

Babies can get accustomed to either a silent home or an average noisy one. So there is no point tiptoeing and whispering around the house at first. The infant and child who, awake or asleep, is used to ordinary household noises and human voices usually sleeps right through a visit of talking laughing friends, a radio or TV tuned to a reasonable volume, even somebody's coming into the room. There are, however, certain infants who appear to be hypersensitive to sounds. They startle easily at the least noise and appear to be happiest when it's quiet. If you have such a baby you'll probably need to keep the house quiet while she sleeps or else she will constantly wake and fuss.

150. On back or stomach? This used to be a hotly debated question. Not any more. Today's slogan is "Back to Sleep." All infants should be put to sleep on their backs, unless there is a medical reason not to do so. This simple change in sleep position from front to back has reduced the number of SIDS deaths by 50 percent. (Discuss with your doctor or nurse practitioner if there is any reason for your baby to sleep on her stomach or side.)

Why the change? Many studies have now shown that the risk for Sudden Infant Death Syndrome (SIDS) is lessened when infants sleep on their backs. And sleeping on your back seems to have no adverse effects on healthy infants. If a baby has never had the opportunity to get used to sleeping on her stomach, she'll easily take to sleeping on her back. These studies also suggest that sleeping on the side isn't as safe as sleeping on the back. So, from the beginning, put your baby to sleep on her back.

151. See if you can train the baby to sleep later or be happy in bed in the morning. In the middle part of the first year, most babies become willing to sleep a little later than the uncivilized hour of 5:00 or 6:00 A.M. However, most parents develop such a habit of listening for their babies in their sleep and jumping out of bed at the first murmur that they never give the children a chance to go back to sleep. As a result, parents may find themselves still getting up before 7:00 A.M. when the child is two or three years old. And a child who has been used to early company for so long will demand it. Some parents like to get up at this early hour and enjoy this morning time with their baby.

152. Co-sleeping (infants and children in bed with parents). Children can sleep in a room by themselves from the time they are born, if convenient, as long as the parents are near enough to hear them when they cry or have an intercom in the bedroom. If they start sleeping in their parents' room, two or three months is a good age to move them. At this age, they begin sleeping through the night and don't need so much care. If they haven't been moved out of the parents' room by six months, it is a good idea to put them in their own room at that time, unless the parents want to have the children in bed with them. Otherwise there is a chance that they may become dependent on this arrangement and be afraid and unwilling to sleep anywhere else. The older they are, the harder it may be to move them. However, in certain cultures co-sleeping is very common (up to 50 percent), and this may be a practice that is culturally dependent.

BREAST- AND BOTTLE-FEEDING

Tips for Breast- and Bottle-Feeding

153. Babies normally lose weight in the first few days. It is perfectly normal for a baby to lose as much as 8 percent of his birthweight in the first few days after birth. That means a 7-pound baby may weigh only 6 pounds, 7 ounces, when he is a few days old.

Breast-fed babies will gain the weight back as soon as their mother's milk comes in. Good-size babies who get formula from the start usually begin to gain it back in a week or so, because they can drink and digest well. Small or premature babies lose weight longer and regain it more slowly, because they can take only small feedings at first. It may take them several weeks just to get back to birth weight. This delay doesn't handicap them. Eventually they will gain rapidly to make up for it.

Some parents worry unnecessarily about this initial weight loss. They can't help feeling that it's unnatural and dangerous for the weight go down instead of up. Concern about the early weight loss not only may upset a mother needlessly but may also cause her to abandon breast-feeding before she has given it a fair chance. It's better for the parents to realize that the weight loss is natural and they should share any concerns with their doctor or nurse practitioner, so that they can be reassured.

154. Infants usually know how much food they need. If they are outgrowing the amount of formula or breast milk they've been getting or if their mother's breast-milk supply has decreased temporarily because of fatigue or tension, they will probably begin to wake earlier and earlier before each feeding and cry with a cry that you now recognize as one of hunger. They will be finishing all their bottles to the last drop and looking around for more. They may try to eat their hands. Sometimes babies who are getting hungry will become constipated, also. If they are getting really hungry, they may cry at the end of some of their feedings, too.

If your baby is showing some of these signs of dissatisfaction and is on a formula, it is time to add more formula to each bottle. If your baby is being breast-fed and waking early, you can nurse early. The more frequent feedings will help to satisfy the baby, and the more frequent emptying of the breasts will stimulate them to produce a larger supply. Remember that the supply of breast milk is made purely by the baby's demands. If you breast-feed more often, you will have more milk. If you have been nursing at only one breast a feeding, give both breasts at each feeding for a while.

155. Burping. You have to hold the bottle with the bottom high enough so the nipple is always full of formula. But all babies swallow some air while they are drinking their milk. It collects as a bubble in the stomach. Some babies' stomachs become uncomfortably full before they're halfway through their feeding and they have to stop. Most never swallow enough air to interrupt the meal. A few, especially breast-fed babies, don't even have a bubble at the end of a feeding.

There are a couple of ways to burp babies. You can find which works best for you. The first is to sit them upright in your lap and gently rub their stomach. Another is to hold them up against your shoulder and massage or pat them in the middle of the back. It's a good idea to put a diaper over your shoulder in case they spit up a little. One kind of stomach lets go of the bubble very easily and promptly. The other kind seems to want to hang on to it. When the bubble doesn't come up easily, it sometimes helps to put these babies in a lying position for a second and then bring them back to your shoulder again.

You need to burp babies in the middle of a feeding only if they swallow so much air that it stops their nursing. But you should at least try to get the bubble up at the end of the feeding. Most babies will become uncomfortable in a little while if put to bed with the bubble still in the stomach; some babies even get colic pains from it. On the other hand, if your baby is hard to burp and always seems just as comfortable whether burped or not, there is no need for you to try for more than a few minutes.

This is as good a place as any to mention the fact that when a young baby has taken a full feeding, the abdomen bulges to an extent that's apt to worry the inexperienced parent. This is only because the amount the baby needs to drink at each feeding is much larger in comparison to the size of the abdomen than it is in an adult. You'd look full too if you weighed 110 pounds and drank 2 quarts of milk at a meal!

Breast-Feeding

The Value of Breast-Feeding

156. Breast-feeding is valuable in a number of ways. Careful studies in recent years have shown that babies receive immunity to a variety of infections through the colostrum (the fluid that comes in before the real milk) and through the milk. Though it contains very little iron, breast milk contains a form of iron that is unusually well digested and absorbed.

A big advantage of breast-feeding is that the milk is always pure; a baby can't catch an intestinal infection from it. From a purely practical point of view, it saves hours of time every week, because there are no bottles to wash or sterilize, no formulas to mix, no refrigeration to worry about, no bottles to warm, and it's less expensive than formula. You appreciate this particularly if you ever have to travel. Breast-feeding is more adapted to satisfying the baby's sucking instinct. At the breast he can suck as long as he feels the need. I think that there is less thumb-sucking among breast-fed babies, for that reason.

The most convincing evidence of the value of breast-feeding comes from mothers who have done it. They speak of the tremendous satisfaction they experience from knowing that they are providing their babies with something no one else can give them, from seeing their devotion to the breast, from feeling their closeness.

Parents don't get to feel like parents or come to enjoy being parents or feel the full parental love for their child just because a baby has been born to them. With their first infant particularly, they become real parents only as they take care of their child. The more success they have in the beginning in doing their part, and the more visibly their baby is satisfied by their care, the sooner and more enjoyably they slip into the role. In this sense, breast-feeding does wonders for a young mother and for her relationship with her baby. She and her baby are happy in themselves, and feel more loving to each other.

Fewer babies have been breast-fed in the twentieth century—all over the world. But in recent years, breast-feeding has increased in America, particularly among women who have attended college. This is partly due to the new knowledge about the physical and emotional advantages, partly to the general respect among the young for nature and the desire to do things the natural way. We are beginning to see more babies from lower-income and minority families being breast-fed. I hope this trend will continue.

Feelings About Breast-Feeding

157. Different feelings about breast-feeding. A few women, usually because of the way they were brought up, feel deeply uncomfortable at the prospect of breast-feeding—it may seem too immodest or too animal-like. Likewise, quite a few fathers, including some very good ones, object to breast-feeding; they can't help feeling jealous. Others feel great pride in their wives' nursing their babies. So the mother has to use her judgment.

It is too seldom mentioned that, after a couple of weeks, breast-feeding becomes definitely pleasurable for the mother. Many nursing mothers say that the pleasurable sensations which they feel in their breasts and in their genital region while they are nursing are very similar to the sensations they experience during sexual excitement. Some women feel confused and guilty about the similarity in these sensations because they don't realize that they are entirely normal. Many nursing mothers have the experience of beginning to leak milk from their breasts when another woman's baby cries hungrily nearby, and this is embarrassing to mothers who don't understand that this, too, is entirely normal. Some mothers and fathers are embarrassed by milk leaking during lovemaking, while others find this quite arousing.

So you can see that it's really important for the parents to try to openly discuss their feelings about nursing with each other. Sometimes, having this discussion with the doctor, nurse practitioner, or lactation specialist present can help the parents get over their trouble in getting started.

How to Give Breast-Feeding a Fair Trial

158. You hear of women who want to nurse their babies but don't succeed. People talk about how complicated our civilization is and how it makes mothers too tense to nurse. It's true that when a nursing mother becomes upset, it sometimes cuts down, for the time being, the amount of milk she can produce. Occasionally it seems to make the baby feel out of sorts, too. But I think breast-feeding most often fails because it isn't given a good trial, not because of nervousness.

There are three factors that make a big difference: (1) keeping away from formula; (2) not getting discouraged too early; and (3) sufficient stimulation of the breasts. Success is increased greatly if mother and baby start breast-feeding in the first hour when the baby is ready, if the baby nurses frequently during the first five days, if the baby is allowed to latch on to the areola by herself, and if there is continuous rooming-in from birth on.

If a baby is given formula for the first three or four days of life, the chance of successful breast-feeding is diminished. It's much easier to express milk from a bottle than from a breast and babies, being as lazy as the rest of us, will usually choose the easiest way. The baby who is satisfied by plenty of formula will not try so hard at the breast. Inexperienced mothers then believe the baby prefers the bottle to the breast, but this is not really the case. The best policy is to avoid formula for as long as possible, certainly until breast-feeding is well established and the baby's preferences are set.

Sometimes a mother becomes discouraged just at the moment when her milk is coming in, or perhaps a day or two later, because she isn't producing very much. This is no time for her to quit. She hasn't given herself half a chance. If a mother has extra help in the home at this stage, it's important to have someone who is encouraging and cooperative. This is also true for her husband and any relatives who may be helping out.

The mother is best off being sure that she is getting enough to eat and drink and enough rest. Then she needs to put the baby to breast more often so as to give the breasts sufficient stimulation and increase her milk supply. The night nursings are as important as the daytime nursings in giving the breasts regular stimulation at first.

159. What about persistent weight loss? Of course, babies cannot be kept off formula indefinitely if they remain miserably hungry for several weeks or continue to lose weight. If a mother is able to keep in frequent touch with the doctor or nurse practitioner, he or she will help her decide at each step such questions as how many days the baby can go on an insufficient amount of breast milk without resorting to formula, how much nursing the mother's nipples can stand and how frequently to nurse. The point is, though, that the doctor or nurse practitioner is influenced in many of these decisions by the mother's attitude toward nursing. If she makes it clear that she is eager to succeed, this will encourage the doctor to give the directions that will make it possible.

160. An insufficiency of confidence. The doubt about sufficiency of the milk supply is common in the new mother, who has had no proof yet of her adequacy in our upside-down society which considers bottle-feeding normal and makes breast-feeding the exception. The doubt also arises in mothers who have had more experience but who have never had much self-confidence. Usually when the mother is worrying about the amount, the doctor finds that there is no insufficiency of milk, only an insufficiency of confidence.

161. Success depends partly on the help of others. The attitudes of the doctor who delivered the baby, the hospital nurses, and the doctor or nurse practitioner who's looking after the baby will have a powerful effect in encouraging or discouraging breast-feeding. So will the attitudes of the mother's relatives and friends. A supportive father can make the difference between a positive experience or an early end to breast-feeding (see Section 164).

162. Don't let friends discourage you. Perhaps this is as good a time as any to mention that a mother who is attempting to breast-feed may occasionally be subjected to a surprising amount of skepticism on the part of friends and relatives who are otherwise quite sympathetic. There are remarks like: "You aren't going to breast-feed, are you?" "Very few can make the grade." "Why in the world are you trying to do that?" "With breasts like yours, you'll never succeed." "Your poor baby is hungry. Are you trying to starve the child to prove a point?" The milder remarks can perhaps be blamed on surprise, but the meaner ones strongly suggest envy. Even later on, if there is any question about continuing to nurse, you'll find several friends who'll urge you to stop.

163. Why some mothers give up after a good start. A good percentage of mothers who are eager to breast-feed are successful in the hospital and for a number of days or weeks afterward (with the possible exception of the first day or two at home when the supply often decreases temporarily). Then, too many of them feel that they are failing and give up. They say, "I didn't have enough milk," or "My milk didn't seem to agree with the baby," or "As the baby grew bigger my milk was no longer sufficient."

Why is it that throughout most of the world a mother's milk takes care of the baby for many months and that it's only in bottle-feeding countries like ours that the breast milk supply seems to fail so early in a majority of cases? I don't believe that American mothers are that nervous. They are certainly as healthy as any. I think there is one main reason. The mother here who is trying to breast-feed, instead of feeling that she is doing the most natural thing in the world and assuming that she'll succeed like everyone else, feels that she's attempting to do the unusual, the difficult thing. Unless she has tremendous self-confidence she keeps wondering whether she won't fail. In a sense, she's looking for signs of failure. If her baby cries one day a bit more than usual, her first thought is that her milk has decreased. If the baby develops indigestion or colic or a rash, she is quick to suspect her milk.

Her anxiety makes her feel sure that the bottle is the answer. And the trouble is that the bottle is always available. Probably she was given formula directions or packs of prepared formula when she left the hospital ("just in case"). Babies on the breast who begin to receive ample amounts of formula several times a day practically always nurse less eagerly at the breast. And milk left in the breast is nature's method of signaling to the glands to make less.

In other words, the combination of a mother lacking confidence in her ability to breast-feed and the availability of bottles of formula is the most efficient method of discouraging breast-feeding.

To put it positively: The way to make breast-feeding a success is to go on breast-feeding and keep away from formula, except possibly for one relief bottle a day after the breast supply is well established (see Sections 204–206).

Under normal conditions the amount of milk supplied by the breasts is not a fixed quantity. The breasts are ready at any time to gradually decrease or increase the amount of milk, depending on whether the baby wants less or more. As a baby grows and her appetite increases, she empties the breasts more completely and sometimes more frequently.

This stimulation encourages an increase in milk production.

164. Community resources for nursing mothers. Many hospitals now have lactation specialists who counsel breast-feeding mothers. Most physicians and nurse practitioners are well versed in supporting breast-feeding also. The La Leche League is composed of mothers who have succeeded at breast-feeding and are eager to give advice and support to inexperienced mothers. Consult your phone book or ask a nurse at the local health department. The **International Childbirth Education Association** instructors in your community can provide support and usually can refer you to a **lactation consultant.** These experienced, knowledgeable consultants, certified by the International Lactation Consultant Association, have a remarkably high rate of success with mothers who are having breast-feeding problems. **The Nursing Mothers' Council** can also help, if there's one near you.

The Nursing Mother's Physical Condition

165. The mother's breasts during pregnancy and nursing. Some mothers shy away from breast-feeding for fear it will spoil their figures. You certainly don't have to eat excessively or get fat in order to make milk. A nursing mother needs enough extra fluid, calories, and calcium to keep her own body from being depleted. She does not need to gain an ounce above her regular weight.

But what about the effect of nursing on the shape and size of the breasts? They enlarge during pregnancy and even more during the first days after birth, whether or not the baby is nursed. Certainly the breasts become much less prominent and firm by the time a baby is a week old, even if the mother continues to nurse successfully, so much so that she may wonder whether her milk has gone.

An important factor—whether nursing is never started or is ended at one, three, six, or twelve months—is the character of the supporting tissue of the breasts in each individual. There are women whose breasts have flattened without their ever having nursed a child. I know from my own medical experience that many women breast-feed several babies with no deleterious effect on their figures. Others end up with even better figures.

There are two precautions that are probably important. First, the mother should wear a well-fitting bra that supports the breasts, not only when she is nursing but also during the later part of pregnancy, day and night, when the breasts are definitely enlarged. This is to prevent stretching of the skin and of the supporting tissues in the breasts during the time the breasts are heavier. It is well worthwhile to buy nursing bras that have changeable washable pads in them to absorb any milk that may leak between feedings (of course, cotton pads may be used instead), and the fronts of which can be opened for nursing (get the kind that can be opened easily with one hand).

The other precaution during pregnancy and nursing is to avoid putting on excess weight. After all, the breasts may sag from obesity, quite apart from pregnancy.

166. Breast size is of no importance. Some women with small breasts assume that they will be less able to produce milk in sufficient quantity. There is no basis for this belief. When a woman is not pregnant and not nursing, the glandular tissue is quiescent and constitutes only a minor part of the breast. The greater part is composed of fat tissue. The larger breast has more fat tissue; the smaller breast has less. As a woman's pregnancy progresses, secretions from the ovaries stimulate the glandular, milk-producing tissue to develop and enlarge. The arteries and veins that serve the glandular tissue enlarge, too, so that the veins become prominent on the surface of the breasts. The milk, when it comes a few days after delivery, causes further enlargement of the breasts. Doctors who have cared for nursing mothers agree that even women who have very small breasts before pregnancy can produce copious amounts of milk.

167. The mother's diet. Some mothers hesitate to nurse their babies because they have heard that they will have to give up too much. Generally speaking this is not so. There is no evidence that it will harm the baby if the mother engages in noncompetitive athletics, and the nursing mother can usually continue to eat a balanced diet. Smoking and alcoholic beverages, however, should be avoided.

Occasionally a baby seems to get upset every time the mother eats a certain food. For example, if a mother drinks cow's milk, which I do not recommend, some of the cow's proteins will actually pass into the breast milk and irritate the baby's stomach. Caffeine, chocolate, and some other foods will sometimes do the same thing after a delay of a day or so. Naturally, if this happens several times in succession, the mother can give up that particular food. Some drugs get into the milk, but usually not in large enough quantities to affect the baby. Check with your doctor about which drugs are safe or unsafe to take while breast-feeding.

A nursing mother does need to be sure that her diet contains plenty of the elements that the baby is withdrawing through her milk. A large amount of calcium is excreted in the milk, to enable the baby's bones to grow rapidly. If the mother takes in too little, it will be withdrawn from her bones. It used to be thought that she would lose calcium from her teeth, too, but this is probably not so. She also should take in as much fluid as the baby is getting from her, plus a little extra for her own needs. This does not have to be milk. I recommend a nondairy beverage and high-calcium foods, such as green leafy vegetables and beans. High-calcium nondairy foods are listed on pages 114–15.

The nursing mother's daily diet should include the following nutrients: (1) plenty of vegetables, especially green leafy vegetables like broccoli and kale, (2) fresh fruit, (3) beans, peas, and lentils, which have vitamins and plenty of calcium, and traces of healthful fats, and (4) whole grains.

Another good reason for getting your nutrition from plant sources is that animals tend to concentrate pesticides and other chemicals in their meat and milk. This is especially true of fish, but chemicals are commonly found in all animal products. Traces of these chemicals can easily end up in a mother's breast milk if she eats these products. Plant foods have much less contamination, even if they are not organically grown. A multivitamin preparation, prescribed by the doctor, is also a good idea. You should avoid using any vitamin in a daily dose larger than the recommended one, unless your doctor has recommended it.

Exercise is the best way to tone the mother's body and help her lose weight if need be. A brisk, thirty-minute walk several times a week, with the baby in a carrier, can be very helpful.

There are two sides to the matter of **fluids.** There is no good to be gained from drinking more fluid than feels comfortable, because the body promptly gets rid of excess water through the urine. On the other hand, a new, excited, busy mother may forget to drink as much as she needs and go thirsty through absentmindedness. A good time to drink something is ten or fifteen minutes before you expect to nurse.

The mother particularly needs to take good care of herself. During this period she can unplug the phone, nap when the baby naps, let the housework go, forget about outside worries and obligations, keep visitors down to one or two comfortable friends, and eat and drink wisely.

CALCIUM REQUIREMENTS

	AGE	CALCIUM
Infants	0–5 months	400 mg
	6–12 months	600 mg
Children	1–10 years	800 mg
Males	11–18 years	1200 mg
Females	11–18 years	1200 mg

Healthful Calcium Sources (in milligrams)*

Black turtle beans (1 cup, boiled)	103	Lima beans (1 cup, boiled)	52

Broccoli			Navel orange	
(1 cup, boiled)	178		(1 medium)	56
Brussels sprouts			Navy beans	
(8 sprouts)	56		(1 cup, boiled)	128
Butternut squash			Onions	
(1 cup, boiled)	84		(1 cup, boiled)	58
Celery			Orange juice, calcium-	
(1 cup, boiled)	54		fortified (1 cup)	300**
Chickpeas			Pancake mix	
(1 cup, canned)	78		($\frac{1}{4}$ cup, 3 pancakes)	140
Collards			Pinto beans	
(1 cup, boiled)	148		(1 cup, boiled)	82
Corn bread			Raisins	
(1 2-ounce piece)	133		($\frac{2}{3}$ cup)	53
English muffin	92		Soybeans	
Figs, dried			(1 cup, boiled)	175
(10 medium)	269		Sweet potato	
Great Northern beans			(1 cup, boiled)	70
(1 cup, boiled)	121		Tofu ($\frac{1}{2}$ cup)	258
Green beans			Vegetarian baked beans	
(1 cup, boiled)	58		(1 cup)	128
Kale			Wax beans	
(1 cup boiled)	94		(1 cup, canned)	174
Kidney beans			Wheat flour, calcium	
(1 cup, boiled)	50		enriched (1 cup)	238
Lentils			White beans	
(1 cup, boiled)	37		(1 cup, boiled)	161

---

*Source: J. A. T. Pennington, Bowes and Church's Food Values of Portions Commonly Used (New York: Harper & Row, 1989).
**Package information.

168. Does nursing tire the mother? You occasionally hear it said that breast-feeding "takes a lot out of a woman." Many women do feel fatigued in the early weeks of nursing, but so do many who are feeding by bottle. They are getting their strength back after the delivery and hospitalization. The nervous tension from caring for a new baby is tiring. But it's also true that the breasts are providing a good number of calories each day for the baby, and so a mother must eat more than usual just to keep her weight up. In the long run there is no more reason for a woman to feel exhausted from breast-feeding than from a vacation on which she is taking a lot of exercise in the form of walks or swimming. Our bodies soon adapt to increasing or decreasing energy needs, and our appetites go up or down accordingly in order to keep our weight stationary. If a nursing mother is healthy and happy, her appetite will naturally take care of the need for extra calories for the baby's milk. Needless to say, a nursing mother who is not feeling well or is losing weight should consult her doctor promptly.

169. Menstruation and pregnancy. Some women never menstruate so long as they continue to nurse. Others menstruate regularly or irregularly. Once in a while a nursing baby will be mildly upset during the mother's menstruation or temporarily refuse to nurse.

Breast-feeding does not always prevent pregnancy, even when the mother is not having periods. It's important to consult your doctor about when to resume the family planning method of your choice.

The Working Mother

170. Breast-feeding and the working mother. What about the woman who hesitates to nurse because she has to go back to work? If you've got the determination to succeed and to gain the emotional support for your breast-feeding at work and at home, then working and breast-feeding can both succeed, no matter what your schedule or situation. Most mothers who best combine work and breast-feeding are those who do frequent feedings after work and don't try to keep their babies on a schedule. Mothers who work can totally breast-feed their babies on their days off. This helps to maintain a good milk supply, which is the main problem. Even if you decide not to nurse after you resume work, it would still be worthwhile for the baby's health to breast-feed the baby temporarily if you have a few weeks at home. You'll probably find it really helpful to talk to some mothers who have nursed after going back to work, before you have your baby.

171. Combining breast- and bottle-feeding. Here are some suggestions offered by experienced mothers who have nursed after going back to work:

1. Wait until the baby is three to four weeks old, if possible, to begin introducing the bottle. By this time the baby should be used to nursing on somewhat of a schedule, and your milk flow should be well established.
2. Begin by giving a bottle of breast milk three times a week. Many babies won't take the bottles from their mothers—they know the difference—so the father or older brother or sister or sitter may need to take over.
3. Warm milk works best. Breast-fed babies aren't used to cold temperatures yet. Some babies will have no difficulty accepting a bottle, but with others it's a struggle and requires patience.
4. If the baby is reluctant to take the bottle, the mother should try leaving the room, or even the house, since some babies will refuse the bottle if they can even hear the mother talking. You can also try holding the baby in a non-nursing position. For example, she can be lying in your lap with her feet toward you and her head toward your knees while you offer her the bottle. Sometimes, babies who really seem to like a sweet taste will at first accept apple juice, diluted half and half with water, from the bottle better than milk.
5. Before the mother returns to work, the baby should be taking at least one bottle a day well. It's important to express your milk during the bottle-feedings to keep your supply up.
6. Try to nurse right before and right after work, and to express your milk at least once if you're working longer than 6 hours.
7. One easy way to express and store milk is to nurse the baby on one breast and use the breast pump on the other. This really helps because the "let-down"

117

reflex from nursing seems to allow the milk to pump easier. *Breast milk keeps a few days in the refrigerator and several months in the freezer.* But smell and taste it, to be sure it's not sour, before giving it to the baby. Once you start a bottle of stored breast milk, discard any unused portion after twenty-four hours. Most good breast pumps allow you to pump directly into small bottles with good sealer caps. These can be labeled and stored in the freezer. Or you can buy ice cube trays with individual cubes. Then you can freeze the breast milk (wrapped in plastic wrap) in $1\frac{1}{2}$-ounce portions for use by the sitter when a bottle is given. Even totally breast-fed babies seem to do fine with one bottle of breast milk and maybe one bottle of diluted apple juice during a normal working day.

Of course, you'll find what works best for you and your baby within a few weeks.

Getting Started at Breast-Feeding

172. Relaxation and letdown. You'll probably notice that the state of your feelings has a lot to do with how easily your milk comes. Worries and tenseness can hold the milk back. So try to get troubles off your mind before beginning. Take some deep breaths and relax your shoulders. If possible, lie down for fifteen minutes before you expect the baby to wake, and do what is most relaxing, whether it's shutting your eyes, or reading, or watching TV.

After you have been nursing for a few weeks, you may notice a distinct sensation of the milk being "let down" or "coming in" at nursing time. It may start leaking from the breasts when you hear the baby beginning to cry in the next room. This shows how much feelings have to do with the formation and release of the milk. The feeling of letdown may not be experienced by all nursing mothers.

173. Finding a comfortable position and getting the baby "latched on." Whichever position you choose, be sure to get the baby properly positioned on your breast. *Incorrect "latch" is the most frequent cause of sore nipples.*

Effective latching on to the breast occurs when part of the areola (the dark area behind the nipple) is inside the baby's mouth. A mother can assist her baby to find a comfortable and effective nursing position by controlling the baby's head with one hand and moving the nipple and areola into the baby's mouth with the other.

Some mothers prefer, even in bed in the hospital, to nurse sitting up. The "cradle hold" works best for most mothers. Hold the baby with his head in the crook of your elbow, facing your breast, with his back supported by your forearm. You can hold his bottom or thigh with your hand. His face, chest, stomach, and knees should all be facing you. A pillow under him and another under your elbow will provide good support. With your opposite hand, support your breast by placing your four fingers under it and your thumb on top, well

Breast-feeding with the cradle hold.

119

behind the areola (the dark skin around the nipple). Gently tickle the baby's lower lip with your nipple until he opens his mouth very wide. (Be patient—this sometimes takes a few minutes.) When the baby's mouth is wide open, pull him in close so his mouth is over the nipple and his gums are well behind the nipple, with most or all of the areola in his mouth. (This is called latching on.) His nose will be touching your breast, but there's usually no need to make an airspace, unless you hear him snuffling as he tries to nurse. If his breathing seems at all obstructed, pull his bottom closer to you or lift up your breast gently with your lower fingers. This will make the extra space he needs to nurse without his nose being plugged.

If you prefer to nurse lying on your side, or if you're more comfortable that way because you've had stitches, have someone help you position pillows behind your back and between your legs. The baby should lie on his side facing you. You may need to experiment with pillows under the baby and under your head and shoulder to bring the nipple to the right height for the baby. Let's say you're on your left side: curl your left arm around the baby in the cradle hold and then get him latched on as described above.

Breast-feeding in bed, lying on the side.

The "football hold" is one you can use if you had a cesarean section birth, or to nurse a small baby, or just for a different position. Sit in a comfortable chair (most prefer a rocking chair) or in bed with lots of pillows keeping you upright. Rest your arm on a pillow and tuck the baby's trunk and legs under your elbow, with his head resting in your hand and his legs pointing straight up the back of the chair or the pillows behind you. The baby is then latched on to the breast as described for the cradle hold.

Breast-feeding with the football hold.

174. How the baby gets the milk. Babies do not get the milk simply by taking the nipple into their mouths and sucking. The milk is formed in the glandular tissue throughout the breast. It then passes through small ducts toward the center of the breast, where it collects in a number of sinuses. These sinuses, or storage spaces, are located in a circle right behind the areola, the dark area around the nipple. A short duct leads from each sinus through the nipple to the outside (there are a number of openings in each nipple). When babies are nursing properly, most or all of the areola area is in their mouths, and the principal action is the squeezing of the sinuses (behind the areola) by the babies' gums. This forces the milk, which has collected in the sinuses, through the nipple and into the mouth. The sucking action of the baby's tongue is not so much to draw the milk through the nipple as to keep the areola drawn into the mouth and also to get the milk from the front of the mouth back into the throat.

175. If babies take only the nipple into their mouths, they get almost no milk. And, if they chew on the nipple, they are apt to make it sore. But if they take most or all of the areola into their mouths, their gums squeeze the areola and cannot hurt the nipple. If babies start to mouth and chew on the nipple alone, they should be stopped promptly. Slip your finger into the corner of the mouth or between the gums if necessary to break the suction. (Otherwise you would have to pull the baby off the breast, which is hard on the nipple.) Then reinsert the areola into the mouth. If the baby persists in chewing the nipple, stop that feeding.

It's common for the breasts to become engorged when the milk first comes in. This may pull the nipple flat and in combination with a firm breast may make it difficult for a newborn to latch on. The baby may get angry and frustrated. Hot compresses and expressing some milk for a few minutes before nursing will pull the nipple out enough to help the baby get the areola into her mouth (see Sections 192–193).

176. There are two things to avoid when putting babies to the breast. The first is holding the head, in trying to direct it toward the breast. Babies hate to have their heads held; they fight to get free. The other is to squeeze them across the cheeks to get the mouth open. Babies have an instinct to turn toward anything that touches their cheeks. This reflex helps them find the nipple. When you squeeze them on both cheeks at the same time, you baffle and annoy them.

When a baby is refusing to take the breast and carrying on, a mother can't help feeling spurned, frustrated, and irritated. She shouldn't let her feelings be hurt by this inexperienced but apparently opinionated newcomer. If she can keep trying for a few more feedings, the chances are that the baby will figure out what it's all about.

177. Inverted nipples. If a mother's nipples are flat or retracted (drawn back into the breast by the supporting tissue), it may further complicate the business of getting a baby started at the breast, especially if the baby is the excitable type. If she searches around and can't find the nipple, she may cry angrily and pull her head back. There are several tactful things you can try. If possible, put her to breast when she first wakes up, before she gets too cross. If she starts crying at the first attempt, stop right away and comfort her before trying again. Take your time. It sometimes makes a nipple stand out better to massage it lightly with the fingers first. A few women have truly inverted nipples which don't become erect, but this doesn't prevent nursing. They sometimes benefit from the use of breast shells or milk cups (see Section 196). Your doctor or her nurse will explain how to use them.

Actually, the nipple is not so important in nursing as it is in guiding the baby to draw the areola into her mouth. However, the supporting tissues that retract the nipple also make it more difficult for the baby to draw the areola forward and shape it to her mouth. Probably the most valuable procedure is for the mother (or nurse) to squeeze some of the milk from the sinuses by manual expression (see Sections 200–202) so that the areolar region will be softer and more compressible. Then press the areola into a more protruding shape, between thumb and finger, when putting it into the baby's mouth.

178. Care of nipples. Some doctors recommend regular massage of the nipples to toughen them during the last month of pregnancy. Or the husband can do this orally. After the baby is born and begins to nurse, no particular care of the nipples, no wiping or ointment, should ordinarily be necessary. (Many women who have breast-fed have a favorite ointment and there is quite a list.) It is sensible for the mother to wash her hands with soap before fingering her nipples to massage or examine them, since infection can enter the breast through the nipple, and babies can easily pick up thrush, a mild yeast infection of the mouth. But hand-washing should not be necessary before an ordinary nursing.

Some experienced mothers are convinced that the most helpful step in healing **sore nipples,** and in keeping them healthy is to allow them to dry in the air for ten or fifteen minutes before closing the nursing flaps of the bra or to leave the flaps open between feedings. Nipples will also stay drier and healthier if there is no waterproof lining in the bra.

Any preparation that causes drying and cracking of the nipples should be avoided, such as soaps or alcohol containing preparations.

179. If soreness starts to develop, the first things to check are the way the baby is latching on to the breast and the nursing position. The frequency of nursing should be increased to promote the emptying of the breasts and to prevent the baby from becoming too hungry. Changing nursing positions so that the pressure of the baby's gums is distributed in different areas of the areola is also helpful.

How the Nursing Pattern Gets Established

180. The early natural feeding pattern. Even though the milk usually doesn't come in for a few days, early, frequent nursings encourage the milk supply and help to prevent engorgement, so rooming-in is of enormous help to a mother in getting started at breast-feeding. Though some babies may be agreeable in adapting to a schedule set by the nursery, others are quite irregular at first in their wakefulness and hungriness. If they wake and cry at a time when they can't be brought from the nursery to their mothers, they may have cried themselves into a deep sleep by the time the schedule calls for a feeding. Whereas with rooming-in, a mother has only to reach over and put her baby to breast whenever she thinks her child is hungry. So the baby never has to cry for long or get overly tired.

Hospitals that favor rooming-in and breast-feeding often let babies be put to breast soon after birth. If allowed, it could even be done in the delivery room, ideally during the time when mothers and fathers have a chance to examine and fondle their new baby.

Some babies tend to be relatively sleepy and not very hungry for the first two or three days, waking only at long intervals. This is particularly apt to be so when their mothers have had a lot of sedation or anesthetic. Then babies are apt to shift over to a pattern of frequent waking as often as every two hours for a few days.

Other babies, though, are hungry and wakeful from the start. They may want to be fed ten or a dozen times in twenty-four hours for the first week or two, before settling down to something like six or seven feedings in the second, third, or fourth week.

181. When the milk comes in. There is considerable variation in the time and manner in which the milk comes in. It most often starts to come in on the third or fourth day of the baby's life. It tends to come in earlier in mothers who have had a child before or who have had rooming-in with their babies and have been able to feed on demand in the hospital. Sometimes it comes so suddenly that the mother can name the hour. In other cases the progress is much more gradual. And it's on about the third or fourth day that many babies become distinctly more wakeful and hungry. This is one of the many examples of how smoothly nature works things out. Studies of babies who have been breast-fed whenever they appeared hungry have shown that a majority of them want to nurse up to ten or twelve times a day between the third and sixth days. (The stools may become frequent on these days, too.) Mothers who are particularly anxious to make a success of breast-feeding are apt to feel disappointed by this frequency, assuming that it means the breast-milk supply is inadequate. This is incorrect. It's more sensible to think that the baby is now settling down to the serious business of eating and growing and is providing the breasts with the stimulation they must have if they are to meet the increasing demands. It is during this latter half of the first week, too, that the breasts are receiving the strongest stimulation from the hormones (the glandular secretions that make the milk come in, in the first place). It is no wonder that in the first few days the breasts sometimes become too full or that sometimes there isn't enough to satisfy the newly hungry baby. Still, the system is generally efficient, much better than you or I could design.

Hormone production calms down at the end of the first week. Then it is how much the baby demands that determines how much the breasts produce. In the changeover period (usually the second week) there may not be quite enough milk until the breasts adjust to the demand. The baby's hunger teaches the breast how much to produce, not just in the second or third week, but on through the succeeding months. In other words, the supply may still be increasing when the baby is several months old, if she wants more.

182. How long to nurse at each feeding. It used to be assumed, since in some cases the nipples became sore, that it was better for the mother to limit the nursing time at first and then gradually increase it as the nipples adjusted. But experience has shown that it's better to let the babies decide from the beginning. If they are always allowed to nurse promptly when hungry and for as long as they wish, they don't get so frantically hungry that they make the nipples sore by not being latched on properly.

Longer nursing from the start allows the letdown reflex, which is slower to respond at first, to come into play. I would still hold babies to twenty or thirty minutes per feeding for the first week or two, because they may be feeding every two hours and the longer duration of nursing would leave the mother with little time to do much else.

183. How often can you nurse? In one sense the answer is "As often as your baby appears hungry and as often as you feel able to accommodate the baby." Mothers in nonindustrialized societies occasionally nurse again as soon as a half hour after the last feeding, though the baby will probably nurse only briefly at one or the other of these feedings. The mother in our society who has successfully nursed a previous baby and has plenty of self-assurance might not hesitate to nurse occasionally after an hour, if she thought there was a special reason for hunger.

But there are several reasons why it wouldn't be helpful for me to tell you to nurse as often as the baby cries. Babies cry for reasons other than hunger—colic, other forms of indigestion, spells of irritability that we don't understand, fatigue that for some reason doesn't bring sleep. An anxious, inexperienced mother can get to a point of frantic fatigue if she's worrying and nursing all day and half the night. This worrying can cut down on the milk supply and interfere with the letdown reflex, too.

So in one way the answer is to nurse as often as you wish. But in another way I think it helps the inexperienced mother to protect herself by generally trying to keep at least two hours between feedings. Let the baby fuss a bit in the hope that she'll go back to sleep. If not, try a pacifier. Try rocking her for a few minutes or carrying her in a carrier on your chest. If you still think she's hungry, nurse her again, but not for more than twenty minutes this time. With a baby who seems to be demanding feedings too frequently, limit each feeding to twenty or, at most, thirty minutes.

But when your nipples have shown they are invulnerable and when you feel confident about your milk supply and your ability to judge your baby's hunger and other discomforts, nurse as often and for as long as you decide it's sensible.

184. One or both breasts? In most nonindustrial parts of the world, where nursing is the only way babies are fed, where mothers carry their babies around with them in slings while they work, and where schedules are unknown, babies wake and are put to breast frequently. They nurse relatively briefly, at one breast, and then fall asleep again. In our society, which runs pretty much according to the clock and in which many babies are put in a crib in a quiet room after a feeding, the tendency is toward fewer and larger feedings. If a mother produces ample amounts of milk, her baby may be quite satisfied with one breast at each feeding. Each breast receives the stimulation of very complete nursing, even though this occurs only once in about four to eight hours.

In many cases, however, the amount of milk in one breast does not satisfy the baby and both breasts are given at each feeding, the left breast being offered first at one feeding, the right breast first at the next. Some mothers and doctors advocate both breasts anyway. To ensure a good milk supply, the baby might be kept on the first breast for twelve to fifteen minutes, if willing, and then allowed to nurse on the second breast for as short or as long a period as desired. A baby who sticks to business will take the greater part of the milk in five or six minutes. (The breasts will always be producing a little new milk, so the baby will always taste something.) Therefore, there is no need for a mother to prolong breast-feeding beyond a total of twenty to forty minutes, depending on how eager the baby is to continue and how much time the mother has to spare. Stop after thirty minutes if your baby is willing.

185. Different babies behave differently at the breast. A physician with a sense of humor, who has studied the behavior of hundreds of babies when first put to breast, has pointed out the different types. The **eager beavers** draw the areola in avidly and suck vigorously until satisfied. The only problem is that they may be too hard on the nipple if they are allowed to chew it. **Excitable babies** may become so agitated and active that they keep losing the breast and then, instead of trying again, they scream. They may have to be picked up and comforted for several minutes before they are calm enough to try again. After a few days they usually settle down. The **procrastinators** can't be bothered to nurse the first few days; they are waiting until the milk comes in. Prodding them only makes them balky. They do well when the time comes. The **tasters** must, for a little while, mouth the nipple and smack their lips over the drop of milk they taste, before they settle down to business. Efforts to hurry them only make them angry. The **resters** want to nurse a few minutes and then rest a few minutes before starting again. They can't be rushed. They usually do a good job in their own way, but it takes them longer.

186. There are several patterns of behavior in the early weeks of nursing that complicate the mother's job and may nearly drive her mad. However, the chances are that the baby will outgrow these inconvenient patterns in a few weeks, no matter how you handle them.

The first is that of the babies who never seem to nurse very vigorously and fall asleep five minutes or so after starting. You don't know whether they have taken a reasonable amount or not. It wouldn't be so bad if they'd sleep for two or three hours, but they may wake and cry again in a few minutes after they're put back to bed. Some of these babies, who find that they're getting little result from the nursing, go back to sleep. Then when they're put back into the harder, cooler bed, their hunger wakes them up again.

We don't really know what causes this inefficient nursing or the prompt waking. One possibility is that the baby's nervous system and digestive system are not yet working well enough together. Perhaps the comfort of their mothers' arms and the breast in the mouth is enough to put them back to sleep. When they're a little older and know what it's all about, their hunger will keep them awake until they're well satisfied.

Other babies, hungrier or more wide awake or more assertive, react with irritation when they find they can't get enough milk. They jerk their heads away from the breast and yell, try again, get mad again. The fact that the baby doesn't nurse well only increases the mother's uneasiness, so a vicious cycle sets in.

If a mother understands how tension can interfere with letting down, she can use all her ingenuity in finding her own best way to relax before and during nursing. It's different for each individual. Music, a magazine, television—whatever works best is what she should adopt.

If your baby gets sleepy or restless after a few minutes at one breast, you can try shifting right away to the other breast, to see if the easier flow of milk will help. Of course, you'd like her to work at least fifteen minutes on one breast to be sure that it is well stimulated, but if she won't, she won't.

If your baby is one of those "resters," who doze off and on, but suck well in between, let her continue. But if she doesn't resume nursing, it works better not to prolong the nursing or to keep trying to wake her up again. In the long run you only take away her enthusiasm and make her an indifferent eater. What do you do if she wakes as soon as you put her to bed or a little later? I think it's better to assume first that if she has nursed for 5 to 10 minutes she's had enough to keep her satisfied for a couple of hours, and try not to feed her again right away. Let her fuss for a while if you can stand it. Give her a pacifier. See if a hot-water bottle on her belly will make her feel cozier (Section 323). The purpose is to teach her that feedings come every few hours and that it's her eagerness that brings the satisfaction. To keep feeding her off and on for an hour and a half tends to teach her that feedings are always chasing her and that sometimes the only way to escape them is to go to sleep. But if she wakes as soon as she's in bed and can't be comforted and gets to crying frantically, you'd better feed her again anyway, and never mind the theory. You can at least give her a second chance. But don't go on to a third and a fourth feeding if you can help it. Make her wait at least an hour or so.

How You Know the Baby Is Getting Enough

187. A reliable guide is the combination of weight gain and satisfaction. It's good to remember that throughout the world, in which there are no scales and no doctors, the mother simply assumes that her baby is receiving plenty if the child acts contented and looks well, and that this system works well in at least nine out of ten cases.

Generally speaking, you and the doctor will decide, on the basis of the baby's behavior over a number of weeks and on the basis of weight gain. Neither alone is conclusive. A baby who is happy and gaining fast is obviously getting enough. A baby who cries hard every afternoon or evening but is gaining weight at the average rate is probably getting plenty to eat but having colic. A baby who gains slowly but is quite contented is, in most cases, a baby who is meant to be a slow gainer. However, there are a few babies who don't protest even when they are not gaining at all. It's the baby who is gaining very slowly and acting hungry most of the time who's probably not getting enough. The baby who is not getting enough to eat may act either unusually upset or lethargic. He'll have fewer than six wet diapers a day, his urine will look dark or smell strong, and he'll have infrequent bowel movements.

Any baby who is not gaining weight well by the end of the second week of life should be awakened every two or three hours and encouraged to feed more frequently. Babies who are sleepy at the breast can be encouraged to feed by being burped and switched to the other breast when they fall asleep. If this routine is repeated four or five times during a feeding most babies will be gaining weight and nursing more vigorously after five to seven days.

130

Breast-fed babies should be seen by their doctor or nurse within two weeks after they leave the hospital—sooner if breast-feeding did not go smoothly in the hospital.

In the long run it's best to assume that the baby is getting enough, unless the baby and the doctor or nurse practitioner definitely tell you differently. Certainly at any one feeding you should be satisfied if the baby seems satisfied.

188. You can't tell from the length of nursing time or the appearance of the breasts or milk. This question of whether the baby's getting enough is likely to baffle the new mother. A good rule of thumb is that by the fifth day of life, babies will usually have six to eight wet diapers and four to ten bowel movements a day, and will be nursing eight to ten times each twenty-four hours.

You certainly can't tell from the length of time the baby nurses. She goes on nursing after she's already obtained most of the milk—sometimes for ten more minutes, sometimes for thirty—because she's still getting a trickle of milk, or because she enjoys sucking, or because she's still awake and having a good time. Careful observation and weighing of slightly older babies have shown that the same baby will appear to be entirely satisfied with 3 ounces at one feeding and by 10 ounces at another.

Most mothers with experience have decided that they can't tell from the apparent fullness of the breasts before feeding how much milk is there. In the first week or two, the breasts are noticeably full and firm as a result of hormonal changes, but after a while they normally become softer and less prominent, even though the milk supply is increasing. A baby can get 6 or more ounces from a breast that to the mother does not seem full at all. You can't tell anything from the color and appearance of the milk either. Breast milk always looks thin and bluish compared to cow's milk and there are no important variations in the composition of the milk from time to time in the same mother, or from one mother to another.

189. Hunger is not the most common reason for crying. The most common reason for a mother to worry is that her baby begins to fret right after feedings or between feedings. Her first thought is that her milk supply is failing. But this assumption is not usually correct. The fact is that almost all babies, especially first babies, have fretful spells, most often in the afternoon or evening. Bottle-fed babies fuss as much as breast-fed babies. Babies who are getting all the milk they can possibly hold have crying spells just the same as babies who are receiving less. (These fretful spells are discussed in Section 312, on colic, and Section 321, on general fretfulness.) If a mother realizes clearly that most of the fussing in the early weeks is not caused by hunger, she won't be so quick to lose confidence in her breast-milk supply.

Though it is much less likely, it is of course possible that a baby is beginning to fret because she's hungry. However, hunger is much more apt to wake a baby a little earlier for the next feeding than to bother her in the first hour or two after the last feeding. If she is hungry, it may be because her appetite has taken a sudden spurt, or it may possibly mean that her mother's milk has decreased slightly because of fatigue or tension. In either case the answer is the same: Take it for granted that she'll wake and want to nurse more frequently and more vigorously for a day or for a few days until the mother's breasts have adjusted to the demand; then she will probably go back to her previous schedule.

The treatment for fretfulness seems clear to me. Any thought of giving a bottle of formula should be postponed for at least a couple of weeks. The baby should be allowed to nurse as often as every two hours (counting from the beginning of one feeding to the beginning of the next), for twenty to forty minutes. If she makes a reasonable weight gain in that week or two, consideration of formula should again be put off, for at least two more weeks. The baby can be comforted during her fretful periods with a pacifier or with a bottle of water or possibly sugar water (Sections 255–256). The mother may occasionally want to nurse her even more frequently than every two hours. It certainly won't do the baby any harm. I'm only thinking of the mother: She can't help becoming frantic if she's nursing all day long, and it won't do that much good. Nursing ten times a day will give the breasts about as much stimulation as they can use. It is also necessary for the mother to have some rest and relaxation. Family and friends can help with holding, rocking and giving the baby a pacifier.

Special Problems During Breast-Feeding

190. Pains during nursing. You may be bothered the first week or so by cramps in your lower abdomen as soon as the baby starts nursing. This is the normal reflex action by which nursing causes the uterus to contract. It is intended to help the uterus get back to its nonpregnant size. These cramps disappear after a while.

During the first few days or weeks, twinges of pain in the nipple that last a few seconds after the baby begins to nurse are very common, mean nothing, and will soon go away.

191. Sore or cracked nipples. Pain that persists throughout the nursing may point to a cracked nipple, and a careful search should be made. (A very few mothers are unusually sensitive and continue to feel pain even though their nipples remain healthy.) If a nipple is cracked (often because a baby has chewed on it instead of taking the areola into her mouth), it is usually recommended that a combination of more frequent nursing, frequent changes of the baby's nursing position, and applications of ice packs be used. The physician or nurse practitioner may prescribe an ointment for the sore nipple. Some mothers find letting some milk dry over the nipples after a feeding to be very soothing. Another method is to let the nipples dry for fifteen minutes before closing the flaps of the brassiere; or leave the flaps open. Remove the waterproof lining from the brassiere. One mother found successful a small tea strainer (the kind that can be detached from the handle) over the nipple, inside an ample bra.

More frequent nursing will provide continued stimulation of the breast and relieve fullness.

Engorged Breasts

192. Areolar engorgement. The most common and simplest cause of engorgement is the overfilling of the sinuses, the storage spaces located behind the areola. This is not uncomfortable for the mother, but it may make the areolar region so firm and flat that the baby cannot take it into her mouth in order to compress it with her gums. The only thing she can get hold of is the nipple, and she is apt to chew on it and perhaps make it sore. It is important, therefore, for the mother or nurse to express sufficient milk from the sinuses so that the areolar region will become soft enough and compressible enough for the baby to take it into her mouth (see Sections 200–202).

It is not necessary to express much milk to soften the areolar region—two to five minutes on each breast should be sufficient. Then the mother can compress the areolar region from above and below as she puts the breast into the baby's mouth, to help her get started. This type of engorgement is most likely to occur in the latter half of the first week, to last two or three days and not to return, as long as nursing continues normally.

193. Peripheral engorgement. This type of engorgement involves not just the areolar region but the whole breast. The entire breast becomes firm and uncomfortable. Most cases are mild, but in the infrequent case that becomes severe, the breast is enlarged, surprisingly hard and very painful.

The usual mild case can be relieved promptly by having the baby nurse. It may be necessary to soften the areolar region first by manual expression if it is too firm for the baby to get it into her mouth. The severe case may require several different kinds of treatment. If the baby cannot consume enough milk to relieve the distension, the entire breast needs to be massaged, starting at the outer edges and working toward the areola. An ointment containing lanolin and petrolatum, or a vegetable oil should be used during the massage to avoid irritating the skin, but the ointment should be kept off the areola, because it makes it too slippery for areolar expression, which comes next. Massage of the entire breast is tiring to the mother and should be carried on only long enough to partially relieve the engorgement. It may be performed once or several times a day. The difficulty usually lasts only two or three days. The application of cloths wet with comfortably hot water seems to help prepare the breasts for massage. If massage and manual expression cannot be used successfully because no one is available to do it or to teach the mother how, a breast pump can be tried (see Section 203). Between nursings or treatments, a firm support should be given to the breasts from all sides by a large, firm brassiere or by a binder that gives support from the shoulders. The binder should be used not to flatten the breasts against the chest but to support them firmly from below and at both sides. An ice bag or hot-water bottle can be applied for short periods. There are various medications that the physician or nurse practitioner may prescribe. This total engorgement practically always occurs, if at all, in the latter half of the first week. It is rare after that.

194. Engorgement due to plugged ducts. A third type of engorgement is similar to total engorgement in that it is outside the areolar region and is painful. But it is confined to only one segment of the breast. This type is due to plugged ducts. It is more likely to occur after the hospital period. Treatment is similar to that for total engorgement:

- hot applications followed by massage of the engorged area
- support by an efficient brassiere or a binder
- ice bag or hot-water bottle between treatments
- increased frequency of nursing
- frequent changes of the baby's nursing position
- adequate rest for the mother

195. Breast infection or abscess. If a sore spot develops inside the breast, this may be an infection, which occasionally leads to a breast abscess. The skin may become red over the sore spot, and fever and chills may develop. You should take your temperature and get in touch with your doctor or nurse practitioner. However, with modern methods of treating infections, it should not be necessary to keep the baby from nursing at that breast, even temporarily.

196. A breast shell or milk cup. Many women have found these valuable in making retracted or inverted nipples stand erect, in lessening engorgement by pressing on the areolar region, and in keeping the nipple dry. The shell is worn under the bra except when nursing. An inner dome with a hole in it fits over the nipple. A more prominent dome, attached to it, protects the nipple from the bra and creates a space which will contain any milk that leaks from the nipple. (Milk leaking directly into a bra keeps the nipple wet.) The pressure of the inner dome and of the rim on the sinuses is believed to lessen engorgement; also, the pressure makes the nipple protrude, and the protrusion continues for a while after the cup is removed. These cups should be worn in the last weeks of pregnancy, if possible.

197. When the mother is ill. In ordinary illnesses during which the mother stays at home, it is customary to allow the baby to continue to nurse as usual. To be sure, there is a chance of the baby's catching the ailment, but this would be true even if the infant weren't being nursed. Besides, most infections are contagious before any symptoms are noticed. Babies on the average have milder colds than older members of the family.

Some mothers notice a decrease in milk supply when they're sick, but it comes right back with increased nursing.

198. Biting the nipple. Once the baby gets teeth, you can't blame her for trying a few bites when her gums are tingling during teething or when a couple of teeth have come in. She doesn't realize it hurts her mother. But it's not only painful; it may make the nipples so sore that nursing has to be stopped.

Most babies can be taught quickly not to bite. Instantly slip your finger between her gums and gently say "No." If she does it again, put your finger in again, say "No," and end the feeding. It's usually late in the feeding anyway when a baby starts to bite.

Manual Expression and Breast Pumps

199. Manual expression or a breast pump can be used to obtain milk for the baby who cannot or will not nurse at the breast, even though the mother has plenty of milk. A small premature baby may be too weak to nurse or to be taken out of the incubator, but he can be fed breast milk from a medicine dropper or a stomach tube. When an ill mother is away in a hospital or when it is considered unwise to expose the baby to her directly, her milk can be collected and given to the baby from a bottle (or discarded) until she can nurse again (see Section 171).

200. Manual Expression. The best way to learn manual expression is from an experienced person while you are in the hospital. It's a good idea to get some instruction even though you don't anticipate using it. A public health nurse or a lactation specialist can teach you at home later on, if necessary. A mother can learn by herself, but this takes longer. In any case, it seems like an awkward business at first, and several practice sessions will be necessary before you become efficient. Don't be discouraged.

The milk produced in the glandular tissue throughout the breast flows through tiny tubes toward the center of the breast and is stored in fifteen to twenty sinuses, or sacs, which are located behind the areola, the dark-colored skin around the nipple. In manual expression, the breast is massaged first and then the milk is squeezed out of the sinuses, each of which has a small tube leading through the nipple to the outside.

If you are going to express only a small amount of milk—for instance, to relieve engorgement in the areolar area—you can use any handy cup or nursing bottle to catch it. If you are going to express as much as you can and will be giving it to the baby right afterward, you should wash the cup with soap, rinse it, and dry it with a clean towel. After expressing the milk, you pour it into a nursing bottle and cap with a nipple, both of which should have been washed with soap and rinsed since the last use. If you are going to save the milk for a number of hours—for instance, if you are a working mother or you're delivering it once a day to the hospital for a premature baby—it should be kept refrigerated.

201. The finger-and-thumb method. First, of course, wash your hands with soap. Then massage the breast to bring the breast milk to the sinuses. In the more common method of manual expression, the sinuses are then repeatedly rolled and squeezed between thumb and finger. To apply the pressure where the sinuses lie, deep behind the areola, it is necessary to place the tips of thumb and finger on opposite sides of the areola (just at the edge where the dark skin meets the normally colored skin). Then press thumb and finger in deeply until they meet the ribs. In this position, squeeze them rhythmically together. The right hand is usually used to express the left breast, and in this instance the left hand holds the cup that catches the milk.

The main thing is to press in deeply enough and at the edge of the areola. The nipple itself is not squeezed or fingered. You may be able to get more milk with each squeeze if you not only press thumb and finger toward each other but pull slightly outward with them (toward the nipple) at the same time, to complete the milking motion.

After a bit, the thumb and finger can be shifted, partway "around the clock," to be sure that all the sinuses are being pressed. If the finger and thumb become tired—and they will at first—you can shift back and forth from side to side.

202. The thumb-and-cup method. Another method, less commonly used but very efficient when learned, is to press the sinuses between the thumb and the inside edge of a teacup that has a flared edge (it's too hard to get the areola and the thumb down inside a cup with straight sides).

First, wash your hands with soap and water. Tuck the lower edge of the cup deep into the left breast, at the lower edge of the areola, and tip the cup up partway, holding it with the left hand. Place the thumb of the right hand on the upper edge of the areola. Now the areola is being pressed between the right thumb and the rim of the cup. Press the right thumb firmly inward (toward the rim) and then downward (toward the nipple). This squeezes the milk from the sacs into the tubes running through the nipple. When you press toward the nipple, don't slide your thumb across the areola; the skin moves with the thumb. It is not necessary to squeeze or even touch the nipple.

With a little practice, you will be able to press the milk out in a fine spray. The first few days your thumb may be tired and lame, but this won't last. If you are expressing a full breast, it may take 20 minutes—more if you are just learning. If you are attempting to express the breasts completely after the baby has finished nursing it will take only a few minutes. When the breast is full, the milk comes in a spray. When it is partly empty, it comes in drops. Stop when no more milk comes. Naturally, if you wait 10 minutes the breast will have made more milk, but you don't have to express it again.

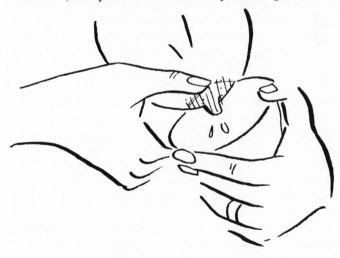

203. Breast pumps. Many mothers who have to express their milk regularly—especially working mothers who may be doing it for many weeks or months—prefer to use a breast pump, which you can rent or buy. There are dozens of different pumps on the market, with a wide range of prices. It's best to talk to your baby's doctor, nurse practitioner or a lactation consultant before your baby is born, to decide which will be best for you. The one type of pump that you should avoid has a plastic cone which fits over the nipple and areola and a rubber bulb, with both the cone and the bulb attached to a rim which can screw on to an ordinary nursing bottle. This type is the cheapest, but can be very hard on the nipple and areola. Also, bacteria will grow in the rubber bulb (see Section 171 on storing pumped milk).

Breast and Bottle Combinations

204. An occasional bottle is all right. Must a mother who wants to continue breast-feeding never give a bottle under any circumstances? No, it isn't that critical. Most of the mothers who want to give a bottle regularly once a day find that they can do so without discouraging the breast-milk supply, provided the supply has been well established for a few weeks and provided it's only one bottle a day. And certainly a mother who has not been giving a bottle regularly can give one occasionally. Perhaps she will have to miss a feeding. Or perhaps she has become extremely tired or upset and the baby has acted entirely dissatisfied with one feeding. One bottle doesn't stop breast-feeding. What I am advising against is giving a bottle in addition to a breast-feeding two or three times a day, if you hope to continue with breast-feeding.

205. Introducing a bottle. A bottle containing breast milk or formula can be given once or twice a week starting at three to four weeks. If a mother plans to wean her baby from breast to bottle sometime between two and nine months, it's a good idea to offer a bottle at least once a week, even though she could nurse just as well. The reason is that some babies become so set in their ways during this age period that they will refuse to take a bottle of milk if they are not used to it, and this can cause quite a struggle. A baby rarely gets this opinionated before the age of two months, and after nine months she can be weaned directly to the cup, if you prefer and she accepts it readily.

It is sometimes recommended that all breast-fed babies get a bottle once or twice a week, even though the mother is planning to nurse until her infant is weaned to the cup. This is on the theory that the mother might have to stop nursing for some unexpected reason. You can decide for yourself, balancing the inconvenience of making the bottle against risking the baby's putting up a struggle if weaned suddenly.

206. Breast and bottle both. If a mother who can't produce enough milk to completely satisfy the baby wants to go on with a combination of breast and bottle, there is no reason why she shouldn't. However, in many cases of mixed feedings, the breast-milk supply gradually decreases. Also, the baby may come to prefer the bottle and reject the breast altogether.

The most sensible thing to do when the mother is producing a reasonable amount of milk—say half or more of what the baby needs—is to make a real effort not to use formula at all. If this does not increase the breast-milk supply sufficiently, the mother can continue a combination of breast- and bottle-feeding, or wean the baby completely to the bottle, knowing that she tried as hard as she could.

Your doctor or nurse practitioner will help you decide the best combination of breast and bottle for your baby.

Bottle-Feeding

Choosing and Preparing Formula

Not so long ago babies were raised on infant formula as a matter of routine. Today we know that there are real health benefits to mother's milk and that formula should be used only when breast-feeding is not an option. If you are using a formula, there are several different brands to choose from.

141

207. Soy formulas have important advantages over those made from cow's milk. They have none of the animal proteins that are linked with colic and insulin-dependent diabetes, and are free of lactose sugar. Soy formulas are available in all hospital nurseries and grocery stores. While they were once reserved for children who were sensitive to cow's milk, they are now regarded as the best choice for infants who are not breast-feeding.

Be sure to use a soy *infant formula,* not regular soy milk. The soy baby formulas are specifically designed with extra nutrients to meet the needs of a rapidly growing child, whereas the soy milk that is intended for older children and adults is not. Soy formula is available fortified with iron. Iron-fortified formula should be used from four months on.

208. Cow's milk formulas are made from milk in which the butterfat has been replaced by vegetable oils. Carbohydrates, vitamins, and minerals have been added, and the protein content has been reduced. Some are iron-fortified. The proteins in cow's milk formulas can cause colic in some infants and are a possible contributor to childhood-onset diabetes. Scientists are still investigating this issue, but evidence suggests that soy is a safer choice.

Both cow's milk formula and soy formulas can cause allergies. About half of those children who have a definite allergy to cow's milk will also be allergic to soy formula. Infants who are allergic to both cow's milk and soy milk are often placed on casein hydrolysate formulas, which contain specially processed cow's milk proteins and are much more expensive. Homemade formulas made from evaporated milk, rice, or other grains, beans, or nuts do not provide adequate nutrition and are not recommended.

209. Prepared commercial formulas, which are most commonly used, are made from cow's milk or from soybeans. They come in three forms: ready-to-use liquid, concentrated liquid, and powder. In order to make them somewhat more like human milk, the percentages of protein and salt have been reduced, the sugar has been increased with the addition of lactose (milk sugar), and the cow's butterfat has been replaced with vegetable oils, and vitamins A, C, and D have been added. Prepared formulas are available with or without iron, according to the doctor's or nurse practitioner's advice, although iron-fortified formulas are almost always preferable.

Sterilization or Washing?

210. Sterilization of formula and bottles is no longer routinely recommended in the United States for people using reliable city or country water supplies. If you are not sterilizing, it's best to prepare one bottle at a time, immediately before feeding. However, if you use well water or for any other reason have any question about your water supply, check with your doctor or public health nurse or health department to see whether or not you have to sterilize.

Those who have to sterilize will find directions in Sections 213–218. Those who don't have to sterilize can substitute a thorough soap-and-water washing and rinsing for sterilization. See Section 211 for details.

211. Washing the nursing bottles, nipples, disks, rings, and, if used, quart storage jars. You can do a quicker and more efficient job of washing the bottle equipment if you do it with soap or detergent, water, and a brush soon after your baby has finished each bottle, before the remaining formula residue has dried in the bottle. But you can just rinse everything and use your dishwasher if it really gets the bottle equipment clean. Nipples should always be washed by hand. Clean a quart storage jar and its lid the same way you clean the nursing bottles. Careful washing of the bottles, nipples, screw rings, disks, and jars is particularly important if you are not sterilizing.

A bottle brush is important for washing the insides of the bottles. A nipple brush is essential for getting the insides of the nipples clean. Then a needle or toothpick should be twisted in each nipple hole, and water squirted through the holes.

212. Plastic holders with sterilized disposable plastic liners. This kind of bottle appeals to parents who are willing to pay a little more to save time washing or sterilizing. You still have to boil the nipples and caps for five minutes if your doctor or nurse practitioner tells you to boil the water and other equipment. (You never use this kind of bottle for terminal sterilization.)

The holder is a cylinder of hard plastic, open at both ends. It has slits on two sides, with ounce markings at the edges, so that you can look through to see how much formula you have put in the inner liner or how much the baby has drunk. You can't use these ounce markings for diluting formula—they're not accurate enough.

To use these bottles you tear a clear plastic liner off the roll and slip it into the holder, slightly folding it lengthwise so that it will go in. Then use the end tabs to stretch it open and fold it back over the upper end of the holder. Try to avoid touching the inside of the nipple and the part that goes into the baby's mouth. In other words, try to handle the nipple by the outside edges.

Be sure to discard the end tabs after assembling each bottle. Even a small baby could pull one off and swallow it.

There are large plastic caps that fit over the nipples while the containers are in the refrigerator or during trips.

Sterilization

Sterilization techniques and equipment may vary, according to your doctor or county health department. If you are uncertain of your water quality, I would suggest that your county health department be consulted for their recommendations on the exact procedures. Also, they can advise you on when it's safe to stop sterilizing. My general rule would be to continue sterilizing as long as you are making a twenty-four-hour supply of formula with unreliable water.

213. If you have to sterilize, there are two methods. One method is called *terminal sterilization.* You put formula made with unsterilized water into unsterilized bottles and then sterilize them all together. This method is used only when you will be filling all your nursing bottles at once. Terminal sterilization is not suitable if you plan to use disposable bottles or store the entire formula in a quart container, filling only one bottle at each feeding time.

The other method (sometimes called *aseptic sterilization)* is to sterilize the bottle equipment by itself, then make a sterile formula with boiled water, and put the sterile formula into the prepared bottles. Using this method, it's fine to fill all your nursing bottles or disposable bottles at once, or you can fill a quart container.

214. Terminal sterilization. Follow the directions for making whichever kind of formula you're using. You don't need to use boiled water or sterilized bottle equipment but the bottles and nipples should be thoroughly cleaned in the regular way. (See Section 211.) Fill all the nursing bottles, insert the nipples upside down, cover them with the disks, and then screw the rings on loosely. Leave the screw rings loose so that there will be a space for the hot air to escape as the bottles heat up, and for the air to reenter as the bottles cool again.

Follow the directions for using your stove top or electric sterilizing kit. Or put 1 or 2 inches of water in a kettle, place the bottles in a rack, lower the rack into the kettle, and cover it. Bring the water to a boil, and boil for twenty-five minutes. Use a timer to be sure. Turn off the heat and let the kettle cool (with the top still on) until the bottles are lukewarm, about an hour or two. Tighten the screw rings and refrigerate all the bottles.

There will be less clogging of the nipple holes when the formula is allowed to cool slowly, for an hour or two, without being shaken at all. This will allow any scum to form into one large, firm piece, which will then stick to the inside of the bottle.

215. Sterilizing the bottles, nipples, disks, and rings. You can buy a stove top sterilizer, which is essentially the same thing as a kettle, or an electric sterilizer that turns itself off at the right time. Sterilizers usually come with all the racks, bottles, disks, nipples, and rings that you'll need to get started, along with bottle and nipple brushes and tongs. Or you can get a kettle large enough to hold, in a wire rack, enough bottles for twenty-four hours—usually six, seven, or eight bottles in the early weeks—along with all the separate bottle equipment.

A pair of tongs sterilized with the rest of the equipment will be helpful in lifting the bottles out of the rack if they are still hot. (You can use a pot holder to pick up the handles of the hot tongs.) The tongs are also helpful in placing the nipples upside down in the bottles after they have been filled with formula, so that you won't handle the nipples where they may dip into the formula. If you don't use tongs, handle the nipples by the edges, not by the tip that may touch the formula and that will later go into the baby's mouth.

Follow the directions that come with your stove top or electric sterilizer. If you're using a regular kettle, put the bottles in the rack upside down so that the steam can more easily get into them and the water can run out. The same goes for the container holding the nipples and other equipment. Put a couple of inches of hot water in the bottom of the kettle, add the racks, put the top on, bring the water to a boil, and boil hard for five minutes, using a timer to be sure. Let the kettle cool.

The bottles are now ready for the formula. Store them in a clean place if you won't be filling them right away. If you want a sterile place to lay nipples, screw rings, and disks while you are bottling the formula, put them on the inverted top of the kettle or sterilizer.

216. To sterilize a quart jar. You can use any glass quart jar for storing formula. (Most plastic containers become misshapen when boiled.) Choose a pan large enough to hold the jar lying down on its side, and the lid, and fill with water. Bring to a boil and boil five minutes. When the jar is cool enough to handle, drain it well and pour the entire amount of sterilized formula into it. Seal loosely, so that air can enter as the formula cools, and refrigerate.

When each feeding time comes around, pour the required number of ounces into a sterilized nursing bottle or into a disposable bottle. Then put the quart jar back in the refrigerator.

146

217. You don't have to boil everything. Even if you have to sterilize the formula and boil the drinking water, you don't have to be so fussy with all the other things that your baby will eat and drink. You don't have to boil dishes and cups and feeding spoons, because germs don't get a chance to grow on clean, dry utensils.

When you first buy teething rings, pacifiers, and toys that babies put in their mouths, you can wash them with soap. But there is no need to keep on washing them afterward, unless they fall on the floor, because the only germs on them will be the babies' own germs that they're used to.

218. When can you stop sterilizing the formula and bottles? Talk to your doctor, public health nurse, or county health department about when it's safe to stop sterilizing. If you absolutely can't consult anyone, I'd go by the general rule that as long as you are making a twenty-four-hour formula that contains water, you have to sterilize the formula and bottles.

Mixing the Formula

If you are using prepared commercial formula, always follow exactly the mixing instructions on the package. A formula that's too strong or too weak isn't well tolerated or satisfying to the baby.

219. Powdered formula comes in 16-ounce cans, with measuring scoops and recloseable plastic lids. It's the cheapest of the prepared formulas, and it's very convenient for an occasional bottle for a breast-fed baby, eliminating waste. It's also very useful for travel. You can take along premeasured amounts of powder and a quart of boiled or distilled water; you can mix the formula at feeding time and avoid the need for refrigeration. The powder and water must be mixed together in the right order to avoid lumps; follow the instructions on the can.

Measure the amount of water needed and mix the formula in a clean pitcher or mixing bowl. A clean whisk or eggbeater is helpful. Pour all the formula into clean nursing bottles, or disposables, or a clean quart jar that you use to fill one bottle at feeding time. Cover and refrigerate.

If you only need to make one bottle, you'll add formula to water, following the instructions on the label. Refrigerate the mixture if you won't be feeding the baby immediately.

220. Concentrated liquid formula comes in cans and must be diluted with an equal amount of water before it can be used. Though this concentrated formula is less convenient than the ready-to-use formula, it costs only about two-thirds as much, and the cans are less bulky to store or to travel with.

Wash and rinse the top of the can and a punch-type can opener, before you open the can. Measure the correct amount of water and mix in the whole can of liquid concentrate. Pour the diluted formula into clean bottles, cap, and refrigerate. Or you can refrigerate the mixture in a clean, covered quart container and fill one clean bottle at a time, as you need it.

To make one nursing bottle at a time, measure equal amounts of water and formula into the bottle. Cap the bottle, and shake it gently to mix. Refrigerate the mixture, unless you'll be feeding the baby immediately.

221. Ready-to-use formula in cans. It's already sterilized and no water needs to be added, so it's very convenient, especially for inexperienced parents.

Wash and rinse the top of the can and a punch-type can opener, before you open the can. Pour the formula directly from the can into clean bottles. Cap the bottles, and refrigerate until you're ready to use them. Or fill one clean bottle at a time, keeping it capped and refrigerated until you feed the baby. The unused portion should be kept refrigerated in the covered can. Plastic snap-on covers are available where formulas are sold.

Ready-to-use formula in disposable bottles comes in 4-ounce and 8-ounce bottles. This avoids all the work and fuss, which makes this product particularly helpful for the inexperienced parent at the start, for the breast-fed baby who needs only an occasional bottle, and for the baby who is traveling. The bottles require no refrigeration if unopened. Bottle formula is more expensive than ready-to-use formula in large cans or concentrated liquid formula. You can also buy these bottles with disposable nipples already attached and capped.

Bottling the Formula

222. How much in each bottle? Most babies want to be fed more frequently at first, especially if they are small (under 7 pounds). Bottle-fed babies may want to be fed six to ten times in twenty-four hours during the first week. You may have discovered your baby's needs in the hospital if you had rooming-in. On the other hand, most babies start off slow and then become more wakeful and hungry after three or four days, so don't be surprised. Generally, from one week to one month, babies want seven to eight feedings in twenty-four hours, decreasing to five to seven feedings from one to three months, four to five feedings at three to six months, and three to four feedings from six months to one year. Keep in mind that it takes up to three hours for a feeding to leave the stomach.

In the first month of life most 7-pound babies will want less than a total of 21 ounces of formula in twenty-four hours; 8-pound babies less than 24 ounces.

Opened cans or bottles of liquid formula should always be tightly covered and refrigerated, and should be kept only as long as is specified on the label. Prepared formula can be kept in the refrigerator for twenty-four to forty-eight hours.

The formulas discussed here provide 26 to 32 ounces, which should be more than enough for twenty-four hours in the early weeks.

If you are using **ready-to-use formula** or **powdered formula,** you will have a total of 32 ounces. Put 4 ounces into each of eight bottles for a start, but don't expect your baby to finish 4 ounces unless she is large and has a large appetite. Later the baby will want fewer bottles and more formula in each. Be careful not to screw on the top too tightly. This will obstruct the air inlet ridges in the nipple and inhibit flow during nursing.

If you are making a formula from cans of **concentrate,** add 13 ounces of water to the 13 ounces of milk for a total of 26 ounces. Put a little over 3 ounces in each of eight bottles. You'll use fewer bottles with more formula in them later on.

223. When you fill the nursing bottles. Pour the right amount of formula into each bottle. Place the nipples upside down in the bottle necks. Handle the nipples with tongs if you're sterilizing or with your fingers on the outside edges. Put the disks on top of the nipples. Screw the rings on. Leave the rings slightly loose if you've poured in a sterilized formula, so that air can enter as the bottle cools. Refrigerate the bottles.

Formula Refrigeration

224. Saving milk or formula. If you use less than a full can of concentrated liquid formula or ready-to-use formula, you can save what is left for the next day. Leave it in the can, cover the top, and keep it in the refrigerator. Use it all up the next day, or discard what's left. *Never keep an opened can longer than the time specified on the label.*

The same rule applies if you make a quart jar of formula or fill all the nursing bottles from one batch of formula: keep it in the refrigerator, and use it all up the next day or discard what's left. *Never keep bottled formula more than twenty-four hours to forty-eight hours, as specified on the label.*

225. How long after a bottle has been taken out of the refrigerator can you still use it? During the time when a bottle is at drinking temperature, room temperature, or pleasant outdoor temperature, any bacteria that may have gotten into the formula will be able to multiply rapidly. I would recommend that you not give your baby a bottle that has been sitting around the house, carriage, or car for more than two hours, whether it's a full bottle or one that has been partly consumed.

If you will need to feed the baby two or three hours after leaving home, put the bottle, as soon as you take it out of the refrigerator, into an insulated bag with a small ice pack or some ice cubes. *Do not use formula that is no longer cold to the touch.*

If you have a young baby who sometimes goes to sleep

after taking a few ounces and then wakes up within sixty minutes for the rest, you can promptly put the half-finished bottle back into the refrigerator. Discard after one hour.

226. If you cannot keep the formula cold. If you ever get into a situation where you can't keep the baby's bottles cold until feeding time—for instance, if your refrigerator stops working or your electricity goes off—use single-serving, ready-to-feed bottles (keep some on hand), and discard anything that remains after feeding. If you find this happening to you often, the easiest solution is to use commercial powdered formula, mixing it with water before each use, one bottle at a time. If you have to sterilize, keep a bottle of distilled water and some disposable bottles on hand, along with powdered formula.

Contrary to popular belief, a bottle from the refrigerator doesn't have to be warmed before feeding. It can be given to the baby straight from the refrigerator.

Giving the Bottle

227. The first few days. Usually the first bottle is offered four to six hours after the baby is born, though it can be started earlier if he seems hungry. Babies are apt to want little the first few feedings. Even if they take only half an ounce, don't try to get more into them. It's often three or four days before they want the amounts you expect them to need, and it may be a week or more. Don't worry; it may be better for their digestion to start gradually. They'll find out what they need when they become more active in a few days.

228. Giving the bottle. You don't need to shake the bottle when you remove it from the refrigerator.

It has been discovered that babies enjoy just as much and do just as well on formula that is warmed, or at room temperature, or right out of the refrigerator, as long as it comes at the same temperature at each feeding. I think many parents still warm the bottles because they have always thought of bottles as being warmed and because breast milk is warm, so it seems unkind to give a baby cold milk. If I were a new parent I'd take advantage of the convenience of the new knowledge and feed always at room temperature.

If you warm the bottle, do it in a saucepan or pitcher of hot water or in a washbasin. If there is no hot water faucet near the baby's room, it's more convenient to use an electric bottle warmer. Body temperature is the right temperature to aim for. The best way to test this is to shake a few drops on the inside of your wrist. If it feels hot, it is too hot.

Microwave warning: Never heat a baby's bottle in a microwave oven. The contents can be hot enough to burn the baby even though the bottle feels cool to your touch. Microwave ovens aren't suitable for sterilizing bottle equipment or formula, either.

Sit in a comfortable chair and hold the baby cradled in your arm. Most parents want a chair with arms, and perhaps a pillow under the elbow. Some find a rocking chair is perfect.

229. Keep the bottle tilted up so that the nipple is always full. Most babies want to work steadily until they have taken all the formula they need. Angle the bottle so that the air pocket is well above the nipple so the baby doesn't swallow a lot of air. Nevertheless, there are some who still swallow a lot of air during nursing and if the air bubble in the stomach gets too big, they feel uncomfortably full and stop nursing in the middle of the bottle. If this happens, burp the baby (see Section 155) and then go on with the feeding. A few babies need to be burped two or even three times in the course of a bottle—others not at all. You will soon find out which type your baby is.

As soon as your baby stops nursing and seems satisfied, let that be the end of the feeding. Babies know better than anyone else how much they need.

230. Can you prop the bottle? It's good for the parent to hold the baby during bottle-feedings. This is the position that nature intended. The baby and parent are as close as can be, and they can watch each other's faces. Feeding is a baby's greatest joy, by far, and it's good for the baby to link this with the parent's presence and face.

231. Making the nipple holes the right size. If the nipple holes are too small, the baby will get too little and start fussing, or become tired and go to sleep long before finishing the bottle. If the holes are too large, the baby may choke or get indigestion and, in the long run, may get too little sucking satisfaction and do more thumb-sucking. For most babies, the right speed is when the bottle takes about twenty minutes of straight sucking time. The holes are generally right for a young baby if, when you turn the bottle upside down, the milk comes out in a fine spray for a second or two and then changes to drops. If it keeps coming in a spray, the holes are probably too large. If it comes in slow drops from the beginning, the holes are probably too small.

There are probably small holes in the rubber shoulders of the nipples you use, or some other channel for letting air into the bottle as the baby withdraws milk, to prevent a vacuum, which would collapse the nipple. (After a while babies learn by themselves to release a collapsed nipple so that air can bubble in.) This air passage is usually designed so that if you screw the nipple ring down tighter, the passage is decreased in size (or closed altogether); so there is a partial vacuum and the baby has to suck harder and take longer to finish the bottle. A looser ring allows faster drinking.

The holes in many new nipples are too small for a young baby but are right for an older, stronger one. If they are too small for your baby, enlarge them carefully as follows: Stick the dull end of a fine (No. 10) needle into a cork. Then, holding the cork, heat the needle point in a flame until it's red-hot. Stick it a short distance into the top of the nipple. You don't have to poke it into the old hole. Don't use too large a needle or poke it in too far, until you can test your results; if you make the holes too large, you'll have to throw the nipple away. You can make one, two, or three enlarged holes. If you have no cork, you can wrap a piece of cloth around the dull end of the needle or hold it with a pair of pliers.

232. Nipple holes clogged with scum. If you have trouble with clogged nipple holes, you can buy nipples that are crosscut instead of having small holes. This means that a small cross has been cut in the tip of the nipple. The milk does not pour out, as you might expect, because the edges of the cut stay together until the baby sucks. You can make small crosscuts in your regular nipples with a sterilized razor blade. First pinch the nipple tip to make a narrow ridge, then cut across it. Then pinch again at a right angle to the first pinch and make another cut. Crosscut nipples should not be used for feeding pureed foods from a bottle.

233. Don't urge babies to take more than they want. The main trouble with bottle-feeding, to my mind, is that the caretaker can see how much formula is left. Some babies always want the same quantity at every feeding of the day, but there are others whose appetites are much more variable. You mustn't get the idea that your baby has to have a certain amount at each feeding. It may help you acquire a more relaxed feeling about this if you realize that breast-fed babies may get as much as 10 ounces at the morning nursing and as little as 4 ounces at the evening feeding and be perfectly happy with each. If you can trust breast-fed babies to take what they need, you can trust your bottle-fed baby.

It is necessary to make this point because quite a number of children develop feeding problems. They lose the natural appetite that they were born with and balk at all or many of their foods. In nine out of ten cases, these problems develop because the parents have been trying, sometimes since infancy, to get their child to eat more than she wants. When you succeed in getting a baby or child to take a few more mouthfuls than she is eager for, it looks to you as if you have gained something. But this isn't so. She will only cut down at her next feeding. Babies know how much they want, and they even know the different kinds of foods that their bodies are calling for. Urging children isn't necessary, and it doesn't get you anywhere. It is harmful because it begins, after a while, to take away the child's appetite, and makes her want to eat less than her system really needs.

In the long run, urging does more than destroy appetite and make thin children. It robs them of some of their positive feeling for life. Babies are meant to spend their first year getting hungry, demanding food, enjoying it, and reaching satisfaction. This lusty success story is repeated at least three times a day, week after week. It builds into them self-confidence, an outgoing nature, and trust in their parents. But if mealtime becomes a struggle, if feeding becomes something that is done to them, they go on the defensive and build up a balky, suspicious attitude toward meals and toward people.

I don't mean that you have to snatch the bottle away for good the first time your baby pauses. Some babies like to rest a bit several times during a feeding. But if she seems indifferent when you put the nipple back in her mouth (and doesn't need to be burped), then she's satisfied, and you should be too.

234. The babies who wake in a few minutes. What about the babies who go to sleep after they've taken 4 of their 5 ounces and then wake up and cry a few minutes later? This is more apt to be due to an air bubble or colic or periodic irritable crying than to hunger. Babies won't notice a difference of an ounce, especially if they've gone to sleep. In fact, babies will often sleep just as well when they've taken only half their usual amount, though they may wake a little early.

It's perfectly all right occasionally to give the rest of the formula a little later, if you feel sure that your baby's hungry for it. But I think it's better to assume first that she's not really hungry and give her a good chance to go back to sleep, with or without a pacifier. In other words, try to postpone the next feeding for two or three hours.

235. The young baby who only half finishes. A mother may bring a baby home from the hospital and find that he stops taking his bottle and falls asleep when it's still half full. Yet they said in the hospital that he was taking it all. The mother keeps trying to rouse him, to wedge another quarter of an ounce in, but it's slow, hard, frustrating work. What's the trouble? He may be a baby who hasn't quite "come to" yet. (An occasional baby stays sluggish like that for the first two or three weeks and then comes to life with a bang.)

The constructive thing to do is to let the baby stop when he wants to, even if he's taken only an ounce or two. Won't he get hungry, then, long before it's time for the next feeding? He may or he may not. If he does, feed him. "But," you say, "I'll be feeding him all day and all night." It probably won't be that bad. The point is that if you let a baby stop feeding when he feels like it and let him come to feel his own hunger, he will gradually become more eager for his feedings and take larger amounts. Then he will be able to sleep for longer periods. You can help him to learn to wait longer and be hungrier by trying to stretch out the interval between feedings to two, two and a half, then three hours. Don't pick him up just as soon as he starts fussing. Wait a while. He may go back to sleep. If he gets to crying hard, though, you'll have to feed him.

236. The baby who fusses soon after starting a bottle or who promptly goes to sleep may be frustrated by a nipple hole that is clogged or too small. See if the milk comes out in a fine spray when the bottle is first inverted. Try enlarging the nipple hole a little anyway, as an experiment.

237. Avoid the bottle in bed. In some cases, babies who drink their bottles in bed develop serious caries (decay) of the teeth when they fall asleep with milk in their mouth. Falling asleep with milk in the mouth can also lead to an ear infection. Some milk can run down the Eustachian tube, which connects the back of the throat to the part of the ear behind the eardrum. Then bacteria can grow in the milk behind the eardrum and start an infection.

After six months, many babies want to sit up, take the bottle away from the parent, and hold it themselves. Practical parents, seeing they're not much use, may put such babies in their cribs, where they drink their bottles and put themselves to sleep all in one operation. This may seem like a handy way to put babies to sleep, but in addition to causing tooth and ear problems, it makes it impossible for some of them to go to sleep without a bottle. (See Section 262.) When the parent tries to withhold a bedtime bottle at nine, fifteen, or twenty-one months, the baby will cry frantically and be unable to fall asleep for a long time. So if you want to prevent bedtime problems later on, let her hold her own bottle, but keep her in your lap or the high chair if that's what she'd prefer.

FEEDING IN THE
FIRST YEAR

What Feeding Means to the Baby

238. A baby knows a lot about diet. She is the one who knows how many calories her body needs and what her digestion can handle. If she's regularly not getting enough, she'll probably cry for more. If there's more in the bottle than she feels like, let her stop when she wants to. Take her word for it.

Think of the baby's first year this way: She wakes up because she's hungry, cries because she wants to be fed. She is so eager when the nipple goes into her mouth that she may shudder. When she nurses, you can see that it is an intense experience. Perhaps she breaks into perspiration. If you stop her in the middle of a nursing, she may cry furiously. When she has had as much as she wants, she is usually groggy with satisfaction and falls asleep. Even when she is asleep, she sometimes looks as if she were dreaming of nursing. Her mouth makes sucking motions, and her whole expression looks blissful.

This all adds up to the fact that feeding is her great joy. She gets her early ideas about life from the way feeding goes. She gets her first ideas about the world from the person who feeds her.

When parents constantly urge their baby to take more than she wants, the baby is apt to become steadily less interested. She may try to escape from the experience by going to sleep earlier and earlier in the feeding or she may rebel and become more balky. She's apt to lose some of her active, positive feeling about life. It's as though she got the idea that life is a struggle, that those people are always after her, that she has to fight to protect herself.

So don't urge babies to take more than they are eager for. Let them go on enjoying their meals, feeling that you are their friend. This is one of the principal ways in which their self-confidence, their joy in life, and their love of people will be firmly established during the first year.

239. The important sucking instinct. Babies nurse eagerly for two separate reasons. First, because they're hungry, and second, because they love to suck. If you feed them a lot but don't give them enough chance to suck, their craving for sucking will go unsatisfied and they will try to suck something else—their fists, or thumbs, or their clothes. It is also true that the sucking need varies greatly in different babies. It's important to give them a long enough nursing period at each feeding and to have a sufficient number of feedings each day.

Schedules

240. During the first half of the twentieth century, babies were usually kept on very strict, regular schedules. Doctors did not know for sure the cause of the serious intestinal infections that afflicted tens of thousands of babies yearly. It was believed that these infections were caused not only by the contamination of milk but also by wrong proportions in the formula and by irregularity in feeding.

Strict regularity worked well enough with a majority of babies. When they took an ample feeding at breast or bottle, it lasted them for about two to four hours, because that is the way a young baby's digestive system usually works.

But there were always a few babies who had trouble adjusting to regularity in the first month or two—babies whose stomachs couldn't seem to hold four hours' worth of milk, babies who went to sleep halfway through feedings, restless babies, colicky babies. They would cry miserably for shorter or longer periods each day, but their mothers and doctors dared not feed them—or even pick them up—

off schedule. This was hard enough on the babies. I think it was harder still on the parents.

Anyway, the serious diarrheal diseases almost disappeared. The chief reasons for this were the pasteurization of milk in the commercial dairy and the availability of clean, safe water. But it took many more years before doctors dared to begin experimenting with flexible schedules.

The first experiments in self-demand feeding were carried out by Dr. Preston McLendon, a psychologist, and Frances P. Simsarian, a new mother, with Ms. Simsarian's new baby. They wanted to find out what kind of schedule babies would establish if they were breast-fed whenever they seemed hungry. The baby awoke rather infrequently the first few days. Then, from just about the time the milk began to come in, he awoke surprisingly often—about ten times a day—in the second half of the first week. But by the age of two weeks he had settled down to six or seven feedings a day, at rather irregular intervals. By ten weeks he had arrived at approximately a two- to four-hour schedule.

They called this an experiment in "self-demand" feeding. Since that experiment led the way, in 1942, there has been a general relaxation in infant feeding schedules, which has had a wholesome effect on babies and parents. It's now realized that the average number of hours between feedings for a breast-fed baby in the first two weeks of life is two. That means that some babies will nurse every three hours and some as often as every hour and a half.

241. What regularity and scheduling are all about. Most babies have a natural tendency to establish a regular pattern of feeding and sleeping. The intervals between feedings may vary within each twenty-four-hour period, but tend to have some consistency from one day to the next. The pattern will change as the baby grows, and the periods of wakefulness will become more prolonged and filled with activity. Through the parents' guidance, this pattern is shaped into a schedule, which helps both baby and parents move into a reasonably comfortable and predictable rhythm.

Scheduling doesn't necessarily mean feeding every four hours, or every three hours, though some babies and families do arrive at that kind of schedule. Some newborns seem to come out of the hospital already set on a two- to four-hour feeding interval. Others seem to fashion a schedule of their own, though it may take a few weeks for them to become consistent about it. At some times in the day, babies seem hungrier than at other times, and want to eat more frequently. For much of the time, they awaken to eat every hour and a half to four hours. They may have a five-hour sleep period, though it may come as easily during the day as at night. They may have a stretch of fretfulness lasting several hours, which usually occurs in the early evening. During these hours, the breast-fed baby is happy if she is almost continually at the breast, crying if she is put down. A bottle-fed baby may act hungry but not eat much if offered a bottle. She may suck avidly at the pacifier. Some unhappy parents say that their newborns "have their days and nights switched." These babies will sleep like a log during the day and are almost impossible to arouse. During the night, they are up to feed and fret every hour and a half (see Section 774 on preventing this problem).

The period of longer sleep tends to shift to nighttime in the early weeks. The evening fussiness gradually improves over the first few months—though it may seem to take forever. In these first few months, times for feeding, playing and even fussing will alternate predictably with daytime sleeping. And the baby will sleep most of the night.

By comparison, a baby approaching her first birthday usually sleeps through the night, though she may awaken early for a breast- or bottle-feeding, only to return to sleep for an hour or two. She eats three meals and a couple of snacks, has a nap or two, and goes to sleep at a reasonable hour, often after a last breast- or bottle-feeding.

How do all these changes happen in a year? It isn't only what the parents do. It's the baby herself, gradually lengthening the time between feedings and shortening the sleep periods. Along with her own maturation, she just naturally tends to fit into the family's schedule.

242. General guide to establishing a schedule. The main consideration for babies is that they not have to cry with hunger for long periods or feel uncared for.

All babies have a tendency to develop a regular schedule of becoming hungry, and this will come much more rapidly if the parents guide them a bit. Babies don't mind at all being awakened for a feeding after an interval of three or four hours.

Smaller babies tend to eat more frequently than bigger babies. But they all tend to gradually lengthen the interval between feedings as they grow bigger and older. Breast-fed babies on average eat more often than bottle-fed babies because breast milk is digested more easily and quickly than cow or soy formulas. By one, two, or three months of age, babies come to realize they don't need the middle of the night feeding and will give it up. Somewhere between the fourth and twelfth month, they will be able to sleep through the feeding at the parents' bedtime, too.

In all these tendencies—to more regular feedings and to fewer feedings—the baby can be greatly influenced by the parents' management. If during the day a mother wakes her baby boy whenever he's still asleep four hours after the last feeding, she is helping him to establish regular daytime eating habits. If, when he stirs and whimpers a couple of hours after the last feeding, she holds back for a few minutes and gives him a chance to go to sleep again or offers a pacifier if he really wakens and cries, she is helping his stomach adjust to a longer interval. If, on the other hand, she always picks him up and feeds him promptly when he stirs, even though it's only shortly after the last feeding, she keeps him accustomed to short intervals and small feedings.

Individual babies differ widely in how soon they can comfortably settle down to regular schedules. A great majority of the ones who are good feeders, who aren't too fussy, and who are getting plenty to drink from breast or bottle, can be eased into a reasonably consistent schedule and will give up the middle of the night feeding a couple of months after birth.

On the other hand, if a baby is a listless, sleepy feeder at first, or a restless, fretful waker (Sections 186, 234–236) or if the breast-milk supply is not yet well established, it will be more comfortable for all concerned to go more slowly. But even in these cases, there will be less perplexity on the part of the parents every day—about whether to give a feeding right away or to wait—and an earlier settling down on the part of the baby, if the parents are always working gently toward more regular feedings, with an average interval of two to three hours for breast-fed babies, and three to four hours for bottle-fed babies.

243. There has been some misunderstanding about the relationship between self-demand feeding and schedules. The main purpose of any schedule is to do right by the baby. But another purpose is to enable the parents to care for their child in a way that will conserve their strength and spirits. This usually means getting down to a reasonable number of feedings at predictable hours and giving up the night feeding as soon as the baby is ready.

Some young parents, eager to be progressive, assume that if they want to get away from the rigid scheduling of the past they must go all the way in the opposite direction, feeding their baby any time she wakes and *never* waking her for a feeding.

This may work out well enough if the baby is a peaceful one with a good digestion, if the parents don't have to worry about their own schedule, and if they don't mind being awakened between midnight and 6:00 A.M. (Of course, very young babies will certainly need to be fed during these hours.) But if the baby happens to be a restless, fretful one, this approach can lead to a great many feedings and very little rest for the parents for several months. And in a few cases it encourages the baby to be still waking for a couple of night feedings even at the end of the first year.

If parents prefer to feed their baby on an irregular, self-demand schedule for many months, there will be no harm done to the baby's nutrition. It does no harm to the parents, either, if they're people who just hate to do anything by the clock. But if they're fairly regular about the rest of their lives and have other things to get done, I only worry that they have gotten the idea that the more they give up for the baby the better it is for the child, or that they have to prove that they are good parents by ignoring their own convenience. These attitudes tend to create difficulties in the long run.

244. Specific suggestions for working toward a regular schedule. The easiest way to begin scheduling a baby is to wake her during the day if she is still asleep four hours after her last feeding. You won't have to urge her to eat; she will probably act starving hungry in a few minutes.

But suppose she wakes an hour after her last feeding. You don't have to feed her the minute she whimpers. She's not sure herself whether she's hungry. But if instead of settling back to sleep she wakens fully and starts crying hard, I wouldn't wait any longer.

245. What if she starts a pattern of waking soon after each feeding? Perhaps she needs more to eat. If she is breast-fed, nursing her more frequently will increase the milk supply in a few days, so she'll be able to take more at each feeding and again lengthen the time between feedings. (It's important for the mother to eat and drink enough and get enough rest, so she can produce more milk as the baby needs it.) If the baby is bottle-fed, increase each feeding by an ounce or more and see if that helps lengthen the intervals.

246. Just how soon should you give another feeding? I have been saying that if the baby who generally can go three or four hours awakens after two or two and a half hours and seems really hungry, it is all right to feed her then. But suppose she wakes an hour or so after her last feeding. If she finished her usual bottle at her last feeding, the chances are against her being hungry again so soon. It is more likely that she has been awakened by indigestion. You can try burping her again, or see whether she will be comforted by a couple of ounces of water or a pacifier. I would not be in a rush to feed her again, though you may decide to try it in a little while if nothing else works. You can't be sure it's hunger just because a baby tries to eat her hand or starts to take the bottle eagerly. Often a baby who is having colic will do both these things. It seems the baby herself can't distinguish between colic pains and hunger pains (see Sections 313 and 321).

In other words, you don't always feed a baby every time she cries. If she is crying at the wrong times, you have to study the situation. She may be wet, or too warm or cold; she may need to burp, or be comforted, or she may just need to let out a few cries to release tensions. If this keeps happening and you can't figure it out, discuss the problem with your doctor or nurse practitioner.

247. Middle-of-the-night feedings. The easiest rule for night feedings is not to waken your baby but to let him wake you if he wants to. A baby who still needs that feeding usually wakes surprisingly close to the hour of 2:00 A.M. Then some night, probably when he's between two and six weeks old, he will sleep through until 3:00 or 3:30 A.M. Feed him then. The next night he might wake still later. Or he might wake but cry in a drowsy way, and go back to sleep if he is not fed right away. When babies get ready to give up the middle-of-the-night feeding, somewhere between six and twelve weeks, they usually do it in a hurry, within two or three nights. In the case of the breast-fed baby, he may nurse longer at his other feedings. In the case of the bottle-fed baby, you can increase the amount in his other bottles to make up for the bottle he's given up, if he wants that extra amount. Night feedings should be given quietly, in a darkened room, in contrast to daytime feedings, which can be accompanied by more stimulation.

248. Giving up the middle-of-the-night feeding. If a baby reaches the age of two or three months and weighs 12 pounds, but still wakes for a middle-of-the-night feeding, it's sensible to try to influence him to give it up. Instead of hurrying to him as soon as he stirs, you can let him fuss for a little while. If he doesn't quiet down but instead is soon crying furiously, apologize to him and feed him promptly. But try again in another week or two. From a nutritional point of view, a 12-pound baby who's eating well during the day doesn't really need this feeding.

The feeding at the parents' bedtime is the one that you can probably time to your own convenience. Most babies, by the time they are a few weeks old, are perfectly willing to wait until 11:00 P.M. or even midnight for it. If you want to get to bed early, wake the baby at 10:00 or even a little before. If a later feeding is more convenient, suit yourself, as long as the baby is willing to stay asleep.

For those babies who are still waking for middle-of-the-night feedings, I would advise against letting them sleep through the 10:00 or 11:00 P.M. feedings, even though they're quite willing to do so. When they're ready to give up one of them, you'll want them to give up the middle-of-the-night feeding first, so that your sleep won't be interrupted.

For those babies who are already off the middle-of-the-night feeding but are still quite irregular about their day-time feeding hours, I'd continue to wake them at 10:00 or 11:00 P.M., provided they're willing to be fed. This at least ends the day on schedule, helps very much to avoid a feeding between midnight and 4:00 A.M., and tends to encourage them to sleep until 5:00 or 6:00 the next morning.

Getting Enough and Gaining Weight

249. Refusal to nurse in later months. Once in a while a baby between four and seven months old acts queerly at feeding time. The mother will say that her baby boy nurses hungrily at breast or bottle for a few minutes. Then he becomes frantic, lets go of the nipple, and cries as if in pain. He still seems very hungry, but each time he goes back to nursing he becomes uncomfortable sooner. He takes his solid food eagerly.

I think that this distress is caused by teething. I suspect that as the baby nurses, the suction engorges his painful gums and makes them tingle unbearably. You can break each nursing period into several parts and give the solid food in the intervals, since the distress comes on only after a number of minutes of sucking. If he is on a bottle, you can experiment with enlarging the holes in a few nipples so that he finishes the bottle in a shorter time with less strenuous sucking. If the baby's discomfort is excessive and comes on very promptly, you could, for a few days, give up the bottle altogether. Give him his milk from the cup if he is skillful enough, or from a spoon, or mix a large amount of it with his cereal and other foods. Don't worry if he doesn't get his usual amount.

An ear infection, complicating a cold, may cause enough pain in the jaw joint so that babies will refuse to nurse even though they may be able to eat solids pretty well. Occasionally, a baby will decline to take the breast during the mother's menstrual periods. They can be offered the breast more often during those days. It may be necessary for the mother to express the breast milk manually in order to relieve the fullness and to keep the supply going. Babies will resume their usual breast-feeding when the period is over and will be able to revive the breast-milk supply.

250. How much weight should babies gain? The best I can say about weight gain is that babies should gain at the rate they seem to want to gain at. Most babies know. If they are offered more food than they need, they refuse it. If they are given less, they show their hunger by waking earlier before feedings and eating their fists.

We can talk about average babies if you remember clearly that no baby is average. One baby is meant to be a slow gainer, and another is meant to be a fast gainer. When doctors talk about an average baby, they mean only that they have added together the fast gainers and the slow gainers and the medium gainers.

If babies are gaining slowly, that doesn't mean for sure that they were meant to. If they are hungry all the time, that is a pretty good sign that they are meant to be gaining faster. Once in a while slow gaining means that a baby is sick. Slow gainers particularly need to be seen regularly by a doctor to make sure that they are healthy. Occasionally you see exceptionally polite babies who are gaining slowly and who don't seem too hungry. But if you give them more to eat, they take it quite willingly and gain more rapidly. In other words, not all babies yell when they are being fed too little.

The average baby's weight is a little over 7 pounds at birth, and 14 pounds between three and five months. That is to say, the average baby doubles its birth weight between three and five months. But in actual practice, babies who are small at birth are more apt to grow faster, as if trying to catch up, and babies who are born big are less apt to double their birth weight by three to five months.

The average baby gains close to 2 pounds a month (6 or 8 ounces a week) during the first three months. Of course, some healthy ones gain less, and others more. Then the baby slows down. By six months the average gain is down to a pound a month (4 ounces a week). That's quite a drop in a three-month period. In the last quarter of the first year, the average gain is down to $\frac{2}{3}$ pound a month (2 or 3 ounces each week) and, during the second year, to about $\frac{1}{2}$ pound a month (2 ounces a week).

As babies grow older, you can see that they gain more slowly. They also gain more irregularly. Teething or illness may take their appetite away for several weeks, and they may hardly gain at all. When they feel better, their appetite revives and their weight catches up with a rush.

You can't decide too much from how babies' weights change from week to week. What they weigh each time will depend on how recently they have urinated, how recently they have moved their bowels, how recently they have eaten. If you find, one morning, that your baby boy has gained only 4 ounces in the past week, whereas before he had always gained 7, don't jump to the conclusion that he is starving or that something else is wrong. If he seems perfectly happy and satisfied, wait another week to see what happens. He may make an extra large gain to make up for the small one. For the breast-fed baby, wetting the diapers at least six to eight times a day, being alert and happy when awake, sleeping well, and having a weight gain from week to week are good indications that he's getting enough to eat. Always remember, though, that the older he gets, the slower he will gain.

251. How often do you need to weigh the baby? Of course, most parents don't have scales, and most babies get weighed only when they go to see their doctor, which is often enough. When a baby is happy and doing well, weighing more frequently than once a month serves no purpose but to satisfy curiosity. If you have scales, don't weigh more often than once a month. On the other hand, if your baby is crying a lot, or having indigestion, or vomiting a great deal, more frequent weighing at the doctor's office may help you and your doctor or nurse practitioner to decide what the matter is. For instance, excessive crying combined with rapid weight gaining points toward colic, not hunger.

252. Fatness in infancy does not necessarily mean that the baby will be fat for life, but it's not a kindness to babies to get them fattened up. It's important to stop feeding your baby when she seems full, in order to prevent feeding problems (Section 233) or poor eating habits (Section 534).

It seems hard for some people to change their feelings that fatness in babies is attractive and desirable. Relatives and friends may compliment the parents on it as if it were proof of superior care. Some parents think of baby fat as a reserve—like money in the bank—against some possible future adversity or illness.

Vitamins in Infancy

253. Babies may need extra vitamin C and vitamin D. These vitamins are discussed in Sections 511 and 512. There are only small amounts of these in milk as it comes from the cow or in solid foods that are given early.

Breast milk usually contains sufficient vitamin C if the mother's diet is rich in citrus fruits and certain vegetables (Section 167).

In the United States, ready-to-use formulas contain 400 units of vitamin D to the quart and to a can of concentrated prepared formula. This should be sufficient to prevent rickets in a normal baby. Breast milk may not contain enough vitamin D, but most babies will get enough vitamin D from brief periods of sun exposure. Natural vitamin D is actually made by a chemical reaction in your baby's skin when it is in sunlight. Your doctor or nurse practitioner may recommend a commercial vitamin preparation with 400 units vitamin D in some situations.

Almost all bottle-fed babies in the United States are given commercially prepared formulas that are vitamin-fortified so they don't need any added vitamins in infancy. Your doctor or nurse practitioner can tell you whether or not your baby needs extra vitamins.

If you are breast-feeding, your doctor may advise you about giving a three-vitamin preparation that contains C, D, and A. The dropper that comes with the bottle has lines showing 0.3 cc and 0.6 cc (three-tenths and six-tenths of a cubic centimeter). Draw the fluid up to the line that's marked 0.3 cc and squirt it directly into the baby's mouth at the beginning of one of the feedings of the day, once a day, winter and summer, starting at one month or earlier. Some doctors prescribe 0.6 cc, but you should not go beyond this amount, since excessive doses of vitamin D can be harmful.

254. Multivitamin preparations contain a number of B vitamins in addition to A, D, and C. However, milk, cereals, and other foods that babies and children eat usually provide sufficient B vitamins. While there is certainly no harm in taking multivitamins, they usually are not worth the added expense.

Drinking Water for a Baby

If there's no fluoride in your drinking water, your doctor will prescribe it, either in the baby's vitamin drops or separately. See Sections 297, 617–618 on why fluoride is important.

255. Some babies want water; others don't. It is sometimes recommended that a baby be offered a few ounces of water between meals once or twice a day. It isn't really necessary, because the amount of fluid in breast milk or formula will satisfy the baby's ordinary needs. It is more important to offer water if the baby has a fever, or during excessively hot weather, especially if his urine turns dark yellow and he appears extra thirsty. Babies who ordinarily refuse water often take it at these times. Some mothers have found that adding small amounts of apple juice to the water gets the baby more interested.

As a matter of fact, a lot of babies don't want any water from the time they are a week or two old until they are about a year. During this age they fairly worship anything with nourishment in it, but they feel insulted by plain water.

If your baby likes it, by all means give it to him once or several times a day when he is awake between meals, but not just before the next meal. You can give him as much as he wants. He probably won't want more than 2 ounces. But don't urge him to take water if he doesn't want it. There's no point in getting him mad. He knows what he needs.

256. Sugar water. You may particularly want your baby to drink water if he is taking little milk because of an illness or if the weather is hot. If he won't take his water plain, you can try giving him sugar water. Add 1 level tablespoonful of granulated sugar to a pint of water, stirring until dissolved.

Weaning from the Breast

Weaning is important not only for the baby but for the mother as well, and not only physically but emotionally. A mother who has set great store by nursing may feel mildly let down and depressed after she stops, as if she has lost some of her closeness to the baby or as if she has become a less worthwhile person. This is an additional reason for making weaning a gradual process whenever possible. Weaning doesn't have to be an all-or-nothing phenomenon. A woman can nurse one or two times a day until her baby is two years old or discontinue nursing entirely.

The ordinary weaning process begins with the introduction of solid foods around four to six months and gradually is completed in the next six to eighteen months, depending on the baby and the mother.

257. Gradual weaning from breast to bottle in the first four months. There are lots of mothers who either aren't able or don't want to nurse until a baby is ready to be weaned to the cup starting at about six to nine months. In some cases the milk supply may become insufficient. The baby cries from hunger and fails to gain sufficient weight. A hungry baby like this seldom puts up any fuss over being weaned to the bottle. How fast the weaning to the bottle goes will depend on how much milk the mother is producing.

If you find that your breast-milk supply is failing rapidly

and the baby is quite hungry, or if, for other reasons, you need to wean from the breast quickly, the simplest method would be to make up a twenty-four-hour supply of formula and divide it into as many bottles as the baby is presently taking breast feedings. Give her a bottle at each feeding, after the breast, letting her take as much or as little of it as she wants. Omit first the breast-feeding when your breasts are the least full. Two days later also omit the breast-feeding when your breasts are the least full. Discontinue the remaining breast-feedings, one every two or three days. If the mother's milk is decreasing only gradually and the baby is only slightly dissatisfied, it will work better to introduce the bottles one feeding at a time.

But suppose there is no problem of the milk supply giving out. Let's say a mother wants to nurse for a few months to give her baby a good start, but not for most of the year. How long is it important to nurse? There's no hard-and-fast answer to this, of course. The physical advantages of breast milk, its purity, its easy digestibility, are most valuable to the baby at first. But there is no age at which they suddenly become of no benefit. The emotional advantages of breast-feeding will not cease at any definite period, either.

One sensible time to wean to the bottle is at about three months. By this age the baby's digestive system will have settled down. She will be about over any tendency to colic. She will be pretty husky and still gaining rapidly. But if a mother would like to stop breast-feeding at one or two months, those are satisfactory times to wean, too.

If you plan to wean to the bottle at some age beyond one month, it is wiser to get the baby accustomed to the bottle from the age of one month on, by giving one bottle regularly two or three times a week, or every day, if you prefer.

If the breasts have been producing a good amount of milk, the weaning should preferably be gradual from the beginning. Begin about two weeks before you want weaning to be complete. First, omit one breast-feeding a day, the one when your breasts are the least full, and give a bottle instead. Let the baby take as much or as little of this as she wants. Wait two or three days until your breasts become adjusted to the change, then omit another breast-feeding and substitute a second daily bottle. Again wait two or three days and then omit another breast-feeding. Now the baby is getting the breast at only two feedings and a bottle at each of the other three feedings. You will probably need to wait three or even four days each time before omitting these last two nursings. Any time your breasts become uncomfortable, use manual expression or a breast pump for a few minutes, just enough to relieve the pressure.

258. If the baby won't take the bottle. A baby of four months or more who has not regularly had a bottle may balk completely. Try for a week offering a bottle once or twice a day, before the breast or solid food. Don't force it; don't get her angry. Take the bottle away if she refuses, and give her the rest of her meal, including the breast. In a few days' time she may change her mind.

If she's still adamant, omit an afternoon breast-feeding altogether and see if this makes her thirsty enough so that she will try the bottle in the early evening. If she still holds out, you will probably have to give her the breast, because the breast will be uncomfortably full. But continue to omit an afternoon nursing for several days. It may work on a subsequent day even though it didn't on the first.

The next step is to try omitting every other breast-feeding throughout the twenty-four hours and reduce the amount of solid foods so that she's pretty hungry—or omit solids altogether.

You can use a breast pump or manual expression (Sections 200–203) just enough to relieve the pressure and discomfort.

259. Gradual weaning from breast to cup between nine and fifteen months. If a mother is producing plenty of milk, how long should she plan to nurse? Best of all, most natural of all, is to nurse until the baby is ready to be weaned to the cup.

I think that a majority of babies start showing signs of decreased need for the breast between nine and twelve months. They stop nursing several times during a feeding and want to play with their mothers. They may have to be nudged back onto the breast. With encouragement they will learn how to take more milk from the cup and will switch over completely in a few weeks without any sign of deprivation or regret.

I make this point about readiness for weaning in the second half of the first year for the benefit of mothers who want to breast-feed for as long as their babies need suckling; they don't want to shift to the bottle. But they don't want to go on beyond what is necessary for "complete" breast-feeding.

But there are many breast-feeding mothers who definitely want to go to at least one year of age or even to two years. I think it's fine to nurse until the age of two if mother and baby want to.

It's a good idea to begin offering a sip of formula or other liquid from the cup from the age of six months, so that your baby gets used to it before she is *too* opinionated. By nine months encourage her to hold the cup herself (see Section 265). If by nine months she is nursing for shorter periods, I would assume she may be ready for gradual weaning. Now offer her the cup at all her meals and increase the amount as she shows her willingness to take more, but continue to breast-feed her at the end of the meal. Next, leave out one of her daily breast-feedings, the one that she seems the least interested in, and give her only the cup. This is usually at breakfast or lunch. In a week, omit another breast-feeding if she seems willing, and in another week, the last one. Her willingness to be weaned may not progress steadily. If she gets into a period when she is miserable from teething or illness, she may want to retreat a little. This is natural enough, and there is no danger in accommodating her.

When weaning is carried out this gradually, there is usually no problem with the mother's breasts. If, however, they become uncomfortably full at any time, the mother needs only to use manual expression for fifteen to thirty seconds to relieve the pressure.

Most mothers are surprised to find they are reluctant to end this emotional tie and some will put off weaning week after week.

Sometimes a mother will be afraid to give up nursing

altogether, because the baby is not taking as much from the cup as she used to take from the breast. This may postpone the weaning indefinitely. I would stop the nursing if the baby is taking an average of 4 ounces from the cup at each meal, or a total of 12 to 16 ounces a day. After the nursing is stopped, she will probably increase the amount she takes from the cup up to a total of 16 ounces or more. This is usually enough, with all the other things she is eating.

260. Sudden weaning from the breast (until you can consult a doctor). You may have to wean the baby from the breast suddenly if, for instance, you become seriously ill or you have to go out of town for an emergency. (It is not usually necessary to wean the baby because of mild or moderately severe illness in the mother. Your doctor is the one to decide this.) In this case, manual expression should be avoided. It may give temporary relief, but it will stimulate the breasts to produce more milk. One method is to apply pressure and ice bags to the breasts. This is a pretty uncomfortable business, and your doctor can prescribe appropriate medication to relieve the pain. "Dry-up" pills don't help and shouldn't be used. They're expensive, have side effects, and often produce a rebound effect, which increases the pressure in the breasts.

Weaning from Bottle to Cup

261. Readiness for weaning. Some parents are eager to get their babies weaned to the cup by a year. Others feel strongly that all babies are entitled to the breast or bottle for two years. The decision depends partly on the parents' wishes and partly on the baby's readiness.

Some breast-fed and bottle-fed babies show less interest in sucking by five or six months. Instead of nursing eagerly for twenty minutes, as they used to, they stop after five minutes to flirt with their parents or play with their bottles or with their own hands. These are the early signs of readiness for weaning. These babies will go on being somewhat casual toward the breast or bottle at eight, ten, or twelve months, though they'll take it as long as it's offered,

174

in most cases. They like to take formula from the cup, and they continue to do so.

262. The baby who becomes more attached to the bottle at six, eight, or ten months. The parent of one of these babies will say, "Oh, how she loves her bottle! She watches it all the time she's taking her solid food. When it's time, she snatches it eagerly. She strokes it lovingly all the time she's drinking it and murmurs to it. She's very suspicious about formula from the cup, though she took it willingly before six months." Many of these babies continue to be very dependent on the bedtime bottle until a year and a half or two years of age. They are unable to settle down or go to sleep without it, and are still firmly opposed to formula in the cup or glass. (It's interesting that they are quite willing to take water or juice from the cup.)

It is the babies who are allowed to take their bottles to bed by themselves who become more attached to their bottles in the second half of the first year. The bottle becomes a precious comforter at bedtime, reminding children of their early months, when their greatest pleasure and security came from their intensely close relationship with their parents. The bottle in this sense becomes a parent substitute. Whereas children who are still taking their bottle in the parent's lap, at five or six or seven months, develop no such attachment to it because their real parent is right there.

So the way to keep babies from forming a lasting dependence on the bottle and delaying final weaning until eighteen to twenty-four months is to refrain from giving them the bottle to take to bed (see Section 237). Other examples of this same kind of dependence—on a soft toy or a pacifier—are explained more fully in Sections 786–811.

263. Starting sips of formula from the cup by five months. It's a good idea to begin offering babies a sip of formula from the cup each day by the time they're five months old. You aren't going to try to wean them to the cup right away. You only want to accustom them, at an age when they're not too opinionated, to the idea that formula comes in cups too.

Pour half an ounce of formula into a small cup or glass

once a day. Your baby won't want more than one sip at a time, and she won't get much at first, but she'll probably think it is fun. Once the baby is comfortable taking formula from the cup, offer her water and diluted juice from the cup, too. This way she'll learn that all liquids can come in a cup.

264. Helping a baby get used to the cup. Once the cup has been introduced, offer it matter-of-factly once or twice at each solid meal, holding it to your baby's lips. Keep the cup in sight so he can indicate if he'd like more. (If you usually give him a bottle at the end of his meal, keep it out of sight until then.) He'll also be interested in anything you're drinking, and you can hold your glass to his lips and let him have a taste, if the contents are suitable.

265. You can let him try his own skills, too. Suppose he's six months old, and wants to grab everything and put it in his mouth. Give him a small, narrow, empty plastic glass or cup that he can hold easily by himself and pretend to drink from. Or a baby's mug with two handles. When he does it fairly well, put a few drops of formula into the cup. Increase the amount as he gains in skill. If he gets balky or loses interest in trying it himself, don't urge him. Drop the matter for a meal or two, then offer the cup again. Remember that in the early months of cup drinking, he'll probably want only one swallow at a time. Many babies don't learn to take several gulps in succession until they are one to one and a half years old. One good place to practice is in the bathtub.

Children between one and two who are suspicious of the old cup they have always been offered may be delighted with a new cup or glass of a different shape or color. Offering them cold milk sometimes changes their minds. Some parents have found that adding a little cereal to the cup of milk makes it different enough to be acceptable for drinking. The cereal can gradually be removed a few weeks later.

There are special cups designed for weaning that have a lid with a flat spout. The lid keeps the milk from spilling, and the spout goes into the baby's mouth. The baby can later use it without the lid and spout. Some parents like them because they prevent spilling for the first few months of cup drinking until the baby gains skill. Other parents object that a baby may first balk at the transition from bottle to weaning cup and then object again as he changes to cup or glass without a spout. There are weaning cups with two handles, which are easier for a baby to hold, and others with a weighted base.

266. Reasons for weaning from the bottle at about one year. The main reason for weaning babies from the bottle by one year is that this is the age when they'll accept the change most easily. By this age, most babies will be holding their own bottles at feeding time, and it's best to let them take over. But you can help them be more grown up, by getting them started with a cup. If the parents have gotten into the habit of letting the baby feed herself and then drop off to sleep with a bottle in bed, this can lead to bedtime problems. See Section 237 for more about avoiding the bottle in bed.

In addition, some parents are bothered by the sight of a toddler wandering around or playing with a bottle in her hand, taking a swig now and then. They think it looks babyish or dopey.

Wean the Baby Gradually

267. Take it easy and follow your baby's lead. Perhaps your baby is nine to twelve months old and is becoming a little bored with her bottle and likes formula from the cup. Gradually increase the amount in the cup. Give her the cup at every meal. This leaves less and less in the bottle. Then leave out the bottle that she takes least interest in— probably the lunch or breakfast one. In a week, give up the second bottle and then the third. Most babies love their supper bottle most and are slowest in giving it up. Others feel that way about the breakfast bottle.

Willingness to be weaned doesn't always increase steadily. Misery from teething or a cold often makes babies want more of the bottle for the time being. Follow their needs. The trend that made them start to give up the bottle before will set in again when they feel better.

268. The reluctant weaner. Babies who are reluctant to give up the bottle at nine to twelve months may take one sip from the cup and push it away impatiently. Or they may pretend they don't know what it's for; they let the formula run out at the sides of their mouths, smiling innocently. They may relent a little at twelve months, but it is more likely that they'll remain suspicious until fifteen months or even later. Put an ounce of formula in a small glass that they can handle and just set it on the tray every day or so, hoping that they'll drink it. If one sip is all they take, don't even try to give them two. Act as if it doesn't make any difference to you.

When suspicious babies do start to take a little formula from the cup, you must still be patient, because it will probably take several more months before they are ready to give up the bottle altogether. This applies particularly to the supper or bedtime bottle. Many late weaners insist on a bedtime bottle till about two years of age, particularly if they have been in the habit of going to bed with a bottle.

269. Sometimes it's the parent who is worried about weaning. Sometimes a baby is kept on the bottle because her parents worry that she isn't taking as much from the cup as she used to take from the bottle. Let's say that at nine to twelve months she's drinking about 6 ounces from the cup at breakfast, 6 ounces at lunch, and about 4 ounces at supper and that she's not especially eager for the bottle, but if her mother gives it to her at the end of the meal she is willing to take a few ounces more that way. I think that a baby of nine to twelve months who is taking as much as 16 ounces a day from the cup and not acting as if she misses the bottle, can be taken off the bottle altogether if the parents wish.

Another problem may develop for the parent who uses the bottle as a pacifier during the second year. Whenever the child has a crying spell in the daytime or wakes at night, mother or father kind-heartedly makes another bottle. The child may get as many as eight bottles in the twenty-four hours—a total of 2 quarts of formula. This naturally takes away most of the baby's appetite for meals. It's important from a nutritional point of view that children not take more than a quart (32 ounces) of formula or milk a day.

Adding Solid Foods

270. Keep a good balance of valuable foods. As your baby begins to eat solid food, he or she is passing a milestone toward independence. In the process, you have a once-in-a-lifetime opportunity to introduce eating habits that will promote good health in the years to come. Children tend to adopt the eating patterns that are presented early. When healthful foods are the order of the day, children follow this pattern easily. This is important, because it is easy for children to learn habits that carry them in the wrong direction. Nutritionists are alarmed—and so am I—at the progressive deterioration of the diet of a majority of American adults and children. They are consuming more and more sweets, highly processed foods, meats, fried foods, and salt. As a result, obesity is much more prevalent today, even in young children. As time goes on, these eating habits lead to other health problems, including heart disease, high blood pressure, and diabetes. Excessive use of fatty or sugary junk foods quickly satisfies hunger so that children then eat too little of the valuable foods—vegetables, fruits, whole grains, beans, and peas—and are thereby deprived of vitamins, minerals, protein, and roughage.

271. Food tastes are formed early in life and then tend to persist, so now is the time to get your child started on good eating habits. For example, an individual's preference for how much table salt she or he wants—and the amount plays a significant role in the causation of high blood pressure—is set in infancy and early childhood. (There are other factors in high blood pressure such as race and heredity.) So when you begin adding salt to your baby's foods (because you like added salt in yours, not because the baby asks for it), you are, in certain cases, encouraging high blood pressure and a shortened life on that account.

Preferences for fatty foods also seem to start early. There is a growing suspicion among students of child development that some, though not all, cases of lifelong obesity are started in infancy by an unnecessarily high caloric diet—too much sugar and fat (see Section 252).

Saturated fats and cholesterol play a part in the development of artery blockages and heart attacks in later life, especially in those with a family history of these problems (see Section 500).

Surgeons concerned with cancer of the large intestine in older adults are now convinced that the main cause of this disease of civilization is the very slow passage of the intestinal contents in people whose diet all their lives has lacked sufficient roughage because they have eaten so little whole grain cereal and bread, and so few vegetables and fruits. Helping children to prefer these natural healthful foods will pay many dividends in the years to come.

The foods to introduce into your baby's diet are similar to those that are important at all stages of life, with some changes that we will cover shortly. Overall, the staples of the diet should be vegetables, grains, fruits, and beans. They are loaded with good nutrition, and children who become accustomed to these foods in childhood carry a tremendous advantage into their adult lives.

272. Our understanding of nutrition has grown enormously over the past several years. While we used to advocate including generous amounts of meat and dairy products in children's diets, we have learned that children are better off getting their nutrients from plant sources. Vegetables, fruits, grains, and beans are rich in vitamins, minerals, and fiber, while at the same time being low in fat, with no cholesterol at all. We have only recently come to appreciate how valuable these seemingly humble plant foods can be and to recognize the range of health problems that can be prevented when they are put front and center in the diet.

It is easiest if the parents join their children in healthful eating practices. While most of us were raised with eating habits that were somewhat distant from those we now understand to be ideal, most of us are rethinking the way we eat and are trying to make healthier choices. As we do so, we help our children make healthier choices too.

Many families are using smaller servings of meat, trimming the fat, and switching to low-fat dairy products. These are steps in the right direction. I would suggest, however, that you go a step further, drawing your family's nutrition from plant foods rather than from animal products or fried, oily foods. Let me encourage you to explore plant-based foods and to have as many meatless meals as you can.

Later in this book, we will look at planning healthful meals for all stages of childhood. Now, let's look at how babies can start their diets in the right direction.

273. There's no set age when it's important to start solid food. At the start of the twentieth century, solid food was introduced when a baby was a year old. As the years passed, doctors experimented with giving it earlier and earlier, even at one or two months. There are two definite advantages in starting in the first half year: babies take to the idea more easily than when they are older and more opinionated; and a variety of solid foods adds to the diet substances, particularly iron, that are scanty in milk.

Nowadays doctors customarily recommend offering the first solid food sometime between four and six months. There is no great advantage in extreme earliness. A baby usually gets all the calories needed from breast milk or formula for the first six months. The immature digestive system doesn't make much use of starch for several months; much of it comes out in the bowel movement.

If you have a family history of allergy, the doctor may advise you to wait considerably longer to introduce foods other than breast milk or formula, because the older a baby is when he receives a new food, the less apt he is to develop an allergy to it.

274. The baby's hunger and digestive system may both influence the age at which the doctor suggests starting solids. Breast-fed babies of eight weeks who are not gaining weight well or who seem to be hungry should be nursed more frequently. This is not the time to introduce solid foods. On the other hand, if the baby's bowel movements have been on the edge of looseness all the time he's been on formula alone, the doctor may advise you to wait longer than usual before introducing solids, for fear of upsetting the digestion further.

275. A big factor in giving solids earlier has been the eagerness of parents who don't want their baby to be one day later than the baby up the street. They put strong pressure on doctors. I think it's sensible to wait till at least four months, possibly longer. You can watch for signs that your baby is ready to eat solid foods. He may be interested in table foods and may try to grab your food. Also, look to see that he can hold his head up well and that his tongue thrust reflex has disappeared.

276. Solids before or after the milk? Most babies who are not used to solids expect their milk and want their milk first when it's feeding time. They become indignant if offered a spoonful of something solid instead. So start with the formula or the breast-feeding. A month or two later, when your baby has learned that solid foods can ward off starvation just as well as milk, you can experiment with moving the solids up to the middle or the beginning of the meal. Eventually almost all babies are happy to take all their solid food first and then top it off with the beverage, the way so many adults do.

277. What kind of spoon? A teaspoon is pretty wide for a small baby's mouth, and most spoons have a bowl so deep that the baby can't scoop all the contents out. A small demitasse spoon is better, preferably one with a shallow bowl. Some parents like to use a flat butter spreader or wooden tongue blades—the kind that doctors use—which can be bought in bulk at the drugstore. There is a spoon with a rubber-coated bowl for a teething baby who wants to bite on the spoon. For the one-year-old self-feeder, there's a spoon with a bowl that swivels to stay level, there's also a wide-bowled, short-handled spoon that works well.

278. How to introduce solid foods. The child should be sitting upright in a sturdy high chair, and wearing a bib. The process will be easier when the child is hungry but not ravenous or overtired. A baby girl taking her first teaspoonful of solid food is quite funny and a little pathetic. She looks puzzled and disgusted. She wrinkles up her nose and forehead. You can't blame her. After all, the taste is new, the consistency is new, the spoon may be new. When she sucks on a nipple, the milk gets to the right place automatically. She's had no training in catching hold of a lump of food with the front of her tongue and moving it back into her throat. She just clacks her tongue against the roof of her mouth, and most of the cereal gets squeezed back out onto her chin. You will have to shave it off her chin and scoop it back into her mouth. Again a lot will ooze out, but don't be discouraged—some goes down inside, too. Be patient until she is more experienced.

It doesn't matter much at which meals you start the solid foods. Just don't give it at the feeding when she's least hungry. If often works well to offer solids an hour or so after a regular breast- or bottle-feeding. The baby should be wide awake, in a good mood, and ready for an adventure—and so should you. Begin with only one meal of solids a day until you're both used to it. I wouldn't suggest more than two solid meals a day until the baby is six months old, because the breast milk or formula is so important for the baby's nutrition in the early months.

279. Cereal. The exact order in which solids are introduced is not important. Cereal is commonly given first. Unfortunately its taste doesn't always have great appeal for a baby. Different babies prefer different ones. There is some advantage in getting a baby used to variety, but do not introduce more than one new food at a time. It often helps to mix cereal with a familiar beverage, either expressed breast milk or formula, whichever the baby is used to.

280. Give the baby time to learn to like it. A doctor or nurse practitioner usually recommends starting with a teaspoonful or less of a new food and working up gradually to two or three tablespoonfuls if the baby wants it. This gradual progression is to make sure the baby learns to like the food and won't be upset. Just give a taste for several days, until the baby shows signs of enjoying it. There's no rush.

It's a good idea, if you are starting with cereal, to mix it thinner than the directions on the box say. Then it will seem more familiar to the baby and be easier to swallow. Also, babies and small children dislike food with a sticky consistency.

281. Which cereals? At first, most parents give the precooked cereals made especially for babies, of which there is a wide variety. They are ready to eat as soon as they're mixed, which is a great convenience. Most of them are fortified with iron, which may otherwise be lacking in a baby's diet. Anemia from insufficient iron is fairly common during the first year. It's wise to start one cereal at a time and offer it for four or five days. Sometimes, if the baby belongs to a family with many allergies, the doctor may prefer to start cereals at a later age than usual, starting with rice, oats, corn, or barley and omitting wheat for several more months, because wheat causes allergy more often than other cereals. Also, the doctor may delay the mixed-grain cereals until the baby has shown a capacity to take each of the separate kinds without trouble.

You may also give the baby the same cooked cereals as you serve the other members of the family. You can start with a white (refined) wheat cereal. This has small grains and little roughage. By the time the baby is six months old, it's wise to shift to the most nutriously valuable cereals— whole wheat and oatmeal—which have the best proteins, vitamins, and roughage. A rice cream can be made from whole grain brown rice and put through a hand food mill.

282. The baby who balks at cereal. You will know within a few days after starting how your baby is going to take to cereal. Some babies seem to decide, "It's queer, but it's nourishment, so I'll eat it." As the days go by they grow more and more enthusiastic. They open their mouths for it like birds in the nest.

But there are other babies who decide on the second day of cereal that they don't like it at all. And on the third day they dislike it more than on the second. If your baby feels this way, be careful. Take it easy. If you try to push the cereal into your baby against his will, he will get more and more rebellious. You will get exasperated, too. In a week or two he may become so suspicious that he will balk at the bottle also. Offer the cereal just once a day. Give only enough to cover the tip of the teaspoon until he is used to it. Add a little fruit to see if he likes it better that way. If in two or three days he is getting more set against it in spite of all these precautions, then stop altogether for a couple of weeks. If he still balks when you try again, report the problem to your doctor.

I think it's a great mistake to get into an argument with babies about their first solid food. Sometimes a long-lasting feeding problem starts in this way. Even if it doesn't last, it's bad for parents and babies to go through an unnecessary fight.

If you have no doctor or nurse practitioner to advise you, I suggest that you start with fruit instead of cereal. Babies are puzzled by fruit, too, the first time they have it. But within a day or two practically all of them decide they love it. By the end of two weeks they are ready to assume that anything that comes on a spoon is wonderful. Then you can add cereal too.

283. Starting fruit. Fruit is often the second or third solid added to the diet, a few weeks after babies have become used to cereal and perhaps vegetables. Some doctors prefer it as the first solid food because babies usually take to it so enthusiastically, while other doctors don't want to encourage a preference for sweet foods.

Apple juice, diluted at first, is often given around the time a baby starts his first solid foods. Your doctor will help you decide when to offer it.

For the first six or eight months of a baby's life, the fruit is stewed, except for raw, ripe banana. Apples, peaches, pears, apricots, and prunes are the usual fruits. You can use fresh or frozen fruit that you have stewed for the rest of the family, but strain or sieve it for the baby. You can also use canned fruit that you serve to other members of the family. Be sure to buy canned fruit packed in water or in its own juice instead of syrup, or you can buy the small jars of strained baby fruits. Look at the label to make sure it is all fruit.

Fruit can be given at any one of the feedings, even twice a day, depending on the baby's appetite and digestion.

Increase each fruit gradually as the baby learns to like it. Most babies are satisfied with half a baby jar. You can give the other half the next day. Fruit can be kept three days if it is well refrigerated. Don't feed the baby out of the jar unless you plan to use it up at one meal. Saliva introduced into the container can spoil food rapidly.

Banana should be very ripe. It should have black spots on the skin and be tan-colored inside. Mash it fine with a fork. Add a little formula or soy milk if it seems too thick for your baby.

Fruit has the general reputation of being laxative. But most individuals, including infants, don't show any definite looseness or cramps from any of the fruits mentioned above, except for prunes, prune juice, and sometimes apricots. Prunes are mildly laxative for almost all babies, and this makes them a doubly valuable food for those who have a chronic tendency to constipation. For the baby who needs a laxative and likes fruit, pureed prunes or prune juice can be given at one feeding and some other fruit at another feeding each day.

If your baby's bowels become loose, you will probably want to omit prunes and apricots for a couple of months and give other fruits only once a day.

In the second half of the first year, you can begin adding or substituting other raw fruits besides bananas: scraped apple, pear, avocado. (Berries and seedless grapes are commonly postponed until the baby is two years of age for fear of choking. Even then you should mash them until the baby's at least three years.)

284. Vegetables. Strained cooked vegetables are commonly added to the diet after the baby has gotten used to cereal or fruit or both. A possible advantage of adding vegetables before fruits is that the baby will not be expecting a sweet taste. The vegetables usually offered first are string beans, peas, squash, carrots, beets, and sweet potatoes.

There are other vegetables—such as broccoli, cauliflower, cabbage, turnips, kale, and onions—which, as usually cooked, are so strong-tasting that some babies don't like them. If your family likes these foods, try straining them and serving them to your baby, perhaps mixed with a little apple juice to counteract their strong taste. Corn is not given initially because of the large husks on the kernels.

You can serve your baby fresh or frozen vegetables, cooked or strained, pureed in a food processor, blender, or grinder, or the ones in jars pureed for babies. Buy the straight vegetables rather than mixtures. Don't feed out of the jar unless you plan to use the whole jar. Saliva spoils foods. Work up to several tablespoonfuls or half a baby jar, as desired. The rest, if refrigerated, can be given the next day. Cooked vegetables spoil fairly rapidly.

Babies are more likely to be choosy about vegetables than about cereals or fruits. You will probably find one or two vegetables that your baby doesn't like. Don't urge them, but try them again every month or so. There's no point in fussing over a few foods when we have so many to choose from.

It's common for undigested vegetables to appear in the bowel movements when the baby first starts them. This is not a bad sign so long as there is no looseness or mucus, but increase the amount of each vegetable slowly until the baby's digestion learns to handle it. If a vegetable causes looseness or much mucus, omit it for the time being and try a very small amount after another month.

Beets may color the urine or show up red in the bowel movement. This is nothing to worry about if you remember that it is caused by beets and not blood. Green vegetables often turn the bowel movement green. Spinach causes chapping of the lips and irritation around the anus in some babies. If this occurs, omit spinach for several months and then try again.

285. Higher-protein foods. Once the baby is familiar with cereals, vegetables, and fruits, you can introduce other foods. Try very well cooked beans, like lentils, chickpeas, and kidney beans. If you use canned beans, put them in a strainer and rinse them well to remove some of the sodium. Start with small amounts of cooked beans. If you notice that your baby develops a rashy bottom and you see bits of undigested bean in his bowel movement, wait a few weeks before reintroducing beans, and make sure they are very well cooked. Tofu is also a good choice. Many babies happily eat it in small cubes or mixed with applesauce, other pureed fruits, or vegetables.

Some people rely on meats, fish, poultry, eggs, or dairy products as protein sources. These products are now seen by many nutritionists in a much less favorable light, however. Children who become habituated to them during their preschool years may pay a price in adulthood for the fat, cholesterol, and animal protein these foods contain. For this reason, I encourage you to explore vegetarian foods and to give your children the advantages these foods offer.

There is a special concern about meats for very small children. Poultry, beef, pork, and other meats often contain bacteria that are not visible to the eye but can cause serious infections. Such illnesses have become alarmingly common in recent years, and infants are much more sensitive to them than adults. Meats must always be thoroughly cooked, and any surfaces or utensils touched by raw meat must be carefully cleaned. Better yet, you can do the whole family a favor by preparing meatless meals.

286. Dinners. There are a variety of "dinners" in jars for babies. They usually consist of small amounts of a meat and a vegetable with a larger amount of potato, rice, or barley. I think it's better to buy vegetables, grains, beans, and fruits in separate jars, so that you will know how much of each food your baby is getting.

When there is a tendency to allergy, these mixtures may be confusing unless the baby has already taken each of the foods included in the mixture without reaction.

287. The meals at six months. By six months of age, your baby will probably be eating cereal and a variety of fruits, vegetables, and beans. He may be taking one, two, or three meals of solids a day (see Section 303). A common arrangement for a moderately hungry baby is cereal for breakfast, vegetable and tofu or well-cooked beans for lunch, cereal and fruit for supper. But there are no hard-and-fast rules. It all depends on your convenience and your baby's appetite. For instance, a not very hungry baby could be given fruit at breakfast, a vegetable and tofu or beans at lunch, and cereal alone at supper. A baby who tends to be constipated can be given prunes every night along with the cereal, and another fruit at breakfast or lunch. You may want the baby to have beans and vegetable at supper with the rest of the family, the cereal and fruit at lunch.

Many breast-fed and some bottle-fed babies are just beginning solids at six months. Their digestion and eating interests are more mature than when they were four months old. You can introduce new foods to these babies more rapidly, and quickly move them up to three meals a day.

288. Finger foods. By the time babies are six or seven months old, they want to and can pick foods up in their hands and suck and munch on them. This is good training for them as preparation for spoon-feeding themselves at about a year. If babies are never allowed to feed themselves with their fingers, they're less likely to have the ambition to try the spoon.

The traditional first finger food is a crust of stale whole wheat bread or toast at six or seven months. Teething biscuits that have added sugar should be avoided. Babies suck at it and chew at it with their bare gums (their gums may be tingling with teething, and in that case they'll enjoy the biting). As it softens gradually with their saliva, some of it rubs or dissolves off into their mouths, enough to make them feel they're getting somewhere. Most of it, of course, ends up on their hands, faces, hair, and the furniture.

Soon you can start putting pieces of fruit or cooked vegetable and tofu chunks on the baby's high chair tray, for her to pick up with her fingers.

Babies love being offered pieces of food from their parents' plates. Some babies, refuse finger foods if the parents offer them, but will happily feed themselves those same foods. Another baby will cram everything into her mouth at once, so you have to offer her only one piece of food at a time, in the beginning.

On average, babies get their first tooth at about seven months, and at one year may have four to six sharp biting teeth. They probably won't get their first molars for grinding until around fifteen months. But somehow they manage

189

most table foods so successfully that by their first birthday, almost all of them can be taken off prepared baby foods and allowed to finger-feed themselves from the family's foods.

289. Mashed and lumpy foods. Sometime after six months, you'll want your baby to get used to lumpy or chopped foods. If a baby goes much beyond that time eating nothing but pureed things, it will get harder and harder to make the change. People have the idea that babies can't handle lumps until they get a fair set of teeth. This isn't true. They can mush up lumps of cooked vegetables or fruit and pieces of whole wheat bread or toast with their gums and tongue.

Some babies seem to be born more squeamish about lumps than others. But some babies and older children who gag easily on particles of food have become that way either because the parents tried to make the change to chopped foods too abruptly or too late or because they have been forcing food when the child didn't want it.

There are two important points to remember when shifting to chopped foods. First, make the change a gradual one. When you first serve chopped vegetables, mash them up pretty fine with a fork. Don't put too much in the baby's mouth at a time. When the child is used to this consistency, gradually mash less and less. And second, allow the baby to pick up a cube of cooked carrot, for instance, in his fingers and put it in his mouth himself. Babies can't stand to have a whole spoonful of lumps dumped into their mouths when they're not used to it.

So start the change at about six months by offering finger foods. You can mash and chop the cooked vegetables and fresh and stewed fruits that you prepare for the rest of the family for the baby or you can buy the chopped (junior) foods in jars prepared for babies.

You don't have to make all the foods lumpy. It is necessary only that the baby get used to eating some lumps each day.

Meats, if they are used, should generally continue to be served ground or minced fine. Most small children dislike chunks of meat that they can't chew up easily. They often chew on such a piece for a long time without getting anywhere. They don't dare try to swallow too big a piece, as adults do when they are desperate. This may lead to gagging (see Section 546). As I mentioned earlier, I would discourage the use of meats, in any case.

Potatoes, pasta, and rice are popular with most children and can be introduced along with other table foods. Try to choose whole grain pasta and brown rice. These contain more fiber and vitamins than more refined products. Also, try other grains, like bulgur and quinoa, for variety.

290. Home preparation of infant foods. Many parents are now interested in preparing their own infant foods, for philosophical or economic reasons. This can be safely done. The advantages are that you have control over the ingredients and the preparation method, that you can use fresh, organically grown foods, and that homemade foods are much cheaper.

There are fine books available on this subject. You'll need a food mill, blender, or food processor. You can reheat individual portions in the small compartments of a cheap egg-poaching pan, double-boiler, or microwave oven. Be sure to stir the food well and test the temperature—especially if it's been heated in a microwave—before feeding it to the baby. Foods can be cooked in quantity and then pureed to a consistency that your baby currently likes. They can be moistened if necessary with water, expressed breast milk, or formula. They can be frozen in serving-size portions in ice cube trays or on cookie sheets and then stored in plastic freezer bags until they're used. Foods for children under a year should not be seasoned.

If your child is to eat table foods, your seasoning habits may have to be modified to avoid excess salt or sugar. This is also when small, handheld food grinders come in so handy.

291. Commercial baby foods. When baby foods in jars were first produced, they consisted of single vegetables, single fruits, and single meats. Since then, the companies have tended toward mixtures of vegetables and starches, fruits and starches, and "dinners" consisting of starches, vegetables, and meats. Most often, the starches are refined rice, refined corn, and refined wheat. And the refining of any grain further reduces its vitamins, proteins, and roughage.

Baby food companies, in order to make their foods appealing to babies and their parents, added sugar and salt for many years. But, because of the complaints of doctors, nutritionists, and parents, this practice has been largely discontinued.

When you buy baby food in jars, read carefully the fine print on the label. (When the big print says "creamed beans," the small print may say "beans with cornstarch.") Buy plain fruits or plain vegetables—in jars—to be sure that your baby is getting enough of these valuable foods and is not being overloaded with deprived starches. Do not buy jars that contain added sugar or salt.

Don't get started on cornstarch puddings and gelatin desserts. They don't have the right food values, and they both contain a lot of sugar. Instead, give your baby plain strained fruits. A baby who has never been exposed to refined sugar will find these to be delightfully sweet.

Many families prepare some or all of their own baby foods. Certainly, this allows you more control over additives. It also allows you to add variety to your baby's diet and to serve your baby many of the same foods the rest of the family is eating.

292. All babies choke a little as they get used to eating lumpy foods, just like they fall when they're learning to walk. Nine times out of ten, they easily bring the food up or down themselves and don't need any help at all. If they can't get it up or down right away, pull the food out with your fingers if you can see it. If you can't see it, put the baby over your lap, with her head down and her bottom up. Hit her firmly between the shoulder blades a couple of times with the palm of your hand. This virtually always solves the problem, and she's ready to go back to her meal. See page 758 for emergency treatment of choking. Some parents worry so much about what to do if their baby chokes that they delay giving finger foods and lumpy foods until way after the baby is old enough for them.

The ten most common foods associated with choking in children under the age of five are hot dogs, round candy, peanuts, grapes, cookies, meat chunks or slices, raw carrot slices, peanut butter, apple chunks, and popcorn. The problem is not caused by young children's inability to chew and swallow these foods. It's the result of the sudden deep inhalation that a child takes when he laughs, giggles, cries, or is surprised. The inhalation can send food from the mouth directly into a lung, blocking off the lung or causing it to collapse.

This doesn't mean that children under five should never have these foods. Though I wouldn't recommend hot dogs—except cut-up veggie hot dogs—or round candy at any age. The child should eat while sitting at a table, under careful adult supervision. Encourage him to chew well, and cut veggie hot dogs, grapes, and similar foods into smaller pieces.

293. Beverages. Bottle-feeding infants should have formula or water in the bottle, rather than juice. Juice contains simple sugars that can promote cavities and spoil a baby's appetite for more nourishing foods.

Once your baby is drinking from a cup, juices can be used. Some are calcium-fortified, which can be helpful. Choose 100 percent juice, rather than mixtures that contain extra sweeteners. Because juices contain simple sugars, it is good to limit them to four to eight ounces a day. You can dilute them with water, if you like. Orange juice is not routinely given until nine to twelve months because some babies don't handle it well and may even be allergic to it. Babies get enough vitamin C in breast milk, formula, or added vitamins. When your doctor does suggest adding orange juice to the diet you can use fresh or frozen, in bottles, cartons, or cans. Orange juice is usually mixed with an equal amount of water so that it won't taste too strong. One way is to start with 1 teaspoon of orange juice and 1 teaspoon of water. The next day give 2 teaspoons of orange juice and 2 teaspoons of water. The third day, 3 teaspoons of each. And so on, up to an ounce of each. Then gradually decrease the water and increase the orange juice, until you are giving 2 ounces of straight orange juice. If your baby is still on the bottle, strain the orange juice so that the pulp won't clog the nipples. As soon as the baby starts using a cup or glass, you can offer her the orange juice that way. You can give it cold, at room temperature, or slightly warmed, but don't let it get hot. Heat destroys vitamin C.

It is good to avoid sodas. They contain sugar, artificial colors, and caffeine that children do not need.

294. Eggs. For a very long time, egg yolk was thought to be important as a valuable source of iron. Recent research has shown, however, that the iron in egg yolk is poorly absorbed by babies' intestines. It has also been found that egg yolk may interfere with iron absorption from other sources—unless the egg yolk is taken with a source of vitamin C. Also, egg yolk contains a large amount of cholesterol, which can play a part in the development of hardening of the arteries and heart attacks later in life, especially in those with a family history of these ailments. It was known long ago that egg white could cause allergies in some babies, especially those with a family history of allergies.

295. Diet by the end of the first year. In case you are mixed up by all the things that have been added to the diet, here is a rough list of what babies are apt to be eating by the end of the first year—a pretty grown-up diet. This is the age at which babies frequently eat less than their parents think they should—and thrive.

Breakfast: Cereal (hot whole wheat or oat cereal, or unsugared cold cereal), toast, pancakes, French toast, fruits, juice, soy milk.

Lunch: vegetable (green or yellow, in lumps), potato, soy foods or beans, fruit, small quarters of sandwiches (such as peanut butter thinned with soy milk and mixed with mashed banana), toast, soy milk, or soy yogurt.

Supper: Cereal, fruit, and soy milk or the family supper.

Or they may have their big meal at supper with the family. Then lunch might be something starchy, such as potato or cereal, and a fruit or vegetable.

Milk: Ordinarily, milk is not given between meals, because it stays in the stomach for 3 or 4 hours and takes away the appetite for the next meal.

Fruit juice: including orange juice, is given daily between meals or at breakfast.

Bread: Whole wheat or rye bread can be given at meals or between.

Frozen foods are just as good for children as fresh and canned foods.

Foods that spoil easily when kept long out of the refrigerator are milk, foods made with milk (puddings, pastry fillings, creamy salad dressings), vegetables, and poultry stuffing.

296. Foods to avoid. Some foods do more harm than good. While your child may eventually discover them despite your best efforts, now is a time when you have more control over what your baby eats. Here are the foods to avoid:

Sugary foods: Candy, sugar-sweetened juices, and sodas promote cavities and can spoil a baby's appetite for more nutritious foods.

Meat: Children who grow up without developing a taste for meat, poultry, or fish will carry a tremendous advantage through life. Their tastes will not be oriented toward these products, all of which contain fat and cholesterol that can contribute to weight problems, heart disease, and some cancers. They will also be at much less risk of infection with the bacteria that often taint meat products.

Dairy products: Nondairy milk, particularly soy milk, has real advantages over cow's milk and other dairy products. These products are free of animal fat, animal protein, and lactose sugar, while still providing excellent nutrition. This is covered in more detail in Section 302.

Artificial flavors and colors: While flavors and colors are added in order to attract children (and their parents), they have no nutritional value. These artificial additives can cause sensitivities, including behavioral problems in a small percentage of children.

Caffeine: Caffeine is found in colas, black tea, and chocolate. Its stimulant effects are best avoided.

Corn syrup and honey: Corn syrup and honey should

never be given to babies under a year old. These sweeteners have been found to contain certain botulism spores, and babies' digestive systems aren't developed enough to kill these spores.

297. Supplements.

Iron: Both breast-fed and formula-fed infants need iron supplements by about four to six months. Children from six months to three years should have a total of 10 milligrams of iron a day including the amount they get from food and whatever vitamin/mineral supplements they may be taking. Iron-fortified formulas are adequate.

Fluoride: Fluoride is recommended for infants if the water supply is not fluoridated. For infants between six months and three years, 0.2 to 0.5 milligram is recommended. For children from three to six years, the recommended amount is 0.5 milligrams. For children from six to twelve years, the recommended amount is 1.0 milligram. If your child drinks fluoridated water, there is no need for extra fluoride.

Vitamin D: Babies can make their own vitamin D if they receive at least two hours of sunshine exposure to head and hands over the course of a week. Dark-skinned babies and those who live in cold climates will need more sunshine exposure to make adequate vitamin D. Because vitamin D deficiency leads to rickets, a condition of soft, fragile bones, supplements should be used if there is any question about whether or not your infant is getting enough sun. Supplements of 400 IU a day are recommended for breast-fed infants and babies with dark skin pigmentation who receive limited sunshine exposure.

Vitamin B_{12}: Vitamin B_{12} supplements should be given to breast-fed infants of mothers on plant-based diets and infants after weaning who are being raised on plant-based diets. Such diets have many health advantages, which is why I recommend them heartily, and adding vitamin B_{12} is a simple way to ensure complete nutrition. For infants between six months and a year of age, 0.5 microgram of vitamin B_{12} is recommended. For children from one to three years, 0.7 microgram is recommended.

298. A low-fat diet is not wise for infants. While low-fat diets are recommended for older children and adults, they are generally not indicated for infants and children under two years of age. Some fat is needed for proper growth and brain development, and children under two years need the concentrated calories provided by the fats in foods like soy products, peanut butter, other nut butters, and avocados. Children do not need animal fat, such as that found in meat and whole milk; the essential fats are those found in vegetable oils. So don't start your baby on a low-fat diet, but do choose plant products that offer something besides just fat. Of course, if your baby has a special medical condition, you should follow the doctor's advice.

Changes in Schedule

299. When to omit the feeding at the parents' bedtime. Giving up this feeding should depend most on when the baby is ready. There are two things to consider.

The first consideration is whether your baby is ready to sleep through the night. You can't be sure that he's ready just because he always has to be waked up at ten or eleven o'clock. If you don't wake him, he may wake by himself around midnight. Better wait until you have had to wake him for several weeks. Then see if he sleeps through. If he wakes up hungry later in the night, go back to feeding him at your bedtime for a few more weeks.

Of course, if your baby is very small, gaining slowly, or having trouble with his digestion, it may be better to keep this feeding going a while longer, even if he is willing to sleep through without it.

The second consideration is whether he is sucking his thumb a lot. If he is, it may mean that he is not getting as much sucking as he'd like from breast or bottle. If you cut out a feeding at this time, you will reduce his sucking time further still. However, if he continues to be a thumb-sucker in spite of all your efforts, you don't have to go on forever giving him the feeding at your bedtime. For one thing, as he gets older he may refuse to wake up, no matter how hard you try, or he may fall asleep again as soon as he has taken a couple of ounces. I'd stop the feeding by this time anyway, whether he is sucking his thumb or not.

In a general way, then, let your baby give up his feeding at the parents' bedtime when he shows that he can sleep through and get enough sucking satisfaction without it. This will probably be between the ages of three and six months. Wait till five or six months if he is sucking his thumb much and is willing to take this feeding.

Most babies get themselves off the feeding at the parents' bedtime as soon as they can. But an occasional one will continue it indefinitely, especially if the mother rushes in as soon as he first murmurs. If your baby is still waking for this feeding at seven or eight months, try to get him over the habit. At this age he certainly doesn't need nourishment at night if he is eating well in the daytime and gaining satisfactorily. Let him fuss for a few minutes without going to him at all and see if he won't go back to sleep.

Sometimes the baby wants more formula in his other bottles to make up for the lost bottle at his parents' bedtime, sometimes not. I wouldn't urge him to take any more than he's interested in.

300. If your baby loses his appetite between six and nine months. A baby may take solids eagerly for the first couple of months and then rather suddenly lose a lot of his appetite. One reason may be that at this age he is meant to slow down in his weight gaining. In his first three months he probably gained close to 2 pounds a month. By six months he is apt to be down to a pound a month; otherwise he would become too fat. Also, he may be bothered by teething. One baby wants to leave out a lot of his solid food; another turns against his formula or breast milk. After six months, some babies refuse to be fed. If you let them have finger food while you're offering food in a spoon, it often will solve this problem.

Go to a three-meals-a-day schedule during the daytime, whether or not he is still on breast or bottle at his bedtime (see Section 303).

If a baby's appetite still doesn't revive with these measures, it's important to get him to the doctor to be sure that he's otherwise healthy.

301. When to switch from formula to soy milk or other milks. Children under one year of age need breast milk or formula. Unmodified milk (as opposed to formula) does not contain the proper ratio of protein, fat, and carbohydrate, or enough of the vitamins and minerals infants need. This is also true of homemade preparations such as soy milk, rice milk, or nut milk intended for older children or adults.

At about one year of age, children can be placed on fortified soy milk. Choose one with added calcium and vitamin D. Vitamin B_{12}–fortified soy milk is a handy source of this vitamin for children who, as I recommend, avoid animal products. Other reliable sources of vitamin B_{12} include fortified breakfast cereals, children's vitamins, Red Star T6635 brand nutritional yeast, and fortified meat analogs.

Children under age two should not use low-fat or nonfat milk. They still need the concentrated calories provided by natural fats. Fortified soy milk is a good choice.

302. What kind of milk? I suggest using soy milk and other plant-derived milks rather than cow's milk. Fortified soy milk has added calcium and vitamin D. It naturally provides essential fats but not animal fat, and is free of animal proteins and lactose sugar. Although virtually any food can cause sensitivities or even allergies, soy milk is less likely than cow's milk to do so.

Some children have respiratory problems, skin conditions, chronic ear infections, or digestive upsets that clear up when they avoid cow's milk. In addition, cow's milk tends to interfere with iron absorption and has virtually no iron of its own.

Soy milks are sold in all health food stores and in many regular groceries, next to the condensed milk. They are also fine for adults.

If you are still using cow's milk in your family, let me encourage you to experiment with various brands and flavors of soy milk and other plant-based milks. Meanwhile, there are some terms you will want to know.

"Pasteurized" means that the milk has been heated high enough for a long enough time to kill the bacteria dangerous to human beings, but not enough to sterilize it (kill all the germs), which would give it a boiled taste. "Homogenized" means that the fat droplets have been divided into very small particles. This makes them easier for babies to digest and keeps the cream mixed in with the milk. "Vitamin D" means that 400 units have been added to each quart of milk. "Whole milk" means that the milk has between 3.25 and 3.5 percent butterfat.

There are a variety of low-fat milks available, in liquid and powdered forms. These are not suitable for children under two, unless your doctor prescribes low-fat milk as part of a special diet for your baby.

303. When to put the baby on three meals a day. This depends on when your baby is ready for it. It may be anywhere between the ages of four and ten months. If your baby is starved an hour before the next meal and crying with hunger, he isn't ready for a three-meal schedule, no matter how old he is. In any case, a baby just starting three meals a day will still be having some breast- or bottle-feedings and some snacks as well.

Babies begin eating solid foods between four and six months, starting once a day and building up at their own pace to three meals a day. During this time they almost invariably still have an early morning breast- or bottle-feeding, but then they go back to sleep for another hour (and so do their grateful parents). Then the whole family gets up and has breakfast.

Before the midmorning nap, younger babies may need another breast- or bottle-feeding or some fruit or juice. Lunch may come very early if the baby is trying to give up his morning nap, so that the morning nap can become the afternoon nap. Younger babies may need breast or bottle before the afternoon nap, and older ones may need fruit or juice. Dinner is usually early. Older babies may join in at the family dinnertime as well. Babies often continue their bedtime breast- or bottle-feeding until weaning. Once weaning is started, the early morning and late night feedings are usually the last to go.

Your baby may show clearly at a certain stage that he is ready for three meals. If he eats well only at every other feeding, then he needs to be changed to a three-meals-a-day schedule, so that he will be hungry at mealtimes. Otherwise feeding problems are apt to develop.

Another consideration is the parents' convenience. Suppose they have their hands full preparing meals for their older children, and their baby is able to go more than four hours between meals, even though still willing to eat that often. These parents naturally want to get her onto the same three meals as the older children now, and there is no reason why they shouldn't, especially if she isn't thumb-sucking much. Other parents, especially with the first baby, find that the approximately four-hour schedule is more convenient than three meals a day. There is no reason why these babies shouldn't stay on the four-hour schedule longer than average as long as they remain hungry for their meals that often. In other words, there is no rule about making such a change in a baby's routine. It's just a matter of reasonableness and common sense. You see what the baby is ready for and fit it in with your convenience.

The hours at which a baby is fed when he goes onto three meals a day will depend largely on the family's habit and somewhat on the baby's hunger. You'll learn how to tell when he's ready for a snack of fruit or juice and how much to give him, so he won't be overly hungry or too filled up between meals.

Ordinarily, milk is not given between meals, because it stays in the stomach for three or four hours and takes away the appetite for the next meal. When a baby is taking milk only three times a day, he is probably getting a smaller total for the day than formerly, because he probably does not want more than his usual 6 to 8 ounces at each meal. Don't worry about this. Don't try to tuck a few extra ounces into him at odd hours to keep up the old 30-ounce total. Most babies are quite safe if they are taking as much as 20 to 24 ounces a day. On the other hand, if your baby is the unusual one who wants as much as 10 ounces a meal, give it to him up to two years.

Changes in Appetite and Habits

304. Babies are apt to change their eating habits. They get more choosy for several reasons. Somewhere around a year old, babies are apt to change their feelings about food. They become choosier and less hungry. This is not surprising. If they kept on eating and gaining the way they did when they were little babies, they'd turn into mountains. Now they seem to feel that they have time to look the meal over and ask themselves, "What looks good today and what doesn't?" What a contrast to their behavior at eight months! In those days they felt starved when mealtime came around. They'd whimper pathetically while their parent tied the bib, and lean forward for every bite. It wouldn't matter much what was served. They were too hungry to care. There are other reasons, aside from not being so hungry, that make them choosy. They're beginning to realize, "I'm a separate person with ideas of my own," so they become definite in their dislikes of a food that they were doubtful about before. Their memory is getting better, too. They probably realize, "The meals here are served up pretty regularly, and they stay around long enough for me to get what I want." Also, teething often takes away a child's appetite, especially when the first molars are on their way. He may eat only half his usual amount for days, or he may occasionally refuse an entire meal.

Finally, and perhaps most important, there is the fact that appetite *naturally* varies from day to day and from week to week. We grown-ups know that one day we grab a big glass of tomato juice and another day split pea soup looks better. It is the same way with children and babies. But the reason you don't see this variation more often in infants under a year is that most of the time they are too hungry to turn anything down.

305. Let them give up certain vegetables for a while. If your one-year-old daughter suddenly rejects the vegetable that she loved last week, let her turn against it. If you don't make a fuss today, she will probably come back to it next week or next month. But if you insist on her taking it when she seems to dislike it, you only make her decide that that particular food is her enemy. You turn a temporary dislike into a permanent hate. If she turns down the same vegetable twice in succession, leave it out for a couple of weeks.

It is naturally irritating to a parent to buy a food, prepare it, serve it, and then have it turned down by an opinionated wretch who loved the same thing a few days ago. It is hard not to be cross and bossy at such a time. But it is worse for the child's feeling about food to try to force her or urge her to eat it. If she turns down half her vegetables for a while, as is common in the second year, serve her the ones that she does like. This is the wise and pleasant way to take advantage of the great variety of fresh, frozen, and canned vegetables that we have. If she turns against all vegetables for a while but loves her fruit, let her have extra fruit. If she is taking enough fruit, soy milk, and good quality grains, she is not missing any of the nutrients in vegetables.

306. What to do if they are tired of cereal. Many babies get fed up with cereal sometime in the second year, especially for supper. Don't try to push it in. There are many substitutes you can offer, which are discussed in Sections 521–523. Even if they give up all starches for a few weeks, it won't hurt them.

307. Expect their tastes to change from month to month. The chances are great that if you don't make a battle of it, your child will eat a reasonably balanced diet from week to week, though it may be somewhat lopsided from meal to meal or from day to day. If it stays unbalanced for weeks, however, you should discuss the problem with your doctor or nurse practitioner.

308. Standing and playing at meals. This may be quite a problem even before the age of a year. It comes about because the baby is less ravenous for food, more interested in all kinds of new activities, like climbing, handling the spoon, messing in the food, tipping the cup upside down, dropping things on the floor. I've seen a one-year-old being fed a whole meal standing up backward in the chair, and even while being followed around the house by a long-suffering parent with a spoon and dish in her hands.

Time to finish the meal.

Fooling around at meals is only a sign that children are growing up and that parents are sometimes more keen about children eating than the children are. This behavior is inconvenient and irritating, and can lead to feeding problems, too. I wouldn't let it go on. You'll notice that children climb and play when they're partly or completely satisfied, not when they're really hungry. So whenever they lose interest in food, assume they've had enough, let them down from the chair, and take the food away. It's right to be firm, but you don't need to get mad. If they immediately whimper for the meal, as if to say they didn't mean they weren't hungry, give them one more chance. But if they show no regret, don't try to give them the meal a little later. If they get extra hungry between meals, give them a little more than usual for their snack, or give them the next regular meal early. If you always stop the meal casually when they lose interest, they will do their part by paying attention when they are hungry.

Now I want to state a reservation. Babies around a year old have a powerful urge to dip their fingers into the vegetable, to squeeze a little cereal in their hands, and to stir a drop of milk around on the tray. This isn't fooling. They may be opening their mouths eagerly for food at the same time. I wouldn't try to stop them from experimenting just a little bit with the feel of food. But if they try to turn the dish over, hold it down firmly. If they insist, keep it out of reach for a while or end the meal.

309. Let them feed themselves early. The age at which babies feed themselves depends largely on the adults' attitude. Some infants are efficiently spoon-feeding themselves before the age of a year. At the other extreme, overprotective parents swear that their two-year-olds can't possibly feed themselves at all. It all depends on when you give them a chance.

Most babies show an ambition to manage the spoon by a year, and if they have opportunity to practice, a lot of them can do a good job without help by fifteen months. Babies get some preparation for spoon-feeding way back at six months when they hold their own bread crusts and other finger foods.

Feeling is learning.

Then at around nine months, when they get chopped foods, they want to pick up each piece and put it in their mouths. Babies who have never been allowed to feed themselves with their fingers are apt to be delayed in taking to spoon-feeding.

A polite baby of ten to twelve months may just want to rest a hand on his mother's or father's hand when being fed. But most babies, when the urge comes, try to yank the spoon out of the parent's hand. Don't think this has to be a tug-of-war; give the baby that spoon and get another one to use yourself. The baby will soon discover that feeding himself is more complicated than just getting possession of the spoon. It may take weeks for him to learn how to get a speck of food on the spoon, and weeks more to learn not to turn it upside down between the dish and his mouth.

When babies become bored with trying to eat, and stir or slop the food instead, it's time to move the dish out of reach, perhaps leaving a few crumbs of meat or bread on the tray for them to experiment with. Even when they're trying very hard to feed themselves correctly, they make plenty of accidental messes, and this you've got to put up with. If you're worried about the rug, put a big plastic tablecloth under the high chair. It also helps to use a hot-water plate with partitions. This keeps the food warm, is harder to pick up, and has straight sides to push the food against. Children's spoons with wide, shallow bowls and short, curved handles work well. Or use a regular teaspoon.

310. When your one-year-old can feed herself, let her take over completely. It isn't enough to let the baby have a spoon and a chance to use it; you've got to gradually give her more *reason* to use it. At first she tries because she wants to do things for herself. But after she sees how complicated it is, she's apt to give up the whole business if you keep on rapidly feeding her anyway. In other words, when she begins to be able to get a speck to her mouth, you ought to let her have a few minutes alone with the food at the beginning of the meal when she's hungriest. Then her appetite urges her on. The better she gets at feeding herself, the longer she should have at each meal to do it.

By the time she can polish off her favorite dish in ten minutes, it's time for you to get out of the picture. This is where parents often go wrong. They say, "She can eat her own cereal and fruit all right now, but I still have to feed her

her vegetable and potato." This attitude is a little risky. If she's able to manage one food, she has skill enough to manage the others. If you go on feeding her the ones she doesn't bother with, you build up a sharper and sharper distinction between the foods she wants and the foods you want her to take. In the long run, this takes away her appetite for your foods. But if you put thought into serving a well-balanced diet from among the foods she is presently enjoying and let her feed herself entirely, the chances are great that she will strike a good balance from week to week, even though she may slight this or that food at certain meals.

311. Don't worry about table manners. Babies want to eat more expertly, more neatly, all by themselves. They want to graduate from fingers to spoon and from spoon to fork, as soon as they feel equal to the challenge, just as they want to try all the other difficult things that they see others doing. Dr. Clara Davis noticed this in the babies she was observing, and they weren't coached at all. She pointed out that puppies show the same urge to learn eating manners without being taught. In the beginning, the puppies stand in a pan of milk and dip their faces. First, they learn to keep their feet out; next, to lap the milk without dipping their faces; finally, to lick their whiskers politely at the end.

I have been making quite a point about letting children learn to feed themselves somewhere between the ages of twelve and fifteen months, because that is the age when they want to try. Suppose a parent keeps a baby from doing it at this age, and then at twenty-one months declares, "You big lummox, it's time for you to feed yourself." Then the child is apt to take the attitude, "Oh, no! It's my custom and my privilege to be fed." At this more advanced stage, trying to manage a spoon is no longer exciting. In fact, the child's whole sense of what's proper rebels against it, and the parents have lost the golden opportunity.

Don't take all this so seriously that you think there is only one right age, don't worry because your baby is not making sufficient progress and don't try to force the issue; that would only create other problems. I'm only making the point that babies want to learn this skill and can do so more easily than many parents realize. It is important for parents gradually to give up feeding the child when he is able to take over.

CARE DURING THE FIRST YEAR

Crying in the Early Weeks

312. What does it mean? This is usually an important question, especially with a first baby. Crying in an infant does not have the same meaning as it does in an older child. It is the baby's only form of communication with the outside, new world and has many meanings, not just pain or sadness. As she grows older, crying is much less of a problem because you worry less, you know what to expect from her at different times of the day, you are able to distinguish between different cries, and she has fewer reasons to cry.

But in the first weeks, baffling questions pop into your mind: Is she hungry? Is she wet? Is she uncomfortable? Is she sick? Does she have indigestion? Is she lonely? (Parents are not apt to think of fatigue, but it's one of the commonest causes.)

It is fairly easy to answer some of these questions, but a lot of fretting and crying can't be so readily explained. In fact, by the time they are a couple of weeks old, almost all babies—especially first babies—get into fretful periods that we can give names to but can't explain exactly. When the crying is regularly limited to one period in the evening or afternoon, we can call it **colic** or **periodic irritable crying.** This crying may be associated with distension of the abdomen and the passing of gas. If the baby is fussing off and on, any old time of the day or night, we can sigh and say that she is just a **fretful baby** at this stage. If she's unusually tense and jumpy, some use the term **hypertonic baby.** But we don't know the meaning of these patterns of behavior. We only know that they gradually peter out—usually by three months of age. Maybe they are different variations of one condition. In a vague way we sense that the age period between birth and about three months is one of adjustment of the baby's immature nervous system and immature digestive system to life in the outside world and that a smooth adjustment is harder for some babies to achieve. Anyway, the important thing to remember is that these most common types of crying in the early weeks are temporary and are not usually a sign of anything serious.

In fact one of your first jobs as a parent is to begin to figure out just what your baby's crying means. You will begin to notice, for example, that her "very hungry" cry is higher-pitched, louder and more insistent than her "slightly uncomfortable" cry, which is softer, lower-pitched and more melodic. Even from another room you will come to learn which cry means "Get in here right this minute!" and which cry means you can wait and see if it stops on its own.

313. Is it hunger? Whether you're feeding your baby on a fairly regular schedule or according to her desire, you soon get an idea of what her pattern is like—at what times of day she wants more to eat, at what times she's apt to wake early. This should help you to decide whether the crying is due to hunger. For example, if your baby took less than half her usual amount at her last feeding, it may be the reason she's awake and crying an hour later, instead of at the usual three hours. Of course, other times a baby who has taken much less than her usual amount may sleep contentedly until her next regular feeding time.

If your baby took an average amount at her last feeding and awakens crying in less than two hours or so, it is even less likely that she is hungry. But if she cries two and a half or three hours after the last feeding, then consider hunger first.

314. Could it be that she has outgrown her formula or the breast-milk supply, or that the supply is decreasing? A baby doesn't outgrow the milk supply all of a sudden. She will have been breast-feeding for a longer time or have been polishing off every bottle for several days and then looking around for more. She begins to wake and cry a little earlier than usual, but not a lot. In most cases, it's only after she has been waking early from hunger for a number of days that she begins crying after a feeding.

I'd sum it up with the following rule of thumb: If a baby has been crying hard for fifteen minutes or more and if it's more than two hours after the last feeding—or if it's less than two hours after a very small feeding—give her another feeding. If this satisfies her and puts her to sleep, you have your answer. If she cries less than two hours after a full feeding, however, it's unlikely that she's hungry.

Listen to the quality of her cry. Does it sound as if she is really unsettled? If so, see if picking her up and holding her does the trick. If she contentedly goes back to sleep, it is less likely she was hungry. If she continues to cry, you can try a feeding or systematically think about other possible causes such as the need to be burped. If her cry is more of a low-pitched whine and she doesn't sound especially upset, leave her alone for ten or fifteen minutes, or as long as you can stand it, and see if she can settle herself down. If not, you can try picking her up and rocking her or give her a pacifier, or whatever usually works and see if she won't go back to sleep. If she's crying harder than ever, there's no harm in feeding her.

315. Is the baby sick? Sometimes babies cry because they just aren't feeling well. Often a baby who is going to become sick first gets very irritable and only later becomes obviously ill. Usually there will be other symptoms aside from crying—like running noise, cough or loose bowels—to tip you off that she's ill. If your baby is not only crying inconsolably, but has any symptoms of illness or looks different in her general appearance, behavior or color, take her temperature and call your doctor or nurse practitioner.

316. Is she crying because she's wet or has had a bowel movement? Most babies don't seem to care especially when they are young infants. But very few seem more fastidious than others. Check the diaper and try changing her.

Check the safety pins; one may be sticking into her. This doesn't happen once in a hundred years, but you can look to be sure. Check for hair and threads wrapped around her fingers or toes.

317. Is it heartburn? Most babies spit up, some more than others. For a few it hurts when the milk comes up because the stomach acid irritates the esophagus (the tube from the mouth to the stomach). Babies who cry from heartburn usually do so soon after feeding, when the milk is still in the stomach. You can try burping the baby again even though you got a burp before. If this kind of crying happens often, you should discuss it with your doctor or nurse practitioner.

318. Is it indigestion? The occasional baby who has a hard time digesting her milk may cry an hour or two after a feeding, when the milk is being most actively digested. If this becomes an early pattern while you are breast-feeding, you should consider changing your own diet—cutting down on milk or caffeine, for example. If you are bottle-feeding, ask your doctor or nurse practitioner if a formula change is worth a try.

319. Is she spoiled? Though older babies can be spoiled, you can be sure that in the first months your baby is not crying because she's spoiled. Something is bothering her.

320. Is it fatigue? Some young babies seem to be made in such a way that they can never drift peacefully into sleep. Their fatigue at the end of every period of being awake produces a tension that is a sort of hump they must get over before falling asleep. They have to cry. Some of them cry frantically and loudly. Then gradually or suddenly the crying stops and they are asleep.

When young babies have been awake an unusually long while or when they have been stimulated more than usual by being with strangers or by being in a strange place or even by being played with by their parents, they may react by becoming tense and irritable. Instead of it being easier for them to fall asleep, it may be harder. If the parents or strangers then try to comfort them with more play, more talk, more jouncing, it only makes matters worse.

So if your baby is crying at the end of a wakeful period and after she has been fed and her diaper changed, try assuming first that she's just tired and put her to bed. If she continues to cry, I'd suggest still leaving her on her own for a few minutes (or as long as you can stand) to give her a chance to settle down by herself. If she can learn early on to put herself to sleep, in the next months she may be able to get to sleep on her own, without too much work on your part, which is a big advantage.

Another baby who has become overfatigued relaxes sooner if kept in gentle motion—by being pushed back and forth in a rocking bassinet, rocked in the carriage, held in your arms or in a carrier and walked quietly, preferably in a darkened room. I would try walking or rocking a baby occasionally during an unusually tense spell, but I wouldn't go on week after week always putting her to sleep this active way. She might become more and more dependent on it and continue to demand it later on. Then you're stuck.

321. Excessive crying after the first two weeks: fretful, hypertonic, colicky or irritable babies. By the time they are a couple of weeks old (in premature infants this usually begins at forty-two weeks gestation) almost all babies have fretful periods that we can give names to but can't explain exactly.

The time babies spend fretting tends to increase until they are six to eight weeks old, and then, mercifully, begins to diminish. For most babies, these fretful periods are brief, happen only once in a while, and quickly cease when the baby's needs are met. But for perhaps one out of ten babies who are healthy and well fed, these crying periods occur more frequently and are much harder to stop. They scream inconsolably, sometimes for long periods. This is the kind of baby people say has "colic." However, colic means pain from the intestines, and it's not at all clear that this is the cause of crying in these infants.

There seem to be two distinct patterns of crying in infants

with colic. For some, the crying is generally limited to one period in the evening—typically 5:00 to 8:00 P.M. The infant is contented and easy to soothe for most of the day, but when evening rolls around, the trouble begins. He cries, sometimes inconsolably, for the next few hours.

This raises a question: what is happening in the early evening that makes him so fretful? If it were indigestion, for example, he would have it at any time of day, not just in the evening. This so-called paroxysmal fussing is a fascinating mystery.

Other infants cry at any and all times of day or night. Some of these infants also seem to be generally somewhat tense and jumpy. Their bodies don't relax well. They startle easily or cry at slight noises or on any quick change of position. If, for instance, a baby is laid on his back on a firm surface and rolls to one side, or if he is held too loosely in the arms, or if the person carrying him moves him too suddenly, he may almost jump out of his skin. He may hate a tub bath for the first couple of months for this reason.

Parents naturally are distressed to have their baby so unhappy and think that something is terribly wrong. They wonder how long the child can keep this up and not become exhausted. They wonder how long they can stand it. The strange thing is that colicky and irritable babies usually prosper from the physical point of view. In spite of hours of crying, they continue to gain weight and appear perfectly healthy.

322. It's hard on the parents of a fretful, hypertonic, colicky, or irritable baby. If your baby is colicky or irritable, she may be soothed when you first pick her up. But after a few minutes she's apt to be screaming harder than ever. She thrashes with her arms and kicks with her legs. She not only refuses to be comforted, she acts as if she were angry at you for trying. These reactions are painful for you. You feel sorry for her, at least in the beginning. Then you feel increasingly inadequate, because you're not able to do anything to relieve her. As the minutes go by and she acts angrier and angrier, you feel that she is spurning you as a parent and you can't help feeling mad at her underneath.

But getting angry at a tiny baby makes you ashamed of yourself, and you try hard to suppress the feeling. This makes you more tense than ever.

We don't really know the reasons for or the meaning of these patterns of crying behavior. We only know that they commonly occur and that they gradually peter out, usually by three or four months of age. There are a lot of theories (each of which may be right some of the time): the baby cries because of an intolerance to the milk (by the way, breast-fed babies have as much colic as bottle-fed infants); the intestinal tract is immature and goes into spasms; the infant is underfed; there is a temporary hormonal imbalance; the nervous system is overly sensitive to the world and is getting too much stimulation; the infant has an intense temperament. . . . You should also know that it is rare for an infant to be colicky because of anything the parent is doing wrong. Generally, colic starts on the inside. The environment can make it better or worse, but it can't cause colic in the first place.

If you have a baby with colic, the first thing to do is have her checked by the doctor or nurse practitioner to make sure there is no obvious medical cause for the crying. Make sure that you are asking all the usual questions when she cries: Could she be hungry? Wet? Sick? Colic is a diagnosis only made after ensuring that the baby is otherwise well fed and healthy.

Once you are told that this is garden-variety colic, you can feel reassured. It almost always goes away by three or four months, for reasons that are as mysterious as why it began in the first place. Additionally, there are no known long-term problems associated with colic. Colicky babies don't grow up to be any more or less happy, smart, or cranky than other babies. The trick for you is to get through the next few months with your confidence and good spirits intact.

323. The treatment of colic. The most important thing is for the mother and father to recognize that the condition is fairly common; that it doesn't seem to do the babies any permanent harm (it seems to occur most often in babies who are developing and growing well) and that it will probably be gone by the time the baby is three or four months old, if not before, leaving the child none the worse for wear. If the parents can accept the condition in a fairly calm and resigned way, the battle is half won.

There are various things you can try to help the situation but first I think you have to come to terms with your feelings about the situation. All parents feel anxious, upset, fearful, and incompetent if they can't calm their infant. Most feel guilty, especially if it is their first baby, as if the baby cries because they are doing something wrong. And most parents also get angry at the baby. This is quite normal. There is no doubt that this squalling creature is turning your life upside down, and it's natural to feel some resentment and anger, even if you know that it's not really your baby's fault, and that he's not crying on purpose, and that he's not really mad at you. Some parents then feel guilty about their angry feelings, as if somehow they are even worse parents because they have these negative feelings. So the first step in dealing with a colicky infant is to come to terms with your feelings about it. You will still experience all the same feelings, but at least you will have some awareness that you are feeling them, and you'll know that all parents go through the same thing. If these negative feelings only intensify, talk to your doctor or nurse practitioner.

Should you hold your baby or rock her gently or carry her around while she has colic? Even if it makes her stop crying, won't it spoil her? We aren't worried nowadays about the danger of spoiling babies, like we used to be. If babies are comforted when they are miserable, they usually don't go on demanding that comfort when they aren't miserable. If babies are screaming with colic or irritability and picking them up or rocking them seems to help them, then do it. If, however, holding them makes them feel no better, it's just as well not to get them used to being held so much.

In consultation with your doctor or nurse practitioner, here are some other things people try with colicky infants (all work some of the time, but none works all of the time): offering a pacifier between feedings (in the immortal words of one pediatrician: "if only to obstruct the orifice from which the cacophonous sound emanates"); swaddling the baby snugly in a receiving blanket; rocking her in a cradle or carriage; using a front carrier for long walks; taking her for a ride in the car; a swing (although most infants get bored and start crying again after a few minutes); giving her a belly massage (with lubricating lotion); placing a hot-water bottle on her belly; trying some herbal tea, a formula change or, if you're breast-feeding, a change in your diet (for example, no milk or caffeine); or playing music. You can also try laying her across your knees or a hot-water bottle and massaging her on the back. You should be able to rest the inside of your wrist against the hot-water bottle without discomfort. Then, as an extra precaution, wrap it in a diaper or towel before laying the baby against it or half on it.

Hypertonic babies often do best on a quiet regime: quiet room, few visitors, low voices, slow movements in handling them, a firm hold in carrying them, a big pillow (with a waterproof cover) to lie on while being changed and sponge-bathed so that they won't roll, or swaddling in a receiving blanket most of the time.

If none of these methods work and if the baby is not hungry, wet, or sick, then what? I think it's perfectly acceptable to put the baby down in his crib, let him cry for a while, and see if he can calm himself. It's hard to listen to a crying infant without trying to do *something,* but realistically what else is there for you to do, except maybe acquire hearing loss from his crying right into your ear? Some even believe it is helpful to allow the baby to try to calm himself during these times so he acquires a knack for it. Some parents can go out for a little walk and let the baby cry; others can't bear to leave the room. Do whatever feels right for you—there is simply no right or wrong way to handle this situation. After a period of time, pick your baby up again if she is still crying and try everything all over again.

Those are things you can do for your baby. You should also ask what you can do for yourself. You may be the kind of parent who isn't bothered too much after you have found out that there is nothing seriously wrong with her and after you have done all that you can to make her happy. That's fine, if you are made that way. But many parents get worn out and frantic listening to a baby cry, especially when it's the first. It is particularly difficult for the mother if she is with the baby constantly. She should make a great effort to get away from home and the baby for a few hours at least twice a week—more often if it can be arranged. It's best if the parents can go out together. Hire a sitter or ask a friend or neighbor to come in and relieve the mother.

If you're like many other parents, you may hesitate to do this. "Why should we inflict the baby on somebody else? Besides, we'd be nervous being away for so long." But you shouldn't think of time off like this as just a treat for you. It's very important for you, for the baby, and for your spouse that you not get exhausted and depressed. If you can't get anyone to come in, the parents can take turns one or two evenings a week to go out to visit friends or see a movie. Your baby doesn't need two worried parents at a time to listen to her. Try also to get friends to come in and visit you. Remember that everything that helps you keep a sense of balance, everything that keeps you from getting too preoccupied with the baby, also helps the baby and the rest of the family in the long run.

Can You Spoil a Baby?

324. This question comes up naturally in the first few weeks at home if a baby is fussing a lot between feedings instead of sleeping peacefully. You pick him up and walk him around and he stops crying, at least for the time being. Lay him down, and he starts all over again. I don't think you need to worry much about spoiling in the first month or even the first six months. The chances are great that such a young baby is feeling miserable. If he stops fussing when picked up, it's probably because the motion and distraction and perhaps the warm pressure on his abdomen from being held make him forget his pain or tension at least temporarily.

The answer to this question really depends on what lessons you think babies are learning in the first months of life. It is unlikely that they are capable of learning to expect their every whim to be attended to twenty-four hours a day. That's what being spoiled would mean. But we know that young infants can't anticipate the future; they live entirely in the here and now. They also can't formulate this thought:

"Well I'm going to make life miserable for these people until they give me everything I want"—another key component of the spoiled child.

What infants are learning during this period is a sense of basic trust (or mistrust) in the world. If their needs are met promptly and lovingly, they come to feel that the world is a benign place, a place where good things generally happen and bad experiences are soon rectified. The famous psychiatrist Erik Erikson felt that this sense of basic trust becomes a core of the baby's character. So the answer to the question "Can a young baby be spoiled?" is no, not until he's old enough to understand why his needs aren't being immediately met—(maybe at nine months of age). I would change the question altogether to ask: How can you instill a sense of basic trust in babies?

325. You can be a little more suspicious by six months. By the time babies are six months old, colic and other causes of physical discomfort are behind them. Naturally, some of these babies who were held and walked a great deal during their colicky period have become accustomed to constant attention. They want their walking and their company to continue.

Let's take the example of a mother who can't stand to hear her baby fret, even for a minute, and who carries him most of the time he's awake. By the age of six months he cries immediately and holds out his arms to be picked up as soon as she puts him down. Housework has become impossible. She can't help resenting her enslavement, but she can't tolerate the indignant crying either. This situation is different from that of a mother in our society, or in a simpler one, who willingly picks up her baby at the slightest whimper or carries him in a sling all day even if he doesn't fret. I suspect that the tense parent's original anxiety was communicated to the baby and made him uneasy, and certainly he feels her increasing resentment. This combination sets up a tug-of-war.

326. Why does a parent get involved in these ordinary types of spoiling? In the first place, it usually happens with the first baby. For most people a first baby is the most fascinating plaything in the world. If an adult can be obsessed for a while with a new car, it's easy to see why a baby is all-absorbing for months.

But delight is not the only factor. Parents are apt to project all the hopes and fears they've had about themselves onto their firstborn. There's the anxiety, too, the unfamiliar sense of being entirely responsible for the safety and happiness of a helpless human being. The baby's crying makes a powerful demand on you to *do something.* But you are not always sure what is the best thing to do. With your second baby you have more assurance and a sense of proportion; you know that children have to be denied some things for their own good and you don't feel guilty about being hard-hearted when you know for sure you're doing the right thing.

But some parents are more easily drawn into spoiling than others—for instance, parents who have had to wait a long time for a baby and suspect that they may not be able to have another; parents with too little confidence in their own worthiness who become willing slaves to a child and expect her or him to be all the things they felt they never could be; parents who have adopted a baby and feel that they have to do a superhuman job to justify themselves; parents who have studied child psychology in college or have worked professionally in the field and feel doubly obligated to prove their capability (actually, it can be a tougher job when you know the theory); parents who are ashamed when they've felt cross at the baby and try to even things up by giving him anything he wants; parents who feel angry or guilty when they hear a baby crying and find the tension unbearable.

Whatever the underlying factor, all these parents are a little too willing to sacrifice their own comforts and their own rights by giving their babies anything they ask for. This might not be too bad if babies knew what was sensible to ask for. But they don't know what's good for them. It's their nature to expect guidance from the parents. This comforts them. When the parents are hesitant, it makes babies uneasy. If parents always anxiously pick babies up whenever they fuss—as if it would be terrible to leave them there—the babies, too, get the feeling that this would be terrible.

And the more parents submit to the babies' orders, the more demanding the children become. Parents then feel like slaves. The trouble is, this is when parents feel cross; later they feel guilty and give in again.

327. How do you unspoil? The earlier you detect the problem, the easier it is to cure. But it takes a lot of willpower and a little hardening of the heart to say "no" to your baby, and in one way or another set limits. To get yourself in the right mood you have to remember that, in the long run, unreasonable demandingness and excessive dependence are worse for babies than for you and get them off kilter with themselves and with the world. So you are reforming them for their own good.

Make out a schedule for yourself, on paper if necessary, that requires you to be busy with housework or anything else for most of the time the baby is awake. Go at it with a great bustle—to impress the baby and to impress yourself. Say you are the mother of a baby boy who has become accustomed to being carried all the time. When he frets and raises his arms, explain to him in a friendly but very firm tone that this job and that job must get done this afternoon. Though he doesn't understand the words, he does understand the tone of voice. Stick to your busywork. The first hour of the first day is the hardest.

One baby accepts the change better if his mother stays out of sight a good part of the time at first and talks little. This helps him to become absorbed in something else. Another adjusts more quickly if he can at least see his mother and hear her talking to him, even if she won't pick him up. When you bring him a plaything or show him how to use it, or when you decide it's time to play with him a bit at the end of the afternoon, sit down beside him on the floor. Let him climb into your arms if he wants, but don't get back into the habit of walking him around. If you're on the floor with him, he can crawl away when he eventually realizes you won't walk. If you pick him up and walk him, he'll surely object noisily just as soon as you start to put him down again. If he keeps on fretting indefinitely when you sit with him on the floor, remember another job and get busy again.

What you are trying to do is to help your baby begin to

build frustration tolerance—a little at a time. If she does not learn this gradually from early infancy, it is a much harder lesson to learn later on.

Letting Babies Cry

I never had a let-them-cry philosophy. In Section 773 I discuss **chronic resistance to sleep,** a relatively uncommon, long-lasting problem that takes months to develop. There are two forms of this problem. In the first, a baby learns how to fight against being put to bed in the early evening in the first half year. In the second form, an older baby learns to fight against being put *back* to bed after waking in the middle of the night; this happens in the last part of the first year or in the early part of the second year. In both cases the resistance to being put to bed is favored by the fact that the parent is unusually kindhearted, perhaps even slightly submissive by nature. He or she keeps trying to put the baby to bed but quickly gives up when the child—who learns by repeated success to be more dominating, more of a bully, despite the great difference in age—objects noisily.

Though I am an advocate of kindness to babies—and to parents—I found through experience that to successfully treat this special problem of chronic resistance to sleep that it was essential to persuade the parent to be less willing to be bullied, to realize that she has to know what is sensible and to be able to apply it. I was further encouraged by the fact that though the problem had been getting worse for weeks and months, it could usually be cured in only a few days or weeks if the parent got up the determination to insist that the baby go to bed or go back to bed at night. Accomplishing this might take twenty minutes of indignant crying at first, then ten minutes, and within a few days or weeks, none.

Another requirement is that the parent not go back into the baby's room, turn on the light, or pick the baby up. These signals to the baby that the parent is about to give in again will stir up fresh determination and crying until the baby is in the parent's arms and being walked again.

I was encouraged further by the relief and delight of the parent who had been carrying the baby first for an hour, then for two or three or even four hours, to find that the problem could be solved so easily.

Stranger Anxiety

328. How a baby feels about strangers. You can get an idea of how your baby goes from phase to phase in development by watching his reaction to strangers at different ages. This is how it goes in a doctor's office for a typical baby until he's about a year old. At two months he doesn't pay much attention to the doctor. As he lies on the examining table, he keeps looking over his shoulder at his mother. The four-month-old is the doctor's delight. He breaks into a body-wiggling smile just as often as the doctor is willing to smile and make noises at him. By five or six months, the baby may have begun to change his mind; by nine months he is certain: the doctor is a stranger and therefore to be feared! When the doctor approaches, he stops his kicking and cooing. His body freezes as he eyes the doctor intently, even suspiciously, maybe for 20 seconds. Then his abdomen begins to rise and fall rapidly. Finally his chin puckers and he begins to shriek. He may get so worked up that he cries long after the examination is over.

This is a sensitive period, when a baby may take alarm at anything unfamiliar, such as his mother's hat or even his father's clean-shaven face if he is used to seeing his father with a beard. This behavior is called *stranger anxiety* and it's very interesting to think about what has changed to make your baby go from loving everyone to being a suspicious worry wart. First, starting around six months of age, babies begin to be able to bring things or people to mind who are not right in front of them. This is called *retrieval memory.* For the first months the baby only had *recognition memory;* that is, he could recognize his parents and preferred them, but didn't really think about them when they were not in his line of sight. With the onset of retrieval memory, he can bring up the image of his mother or father, even if they are not in his line of sight, and compare it to the unknown person in front of him. If the baby can't retrieve a memory of the stranger in front of him, he becomes worried: who is this guy anyway?

At six to nine months the infant still can't formulate reasonable hypotheses of what might happen next, based on past experience. He lives pretty much in the present. So when there is a stranger right in front of him, he can't understand why it's not a familiar person, and he can't figure out any good that will come of this situation. Finally, the non-ambulatory infant has few options for resolving his uncertainty. He can't run and he can't hide. He becomes anxious and cries.

By fifteen months, when stranger anxiety is generally gone, the infant has the ability to learn from the past and anticipate the future: "Maybe I don't know who this person is but in the past my mother has come back and everything has been OK, so I can handle this stranger without panicking."

So stranger anxiety is a common and developmentally predictable phase that peaks at about nine months and goes away at about fifteen months. If your baby seems especially sensitive about new people and new places in the middle of the first year, I'd protect him from too much fright by making strangers keep at a little distance until he gets used to them. Don't keep him from seeing strangers, though.

Developmental Gains

Play Is the Work of Babies

329. Be companionable with your baby. Be quietly friendly with your baby whenever you are with him. He's getting a sense of how much you mean to each other all the time you're feeding him, burping him, bathing him, dressing him, changing his diapers, holding him, or just sitting in the room with him. When you hug him or make noises at him, when you show him that you think he's the most wonderful baby in the world, it makes his spirit grow, just the way food makes his bones grow. That must be why we grown-ups instinctively talk baby talk and waggle our heads when we greet a baby.

One trouble with being an inexperienced parent is that part of the time you take the job so seriously that you forget to enjoy it. Then you and the baby are both missing out on something. Your baby will be fully grown and out of the house before you know it, and you'll wonder why you didn't spend more time just enjoying him.

Naturally I don't mean that you should be talking a blue streak at him all the time he's awake, or constantly joggling him or tickling him. That would tire him out and, in the long run, would make him tense and spoiled. You can be quiet nine-tenths of the time you are with him. It's the gentle, easygoing kind of companionship that's good for him and good for you. It's the comfortable feeling that goes into your arms when you hold him, the fond, peaceful expression on your face when you look at him, and the gentle tone in your voice.

330. Companionship without spoiling. It's good for a baby during his play periods to be somewhere near his parents (and brothers and sisters, if any) so that he can see them, make noises at them, hear them speak to him, have them show him a way to play with something occasionally. But it isn't necessary or sensible for him to be in a parent's lap or arms or to have his mother or father amusing him much of the time. He can be enjoying their company, profiting from it, and still be learning how to occupy himself. When new parents are so delighted with their baby that they hold him or make games for him most of his waking hours, he may become quite dependent on these attentions and demand more and more of them.

331. Things to watch and things to play with. Young babies begin waking earlier and earlier, especially at the end of the afternoon. At such times they want something to do and they want some companionship. At two to four months, they enjoy looking at brightly colored things that move. Outdoors, they are delighted to watch leaves and shadows. Indoors, they study their hands, pictures on the wall. There are brightly colored plastic shapes on strings that you can suspend between the top rails of the crib. Place them just within arm's reach—not right on top of baby's nose—for the time when he begins reaching. You can make mobiles yourself—cardboard shapes covered with colored paper that hang from the ceiling or from a lighting fixture and rotate in slight drafts (they aren't strong enough for playing with or healthful for chewing)—or you can hang suitable household objects, like spoons or plastic cups, within reach.

Remember that eventually everything goes into the mouth. As babies get toward the middle of their first year, their greatest joy is handling and mouthing objects: collections of plastic objects linked together (made for this age), rattles, teething rings, animals and dolls of cloth, household objects that are safe in the mouth. Don't let a baby or small child have objects or furniture that have been repainted with outdoor paint containing lead, or thin celluloid toys that can be chewed into small, sharp pieces, or small glass beads and other small objects that can be choked on.

Clothes and Equipment

332. Shoes: when and what kind? In most cases there's no need to put anything on your baby's feet until he is walking outdoors. Indoors their feet stay cool just the way their hands do, so they aren't uncomfortable barefoot. In other words, there's no necessity for knitted booties or soft shoes in the first year unless the house or the floor is unusually cold.

After a baby is standing and walking there's a real value in leaving the child barefoot most of the time when conditions are suitable. The arches are relatively flat at first. The baby gradually builds the arches up and strengthens the ankles by using them vigorously in standing and walking. (I suppose the reason that the soles of the feet are ticklish and sensitive under the arch is to remind us to keep that part arched up off the ground.) Walking on an uneven or rough surface also fosters the use of the foot and leg muscles.

Of course, a child who is walking needs shoes outdoors in cold weather and when walking on pavements and other surfaces that are hazardous. But it's good for a child to continue to go barefoot (or with socks) indoors till the age of two or three and outdoors, too, in warm weather at the beach, in the sandbox, and in other safe places.

Semi-soft soled shoes are best at first, so that your child's feet have a better chance to move. Shoes with fancy "supports" are pretty much a waste of money. The important thing is to have the shoes big enough so that the toes aren't cramped, but not so big that they almost slip off.

Small children outgrow their shoes at a discouragingly fast rate, sometimes in two months, and parents should form the habit of feeling the shoes every few weeks to make sure they are still large enough. There must be more than just enough space for the toes, because as the child walks, the toes are squeezed up into the front of the shoe with each step. There should be enough empty space in the toe of the shoe, as the child stands, so that you can get about half your thumbnail (about $\frac{1}{4}$ inch) onto the tip of the shoe before running into the child's toe. You can't judge while the child is sitting down since the feet fill more of the shoe when a person is standing up. Naturally, the shoes should be comfortably wide, too. There are soft adjustable shoes which can be let out a full size. It's helpful to have a nonskid sole so your child learns to walk before he learns to skate. You can rough up a smooth sole with coarse sandpaper.

I recommend inexpensive shoes if they fit well. Sneakers are just fine as long as they don't cause excessive sweating. The feet are pudgy the first couple of years, and as a result, low shoes sometimes do not stay on as well as high-top shoes. There isn't any other reason for ankle-high shoes; the ankles don't need the support.

333. Use of the playpen. I think a playpen is a great help, especially for the busy parent, from about three months on. Set up in the living room or the kitchen, where the caregiver is working, it gives babies the company that they can't have in their own rooms and a chance to see everything that is going on without the danger of being stepped on or spilled on. When they are old enough to stand up, the pen gives them a railing to hold onto and a firm foundation under their feet. In good weather they can sit safely in the playpen on the porch and watch the world go by.

Each afternoon when the baby becomes bored with his crib, put him in the playpen near where you are working or sitting. If you are going to use a pen, the baby should become accustomed to it at three or four months, before he has learned to sit and crawl and before he has had the freedom of the floor. Otherwise he might consider it a prison from the start. By the time he can sit and crawl, he has fun going after things that are a few feet away, handling larger objects like cooking spoons, saucepans, strainers. When he becomes bored with the playpen, he can sit in a bouncing chair or a chair-table arrangement. It's good for him to end up with some free creeping.

Even if they are willing, babies should not be kept in pens all the time. They need time for explorative crawling, while the parent pays attention. They should, every hour or so, be played with, hugged, perhaps carried around in a chest carrier for a spell while the parent works. Between twelve and eighteen months they will tolerate the playpen for shorter and shorter periods.

334. Swings. A swing is useful after babies have learned to sit and before they learn to walk. Some swings are for indoors or out, some have windup motors, some are for use in doorways, others have springs so the baby can bounce. The springs should have covers to prevent finger injury, or the coils should not be more than $\frac{1}{8}$ inch apart. A swing may keep your baby happy for a period of time—some for quite a while and others soon grow bored. A swing keeps her from getting into as much trouble as she would creeping, but she shouldn't be kept in it all the time she's up. She needs lots of opportunities to creep, explore, stand, and walk.

335. Walkers used to be very popular, because they're a kind of baby-sitter and some people think they help babies learn to walk earlier. Actually walkers thwart learning to walk because all the infant has to do is thrash her legs and not worry about balance. Very different skills are needed to walk, but the baby may be less motivated to learn them. After all, she gets around fine under her own steam. Why learn something new, like walking, that is more difficult to do and, initially, less efficient?

Walkers are also dangerous and have been responsible for many injuries. They raise the baby's height, so that she can reach objects that may hurt her; they raise her center of gravity so that it's easier for her to tip over; and they allow her to move forward at an amazingly fast rate. The worst injuries have come from babies falling down flights of stairs in their walkers.

As far as I'm concerned the manufacture of baby walkers should be discontinued. I don't recommend one.

Common Physical Issues in the First Year

Consult your doctor or nurse practitioner promptly about any change in your baby's health. Don't try to diagnose it yourself—there is too much chance of error. There are many other causes of the problems mentioned here. This discussion is primarily to help parents to adjust to a few common types of mild physical concerns of early infancy, after the doctor or nurse practitioner has made a diagnosis.

336. Hiccups. Most babies hiccup pretty regularly after meals in the early months. In fact many babies can be seen hiccuping on the prenatal ultrasound and can be felt hiccuping during the end of pregnancy. It doesn't seem to mean anything, and there is nothing that you need to do, aside from seeing if they have to burp. A drink of warm water occasionally stops the hiccups if you want to try something.

337. Spitting up and vomiting are common. The term "spitting up" is popularly used when the stomach contents spill gently out of the baby's mouth, usually in small amounts. The muscle valve at the upper end of the stomach just doesn't hold the contents down well, the way it does in an older child or adult. Any movement may cause the spitting: joggling, squeezing too tightly, laying the baby down, or just the digestive motions of the stomach itself. Most babies do considerable spitting up during the early months, and this is usually of no significance. Some spit up several times after every feeding. Others do it only occasionally. (Remember: milk stains can be more easily removed from sheets, diapers, and clothing if they are first soaked in cold water.)

In most babies the tendency to spit up is greatest in the early weeks and months, and decreases as they get older. Most have stopped it altogether by the time they can sit up. Occasionally it goes on until the child is walking. Once in a while babies only start spitting when they are several months old. Sometimes teething seems to make it worse for a while. Spitting is messy and inconvenient but not important if the baby is gaining weight well, isn't bothered by coughing or gagging, and is happy.

The word "vomiting" is used when the stomach contents are ejected with enough force to propel them at least a few inches away from the mouth. It alarms new parents when their baby first vomits a large amount of milk. But this is not serious in itself if the baby seems otherwise happy and healthy and is infrequent. There are a few babies who vomit a large amount as often as once a day, especially in the early weeks. Naturally, if your baby spits or vomits regularly even though continuing to gain weight, you should discuss it with the doctor or nurse practitioner—particularly if there are other signs of indigestion. It is worthwhile taking extra care to burp the baby, but in most cases the spitting or vomiting goes right on, no matter how you change the formula, decrease the quantity, or burp him.

If babies have vomited what seems like their whole feeding, should they be fed again right away? If they seem happy enough, don't feed them, at least until they act very hungry. The stomach may be a little upset, and it is better to give it a chance to quiet down. Remember that the amount vomited usually looks larger than it actually is. There are babies who you would swear are vomiting most of every feeding but who still go on gaining satisfactorily.

338. Whether or not the spit-up milk is sour and curdled is not important. The first step in digestion in the stomach is the secretion of acid. Any food that has been in the stomach for a while is acidified. The effect of acid on milk is to curdle it.

Occasionally the valve between the esophagus (the tube that leads from the mouth to the stomach) and the stomach isn't as strong in some babies as it is in others. Such a baby might then be more likely to spit up frequently (and less commonly to vomit) if you lay her down right after a feeding, because the milk leaks out from the stomach back up into the esophagus *(gastro-esophageal reflux, or GER)*. In these situations, the baby may not be gaining weight as well as you want her to and the doctor may suggest keeping her on her stomach with her head above her tummy after each feeding and thickening the feedings with rice cereal. In some cases, medication is necessary to prevent the milk from escaping up the esophagus, causing pain, irritability, poor weight gain, and possibly pneumonia.

All that I have been saying about how common it is for babies to spit and to vomit occasionally doesn't mean that you never have to take vomiting seriously. A baby who begins vomiting all feedings right after birth must be watched carefully by the doctor. Usually it's due to mucus in the stomach and clears up in a few days, but once in a great while it's more serious, especially if there is green bile in it, and requires prompt medical or surgical treatment.

If your baby has not been a vomiter and then suddenly vomits a large amount for the first time, it's a good idea to take his temperature to make sure he doesn't have an infection. If there is no fever and the baby looks entirely normal, don't worry. If the baby seems sick in any other way or vomits again, call the doctor or nurse practitioner.

Any persistent vomiting that comes on suddenly later in infancy, especially if there is pain or if there is green bile in the vomitus, may indicate an obstruction of the intestines. It requires immediate attention.

339. Worrisome vomiting in pyloric stenosis. An uncommon form of vomiting is most apt to begin when the baby is several weeks old. It is called *pyloric stenosis.* In this condition, the valve leading from the far end of the stomach into the intestines will not open up satisfactorily to let the food through. It is more common in boy babies. The food is vomited out with great force *(projectile vomiting),* so that it lands at a distance from the baby's mouth. The vomiting may occur during or shortly after the feeding. It doesn't mean that your baby has this condition if he has projectile vomiting once in a while. But if he has projectile vomiting as often as twice a day, call your doctor or nurse practitioner for an evaluation. If the diagnosis is definite, a simple operation will probably be necessary.

340. Mild indigestion and gas. Occasionally, babies may develop a spell of indigestion that is chronic. Common symptoms are discomfort and fretting, passing gas by rectum, increased spitting up and vomiting, bowel movements that are partly loose, partly curdy, and perhaps greenish. These are cases where a change in formula can be considered. It is absolutely necessary to consult a doctor or nurse practitioner if a baby is having trouble and not gaining weight.

341. Changes in the color of the stool. Nothing seems to upset some parents as much as a change in the color of bowel movements. Brown, yellow or green—it simply doesn't matter. Like designer fashions, bowel movements come in many colors. None is healthier than the next. You should be concerned if the bowel movement turns black (this could indicate lots of blood, which turns black and tarry-looking as it goes down the intestines), red, or chalk white, which can indicate a problem with the bile.

Constipation

342. What's constipation and what isn't? Generally speaking, constipation refers to hard, dry stools that are difficult to pass. It's not the number of bowel movements each day which determines whether or not a baby (or older child or adult) has constipation. Occasionally, passing hard stools can cause small streaks of red blood on the stool. While not uncommon, any blood in the stool should be discussed with your doctor or nurse practitioner.

One baby always has a bowel movement at the same time of day, another at a different time each day. Some babies do have more than one bowel movement a day, and others go days without having a bowel movement. One is just as healthy as the other. There is no advantage to be gained by trying to make the irregular baby regular. In the first place, it usually can't be done. In the second place, there's a danger, in the long run, of upsetting babies emotionally if you keep trying to get a movement out of them when they aren't ready.

343. Constipation in the breast-fed baby. It isn't constipation when a breast-fed baby has a movement only every other day, or even every several days, as long as the movement is still very soft. There is no reason why a baby needs to have a movement every day. Breast-fed babies more than formula-fed babies commonly have infrequent movements after the first few months.

Constipation may occur when the older breast-fed baby is first begun on solid foods. It seems as though his intestine has had such an easy time with the breast milk, it doesn't know what to do with more complicated foods. The baby develops firm, infrequent stools and seems uncomfortable. You can offer a little sugar water (1 teaspoon of granulated sugar to 2 ounces of water) or prune juice (start with two ounces and work your way up) or stewed prunes (start with two teaspoons a day and work your way up). Some babies get cramps from prunes but most take it well. Usually constipation is a temporary problem, but if it lasts longer than a week, check with the doctor or nurse practitioner.

344. Hard movements with the bottle-fed baby. Constipation also occurs when the movements of a baby on commercially prepared formula become hard and formed. They may be uncomfortable for the baby to pass. Consult your doctor or nurse practitioner about this. You can try the same two remedies as suggested above for breast-fed babies.

Diarrhea

345. Mild diarrhea is common in babies. A baby's intestine is sensitive during the first year or two, and may be upset not only by the germs that cause diarrhea but also by other mild germs, or by a new food, or by too much fruit juice. Fortunately, this kind of upset is usually mild and of no great consequence. There are a couple of extra stools that are looser than usual. Commonly they are greenish and the odor may be different. The most important characteristic of this kind of mild diarrhea is that the baby acts well or almost well. He is playful, active, urinating as often as usual, and doesn't have more in the way of illness than perhaps a slightly stuffy nose or a mild decrease in appetite. In a couple of days, without any special treatment, the symptoms usually disappear. You can offer some extra water or diluted juice, or remove a food that has been added recently. If the diarrhea lasts more than two or three days, you should consult your doctor or nurse practitioner, even if the baby continues to act healthy.

It used to be that a baby with mild diarrhea would be taken off solids and formula and instead given a lot of liquids that are high in sugar (such as Jell-O water, soda, or apple juice). But now research has shown that this traditional "diarrhea diet" actually increases and prolongs diarrhea. So for mild, brief infant diarrhea, offer breast milk or formula and the baby's regular diet, and let him eat as much as he seems hungry for. This is what works best.

346. Severe diarrhea in babies. If a baby with diarrhea isn't back to normal in a couple of days, or has more than a few extra stools a day, has pus or blood in his stools, or is vomiting, has fever, or seems generally ill, you must contact your doctor or nurse practitioner promptly.

Vomiting and severe diarrhea are potentially dangerous, especially in infants, because of the possibility of *dehydration.* This occurs when the baby has not been able to take in as much water as he has lost through diarrhea or vomiting. As a result there is less and less water available for his body's needs.

When dehydration is mild, the baby has lost up to about 5 percent of his weight. His mouth may be a little dry and his tears not as abundant. He may urinate less often than usual but generally looks alert and restless. He often acts thirsty.

When dehydration is moderate, the baby may have lost up to 10 percent of his weight. The mouth is very dry, tears are diminished in volume or absent, the skin feels dry and doughy, the eyes look sunken in, and there is little urine output. At this stage, which is quite serious if the dehydration progresses, the infant is irritable or lethargic.

When dehydration is severe, the baby has lost more than 10 percent of his weight. This is a life-threatening emergency because there is not enough water in the blood system to maintain a normal blood pressure—a condition known as *shock.* The infant looks very ill and is pale with cool, clammy skin, very dry mouth, no tears, and appears very lethargic. Urine output is absent or very low. Breathing becomes rapid and shallow.

If your baby has ongoing diarrhea and/or vomiting, it's wise to stay in close touch with your doctor or nurse practitioner, especially if there is any question of dehydration. Usually babies will not get dehydrated if they are frequently offered plenty of liquids. Their thirst tells them to drink as much as they need so as not to get dehydrated. You might consider purchasing an oral rehydration solution from your pharmacy if the diarrhea seems severe or prolonged and you are concerned that he might be getting dehydrated. This is sugar water with the right proportion of minerals and sugar to replenish the body during times of diarrhea or vomiting. If your baby is not particularly ill, however, the usual formula and diet should work just fine.

Rashes

Consult your doctor or nurse practitioner about all rashes. It's easy to be mistaken.

347. Simple diaper rash. Most babies have sensitive skin in the early months. The diaper region is particularly apt to suffer because diapers retain water next to the tender skin and don't allow the area to "breathe." In fact, any of us would get a rash in the groin if we had to wear a diaper twenty-four hours a day.

That's why the best treatment for almost any diaper rash is usually to allow the baby to go diaperless for as long as is possible—a few hours a day is ideal. Right after a bowel movement, for example, is a good time to let him hang in the breeze, since there is less likelihood of action in that area in the near future. Fold a diaper underneath your baby or put him on a large waterproof pad and try to keep the diaper under him. The warm air and lack of contact with any material usually does the trick. Almost all babies develop a few spots of diaper rash from time to time. If it is slight and goes away as fast as it came, no special treatment is necessary, except air drying.

Don't wash the diaper area with soap while there is a

rash, because soap can be irritating. Use plain water instead of diaper wipes. You can give the skin a protective coating by slathering on petroleum jelly or any of the diaper ointments. Diaper services use special rinses in the case of diaper rash, and it may be worthwhile to use a diaper service while the rash is bad. If you wash the diapers at home, you can add $\frac{1}{2}$ cup of clear white vinegar to the last rinse.

348. Urine irritation. Most diaper rash in older babies is caused by the baby's skin being in prolonged contact with the warm, acidic urine. It used to be thought that ammonia, which is manufactured out of the urine by bacteria, was usually the cause of diaper rash, especially in older babies. But recent research has shown that it's the urine itself, not the ammonia, that causes the rash.

349. Seborrheic rash. If there is a bright red rash, worse in the skin folds than on the prominences, it may be a seborrheic rash. Seborrheic rashes usually also occur behind the ears and on the neck and the baby may also have obvious crusts in the scalp *(cradle cap,* see Section 358). This usually responds to a steroid cream or ointment, which your doctor or nurse practitioner may prescribe.

350. Bacterial and yeast rash. If there are many pimples with pus in them, and especially if the baby develops fever, this may be a rash caused by bacteria for which your doctor may need to prescribe an antibiotic. A yeast rash will have bright red spots that often come together to form an area which is solidly red, bordered by the red spots. The folds in the diaper area usually have a bright red color, with bright red spots on the prominences. The doctor will prescribe a special anti-yeast cream for this rash.

351. Diarrhea rash. Irritating bowel movements during an attack of diarrhea sometimes cause a very sore rash around the anus or a smooth, bright red rash on the buttocks. The treatment is to try to change the diaper just as soon as it is soiled—which is no small task. Then clean the area with oil or if the area is too sore to wipe, hold the baby's bottom under warm water from a running faucet, pat him dry, and apply a thick covering of an ointment made with petroleum jelly and lanolin. If this doesn't work, the diaper should be left off and the diaper area exposed to the air. Sometimes it seems that while the baby has diarrhea, nothing helps very much. Fortunately, this rash cures itself as soon as the diarrhea is over.

352. Mild face rashes. There are several mild face rashes that babies have in the first few months that aren't definite enough to have names but are very common.

353. Milia. These are minute shiny white pimples without any redness around them. They look like tiny pearls in the skin. In this case, the oil glands in the skin are making oil but they haven't opened up to the skin yet, so the oil packets just sit there. Over the next weeks or months, the oil ducts open up and the oil is expressed.

354. Acne. Some babies have collections of a few small red spots or smooth pimples on the cheeks and forehead. They look like acne, and that's exactly what they are. They are caused by exposure to the mother's hormones in the womb. These may last a long time and get a parent quite upset. At times they fade and then get red again. Different ointments don't seem to do much good, but these spots always go away eventually.

355. Erythema toxicum. There may also be splotchy red patches that are $\frac{1}{4}$ inch to $\frac{1}{2}$ inch in diameter, some of them with a tiny white pimple head. They come and go on different parts of the face and body. We don't know what causes this common rash, but once it goes away, it doesn't come back. Larger, pus-filled blisters or pimples could be infections and should be reported promptly to the doctor or nurse practitioner.

356. Sucking blisters. Some babies are born with blisters on their lips or hands or wrist, caused by finger-sucking in the womb. Other babies develop white dry blisters in the middle part of their lips from sucking. Sometimes the blisters peel. These clear up in time with no special treatment.

357. Prickly heat. Prickly heat is very common in the shoulder and neck region of babies when hot weather first begins. It is made up of clusters of very small pink pimples surrounded by blotches of pink skin. Tiny blisters form on some of the pimples. When they dry up they can give the rash a slightly tan look. Prickly heat usually starts around the neck. If it is bad, it can spread down onto the chest and back and up around the ears and face, but it seldom bothers a baby. You can pat this rash several times a day with a bicarbonate of soda solution (1 teaspoon bicarbonate of soda to 1 cup water) on absorbent cotton. Another treatment is dusting with cornstarch powder (we don't recommend talcum powder anymore because it is very irritating to the lungs if accidentally inhaled). Most forms of prickly heat do not need any treatment. It goes away eventually. It is more important to try to keep the baby cool. Don't be afraid to take off the baby's clothes in hot weather. After all, there's no evidence that early experiences with nakedness lead to children growing up to be nudists.

358. Cradle cap. Cradle cap *(seborrhea)* is a mild disorder of the skin of the scalp caused by making too much oil, which crusts over and may irritate the skin. It is quite common in the early months. It appears as scalp patches that look like honey colored crusts. The best treatment is daily washing with soap and water. You can try oiling the patches to soften them and then washing with a mild dandruff shampoo and brushing out the scales that come from the patches. Don't leave the oil on for too long before shampooing it out, since the problem is caused by too much oil in the first place. Cradle cap rarely persists beyond the early months.

359. Impetigo. Impetigo is a bacterial infection of the skin. It's not generally serious, but it is contagious and should be treated promptly by your doctor or nurse practitioner. It starts with a very delicate small blister that contains yellowish fluid or white pus and is surrounded by reddened skin. The blister is easily broken and leaves a small raw spot. It does not develop a thick crust in infants as it does in older children. It's apt to start in a moist place, such as the edge of the diaper or in the groin or armpit. New spots may develop. If you cannot reach your doctor, the best method is to carefully wipe off the blister with a piece of cotton, so as not to spread the pus onto the surrounding skin, and then leave the raw spot exposed to the air. Do not pop the blisters. You can also rub a little antibacterial ointment on it. Arrange the clothing and bedclothes so that they do not cover the spot or spots, and keep the room warmer than usual if necessary. During impetigo, disinfect the diapers, sheets, underclothing, nighties, towels, and washcloths. Using ordinary hypochlorite bleach in the wash, according to the directions on the bottle, works well.

Birthmarks and Other Skin Conditions

Birthmarks

360. Salmon patches. Many babies have a collection of red, irregularly shaped spots on the nape of the neck ("stork bites"), upper eyelids ("angel's kiss"), or between the eyebrows when they are born. These blotches are nests of little blood vessels that have grown because of exposure to the mother's hormones in the womb. Most disappear gradually (although "stork bites" may persist) and nothing needs to be done for them.

361. Port wine stains. Areas of skin that are flat and have a deep purplish-red coloring may occur on the temples and cheeks or on other parts of the body. Some of these stains do fade, particularly the lighter ones, but others are permanent. Laser treatments are now used for some of the larger permanent port-wine stains. Occasionally, this rash can be associated with other problems.

362. Mongolian spots. These are slate-blue patches in the skin of dark-skinned babies. They're usually around the buttocks, but may be scattered anywhere. They are simply little areas of increased pigment in the top layer of the skin.

They almost always disappear completely in the first two years.

363. Strawberry marks. These fairly common marks are growths of very small blood vessels *(capillaries)* which are not connected to the rest of the blood system of the body. They are rarely seen in the immediate newborn period. Usually a strawberry mark starts off as a pale area that, over time, changes dramatically to become a raised mark of an intense, deep-crimson color which looks very much like a piece of the outside of a shiny strawberry. These marks usually start small and then grow for a year or so, and then stop. Strawberry marks almost always disappear on their own, so treatment is rarely needed. The general rule is that half are completely gone by age five, 70 percent by age seven, and 90 percent by nine years. Some marks may bleed easily. Many parents have a hard time letting nature take its course when the strawberry is cosmetically unsightly (such as at the tip of the nose), but in the long run, they look much better if they are left to shrink on their own. Surgery tends to cause scars, but some newer treatments, including laser surgery and medications, hold promise for better treatment. In the rare case, however, surgery is necessary.

364. Cavernous hemangiomas are fairly large blue-and-red marks caused by a collection of distended veins deep in the skin. They may or may not disappear completely on their own. Sometimes they need to be removed if they are disfiguring or in a perilous place, such as near the windpipe.

365. Moles can be of all sizes, smooth or hairy. All moles should be checked by your doctor or nurse practitioner, especially if the mole starts to grow or change color. Most are entirely benign, but a few have the potential for cancerous transformation later in life. They can be removed surgically if they are potentially dangerous, disfiguring, or irritated by clothing.

Jaundice

366. Blueness of the skin. The hands and feet of many newborns look blue. This condition *(acrocyanosis)* usually occurs when the hands or feet get a little cold and the blood vessels clamp off a little bit. Some babies with pale skin often show a bluish mottling all over their bodies when undressed. In both cases this phenomenon is insignificant, and it disappears as the baby gets older. If blueness of the body or around the mouth occurs in combination with difficulty breathing or any other signs of illness or abnormality, call your doctor or nurse practitioner.

367. Jaundice. Many newborn babies develop a yellow tinge to their skin called jaundice. The yellow color is due to a substance called *bilirubin* which is produced when red blood cells are broken down. Usually the bilirubin is taken up by the liver and then excreted. The liver of newborn babies, however, is still immature and can't do a very good job of handling it, so the bilirubin remains in the blood and makes the skin appear yellow.

A little jaundice is very common. Occasionally the level can be high enough to be worrisome, especially if there are reasons why it might be expected to go higher—for example, if the mother's and baby's blood types are different. The degree of jaundice can then be measured by a simple blood test. On rare occasions, treatment is felt to be necessary—for example with fluorescent lights.

368. Jaundice after the newborn period. Sometimes jaundice persists beyond the newborn period. This usually occurs in a mother who is breast-feeding. This type of jaundice is rarely dangerous, but doctors handle it differently. Some recommend stopping breast-feeding altogether for a day or two and then restarting. Others recommend continuing or even increasing breast-feeding. In either case the baby invariably does well. Very rarely persistent jaundice signifies a chronic problem with the liver, a condition that needs to be diagnosed through special tests.

Other Common Newborn Conditions

369. Umbilical hernia. After the skin of the navel heals over, there is usually still an opening in the deeper, muscular layer of the abdomen where the umbilical vessels passed through. When the baby cries, a small part of the intestine is pushed through this hole (umbilical ring), and it makes the navel puff out somewhat. This is called an umbilical hernia. When the ring is small, the protrusion of the hernia is never much larger than a pea and the ring is likely to close over in a few weeks or months. When the ring is large, it may take months or even years to close and the protrusion may be larger than a cherry.

It used to be thought that the closing of the umbilical ring could be hastened by putting a tight strap of adhesive and a coin across the navel to keep it from protruding. It is now believed that strapping makes no difference. It is much easier not to bother with the adhesive, which always became soiled, soon loosened, and left raw places on the skin.

You don't have to worry about the protrusion of the hernia. For example, there is no need to try to keep the baby from crying. Umbilical hernias almost never cause any trouble, as other hernias sometimes do.

If an umbilical hernia is still large at six or eight years and shows no decrease, surgical repair may be recommended.

370. Swollen breasts. Many babies, both boys and girls, have swollen breasts for some time after birth. In some cases a little milk (in olden times this was called "witches' milk") runs out. This is caused by the mother's hormones, which passed through the umbilical cord to the baby in the womb. Nothing needs to be done for swollen breasts in the baby, as the swelling will surely disappear in time. The breasts should not be massaged or squeezed, since this is likely to irritate and infect them.

371. Vaginal discharge. Girl babies may have a vaginal discharge at birth. This is very common, and the mucus is usually white, thick, and sticky. It's not significant, doesn't require any treatment, and is caused by the mother's hormones (the same ones that can cause a baby to have swollen breasts).

At a few days of age, many girl babies have a little bit of bloody discharge. This is similar to a period and is caused by the withdrawal of maternal hormones after delivery. It usually lasts only a day or so. If a bloody discharge persists after the first week, it should be reported to your doctor or nurse practitioner.

372. Undescended testicles. In a certain number of newborn boys, one or both testicles are not in the scrotum (the pouch in which the testicles normally lie), but are farther up in the groin or even inside the abdomen. Many of these undescended testicles come down into the scrotum soon after birth. Sometimes, on casual examination, the testicles may appear not to have descended, but they are actually down. They are only more lively than the average in retreating back into the abdomen.

The testicles are originally formed inside the abdomen and move down into the scrotum only shortly before birth. There are muscles attached to the testicles that can jerk them back up into the groin or even back into the abdomen. This is to protect the testicles from injury when this region of the body is struck or scratched.

There are lots of boys whose testicles withdraw on slight provocation. Even chilling of the skin from being undressed may be enough to make them disappear into the abdomen. Handling the scrotum in an examination frequently makes them disappear. Therefore, a parent shouldn't decide that the testicles are undescended just because they are not usually in sight. A good time to look for them is when the boy is in a warm bath.

Testicles that have been seen at any time in the scrotum, even if only rarely, need no treatment; they will surely settle down in the scrotum by the time puberty development is under way.

Sometimes just one testicle is definitely undescended.

373. If one or both testicles have never been seen in the scrotum by the time a boy is nine to twelve months old, he should be examined by a competent pediatric surgeon. If one or both are found to be truly undescended, the surgeon may recommend watchful waiting or a medication that sometimes brings the testicles down or an operation. The goal is to avoid potential damage to the undescended testicle if it remains inside the warm body for longer than it should. Though this may require treatment, there is no cause for great concern because one testicle is sufficient to make a boy develop properly and become a father, even if the other one doesn't appear later.

Mouth Troubles

374. Thrush. Thrush is a very common mild yeast infection of the mouth. It looks like patches of milk scum were stuck to the cheeks or tongue or roof of the mouth. But, unlike milk, it does not wipe off easily. If you do rub it off, the underlying skin may bleed slightly and look inflamed. Thrush may make babies' mouths sore and they may appear uncomfortable when they are trying to nurse.

Thrush occurs in all babies and has nothing to do with poor hygiene on your part. If you suspect it, consult your doctor or nurse practitioner promptly for diagnosis and treatment. They will prescribe oral medications that work very well. If there is a delay in getting medical advice, it is helpful to have the baby drink half an ounce of water after the milk. This washes the milk out of the mouth and gives the thrush fewer nutrients to live on.

Don't be fooled by the color of the inner sides of the gums where the upper molar teeth are going to be. The skin color here is normally very pale and is sometimes mistaken for thrush by mothers who are on the lookout for it.

375. Cysts on the gums and the roof of the mouth. Some babies have one or two little pearly white cysts on the sharp edge of their gums. They may remind you of teeth, but they are too round and they don't make a click on a spoon. Similar cysts can often be seen on the roof of the mouth, along the ridge that runs from front to back. They have no importance and eventually disappear.

Eye Troubles

376. Eye discharge and tearing. Many babies develop a mild inflammation of the eyes a few days after birth. This is probably caused by an immature tear duct that may be partially obstructed. It doesn't require any treatment, as it usually clears up by itself.

377. Obstructed tear duct. Another kind of very mild but chronic infection of the eyelids develops off and on in the early months in quite a number of babies, most commonly in only one eye. The eye waters and tears excessively, particularly in windy weather. White matter collects in the corner of the eye and along the edges of the lids. This discharge may keep the lids stuck together when the baby first wakes up. A plugged tear duct does not cause inflammation of the white of the eye.

This condition is caused by an obstructed tear duct. The tear duct leads from a small opening at the inner corner of the eyelid, first toward the nose, then down the side of the eye socket and into the nose cavity. When this duct is partly plugged, the tears are not drained off as fast as they form. They well up in the eye and run down the cheek. The lids keep getting mildly infected because the eye is not being cleansed sufficiently by the tears. Your doctor or nurse practitioner should, of course, see the eyes and make the diagnosis. The usual treatment is a combination of eye ointment or drops and gentle massage of the tear ducts to try and open them up. Your doctor or nurse practitioner will show you how to do this.

Blocked tear ducts are fairly common, not serious, and do not injure the eye. The condition may last for many months. The tendency is outgrown in most cases even if nothing is done. If by a year it is still bothersome, an eye doctor may clear the duct with a simple procedure. When the lids are stuck together, you can soften the crust and open them by gently applying water with your washed fingers or a clean washcloth and warm water—not hot, because the eyelid skin is very sensitive to temperature.

378. Conjunctivitis. This bacterial or viral infection of the lining of the white of the eye causes the whites of the eyes to look bloodshot or even pink. Usually there is a discharge of yellow or white pus from the eye. The doctor or nurse practitioner should be called promptly.

379. Crossed eyes. It is common for a baby's eyes to turn in or out too much at moments in the early months. In most cases they become steady and straight as the child grows older, usually by three months. If, however, the eyes turn in or out all the time or much of the time, even in the first month, or if they are not steady by three months, an eye doctor should be consulted.

Many times parents think their baby's eyes are crossed when they are really straight. This is because the skin between the eyes (over the bridge of the nose) is relatively wider in a baby than in an older person. This extra skin covers a little of the white of the eye (toward the nose), which then appears to be much smaller than the white on the outer side (toward the ear). It's also not uncommon in a newborn baby for the lid of one eye to droop a little lower than the other or for one eye to look smaller. In most cases, these differences become less and less noticeable as the baby grows older. The baby's eyes should be examined, though, to be sure that they are straight.

Another reason babies' eyes sometimes appear crossed is that when they are looking at something in their hands they have to converge (cross) the eyes a lot to focus on it, because babies' arms are so short. They are only converging their eyes normally, the way we adults do to a lesser extent. Their eyes won't get stuck that way. Parents often ask whether it is safe to hang toys over the crib, since the baby sometimes is cross-eyed looking at them. Don't hang a toy right on top of a baby's nose, but it's perfectly all right to hang it a foot away or more.

If you think your baby's eyes may be crossed, you can check the image of a light as it's reflected in the baby's pupils. If the image of the light always falls in the same spot on each of the baby's pupils (black central part), it's unlikely that the eyes are truly crossed.

It is important for infants' eyes to be examined promptly if there is a question about whether they are straight because an eye that is always crossed will gradually become non-seeing if efforts are not begun early to make the child use it. When the two eyes do not coordinate and converge on an object, each eye will be seeing a somewhat different scene; the child will be seeing double. This is so confusing

245

and uncomfortable that the brain automatically learns to ignore and suppress the vision of one eye. Over the first couple of years, the brain will lose the capacity to process visual information from that suppressed eye and the eye will, for all intents and purposes, be blind. If this goes on too long, it will become impossible ever to bring back the vision in that eye. This condition is known as "lazy eye."

The eye doctor's job is to promptly put the lazy eye back to work, usually by having the child wear a patch over the good eye for long periods of time. The eye doctor may also prescribe glasses to further encourage the coordinated use of both eyes. Then comes the decision as to whether there should be an operation. Occasionally several operations have to be performed before the result is satisfactory.

Breathing Troubles

380. Sneezing. Babies sneeze easily. Sneezing doesn't usually mean a cold unless the nose begins to run, too. It is most often caused by dust and dried mucus that has collected in the front of the nose and tickles.

381. Faint breathing. New parents usually worry a little about a new baby's breathing because it is often irregular and at times so shallow that they can't hear it or see it. They may worry, too, the first time they hear their baby snoring faintly while asleep. Both of these conditions are normal.

382. Chronic noisy breathing. This occurs in a certain number of young babies. Although it's usually without significance, every baby with noisy breathing should be examined by a doctor or nurse practitioner.

Many babies make a soft snoring noise in the back of the nose. It's just like a grown-up snoring, except that babies do it while they are awake. It seems to be caused by the fact that they haven't yet learned to control their soft palates. They'll outgrow it.

The commoner type of chronic noisy breathing is caused around the larynx (voice box). The cartilage (firm tissue that supports the airway around the larynx) is underdeveloped. This causes a loud rattling, snoring noise during breathing in, which doctors call *stridor.* It sounds as if the babies were choking, but they can breathe that way indefinitely. In most cases the stridor occurs only when the babies are breathing hard, especially during a cold. It usually goes away when they are quiet or asleep. It may be better when they lie on their abdomen. It should be discussed with your doctor or nurse practitioner, but usually no treatment is necessary or helpful. Mild stridor goes away as the baby grows older.

383. Noisy breathing that comes on *acutely,* particularly in an older infant or child, has an entirely different significance from the chronic variety. It may be due to croup, asthma, or other infection, and requires prompt medical attention.

384. Breath-holding spells. Some babies get so furiously angry when they are frustrated that they cry and then hold their breath and turn blue. When this first happens, it's bound to scare the wits out of her parents. It seldom means anything except that she has that kind of temperament. (It's often a baby who's unusually happy at other times.) You should be reassured that no one can hold her breath to death. In the worst-case scenario, the baby holds her breath for so long that she blacks out and her body assumes control and starts breathing again. The occasional baby holds her breath so long she not only blacks out but also has seizure-like movements! Again, this is terrifying to watch but not really dangerous.

Your doctor or nurse practitioner should be told initially about any breath-holding episodes, and subsequently about particularly bad breath-holding spells so he or she can make sure that everything is all right physically. Otherwise nothing much needs to be done. If you want to try to prevent your baby from having a breath-holding spell, you can try to divert her attention. When she begins to cry, try to distract her by encouraging another activity. Even distraction may not prevent breath-holding, however. Most breath-holding spells occur between one and three years, and stop happening by the time the child starts kindergarten. Breath-holding spells do not cause brain injury.

Other Common Issues in the First Year

385. Babies who startle easily. Newborn babies are startled by loud noises and by sudden change in position. Some are much more sensitive than others. When you put babies on a flat, hard surface and they jerk their arms and legs, it's likely to rock the body a little. This unexpected motion is enough to make sensitive babies nearly jump out of their skins and cry with fright. They may hate the bath because they are held so loosely. They need to be washed in their parent's lap and then rinsed in the tub, while held securely in both hands. They should be held firmly and moved slowly at all times. They gradually get over this uneasiness as they grow older. See Section 321 on the hypertonic baby.

386. The trembles. Some babies have trembly or jittery moments in the early months. The chin may quiver, or the arms and legs may tremble, especially when the baby is excited or is cool just after being undressed. This trembling is usually nothing to be disturbed about. It is just one of the signs that the baby's nervous system is still young. The tendency passes away in time.

387. Twitching. Some babies twitch occasionally in their sleep, and once in a while there is one who twitches frequently. This, too, usually disappears as the baby grows older. Mention it to the doctor or nurse practitioner as something to check.

Physical Development and Motor Skills

388. A baby starts by using his head. In a gradual process a baby learns to control his body. It starts with the head and gradually works down to the hands, trunk, and legs. A lot of early motor movements are programmed into the tracks of the brain. I guarantee, for example, that you will not have to teach your baby how to suck and swallow, how to cry, how to follow objects with his eyes, or how to reach for objects. Just as soon as he's born, he knows how to suck. And if something touches his cheek—the nipple or your finger, for example—he tries to reach it with his mouth. After a few days he's more than ready to do his part in nursing. If you try to hold his head still, he becomes angry right away and twists to get it free. (Probably he has this instinct to keep from being smothered.)

389. Using his hands. As soon as they are born, some babies can put their thumbs or fingers in their mouths any time they want to. Ultrasound examinations during pregnancy show they were probably doing it prior to delivery. But most can't get even their hands to their mouths with any regularity until they are two or three months old. And because their fists are still clenched tight, it usually takes them longer still to get hold of a thumb separately. But at about two or three months, many babies will spend hours just looking at their hands, bringing them up until, surprised, they bang themselves in the nose—only to stretch their arms out and start all over again. This is the beginning of eye-hand coordination, which has been important for human survival since man first stood on his two feet.

The main business of hands is to grab and handle things. A baby seems to know ahead of time what he's going to be learning next. Weeks before he can actually grab an object, he looks as if he wants to and is trying to grab it. At this stage, if you put a rattle into his hand, he holds on to it and waves it. Around the middle of the first year, he learns how to reach something that's brought within arm's reach. At about this time, he'll learn how to transfer an object from one hand to the other. Gradually he handles things more expertly. In the last quarter of his first year, he loves to pick up tiny objects, especially those you don't want him to (like a speck of dirt), carefully and deliberately.

390. Right- and left-handedness. The subject of handedness in children is a somewhat confusing one. Most babies stay ambidextrous for the first year or two and then gradually become right- or left-handed. It is unusual for a baby to have a preference for the right or left hand in the first six to nine months.

Right- or left-handedness is an inborn trait that will sooner or later become evident in each individual, with approximately 10 percent of all people being left-handed. Handedness tends to run in families, so that some families will have several lefties and others may have none. Since handedness is an inborn trait, it's a real mistake to try to force a left-handed child to become right-handed. This is confusing to the brain, which has been set up to work by a different scheme. Incidentally, handedness also applies to a preference for the right or left leg and eye.

391. Rolling over and sitting up. The age when babies roll over, sit up, creep, stand up, or walk is more variable than the age when they get control of their head or arms. A lot depends on temperament and weight. A wiry, energetic baby is in a great rush to get moving. A plump, placid one may be willing to wait until later.

A baby, by the time he first tries to roll over, shouldn't be left unguarded on a table for even as long as it takes you to turn your back, unless he is secured with a strap. By the time he can actually roll over, anywhere from two to six months, it is not safe to leave him even in the middle of an adult's bed. It is amazing how fast such a baby can reach the edge, and many do fall from an adult bed to the floor, which makes a parent feel very guilty. (I've assured parents whose baby has fallen, that many who haven't fallen have probably been watched too anxiously, which isn't too good either.) If a baby cries immediately after a fall from a bed, then stops crying and regains his normal color within fifteen minutes, he probably has not injured his brain. If he falls asleep he should be awakened in an hour to be sure he is conscious. Call your doctor or nurse practitioner and describe the event; in most cases, you will be reassured that your baby is well.

Most babies learn to sit steadily, after being helped up, without support at seven to nine months. But before babies have the coordination to succeed, they want to try. When you take hold of their hands, they attempt to pull themselves up. This eagerness always raises the question in the parents' mind: how young can I prop my baby up in the carriage or high chair? In general it's better not to prop babies straight up until they can sit steadily by themselves for many minutes. This doesn't mean that you can't pull them up to a sitting position for fun, or sit them in your lap, or prop them on a slanted pillow in the carriage, just as long as the neck and back are straight. It's a curled-over position that's not so good for long periods.

This brings up the question of a **high chair.** It is of greatest advantage when babies are eating meals with the rest of the family. On the other hand, falling out of a high chair is worrisome and not uncommon. If babies are to be eating most of their meals by themselves, I think it is preferable to buy a low chair-and-table arrangement. If you are going to use a high chair, get one with a broad base (so that it doesn't tip over easily) and always use the strap to buckle the baby in. Don't ever leave a baby alone in a high or low chair.

392. A toy or food while being changed. One of the things babies never learn is that they ought to lie still while being changed or dressed. It goes completely against their nature. From the time they learn to roll over until about one year, when they can be dressed standing up, they may struggle or cry indignantly against lying down, as if they have never heard of such an outrage.

There are a few things that help a little. One baby can be distracted by a parent who makes funny noises, another by a small bit of cracker or cookie. You can have an especially fascinating toy, like a music box, that you offer at dressing time only. Distract your baby just before you lay her down, not after she starts yelling.

393. Creeping and crawling. Creeping, when your baby begins to drag himself across the floor, can begin any time between six months and one year. Crawling, when your baby gets up on his hands and knees and moves about, usually starts a few months after creeping. Occasionally, some perfectly normal babies never creep or crawl at all; they just sit around until they learn to stand up.

There are a dozen different ways of creeping and crawling, and babies may change their style as they become more expert. One first learns to creep backward, another somewhat sideways, like a crab. One wants to crawl on her hands and toes with her legs straight, another on his hands and knees, still another on one knee and one foot. The baby who learns to be a speedy creeper may be late in walking, and the one who is a clumsy creeper, or who never learns to creep at all, has a good reason for learning to walk early.

394. Standing. Standing usually comes in the last quarter of the first year, but a very ambitious and motorically advanced baby may stand as early as seven months. Occasionally you see one who doesn't stand until after one year, but who seems to be bright and healthy in all other respects. Some of these are plump, easygoing babies. Others just seem to be slow getting coordination in their legs. I wouldn't worry about such children so long as your doctor or nurse practitioner finds that they are healthy and so long as they seem bright and responsive in other ways.

Quite a number of babies get themselves into a jam when they first learn to stand up but don't yet know how to sit down again. The poor things stand until they are frantic with exhaustion. The parents take pity on their boy and unhitch him from the railing of his playpen and sit him down. But instantly he forgets all about his fatigue and pulls himself to his feet again. This time he is crying within a few minutes. The best a parent can do is to give him especially interesting things to play with while he's sitting, wheel him in the carriage longer than usual, and take comfort in the fact that he'll probably learn how to sit down within a week.

One day he tries it. Very carefully he lets his behind down as far as his arms reach and, after a long moment of hesitation, plops down. He finds that it wasn't such a long drop and that his seat is well padded.

As the weeks go by, he learns to move around while hanging on, first with two hands, then with one. This is called cruising. Eventually he has enough balance to let go altogether for a few seconds when he is absorbed and doesn't realize what a daring thing he's doing. He is getting ready for walking.

395. Walking. Lots of factors determine the age at which a baby walks alone: inheritance probably plays the largest role, followed by ambition, heaviness, how well she can get places by creeping, illnesses, and bad experiences. A baby who is just beginning to walk when an illness lays her up for two weeks may not try again for a month or more. One who is just learning and has a fall may refuse to let go with her hands again for many weeks.

Most babies learn to walk between twelve and fifteen months. A few muscular, ambitious ones start as early as nine months. A fair number of bright children do not begin until eighteen months or even later.

You don't have to do anything to teach your child to walk. When her muscles, her nerves, and her spirit are ready, you won't be able to stop her. I remember a mother who got herself into a jam by walking her baby around a great deal before he was able to do it by himself. He was so delighted with this suspended walking that he demanded it all day long. Needless to say, she was tired and bored long before he was.

A parent of an early walker may worry that it's bad for the baby's legs. As far as we know, children's physiques are able to stand whatever they're ready to do by themselves. Babies sometimes become bowlegged or knock-kneed in the early months of walking, but this happens with late walkers as well as with early walkers. Most babies toe out to some degree when they start to walk and then gradually bring the front part of the feet in as they progress. One starts with the feet sticking right out to the sides, like Charlie Chaplin, and ends up toeing out only moderately. The average baby starts toeing out moderately and ends up with the feet almost parallel. The baby who starts out with feet almost parallel is more apt to end up toeing in. Toeing in and bowlegs often go together.

How straight the legs, ankles, and feet grow depends on several factors, including the pattern of development babies

are born with. Some babies seem to have a tendency to knock-knees and ankles that sag inward. The heavy child is more apt to develop these conditions. Other babies seem to be born with a tendency to bowlegs and toeing in. I think this is especially true of the very active, athletic ones. Another factor may be the position babies keep their feet and legs in. For instance, you occasionally see a foot that becomes turned in at the ankle because the baby always sits with that foot tucked under him in that position. It is suspected that some babies have been made to toe in by always lying on their stomachs with their feet pointed toward each other.

Your doctor or nurse practitioner, during the regular examinations, will watch the ankles and legs from the time the baby begins to stand up. This is one reason why regular visits are important during the second year. If weak ankles, knock-knees, bowlegs, or toeing in develop, corrective measures may be recommended, but most of these conditions resolve themselves over time.

(See Part 2, "The Child's Part," for more on children's temperament, language, and cognitive development.)

254

ONE-YEAR-OLDS

What Makes Them Tick?

396. Feeling their oats. One year is an exciting age. Babies are changing in lots of ways—in their eating, in how they get around, in how they understand the world, in what they want to do, and in how they feel about themselves and other people. When they were little and helpless, you could put them where you wanted them, give them the playthings you thought suitable, feed them the foods you knew were best. Most of the time they were willing to let you be the boss, and took it all in good spirit.

It's more complicated now that they are around a year old. They seem to realize that they're not meant to be baby dolls the rest of their lives, that they're human beings with ideas and wills of their own.

By fifteen to eighteen months, your child's behavior makes it clear that he's heading for what is often called the terrible twos—a slanderous term, because two years is a really marvelous and exciting, if challenging, age. When you suggest something that doesn't appeal to him, he feels he must assert himself. His nature tells him to. It's the beginning of the process called individuation, when he begins to become a person in his own right. The honeymoon with you is over, at least partly, because to become his own person he needs to rebel against your control.

So he may begin to say no in words or actions, even about things that he likes to do. Some call this "negativism," but stop and think what would happen if he never felt like saying no. He's getting smarter all the time, and more and more able to make some of his own decisions (even if they are wrong). Really, he'd have to become a compliant robot if he never disagreed with you, and he'd never really learn anything through trial and error, which is the best way to learn. He'd just have to memorize everything you said.

The process of separating from you begins at this stage. While it can be painful, and you may feel rejected, and it's hard to give up control, this separation is absolutely necessary for your child's growth as a human being. So say goodbye to that special bond of unquestioning, unconditional love that your infant once gave you and say hello to a more complicated relationship with this newly emerging person.

397. The passion to explore. One-year-olds are demon explorers. They poke into every nook and cranny, finger the carving in the furniture, shake a table or anything else that isn't nailed down, want to take every single book out of the bookcase, climb onto anything they can reach, fit little things into big things, and then try to fit big things into little things. In short, they are into *everything.*

Like everything else, their curiosity is a dual-edged sword. On one hand, it's the way your child learns. He has to find out about the size and shape and movableness of everything in his world and test his own skill before he can advance to the next stage, just the way he'll have to go through the grades before he can go to high school. His incessant explorations are a sign that he's bright in mind and spirit.

On the other hand, this can be a physically exhausting and trying time for you, requiring your constant attention to allow him to explore but at the same time make sure that he is safe and that his experiences are beneficial to his growth and development.

Avoiding Injuries

398. One year is a dangerous age. Parents cannot prevent all injuries. If they were careful enough or worried enough to try, they would only make a child timid and dependent. All children will get some cuts and bruises as a natural part of their active, healthy play. But if you keep your guard up and take a few simple precautionary measures, you can protect your children from serious injury. See pages 368–401 on **Preventing Injuries.**

Fears Around One Year

399. Protect them from frightening sounds and sights. Your baby at a year may become fascinated with one thing for several weeks on end—the telephone, for instance, or planes overhead, or electric lights. Remember that she learns best by touching, smelling, and tasting things and that as a little scientist she needs to conduct her experiments over and over again. Let her touch and become familiar with objects that are not dangerous or disturbing.

But the hardy explorer also begins to develop fears of certain things at this time. She may be frightened by strange objects that move suddenly or make a loud noise, such as folded pictures that pop up from a book, the opening of an umbrella, a vacuum cleaner, a siren, a barking dog, a train, even a vase of rustling branches.

All children have fears; this is a normal element of the developmental process. It's not hard to understand why. Fears occur when the child's understanding of an object or event is too poorly developed to really explain why this object has suddenly come into her life, why this startling event has occurred, and if the situation is really safe. We all fear that which we do not understand. In the second year of life that covers a lot of territory. I'd suggest simply avoiding as much as possible these startling things until she figures them out. If the vacuum cleaner bothers her, try not to use it for a while, at least while she's nearby. Always be comforting and sympathetic. Don't try to convince her it's a ridiculous fear; her terror makes perfect sense to her at her level of understanding.

400. Fear of the bath. Between one and two years, your child may become frightened of the bath. She may fret

257

about slipping underwater or getting soap in her eyes or even seeing and hearing the water go down the drain. She has to have a bath, so you need to figure out how to make it a less traumatic experience and allow her to come to terms with it. To avoid soap in the eyes, soap her face with a washcloth that is not too wet and rinse several times with a damp but not dripping washcloth. Use baby shampoo that won't sting her eyes. Babies who are afraid to get into the bathtub shouldn't be forced to. You can try using a dishpan, but if she is afraid of that too, give her sponge baths for several months, until her courage returns. Then start with just an inch of water and remove the baby before you pull the stopper.

Independence and Outgoingness

401. A baby gets more dependent and more independent at the same time. This sounds contradictory, and of course it is. But so are babies! A parent complains of a year-old boy, "He's begun to cry every time I go out of the room." This doesn't mean that he is developing a bad habit, but that he's growing up and realizing how much he depends on his parents. It's inconvenient, but it's a good sign. Yet at this very age he is also becoming more independent, he is developing the urge to be on his own, discover new places, befriend unfamiliar people.

Watch a baby at the crawling stage when his parent is washing the dishes. He plays contentedly with some pots and pans for a while. Then he gets a little bored and decides to explore in the dining room. He creeps around under the furniture there, picking up little pieces of dust and tasting them, carefully climbing to his feet to reach the handle of a drawer. After a while he seems to feel the need of company again, for he suddenly scrambles back into the kitchen. At one time you see his urge for independence getting the upper hand; at another, his need for security. He satisfies each in turn.

As the months go by, he becomes bolder and more daring in his experiments and explorations. He still needs his parents, but not so often. He is building his own independence, but part of his courage comes from knowing he can get security when he needs it.

I am making the point that independence comes from security as well as from freedom, because a few people get it twisted around backward. They try to "train" independence into children by leaving them in a room by themselves for long periods even though they are crying for company. I think that when the issue is being forced this hard, a child is learning that the world is a mean place, which makes him even more dependent in the long run.

So your baby at around a year old is at a fork in the road. Given a chance, he will gradually become more independent: more sociable with outsiders (both grown-ups and children), more self-reliant, and more outgoing. Stranger anxiety, so intense at nine months, begins to wane. If he's confined a great deal, kept away from others, and used to having only his parents around, it may take longer for him to become sociable outside of the home. The most important thing is for a one-year-old to have a strong attachment to his consistent caregivers. With a solid foundation of emotional security, outgoingness will eventually come.

402. How is independence encouraged? When a baby has learned to walk, it's time to let him out of his carriage or stroller on his daily outings. Never mind if he gets dirty; he should. Try to go to a place where you don't have to be after him every minute and where he can get used to other children. If he picks up cigarette butts, you have to jump, take them away, and show him something else that's fun. You can't let him eat handfuls of sand or earth because it will irritate his intestines and may give him worms. If he puts everything in his mouth, try giving him a hard cracker or some clean object to chew on, to keep his mouth busy.

Such are the ordinary risks of independence at this age. Keeping an able-bodied walking baby tucked in his carriage may keep him out of trouble, but it also cramps his style, hinders his development, and dampens his spirit.

403. Harness or wrist leads? Some parents find a harness or a leash attached to their wrist to be very practical for shopping and walks at this age. Others worry that they will be accused of treating their toddler like a leashed dog. It seems to me that the parent who happens to have an especially active toddler, particularly if there is also a younger child in the family, can use such a harness arrangement as a very effective safety measure while shopping in supermarkets or other places where toddlers can easily do damage to themselves or the merchandise! Naturally, the harness lead should never be used to tie the toddler to something while the parent goes off in another direction. Safety comes before all else and toddlers get used to these restraints very quickly.

404. Let them out of the playpen when they insist. One child is willing to stay in the playpen, at least for short periods, as late as a year and a half. Another thinks it's a prison by the time she's nine months. Most accept it well enough until they learn to walk, around the age of fifteen months. I'd say let your baby out of the playpen when she feels unhappy there. I don't mean at the first whimper; if you give her

Let her out when she's had enough.

something new to play with, she may be happy there for another hour. Outgrowing the pen is a gradual process. At first she gets sick of it only after a long spell. Gradually she gets impatient earlier. It may be months before she objects to being put in at all. In any case, let her out each time she's sure she's had enough.

405. Get them used to outsiders. At this age a baby's nature tells her to be leery and suspicious of strangers till she has had a chance to look them over. But then she wants to get closer and eventually make friends—in one-year-old fashion, of course. She may just stand close and gaze, or solemnly hand something to the newcomer and then take it back, or bring everything movable in the room and pile it in the person's lap.

Many adults don't have the sense to let a small child alone while she sizes them up. They rush up to her, full of talk and enthusiasm, while she beats a hasty retreat to her parent for protection from this uninvited invader. Then it takes longer for her to work up her courage to be friendly. I think it helps for a parent to remind a visitor in the beginning, "It makes her shy when you pay attention to her right away. If you ignore her for a while, she'll try to make friends sooner."

When your baby is old enough to walk, give her plenty of chances to get used to seeing strangers. Take her to the grocery store a couple of times a week. As often as you can, take her someplace where other small children play. She won't be very interested in actually playing with the others yet, but at times she will want to watch. As she gets used to seeing others play, she will be more ready for cooperative play when the time comes, between two and three.

Handle Them Matter-of-Factly

406. They're very distractible, and that's a big help. Year-old babies are so eager to find out about the whole world that they aren't particular where they begin or where they stop. Even if they're absorbed in a ring of keys, you can make them drop it by giving them an empty plastic cup. If your baby, toward the end of the first year, begins to fight against having the food washed off his face and hands with a cloth after meals, set a pan of water on the tray and let him dabble his hands while you wash his face with your wet hand.

Distractibility is one of the handles by which wise parents guide their children.

407. Arranging the house for a wandering baby. When I tell parents that their toddler has outgrown the playpen or the crib and that they ought to let her on the floor, they are apt to look unhappy and say, "But I'm afraid she'll hurt herself. At the least, she'll wreck the house." Sooner or later she must be let out to roam around, if not at ten months, at least by fifteen months, when she's walking. And she's not going to be any more reasonable or easier to control then. At whatever age you give her the freedom of the house, you will have to make adjustments, so it's better to do it when she is ready.

How do you keep a year-old baby from hurting herself or the household furnishings, anyway? First of all, you can arrange the rooms where she'll be so that she's allowed to play with most of the things she can reach. Then you'll rarely have to tell her she can't play with something. Whereas, if you forbid her to touch most of the reachable objects, you will drive her and yourself mad. If there are plenty of things she *can* do, she's not going to bother so much about the things she *can't* do. Practically speaking, this means taking breakable ashtrays and vases and ornaments off low tables and shelves and putting them out of reach. It means taking the valuable books off the lower shelves of the bookcases and putting the old magazines there instead. Jam the good books in tight so that she can't pull them out. In the kitchen, put the pots and pans and wooden spoons on the shelves near the floor and put the china and packages of food out of reach. Fill a lower bureau drawer with old clothes, toys, and other interesting objects and let the baby explore it, empty it, and fill it to her heart's content.

408. How do you make them leave certain things alone? This is a significant dilemma between one and two years. There will always be a few things that your toddler will have to leave alone. After all, there have to be lamps on tables. She mustn't pull them off by their cords or push the tables over. She mustn't touch the hot stove or turn on the gas or crawl out a window.

409. "No" isn't enough at first. You can't stop a toddler just by saying no, at least not in the beginning. Even later it will depend on your tone of voice, how often you say it, and whether you really mean it. It's not a method to rely on heavily until she has learned from experience what it means—and that you mean it. Don't say "No" in a challenging voice from across the room. This gives her a choice. She says to herself, "Shall I be a wimp and do as she says, or shall I be mature and grab this lamp cord?" Remember that her natural instinct is egging her on to try things and to balk at directions. Chances are, she'll keep on approaching the lamp cord with an eye on you to see how angry you get. It's much wiser, the first few times she goes for the lamp, to go over promptly and whisk her to another part of the room. You can say "No" at the same time to begin teaching her

*Better to remove and distract him
than just to say, "No, no!"*

what it means. Then quickly give her a magazine or an empty box, anything that is safe and interesting.

Suppose she goes back to the lamp a few minutes later? Remove her and distract her again, promptly, definitely, cheerfully. Say, "No, no," at the same time that you remove her, adding it to your action for good measure. Sit down with her for a minute to show her what she can do with the new plaything. If necessary, put the lamp out of reach this time, or even take her out of the room. You are cheerfully but firmly showing her that you are absolutely sure in your own mind that the lamp is not the thing to play with. You are keeping away from choices, arguments, cross looks, scoldings—which may not do the job and which are likely to make her irritable.

You might say, "But she won't learn unless I teach her it's naughty." Oh, yes, she will. In fact, she can accept the lesson more easily if it's done in this matter-of-fact way. When you disapprovingly waggle a finger from across the room at babies who haven't yet learned that no really means no, your crossness rubs them the wrong way. It makes them want to take a chance on disobeying. And it's no better if you grab them, hold them face-to-face, and give them a talking-to. You're not giving them a chance to give in gracefully or forget. Their only choice is to surrender meekly or to defy you.

I think of a Mrs. T. who complained bitterly that her sixteen-month-old daughter was "naughty." Just then Suzy toddled into the room—a nice girl with a normal amount of spunk. Instantly Mrs. T. looked disapproving and said, "Now, remember, don't go near the radio." Suzy hadn't been thinking of the radio at all, but now she had to. She turned and moved slowly toward it.

Mrs. T. gets panicky just as soon as each of her children in turn shows signs of developing into an independent person. She dreads the time when she won't be able to control them. In her uneasiness, she makes an issue when there doesn't need to be any. It's like the boy learning to ride a bicycle who sees a rock in the road ahead. He is so nervous about it that he keeps steering right for it.

Take the example of a baby who is getting close to a hot

stove. A parent doesn't sit still and say "No-o-o" in a disapproving voice, but jumps and gets the baby out of the way. This is the method that comes naturally if the parent is really trying to keep the child from doing something, and not just engaging in a battle of wills.

410. Take lots of time or be masterful. A mother of an eighteen-month-old boy walks with him every day to the grocery store. But she complains that instead of walking right along, he wanders across the sidewalk and climbs the front steps of every house they pass on the way. The more she calls to him, the more he lingers. When she scolds him, he runs in the opposite direction. She is afraid he is developing a behavior problem.

This baby doesn't have a behavior problem, though he may be made to have one. He's not at an age when he can keep the grocery store in mind. His natural instincts say to him, "Look at that sidewalk to explore! Look at those stairs!" Every time his mother calls to him, it reminds him of his new-felt urge to assert himself. What can the mother do? If she has to get to the store promptly, she can take him in his stroller. But if she's going to use this time for his outing, she should allow four times longer than if she were going alone, and let him make his side trips. If she keeps moving slowly, he'll want to catch up to her every once in a while.

Here's another tight spot: It's time to go in for lunch, but your small daughter is digging happily in the dirt. If you say, "Now it's time to go in," in a tone of voice that means, "Now you can't have any more fun," you will get resistance. But if you say cheerfully, "Let's go climb the stairs," you may give her a desire to go.

But suppose she's tired and cranky that day, and nothing that's indoors has any appeal. She just gets disagreeably resistant right away. I'd pick her up casually and carry her indoors, even if she's squealing and kicking. Do this in a self-confident way, as if you were saying to her, "I know you're tired and cross, but when we have to go in, we have to." Don't scold her; that won't make her see the error of her ways. Don't argue with her, because that won't change her mind; you will only get yourself frustrated. A small child who is feeling miserable and making a scene is comforted underneath by sensing that the parent knows what to do without getting angry.

411. Dropping and throwing things. Around the age of one year, babies learn to drop things on purpose. They solemnly lean over the side of the high chair and drop food on the floor, or toss toys, one after the other, out of the crib. Then they cry because they haven't got them. Are these babies deliberately trying to annoy their parents? No. They aren't even thinking about their parents. They are fascinated by a new skill and want to practice it all day long, the way an older child wants to ride a new two-wheeler. If you pick up the dropped object, they realize it's a game that two can play and are more delighted. It's better not to get in the habit of picking up dropped toys right away. Put babies on the floor or ground when they get in this dropping mood. You don't

Dropping is a new skill.

want them throwing food out of the high chair in any case, but they won't start until their appetite is pretty well satisfied. Take the food away promptly and firmly when they start dropping, and put them down to play. Trying to scold a baby out of dropping things leads to nothing but frustration for the parent. Children have to learn about object permanence (see Sections 34 and 35), but that doesn't mean it has to happen at the dinner table.

Nap Hours Are Changing

412. Nap times are shifting in most babies around the age of a year. Some who were taking a nap at about 9:00 A.M. may refuse it altogether or show that they want it later and later in the morning. If they take it late, they are unready for their next nap until the middle of the afternoon, and this probably throws off their bedtime after supper. Or they may refuse the afternoon nap altogether. A baby may vary a lot from day to day at this period, and even go back to a 9:00 A.M. nap after two weeks of refusing it, so don't come to a final conclusion too soon. You have to put up with these inconveniences as best you can, realizing that they are temporary. With some babies who are not ready to sleep in the first part of the morning, you can remove the need for the before-lunch nap by putting them in their beds anyway, around nine in the morning, if they are willing to lie or sit quietly for a while. Of course, another kind of baby only gets in a rage if put to bed when she's not sleepy, and nothing is accomplished.

If a baby becomes sleepy just before noon, it's the parent's cue to move lunch up to 11:30 or even 11:00 for a few days. Then the long nap will come after lunch. But for a while, after cutting down to one nap a day, whether morning or afternoon, the baby may get frantically tired before suppertime.

Don't get the idea from this section that all babies give up their morning nap in the same way or at the same age. One is through with it at nine months; another craves it and benefits from it as late as two years. There is often a stage in a baby's life when two naps are too many and one is not enough! You can help babies through this period by giving them supper and putting them to bed for the night a little earlier for the time being.

TWO-YEAR-OLDS

What They're Like

413. A tumultuous time. Some refer to this period as "the terrible twos." It's not really a terrible time though; it's a terrific time, although few call it the "terrific twos." It's a time when your child is beginning to come into her own and learn what it's like to be an independent person, when her language skills are increasing at a breathtaking pace, but when her understanding of the world is still so limited that the world appears a scary place.

For two-year-olds, both sides of the coin are simultaneously true: she is both independent and dependent, loving and hateful, generous and selfish, mature and infantile. The two-year-old always has her feet in two worlds—that of the warm cozy dependent past and the exciting prospect of independence and autonomy. With so much excitement going on, it's no wonder it's a challenging time for parent and child alike. But terrible it isn't. It's really pretty amazing.

414. The two-year-old learns by imitation. In a doctor's office a two-year-old girl solemnly places the stethoscope bell on different spots on her chest. Then she pokes the ear light in her ear and looks a little puzzled because she can't see anything. At home she follows her parents around, sweeping with a broom when they sweep, dusting with a

268

cloth when they dust, brushing her teeth when they do. It's all done with great seriousness. She is making giant strides forward in skill and understanding by means of constant imitation.

In some ways she may be quite dependent around age two. She seems to realize clearly who it is that gives her a sense of security, and she shows it in different ways. A mother complains, "My two-year-old seems to be turning into a mama's girl. She hangs on to my skirts when we're out of the house. When someone speaks to us, she hides behind me."

Two is a great age for whining, which is a kind of clinging. A two-year-old may keep climbing out of bed in the evening to rejoin the family, or calling from her room. She may be timid about being left anywhere by her parents. She's apt to be upset if a parent or other member of the household goes away for a number of days or if the family moves to a new house. It's wise to take her sensitivity into account when changes in the household are being considered.

415. Parallel play. At two, children don't play cooperatively with each other very much. Although they may love to watch each other's occupations, mostly they enjoy playing alongside each other in what is called parallel play. "Sharing" is not a word in their vocabulary: what's theirs is *theirs.* There is no point in trying to teach a two-year-old to share; it goes against his very nature. The fact that he won't share at two has nothing to do with how generous a person he will become when he is older. But this doesn't mean you have to accept bad manners, even if he hasn't a clue why you consider his grabbing a toy away from a companion to be bad form. You can firmly but cheerfully take the toy away from him, return it to its rightful owner, and quickly try to distract him with another object of interest. Long harangues about why he should share things are wasted breath. He will start to share when he understands the *concept* of sharing, and not before.

Playing near and watching come before playing together.

Negativism

416. Balkiness between two and three. In the period between age two and age three, children are apt to show signs of balkiness and other inner tensions. Your baby probably began to be balky and "negativistic" way back when she was fifteen months old, so this is nothing new. But it reaches new heights and takes new forms after two. One-year-old Petunia contradicts her parents. Two-and-a-half-year-old Petunia even contradicts herself. She has a hard time making up her mind, and then she wants to change it. She acts like a person who feels she is being bossed too much, even when no one is bothering her and even when she tries to boss others. She insists on doing things just so, doing them her own way, doing them exactly as she has always done them. It makes her furious to have anyone interfere in one of her jobs or rearrange her possessions.

The child's nature between two and three seems to be urging her to decide things for herself, and to resist pressure from other people. Trying to fight these two battles without much worldly experience seems to get her tightened up inside. For that reason it's often hard to get along with a child between two and three.

417. Parents have to be understanding. The parents' job is to keep from interfering too much, from hurrying him. Let him help to dress and undress himself when he has the urge. Start his bath early enough so that he has time to dawdle and scrub the tub. At meals let him feed himself without urging. When he is stalled in his eating, let him leave the table. When it's time for bed, or going outdoors, or coming in, steer him while conversing about pleasant things. Get things done without raising issues. Your goal is not to let him be a little tyrant, but not to "sweat the small stuff."

You need to set firm, consistent limits, but you should choose where and what those limits are very carefully. If you find yourself saying no a lot more than yes, you're probably setting too many arbitrary limits. A battle of wills with a two-year-old is exhausting. On the one hand, I wouldn't advise it except when an issue is really important to you. On the other hand, if you never say no, you may be overindulgent. Finding the right balance is the key.

418. Favoritism toward one parent. Sometimes a child around thirty to thirty-six months can get along with either parent alone, but when the other one comes onto the scene she flies into a rage. It may be partly jealousy, but at an age when she's sensitive about being bossed around and trying to do a little bossing herself, I imagine she feels outnumbered when she has to take on two important people at once. It's more often the father who is particularly unpopular at this period; he sometimes gets the feeling he's pure poison. He shouldn't take the child's reaction too seriously, or feel hurt and turn away from her. It will help if he regularly cares for her by himself, doing things that are fun, as well as everyday chores such as feeding and bathing. That way she gets to know him as an enjoyable, loving, and important person, not just an intruder. If she objects at first when he takes over from her mother, the father should cheerfully but firmly carry on, and the mother should be firm and cheerful as she hands her over and leaves. This is a good chance for a mother to have some time to herself. But the child must also learn that the parents love each other, want to be with each other, and will not be bullied by her.

Worries Around Two

419. Fear of separation. Many normal children develop a fear of being separated from the parent beginning around the age of a year. This expresses, I suspect, their new recognition of how much their sense of security depends on being near the parent. This is probably the same instinct that makes the young of other species, such as sheep and goats, follow close after their mothers and bleat when separated. It's natural that lambs and kids feel this anxiety from birth, because they can walk right away. But human babies acquire the anxiety at about the age of a year when they finally learn to walk, so that if they wander away, they'll soon feel the urge to get back.

Here's what happens occasionally when a sensitive, dependent child of two years, particularly an only child, is separated abruptly from the parent who has spent the most time with him. Perhaps it is the mother and she has to go out of town unexpectedly for a couple of weeks. Or she decides that she has to go to work, and arranges for a stranger to come in and take care of the child during the day. Usually the child makes no fuss while the mother is away, but when she returns, he hangs on to her like Velcro and refuses to let the other person come near. He becomes panicky whenever he thinks his mother may be leaving again.

Separation anxiety is worst at bedtime. The terrified child fights against being put to bed. If his mother tears herself away, he may cry in fear for hours. If she sits by his crib, he lies down only as long as she sits still. Her slightest move toward the door brings him instantly to his feet.

In some of these cases there is also worry about urinating. The child keeps saying "Wee wee"—or whatever word he uses. His mother takes him to the bathroom, he does a few drops, and then cries "Wee wee" again just as soon as he is back in bed. You might say that he just uses this as an excuse to keep her there. This is true, but there is more to it. Children like this one are really worried that they might wet the bed.

They sometimes wake every two hours during the night thinking about it. This is the age when the parents are apt to be showing disapproval when there is an accident. Maybe the child figures that if he wets, his parents won't love him so much and will therefore be more likely to go away. If so, he has two reasons to fear going to sleep. If your child is worried about wetting, keep reassuring her that it doesn't matter if she does wee-wee in bed—that you'll love her just the same.

420. If your two-year-old child has become terrified about going to bed, the safest advice, but the hardest to carry out, is to sit by her crib in a relaxed way until she goes to sleep. Don't be in a hurry to sneak away before she is asleep. That will alarm her again and makes her more wakeful. This campaign may take weeks, but it should work in the end. If your child was frightened because one of you left town, try to avoid going away again for many weeks. If you have taken a job for the first time since the child was born, say good-bye each day affectionately, but cheerfully and confidently. If you have an anguished, *unsure-whether-you're-doing-the-right-thing* expression, it adds to the child's uneasiness.

Making the child more tired by keeping her up later or omitting her nap may help a little but usually won't do the whole job. A panicky child can keep herself awake for hours even though she's exhausted. You have to take away her worry, too.

421. Avoiding drastic changes at this age. Children who, from infancy, have been around different people and who have been allowed to develop independence and outgoingness are less apt to develop separation fears.

If your child is between fifteen and twenty-four months, be careful about drastic changes. If it's almost as easy to postpone a long trip for six months or for the nonworking parent to delay in taking a job, it will be better to wait, especially if it's your first child.

If neither parent can be at home with the child, arrange for her to get thoroughly used to the person who is going to take care of her, whether it's a friend, a relative, a sitter, or family day-care worker. If the child is going to be staying at the other person's house, it's even more important for her to get used to the new person and the new place by gradual

273

steps. Allow two weeks anyway. Let the new person just be around the child for a number of days without trying to take care of her, until she trusts and likes her or him. Then let the caretaker take over gradually.

Don't leave the child for a full day at first. Start with half an hour and work up. Your quick reappearance will reassure her that you always come back soon. Don't go away at all for a month or so after you have moved or after another member of the household has left. A child at this age needs a long time to adjust to each of these changes separately.

422. Overprotectiveness increases children's fears. A child who is frightened by separation—or anything else—is very sensitive to whether her parents feel the same way about it. If they act hesitant or guilty every time they leave her side, if they hurry into her room at night, their anxiety reinforces her fear that there really is great danger in being apart from them.

This may sound contradictory after I've said that a parent must reassure a frightened two-year-old by sitting by her bed as she goes to sleep and by not going away on any more trips for a number of weeks. I mean that parents must give her this special care the way they give special consideration to a sick child. But they should try to be cheerful, confident, unafraid. They should be looking for signs of the child's readiness to give up her dependence, step by step, and encourage her and compliment her. This attitude of theirs is the most powerful factor in getting her over her fear. That and the maturational forces which, with time and maturity, will allow the child to better understand and master her fears.

423. Some causes of overprotectiveness. Overprotective feelings occur mostly in very devoted, tenderhearted parents who are inclined to feel guilty when there is no realistic need for it. Sometimes, the most important factor in overprotectiveness is the parent's inability to admit that she or he sometimes feels resentful or angry toward the child.

The parent and child who are afraid to recognize that there are naturally moments when they have mean feelings toward each other, when each wishes that something bad would happen to the other, have to imagine instead that all the dangers in the world come from somewhere else, and grossly exaggerate them. The child who is denying the meanness in her parents and in herself places it all in monsters or robbers or dogs or lightning, depending on her age and experience. And she clings tightly to her parents—for protection and to reassure herself that nothing is really happening to them. And a mother, for instance, may suppress her occasional mean thoughts and exaggerate the dangers of kidnappers or home accidents or inadequate diet. She has to stay close to the child to make sure the dangers don't strike, and her anxious expression convinces the child that her own fears are well founded.

Of course, the answer is not for parents to take out all their angriest feelings on the child or to let her be abusive toward them. But it certainly is helpful for parents to recognize the inevitability of their occasional mean feelings toward their child and to admit them to each other and to themselves. It helps to clear the air if parents occasionally admit to a child how angry they felt—especially if the anger was not quite fair. It's good to say to a child once in a while, "I know how angry you feel toward me when I have to make rules like this for you."

424. How to help a fearful two-year-old. When it comes to the management of children's fear, a lot depends on how important it is for them to get over it in a hurry, from a practical point of view. There's no great necessity for anxious children to be hurried into making friends with dogs or going into deep water in the lake. They'll want to do these things as soon as they dare. On the other hand, if they have already started preschool, I think it's better to insist that they go unless they're deeply terrified. Children should not be allowed to come into the parents' bed every single night; they should be comforted and soothed in their own beds so that sleeping with the parents doesn't become a pleasant habit for which there is no motivation (for the child at least) to stop. A child with a school-refusal problem must get back to school sooner or later; the longer it is put off the harder it is. It is wise for parents to try to see whether their protectiveness is playing a part in these various separation fears, and to overcome it. Both steps are difficult to accomplish alone, and the parents are certainly entitled to help from a child guidance clinic, a family agency, or some other professional.

425. Children may use separation anxiety to control. A child clings to his mother because he has developed a genuine fear of being separated from her. But if he finds that she is so concerned about his fear that she will always do anything he wants for reassurance, he may begin to use this as coercion. There are three-year-olds, for instance, who are anxious about being left at preschool and whose parents not only stay at school for days but stay close to the children and do what they ask, to reassure them. After a while you begin to see that such children are exaggerating their uneasiness because they have learned to enjoy using it to boss their parents around. A parent can say, "I think you are grown up now and aren't afraid to be in school. You just like to make me do what you want. Tomorrow I won't need to stay here anymore."

THREE- TO SIX-YEAR-OLDS

Devotion to the Parents

426. Children at this age are usually easier to lead. Boys and girls around three have reached a stage in their emotional development when they feel that their fathers and mothers are wonderful people, and they want to be like them. The automatic resistance and hostility that were just below the surface in the two-year-old seem to lessen after three in most children.

The feelings toward the parents aren't just friendly now; they are warm and tender. However, children are not so devoted to their parents that they always obey them and behave well. They are still real people with ideas of their own. They want to assert themselves, even if it means going against their parents' wishes at times.

While I'm emphasizing how agreeable children usually are between three and six, I ought to make a partial exception for four-year-olds. A lot of assertiveness, cockiness, loud talk, and provoking comes out around four years in many children, when they come to the realization that they know everything—a realization that mercifully soon fades.

427. Children strive now to be like their parents. At two years of age children were eagerly imitating their parents' activities, whether it was mopping the floor or hammering a pretend nail. The focus was on the use of the mop or the hammer. By three years of age they want to be totally like their parents as people. They play at going to work, tending house (cooking, cleaning, laundering), caring for children (using a doll or a younger child). They pretend to go for a drive in the family car or to step out for the evening. They dress up in their parents' clothes, mimic their conversation, their manners, and their mannerisms. This process is sometimes called *identification.*

Identification is a lot more important than just playing. It's how character is built—much more by what children perceive in their parents, and model themselves after, than by what the parents try to teach them in words. This is how their basic ideals and attitudes are laid down—toward work, toward people, toward themselves—though these will be modified later as they become more mature and knowing. This is how they learn to be the kind of parents they're going to turn out to be twenty years later, as you can tell from listening to the affectionate or scolding way they care for their dolls.

It's at this age that a girl becomes more aware of the fact that she's female and will grow up to be a woman. So she watches her mother with special attentiveness and tends to mold herself in her mother's image: how her mother feels about her husband (lord and master, worm, or beloved partner) and about the male sex in general; about women (confidantes or competitors); about girl and boy children (if the child of one sex is more favored than the other or if each individual is appreciated for herself or himself); toward work and housework (chore or challenge). The little girl is not about to become an exact replica of her mother, but she will surely be influenced by her in many respects.

A boy at this age realizes that he is on the way to becoming a man, and he therefore attempts to pattern himself predominantly after his father: how his father feels toward his wife and the female sex generally, toward other men, toward his boy and girl children, toward outside work and housework.

Though the predominant identification is with the parent of the same sex, there's also a degree of identification with the parent of the opposite sex. This is how the two sexes come to understand each other well enough to be able to live together.

428. Boys and girls now become fascinated with all aspects of babies. They want to know where babies come from. When they find out that babies grow inside their mothers, they are eager to carry out this amazing act of creation themselves—boys as well as girls. They want to take care of babies and love them, the way they realize they were cared for and loved. They will press a younger child into the role of a baby and spend hours acting as father and mother to him, or they'll use a doll.

It's not generally recognized that little boys are as eager as girls to grow babies inside themselves. When their parents tell them that this is impossible, they are apt to refuse to believe it for a long time. "I will too grow a baby," they say, really believing that if they wish something hard enough they can omnipotently make it come true. In some nonindustrial, isolated parts of the world, when a woman goes into labor her husband does, too, and is taken to the men's labor hut, moaning and writhing, by his sympathetic male friends.

429. Boys become romantic toward their mothers, girls toward their fathers. Up to this age, a boy's love for his mother has been predominantly of a dependent kind, like that of a baby. But now it also becomes increasingly romantic, like his father's. By the time he's four, he's apt to insist that he's going to marry his mother when he grows up. He isn't clear just what marriage consists of, but he's absolutely sure who is the most important and appealing woman in the world. The little girl who is growing in her mother's pattern develops the same kind of love for her father.

These strong romantic attachments help children to grow spiritually and to acquire wholesome feelings toward the opposite sex that will later guide them into good marriages. But there is another side to the picture that creates unconscious tension in most children at this age. When people, old or young, love someone very much, they can't help wanting that person all to themselves. So, as a little boy of three or four or five becomes more aware of his possessive devotion to his mother, he also becomes aware of how much she already belongs to his father. This irritates him, no matter how much he loves and admires his father. At times he secretly wishes his father would get lost, and then he feels guilty about having such disloyal feelings. Reasoning as a child does, he imagines that his father has the same jealous and resentful feelings toward him.

The little girl develops the same possessive love for her father. She wishes at times that something would happen to her mother (whom she loves so much in other respects) so that she could have her father for herself. She may even say to her mother, "You can go away for a long trip, and I'll take good care of Daddy." But then she imagines that her mother is jealous of her, too, and subconsciously worries about this.

Children try to push these scary thoughts out of their minds, since the parent, after all, is so much bigger and stronger, but they are apt to come to the surface in their symbolic play and dreams. We believe that these mixed feelings—of love, jealousy, and fear—toward the parent of the same sex are sometimes the root of the bad dreams that little children of this age are so apt to have—dreams of being chased by giants, robbers, witches, and other frightening figures.

430. The attachment isn't meant to become too complete. This romantic attachment to the parent of the opposite sex in the years between three and six is what you might call nature's way of molding children's feelings in preparation for their eventual life as spouse or parent. But it wouldn't do for the attachment to go so far or get so strong that it lasts throughout life or even throughout childhood.

Nature expects that children by six or seven will become quite discouraged about the possibility of having the parent all to themselves. The unconscious fears about the parent's supposed anger and about genital differences will turn their pleasure in dreaming about romance into an aversion. From now on, children will shy away from kisses by the parent of the opposite sex. Their interests turn with relief to impersonal matters such as schoolwork and science. They try now to be just like the other children of their own sex rather than like their parents. (Freud regarded this shift as the resolution of the Oedipus complex.)

A father who realizes that his young son sometimes has unconscious feelings of resentment and fear toward him does not help the boy by trying to be too gentle and permissive with him or by pretending that he, the father, doesn't really love his wife very much. In fact, if a boy becomes convinced that his father is afraid to be a firm father and a normally possessive husband, the boy will sense that he is having his mother too much to himself and will feel really guilty and frightened. And he will miss the inspiration of a confident father, which he must have in order to develop his own self-assurance.

In the same way a mother, even though she knows that her young daughter is sometimes jealous of her, best helps her daughter to grow up by being a self-confident mother who doesn't let herself be pushed around, who knows how and when to be firm, and who isn't at all afraid to show her affection and devotion to her husband.

It complicates life for a boy if his mother is a great deal more permissive and affectionate toward him than his father is. The same is true if she seems to be closer and more sympathetic to her son than she is to her husband. Such attitudes have a tendency to alienate a boy from his father and to make him too fearful of him. In a corresponding manner, the father who is putty in his daughter's hands and is always undoing the mother's discipline, or the father who acts as if he enjoys his daughter's companionship more than his wife's, is being unhelpful not only to his wife but to his daughter as well. This interferes with the good relationship that a daughter should have with her mother in order to grow up to be a happy woman.

Incidentally, it is entirely normal for a father to be a bit more lenient toward his daughter and a mother toward her son, and for a son to feel a little more comfortable with his mother and a daughter with her father, because there is naturally less rivalry between male and female than between two males or two females.

In the average family there is a healthy balance among the feelings of father, mother, sons, and daughters that guides them through these stages of development without any special effort or conscious thought. The discussion here is intended only to offer a Freudian view of the development of three- to six-year-olds and to give some clues for a family whose relationships have gotten out of kilter.

431. Parents can help children through this romantic but jealous stage by gently keeping it clear that they do belong to each other, that a boy can't ever have his mother to himself and a girl can't have her father to herself, but that the parents aren't shocked to realize that their children are mad at them sometimes on this account.

When a girl declares that she is going to marry her father, he can act pleased with the compliment, but he can also explain that he's already married and that when she grows up she'll find a man her own age to marry.

When parents are being companionable together, they needn't and shouldn't let a child break up their conversation. They can cheerfully but firmly remind her that they have things to talk over and suggest that she get busy, too. Their tactfulness will keep them from prolonged displays of affection in front of her, just as it would if other people were present, but they don't need to spring apart guiltily if she comes into the room unexpectedly when they're hugging or kissing.

When a boy is being rude to his father because he's feeling jealous, or to his mother because she's the cause of his jealousy, the parent should insist on politeness. And the converse is equally true if a girl is being rude. But at the same time the parents can ease the child's feelings of anger and guilt by saying that they know the child is cross at them sometimes. (See Section 657.)

432. Sleep problems. Many of the sleep problems in three-, four-, and five-year-old children have been found to be caused by romantic jealousy. The child wanders into the parents' room in the middle of the night and wants to get into their bed because subconsciously she doesn't want them to be alone together. It's much better for her as well as for the parents if they promptly and firmly, but not angrily, take her back to her own bed. (See Section 769.)

Curiosity and Imagination

433. Children's curiosity at this age is intense. They want to know the meaning of everything they encounter. Their imagination is rich. They put two and two together and draw their own conclusions. They connect everything with themselves. When they hear about trains, they want to know right away, "Will I go on a train someday?" When they hear about an illness, it makes them think, "Will I have that?"

434. A little imagination is a good thing. When children of three or four tell a made-up story, they aren't lying in our grown-up sense. Their imagination is vivid to them. They're not sure where the real ends and the unreal begins. That is why they love stories that are told or read to them. That is why they are scared of violent TV programs and movies and shouldn't see them.

You don't need to scold a child or make him feel guilty for making up stories occasionally. You needn't even be concerned yourself, so long as he is outgoing in general and happy with other children. On the other hand, if he is spending a good part of each day telling about imaginary friends or adventures, not as a game but as if he believes in them, it raises the question as to whether his real life is satisfying enough. Part of the remedy may be finding him children the same age to play with and helping him to enjoy them. Another question is whether he is having enough easygoing companionship with his parents.

Children need hugging and piggyback rides. They need to share in parents' jokes and friendly conversations. If the adults around them are undemonstrative, children dream of comfy, understanding playmates as the hungry man dreams of chocolate bars. If the parents are always disapproving, the children invent a wicked companion whom they blame for the naughty things they have done or would like to do. If children are living largely in the imagination and not adjusting well with other children, especially by the age of four, a child psychiatrist, child psychologist, or other mental health counselor should be able to find out what they are lacking.

Fears Around Three, Four, and Five

435. Imaginary worries are common at this age. In earlier sections I discussed how anxieties are different at different age periods. New types of fear crop up fairly often around the age of three and four—fear of the dark, of dogs, of fire engines, of death, of crippled people. Children's imaginations have now developed to the stage where they can put themselves in other people's shoes and picture dangers that they haven't actually experienced. Their curiosity is pushing out in all directions. They want to know not only the cause of everything but what these things have to do with them. They overhear something about dying. They want to know what "dying" is. As soon as they get a dim idea they ask, "Do I have to die?"

These fears are more common in children who have been made tense from battles over such matters as feeding and toilet training, children whose imaginations have been overstimulated by scary stories or too many warnings, children who haven't had enough chance to develop their independence and outgoingness, children whose parents are too protective. The uneasiness accumulated before now seems to be crystallized by the child's new imagination into definite dread.

It sounds as if I mean that any child who develops a fear has been handled mistakenly in the past, but I don't mean that at all. *All* children have fears. The world is still full of things they do not understand, and no matter how lovingly they have been raised, they recognize their own weakness and vulnerability. I think that some children are born more sensitive than others; and all children, no matter how carefully they are brought up, are frightened by something.

It is not your job as a parent to banish all fears from your child's imagination. In fact, learning to face and conquer one's fears is an important lesson. Your job is to help your child learn constructive ways to cope with and conquer those fears. In the eloquent words of Selma Fraiberg in *The*

Magic Years: "The future mental health of the child does not depend on the presence or absence of ogres in his fantasy life. It depends on the child's solution to the ogre problem."

436. Fear of the dark. If your child develops a fear of the dark, try to reassure her. This is more a matter of your manner than your words. Don't make fun of her or be impatient with her or try to argue her out of her fear. If she wants to talk about it, as a few children do, let her. Give her the feeling that you want to understand but that you are *absolutely certain* that nothing bad will happen to her. Naturally you should never threaten her with monsters or policemen or the devil.

Avoid scary movies and TV programs and cruel fairy tales. The child is afraid enough of her own mental creations. Call off any battle that you might be engaged in about eating or staying dry at night. Keep her behaving well by firm guidance rather than by letting her misbehave and then making her feel guilty about it afterward. Arrange to give her a full, outgoing life with other children every day. The more she is absorbed in games and plans, the less she will worry about her inner fears. Leave her door open at night if that is what she wants, or leave a dim light on in her room. It's a small price to pay to keep the goblins out of sight. The light, or the conversation from the living room, won't keep her awake so much as her fears will. When her fear subsides, she will be able to stand the dark again.

437. Questions about death. Realize ahead of time that questions about death are apt to come up at this age. Try to make the first explanation casual, not too scary. You might say, "Everybody has to die someday. Most people die when they get very old and sick, and their body just stops working."

You have to tailor your answer to your child's developmental level. For example, "We lost Uncle Archibald" can strike terror into the heart of any child who himself has gotten lost. Since this is the age when children take everything quite literally, it's especially important not to refer to death as "going to sleep." Many children will then become terrified of going to sleep and dying themselves or else say: "Well, wake him up."

I think it's much better to explain as simply as possible—and without sugar coating the facts—that death is a state where your body "stops working completely." You can then use the opportunity to discuss your family's beliefs about death. Most adults have some degree of fear and resentment of death; there is no way to present the matter to children that will get around this basic human attitude. But if you think of death as something to be met eventually with dignity and fortitude, you'll be able to give somewhat the same feeling about it to your child. Also remember to invite questions and answer them simply and truthfully. Remember to hug her and remind her that you're going to be together for a very, very long time.

438. Funerals. Many parents wonder what to do about allowing a three- to six-year-old child to attend the funeral of a relative or close friend of the family. I think that if a child wants to attend a funeral, if the parents are comfortable with the idea, and if the parents prepare him for what will happen at the funeral, then children from the age of three onward can attend funerals. They can even accompany the family to the cemetery for the burial. It's important that an adult whom the child knows well is with the child and emotionally available to him at all times, to answer questions and if necessary, to take the child home if he becomes too upset.

439. A fear of an animal is common at this period, even in children who have had no bad experiences. Don't drag them to a dog to reassure them. The more you pull them, the more you make them feel they have to pull in the opposite direction. As the months go by, they themselves will try to get over their fear and approach a dog. They will do it faster by themselves than you can ever persuade them.

440. Fear of the water. Don't ever pull a child, screaming, into the ocean or a pool. It is true that occasionally a child who is forced in finds that it is fun and loses the fear abruptly, but in more cases it works the opposite way. Remember that the child is longing to go in, despite the dread she feels.

With fears of dogs and fire engines and policemen and other concrete things, a child may try to get used to the worry and overcome it by playing games about it. This playing out of a fear is a great help if the child is able to do it. A fear is meant to make us act. Our bodies are flooded with adrenaline, which makes the heart beat faster and supplies sugar for quick energy. We are ready to run like the wind or to fight like wild animals (fight or flight). The running and the fighting burn up the anxiety. Sitting still does nothing to relieve it. If children with a fear of a dog can play games in which they pound the stuffing out of a toy dog, it partly relieves them. If your child develops an intense fear or a number of fears that begin to cross over into other parts of his daily life, you ought to get the help of a children's mental health professional.

441. Fear of injury. I'd like to discuss separately the fear of bodily injury in the age period between two and a half and five, because there are special things you can do to prevent or relieve it. Children at this age want to know the reason for everything, worry easily, and apply dangers to themselves. If they see a crippled or deformed person, they first want to know what happened to that person; then put themselves in the person's place and wonder if that injury might happen to them.

This is also the age period in which there is naturally a great interest in physical mastery of all kinds (hopping, running, climbing), which makes body intactness very important and being broken very upsetting. This explains why a child at the age of two and a half or three can get so upset about a broken cookie, refusing a cookie that's in two pieces and demanding a whole one.

Children develop these fears not only about real injuries. They even get mixed up and worried about the natural differences between boys and girls. If a boy around the age of three sees a girl undressed, it may strike him as queer that she hasn't got a penis like his. He's apt to say, "Where is her

287

wee wee?" If he doesn't receive a satisfactory answer right away, he may jump to the conclusion that some accident has happened to her. Next comes the anxious thought, "That might happen to me, too." The same misunderstanding may worry the little girl when she first realizes that boys are made differently. First she asks, "What's that?" Then she wants to know anxiously, "Why don't I have one? What happened to it?" That's the way a three-year-old's mind works. Children may be so upset that they're afraid to question their parents.

This worry about why boys are different from girls shows up in different ways. I remember a boy just under three who, with an anxious expression, kept watching his baby sister being bathed and telling his mother, "Baby is boo-boo." That was his word for hurt. His mother couldn't make out what he was talking about until he got bold enough to point. At about the same time he began to hold on to his own penis in a worried way. His mother was unhappy about this and assumed it was the beginning of a bad habit. It never occurred to her that there was a connection between these two developments. I also remember a little girl who became worried after she found out about boys, and kept trying to undress different children to see how they were made, too. She didn't do this in a sly way; you could see she was fearful. Later she began to handle her genitals. A boy three and a half first became upset about his younger sister's body and then began to worry about everything in the house that was broken. He would ask his parents nervously, "Why is this tin soldier broken?" There was no sense to this question, because he had broken it himself the day before. Everything that was damaged seemed to remind him of his fears about himself.

It's wise to realize ahead of time that normal children between two and a half and three and a half are likely to wonder about things like bodily differences and if they aren't given a comforting explanation when they first get curious, they're apt to come to worrisome conclusions. It's no use waiting for them to say, "I want to know why a boy isn't made like a girl," because they won't be that specific. They may ask some kind of question, or they may hint around, or they may just wait and get worried. Don't think of this as an unwholesome interest in sex. To them it's just like any other important question at first. You can see why it would work the wrong way to shush them, or scold them, or blush and refuse to answer. That would give them the idea they are on dangerous ground, which is what you want to avoid. On the other hand, you don't need to be solemn as if you were giving a lecture. It's easier than that. It helps, first of all, to bring the child's fear out into the open by saying that he probably thinks a girl had a penis but something happened to it. Then you try to make it clear, in a matter-of-fact, cheerful tone, that girls and women are made differently from boys and men; they are *meant* to be that way. A small child gets an idea more easily from examples. You can explain that Johnny is made just like Daddy, Uncle Harry, David, and so on, and that Mary is made like Mommy, Mrs. Jenkins, and Helen (listing all the individuals that the child knows best). A little girl needs extra reassurance because it's natural for her to want to have something that she can see. (I heard of a little girl who complained to her mother, "But he's so fancy and I'm so plain.") It will help her to know that her mother likes being made the way she is, that her parents love her just the way she is. This may also be a good time to explain that girls when they are older can grow babies of their own inside them and have breasts with which to nurse them. That's a thrilling idea at three or four.

442. The fear of nuclear war or nuclear accident. Children who have heard their parents discussing nuclear war or nuclear accidents are apt to pick up such worries. Young children express these worries as fear that their parents will be killed, and they worry about who will take care of them then. Older children see the direct danger to themselves. Adolescents are moved to pessimism, asking what is the use of studying or maintaining their health if they are to die before they become workers and parents.

Parents can give their children partial reassurance if they can say, "Yes there is a danger but it need not happen if we all work politically for peace. We vote for the candidates for president, senator, and congressman who are for a nuclear freeze, disarmament, and peaceful settlement of disputes. We write to our officials, not just once but often. We belong to peace groups and attend demonstrations. You can help by writing letters and attending demonstrations, too."

Children who are too young to write letters or understand demonstrations can be reassured by being told that their parents and other adults are working hard to prevent nuclear war from ever happening.

SIX- TO ELEVEN-
YEAR-OLDS

Fitting into the Outside World

443. Changes after age six. Children become more independent of their parents, even impatient with them. They're more concerned with what the other children say and do. They develop a stronger sense of responsibility about matters they think are important. Their conscience may become so stern that it nags them about senseless things like stepping over cracks. They are interested in impersonal subjects like arithmetic and engines. In short, they're beginning the job of emancipating themselves from the family and taking their places as responsible citizens of the outside world.

In Section 430, I mentioned Freud's explanation of what makes children change so much. Between three and five years they were generally cozy, affectionate family members who proudly patterned their activities, table manners, and speech after their parents. The girl was trying to be like her admired mother, and she had a strong romantic attachment to her father. For the boy it was the other way around.

But the possessive, romantic feelings brought about an increasingly uncomfortable sense of rivalry with the parent of the same sex. The unconscious fear of incurring the parent's resentment eventually caused a turning-away from open expressions of feeling and a reversal of many feelings. The former pleasure in romantic daydreaming now turns to aversion. Children may now squirm when a parent tries to kiss them. Their aversion spreads to include children of the opposite sex. They groan when there are love scenes in movies. This is what makes them so eager to turn to such impersonal and abstract subjects as reading, writing, arithmetic, mechanics, science, nature study. This is part of the explanation of why children are so emotionally ready for schoolwork at this age.

Another way of viewing the psychological changes that take place in children of about six or seven is to see how these changes are related to the evolution of humans from their pre-human ancestors. Each individual passing through the six- to twelve-year-old period is retracing, I think, that particular stage of evolution. Millions of years ago our pre-human ancestors used to acquire full growth and full instincts by about five years of age. In their attitude toward family life, when full grown, they were probably much like our five-year-old children: happy to continue to live with their family, happy to be obedient to the elders of the family, striving to be like them and learn from them.

In other words, these prehumans were tied together for life by close personal family ties. It was only much later in the course of evolution that our ancestors developed the ability to become more independent of their parents and learned to live in a larger society by means of cooperation, rules, self-control, thinking things out.

It takes years for each individual to learn how to get along in this complicated adult way. Probably that's the reason human beings are held up so long in their physical growth. The infant increases rapidly in size like an animal, and so does the older child in the puberty period. But in between they slow down more and more, particularly in the two years just before puberty development begins. It's as if their nature were saying, "Whoa! Before you can be trusted with a powerful body and full-grown instincts, you must first learn to think for yourself, control your wishes and instincts for the sake of others, learn how to get along with your fellows, understand the laws of conduct in the world outside your family, and study the skills by which people live."

444. Independence from parents. Children after six go on loving their parents deeply underneath, but they usually don't show it so much on the surface. They're often cooler toward other adults, too. They no longer want to be loved as a possession or as an appealing child. They're gaining a sense of dignity as individuals and want to be treated as such.

From their need to be less dependent on their parents, they turn more to trusted adults outside the family for ideas and knowledge. If they mistakenly get the idea from an admired science teacher that red blood cells are larger than white blood cells, there's nothing their parents can say that will change their minds.

The ideas of right and wrong that their parents taught them have not been forgotten. In fact, they have sunk in so deep that they now think of them as their own creations. Children are impatient when their parents keep reminding them of what they ought to do, because they know already and want to be considered responsible.

445. Bad manners. Children drop the grown-up words out of their vocabulary and pick up a little tough talk. They want the style of clothes and haircut that the other kids have. They may leave their shoelaces untied with the same conviction with which people wear party buttons during a political campaign. They may lose some of their table manners, come to meals with dirty hands, slump over the dish, and stuff too much food into their mouths. Perhaps they kick the leg of the table absentmindedly. They throw their coats on the floor. They slam doors or leave them open.

Without realizing it, they are really accomplishing three things at once. First, they're looking to children of their own age as models of behavior. Second, they're declaring their right to be more independent of parents. Third, they're keeping square with their own conscience, because they're not doing anything that's morally wrong.

These bad manners and bad habits are apt to make their parents unhappy. They imagine that the child is forgetting all that they so carefully taught. Actually, these changes are proof that their child has learned what good behavior is—otherwise he wouldn't bother to rebel against it. When he feels he has established his independence, he will probably revisit his family values.

Manners may seem to be lost.

I don't mean that every child is a hellion during this age period. One who gets along happily with easygoing parents may show no open rebelliousness at all—most girls show less than boys. But if you look carefully, you will see signs of a change of attitude.

What do you do? After all, children must take a bath once in a while, get neatened up on holidays. You may be able to overlook some of the minor irritating ways, but you should be firm in matters that are important to you. When you have to ask them to wash their hands, try to be matter-of-fact. It's the nagging tone, the bossiness, that they find irritating and that spurs them on unconsciously to further balkiness.

446. Clubs. This is the age for the blossoming of clubs. A number of kids who are already friends decide to form a secret club. They work like beavers making membership buttons, fixing up a meeting place (preferably hidden), drawing up a list of rules. They may never figure out what the secret is. But the secrecy idea probably represents the need to prove they can govern themselves, undisturbed by grown-ups and unhampered by other more dependent children.

It seems to help children, when they're trying to be grown-up, to get together with others who feel the same way. Then the group tries to bring outsiders into line by making them feel left out or by picking on them. This sounds conceited and cruel to grown-ups, but that's because we are accustomed to using more refined methods of disapproving of each other. The children are only feeling the instinct to get community life organized. This is one of the forces that makes our civilization click.

447. Helping children to be sociable and popular. These are some of the early steps in bringing up children to be sociable and popular: not fussing over them in their first years; letting them be around other children their size from the age of a year; allowing them freedom to develop independence; making as few changes as possible in where the family lives and where the children go to school; letting them, as far as possible, associate with, dress like, talk like, play like, and have the same allowance and other privileges as the other average children in the neighborhood. Of course, I don't mean letting them take after the town's worst scoundrel. And you don't have to take your child's word about what the other children are allowed to do.

How happily people get along as adults in their jobs and in family and social life depends a great deal on how they got along with other children when they were young. If parents give children high standards and high ideals at home, these form part of their character and show up in the long run, even though they go through a period of bad English and rough manners in the middle period of childhood. But if parents are unhappy about the neighborhood they live in and the companions their children have, give their children a feeling that they are different from the others, or discourage them from making friends, the children may grow up unable to get along comfortably with anyone. Then the high standards won't be of much use to the world or to themselves.

If a boy is having trouble making friends, it helps most if he can be in a school and in a class where the program is flexible. Then the teacher can arrange things so that he has chances to use his abilities to contribute to class projects. This is how the other children learn to appreciate his good qualities and to like him. A good teacher who is respected by the class can also raise a child's popularity in the group by showing that she appreciates that child. It even helps to put him in a seat next to a very popular child, or to let him be partners with that child in activities, going on errands around the school, etc.

There are things that the parents can do at home, too. Be friendly and hospitable when your child brings others home to play. Encourage him to invite friends to meals and then serve the dishes that they consider "super." When you plan weekend trips, picnics, excursions, movies, and other shows, invite another child with whom your child wants to be friends—not necessarily the one you would like him to be friendly with. Children, like adults, have a mercenary side and they are more apt to see the good points in a child who provides treats for them.

Naturally, you don't want your child to have only "bought" popularity; that kind won't last anyway. What you are after is to prime the pump, to give him a chance to break into a group that may be shutting him out because of the natural clannishness of this age. Then, if he has appealing qualities, he can take over from that start and build real friendships of his own.

448. Avoid too many organized activities. By the time they're seven years old, some children are involved in organized after-school activities every day. This is particularly true in single-parent families and those in which both parents work outside the home. There's nothing wrong with sports, gymnastics, music, and dance, if they're done in moderation and without excessive competitiveness. But all children need some time to just hang out, alone or with friends, using their own creative imaginations to decide what to do. For working and single-parent families this is hard to arrange, but I think it's important to make the effort.

449. Allowance should be separate from chores. An allowance is a way for children to learn about handling money and about saving or spending. Most children can begin to understand these ideas at about age six or seven, so that's a good time to start giving an allowance. The amount will depend on your family custom and finances, as well as the pattern in your community. I think children should make their own choices about how to spend their allowance, as long as it isn't for something the parents have ruled out, like excessive sweets.

I don't think allowance should be used as payment for chores, because chores serve a different purpose. They are one of the ways children learn about doing their share in the household, the same way they will later participate in the larger society. There should be routine chores for each child, such as setting or clearing the table, washing the dishes, or taking out the garbage. If you are consistent and matter-of-fact about their responsibilities, the children will be, too. Try not to keep making exceptions, or letting them get away without finishing their tasks.

There are always some extra chores, and these may be a way for children to earn money at home. Whether or not a teenager should be paid for baby-sitting at home is up to each family to decide. I think the same is true for some of the heavier jobs, like lawn-mowing or car-washing.

Self-Control

450. Children after six become strict about some things. Think of the games children enjoy at this age. They're no longer so interested in make-believe without any plan. They want games that have rules and require skill. In hopscotch, jacks, and jump-rope, you have to do things in a certain order, which becomes harder as you progress. If you miss, you must penalize yourself, go back to the beginning, and start over again. It's the very strictness of the rules that appeals to children. This is the age for starting collections, whether it's stamps or cards or stones. The pleasure of collecting is in achieving orderliness and completeness.

At this age children have the desire at times to put their belongings in order. Suddenly they neaten their desk, put labels on the drawers, or arrange their piles of comic books. They don't keep their things neat for long, but you can see that the urge must be strong just to get them started.

451. Compulsions. The tendency toward strictness becomes so strong in many children around eight, nine, and ten that they develop nervous habits. You probably remember them from your own childhood. The commonest is stepping over cracks in the sidewalk. There's no sense to it; you just have a superstitious feeling that you ought to. Other examples are touching every third picket in a fence, making numbers

A Compulsion May Have a Meaning

"Step on a crack, break your mother's back."

298

come out even in some way, saying certain words before going through a door. If you think you have made a mistake, you must go way back to where you were absolutely sure that you were right, and start over again.

The hidden meaning of a compulsion pops out in the thoughtless childhood saying, "Step on a crack, break your mother's back." Everyone has hostile feelings at times toward the people who are close to him, but his conscience would be shocked at the idea of really harming them and warns him to keep such thoughts out of his mind. And if a person's conscience becomes excessively stern, it keeps nagging about such "bad" thoughts even after he has succeeded in hiding them away in his subconscious mind. He still feels guilty, though he doesn't know what for. It eases his conscience to be extra careful and proper about such a senseless thing as how to navigate a crack in the sidewalk.

The reason a child is apt to show compulsions around the age of nine is not because his thoughts are more wicked but because his conscience is just naturally becoming stricter at this stage of development. He is now worrying, perhaps, about his suppressed desire to hurt his brother or father or grandmother when they irritate him. We know that this is an age when the child is also trying to suppress thoughts about sex, and these sometimes play a part in compulsions, too.

At this age compulsions are also a way of keeping the world of one's playmates under control. Children are now free of constant adult supervision and control, and while this feels great in many ways, it's also scary in many ways.

Mild compulsions are so common around the ages of eight, nine, and ten years that it's a question whether they should be considered normal or a sign of nervousness. I wouldn't worry too much about a mild compulsion, like stepping over cracks, in a child around nine years who is happy, outgoing, and doing well in school. On the other hand, I'd call on a mental health professional for help if a child has compulsions that occupy a lot of his time (for instance, excessive hand-washing, precautions against germs) or if he is tense, worried, or unsociable.

452. Tics. Tics are nervous habits such as eye-blinking, shoulder-shrugging, grimacing, neck-twisting, throat-clearing, sniffing, dry coughing. Like compulsions, tics occur most commonly around the age of nine, but they can begin at any age after two. The motion is usually quick, repeated regularly, and always in the same form. It is more frequent when the child is under tension. A tic may last off and on for a number of weeks or months and then go away for good or be replaced by a new one. Blinking, sniffing, throat-clearing, and dry coughing often start with a cold but continue after the cold is gone. Shoulder-shrugging may begin when a child has a new loose-fitting garment that feels as if it were falling off. Children may copy a mannerism from another child with a tic, especially from a child they look up to, but these mannerisms don't last long.

Tics are more common in tense children with fairly strict parents. There may be too much pressure at home. Sometimes the mother or father is going at the child too hard, directing him, correcting him, whenever he is in sight. Or the parents may be showing constant disapproval in a quieter way, or setting standards that are too high, or providing too many activities such as dancing, music, and athletic lessons. If the child were bold enough to fight back, he would probably be less tightened up inside. But being, in most cases, too well brought up for that, he bottles up his irritation, and it keeps backfiring in the form of a tic.

No child should be scolded or corrected on account of his tics. They are out of his control. The parents' whole effort should go into making his home life relaxed and agreeable, with the least possible nagging and making his school and social life satisfying.

I am speaking here about the mild tics of childhood, which one child in ten will show. These almost always go away with benign neglect. Maybe one out of a hundred children will continue to have multiple tics that persist for over a year. This one child may have Tourette's Disorder (see Glossary) and should be checked by the doctor or nurse practitioner.

Posture

453. The treatment of bad posture depends on the cause.
Good or bad posture is made up of a number of factors.

One—perhaps the most important factor—is the skeleton the child is born with. You see individuals who have been round-shouldered from babyhood, like their mother or father before them. Some children seem to be born with a relaxed set of muscles and ligaments. Other children look tightly knit, in action or at rest. It's hard for them to slump.

There are also rare diseases that affect posture, and chronic illness and chronic fatigue (from any cause) can cause children to slump and sag. Overweight sometimes exaggerates sway back, knock-knees, and flat feet. Unusual tallness makes the self-conscious adolescent duck the head. A child with poor posture needs regular examinations to make sure that there is no physical reason.

Many children slouch because of a lack of self-confidence. This may result from too much criticism at home, from difficulties in school, or from an unsatisfactory social life. People who are buoyant and sure of themselves show it in the way they sit and stand and walk. When parents realize how much the child's feelings have to do with his posture, they can handle the problem more wisely.

The natural impulse of a parent, eager to have a child look good, is to keep after posture: "Remember the shoulders," or "For goodness' sake, stand up straight." But children who are stooped over because their parents have always kept after them too much won't be improved by more nagging. Generally speaking, the best results come when the child receives posture work through dance or other body-movement classes, from a physical therapist, or in a doctor's office. In these places the atmosphere is more business-like than at home. The parents may be able to help a boy greatly in carrying out his exercises at home, if he wants help and if they can give it in a friendly way. But their main job is to help the child's spirit by aiding his school adjustment, fostering a happy social life, and making him feel adequate and self-respecting at home.

Stealing

454. Taking things in early childhood. Small children of one, two, and three take things that don't belong to them, but this isn't really stealing. They don't have any clear sense of what belongs to them and what doesn't. They just take things because they want them very much. It's better not to make small children feel wicked. The parent needs only to remind them that the toy is Peter's, that Peter will want to play with it soon, and that "you have lots of toys at home."

455. What stealing means in the child who knows better. Problem stealing occasionally crops up in the period between six and adolescence. When children at this age take something, they know they are doing wrong. They are more apt to steal secretly, to hide what they have stolen, and to deny that they have done it.

When parents or teachers find that a child has stolen something, they are understandably pretty upset. Their impulse is to jump hard on the child and fill her with a sense of shame. This is natural enough, since we have all been taught that stealing is a serious crime. It scares us to see it coming out in our child.

It is essential that children know clearly that their parents disapprove of any stealing and insist on immediate restitution. On the other hand, it isn't wise to scare the daylights out of them or act as if you will never love them again.

Let's take first the boy around seven who has been carefully brought up by conscientious parents, who has a reasonable number of toys and other possessions, and who gets an allowance. If he steals something, it's apt to be small amounts of money from his mother or from classmates, his teacher's pen, or a comic book from another child's locker. Often there's no sense to the stealing because he may own these things anyway. We can see that he's mixed up in his feelings. He seems to have a blind craving for something and tries to satisfy it by taking an object he doesn't really need. What does he really want?

In most cases, the child is at least slightly unhappy and lonesome. He probably doesn't have as close a relationship with his parents as he used to. He may not feel completely successful in making friends with children his own age. (He may feel this way even though he is actually quite popular.) I think the reason that stealing occurs more often around seven is that children at this age may be feeling particularly distant from their parents. Then, if they haven't the knack of making equally warm and satisfying friendships, they get into a no-man's-land and feel isolated. This explains why some children who steal money use it all to try to buy friendship. One passes out dimes and nickels to classmates. Another uses it to buy candy for the class. Remember that children are drawing away a little from the parents, and the parents are apt to be more disapproving of them during this trying period.

The early part of adolescence is another period when some children become more lonely because of increased self-consciousness, sensitivity, and desire for independence.

A craving for more affection probably plays some part in stealing at all ages, but there are usually other individual factors, too, such as fear, jealousy, resentment. A girl who is deeply envious of her brother may repeatedly steal objects that are linked in her unconscious mind with boys.

456. What to do for the child who steals. If you are pretty sure that your child (or pupil) has stolen something, tell him so, be firm about wanting to know where he got it, insist on restitution. In other words don't make it easy for him to lie. (If parents accept lies too easily, it's as if they were condoning the theft.) The child should take the object back to the child or store from which it was taken. If it's a store, it may be tactful for the parent to go along to explain to the salesperson that the child took it without paying and wants to return it. A teacher can return an article to its owner to spare the child from public shame. In other words, it's not necessary to humiliate the child, only to make it crystal clear that stealing will not be permitted.

It is time to think about whether the child needs more affection and approval at home and more help in making closer friendships outside. This is the time to give him, if possible, an allowance of about the same size as that of the other children he knows. This will help him to establish himself as one of the group. The parents should get help from a child guidance clinic or a child psychiatrist or psychologist if the stealing persists or if the child seems maladjusted in other ways.

The next type of stealing is entirely different. There are plenty of neighborhoods where the kids think of swiping things as the daring thing to do. It's not proper, but it's not vicious and it's not a sign of maladjustment. I think of this as a sort of group testing-out of the individual conscience. The children of conscientious parents who live in such a neighborhood may need an understanding talk, but they should not be treated like criminals because they joined in one of these adventures. They were only obeying a normal instinct to make their place in the group. The cure lies in a clear-cut reprimand and making sure that the parents aren't modeling this kind of behavior by talking—even boasting at times—about cheating on their income taxes or charging personal phone calls to their business phone.

Finally, there is the stealing of the aggressive child or adult who has little conscience or sense of responsibility. A person gets this way only through a childhood quite lacking in love and security. The only hope is in good psychological treatment and being able to live with kind, affectionate people.

Lying

457. Why does an older child lie? Everyone, grown-up or child, gets in a jam occasionally when the only tactful way out is a small lie, and this is no cause for alarm. But if a child tells a lie to deceive, the first question to ask yourself is: Why does the child feel she has to lie?

458. A child isn't naturally deceitful. When a girl lies regularly it means that she is under too much pressure of some kind. If she is failing in her schoolwork and lying about it, it isn't because she doesn't care. Her lying shows that she does care. Is the work too hard for her? Is she confused in her mind by other worries so that she can't concentrate? Are her parents setting too high standards? Your job is to find out what is wrong, with the help of the teacher, a guidance counselor, a school psychologist, or a psychiatrist. You don't have to pretend that she has pulled the wool over your eyes. You might say gently, "You don't have to lie to me. Tell me what the trouble is and we'll see what we can do." But she won't be able to tell you the answer right away because she probably doesn't know it herself. Even if she knows some of her worries, she can't break down all at once. Helping her to express her feelings or worries takes time and understanding.

ADOLESCENCE

Adolescence is a two-way street. Teenagers and their parents both have to find a way to let go of each other gradually and as gracefully as possible. In some families, this happens very smoothly. In many others, there are struggles, often caused by parents not being aware of the normal developmental issues in adolescence. I think that the whole process is much more comfortable when parents remember that their teenagers aren't really out to get them, but in fact are just trying to establish their own adult identity.

Puberty

459. Physical changes. Pubertal development marks the beginning of adolescence. It consists of the two to four years of rapid physical growth and development that precede the appearance of reproductive capabilities.

460. Timing. The first thing to realize is that there is a wide age range at which puberty begins. The largest number of girls begin their development at around the age of ten and have their first period at about twelve and a half. The average boy starts puberty two years later than the average girl.

Pubertal timing is influenced by heredity, nutrition, and general health. Usually, by the time a girl is twelve and a half or a boy is fourteen the early stages of puberty have begun. Conversely, pubertal development prior to eight years of age for girls and ten years of age in boys should be discussed with your child's physician.

461. General pubertal developments. Although they mature at different rates, there are common elements to puberty in both boys and girls which have a predictable progression and are triggered by hormonal changes. The development of height, muscle growth, pubic, armpit, and facial hair, as well as changes in the genitalia occur in a sequence that is remarkably consistent from one adolescent to another. Your doctor or nurse practitioner will examine your teenager to see that this developmental sequence is progressing normally.

There are five stages of pubertal development in adolescence. These stages are referred to as the "sexual maturational rating" or Tanner staging, and should be a part of every physical exam. This is important to know since most parents no longer see their children naked to be able to assess this themselves, nor do they have the experience that enables the clinician to make an informed evaluation. For example, in boys, a growth spurt and the lowering of the voice are often the first outward signs of pubertal development that has already been under way for a year.

462. Puberty development in girls. Let's trace what happens in the case of the average girl who starts puberty at age ten. When she was seven years old, she was growing 2 to $2\frac{1}{2}$ inches a year. When she was eight, her rate of growth slowed down to perhaps $1\frac{3}{4}$ inches a year. Nature seemed to be putting on the brakes. Suddenly, at about ten, the brakes let go and she begins to shoot up at the rate of 3 or $3\frac{1}{2}$ inches a year for the next two years. Instead of putting on 5 to 8 pounds a year, as she used to, she now gains between 10 and 20 pounds a year. Her appetite increases significantly to make this gain possible.

But other things are happening, too. At the beginning of this period her breasts begin to develop. The first thing noticed is a hard lump under the nipple. This may be frightening to parents because of the fear of breast cancer, but this is the normal onset of breast development. Then the whole breast begins to take shape. For the first year and a half it has a conical shape, but as her first menstrual period nears, it rounds out into more nearly a hemisphere. Occasionally one breast begins to develop months before the other. This is fairly common and nothing to worry about. The earlier developing breast tends to stay larger throughout puberty and may on occasion remain so permanently.

Soon after the breasts begin to develop, the pubic hair starts to grow. Later, hair appears in the armpits. The hips widen. The skin texture changes.

At twelve and a half the average girl has her first menstrual period. This event is called *menarche*. By now her body has begun to look more like a woman's, and she has acquired most of the height she will ever have. From this time on, her growing slows down rapidly. In the year after her first period she will grow perhaps $1\frac{1}{2}$ inches, and in the year after that, perhaps $\frac{3}{4}$ inch. In many girls, menstrual periods are irregular and infrequent for the first year or two. This is not a sign that something is wrong; it only shows that full maturity was not reached by the first period.

There is no one age at which puberty begins. We have been talking about the average girl, but each girl has an individual maturational rate and timetable. The fact that a girl starts her puberty development much earlier or later than average usually doesn't mean that her glands aren't working right. It only means that she is on a faster or slower timetable. This individual timetable seems to be an inborn trait: parents who were late developers are more apt to have children who are late developers, and vice versa. The thirteen-year-old who has shown no signs of pubertal development can be assured that she will develop, even though it may take her longer to do so.

Adequate nutrition throughout childhood is another factor. In earlier times, when many poorer families had inadequate diets, the average age of menarche in girls was sixteen.

463. There are other variations besides the age at which puberty development begins. In some girls the pubic hair appears months before the breasts start to develop. And once in a while hair in the armpits is the earliest sign of change instead of a late one. The length of time between the first signs of puberty development and the coming of the first period is usually about two and a half years. If a girl has been fully mature for over two years or is over 16 years of age and has not had her first period, she should be evaluated by her physician.

464. Puberty brings psychological reactions. Regardless of the age at which she reaches puberty, a girl is bound to have some emotional reactions, even if she does not show them. The girl who gets along well with her mother and wants to

Puberty comes at different ages.

be like her may be pleased when she sees that she is growing up, whether or not she is ahead of her classmates. But the girl who resents being a girl—because she is jealous of her brother and would like to have a boy's body, because she doesn't get along well with her mother and doesn't want to be like her, or because she is afraid of growing up—is apt to feel resentful or alarmed by early signs of womanhood.

When the onset of puberty is later or earlier than average, there can be psychological effects. The girl who begins puberty at eight may feel awkward and self-conscious when she finds herself the only girl in her class who's shooting upward and acquiring the shape of a woman. This experience isn't painful to every early developer. It depends on how well adjusted the girl was before and on how ready and eager she is to grow up.

Also bothered is the girl who's on a slow timetable. The thirteen-year-old who has shown no signs of puberty development has seen her classmates grow rapidly taller and develop bodies more like those of women while she still has the body of a child and remains in a period of slow growth. She may think she's abnormal. She needs to be assured she will grow and develop just as surely as the sun rises and sets. If her mother and other relatives were late developers, she needs to be told that. She can be promised that when her time comes, she too will grow taller and develop a woman's body.

465. Puberty development in boys. The first thing to realize about puberty development in boys is that the average boy begins two years later than the average girl, at twelve in contrast to her ten. The earlier developers among boys begin as early as ten, a few younger still. Plenty of slow developers start as late as fourteen, and there are a few who wait longer.

During puberty a boy may grow in height at double the rate as before. The penis, testicles, and scrotum (the sac in which the testicles lie) all develop rapidly. Pubic hair begins to grow first, then the testicles grow, and finally the penis begins to increase, first in length and then in diameter.

All these events begin prior to the growth spurt and may be known only to the boy himself, in contrast to a girl's development where the first sign of puberty, breast development, is obvious to others. Later comes the hair in the armpits and on the face. Then the voice cracks and deepens.

In some boys, a small area under the breast nipples enlarges and may become tender; this is normal.

After about two years the boy's body has fairly well completed its transition. In the following few years, he will continue to grow more slowly and finally stop at around age eighteen. Some later-developing boys will continue to grow even into their early twenties.

466. The awkward stage. Boys, like girls, often go through a period of some physical and emotional awkwardness as they come to terms with a new body and new feelings. A boy's voice may keep breaking as an example of how he is both boy and man and yet not either. In addition, girls of the same age are, on the average, two years ahead of the average boy's development physically and often socially as well.

467. The boy who is on a slow timetable of development, who is still a "shrimp" at fourteen when most of his friends have turned almost into grown men, usually needs reassurance. Size, physique, and athletic ability count for a lot at this age. Some parents, instead of reassuring their son that he will start developing in time and grow 8 or 9 inches in the process, take him on a hunt for a doctor who will give him growth hormone treatment. This only convinces him that something is *really* wrong with him. True, there are hormone preparations that bring on the signs of puberty, at whatever age they are given. However, these may well cause a boy to end up shorter than he normally would have been by stopping his bone growth prematurely. I'm opposed to tampering with nature in such a vital matter. For the rare occasion when there might be too little or too much growth hormone production, a pediatric endocrinologist (hormone specialist) should be consulted before any decision is made about giving hormones to a boy or a girl.

Other Changes in Adolescence

468. Body odor. One of the earliest changes of adolescence is more profuse and stronger-smelling perspiration in the armpits. Some children (and parents too) are not aware of the odor, but it can cause unpopularity with schoolmates. Now hygiene becomes especially important. Daily washing with soap and perhaps the regular use of a suitable deodorant will control the odor.

469. Acne. Our understanding of the cause and treatment of pimples (acne) has changed a lot in recent years. The texture of the skin becomes more coarse at puberty. The pores enlarge and secrete up to ten times more oil than previously. Some of the pores may become clogged with a combination of oil (sebum) and dead skin cells. (The skin cells that line the pores naturally die and peel off at regular intervals and are replaced by new ones.) When this plug of cells and oil comes into contact with the air, it oxidizes and turns black. This is how blackheads form. The germs that are normally on the skin may get into these enlarged, plugged pores and cause a pimple, which is a small infection. The same basic process that causes the usual acne pimples can also cause a deeper, scarring type of acne, which tends to run in families.

Two misconceptions about acne have been cleared up by recent research. We now know that the pimples of acne are not caused by dirt, and we have also learned that certain foods, such as chocolate and fried foods, do not effect this skin condition. Pimples occur as a natural part of puberty in nearly all teenagers, whether or not they have dry or oily skin. Since squeezing a pimple can make the infection worse, teenagers should be encouraged to avoid squeezing.

Some adolescents, worried about sex, imagine that their pimples are caused by sexual fantasies or masturbation, and they need to be reassured that that isn't true.

Children are entitled to all the help they can get with pimples, from their regular doctor, nurse practitioner, or a skin specialist, for the sake of improving their present appearance and spirits, and to prevent the permanent scars that sometimes develop. With modern methods of treatment, great improvement can be made in most cases and even the deeper, scarring type of acne can be kept under control. In some cases, a physician or nurse practitioner may prescribe an antibiotic, a topical benzoyl peroxide cream, or a medicine related to vitamin A.

Whatever the specific methods are prescribed, there are also general measures that are believed to be helpful. Vigorous daily exercise, fresh air, and direct sunshine (wearing a suitable sunscreen to avoid sunburn, see Section 638) seem to improve many complexions. And it's generally a good idea to wash the face with a mild soap or soap substitute and warm water in the morning and again at bedtime. There are soaps and topical medications that contain 5 to 10 percent benzoyl peroxide that can be purchased without a prescription. And there are many water-based cosmetic preparations (the oil-based ones should be avoided) available for covering up pimples and blemishes while nature takes its course.

Psychological Changes

Pubertal physical development has a distinct onset and end point. The psychological changes of adolescence are a little bit more difficult to categorize. One way to look at adolescent emotional development is to think of the psychological tasks or milestones that must be achieved in order to be able to function effectively in the adult world. At each stage of adolescence—early adolescence, from twelve to fourteen years; middle adolescence, from fifteen to seventeen years; and late adolescence from eighteen to twenty-one years—young people struggle toward and eventually reach these milestones. The support and guidance that parents need to give—and the ways in which they need to give—also vary with each stage.

Psychological Milestones of Adolescence

- Coming to terms with their new physical identity
- Developing a new male or female emotional identity that is separate from their parents
- Coming to terms with the difference between the norms and values of their peers and those of their parents, and establishing and expressing their own moral convictions
- Developing a sense of self-responsibility and demonstrating at least the potential for financial self-sufficiency

A central problem for adolescents and young adults is to find out or investigate what kind of people they are going to be, doing what work, living by what principles. This is partly a conscious, but even more an unconscious, process. Erik Erikson has called this the identity crisis: the search to find the real inner self. In groping to find this identity adolescents may try out a variety of roles: dreamer, cosmopolitan, cynic, leader of lost causes, ascetic, and so on.

Adolescents have to separate themselves emotionally from their parents in order to find out who they are and what they want to be. Yet they are basically made from their parents—not because they have inherited their genes from them but also because they have been deliberately patterning themselves after them all their lives. So they must now pry themselves apart. The eventual outcome will be influenced by three circumstances: the extent of their dependency, the intensity of their rebelliousness and rivalry, and the kind of outside world they live in and what it asks of them.

470. Risk-taking behavior. One way for the adolescent to reach these milestones is by taking risks. Risk-taking can foster a mastery of life skills, enhance self-esteem, and develop decision-making strategies. As adults we are able to calculate risks and weigh benefits because as adolescents we learned, through trial and error, how much risk we were willing to take and what the cost of those risks might be.

As parents, your role is to help your children to safely take risks through providing limits. But what limits are appropriate to set and at what age? This depends in large part on the stage of adolescent development the child is in.

471. When the risks are beyond average. Over the years, the world has become a more dangerous place in which to grow up. Adolescent pregnancy, drug use, violence and suicide are ever-present in the media. Discussions of the complicated origins of these behaviors—which represent the severe end of the risk-taking spectrum—lie beyond my discussion of the *average* adolescent. However, parents should be aware that help for excessive risk-taking and other concerns of adolescence is more available now than ever.

In response to the complex needs of today's adolescents, clinicians are being trained to address specific problem behaviors. There is also a recognized subspecialty of Adolescent Medicine, providing additional training and certification to physicians interested in primarily caring for this age group.

The Three Stages of Adolescence

472. The psychological tasks of early adolescence. The years from age twelve to age fourteen are characterized by the adolescents' need to come to terms with their developing bodies. In this age group there is a wider variation in the physical stages of development than any other age. Between ten and fourteen, the average girl is two full years ahead of the average boy in development—towering over him in height and more sophisticated in her interests. She's beginning to want to go to dances and be treated as if she were glamorous, while he is still an uncivilized little boy who thinks it would be shameful to pay attention to her. During this whole period it may be better for social functions to include different age groups for a better fit.

As a result of all the physical and emotional changes, adolescents at this stage become acutely self-conscious about their body. They may exaggerate and worry about any defect. If a girl has freckles, she may think they make her look "horrible." A slight peculiarity in the body or how it functions easily convinces them that they are "abnormal."

They may not be able to manage their new body with as much coordination as they used to, and the same is true of their new feelings. They are apt to be touchy, easily hurt when criticized. At one moment they feel like grown-ups and want to be treated as such. The next moment they feel like children again and expect to be cared for.

Adolescents often become ashamed of their parents for a few years, particularly when their friends are present. This is partly related to their anxious search for their own identities and partly it reflects the extreme self-consciousness of the age period. They have an intense need to be just like their friends and to be accepted totally by their friends. They fear that they could face ridicule and rejection by their friends if their parents deviate in any way from the neighborhood pattern.

In trying to establish their own identity, early adolescents often turn away from their parents. This may make them feel an intense sense of loneliness. As a result they are apt to have a great need to find compensation in intimate ties to friends of the same age—more often ties to those of the same sex at first. These friendships, within or across the sexes, help to lend the youths some external support, like the timbers that are sometimes used to prop a building up during alterations, while adolescents are giving up their identity as their parents' child and before they have found their own.

Sometimes a boy finds himself through finding something similar in his friend. He mentions that he loves a certain song or hates a certain teacher or craves a certain article of clothing. His friend exclaims with amazement that he has always felt the very same way. Both are delighted and reassured. Each has lost a degree of his feeling of aloneness, of peculiarity, and gained a pleasurable sense of belonging.

As another example, two girls may talk constantly all the way home from school, talk for another half hour in front of the house, and finally reluctantly separate. But as soon as the second reaches her home she telephones her friend and they resume the mutual confidences.

473. The importance of appearance. A majority of adolescents help to overcome their feelings of aloneness by slavishly conforming to the styles of their classmates—in clothes, hairdos, language, reading matter, songs, entertainers. These styles have to be different from those of their parents' generation. And if their own styles irritate or shock their parents, so much the better. It is revealing, though, that even those youths who adopt an extreme style to differentiate themselves from their parents must still conform to the style of at least a few of their friends, or perhaps of some idolized figure such as a rock star.

Parents can be most helpful to teenagers by trying to understand their behavior and then helping them to understand themselves. If you explain why you object to certain styles, you may be able to persuade your children to change without your having to issue an "or else" order. But the teenager who feels free to discuss and argue with her parents may end up persuading them to accept her teenager point of view. Adults tend to be slower than youths in accepting new styles. What may horrify or disgust us one day may later become quite acceptable for us as well as for our children. This was true with the long-hair styles and dungarees introduced by youths in the 1960s, and the pants for girls that so upset school authorities at one time.

474. The psychological tasks of middle adolescence. At fifteen to seventeen, having come to terms with their mature bodies, middle adolescents have two important tasks. First, they must come to terms with their sexuality and the conflicting emotions aroused as they begin romantic encounters with the same or opposite sex partners. Second, they must separate emotionally from their parents and find that they can function independently. As a part of this process the dependence-independence struggles intensify.

A common complaint by adolescents is that their parents don't allow them enough freedom. It's natural for children nearing adulthood to insist on their rights, and their parents need to be reminded that they are changing, but parents don't have to take every complaint at face value. The fact is that adolescents are also afraid of growing up. They are unsure of their capacity to be as knowledgeable, masterful, sophisticated, and charming as they would like. But their pride won't allow them to recognize this doubt. When they unconsciously doubt their ability to carry off some challenge or adventure, they're quick to find evidence that it is their parents who are blocking their way, not their own fears. They reproach their parents indignantly or blame them when talking with friends. Parents can particularly suspect this unconscious maneuver when their children suddenly announce a plan of their group for some escapade which is way beyond anything they've done before. They may be asking to be stopped, or perhaps they're looking for clear rules and consistency. Yet they are also on the lookout for evidence of hypocrisy in their parents. To the extent that their parents are obviously sincere about their rules and ideals, their children feel obligated to continue to adhere to them. But if they can uncover hypocrisy in their parents, this relieves them of the moral duty to conform and offers a welcome opportunity to reproach their parents. At the same time, however, it may undermine their sense of safety.

475. The psychological tasks of late adolescence. By age eighteen to twenty-one, most conflicts are beginning to subside, as the adolescent has developed an individual emotional, physical, and moral identity. If these youths had never experienced rebelliousness, they might lack the motivation to leave home and make their own way in the world. One of the most important tasks for the late adolescent is to separate from his family and find true independence by beginning to take responsibility for himself and his actions.

With this independence comes the desire to improve the world, find new methods that will supersede the old, make discoveries, create new art forms, displace tyrants, and right wrongs. A surprising number of scientific advances have been made and masterpieces of art created by individuals just on the threshold of adulthood. They were not smarter than the older people in their fields and they were certainly less experienced. But they were critical of traditional ways, biased in favor of the new and the untried, and willing to take risks, and that was enough to do the trick. This is how the world makes progress.

It sometimes takes youths five to ten years to truly find their own positive identity. Meanwhile they may be stalled at a halfway stage, characterized by passive resistance to and withdrawal from mainstream society (which they equate with their parents) or by excessively rebellious radicalism.

They may decline to take an ordinary job like their parents and instead adopt unconventional dress, grooming, acquaintances, residence. These decisions seem like evidence of vigorous independence to them. But these things by themselves don't add up yet to a positive stand on life or a constructive contribution to the world. They are essentially a negative protest against the parents' conventions. Even when the striving to be independent shows up only in the form of eccentricities of appearance, it should be recognized as an attempted step in the right direction, which may later lead to a constructive, creative stage. As a matter of fact, the young people who have to strain so visibly to be free are apt to come from families with unusually strong ties and high ideals.

Other youths, who are idealistic and altruistic in character, often take a sternly radical or purist view of things for a number of years—in politics or in the arts or in other fields. Various tendencies of this age period operate together to draw them into these extreme positions: heightened criticalness, cynicism about hypocrisy, intolerance of compromise, courage, and a willingness to sacrifice, in response to their first awareness of the shocking injustices of the society they live in.

A few years later, having achieved a satisfactory degree of emotional independence from parents and having found out how to be useful in their chosen field, they are more tolerant of the frailties of their fellow men and more ready to make constructive compromises. I don't mean that they all become complacent conservatives. Many remain progressive, some remain radical. But most become easier to live and work with.

Anticipatory Guidance for Parents

Being a wise parent to adolescents has always been a difficult job at best. Some unknown parent once said, "Oh, to be only half as wonderful as my child thought I was, and only half as stupid as my teenager thinks I am."

As I have discussed, most adolescents are bound to feel rivalrous and rebellious at least some of the time, whether or not the parent is being reasonable. The first and most important point, by far, is that adolescents need and want guidance—and even consistent rules—from their parents, no matter how much they argue against them. Their pride won't let them admit the need openly, but in their hearts they often think, "I wish my parents would make definite rules for me, like my friends' parents do." They sense that it is one aspect of parents' love to want to protect their children from misunderstandings and embarrassing situations out in the world, from giving the wrong impression and gaining an unfortunate reputation, from getting into trouble through inexperience.

This doesn't mean that parents can be arbitrary, inconsistent, or overbearing. Adolescents have too much dignity and indignation for that; they want to discuss the issues on what they feel is an adult-to-adult basis. If the argument ends in a draw, though, the parents shouldn't be so scrupulously democratic that they assume the child is as likely to be right as they are. The parents' experience should be presumed to count for a lot. In the end, the parents should confidently express their judgment and, if appropriate, their explicit request. They owe their child this clarity and certitude.

Parents should indicate, without necessarily saying so in words, that they realize the youth will be out of their sight most of the time and will therefore comply because of her conscience and respect for her parents, not because the parents can make her obey or because they can watch her at all times.

I think parents need to discuss with their young adolescent children the hour at which they are expected to come home from parties and dates, where they are going and with whom, and who is to drive. If the child asks why they want to know, they can answer that good parents feel responsible for their children. "Suppose there is an accident," parents can say. "We ought to know where to inquire or to search." Or the parents can say, "If there were a family emergency we would want to be able to reach you." (Parents should tell their children where they're going and when they expect to be home, for the same reasons.) Incidentally, if there is a delay or a change in plan, adolescents (and parents) should call home to explain, before they are overdue. With the agreement of their children, the parents can set a certain hour and be waiting for them. This reminds children that the parents are genuinely concerned with their conduct and safety. When children have a party at home, the parents should be there.

Parents can't dictate to their adolescent children or talk down to them. But they can have mutually respectful, adult-to-adult discussions. Young people never have been willing to be guided beyond a certain point by their parents, but that doesn't mean that they haven't benefited from discussions.

It should be helpful for parents to understand that there is a sharp contradiction in adolescents' attitudes toward their parents' opinions. On the one hand adolescents have a strong urge to become progressively more independent of their parents (and their teachers) in their opinions and in their actions. They don't want to be told what to believe. They don't want to be talked down to. On the other hand they are quite unsure of their own beliefs at first and have a real need to hear what their parents and other respected adults think.

Many parents, aware of their adolescent children's impatience with their parents' views and respectful of their drive for independence, carefully conceal their own opinions, and refrain from criticizing adolescent tastes and manners, for fear of seeming old-fashioned or oppressive.

The solution, I think, is for parents to allow themselves to talk easily about their views and about how things were in their youth, but to do so as if they are talking to a respected adult friend, not as if they are laying down the law or as if they think their opinions are right simply because they are older.

476. But, parents ask, what if the child openly defies a request or quietly disobeys? If the child-parent relationship is halfway sound, the child will not defy or disobey in the early years of adolescence, and may not even in the later years. In the later years the parents may even consider it wise on occasion to give permission to go against the parents' judgment.

Even if an older adolescent defies or disobeys a parental direction, this does not mean that the direction did no good. It certainly helps inexperienced persons to hear all sides. If they decide not to take their parents' direction, they may of course be making a reasonably sound decision, perhaps being in possession of knowledge or insights that the parents lack. Certainly as they progress into adulthood they must be prepared to reject advice on occasion and to take responsibility for their decisions. If young people reject their parents' direction and get into trouble, this experience will increase their respect for their parents' judgment, though they probably won't admit it.

Suppose parents don't know what to say or think about some issue? They can discuss it not only with their child but with other parents. But individual parents should not feel bound in advance to adhere to other people's codes even if they are the only parents who disagree. In the long run parents can do a good job only if they are convinced they are doing the right thing. And what is right for them is what they feel is right, after hearing the arguments.

I have strong opinions about the general principles of parental guidance but I'd be hesitant to convert these into arbitrary specifics. Times change. Customs vary in different parts of the country and in different groups in the same community. Individual children vary greatly in their maturity and reliability.

477. There are two simple rules, I think:

1. Individually and in groups, adolescents should be expected to behave civilly to people and to be cordial to their parents, family friends, teachers, and the people who work with them. At times it is natural for youths to have at least a mildly hostile attitude underneath toward adults, with whom they are inevitably rivalrous, whether or not they are aware of this. But it does them no harm to have to control this hostility and be polite anyway. Their politeness certainly makes a great difference to the adults concerned.

2. Adolescents should have serious obligations in helping their families—by doing regular chores and special additional jobs. This benefits them by giving them a sense of dignity, participation, responsibility, and happiness, as well as helping the parents.

You can't enforce these rules. I'm only saying that parents are entitled to express them in discussions with their children. It will help adolescents to hear their parents' principles, even if they don't conform.

Gay and Lesbian Sexuality and Bisexuality

In Section 45, I talked about parents' fears of their children being gay or having contact with gays. How should you react if you think your teenager might be gay, lesbian or bisexual? The first thing to do is to get your own fears and anxieties under control.

Adolescence is a complex time for any youngster, and the pressure of school activities, proms and dating can create a powerful sense of exclusion or "differentness" for gay and lesbian teens, which may make them feel troubled or unhappy. If you think your child is struggling with issues surrounding sexual identity, it's very important to let him or her feel that there is a place to turn to for help. Sadly, statistics show that a high percentage of teenage suicides and attempted suicides are related to issues of sexual identity.

Heterosexual parents might not know where to begin talking to a teenager about sexual orientation. Remember, it's likely that your child is as afraid of the subject as you are and might feel very threatened if confronted abruptly. To start with, try to make the subject of sexual orientation something that the family can casually discuss. Introducing books, videos, and music into the family collections that are created by openly gay, lesbian, or bisexual artists or that deal with those themes could be a place to start. To follow up, you can begin using words like "bisexual," "gay," and "lesbian," so that they lose their taboo connotation. It's also important to be aware of, and critical of, homophobia (see Sections 46 and 996). It's no help to a gay or lesbian teenager to hear their own family members tell insulting jokes or tolerate prejudiced comments made by friends or relatives.

For some adolescents, their sexual orientation becomes very clear to them quite quickly and they embrace that as a strong identity. But other teenagers might go through a phase of experimentation before settling on an identity they feel most comfortable with. Teenagers shouldn't be pressured into assuming a gay or lesbian identity before they are ready. If a teenager expresses a sense of alienation, isolation or deep confusion about his or her sexual orientation, parents should suggest professional counseling, not to change their teen's orientation but to help the boy or girl deal with any shame or anxiety that might undermine his or her self-esteem. The greatest gift a parent can give a child is a sense of self-pride and dignity. For a gay or lesbian teen, having access to positive role models, and the ability to deal with sexual diversity frankly and honestly, will go a long way toward building self-esteem.

If you're raising a gay or lesbian adolescent, you might want to seek support too. Organizations such as Parents and Friends of Lesbians and Gays, which have chapters all across the country, provide information and advice and hold events. Most cities and large towns have gay and lesbian switchboards or hot lines that can provide useful information, and gay and lesbian community centers have outreach programs for gay and lesbian youths and their parents. These facilities are listed in telephone directories under "Gay and Lesbian" or under "Social and Human Services" in the Yellow Pages.

Diet in Adolescence

478. Diet and peer pressure. After the age of ten or twelve it may become increasingly difficult to get children to accept a diet that is different from that of their friends and age-mates. Up to then they usually go along with their parents' ideas, especially if both parents are in agreement. In fact they don't think of such meals as a diet; they are just foods that regularly appear at mealtime. But after they have eaten with friends or at school for a few months they may want to eat hamburgers, potato chips, french fries, cheese, ice cream, and other sweet and creamy desserts.

479. A plant-based diet. If you are strongly in favor of a plant-based diet, as I am, what can you do? There's often no easy answer. My own inclination is to continue to serve the plant-based foods at home, without comment or argument. (I'm generally in favor of enjoyable, polite meals, without scoldings. Save the correction of table manners for brief private sessions, after meals.) If your children ask why you don't serve animal-based foods, including dairy products, explain matter-of-factly and cheerfully, not defensively, that a plant-based diet has been shown to be helpful for athletic success, long life, and low level of disease; you naturally want your children to have these advantages. Don't get into a long argument. If they demand to know why other parents don't follow similar rules, you can say truthfully that you don't know; maybe they never read medical articles. If your children wonder what would happen if they broke your rules at school or at other children's homes or at restaurants, you can point out that they will be increasingly out of your sight and must decide more things for themselves. And you don't want to snoop or to punish them, you only want to serve them the best possible foods.

Certainly the most powerful influence is for both parents to eat, politely, the thoughtful meals that have been prepared. No holding back on the children's favorite dishes until they have eaten what you consider the most healthful items—that's *always* counterproductive.

It sounds as if I would always let adolescents decide for themselves whether to follow their parents' diet. In general I would advise that, instead of constant arguments. But if teenagers are proposing to eat dangerous or weird foods—or to do anything else dangerous or weird—a sensible parent may have to put his foot down in a determined or even angry manner to show that he is truly alarmed.

There is an important reason why I'm urging you to avoid food arguments and to stick to a plant-based diet during adolescence, for this is when the rebellion against the plant-based diet is apt to be strongest and when the desire to eat just the same foods as classmates and friends is also strongest. Parents and nutritionists who have gone through this phase with adolescent children testify that there is a better chance that the children will revert to their parents' diet in time *if no issue is made of the rebellion.* To put it the other way around, when a long, bitter conflict has occurred over diet in adolescence, its pattern is more likely to persist—for years.

480. Anorexia and bulimia. Eating disorders that may lead to excessive weight loss in adolescent girls and boys can seriously affect physical and psychological health. *Anorexia nervosa* is a progressive loss of weight due to self-imposed dieting. An overwhelming fear of fatness, a persistent concern about body shape, and a determined, inflexible drive to be thin result in a restriction of food intake and a fall in weight. *Bulimia* is a problem in which adolescents periodically gorge themselves on enormous amounts of food (binge eating) and then either vomit it all up in secret, take large amounts of laxatives to expel everything they have eaten, or exercise excessively.

These problems are not rare. At least 1% of adolescent girls have anorexia nervosa. Our society's focus on thinness (movies, television, and fashion advertising), especially for women, challenges many of the changes young girls experience during puberty when the hips widen and increased fatty areas are seen in most young girls. For some, these normal body changes lead to a preoccupation with weight and a dissatisfaction with a changing body image. It is hard to know why some teenagers respond to these changes in maturity by starving themselves. Many youth with anorexia nervosa have a difficult time separating from their family and finding their own identity (see Section 472). The family may be overprotective, unable to express emotions or resolve conflicts.

A pediatrician or nurse practitioner should be consulted whenever an adolescent is losing an excessive amount of weight. Anorexia nervosa and bulimia will be considered by the clinician, as well as other conditions that are associated with loss of weight. Parents should be concerned with a potential eating disorder when food intake is minimal, physical appearance is thin, and when their teen exhibits behavior including irritability, lethargy, dizziness, or sleep problems. Most teenagers with an eating disorder will not disclose their behavior to you, their doctor or nurse practitioner. They deny their hunger as well as weight loss, bingeing, forced vomiting, or use of laxatives. Girls with anorexia nervosa early in adolescence do not gain the expected weight during puberty and may experience a delay in menstruation and the development of normal sexual characteristics (see Section 462).

Both anorexia nervosa and bulimia are serious illnesses which can be life-threatening and which represent major emotional disorders involving both the adolescent and the parents. A doctor should be consulted as soon as there is any suspicion of one of these problems. In the mild form and with early detection, treatment is usually successful when it is directed toward nutritional education, behavioral interventions, and counseling for the adolescent and family. If the illness progresses and the youth loses more than 25 percent of her body weight, additional treatment by a child psychiatrist or specialist in adolescent medicine is necessary.

RAISING PHYSICALLY
HEALTHY CHILDREN

Nutrition

The Importance of Good Nutrition

I'm beginning this section with a discussion on nutrition because I have become convinced, partly from my own life experience, that it is of critical importance for our children's well-being, as well as for our own.

481. What is good nutrition? The evidence in adults couldn't be more compelling: excessive animal fat, cow's milk, protein, and the high number of calories in the typical American diet have been linked to high cholesterol levels, coronary heart disease, strokes, high blood pressure, diabetes, and some cancers. We have also learned that many of these diseases have their roots in childhood. Fatty deposits are now commonly found in the coronary arteries of children on a typical American diet by age three. And by age twelve, they are found in 70 percent of children. Teenagers, not surprisingly, have more and thicker deposits. And, finally, virtually all young adults have them by age twenty-one. Before long, high blood pressure and other problems start taking their toll. Moreover, obesity, with all its associated problems, is on a sharp rise among our children.

But there is hope especially with regard to our children. First, food preferences are learned early. Children who are cheerfully and regularly offered a variety of healthy foods (vegetables, fruits, whole grains, and beans) learn to eat and even prefer these foods. The trick is to make these foods a regular part of the family diet, without giving the child the message that they are "good for you" (with the clear implication that "nobody really likes to eat this stuff"), followed by "If you eat your broccoli, I'll give you some dessert." If healthful foods are part of the family routine, children accept most of them naturally.

Guiding our children toward healthy eating habits can sometimes be a challenge. Children are not particularly concerned about the problems that come from unhealthful diets. At school, the foods served may not be what you would offer at home. The media may also give children the wrong message. Just think about the kinds of foods that are the subjects of flashy advertisements for children—they're not vegetables and fruit. There are plenty of ads for potato chips, but none for baked potatoes. Children watching Saturday morning cartoons are bombarded with commercials for sugar-coated cereals and high-fat junk foods. They know these commercial jingles even before they can read. It's no wonder they grow up with the message firmly implanted that high-fat foods are best.

If we want our children to get a healthy start in life—and to maintain it by continuing to eat nutritious foods—there should be a shift in the whole family's diet, starting with the parents.

Plant-Based Diets

482. Nutrition today. In the past few decades, we have learned quite a lot about how to use nutrition to help children stay healthy. We used to think of vegetables, grains, and beans as side dishes. We kept meat and dairy products as our favored foods, and we were not particularly concerned about fat and cholesterol in children's diets. We now know better. Research shows us very clearly that vegetables, grains, beans, and fruits should take center stage. They provide the nutrition children need to grow, and avoid the cholesterol and animal fat that can cause so many problems.

Unfortunately, not many of us were raised on diets that

emphasized vegetables, grains, and beans, so we are not always sure how to go about planning complete meals. Here are some steps to simplify things. Some will sound like basic common sense, and others may be new to you, as they were to me at one time. But each step is important.

483. Green leafy vegetables. Broccoli, kale, collards, watercress, Swiss chard, Napa, Chinese cabbage, and Bok Choy, and other green vegetables are loaded with the absorbable calcium, iron, and many vitamins that your child needs. Include two to three servings of a green leafy vegetable every day. Leafy greens should always be cooked very quickly, some just one or two minutes, so that they come out bright green. They can be seasoned with a little sea salt when your child is older, but I recommend limiting the sea salt for the younger child.

484. Other vegetables. Vegetables should make up 25 to 30 percent of the diet. Select the freshest organic vegetables at a farmers' market or a local garden or, best of all, grow your own. Vegetables selected from an organic farm, in the organic foods section of the supermarket, or at the local farmers' market carry the added advantage of being free of pesticides. I prefer to go to the farmers' market myself every Saturday morning and select my own organic food from local farmers whom I know and can trust. Growing some of your own produce with your children is an excellent way to have fresh, healthy food, and a great experience to share.

Freshness is always the key to good nutrition in vegetables. Vegetables should be washed, cut, and cooked, emphasizing variety in both your choice of vegetables and in preparation. Cooking vegetables correctly will enhance your child's appetite and make the meal more appealing. I recommend and use *Fresh from a Vegetarian Kitchen* by Meredith McCarty.

It helps to offer more than one vegetable at a meal, selecting those your child likes. Your child may prefer vegetables prepared a certain way—fresh watercress leaves in a salad, for example, as opposed to cooked watercress. Pushing children to eat vegetables they do not care for is likely to do more harm than good.

485. Beans and bean products. Beans are rich in protein, calcium, and many other nutrients and should be a regular part of the diet. Tofu and tempeh, made from soybeans, can be used in many main dishes and soups. A meal of beans and brown rice—or any bean and grain combination, for that matter—will give your child plenty of protein without the harmful effects of animal protein or animal fat.

486. Fruits, seeds, and nuts. These foods can be delicious treats and additions to the diet. Fruits are better digested when cooked, such as applesauce. Apples, pears, and other fruits in season and grown locally are preferred, and organic produce is much better than pesticide-treated brands. Seeds and nuts can be dry-roasted and ground to make digestion easier. Almond butter and organic peanut butter make delicious treats for children and are a healthy substitute for candy or ice cream.

487. Whole grains. A generous portion of a child's diet should be composed of whole grains. Short grain brown rice, barley, oats, millet, whole wheat noodles and pasta, and whole grain bread contain complex carbohydrates, which are filling, nutritious, and a great energy source for growing children. They also have protein, fiber, and important vitamins.

These four groups—vegetables, beans, fruits, and grains—provide the basics of healthy nutrition. If they are part of your child's daily routine, you have the main nutritional bases covered.

In addition, two simple but important nutrients deserve particular attention: vitamin D and vitamin B_{12}.

488. Vitamin D. Your child needs vitamin D to help build strong bones. Normally, it is formed in the skin by the action of the sun and is then stored in the body. Fifteen minutes of sun on the face and hands each day will provide enough vitamin D for the body's needs. However, children in northern climates and those who tend to stay out of the sun may not get enough vitamin D from the sun alone. Fortified cereals contain vitamin D, and all common chil-

dren's multivitamins provide enough vitamin D, without
the risk of excess.

489. Vitamin B$_{12}$. A reliable source of vitamin B$_{12}$ is needed
for healthy nerves and blood cells. It is not made by plants
or animals but by bacteria. In less developed countries,
traces of bacteria in the soil or on plants provide B$_{12}$, but in
the modern world, these are not reliable sources. Animal
products contain vitamin B$_{12}$ formed by bacteria in animals' intestinal tracts, but the fat and cholesterol they
contain make them undesirable. Good sources include
fortified products such as soy milk or cereal (check the label
for cobalamin or cyanocobalamin, which are vitamin B$_{12}$'s
technical names). Probably the most convenient source is
any common children's multivitamin. They all contain
more than enough vitamin B$_{12}$.

490. The question of cow's milk after two years. I no longer
recommend dairy products after the age of two years. In the
section "Feeding Young Children" on page 335, we consider the reasons for this. Of course, there was a time when
cow's milk was considered very desirable. But research,
along with clinical experience, has forced doctors and
nutritionists to rethink this recommendation. It is an area
where there are still disagreements among scientists, but
there are several points that most everyone agrees on.

First of all, other calcium sources offer many advantages
that dairy products do not have. Most green leafy vegetables
and beans have a form of calcium that is absorbed as well as
or even a bit better than that in milk. Along with this
calcium come vitamins, iron, complex carbohydrates, and
fiber, all of which are generally lacking in cow's milk.
Calcium-enriched soy or rice milk is just as tasty on cereal
as cow's milk, and it has no animal proteins, animal fats,
milk sugars, or dairy contaminants. You can refer to the list
of calcium-rich foods on pages 114–15.

At first it may be surprising to learn of the range of
problems that dairy products can cause. The best known, of
course, relate to fat and cholesterol. While milk and yogurt
are available in low-fat versions, most cheeses, ice cream,

and other dairy products are very high in fat—and it is the wrong kind of fat. The essential fats that are needed for brain development are found in vegetable oils. Milk is very low in these essential fats and high in the saturated fats that encourage artery blockage and weight problems as children grow.

There are other concerns about dairy products, too—concerns that relate even to low-fat products. Dairy foods can impair a child's ability to absorb iron and can cause subtle blood loss from the digestive tract in small children. These problems, combined with the fact that milk has virtually no iron of its own, can lead to iron deficiencies.

Pediatricians often find that certain health problems are aggravated, or even caused, by milk products. These include asthma and other respiratory problems, chronic ear infections, and skin conditions. The reason is not necessarily an allergic reaction. Exactly why these problems occur is not known. Nonetheless, removing dairy products from the diet often eliminates them.

Finally, as children grow up, many will develop stomachaches, bloating, diarrhea, and gas caused by the milk sugar (lactose). These symptoms are not abnormal. They are simply a result of the fact that the ability to digest milk sugar disappears for many people in late childhood. In nature, animals do not drink milk after infancy, and that is the normal pattern for humans, too.

Vegetables and legumes provide a healthy source of calcium, along with many other nutritional advantages, and they really make milk consumption unnecessary.

491. Eliminate meat and poultry, and cut down on fish. Most families have become more conscious about the fat content of meats, and many are choosing the lower-fat cuts. The healthiest diets of all, however, go a step further, and get their nutrients from beans, grains, vegetables, and fruits, rather than from meats.

Children can get plenty of protein from beans, grains, and vegetables, and when they do, they avoid the animal fat and cholesterol found in meats. Unfortunately, switching from red meat to chicken does not help very much. Chicken actually has just as much cholesterol as beef (about 100 milligrams of cholesterol in a 4-ounce serving) and almost as much fat. Researchers have also learned that the cancer-causing chemicals that form in beef as it cooks also tend to form in chicken.

Children who grow up getting their nutrition from plant foods rather than meats have a tremendous health advantage. They are less likely to develop weight problems, diabetes, high blood pressure, and some forms of cancer.

There are other reasons why families are looking more favorably at plant-based choices. In recent years, the prevalence of disease-causing bacteria in meat, poultry, and eggs has risen sharply, which is why health authorities insist that these products be carefully handled and thoroughly cooked, if they are used at all.

Meatless meals also help your child to keep stronger bones. Children stay in better calcium balance when their protein comes from plant sources. My siblings and I were given no red meat until we were twelve years of age, and we were all oversize and healthy. We should have continued to avoid meat through adolescence and adulthood.

Many families are gradually changing their diets as they come to learn of the advantages to doing so. If you are still serving meats regularly, you will want to try as many meatless meals as possible, explore new cookbooks, and experiment with new products that take the place of meats. Some of these, such as meatless burgers and meatless hot dogs, are in the freezer case of your grocery or health food store.

I have personally been on a nondairy, low-fat meatless diet since 1991 when I was eighty-eight years old. Within two weeks of beginning this diet, my chronic bronchitis went away after years of unsuccessful antibiotic treatments. I have several middle-aged and older friends who have halted heart disease by eliminating dairy products, meats, and other high-saturated-fat foods from their diet. To achieve this kind of success, it's important to substitute whole grains and a variety of vegetables and fruits and to become more active.

492. Fats and oils. I recommend using sesame oil, olive oil, corn oil, flaxseed oil, and polyunsaturated vegetable oils.

Use only a small amount, for brushing the bottom of the skillet, or use a vegetable oil spray. Vegetable fats are much healthier than animal-derived fats, but use only a modest amount of whatever oil you choose. Margarine is only slightly less harmful than butter because the processing creates a type of fat that may be as bad for our arteries as saturated fats. Instead of using margarine or butter on a baked potato, try Dijon mustard, salsa, or steamed vegetables. Jam and cinnamon work well on toast without the layer of butter in between, and whole grain bread can be delicious with no topping at all.

493. Avoid sugar. Refined sugar is a *simple carbohydrate,* full of empty calories that have no nutritional value. Instead, a child's diet should be rich in *complex carbohydrates,* which are found in grains, beans, and vegetables. For a sweet treat, the healthiest choices are fresh fruits and fruit juices. Use apple juice when cooking fruits instead of water and sugar. Or you may want to boil some raisins and use the juice, which is very sweet. You can also substitute rice syrup or barley malt for sweetness. When you use sweet vegetables such as pumpkin, corn, squash, and carrots, you don't need to add sugar. At first these foods don't taste sweet in the sense that they don't taste like sugar. But when you take sugar out of your cooking, you will notice the real taste of sweet vegetables and fruits.

494. Limit salt intake. Cook grains with a pinch of sea salt and don't use salt at the table. The only advantage of typical table salt is that it is fortified with iodine, an essential nutrient. Plants vary in their iodine content, although sea vegetables are very rich in it. Substitutes for sea salt may be soy sauce, miso, or ground-up sesame seeds mixed with a pinch of sea salt. Excess salt intake can make it harder to stay in calcium balance; salt actually causes calcium to pass through the kidneys into the urine.

495. Avoid caffeine. Chocolate contains a fair amount of caffeine, as do black tea and coffee. Instead, substitute teas with no caffeine. Drink a grain "coffee" made from roasted barley. Tea can be made from twigs of the bancha plant, which has no caffeine. The beverage children really need is pure, clean water. For variety, they can have "teas" made from grains, herbs, or fruit juices, and they can also enjoy sweet vegetable drinks made from squash, onion, carrots, and cabbage.

496. Have fun with foods. Wide variety in foods is crucial to the success of any cook, and it is also makes meals more appealing. Give your child a wide variation of foods in colors, textures, and taste. The plate should look balanced with colors. Balance is one key to your child's diet.

I like to keep mealtime free of the distractions of television and telephone. Some families say grace or meditate for a few minutes, which can establish a spirit of thankfulness and togetherness for the meal. Scoldings should not be part of the dining experience, even though spills and lapses of manners will inevitably occur.

Feeding Young Children

497. Ensuring complete nutrition. Before we talk about the everyday foods that children can eat, we ought to discuss the more important chemical substances that foods are composed of and what the body uses them for.

You can compare a child's body to a building under construction. A lot of different materials are needed to build it and to keep it in repair. But a human being is also a machine that's running. It requires fuel for energy and other substances to make it work properly, just as an automobile needs gasoline and oil.

498. Protein. The main building material of the body is protein. The muscles, heart, brain, and kidneys, for instance, are largely made of protein (aside from water). The structure of bones is protein filled in with minerals, much the way a collar is made stiff with starch. The child needs protein to continually increase the size of every part of the body and also to repair wear and tear.

The healthiest way to provide your child with plenty of good-quality protein is to serve a variety of vegetables, grains, beans, and fruits every day. Soy milk and other soy products are also protein-rich. The U.S. government and the American Dietetic Association hold that those foods provide more than enough protein, provided you serve a variety of them, as opposed to sticking only to corn or rice. An added advantage of plant sources of protein is that they also contribute plenty of complex carbohydrate, fiber, and vitamins. Animal products—meats, dairy products, and eggs—do have protein and lots of it, but they tend to cause more problems than they solve because of the animal fat and cholesterol they contain. They lack complex carbohydrates and fiber, and they are low in some vitamins.

499. Complex and simple carbohydrates. These are the starches that supply most of your child's energy requirements. *Complex carbohydrates,* such as vegetables, fruits, grains, and legumes, burn slowly as fuel. *Simple carbohydrates,* such as sugar and honey, are burned as fuel at a much faster rate. Both can be stored in the liver as *glycogen* to be used at a later time.

500. Fat. This rich source of fuel for the body contains more than twice as many calories as the same weight of carbohydrates. It is harder to convert fat to fuel, however, so it is more easily stored under the skin and around body organs. If inadequate carbohydrates are consumed to meet the body's needs, then the fat is metabolized into fuel. There are two kinds of fats: *saturated fat,* primarily found in meat and dairy products, and *unsaturated* or *polyunsaturated fat,* found primarily in plant-based foods. The saturated fats are implicated in heart disease and strokes, while unsaturated fats do not appear to have this effect. This is why a vegetarian or low saturated fat diet appears to be the most beneficial.

501. Fiber is the roughage in vegetables, fruits, grains (bran, for instance), and legumes that our intestines can't digest and absorb. Meat, dairy products, fish, and poultry have no fiber at all. Fiber appears to play an important role in promoting normal bowel movements by providing part of the bulk that helps to stimulate the intestines to function. A person who stays on a bland diet—let's say, milk and broth and eggs, is apt to become constipated from having too little substance left in the lower intestines. Fiber also appears to be helpful in maintaining the health of the intestines and colon. It is now suspected that the major factor in cancer of the large intestine is the slow passage of food caused by the lack of roughage in our overly refined diet. Fiber also helps lower cholesterol levels.

502. Calories. The fuel energy value of food is measured in calories. Water and minerals have no calories—that is, they have no fuel or energy in them. Fat is rich in calories; an ounce of it has more than twice as many calories as an ounce of starch, sugar, or protein. Butter, margarine, and vegetable oil, which are essentially pure fat, and cream and salad dressings, which contain a lot of it, are therefore very high in calories. Meats, poultry, fish, eggs, and cheese are high in calories because of their combination of protein and fat. Sugars and syrups are also high in calories, because they are concentrated simple carbohydrates and contain no water or roughage.

Whole grains, which have a high proportion of fiber, are much less calorically dense than are fatty foods. Most vegetables are composed mostly of water, carbohydrate, protein, and fiber, with very little fat, and are therefore also low in calories.

503. Minerals. Many different minerals play a vital part in the structure and in the working of every part of the body. The hardness of bones and teeth depends on calcium and phosphorus. The substance in red blood cells that carries the oxygen to all regions of the body is made partly of iron and copper. Iodine is necessary in the functioning of the thyroid gland. (See Section 618 on Flouride.)

All natural, unrefined foods contain a variety of valuable minerals. But the refining of grains and the prolonged cooking of vegetables in water remove a great deal of the mineral content.

504. Calcium. An ample source of calcium is important during periods of rapid bone growth, especially during infancy and adolescence. Adolescent girls who consume a lot of calcium appear to be protected somewhat against thinning of the bones (*osteoporosis*) in later life. Green leafy vegetables, beans, and fortified orange juice are healthful calcium sources, and plant-based diets help keep calcium in the bones and may actually reduce calcium loss via the kidneys. While milk is often used as a calcium source, parents should consider the disadvantages of dairy products, which are discussed in Section 524.

505. Iron. Iron can be obtained in quantities sufficient for normal growth and development from vegetable sources (especially broccoli, collards, and squash) and beans (especially soy, navy, and Great Northern) without overloading the child with the saturated fat found in most meats and dairy products.

Babies begin to need more iron for their red blood cells around the middle of the first year, because with their rapid growth, they begin to deplete the limited supply that was in their bodies at birth. Since cow's milk contains practically no iron, infants who consume lots of milk, often eating little else, may become profoundly anemic. That's why it's important to seek out iron-fortified cereal for your infant and use an iron-fortified formula if you are bottle-feeding. It has recently been found that breast milk, though it contains very little iron, contains a form of iron that is unusually well digested and absorbed. Breast milk contains sufficient iron for the first six months of a baby's life.

506. Iodine. Iodine is missing in some inland regions where the drinking water, vegetables, and fruits lack it, and seafood is less available. However, table salt is iodized for people in those areas, to prevent goiter.

507. Vitamins. These are special substances that the body needs in small amounts in order to work right, somewhat the way any machine needs a few drops of oil, or a gasoline motor depends on a tiny electric spark.

All vitamins can be obtained from a well-balanced diet of vegetables, whole grains, fruits, beans and peas, except vitamin B_{12}, which is found only in animal sources, supplemented cereals, and a few other fortified products. There-fore, if children consume no meat or dairy products, which is actually the healthiest diet, a vitamin supplement is prudent. I'd also recommend a vitamin for any child who appears to be a picky eater, who refuses all fruits or vegetables, or who just doesn't appear to be growing well. One vitamin pill a day is far preferable to fighting with your child to finish his vegetables or eat more raw fruit!

508. Vitamin A. Made in the body from beta-carotene, this vitamin is necessary to keep healthy the linings of the bronchial, intestinal, and urinary systems and various parts of the eyes, including the part that enables us to see in dim light. Vegetables, especially yellow and orange ones, supply all of the vitamin A a child will need. Probably the only children with vitamin A deficiency are those with a chronic intestinal illness or chronic malnutrition. Excessive amounts of vitamin A can be harmful to children and adults, but this will not happen by eating a lot of vegetables.

509. Vitamin B complex. Scientists used to think that there was just one vitamin B, which had several actions in the body. But when they studied "it," it turned out to be a dozen different vitamins, occurring mostly in the same foods. Since the B vitamins are not yet all known or understood, it is more important for people to eat plenty of the natural foods they mostly occur in than to take them separately in pill form. The four known to be most impor-tant for human beings are called by their chemical names now: thiamin, riboflavin, niacin, and pyridoxine. Every tissue in the body needs these four vitamins.

Thiamin (B_1), *Riboflavin* (B_2), and *Niacin* (B_3 or nicotinic acid) occur in fair amounts in milk, eggs, liver, and meat, but since these foods often contain excessive saturated fats, the vitamins can also be obtained from brown rice, whole grains, peas, beans, peanuts, fortified breads, pasta and cereals. Deficiencies of these vitamins in children are un-likely unless the diet consists mainly of refined starches and sugar.

Pyridoxine (B_6) is found in bananas, cabbage, corn, oats, split peas, wheat bran, cantaloupe, and blackstrap molasses. These, along with most grains, supply the child's daily needs.

Cobalamin (B_{12}) is widely distributed among animal foods, including milk, but absent in most foods from the vegetable kingdom. Children who avoid animal products can get B_{12} from cereals and soy milk products fortified with it (check the label for cobalamin or cyanocobalamin). It's a good idea to take any common children's multivitamin to ensure vitamin B_{12} among children who avoid animal products.

510. Folic acid. Important in the manufacturing of DNA and red blood cells, folic acid is found in spinach, broccoli, turnip greens, whole grains, and fruits, such as cantaloupe and strawberries.

511. Vitamin C (*ascorbic acid*). Most abundant in oranges, lemons, grapefruit, raw and properly canned tomatoes and tomato juice, and raw cabbage, vitamin C is also present in fair amounts in other fruits and vegetables, including potatoes. Vitamin C is easily destroyed in cooking, however. It is necessary for the development of bones, teeth, blood vessels, and other tissues, and plays a part in the functioning of most of the cells in the body. Deficiency of vitamin C shows itself in painful hemorrhages around the bones and in swollen, bleeding gums. People whose diets contain lots of vitamin C–rich vegetables and fruits tend to have lower cancer rates, although some of the credit for this may go to other nutrients in these foods.

512. Vitamin D. Needed in large amounts for growth, particularly of the bones and teeth, vitamin D helps calcium and phosphorus, which are present in the food in the intestines, to be absorbed into the blood and deposited in the growing parts of the bones. That's why it should be added to the diet of children, especially in the period of rapid growth in infancy. The amount in common children's multivitamins is adequate, although ordinary foods contain only a small amount.

The sun's rays shining on people's skin manufacture

vitamin D right there, so people naturally get this vitamin when they spend time outdoors on a regular basis. In colder weather, however, they cover up their bodies with clothes and stay indoors. Most children who are exposed to sunlight for about thirty minutes per week will not become vitamin D deficient. African-American and other children with darker skin need more sun exposure because the pigment in their skin blocks some of the rays. Mothers need extra vitamin D during pregnancy and breast-feeding. Darker skinned babies who are exclusively breast-fed need a vitamin D supplement.

513. Vitamin E. This vitamin is found in nuts, seeds, many vegetable oils, and other vegetables such as corn, spinach, broccoli, cucumbers, and whole gain cereals.

514. Vitamin toxicity. Megavitamins—vitamins in doses hundreds of times higher than the minimum daily allowance recommended by the Food and Drug Administration—can be dangerous to children. The fat-soluble vitamins, A and D, are most likely to cause serious toxicity, but even water-soluble vitamins such as pyridoxine (B_6) and niacin can cause severe negative effects. Don't give your child vitamins in higher doses than those recommended by your doctor or nurse practitioner.

515. Water. Although it provides no calories or vitamins, water is vital to the makeup and working of the body. (A baby's body is 60 percent water.) It's the most important beverage for children and adults, especially in hot weather when the body loses a lot of water through sweating and evaporation. Most foods (and breast milk) are largely composed of water and that is how people receive most of their daily needs.

Foods for a Sensible Diet

516. Keep a balanced attitude. Don't judge foods on calories, vitamins, or minerals alone. Other important considerations are fat, protein, carbohydrates, fiber, sugar, and sodium, all of which take care of themselves when a child eats a well-balanced diet. Remember that not all essential foods need to be eaten at any one meal. What's important is what is taken in over a day or two.

Everybody in the long run needs a balance of low- and high-calorie foods as well as a balance in other respects in the diet. If a person takes one aspect of diet too seriously and forgets the others, it's apt to lead to trouble. An adolescent girl, for example, acquires a fanatical zeal to reduce. She leaves out all the foods in which she has heard there are more than a few calories, and she tries to live on salad, juice, fruit, and coffee. She is bound to be sick if she keeps on. Serious-minded parents who have the mistaken idea that vitamins are the whole show and that starches are inferior may serve their child carrot salad and grapefruit for supper. The poor child can't get enough calories out of that to satisfy a rabbit. A plump mother from a plump family, ashamed of her son's scrawniness, may serve him only rich foods, crowding out the vegetables, beans, and grains. In the process, he is apt to be deprived of minerals and vitamins.

517. Vegetarian diets. A vegetable-based diet for children is generally more healthful than a diet containing the cholesterol, animal fat, and excessive protein found in meat and dairy products. But a vegetarian diet should not be a low-calorie diet. Calories should come from a broad variety of leafy green vegetables, fruits, whole grains, beans, and bean products. Studies have shown that a well-balanced vegetarian diet has many advantages and does not interfere with a child's growth and development. A reliable vitamin B_{12} source such as a children's vitamin or cereal or soy milk fortified with B_{12} is recommended for vegetarians.

Children and adolescents will get plenty of protein, as long as they eat a variety of whole grains, legumes, vegetables, fruits, and nuts. If you are a strict vegetarian (vegan), you can still get plenty of calcium. Nondairy calcium sources include green leafy vegetables, beans, and calcium-fortified soy milk and orange juice. A number of good books are available on vegetarian diets; some of these books include a variety of recipes.

518. Vegetables. Vegetables are so important that they deserve featured status on a child's plate. The baby during the first year has probably had most of the following cooked vegetables: spinach, peas, onions, carrots, asparagus, chard, squash, tomatoes, beets, celery, potatoes. By six months of age, most table vegetables eaten by the rest of the family can be fed to your infant after placing them in the blender and serving them in finely pureed form. These same vegetables can be bought in a jar of baby food. Be sure to read the nutritional information on the label and choose the one that appears to be the most unadulterated. Beware of baby foods that are diluted with water or starch or tapioca. This makes them nutritionally inferior to what you can make at home in your blender.

By the end of the first year the vegetables can be offered in a more coarsely pureed, lumpy consistency. Peas should be mashed slightly to avoid their being swallowed whole. Steamed vegetables such as carrots, potatoes, and green beans cut into pieces make good finger foods.

Sweet potatoes or yams can be used at times instead of white potatoes. If you have been sticking to the easily digested vegetables up to the age of a year, you can try gradually the less popular and sometimes less digestible ones such as lima beans (mashed), broccoli, cabbage, cauliflower, turnips, and parsnips. If you persist in offering them, without trying to force it, over time your child will develop a taste for them.

Wait until two years to serve corn in the kernel. Young children don't chew it; it passes through them unchanged. Use only tender corn. When cutting it off the cob, don't cut too close. Then each kernel will be cut open. At three or four, when you start corn on the cob, slice down the center of each row of kernels, so that they are all open.

The more easily digested raw vegetables are usually started between one and two years. The best are peeled tomatoes, sliced string beans, shredded carrots, scraped chopped celery. They should be well washed. Go slowly at first and see how they are digested. You can use orange juice or sweetened lemon juice as a dressing.

Vegetable and fruit juices can be started at the same time. These are not as healthful as the whole food because the juice lacks the fiber contained in the fruit or vegetable. Juicers that keep the fiber in the juice are preferable, if you have one. One advantage of juice over cooked vegetables is that no vitamins are destroyed in cooking. If a child has temporarily turned against plain vegetables, remember vegetable soups: pea, tomato, celery, onion, spinach, beet, corn, and the soups that contain large amounts of mixed vegetables. Some commercially prepared vegetable soups are very high in salt however, so you need to read the label carefully. Almost all commercially prepared soups need to be diluted with equal amounts of water. If they're given to children in the undiluted form, right out of the can, they can be harmful because the salt is too highly concentrated.

Vegetables are among the most nutritious foods you can feed your child.

519. Temporary substitutes for vegetables. Suppose a child has refused vegetables in any form for weeks. Will her nutrition suffer? Vegetables are particularly valuable for various minerals, vitamins, and fiber. But various fruits also supply many of the same minerals, vitamins, and fiber. Whole grains also offer some proteins and many of the vitamins and minerals found in vegetables. So if your child refuses to eat vegetables for a period of time, don't make a big issue out of it. Continue to keep mealtime relaxed and fun. If you are really concerned, give your child a daily multivitamin. Her taste for vegetables will return, unless you turn eating them into a power struggle, in which case she may refuse to eat them just to show you who is the boss!

520. Fruits. A baby during the first year has probably had stewed or canned peaches, pineapple, applesauce, apricots, prunes, pears, and raw ripe banana, apple, pear, and avocado. By a year some of these should be served in a lumpy consistency. Canned fruits such as pears, peaches and pineapple are not desirable if they are heavily sweetened with syrup. Look for canned fruits that contain nothing but fruit and their own juices.

Raw fruits such as oranges, peaches, apricots, plums, and melons are usually added between the ages of one and two years. When the peel is left on, the fruit should be washed to remove chemicals used in spraying.

I'd hold off until age three to offer cherries and raw

berries because of the risk of choking and blocking the airway. These can be given earlier if they are mashed and any seeds or pits are removed. Dried fruits, such as pitted prunes and dates, raisins, apricots, and figs, can be given unstewed at age three or earlier if they are chopped in salads. Whole pieces can cause choking in infants. Dried fruits stick to the teeth for a long time, so they should not be eaten frequently, and the child's teeth should be brushed promptly.

521. Cereals. At one year of age, babies should be taking one or a variety of the precooked whole grain cereals and also cooked oatmeal and cooked whole wheat cereals that the rest of the family eats. Most infants like their cereal either firm or thin but not pasty. If you see signs of boredom with one, try another that your child may not have been so keen about before.

Dry cereals, especially the whole wheat and oat varieties, are excellent sources of nutrition. Those made from corn and rice are generally less nutritious. Just remember to buy whole grain cereals and read carefully the nutritional information on the label. Sugar-coated cereals are junk foods. They are also heavily advertised on children's television programs. Don't buy them, and use your children's requests as an opportunity to discuss good nutrition and junk food.

The four things to look for in a dry cereal are low fat, high fiber, low sugar and low sodium. As always, read the nutritional information on the label carefully.

522. Bread is cereal in baked form, and it's just as valuable as cooked cereal. If your child is no longer interested in cereal for breakfast, you can serve bread, toast, or buns made from whole grains. Spread pureed fruit on the bread; there is really no reason to use margarine or butter. A wonderful low-fat spread can be made with one teaspoon of natural peanut butter and two tablespoons of cooked sweet potato. This "peanut butter stretcher" contains all of the essential nutrients, and children love it.

523. Whole grains are more nutritious than refined grains. Brown unrefined rice is superior to the white variety because it contains more fiber, vitamins, and minerals. When any grain is refined, nutrients are lost. That's why whole grains are always preferable to refined grains. So choose the darker, whole grain product whenever possible.

524. Milk. We used to think of cow's milk as a nearly perfect food. However, over the past several years, researchers have found new information that has caused many of us to change our opinion. This has provoked a lot of understandable controversy, but I have come to believe that cow's milk is not necessary for children.

First, it turns out that the fat in cow's milk is not the kind of fat ("essential fatty acids") needed for brain development. Instead, milk fat is too rich in the saturated fats that promote artery blockages.

Also, cow's milk can make it harder for a child to stay in iron balance. Milk is extremely low in iron and slows down iron absorption. It can also cause subtle blood loss in the digestive tract that causes the child to lose iron.

The proteins in cow's milk are an occasional cause of colic in infants (see Section 323). Now researchers are studying the links between cow's milk proteins and childhood-onset diabetes; at the present time, this association is uncertain. Some children have sensitivities to milk proteins, which show up as ear problems, respiratory problems, or skin conditions. Milk also has traces of antibiotics, estrogens, and other things a child does not need.

There is, of course, nothing wrong with human breast milk—it is perfect for infants. For older children, there are many good soy and rice milk products and even nondairy "ice creams" that are well worth trying. If you are using cow's milk in your family, I would encourage you to give these alternatives a try.

525. Meat, poultry, and fish. We used to recommend meat, poultry, and fish for children because they are rich in protein and iron. However, we now know that there are harmful effects of a meaty diet, particularly changes in the arteries and weight problems, and that these changes begin in childhood. When children develop a taste for meats, it is hard to break this habit later on.

It turns out that children can get plenty of protein and iron from vegetables, beans, and other plant foods that avoid the fat and cholesterol that are in animal products. Small children do need somewhat more fat in the diet than they will need later on, but this should not be animal fat. The essential fats used for growth and brain development come from vegetable oils. Vegetable-based meals are also much more likely to be free of the bacteria, such as salmonella and E. coli, that are common in meat and poultry products.

Dietitians now recommend leaner, smaller servings of meat, fish, and poultry, with all visible fat cut off. They also suggest cooking all meats thoroughly. That's good advice as far as it goes, but I recommend that you go a step further.

If you are including meats, poultry, or fish in your regular family routine, let me encourage you to explore vegetarian meals and to serve as many meatless meals as possible. You might also wish to try the new meat substitutes. Health food stores carry burgers, hot dogs, deli slices, and other products that taste like meats but are made from soy or wheat, and many of them are really delicious.

526. Eggs contain a substantial amount of animal protein in the white, and cholesterol and fat in the yolk, and are not necessary for children.

527. Sweets. Cookies, cakes, rich crackers, pastries quickly satisfy a child's appetite for a short time, but give him practically no minerals, vitamins, fiber, or protein. These sweets and snacks are also the greatest source of invisible fat. They cheat children by making them feel well fed when they are being partly starved, and by spoiling their appetite for better foods.

You don't have to be so suspicious of rich refined foods that you stop your children from eating cake at a birthday party or on other special occasions. It's the steady diet of such foods that deprives them of nutrition. There's no sense starting them at home when there is no need, and there is no reason to train your child to expect a big, fat, rich dessert after every dinner.

Highly sweetened foods such as jams, jellies, and candy contain excessive sugar. They quickly satisfy the appetite, but take it away for better foods, and they promote obesity and tooth decay. Give children their cereal and fruits without extra sugar. If occasionally it is convenient to give them canned fruit because the rest of the family is having it, pour off the syrup or buy canned fruit packed in fruit juice without added sugar. Children should brush their teeth after meals, anyway.

Candy, sodas, sundaes are usually eaten between meals while children are away from home with their friends. These snacks can spoil their appetites for regular meals and promote tooth decay. If your child is not trained to love these foods at home, he is less likely to eat a lot of them when away from home. Studies have shown that children by the age of five can learn the basics of good nutrition, if given the chance.

528. Craving for sweets and fatty foods often starts at home. Children often learn these tastes at home where there is a rich dessert with every meal, where candy is always offered between meals, and where the highest reward is considered to be a junk food splurge. When parents say, "You can't have your ice cream until you finish your vegetables," they are giving the wrong message and basically using junk food as a bribe. Teach your young child, instead, that a banana or a peach is the greatest treat of all!

For many children, a taste for fatty foods is determined by the foods they are given and the messages around those foods. Dr. Clara Davis, in 1939, in her experiments in letting children choose their own diets from a variety of natural foods, found that in the long run they wanted only a reasonable amount of the sweeter, high-fat foods.

Your children will also tend to eat whatever you eat. If you drink a lot of soda, eat a lot of ice cream or candy, or have chips around all the time, your children will want these things too. (I think that sweets brought by a grandparent who visits occasionally can be regarded as a special treat.)

529. Coffee, tea, cola drinks, and chocolate are not good drinks for children because they contain lots of sugar and the stimulant caffeine. These drinks also tend to replace the healthier beverages such as fruit juice and water. Even soft drinks without sugar or caffeine still take away the appetite and should be avoided. Herbal teas are fine as an occasional treat.

Meals

530. A simple guide to healthful diet. The whole business of diet sounds complicated, but it needn't be. Actually, it's probably much simpler than we used to think. The ideal diet is based on fruits, vegetables, whole grains, peas, and beans. Meat, poultry, and fish are not necessary and can be eliminated. The experiments of Dr. Clara Davis and Dr. Birch suggest that, left to their own devices, children will seek a well-balanced diet in the long run if they are raised on plant-based foods and if they haven't been taught to favor fatty foods.

Roughly speaking, the following foods are required every day:

- Vegetables, green or yellow, three to five servings. Ideally some of these are raw.
- Fruit, two or three servings, at least half of them raw. Fruit and vegetables may be interchanged.
- Legumes (beans, peas, and lentils), two to three servings.
- Whole grain bread, crackers, cereals, or pasta, two or more servings.

531. A suggested guide for meals. These are only guidelines, and you can vary the meals according to your child's preferences and your family's routines. Fruit and tomato juice can be given between meals if needed. Whole grain sourdough bread can be given with meals if desired. Once you've decided on the kind of diet you want for your child, check with your child's day care provider or school; you may have to supply your child's food.

Breakfast

Fruit or fruit juice or green leafy vegetables
Whole grain cereal, bread, toast, or pancakes

Scrambled tofu with greens
Soy milk
Vegetable soup

Lunch

A filling dish, such as baked beans; soup with crackers, toast, or barley; whole wheat or oat cereal, millet, or barley soup with vegetables; whole grain bread or sandwiches with tofu spread or nut butter; potato; soup with crackers, toast, barley, or a milk pudding; steamed, boiled, or stir-fried leafy greens
Vegetable or fruit, raw or cooked
Dry-roasted sunflower seeds
Soy milk, non-caffeine tea, or apple juice

Dinner

Green leafy vegetables, fast-cooked with a little water
Beans or bean product such as tofu or tempeh
Rice, bread, pasta, or other grain
Raw fruit or applesauce
Juice or water

532. It's not hard to vary lunch. Many parents complain that they don't know how to vary lunch. A good rough rule is to serve three items.

1. A filling dish with plenty of calories
2. A fruit or a vegetable
3. A green leafy vegetable (kale, broccoli, collards, scallions) cooked in a variety of ways

Breads and sandwiches of several kinds can be the filling dish as children approach the age of two. You can use rye, whole wheat, oatmeal, sourdough, or banana bread to start with. In general, avoid butter, margarine, and mayonnaise, which are full of fat and low on nutrition. Nut butters, used sparingly, are preferable. Mustard is a fat-free, well-accepted spread for sandwiches and potatoes.

Sandwiches can be made with a wide variety of other foods, plain or in combination: raw vegetables (lettuce, tomato, grated carrot, or cabbage), stewed fruit, chopped dried fruit, peanut butter, or tofu mashed with an eggless, low-fat mayonnaise.

A fairly substantial dish is a broth or soup containing lots of barley or brown rice, or a vegetable soup, plain or creamed, with a couple of handfuls of whole wheat toast cut into small cubes to toss in. Also lentil, split pea, and bean soups are a good balance with a grain dish and a green vegetable.

Simple unsalted whole grain crackers can be served plain or with one of the spreads mentioned above.

Potato is a good, filling, low-fat dish. A baked potato can be topped with vegetables, baked beans, mustard, black pepper, or salsa. A small amount of ketchup entices many a child to eat a greater variety of vegetables.

Cooked, precooked, or dry cereal can be made more exciting by adding sliced raw fruit, stewed fruit, or chopped dried fruit. But I recommend that you avoid adding sugar.

Instead of a filling first course followed by stewed or raw fruit, you can serve first a cooked green or yellow vegetable or a vegetable or fruit salad. A banana makes an excellent, filling dessert.

Pasta, hot or cold, is an excellent source of complex carbohydrates and fiber. It may be mixed with steamed vegetables and tomato sauce. Some children don't seem to like grains and pasta. They will do just fine nutritionally on a variety of fruits, vegetables, and beans. Their taste for grains will develop later if it's not forced on them early on. Pasta noodles made without eggs are available in most health food stores. Noodles made with whole grains are best. I like to add noodles to a stir-fry or have noodles in a broth of soup with greens added.

Feeding Between Meals

533. Use common sense between meals. Many young children, and some older ones, too, want a snack between meals, although others never snack. If it's the right kind of food, given at a sensible hour, presented in the right way, a snack shouldn't interfere with meals or lead to diet problems. When the regular meals contain plenty of carbohydrates in the grains and vegetables, children are much less likely to feel ravenous between meals.

Milk isn't a good snack food since it is more likely to take away the child's appetite for the next meal. A snack shouldn't contain that much fat or protein. Fruits or vegetables are the best bet. Occasionally, though, you see children who never can eat very much at one meal and get excessively hungry and tired before the next; they may thrive when given more caloric and rich snacks between meals. Its slow digestibility is what keeps them going, and they have a better appetite for the next meal because they're not exhausted.

Cakes, cookies, pastries, and salty and fried snack foods have three disadvantages: they are rich in calories and fat, poor in other food values, and bad for the teeth.

For most children the snack is best given midway between meals, and no closer than an hour and a half before the next one. Even here there are exceptions. There are children who receive juice in the middle of the morning but still get so hungry and cranky before lunch is ready that they pick fights and refuse to eat. Getting a glass of orange or tomato juice the minute they get home, even though it is twenty minutes before lunch, may improve their disposition and their appetite. So you see that what and when to feed a child between meals is a matter of common sense and doing what suits the individual child.

Parents may complain that their child eats badly at meals but is always begging for food between meals. This problem doesn't arise because the parents have been lenient about offering snacks between meals. Quite the contrary. In every case I have seen, the parents have been urging or forcing the child to eat at mealtimes and holding back on food at other times. It's the pushing that takes away the appetite at meals. After months of it, the very sight of the dining room is enough to make the child's stomach revolt. But when the meal is safely over (though little has been eaten), the stomach feels natural again. Soon it's acting the way a healthy empty stomach is meant to act—it's asking for food. The treatment, then, is not to deny children food between meals but to let mealtime be so enjoyable that their mouths water then, too. After all, what is a meal? It's food specially prepared to be appetizing. When a child finds it less appealing than snacks, something has gone wrong.

Feeding Problems

534. Where feeding problems begin. Why do so many children eat poorly? Most commonly because so many parents are conscientious about trying to make them eat well. You don't see many feeding problems in puppies or among young humans in places where mothers don't know enough about diet to worry.

Some children seem to be born with a wolf's appetite that stays big even when they're unhappy or sick. Others have appetites that are more moderate and more easily affected by their health and spirits. Almost without exception, babies are born with enough appetite to keep them healthy and to keep them gaining at the proper rate.

The trouble is that children are also born with an instinct to get balky if pushed too hard, and an instinct to get disgusted by food with which they've had unpleasant experiences. There's a further complication: children's appetites change, almost by the minute. For a while a child may feel like eating a lot of squash or a new breakfast cereal, but next month the same foods disgust her. If you understand this, you can see how feeding problems might begin at different stages in a child's development. Some babies become balky in their early months if their parents often try to make them finish more of their bottle than they want or if, when the first solid food is introduced, they aren't given a chance to get used to it gradually or if they are pressured to eat when they are not in the mood. Many become more picky and choosy after the age of eighteen months because they aren't meant to be gaining so fast, because they are more opinionated, or perhaps because of teething. Urging them to eat reduces the appetite further and more permanently. A very common time for eating problems to begin is at the end of an illness. If an anxious parent begins pushing food before the appetite returns, the pressure may quickly increase the child's disgust and get it firmly fixed.

All eating problems don't start from mere urging. A child may stop eating because of jealousy of a new baby or worries of many kinds. But whatever the original cause, the parents' anxiety and urging usually make the problem worse and keep the child's appetite from returning.

535. A cure takes time and patience. Once an eating problem is established, it takes time and understanding and patience to undo. The parents have become anxious. They find it hard to relax again as long as the child is eating poorly. And yet their concern and insistence are the main things that are keeping the child's appetite down. Even when they reform, by a supreme effort, it may take weeks for the child's timid appetite to come back. She needs a chance to slowly forget all the unpleasant associations with mealtime.

Her appetite is like a mouse and the parents' anxious urging is the cat that has been scaring it back into its hole. You can't persuade the mouse to be bold just because the cat looks the other way. The cat must leave the mouse alone for a while.

536. Parents have feelings, too. And they are strong feelings by the time they have a chronic feeding problem on their hands. The most obvious one is anxiety—that the child will develop some nutritional deficiency or lose resistance to ordinary infections. The doctor tries to reassure them again and again that children with eating problems are not more susceptible to diseases than other children are, but this is hard for them to believe. They are apt to feel guilty, imagining that their relatives, their in-laws, the neighbors, the doctor, consider them neglectful parents. They don't, of course. It's more likely that they understand because they have at least one child in the family who's a poor eater, too.

Then there's the parents' inevitable feeling of frustration and anger at a whippersnapper who can completely foil their efforts to do right by her. This is the most uncomfortable feeling of all, because it makes conscientious parents feel ashamed of themselves.

It's an interesting fact that many parents whose children have eating problems recall having had an eating problem themselves in their own childhood. They remember only too well that urging and forcing worked in the wrong direction, but they find themselves powerless to do otherwise. In such cases, the strong feelings of anxiety, guilt, and irritation are partly leftovers from the same feelings implanted in their own childhood.

537. There's rarely danger for the child. It's important to remember that children have a remarkable inborn mechanism that lets them know how much food and which types of food they need for normal growth and development. It is extremely rare to see serious malnutrition, or vitamin deficiency, or infectious disease result from a child's picky eating habits. The child's eating pattern should be discussed with the doctor at the time of checkups, of course.

538. Make mealtime pleasant. The aim is not to make the child eat but to let her natural appetite come to the surface so that she wants to eat.

Try hard not to talk about her eating, either threateningly or encouragingly. I wouldn't praise her for taking an unusually large amount or look disappointed for eating little. With practice, you should be able to stop thinking about it, and that's real progress. When she feels no more pressure, she can begin to pay attention to her own appetite.

You sometimes hear the advice, "Put the food in front of the child, say nothing, take it away in thirty minutes, no matter how much or how little has been eaten. Give nothing else until the next meal." It is true that usually when children are hungry they will eat. So this is all right if it is not done in anger or as a punishment and if it's carried out in the right spirit—that is to say, if the parent is really trying not to fuss or worry about the child's eating and remains agreeable. But angry parents sometimes apply the advice by slapping the plate of dinner in front of the child, saying grimly, "Now, if you don't eat this in thirty minutes,

I'm going to take it away and you won't get a thing to eat until supper!" Then they stand glaring at her, waiting. Such threatening hardens her heart and takes away any trace of appetite. The balky child who is challenged to an eating battle can always outlast a parent.

You don't want your child to eat because she has been beaten in a fight, whether you have been forcing her or taking her food away. You want her to eat because she feels like eating.

Start by offering the foods she likes best. You want her mouth to water when she comes to meals so that she can hardly wait to begin. The first step in building up that attitude is to serve for two or three months the wholesome foods she likes best, offering as balanced a diet as possible, and to omit all the foods that she actively dislikes.

If your child dislikes only one group of foods or another but eats most kinds fairly well, read Sections 519 and 532, which explain how one food can be substituted for another until a child's appetite swings around or until her suspiciousness and tenseness at meals abate.

539. The child who likes few foods. A parent might say, "Those children who dislike just one type of food aren't real problems. Why, my child likes only peanut butter, bananas, oranges, and soda pop. Once in a while he'll take a slice of white bread or a couple of teaspoons of peas. He refuses to touch anything else."

This is a more difficult feeding problem, but the principle is the same. You could serve him sliced bananas and a slice of enriched bread for breakfast; a bit of peanut butter, 2 teaspoons of peas, and an orange for lunch; a slice of enriched bread and more banana for supper. Let him have seconds or thirds of any of the foods if he asks for them. Give him a multivitamin as nutritional insurance. Serve different combinations of this diet for days. Hold down firmly on soft drinks and other junk foods. If his stomach is awash with syrup, it takes away what little appetite he has for more valuable foods.

If at the end of a couple of months he is looking forward to his meals, add a couple of teaspoons (no more) of some food that he sometimes used to eat—not one he hated. Don't mention the new addition. Don't comment, whether he eats it or leaves it. Offer this food again in a couple of weeks, and meanwhile try another. How fast you go on adding new foods will depend on how his appetite is improving and how he's taking to the new foods.

540. Make no distinctions between foods. Let him eat four helpings of one food and none of another if that's the way he feels, as long as the food is wholesome. If he wants none of the main course but does want dessert, let him have dessert in a perfectly matter-of-fact way. If you say, "No dessert until you've finished your vegetables," you further take away his appetite for the vegetable or the main course and you increase his desire for desserts. These results are the exact opposite of what you want. The best way to handle the dessert problem is not to serve any dessert except fruit more than a night or two a week. If a non-fruit dessert is served, it should be given to all family members without exception.

It's not that you want children to go on eating lopsided meals forever. But if they have a feeding problem and are already suspicious of some foods, your best chance of having them come back to a reasonable balance is to let them feel that you do not care one way or the other about what they eat.

I think it's a great mistake for the parent to insist that children who have feeding problems eat "just a taste" of a food they are suspicious of, as a matter of duty. If they have to eat anything that disgusts them, even slightly, it lessens the chance that they will ever change their minds and like it. And it lowers their enjoyment of mealtimes and their general appetite for all foods.

Certainly, never make them eat at the next meal food that they refused at the last meal. That's looking for trouble.

541. Serve less than they will eat, not more. For any child who is eating poorly, serve small portions. If you heap her plate high, you will remind her of how much she is going to refuse and you'll depress her appetite. But if you give her a first helping that is less than she is going to eat, you will encourage her to think, "That isn't enough." You want her to have that attitude. You want her to think of food as something she is eager for. If she has a really small appetite, serve her miniature portions: a teaspoon of beans, a teaspoon of vegetables, a teaspoon of rice or potatoes. When she finishes, don't say eagerly, "Do you want some more?" Let her ask, even if it takes several days of miniature portions to give her the idea. It's a good idea to serve the miniature portions on a very small plate, so that the child doesn't feel humiliated by sitting in front of tiny portions of food on a huge plate.

542. Getting them to feed themselves. Should the parents feed a poor eater? A child who is given proper encouragement (Sections 309 and 310) will take over his own feeding somewhere between twelve and eighteen months. But if overworried parents have continued to feed him until age two or three or four, probably with a lot of urging, it won't solve the problem simply to tell him, "Now feed yourself."

The child now has no desire to feed himself; he takes being fed for granted. To him it's now an important sign of his parents' love and concern. If they stop suddenly, it hurts his feelings and makes him resentful. He is liable to stop eating altogether for two or three days—and that's longer than any parents can sit by doing nothing. When they feed him again, he has a new grudge against them. When they try another time to give up feeding him, he knows his strength and their weakness.

A child of two or more should be feeding himself as soon as possible. But getting him to do it is a delicate matter that may take several weeks. You mustn't give him the impression that you are taking a privilege away. You want him to take over because he wants to.

Serve him his favorite foods, meal after meal and day after day. When you set the dish in front of him, go to the kitchen or into the next room for a minute or two, as if you had forgotten something. Stay away a little longer each day. Come back and feed him cheerfully with no comments, whether or not he has eaten anything in your absence. If he gets impatient while you are in the next room and calls you to come and feed him, come right away, with a friendly apology. He probably won't progress steadily. In a week or two he may get to the point of self-feeding one meal and insisting that you feed him at others. Don't argue at all during this process. If he eats only one food, don't urge him to try another. If he seems pleased with himself for doing a good job of self-feeding, compliment him on being a big boy, but don't be so enthusiastic that he gets suspicious.

Suppose for a week or so you have left him alone with good food for as long as 10 or 15 minutes and he's eaten nothing. Then you ought to make him hungrier. Gradually, over three or four days, cut down to half what you customarily feed him. This should make him so eager that he can't help starting to feed himself, provided you are being tactful and friendly.

By the time the child is regularly feeding himself as much as half a meal. I think it's time to encourage him to leave the table rather than feed him the rest of the meal. Never mind if he has left out some of his foods. His hunger will build up and soon make him eat more. If you go on feeding him the last half of the meal, he may never take over the whole job. Just say, "I guess you've had enough." If he asks you to feed him some more, give him two or three more mouthfuls to be agreeable and then suggest casually that he's through.

After he has taken over completely for a couple of weeks, don't slip back into the habit of feeding him again. If someday he's very tired and says, "Feed me," give him a few spoonfuls absentmindedly, and then say something about his not being very hungry. I make this point because I know that a parent who has worried for months or years about a child's eating, who spoon-fed him much too long, and finally let him feed himself, has a great temptation to go back to feeding him again the first time he loses his appetite or the first time he is sick. Then the job has to be done all over again.

543. Should the parents stay in the room while the child is eating? This depends on what the child is used to and wants, and how well the parents can control their worry. If they have always sat there with him, they can't suddenly disappear without upsetting him. If they can be sociable and relaxed, and get their minds off the food, it's fine for them to stay, whether or not they are eating their own meal. If they find that even with practice they can't get their minds off the child's eating or can't stop urging him, it may be better for them to retire from the picture at the child's mealtime, not crossly, not suddenly, but tactfully and gradually, a little more each day, so that he doesn't notice the change.

544. No acts, bribes, or threats. Certainly the parents shouldn't put on an act to bribe the child to eat—a little story for every mouthful or a promise to stand on their heads if the spinach is finished. Although this kind of persuasion may seem at the moment to make the child eat a few more mouthfuls, in the long run it dampens his appetite more and more. The parents have to keep upping the ante to get the same result. They end up putting on an exhausting vaudeville act for five mouthfuls.

Don't ask a child to eat to earn his dessert or a piece of candy or a gold star or any other prize. Don't ask him to eat for Aunt Minnie, or to make his mother or father happy, or to grow big and strong or to keep from getting sick or to clean his plate. Children should not be threatened with physical punishment or loss of privileges in an attempt to get them to eat.

Let's state the rule one more time: **Don't ask, bribe, or force a child to eat.**

There is no great harm in a parent's telling a story at suppertime or playing music, if that has been the custom, so long as it is not connected with whether the child is eating or not.

545. It isn't necessary to be a doormat. I have said so much about letting a child eat because he wants to that I may have given the wrong impression to some parents. I remember a mother who had been embroiled in a feeding problem with her seven-year-old daughter—urging, arguing, forcing. When the mother understood that the child probably had, underneath, a normal appetite and a desire to eat a well-balanced diet, and that the best way to revive it was to stop battling over meals, she swung to the opposite extreme and became apologetic. The daughter by this age had a lot of resentment in her from the long struggle. As soon as she realized that her mother was all meekness, she took advantage of her. She would pour the whole sugar bowl on her cereal, watching out of the corner of her eye to see her mother's silent horror. The mother would ask her before each meal what she wanted. If the child said, "Hamburger," she obediently bought and served it. Then the child, as like as not, would say, "I don't want hamburger. I want frankfurters," and the mother would run to the store to buy some.

There is a middle ground. It's reasonable for a child to be expected to come to meals on time, to be pleasant to other diners, to refrain from making unpleasant remarks about the food or declaring what she doesn't like, to eat with the table manners that are reasonable for her age. It's fine for the parents to take her preferences into account as much as is possible (considering the rest of the family) in planning meals, or to ask her occasionally what she would like, as a treat. But it's bad for her to get the idea that she's the only one to be considered. It's sensible and right for the parents to put a limit on sugar, candy, soda, cake, and the other less wholesome foods. All this can be done without argument as long as the parents act as if they know what they are doing.

546. Gagging. The child beyond the age of a year who can't tolerate anything but pureed food has usually been fed forcibly, or at least urged vigorously. It isn't so much that she can't stand lumps. What makes her gag is having them pushed into her. The parents of gagging children usually say, "It's a funny thing. She can swallow lumps all right if it's something she likes very much. She can even swallow big chunks of meat that she bites off the bone."

There are three steps in curing a child who gags. The first is to encourage her to feed herself completely (Sections 309 and 310). The second is to get her over her suspicion of foods in general (Section 534). The third is to go unusually slowly in coarsening the consistency of her food. Let her go for weeks or even months, if necessary, on pureed foods, until she has lost all fear of eating and is really enjoying it. Don't even serve her meats, for instance, during this time if she cannot enjoy them finely ground.

In other words, go only as fast as the child can comfortably take it.

A few babies have such sensitive throats that they gag even on pureed foods. In some of these cases, the cause seems to be the pasty consistency of the food. Try diluting it a little with milk or water. Or try chopping vegetables and fruits fine without mashing them.

Thin Children

547. Thinness has various causes. Some children seem to be thin by heredity. They come from thin stock on one or both sides of the family. From the time they were babies they have been offered plenty to eat. They aren't sickly, and they aren't nervous. They just never want to eat a great deal, especially of the rich foods.

Other children are thin because their appetites have been taken away by too much parental urging (see Section 534). Other children can't eat for other nervous reasons. Children who are worrying about monsters, or death, or a parent's going away and leaving them, for example, may lose a lot of their appetite. The jealous younger sister who is driving herself all day long to keep up with her older sister burns up a lot of energy and gives herself no peace at mealtime, either. As you can see, the tense child is thinned out by a two-way process: the appetite is kept down, and the restlessness uses up extra energy.

Many children throughout the world are malnourished because their parents can't find or afford the proper food. Some chronic physical diseases cause malnutrition, but children who become thin during an acute illness usually recover their weight promptly if during convalescence they are not urged to eat until their appetite recovers.

548. Sudden loss of weight is serious. If a child abruptly or slowly loses a lot of weight, he must have a careful checkup—promptly. The most common causes of weight loss are diabetes (which also produces excessive hunger and thirst and frequent urination), worry about serious family tensions, tumors, and obsession in adolescent girls with the need to diet. (See Section 480 on anorexia nervosa.)

549. Care of a thin child. A thin child should, of course, have regular medical checkups. This is more important if the child acts tired or has lost weight or has failed to gain a reasonable amount. Thinness, failure to gain weight, and fatigue come more often from emotional troubles than from physical causes. If your child is nervous or depressed, consult a child guidance clinic or a family social agency. Talk over his situation with his teacher. In any case, it's wise to think over again his relations with parents, brothers, sisters, friends, and school. If you have gotten involved in a feeding problem, try to undo it (see Section 535).

Eating between meals is helpful for those thin children whose stomachs never seem to want to take much at a time but who are quite willing to eat often. It doesn't help to allow constant snacking. Children who do that develop poor eating habits. I am suggesting one nutritious snack after breakfast and lunch, then one at bedtime. You have to avoid the temptation of feeding the thin child high-calorie, low-nutrition junk foods for snacks, either as a bribe or to have the comfort of seeing him eat something.

A healthy child may stay thin despite a large appetite, and this is probably the way she or he was meant to be. In many of these cases, the child prefers relatively low-calorie foods, like vegetables and fruit, and shies away from rich desserts. If your child doesn't seem to have any kind of problem, has been slender since infancy, but gains a reasonable amount of weight every year, relax. She or he is meant to be that way.

Fat Children

550. The treatment depends on the cause. Many people think the cause of obesity is thyroid or other hormonal trouble, but actually this is rarely the case, especially if the child's height is within the normal range. Several factors can increase a child's chances of becoming overweight, including heredity, temperament, appetite, and unhappiness. If both parents are overweight, the child's chance of becoming obese is as high as 80 percent. This has led many to think of genes or heredity as the principal cause of obesity. In my opinion, lifestyle patterns such as excessive fat intake and inactivity play an equally important role. In the fifty years since this book was first published, children's genes have not changed, but obesity has increased significantly.

The placid child who takes little exercise and watches a lot of television has more food calories left over to store in the form of fat.

Another key factor is appetite. The child who has a tremendous appetite that runs to rich foods like potato chips, meats, cheese, cake, cookies, and pastry is naturally going to be heavier than the child whose taste runs principally to vegetables, fruit, and grains. But this only raises the question of why one child craves large amounts of rich foods. We don't understand all the causes of this, but we recognize the children who seem to have been born to be big eaters. They start with a huge appetite at birth and never lose it, whether they're well or sick, calm or worried, whether the food they're offered is appetizing or not. Perhaps they learn to appreciate fatty foods because they are offered as treats and rewards for good behavior or to express their parents' love for them. They're fat by the time they're two or three months old and stay that way at least through childhood, so the time to establish healthy eating patterns is right then, as soon as the tendency to overweight is evident (see Section 252).

551. Unhappiness is sometimes a factor. Of the excessive appetites that develop later in childhood, some at least are due to unhappiness and depression. This can happen, for instance, around the age of seven in children who are somewhat unhappy and lonely. This is the period when children are drawing away from their close emotional dependence on their parents. If they don't have the knack of making equally close friendships with other children, they feel left out in the cold. Eating sweet and rich foods seems to serve as a partial substitute. Worries about schoolwork or other matters sometimes make children seek comfort in overeating, too.

Overweight often develops during puberty. The appetite normally increases at this time to compensate for the increased rate of growth, but it's probable that loneliness plays a part in some cases, too. This is the period when children may become more turned-in and self-conscious because of all the changes they are experiencing, and this may lessen their ability to get along enjoyably with their fellows.

Obesity may become a vicious circle, no matter what caused it in the beginning. The fatter the child, the harder it is for her to enjoy exercise and games. And the quieter she is, the more energy her body has to store as fat. It's a vicious circle in another way, too: the fat child who can't comfortably enter into games may come to feel even more like an outsider, and is liable to be kidded and ridiculed.

Obesity is a most serious problem for any child. Since it's apt to be associated with physical and mental problems, it should be combatted as soon as it appears. If a baby is becoming unusually plump during his first year, this shouldn't be considered cute. It should be treated with dietary shifts right away. Often it's possible to satisfy such a child fairly well with a lot of vegetables, fruits, whole grains, and beans, and to cut way down on starches and fats.

552. Mild overweight is common between seven and twelve. I don't want to leave the impression that every child who turns plump is unhappy. There seems to be a normal tendency for many children, including the cheerful and successful ones, to put on extra weight in the seven- to twelve-year-old period. Very few of these children become excessively obese; they are just slightly overpadded. Most of them stay plump during the two years of very rapid puberty development and then slim down as they get further into adolescence. Many girls, for instance, become slimmer around fifteen years of age without great effort. It's good for parents to know that this mild school-age obesity is common and that it often goes away later, so that they won't make an issue of it.

553. Dieting is difficult. What can you do about fat children? Right away you would say, "Put them on a diet." It sounds easy, but it isn't. Think of the grown-ups you know who are unhappy with their weight and who still aren't able to stick to a diet. A child has less willpower than an adult. But if the parents serve the child lower-fat foods, it means either the whole family must go without the richer dishes or the overweight child must be kept from eating the very things that his heart craves most while the rest of the family enjoys them. Very few children are mature enough to think that that's fair, and the feeling of being treated unfairly may further increase the craving for sweets. Whatever is accomplished in the dining room may be undone at the refrigerator or fast-food counter between meals.

But the prospect of dieting is not so dismal as I have made out. Tactful parents can do a good deal to keep temptation away from their overweight child without making an issue of it. They can eliminate rich, fatty desserts. They can stop keeping cake and cookies around in the kitchen and provide fresh fruit for between-meals nibbling. They can serve low-fat foods for the whole family, with plenty of vegetables, fruits, grains, beans, and peas. When families adopt a vegetarian diet and keep vegetable oils to a minimum, too, weight problems generally improve, as do other health conditions. This is not a diet in the usual sense. It is meant to be a permanent change in the way the entire family eats, a new way of eating that is more nutritious and that the child will accept in time. Any additional weight loss is simply a bonus of healthier eating habits.

A child should be encouraged to learn about various nutritious foods, where they come from, how they are prepared, their ethnic origins. She should also participate in choosing and purchasing the foods. The supermarket provides a wonderful opportunity to teach children about various foods and good nutrition.

A child who shows any willingness to cooperate in a diet should certainly be encouraged to visit the doctor, preferably alone. Talking to the doctor or nurse practitioner, person to person, may give the child the feeling of running her own life like a grown-up. Anyone can take dietary advice better from an outsider. Children do not need any medicine for reducing. The "treatment" is a change in eating patterns, from fatty foods to healthy foods.

Since overeating is often a symptom of loneliness or maladjustment, the most constructive thing is to make sure that the child's home life, schoolwork, and social life are as happy and satisfying as possible (see Section 447).

If, despite your efforts to help, the extra weight is more than mild, or if the child is gaining weight too rapidly, you should certainly get medical assistance.

554. Dieting should be supervised by a doctor. Self-dieting sometimes becomes a problem and a danger in the adolescent period. A group of girls excitedly work themselves up to going on some wild diet that they have heard about. Within a few days, hunger makes most of them break their resolutions, but one or two may persist with fanatical zeal. Occasionally a girl loses alarming amounts of weight and can't resume a normal diet even when she wants to (see Section 480 on anorexia nervosa). The group hysteria about dieting seems to have awakened in her a deep revulsion against food, which is usually a hangover from some unresolved worry of early childhood. Another girl in the early stages of puberty declares, "I'm getting much too fat," even though she is so slender that her ribs are showing. She may be emotionally unready to grow up and secretly disturbed by the development of her breasts. The child who becomes obsessed with dieting should have the help of a children's psychiatrist or psychologist.

Weight-loss diets should be mainly based on changing the *type* of food children eat, rather than focusing on the amount of food. When the family brings in low-fat plant-based foods—pasta, beans, vegetables, rice dishes—in place of oily fried foods, meats, and dairy products, weight loss typically occurs without anyone going hungry and without the risk of anorexia, which can result from a severe low-calorie diet.

If dieting is being considered, the first step, for a number of reasons, is to consult a doctor. The doctor's first task is to determine whether dieting is either necessary or wise.

Adolescents are more apt to accept the doctor's advice than that of their parents. If it is agreed that diet is wise, it should certainly be prescribed by the doctor or dietitian who will take into account the child's food tastes and the family's usual menus in order to work out a diet that is not only sound nutritionally but practical in that particular home. Finally, since weight loss puts some strain on the dieter's health, anyone who is planning to reduce should be examined at regular intervals to make sure that the rate is not too fast (a pound a week is usually safe) and that the dieter remains strong and healthy.

Preventing Injuries

Principles of Prevention

555. Injuries cause more deaths in children over the age of one year than all illnesses combined. According to the National SAFE KIDS Campaign, each year an estimated 7,000 children between ages one and fourteen die from injuries. An additional 120,000 are permanently disabled. The leading causes of injuries to children, in order of frequency, are traffic injuries, which include children as passengers, pedestrians, and bicyclists; fire and burns; drowning; suffocation; poisoning; choking; unintentional shootings; and falls.

When you say "accident" everyone assumes it's something unavoidable—just one of those things you can't control in life. In some situations this is true. However, many of what we call accidents are really injuries that could be easily prevented. Even when accidents aren't preventable, the injuries that result from them often are. And most of us know how to do it: using car seats, seat belts, and bicycle helmets; practicing pedestrian and water safety; installing smoke detectors; and lowering temperatures in water heaters. These simple measures could prevent most of these tragedies.

556. Why do we all have so much trouble taking the necessary actions regularly? I think it's because of a natural human tendency to go through life with an attitude of "It can't happen to me." So the first step is to stop denying the possibility of an injury. Then practice the two basic principles of effective injury prevention.

557. Child-proof the environment. Be aware of your environment in order to identify and reduce hazards as much as possible. To prevent injuries, it is necessary to remove dangerous objects from your child's grasp. Begin to teach good safety habits and change hazardous environments that contribute to injuries, such as coffee tables with sharp corners, unguarded stairs, and furniture and beds next to open windows.

Be particularly careful during stressful times. In trying to juggle greater and greater demands upon your time, take care to remember where you left the scissors, razor, hedge trimmer or any other sharp item you may have been using before being interrupted or distracted.

558. Supervise your child closely. The second principle of injury prevention is vigilant supervision of your child. Even in a childproofed environment, children require close supervision. Toddlers especially, take chances, lack judgment, and need the protection of an adult. Of course you can't spend every waking minute keeping track of your child, but some environments are inherently more dangerous than others. If a playroom has been well childproofed, you can relax a little. But out in the big world you must be more vigilant.

Traffic Injuries

Children are vulnerable to traffic injuries as auto occupants, as pedestrians, and as bicycle riders. I'm including bikes in this category because nearly 90 percent of fatal bike injuries are motor-vehicle related.

559. Car safety seats and seat belts. Your baby's first ride home after birth and every ride should be in a car safety seat conforming to Federal Motor Vehicle Safety Standards.

This is not to be confused with an infant carrier which is not designed to withstand the impact of an automobile crash. Infant-only safety seats are used for infants who weigh less than twenty pounds and they must *face rearward* in the back seat of the car. This is to protect an infant's neck in the event of an impact or sudden stop.

A car seat is safest in the back seat. An infant weighing less than 20 pounds should face the rear of the vehicle and be placed in the center of the back seat.

560. When your baby weighs 20 pounds at about a year, he should be moved to a toddler or convertible car safety seat for children weighing up to 40 pounds or the convertible seat he used as an infant should be turned to face forward. A five point harness provides more protection than the three point harness. The three point harness or shield is also not recommended if you are using the convertible seat for an infant because the shield often can potentially cause too much pressure on an infant's chest and torso.

561. Booster seats are for children who have outgrown child safety seats. A booster seat can be used once the child

A baby over 20 pounds may be placed in a toddler seat, facing forward in the back seat of a car with attention to proper harnessing.

weighs 40 pounds and should be used until he weighs approximately 60 pounds or until the shoulder strap rests on his shoulder (and not across his neck or chin). A booster seat used with a lap belt only or with a shoulder-lap belt will give the child more protection if it is fitted over the child's pelvis bone instead of the tops of his thighs and groin. Many parents skip the booster seat because they don't want to buy another restraint system. This is a mistake because the injuries sustained by young children in seat belts tend to be worse than those in a booster seat.

562. Car safety seats and seat belts offer no protection unless they're installed and used properly. As many as nine out of ten car seats are misused in some way. Be sure your baby's seat is correctly secured to the car. Secondhand car seats must be carefully checked for any missing parts. Seats that have been in a crash should be discarded.

All fifty states have laws requiring that children under age four be properly restrained in a child safety seat when a car is in motion. More than half the states now require that

A child weighing over 60 pounds may use a rear-seat shoulder strap restraint (if it is not across her neck or chin).

everyone riding in the front seat be buckled up. Some parents claim that their children refuse to wear them. This excuse isn't worth a nickel. All children will do whatever their parents really insist on. If you begin making exceptions, a child will argue every time, and that's exhausting for both child and parent. *The safest policy is not to operate any vehicle unless everyone in it is secured in a car seat or seat belt.*

There's an added benefit to keeping children in car seats or seat belts: They behave better when they're secured than when they're not!

563. Keep your children in the back seat. The safest place in the car is the middle of the back seat. All infants and children should ride in the back seat. Unless a child's feet can reach the floor of the vehicle at the age of twelve, he should not be placed in the front seat if there is a passenger-side airbag. Children should sit in the back seat whenever an airbag is present. Airbags implode upon impact, and this force could seriously injure or kill a child who is not properly restrained or too close to the airbag.

A rear-facing safety seat should never be placed in the front seat if an airbag is present. Likewise a child in a toddler seat or booster seat would not be sufficiently anchored to withstand the impact of an airbag without injury. If a child must ride in the front, make sure he is properly restrained and the seat is moved back as far as possible. I'd suggest your child continue to ride in the back seat for as long as possible. Don't use one seat for two children together or for an adult holding a small child or infant in her arms.

564. On airplanes. The recommendations for safe travel and the use of child safety seats on airplanes are confusing. Children under age two can fly for free, but they are not given a seat. As a result you may not be able to use a child safety seat unless there is a vacant seat next to you. Of course, holding a child in one's arms on an airplane is never as safe as securing a child into a safety seat (see Section 915); however, air travel is much safer than driving. If you don't want to pay for an extra seat for your baby on the plane, it's still safer to fly than drive to your destination. Take your car safety seat along, whether or not you use it on the plane so you'll have it for travel when you reach your destination.

Beds are available for use on airplanes by infants under two, but they can be used in the bulkhead seats only. For children over age two, a ticket is required, and it is recommended that you bring a toddler seat on board for children under 40 pounds. Harnesses and inflatable seat vests are not recommended by the FAA for safe travel.

Pedestrian Injuries

565. The most common cause of death by injury in children between the ages of five and nine is getting hit by a car. School-age children are especially at risk because they are frequently exposed to traffic but do not have enough skill to handle it. Their peripheral vision isn't fully developed. They can't accurately evaluate the speed and distance of oncoming cars. Many don't have the judgment to know when it's safe to cross.

Research shows that adults generally give their children credit for more street smarts than they actually have. Here are some guidelines for pedestrian safety:

1. From the time your child begins to walk on the sidewalk, teach him that he can step off the curb only when you are holding his hand.

2. Always supervise the outdoor play of pre-schoolers, and make sure they never play in driveways or streets.

3. Explain to five- to nine-year-olds over and over again the rules about crossing residential streets. Model safe pedestrian behavior yourself, as you walk with them. Point out how traffic lights and crosswalks work, and why it's so important to look left, right, and left again, even when they have the traffic light in their favor and even when they are in a crosswalk. The hardest job for parents is to teach children that drivers regularly ignore red lights and that crosswalks are not automatic safety zones. One-third of pedestrian injuries occur when the child is in a marked crosswalk!

4. Remember that children aren't developmentally ready to cross a heavily traveled street without adult supervision until they're at least nine or ten years old.

5. Together with your child, find the safe places to play in your neighborhood. Explain repeatedly that he must never run into the street when playing, no matter how important the game may seem.

6. Think about where your child walks, especially on the way to school, to the playgrounds, and to playmates' houses. Walk with him, as if you are explorers, and find the safest route with the easiest street crossings. Then help him learn that the safest route is the only route he should use.

7. Try to find the time to get involved in community safety. Find out if there are enough traffic signals and crossing guards on the way to your child's school. If a new school is being built, look into the traffic pattern in that area. Will there be enough sidewalks, lights, and guards?

8. Be particularly cautious with toddlers in parking lots and insist that they hold your hand. Keep toddlers in wagons or put them in the car while loading bags.

Bicycle Injuries

566. For children ages fourteen and under in the United States, bicycle injuries cause more than 250 deaths and 350,000 emergency room visits every year. These injuries are especially common in the after school hours before darkness. Following basic safety rules can prevent the majority of serious injuries. Remember that 60 percent of all serious bike injuries are head injuries. And a head injury means a potential brain injury, which always carries the possibility of permanent brain damage. *Proper use of bicycle helmets can reduce the incidence of head injuries by 85 percent.*

A helmet should meet voluntary ASTM, ANSI or SNELL standards for safety or mandatory federal standards after February 1999. It should have a solid, hard outer shell and a firm polystyrene liner. The chin strap should be attached to the helmet at three points: beneath each ear and at the back of the neck.

A bicycle helmet is an important part of every ride. Start early, when using training wheels.

567. The helmet must fit properly. It should sit on top of the child's head in a level position and should not rock back and forth or from side to side. Measure your child's head with a tape measure and select the appropriate size according to the information on the box. Be sure the box tells you the head size in inches to ensure proper fit—do not rely entirely on the age recommendations on the box. A general guideline to follow is that infant-sized helmets are recommended for children ages one and two years, a child's size will fit a child between three and six, a youth helmet can be used from age seven to eleven, and then an adult size will be required. Adult helmets come in small, medium, large, and extra-large sizes.

Replace the helmet if it is involved in any crash or serious head thump. Most companies will replace the impact absorbing liner free if you send them the helmet. Competition is bringing prices down. You should be able to get a safe helmet for $20 or less.

For biking safety, go by these rules:

1. No riding without a helmet—ever.
2. When parents ride, they must wear helmets too. You can't expect your children to follow this rule if you don't set an example.
3. Always get your child a tricycle or bicycle that fits her, not one that she will have to grow into.
4. Don't start your child on a two-wheeler until she's developmentally ready, usually between ages five and seven.
5. Use bikes with coaster brakes for children up to age nine or ten, when they have developed the strength and coordination to manage hand brakes.
6. Allow children to ride only on sidewalks until age nine or ten (when judgment matures enough to handle traffic while riding in the street). Then teach them the basic rules of the road so they can obey all the same traffic rules that automobile drivers follow.
7. Put reflective materials on the bike, the helmet, and the child for better visibility. This is especially important for children who ride at dawn or dusk, and from school or playmates' houses.
8. Headlamps are required for any night riding, although night riding is not recommended for children.

568. Bicycle carrier seats. Parents bicycling with a child in a carrier should follow these additional rules:

1. Select a child carrier with headrest protection, spoke guards, and shoulder straps. Never use a backpack to carry your child on a bike.
2. Practice with your bike and a weighted carrier before biking with your child. Practice riding in an open area, free of traffic and other cyclists, to get used to

the extra weight and to gain confidence with balancing a child in a carrier.

3. Never carry a child who's less than one year old or who weighs over 40 pounds.
4. A child should wear a helmet at all times while strapped in the carrier seat.
5. Never leave your child unattended in the carrier. Bikes are not made to stand with loaded carriers, and many injuries are caused by falls from a standing bike.
6. Adults should also wear helmets while riding.
7. Ride on safe, uncongested bike paths, not in the street.
8. Don't ride after dark.

Fire, Smoke, and Burns

Take these simple, one-time-only steps to ensure long-term protection:

1. Install smoke detectors on each floor of your house. Install them in the hallways just outside sleeping areas and outside the kitchen. Change batteries yearly.
2. Keep a dry chemical fire extinguisher in the kitchen.
3. Turn the temperature of your water heater down to 120°F. At 150° to 160°F (most manufacturers' preset temperature) a small child will receive third-degree burns in less than two seconds! But at 120°F, it takes five minutes to produce a scald burn. (You'll also reduce your energy bill.) If you live in an apartment or condominium ask your landlord or condominium association to turn the water heater down. You can still get your dishes clean in water temperature less than 130°F. Anti-scald devices can be installed in your shower, bathtub and sink fixtures to stop the flow of water when the temperature exceeds 120°F.
4. As a matter of habit, always feel the temperature of bathwater even if you remember doing it earlier.
5. Hot faucets sometimes cause burns.
6. Don't touch or let a child touch electrical equipment while in a bath or while holding on to a faucet.

Water temperature below 120°F prevents scald burns.

7. Teach your children that if they smell smoke and suspect a fire, the first thing they should do is *get out of the house.* They can call the fire department from a neighbor's phone.
8. Make a fire escape plan with two escape routes from each bedroom, and choose a designated meeting place outdoors. Have the whole family practice the plan.

569. Fire is the second most common cause of death from injury in childhood. Children under five are at the greatest risk. *Some 75 percent of fire-related deaths are actually due to smoke inhalation, not burns. Approximately 80 percent of all fire-related deaths occur in house fires.* (Half of all house fires are due to cigarettes.) Fire spreads rapidly, so don't leave young children alone in a house, even for a few minutes. Take them with you if you have to go out.

570. Scalding. The most common non-fatal burn injuries result from scalding. About 20 percent of these cases result from tap water; 80 percent are from spilled foods and liquids. Half of all scald burns are serious enough to require skin grafting.

571. Other safety tips to prevent fires and burns. Coffee burns are the most common ones seen by doctors. Never drink hot coffee or tea with a small child in your lap. And be sure that cups of hot coffee aren't near the edge of the table where a small child can reach up to pull them off.

Avoid using tablecloths or placemats, which a small child can pull off the table.

Never heat a child's bottle in a microwave oven. The milk can be scalding hot even when the container feels cool.

Children's sleepwear is required by law to be flame-retardant. It is important to chose this sleepwear and not "all cotton" underwear for sleeping. But the fire-retardant chemical will be washed away if non-phosphate detergent or soap or chlorine bleach is used. Sleepwear may need to be discarded if washed repeatedly with non-phosphate soap or bleach.

Always turn pot handles toward the rear of the stove. Using the back burners is preferable.

Keep matches in containers in high places that are impossible for even a determined three- or four-year-old to reach. Starting at this age, many children go through a phase of being fascinated by fire, and it's very hard for them to resist the temptation to play with matches.

Open heaters, woodstoves, fireplaces, poorly insulated ovens, and easily opened broilers are dangerous. Place grilles or guards around woodstoves, fireplaces, and wall heaters. Install radiator covers to prevent burns. Talk to toddlers about what is hot and warn them not to touch these things.

Don't allow curtains, bedclothes, or towels to touch a heater or space heater. This could start a fire.

Replace worn electric cords. Tightly tape the connections between cords and extension cords. Don't run cords under rugs or across walkways.

Put electric outlet covers on all outlets to prevent children from shock if they insert something into the outlet. Don't overload outlets.

Discuss fire safety with young children. Include instructions to "Stop, drop, roll" and "crawl low under the smoke."

Drowning and Water Safety

572. Drowning takes the lives of more than 1,000 children under age fourteen each year, ranking as the second leading cause of injury death to children in this age group. For every child who drowns, an additional four are hospitalized after nearly drowning. Children under age four have a two to three times greater drowning rate than other age groups.

Among preschoolers, *the bathtub is a major cause of drowning.* Young children can also drown in toilets or buckets of water. Five gallon buckets should not be left emptied outside because they collect rain water and a child can drown if he falls in. Keep toilet seats down. Children can fall into a toilet or a pail of water headfirst, facedown, and drown in just a few inches of water.

There's no research to show that early swimming lessons (infant, toddler, and preschool swim classes) protect children from drowning in bathtubs, swimming pools, ponds, lakes, or rivers. Children up to age five just don't have enough strength and coordination, even with lessons, to float or swim out of danger. These early lessons may even increase the risk of drowning by giving parents and children a false sense of security.

573. Water safety. Prevention of drowning requires constant parental awareness and supervision. Emphasize these points with any baby-sitter as well:

1. Never leave a child age five or younger alone in the bathtub, even for an instant. A child can drown in as little as one inch of water. Do not leave her in the tub in the care of another child under age twelve. If you absolutely must answer the phone or the doorbell, wrap up the soapy child in a towel and cart her along with you.
2. Children should learn to swim, but do not assume your child is drown-proof if he has had lessons. Do

not rely on pool alarms to warn you; they don't go off until the child is in the water and this is often too late. Also, they tend to be shaped like animals and look appealing to young children. A better warning system would be an alarm on the pool gate.

3. Keep your eyes on your child when he is near the water, even when a lifeguard is present. Here is the best rule I know: children must wear personal flotation devices (PFD) at the beach, at a lake, near a wading or swimming pool, and on a boat, until they can swim a quarter mile. You can expect them to fight like steers against this rule, until they see that you make no exceptions. When your child is an accomplished swimmer with enough skill and judgment to stay out of trouble, at ages ten to twelve, she can swim without adult supervision as long as she always swims with a buddy. Do not permit her to dive unless the water is 5 feet deep and an adult is present.

4. Stay away from frozen ponds and lakes unless the ice has been authorized safe for skating.

5. Keep everyone away from pools or other bodies of water during thunderstorms.

6. Do not allow children to sled near water. Golf courses, a popular spot for sledding, often have bodies of water that are potentially dangerous.

7. Wells and cisterns should be well protected.

8. If you have a swimming pool, it should be fenced on all four sides. The fence should be at least 5 feet high, with a lock on the gate. The gate should be self-closing and self-latching with slats no more than 4 inches apart. Don't consider the house as one side of the fence; it's too easy for a child to slip out through a door or window.

9. Adult supervision is required at all times around water. Backyard wading pools should be emptied and turned upside down to prevent small children from drowning. Remember: If a child drowns, CPR should be immediately instituted.

Poisons

574. Now is the time to inspect your house with an eagle eye—or rather with a baby's eye. Put all medicine safely out of reach *immediately after each use.* A cabinet or drawer with a childproof latch is best. Put bold, clear labels on all medicines so that you won't use the wrong one. Flush medicine down the toilet after an illness is over. It's unlikely you'll use it again and it may deteriorate anyway. It's confusing to have old medicines mixed in with others still in use. Keep the telephone number of the nearest poison control center attached to your phone. Every household where children live or visit regularly should have on hand a bottle of syrup of ipecac for each child in the house. But give syrup of ipecac to your child only if you're instructed to do so by your doctor, nurse practitioner, or the poison control center; amounts will vary based on a child's weight. (See Sections 1085 and 1086 for emergency treatment of poisoning.)

More than one-third of medicine poisonings are due to children taking their grandparents' prescription drugs. Check to be sure the grandparents' medicines are locked away or completely out of reach before the children arrive for a visit.

575. Federal and state laws now require that all medicines dispensed by a pharmacist come in childproof containers. Don't change a medicine to another container. Also, don't change any substance from the container it came in to a container in which something else came—in other words, don't put plant spray in a soft drink bottle or oven cleaner in a cup. This is a frequent cause of serious injuries.

576. Now is the time to put poisons out of reach. One-fifth of all accidental poisonings occur in the second year of life. Recently the poison control center in a medium-size city received 50,000 assistance calls, 90 percent of which were for children. Children in this exploring and tasting age will, when the spirit moves them, eat almost anything, no matter how it tastes. They especially love pills, good-tasting medicines, cigarettes, and matches. You will be surprised to read this list of the substances that most frequently cause dangerous poisoning in children: aspirin and other medicines, insect and rat poisons, kerosene, gasoline, benzene, cleaning fluids, liquid furniture polish, auto polish, lye, other alkalis used for cleaning drains, bowls, ovens, oil of wintergreen, and plant sprays.

577. Potentially harmful substances in the bathroom include: perfume, shampoos, hair tonics, home permanent and beauty preparations.

578. Find inaccessible places in the kitchen and utility room to store cleaning fluids and powders; detergents; drain, toilet bowl, and oven cleaners; ammonia; bleach; wax remover; metal polish; borax; mothballs; lighter fluid; shoe polish, and other dangerous substances. Get rid of rat poisons and insect pastes and poisons. They are just too dangerous.

579. In the basement or garage find truly safe places for turpentine, paint thinners, kerosene, gasoline, benzene, insecticides, plant sprays, weed killers, antifreeze, and car cleaners and polishes. Before you discard containers, be sure they are completely empty and then rinse them out. Potentially hazardous household cleaners and medications in the bathroom and kitchen should be stored out of reach or in cabinets with childproof locks or latches. Simple hook and eye latches can be installed on bathroom doors to prevent a child from exposure to all of the hazards associated with the bathroom, from poisoning to drowning to hot water burns.

580. Plant poisons. We think of plants and flowers as merely beautiful. Crawling babies and small children think of them as a tasty snack. This is a dangerous combination of attitudes, for many plants and flowers—over seven hundred of them in all—can cause illness or death. The best rule is to have no plants or flowers in the house until children are past the "eat everything" stage and can accept prohibitions. At least place plants high out of reach. Watch small children when they are around plants and flowers in the garden or away from home.

Here is a partial list of potentially fatal plants: caladium, diffenbachia, philodendron, elephant's ear, English ivy, hyacinth, daffodil, narcissus, mistletoe, oleander, poinsettia, rosary pea, castor bean, delphinium, larkspur, belladonna, foxglove, lily of the valley, azalea, laurel, rhododendron, daphne berries, golden chain, hydrangea, jessamine berries, privet (hedges), yew, jimsonweed (thorn apple), morning glory seeds, mushrooms, nightshade, holly berries.

Some plants are toxic but not fatal; they will cause skin irritation if touched or swelling of lips and tongue if ingested. Be prepared to identify poison ivy, poison oak, and poison sumac to avoid the painful irritation of an allergic reaction.

Your local poison control center or health department can tell you whether a plant in your house or yard is poisonous or toxic.

Lead Poisoning

581. Approximately 3 million children in the United States suffer from lead poisoning. If your home was built before 1978, chances are the paint contains lead. The areas in the home of most concern are the mouthing surfaces, windowsills, baseboards, and all doors and doorways below six feet. Even if paint is not chipped, the very act of opening and closing a window can loosen paint chips and dust that may contain lead.

Lead poisoning affects children under the age of six who ingest lead paint or soil that contains lead from peeling house paint or, as in the case of many urban areas, from lead gas deposited in the soil. Lead in drinking water can also be a source. Lead poisoning can affect the developing brains of children under the age of six and cause a variety of neurological problems, including learning disabilities, behavioral difficulties, or, rarely, brain damage.

Lead poisoning requires medical attention if levels are above 10, even though a child does not show symptoms. Typically the levels must be much higher for learning or neurological problems to occur. Mild lead poisoning is treated with oral therapy; more significant lead poisoning requires intravenous medications. Your home or play environment can be tested for potential levels of lead. Your child can be tested for lead beginning at nine months of age. The test may be repeated periodically until your child reaches six years old.

Choking

582. Choking is the fourth leading cause of death in young children. A baby or small child who puts things in her mouth should not have any small objects (like buttons, beans, beads) within reach. These are easily breathed into the windpipe (*aspirated*) and cause choking (see Sections 1090–1091).

One of the most common items to cause choking are broken balloon pieces which can be easily inhaled. Children have also choked on pieces of a balloon they have been blowing up. The balloon burst and they breathed in pieces of the balloon. Small balls (from children's toys and games) are also a common item that children under the age of three choke on.

Food items that cause choking include hot dogs, which should be cut lengthwise so as not to act as a stopper in the windpipe once moisture is absorbed by the hot dog. Round, hard slippery foods such as nuts, hard candies, carrots, popcorn, grapes and raisins are especially dangerous to young children.

It has been traditional to begin the main meal with warm soup. It helps to relax the esophagus and to move things along. A liquid also helps to keep the food moist, making it less likely to stick and cause choking. For similar reasons, many nutritionists are now recommending sips of warm water along with meals. (I follow this advice from Deepak Chopra myself, and have found it very helpful to moisten and relax the esophagus.) Usually ice water is served in American restaurants, but ice can cause tightness or constriction, whereas the warmer drink will relax and soothe. The water can keep the solid foods moist so that they will go down more easily than dry food.

An excellent preventive for choking on large pieces of food is to chew, and chew well. Children can be taught to chew; and if you set an example, they will most likely follow, especially if they are not rushed.

Take away lollipops and Popsicles if small children keep

them in their mouths while running. Don't let your child lie down while eating, and never leave a baby alone with a propped-up bottle.

One of the most dangerous foods is peanut butter eaten directly off a spoon or knife. When aspirated, nothing can remove the peanut butter from the lungs. It should always be spread thinly on bread.

583. Age-appropriate toys should be selected for children. For children under three years, "age-appropriate" means that the toy does not contain small parts. Children as old as five who continue to put things in their mouths should also refrain from playing with toys with small parts without supervision. Keeping an older child's toys away from a younger sibling or visitor to your home is always a challenge.

Items that fit into a No Choke Test Tube (a tool smaller than a toilet paper roll developed by the Consumer Products Safety Commission to identify objects that can choke children age three and under) are potentially dangerous. However, even items that a child does not ingest completely, such as a pencil, can cause choking. Take these items away from a young child.

Suffocation

584. For children under age one, suffocation is the leading cause of unintentional injury-related death. An infant spends a majority of his time in his crib, so steps should be taken to make sure this is a safe environment. To prevent suffocation in the crib, follow these recommendations:

1. All infants should be put to sleep on their backs.
2. The crib mattress must fit snugly so that the infant will not become trapped between the mattress and the side of the crib.
3. An infant should not be put to bed with a large stuffed animal or placed face down on a sheepskin blanket or a pillow. An infant often does not have the neck strength to lift his head for air if his face is enveloped in material.
4. If an infant sleeps or naps on an adult bed, not only

should precautions be taken for falls, but there should be no space between the mattress and head board or baseboard. If a parent sleeps with an infant, special care should be taken not to roll onto the infant. (This is a very rare event.)

5. Water beds should be avoided for infants. On occasion the baby's face can become trapped within the contours of the mattress.

6. Once an infant begins to creep and crawl, care should be taken to remove diaper packs from the floor. Plastic dry-cleaner bags should be removed from closets where the baby could pull them down over her face.

Guns in the Home

585. Guns continue to be more and more prevalent in our society. As a pediatrician, I would discourage any family from owning a gun if there are children at home. Every day in this country a child is killed unintentionally by a gun.

For different reasons, children at all stages of life are susceptible to unintentional and intentional gun-related injuries when there is a gun in the home. We also know that a gun will more likely be used to injure or kill a family member than an intruder. A gun purchased for self-defense is rarely put to its original purpose.

If you do own a gun or guns, it must be stored unloaded, with the ammunition locked away in a separate place. In addition to completing a gun safety program offered by local police or a gun club, gun owners should investigate newer safety technologies such as trigger locks or "smart" guns, which can only be fired by the gun owner.

Very young children can become victims of unintentional gun-related deaths if they play with a loaded gun or if they are with another child who is playing with a loaded gun. Children ages seven to ten will want to show off a gun to their friends and may inadvertently end up as shooter or victim.

Older children and adolescents, especially as they begin to experiment with drinking, may lack self-control and take gratuitous risks if a gun is accessible. In addition, teenagers who are depressed or using drugs are at higher risk for suicide if there is a gun at home. You may not be eager to ask the parents of your children's playmates if there is a gun in their home and if it is stored safely, but tragic statistics tell us that you should do so.

Falls

586. Falls are the sixth leading cause of injury death, and are the leading cause of nonfatal injury. Each year approximately 120 children ages fourteen and under die from falls. The highest death rate due to falls is during the first year of life. Three million children are treated in emergency rooms for fall-related injuries every year, and for every child who is treated, at least ten children fall but never seek medical attention.

Falls occur from as many places as you can imagine: from beds, changing tables, down the stairs, from windows and porches, out of trees, off bicycles and play equipment, on ice, and so on. Toddlers are especially at risk for falls from windows and down stairs; older children are at risk of falling from rooftops and playground or recreational equipment. The majority of falls in the home occur to children age four and under. The peak hours for falls in the home are around mealtimes, with 40 percent occuring between 4:00 and 8:00 P.M.

To prevent toddlers from falling down stairs, gates should be installed at the top and bottom of stairs, including porch steps, until the child can go up and down steadily.

To avoid falling in winter, keep walkways free of ice by using rock salt or sand.

587. Window falls occur most frequently during spring and summer months and in urban environments. Window falls are most common from the second and third story, with the most serious falls occurring above the third story. Prevention tips include:

1. Remove all furniture and beds from in front of the window.
2. Lock all unused windows.
3. Restrict the opening of the window to 4 inches.

4. Open the window from the top.
5. Install window guards. Window guards are metal gates that have a maximum of four inches between the bars and are strong enough to withstand 150 pounds of pressure. Window guards can be placed on the inside of all windows, but at least one window in every room must have an operable or removable guard in the case of an emergency or fire. This operable guard must not require the use of a key or special tool to remove. Child safety window guards are a recent phenomenon. They should not be confused with burglar bars that are meant to keep people from getting in. Some states have laws requiring the use of window guards.

Window guards, properly installed on windows on the second story and above, prevent serious injuries from falling.

588. Baby walkers. Once considered a necessary piece of infant equipment, the walker is now seen as a potential hazard. Accidents in baby walkers contributed to an estimated 23,000 emergency room visits a year for children six to twelve months. Some 80 percent of these injuries involved falls down stairs. Baby walkers should not be used in homes with stairs. I strongly discourage the use of walkers because they increase a child's mobility and raise her center of gravity beyond safe limits. There is also no developmental benefit from walkers.

Stationary walkers, which don't go anywhere, are becoming more popular. They can give a child a sense of independence without the risk of falls. Make sure there are no exposed springs to pinch the baby's fingers.

Infant Equipment

If you use a **high chair,** it should have a broad base so that it won't tip over, a harness to hold a climbing baby, and a latch to keep the child from raising the tray. Low chair-and-table combinations are safer than high chairs.

A **baby carriage** or **stroller** should have a safety strap for a baby who has reached the climbing age and should be used at all times.

A **"jolly-jumper"** placed in a doorway serves to exercise and entertain. To prevent finger injuries, coils should be no more than $\frac{1}{8}$ inch apart.

A **swing** is useful to have after a baby has learned to sit and before she is mobile. Watch that the child keeps her hands and arms inside the swing to prevent hitting the frame while in motion. A child should be supervised while using infant equipment, such as jolly jumpers and swings. Children can suffocate by sliding down too far in seats or folding over in swings without being able to sit back up.

Start with a **crib** with bumpers all around the sides. Crib slats should be no more than $2\frac{3}{8}$ inches apart. The mattress must fit snugly to avoid a child getting trapped between the mattress and the slats, and the crib must be free of lead paint. It should have a side locking mechanism and the top of the rail should be at least 26 inches above the mattress when set at its lowest setting. Gyms and mobiles should be removed from the crib as soon as a child can pull himself up, at about five months.

A **child gate** installed in a doorway or opening should be easy for an adult to use and designed to well protect a child from falls. Gates are either mounted to the wall and swing open, or are pressure mounted and have to be removed with each use. A gate should be removed once a child can climb over or dislodge it.

589. A note on siblings. Brothers and sisters should really carry warning labels! Even the most loving toddler can unintentionally injure an infant or younger sibling. Never leave a child under five alone with an infant or allow him to pick up a baby without adult supervision. More often than not an older sibling will remove a safety gate from the stairs, inadvertently hold something over a baby's face, discover the unlocked gun in the home, or leave a chair in front of an open window.

Playground Injuries

590. More than 200,000 children are seen in hospital emergency rooms each year as a result of playground injuries. About 75 percent of these are the result of falls. Children under age six are at greatest risk for head injuries from the impact of moving swings. For children older than six, limb fractures from falls are most common.

Because falls are the most common type of playground injury, the surfacing under equipment is one of the most important safety features on the playground. Surfacing should consist of 9 to 12 inches of resilient material including sand, pea gravel, and wood chips. The surface needs to be regularly maintained because it becomes packed down or dispersed with use. Rubber mats manufactured specifically for playgrounds, which meet the standards of the Consumer Product Safety Commission, may also be used. Parents should check their playground for safe surfaces and for well built and maintained equipment. You should notify the local parks department or school district if you are concerned about the safety of a public or school playground.

591. One-half of all playground fatalities are a result of strangulation due to entanglement with an article of clothing or head entrapment. All loose clothing should be removed. Drawstrings on hoods of jackets and sweatshirts should also be removed. Several clothing manufacturers have voluntarily discontinued using drawstrings in children's garments based on recommendations by the Consumer Product Safety Commission.

592. Toddlers are in the process of testing their limits and learning new skills on the playground. Many sustain injuries on playgrounds because of their lack of balance and coordination; adult supervision is a must. For those fearless toddlers who take physical risks, an adult should always be monitoring their activity on the equipment.

Sports and Recreation Safety

It is estimated that 20 million children play organized sports outside of school and 25 million participate in competitive school sports. Participation in sports is beneficial in many ways to improve physical fitness, coordination, self-discipline, and teamwork; however, young children are highly susceptible to sports-related injuries because they are still growing.

593. Young children are at high risk of injury while training and competing. Collision and contact sports have the highest rate of injury, with football, basketball, baseball and soccer topping the list for boys and softball, gymnastics, volleyball, and field hockey topping the list for girls. Boys incur 75 percent of all sports injuries; however, prior to puberty the risk of sports-related injury between boys and girls is the same. At puberty, as boys grow in strength and size, they are more frequently and severely injured than girls. Overuse injuries from playing while injured or tired may cause chronic conditions like tendonitis and arthritis. Head injuries, though less frequent, can result in more serious problems.

To prevent sports injuries, I strongly encourage the use of protective equipment to protect the eyes, head, face, and mouth.

594. Baseball safety includes wearing the proper protective equipment to prevent eye, head, face, and mouth injuries. Ball players should wear shoes with rubber, not metal, spikes. Injuries can be reduced by using safety bases and safety fencing by the dugouts and benches. Youngsters should be taught to slide properly and should not be allowed to slide headfirst. "Softer than standard" baseballs and softballs can reduce the risk of impact injuries to the head and chest. Young players should be restricted in the amount of pitching they do so as to prevent permanent elbow injury.

595. Heading in soccer is not recommended for young children just learning to play the game. Moveable soccer goals can tip over on children, causing serious injury, and should be anchored to the ground. Children should not be allowed to climb on moveable goals.

596. Mouth guards help to prevent dental injuries, which are the most common type of sports-related facial injury. Mouth guards also cushion blows that could cause a concussion or a jaw fracture.

Skateboard injuries can be prevented with wraparound guards on the elbows, wrists and knees, and a bicycle helmet.

393

597. In-line skating. Thousands of children are injured each year on in-line skates. The majority of these injuries are to the wrist, elbows, ankles, and knees. These can be minimized by wearing the proper protective gear—knee pads, elbow pads, and wrist guards. Head injuries, which tend to be more serious, can be prevented by wearing a helmet. A multisport helmet is now available and provides extra protection to the back of the head. The current safety label to look for on a multisport helmet is "N-94." If your child does not own a multisport helmet, a bicycle helmet worn while in-line skating or skateboarding will provide adequate protection. Be sure your child always skates on smooth, paved surfaces without any traffic; warn her to avoid streets and driveways. Make sure she learns to stop safely using the brake pads on the heels of most in-line skates.

598. Sledding. Wintertime fun includes sledding down snowy hills. Before you begin, review these safety tips:

1. Survey sledding areas before letting children use them. Look for hazards such as trees, benches, ponds, rivers, rocks, and excessive elevation.
2. The bottom of the hill should be far from traffic or bodies of water.
3. Inflatable snow tubes are fast and unsteerable; use extra caution when children are using them. Sleds with steering mechanisms are safer.
4. Never allow a child under four years to sled unsupervised. The steepness of the hill should be your guide as to whether older children should be allowed to sled alone.
5. Avoid crowded hills and don't overload a sled with children.
6. Do not sled alone or after dusk without adequate light.
7. Consider having your child wear a helmet for head protection, but warn him not to let it be an excuse for recklessness.

Cold Weather–Related Illnesses

Dress warm and stay dry, preferably in multiple layers with special attention to hands and feet. Infants should remain outdoors only for short periods of time when the weather is below 40°F. Do not ignore shivering. Persistent shivering is a sign to head indoors. Serious health risks from cold weather include hypothermia and frostbite.

599. Hypothermia is a result of loss of body heat due to prolonged exposure to cold temperatures. Infants will exhibit warning signs which include bright red, cold skin and very low energy. Older children will exhibit shivering, drowsiness, and confusion or slurred speech. If a child's temperature falls below 95°F, seek medical attention immediately and begin warming the child.

600. Frostbite causes a loss of feeling and color in the affected part of the body due to freezing. It most often affects the nose, ears, cheeks, chin, fingers, or toes. A white or grayish yellow patch may appear. Frostbite can permanently damage the body. To treat frostbite immerse the affected area in warm—not hot—water, or warm the affected area with your body heat. Do not massage, rub, or, in the case of feet, walk on the affected area. Do not use heat of a stove, fireplace, radiator, or heating pad to warm the affected area.

Heat-Related Illness

Infants and children up to the age of four are sensitive to high temperatures. Be sure they drink frequent liquids, wear a hat, avoid overexertion, and stay indoors during the hottest part of the day if possible. All children should wear sunscreen no matter what the color of their skin to protect them from the harmful rays of the sun (see Sections 635–639). Sunburn and heat rash are the most common heat-related illnesses for young children (see Section 1075).

601. Heat rash is an irritation caused by excessive sweating during hot, humid weather. It looks like a red cluster of pimples or blisters. The best treatment is to keep the area dry and avoid creams—they keep the skin moist and make the condition worse.

Bug Bites

Protect your child against all insect bites by making sure his clothing covers as much skin as possible when the bugs are out in full force. Light-colored clothing is less attractive to bugs. Avoid heavily scented detergents and shampoos during the bug season. Use insect repellents designed for children. If the product contains DEET, the concentration for children should not exceed 10 percent. Try to keep the child's hands free of repellent so it doesn't get in his eyes or mouth. DEET may be harmful if ingested. Wash all repellent off once the child is back indoors.

602. Beehives or wasps' nests should be removed professionally. When bees are about, avoid snacking outdoors. Wash your children's hands after snacks to avoid attracting bees.

603. Drain any still water on your property to cut down on mosquitoes. Keep toddlers indoors at night when mosquitoes arrive in full force. Keep doors closed and repair damaged or missing screens.

604. Check skin clothing and hair for ticks after playing outside especially in tall grass or near wooded areas. Deer ticks are very tiny creatures—the size of a pinhead—found in certain parts of the United States, which can carry Lyme disease. Treatment is available, but removing the tick before infection is the best prevention. Wood ticks, about the size of a nail head, are more common and not harmful.

605. Remove spiderwebs and do not encourage children to play with spiders.

Dog Bite Prevention

606. Don't let children go close to a strange dog, especially when they are at an age when they are likely to startle or hurt the animal. Hundreds of thousands of people are injured each year by dog bites; the majority of victims are ten years old and younger. The breeds most commonly associated with dog-related injuries, in order of frequency, are pit bulls, Rottweilers, and German shepherds. A combination of events contributes to these injuries including the behavior and upbringing of the dog, whether or not the dog is leashed, and the behavior of the child. Tips for children include:

1. Never go near a dog you don't know or one who is tied up.
2. Do not run away from a dog that comes near you. Just stay calm; he probably just wants to sniff you.
3. If a dog knocks you over, just curl up in a ball and stay still.
4. Never touch, pet, or play with a dog unless the owner says it's okay.
5. Never tease a dog.
6. Don't stare into the eyes of a dog you do not know. Most dogs perceive this as aggressive.
7. Don't disturb a dog who is sleeping, eating, or caring for puppies.
8. Beware of dogs while biking or skating.

607. Additional tips for parents:

1. Read about the various breeds before you choose a family dog. Aggressive and high-strung dogs are not appropriate for families.
2. Spay or neuter your dog to reduce aggressive tendencies related to territorialism.
3. Never leave infants or young children alone with any dog.

Holiday Safety

608. Fourth of July. The use of fireworks on the Fourth of July results in almost 6,000 injuries to children each year. These injuries usually involve hands, fingers, eyes, or head and sometimes result in amputation and blindness. Children and fireworks are a bad combination. I'd avoid them altogether. Fireworks are illegal in many states and are not recommended for personal use. In viewing public fireworks displays, keep far enough away from the source and protect the ears of small children from loud explosions.

609. Halloween. Injuries sustained during Halloween are often caused by falls, pedestrian mishaps and burns. Most importantly, make sure that costumes and masks don't obstruct your child's vision. Face paint or makeup is often safer than a mask. Trick-or-treaters should carry flashlights and not cut through yards where they may trip on items they cannot see. Shoes and costumes should fit to prevent tripping, and all items such as fake swords and knives should be of flexible material that cannot cause injury.

To prevent burns, which often occur on Halloween, choose flame-resistant costumes, masks, beards, and wigs. Very loose clothing is likely to come in contact with candles and should be avoided.

Make sure that cars can see trick-or-treaters by putting reflective tape on bags and costumes and by having your children carry flashlights. Remind children to obey all traffic rules and not to dart out between parked cars. Accompany young children and wait until arriving at home before eating any treats. Children under age eight should not trick-or-treat without the supervision of an adult or older sibling. Instruct children to travel only on well-established routes, stopping only at homes with outside lights on and never to enter a home unless accompanied by an adult. In many neighborhoods, trick-or-treating is no longer considered safe, and Halloween parties have become a popular alternative.

610. Christmas/Hanukkah toy safety. Parents should always observe age recommendations when purchasing toys for children. Manufacturers are now required by federal law to place warning labels on toys with small parts. Toys such as marbles, balloons, and small blocks present a choking hazard for children age three and under. Toys with sharp points or edges may cause a young child to stab or cut himself or another person. Propelled toys, such as toy darts and projectiles, should be avoided to prevent eye injury. Electric toys should only be used by children eight or older.

Home Alone: Children in Self-Care

About 60 percent of parents work outside the home. It's now more common for children to spend time in an after-school program or to return home alone after school. After-school programs are recommended, but if children are alone, here are some commonsense suggestions:

- Make sure your child knows how to reach you or another adult, and check in regularly with each other.

- Teach your child basic safety rules: not to open the door to strangers, never to use the stove alone, and how to respond in the case of an emergency.
- Talk with your child about being home alone and address her fears or uncertainties.
- Keep important phone numbers by the phone. Keep the list current.
- Make sure your child knows his complete name, address, and phone number.
- Learn and practice simple first aid. Keep a first aid kit handy.
- Select appropriate chores to be completed.
- Limit television watching. Encourage reading and other activities.
- Investigate community activities and car pools your child can join.

Childproofing Your Home

In addition to practicing safe behavior and making a child's environment as safe as possible, home safety supplies are important devices to help you to protect young children from serious injury. The following safety items will buy you some time while teaching children important safety messages or until the child loses interest in getting into something that is off limits. These safety supplies do not under any circumstances replace the need for adult supervision.

- Use cabinet **latches and locks** in the kitchen and bathroom to keep young children out of cabinets where harmful substances may be stored. **Velcro latches** can be used to keep toddlers out of hard-to-lock objects such as refrigerators, toilets or sliding cabinets. **Toilet lid locks** are designed to lock children out of the toilet bowl with a spring-loaded lever that holds the lid shut.
- A **toy box lid support** will prevent a toy box from slamming shut and injuring a child's hands, head, or neck.
- A **hook and eye door latch** will keep a young child from opening doors that lead to stairs or areas where dangerous cleaners or tools are stored. Bathroom doors can also be latched to keep children away from toilet bowls

and stored items like razors, medications, and harmful substances.

- **Cord shorteners** will prevent children from putting long cords around their necks. Use them on accordion blind cords (many unintentional strangulations are cause by blind cords), appliance cords, telephone cords and lamp cords. **Window blind devices** that resemble a large wing nut around which you wrap excess cord can be attached to the window frame to prevent strangulation.
- A reusable **water temperature gauge** can test hot water to ensure that water is no hotter than 120°F.
- **Corner cushions** can be attached to coffee tables and countertops that are the perfect height to cause injury to the forehead or face of a young child. They offer some protection for children through age two, but can be easily removed by an older child.
- **Bathtub spout covers** inflate and fit over tub spouts to cushion any impact.
- **Outlet covers** should be placed on all outlets, used or unused, as a permanent solution to the risk of electrical shock caused by a child placing a metal object into a socket. The outlet cover contains a spring-loaded mechanism allowing the plug to be inserted when necessary and covering the opening when it is not in use. Unlike shock stoppers, these covers do not need to be removed each time the outlet is used. If shock stoppers are used, make sure they are too large for a child to easily swallow.

Other childproofing items such as window guards, stair gates, syrup of ipecac, smoke detectors, fire extinguishers have been mentioned elsewhere in this chapter. In addition:

- Put bulbs into empty lamp sockets if they are within reach.
- Put broken glass and opened cans into a covered, hard-to-open receptacle. Use a can with a slot in the top for used razor blades.
- Keep dangerous tools and power tools out of your child's reach.
- Be extremely cautious in backing a car into or out of a driveway.

- Take the doors off of all unused refrigerators and freezers.
- Power mowers amputate fingers and toes and throw stones viciously. If you have a rotary mower, trade it in.

The U.S. Consumer Product Safety Commission can answer your questions or respond to your concerns about the safety of any product you own or are considering buying. Their telephone number is (800) 638-2772.

Dental Development and Oral Health of Children

When I was a young man, I asked a wise old gentleman what the secret to a happy life was. "Take care of your teeth!" was his reply. It was as good advice as I ever got.

As a parent, you can follow that same advice for your children and ensure that their teeth are healthy and a joy to behold. *Prevention* is the key. What makes for healthy teeth? Can decay be prevented? What about teething? Fluoride? When should a child first visit the dentist? What about permanent teeth and braces? With the information here, supplemented by advice from your child's dentist and staff, you'll easily be able to sort it all out.

The dental topics of most concern to parents include—in a kind of chronological order—teething, tooth development, what makes good teeth, tooth decay, and avoiding traumatic injuries to the mouth. Most important of all is your ability to get your child's teeth off to a healthy start, an advantage that can last a lifetime!

Tooth Development

611. How and when will your baby's teeth come through? The average baby gets his first tooth at around seven months, but this is quite variable. One baby may get her first tooth at three months, another not until eighteen months. Yet both are perfectly healthy, normal infants. It is true that certain diseases can influence the age of teething, but this is rare. The age of teething is simply a matter of the pattern of development the child was born with, like when she first begins to walk.

Since babies get twenty teeth in their first three years, it's easy to understand why they seem to be teething for most of the infant and early childhood years! This also explains why it's so easy to blame every ailment on teething. It once was believed that teething caused colds, diarrhea, and fevers. Of course, these conditions are caused by germs (bacteria and viruses) and not by teething. Mainly, teething causes teeth and not much else. If your baby has a fever or appears ill, don't assume it's because of teething. Call her doctor or nurse practitioner.

612. Usually the first two teeth to appear are the lower central incisors. "Incisor" is the name given to the eight front teeth (four on the bottom and four on the top), which have sharp cutting edges to tear off (or incise) food. After a few months come the four upper incisors so that the average baby has these six teeth, four above and two below, at about a year old. After this, there's usually a lull of several months before the next onslaught. Then, six more teeth quickly appear: the two remaining lower incisors and all four first primary (baby) molars. The molars don't come in next to the incisor teeth but farther back, leaving space for the canine teeth.

After the first molars appear, there is a pause of several months before the canines (the pointed "dog" teeth or eye teeth) erupt in the spaces between the incisors and the molars. The most common time for this to happen is in the second half of the second year. The last four teeth in the baby set are the second primary molars, which come in right behind the first primary molars, usually in the first half of the third year. Remember that these are all average times. You don't need to worry if your baby is ahead of or behind the schedule.

613. Permanent teeth begin to appear at about six years of age. The six-year (first permanent) molars come through behind the baby molars. The primary teeth to be lost first are usually the lower central incisors. The permanent incisors, pushing up underneath, come into position where the baby tooth roots have been dissolved away. Eventually, all the primary teeth become loose and fall out. The baby teeth are lost in about the same order in which they came in. Your toughest decision will be figuring out the monetary value of these baby teeth when the Tooth Fairy makes her appointed rounds.

614. The permanent teeth that take the place of the baby molars are called bicuspids or premolars. The twelve-year molars (second permanent molars) come in behind the six-year molars. The third molars (eighteen-year molars, or wisdom teeth) may be impacted in the jaw. Sometimes they need to be removed so they won't do any damage to neighboring teeth or the bone of the jaws. Permanent teeth often appear with jagged edges (called *mammelons*). They either wear down or the dentist can trim them. Also, permanent teeth are more yellow than primary teeth.

Permanent teeth sometimes come through crooked or out of place, but they may eventually straighten out by the muscular action of the tongue, lips, and cheeks. If teeth don't straighten out, or are crowded or crooked, or if the jaw alignment is abnormal, then orthodontic treatment (braces) may be required for bite improvement.

Teething

615. Teething has different effects on different babies. One chews things, frets, drools, has a hard time getting to sleep and generally makes life miserable for the family for a month or two as each tooth comes through. In another baby, a tooth is discovered without any idea that he was teething. In either case, most babies start to drool at around three to four months, as their salivary glands become more active. Don't be fooled into thinking that drooling always means that teething has started.

616. Let your baby chew! The first four molar teeth, at around twelve to eighteen months, are more likely to cause trouble than the others, but any teeth may distress a baby. What to do? First, let her chew! Provide chewable objects that are dull and soft enough so that when she falls with them in her mouth they won't do any damage. Rubber teething rings of various shapes are good. You should be careful about toys made from thin, brittle plastic, which could break and cause choking. You also need to be careful that your baby doesn't gnaw the paint off furniture and other objects if there is any danger that the paint is made with lead. Fortunately, nowadays practically all baby furniture and painted toys are painted with lead-free paint.

Some babies prefer to chew on a certain kind of cloth. You can try tying an ice cube or a piece of apple in a square of cloth. Some parents swear by frozen bagels. Many babies love to have their gums firmly rubbed at times. Be creative! Let your baby chew what she wants as long as it's not dangerous. And don't fret about germs on the teething ring or piece of cloth. Your baby is putting all sorts of things in her mouth anyway, none of which are germ-free. Of course, it's a good idea to wash the teething ring after it has fallen on the floor or after the dog has slobbered over it, and you should wash or boil the piece of cloth occasionally. There are lots of teething medicines on the market that occasionally offer some relief, but you should talk to your doctor or nurse practitioner before using them.

What Makes Good Teeth?

617. The crowns (the parts that show) of a baby's teeth are formed in the gums before birth. Additionally, many of her permanent teeth begin forming within a few months after birth, and some even before! We know that these growing teeth are sensitive to proper nutrition. Among the food elements necessary to make strong teeth, the following are particularly important: calcium and phosphorus (in vegetables, cereals, and milk—although I don't recommend milk after age two), vitamin D (in fortified milk, vitamin drops, and sunshine), and vitamin C (most fruits, especially citrus, vitamin drops, raw tomatoes, cabbage). An adequate amount of vitamin C is found in breast milk. If you are breast-feeding and your baby's sun exposure is limited, a vitamin D supplement may be prescribed. Other vitamins are also helpful, including vitamin A (in yellow, orange, and red fruits) and some of the B vitamins (in grains). So, as in so many other areas, good nutrition sets the stage for healthy teeth.

618. Fluoride. One element known to be valuable in forming strong, decay-resistant teeth is fluoride. A small amount in the diet of the mother while she is pregnant and in the diet of your child greatly decreases the possibility of later tooth decay. There is, for example, much less tooth decay in areas with a high natural fluoride content in the drinking water. When the enamel of a tooth is formed with fluoride, it resists the action of acid much better. In addition, fluoride in the mouth discourages the activity of the bacteria that cause tooth decay.

There are two major ways that children receive the benefit of fluoride: in the body system and on the surface of the teeth. If there is little or no fluoride in the community water system, a child can receive fluoride in prescribed vitamins or tablets. That fluoride goes into the system and is taken up by the permanent teeth, which are developing in the jaws. Another way for fluoride to benefit teeth is by direct application. Fluoride can be introduced into the mouth in toothpastes, mouth rinses, or special preparations that will saturate the outer layer of enamel and help to fight the action of acid.

For decades, fluoride has been added in very small, safe amounts to the water of many communities as a public health measure. If you're not sure about whether or not your water has enough fluoride, you can call the information number on your water bill and request that information. Adequate fluoridation is 0.7 to 1.0 ppm (parts per million). If you have your own well, call the county health department for advice.

Some clinicians recommend supplemental fluoride for breast-fed babies, depending on whether the baby gets fluoride in water. Most babies do not need fluoride until after 6 months of age. Formulas do not contain much fluoride. If you use fluoridated tap water to mix the formula, then your baby will not need other fluoride supplements.

Fluoride is a naturally existing element; we all have it in our teeth and bones. Your child's doctor or nurse practitioner and dentist will ensure that your child gets the correct amount. If there is no fluoride in your water supply, your doctor or nurse practitioner may prescribe the appropriate daily dose for your infant, which will vary depending on your community and your child's age and weight. Too much fluoride can cause unattractive white and brown specks on the teeth, so it's important to give the correct amount. Your child may also periodically receive topical applications of special fluoride solutions in the dentist's office. Fluoridated toothpastes are also quite beneficial for their surface effect on the enamel. But be careful: children who eat toothpaste, as most young children will, are at risk of getting too much fluoride. So use very small amounts (pea-size) and keep the toothpaste away from very young children so it won't become a convenient bathroom snack.

Tooth Decay

619. Some children end up with a lot of cavities, others with almost none. Why should this be so? We still don't know all of the factors leading to tooth decay *(dental caries),* but we do know that the diet of the pregnant mother and later of the child, is important in the proper mineral formation of the baby's teeth. Heredity also certainly plays some role in tooth decay.

620. The principal cause of tooth decay is acid produced by bacteria in the mouth, which thrive on the sugars and starches of a child's diet. The bacteria and food debris combine with saliva to form a sticky material called *dental plaque* that sticks to tooth surfaces. The more hours of the day that this plaque remains on the teeth, the greater the number of bacteria and the more acid is produced. This acid dissolves the mineral content of the tooth structure (enamel and dentin) and, once weakened, the tooth structure is eaten away by the invading bacteria. The process of acid formation is also what causes the gum bleeding of inflamed gum tissues *(gingivitis)* and bad breath. That is why frequent between-meal sucking of lollipops, eating of sticky candy and dried fruit, drinking of soda pop, nibbling of cookies and crackers (which cling to the teeth) are particularly likely to promote decay.

An especially devastating type of tooth decay is "nursing caries," or "baby-bottle tooth decay." When children nurse or use the bottle excessively, especially while going to sleep, the pooling of fluid around the upper front teeth can result in much acid formation and rapid decay of the teeth. Some babies even develop such decay before their first birthday! Sometimes nursing caries is so severe that the infected teeth have to be removed. For this reason, a baby should not be put to bed with a bottle of milk, juice, or any other sweetened fluid. The only acceptable fluid for a sleep time is water. Even diluted sweet fluids can promote decay.

Tooth Brushing and Flossing

621. How can tooth decay be prevented? The secret is daily, consistent removal of dental plaque before it can do its nasty work. First, a tip about cleaning baby's teeth. Use a soft-bristled toothbrush! There is a myth that one should use a soft gauze or cloth to wipe a baby's teeth and gums so as not to damage the delicate gum tissue. But those "delicate" gum tissues chew on table legs, cribs, coffee tables, siblings, and anything else in their way. A baby's gums are as delicate as alligator hide. Brush, don't wipe! Babies love it.

I recommend that a child's teeth be carefully brushed after breakfast and before bedtime, with a daily flossing between adjoining teeth, usually before the evening brushing. If possible, an after lunch brushing is helpful too, to remove food residue. Starting at about two, your child may insist on doing everything herself, but most young children do not have the manual dexterity required for proper brushing and flossing until they are nine or ten years old. You can let your young child begin the brushing by herself from the earliest ages, but you will probably need to finish up to ensure that all dental plaque has been eliminated. You can gradually let your child take over completely when she proves capable, usually between six and ten years.

Children want to do grown-up things.

Some parents question the need to floss a child's teeth, but in most cases, teeth in the back of a child's mouth contact each other on the sides. Even some front teeth may tightly contact neighboring teeth. Such teeth are so close together that food and dental plaque get wedged in between them. No matter how vigorously or carefully those areas are brushed, the toothbrush bristles cannot penetrate and clear out the food and plaque. Dental floss disrupts and dislodges all that debris so that the toothbrush can sweep it away.

I recommend getting your child used to gentle flossing as soon as you notice food wedged between her teeth. Your child's dentist or dental hygienist can demonstrate all the methods used to hold a child for perfect brushing and flossing. And best of all, when your child is ready to brush and floss perfectly without your help, she will already be accustomed to the daily habit.

A dentist will teach a child about the importance of flossing.

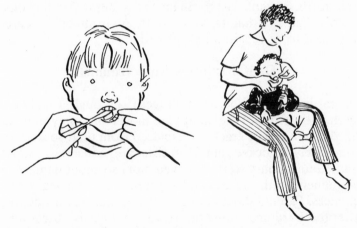

A parent can assist a small child in brushing and flossing teeth by distraction (e.g. singing or telling a story) and gentle manipulation of the toothbrush and dental floss.

Sealants

Sealants are another important part of preventive dentistry. Many teeth have small grooves or pitted areas in the enamel, where bits of food and dental plaque accumulate. Most of these tooth surface imperfections are too small for toothbrush bristles to enter, so the food material and bacterial plaque cannot be brushed or flossed away. Tooth decay, called "pit and fissure caries," usually results. However, the dentist or hygienist can often prevent such tooth decay. A sealant consists of a liquid resin that flows across the tooth surface and fills the grooves and pits. The resin then completely hardens and the enamel imperfection is "sealed" off. Food debris and dental plaque cannot enter a groove or pit that has been sealed with bonded resin. Other dental materials, such as glass-ionomer cements, are also used as sealants as dentists continue to seek the ideal method of protecting enamel pits and fissures. Certain primary molars can also receive the protection of sealants, but dentists are very selective in sealing baby molars. Clinical experience has shown that sealants don't seem to stay bonded to primary teeth as well as they do on permanent teeth. Sealants last for many years, but depending on a child's diet, oral habits, and mouth environment, eventually need to be repaired or replaced.

Dental Injuries from Trauma

Dental injuries can occur in all teeth, although usually the teeth in the front of the mouth are most commonly traumatized. Teeth can be cracked, displaced from their sockets, or completely knocked out. Dentists are concerned about trauma to primary teeth, but even more so about damage to permanent teeth, which can have important lifelong consequences. Parents should always consult their child's dentist after tooth trauma. Some injuries are not easily observable, but a dentist is trained to make a complete diagnosis and perform the proper treatment.

622. Cracked teeth. A tooth is composed of three layers: the outer protective *enamel,* the internal supportive structure called *dentin,* and the soft tissue center of the tooth containing the nerves, which is called the *dental pulp.* A crack (fracture) in a tooth can affect any or all of these layers. A small fracture may require only smoothing by the dentist using a sandpaper-type of instrument. A more extensive crack may require a dental restoration to reestablish the form, function, and appearance of the tooth. If a dental fracture affects the hollow portion in the center of the tooth, and exposes the dental pulp (there is usually bleeding from the exposed region), a dentist needs to be consulted as soon as possible, to repair the damage and hopefully prevent loss of the pulp. If the pulp does become devitalized, the tooth can still be saved with endodontic (root canal) therapy. That simply means removing the nonvital pulp tissue and filling the root canal space with a sterile filling material. Then the tooth can be repaired in the usual manner.

623. Loosened teeth. Most times, without any treatment, slightly loosened teeth will reattach themselves and become stable after a few days' rest. Sometimes, however, teeth are so loose that the dentist needs to splint them together to stabilize them while healing occurs. Antibiotics, to prevent infection of the dental pulp and attachment tissues, are sometimes beneficial. Dentists will advise a soft diet for a period of time, to help the healing process.

624. Avulsed teeth. Sometimes, a tooth can be completely knocked out of the mouth. Dentists call this the "avulsion" of the tooth. If a baby tooth is avulsed, dentists usually recommend not to reimplant it. There is a good possibility that underlying permanent teeth can undergo developmental damage if a traumatized primary tooth is reimplanted. A permanent tooth should be reimplanted as quickly as possible however, usually within thirty minutes, to maximize the chance of preserving pulp vitality. First, make sure that the tooth is indeed permanent and that it is intact. Gently hold the tooth by the crown (the part that shows in the mouth), not by the pointed roots. Rinse the tooth very gently under tap water. Do not scrub or rub the root in any way; that will damage the attached tissue, which is required for reattachment. Insert the tooth back into its normal position. If you cannot reimplant the tooth, place it in a glass of milk or in a commercially available "tooth rescue" container. Then take the child to the nearest dentist or seek dental emergency service at a hospital emergency room.

Time is important with permanent tooth avulsions. After a tooth has been out of the mouth for 30 minutes the chances for successful reimplantation decline dramatically.

Preventing Traumatic Injuries to the Mouth

Some injuries cannot be prevented. Parents, however, should realize that young children stumble often and their teeth are located at a perfect height to crash into the edge of a coffee table. So crashproof your child's cruising area. Take extraordinary care to make sure he doesn't have the opportunity to bite any electrical wires! Electrical wall sockets also need to be kidproofed. Don't let your child parade around the house with a toothbrush in her mouth. The brush can do serious damage if she falls. Later on, youngsters in all sports are at risk of dental injuries. A Little Leaguer can be kicked in the mouth, struck with a ball, hit with a bat, or collide with a team member or opposing player running the bases. Such catastrophes can happen to both girls and boys in soccer, field hockey, basketball . . . all sports! Children in organized sports generally need to wear a comfortable protective mouth guard—sort of a crash helmet for the teeth. Mouth guards are sold at sporting goods stores or pharmacies, or your child's dentist can make a custom-fitted mouth guard. Rough individual activities such as in-line skating, skateboarding, and martial arts also call for mouth guards.

Dental Office Visits

Getting to know the dentist and the dental office staff is very important. I recommend that you take your child to the dentist shortly after the first tooth erupts, usually by twelve months of age. You can ask the dentist questions about your child's dental care and learn more about dental problems. With early preventive visits the dentist is able to detect developing problems in the early stages, when they are solved more easily, painlessly, and inexpensively. More important, your child will have positive early experiences in the dentist's office. By the time she is three, she will be a dental-office veteran. Most future visits will be preventive in nature, rather than the traditional "drill and fill" sessions that haunt the childhood memories of so many adults.

Immunizations

I grew up in a time when every parent was worried sick about their child contracting polio, a paralytic virus. This illness killed about 25,000 people, mostly children, each year. We were warned not to drink from drinking fountains, to avoid crowds in the summer, and to fret about every viral infection. But no more. There has not been a naturally occurring case of polio in the United States since 1979. The rest of the world is a little behind us, but on the same track. Smallpox has been totally eradicated from our planet.

The elimination of these illnesses is nothing less than a medical miracle, one of mankind's proudest achievements, and it came to pass because of *vaccines*. Many vaccines are made from bacteria or viruses that have been killed or weakened so that they won't cause the disease itself but will still stimulate the body's immune system to be ready to fight the particular disease-causing virus or bacteria. After a child has been *immunized* with a vaccine, either by swallowing it or by being given a shot, his body makes antibodies to fight off that bacteria or virus if it should try to invade.

625. Keep a record with you. It's a good idea to keep a record (signed by your doctor or nurse practitioner) of all your children's immunizations (and sensitivity to drugs, if any) and to carry it with you when the family goes on trips, moves, or changes doctors. The commonest emergency occurs when a child away from home receives a wound that calls for extra protection against tetanus (lockjaw). Then it is very important for the attending doctor to know for certain whether the child has received tetanus immunizations. If a child has been fully immunized, very few wounds will require extra protection against tetanus. Immunization records are also needed for children entering day care, school, and college.

626. Prepare your child. The best way to get your child ready for each immunization is to be as honest and simple in your explanations as possible, considering his age and understanding. Tell him that the shot will hurt a little ("like a hard pinch"), but that it will protect him from sickness that would hurt much more than the shot. Reassure him that it's okay to cry if he wants to and it's okay to feel angry at the doctor and you. I think that even little babies, who won't understand your words, are still soothed by your tone of voice when you're holding them and explaining why they have to have a shot.

627. From time to time, some parents are alarmed and confused by stories in the newspapers and on television about a few children who have had bad reactions to a particular vaccine, especially the pertussis (whooping cough) and polio vaccines. Some of these parents then decide not to give their children *any* immunization, for fear that the immunization will make the child sicker than the disease would have. I think this is a mistake, because we know that in the vast majority of cases the disease is much more dangerous to many more children than is the rare bad reaction to an immunization. If you hear a story that worries you, talk to your doctor or nurse practitioner.

628. The vaccines. A vaccine may contain a *live virus* (e.g., the polio, measles, mumps, German measles, and chicken pox vaccines). The virus in these vaccines has been altered and weakened so that it no longer makes the person sick (except on rare occasions) but still activates the immune system to fight it off. Other vaccines may be made from a *killed bacteria or virus* (e.g., diphtheria, tetanus, whooping cough, hepatitis B), which is usually a part of the whole virus or bacteria which can stimulate an immune response but, since it is not alive, cannot infect the person. In both cases the body becomes relatively immune when exposed to the virus or bacteria by successfully fighting it off with the extra antibodies.

629. DTP: diphtheria, tetanus, pertussis. The vaccines against these three bacterial diseases are combined and given in a series of three shots, two months apart, starting at age two months. The protection from the three shots gradually tapers off, so a booster shot is given a year later, at fifteen to eighteen months of age, and again at age four to six. Further immunizations against diphtheria and tetanus are given every ten years thereafter, but no pertussis (whooping cough) immunization is given after the seventh birthday. The DPT vaccine may be given as a combined shot with another vaccine, such as HIB.

The soreness and fever associated with these vaccines can be significantly reduced by giving your child acetaminophen just before they receive the shot, instead of waiting to see if there's a reaction. If your baby does develop fever, crankiness, loss of appetite, or soreness at the injection site, your doctor or nurse practitioner can prescribe medications to relieve the symptoms. Your baby should feel better the next day. If he has a fever after that, I wouldn't necessarily blame it on the immunization; it could be due to some new infection. These shots do not cause cough or cold symptoms.

It is common for a small, firm lump, or knot, to form in the thigh or arm where the child has received a shot. It may remain for several months and is nothing to worry about. These knots almost always go away.

630. Polio vaccine. OPV (oral polio vaccine, or Sabin vaccine) or IPV (inactivated polio virus, or Salk vaccine) is given to all babies in the United States, beginning at two months of age or as soon thereafter as possible. OPV is a live but weakened virus that has been grown on living cells in a laboratory and is taken by mouth. This oral vaccine is tasteless and is dropped directly onto the tongue. IPV is a killed polio virus that is given by shot.

It's recommended that a child begin the polio vaccine at two months of age, the second at four months and a third dose is given between six and eighteen months, and the fourth when she enters school at four to six years.

If there has been delay between the doses, the only risk is during the period of delay; the protection will eventually be just as high, provided the correct number of doses is given. The vaccine can be given at the same time as shots against diphtheria, tetanus, pertussis, *Haemophilus influenzae* B, and hepatitis B.

When the oral vaccine is used, some live polio virus comes out in the bowel movements of the vaccinated child for many weeks following vaccination. This can be a problem if a family member or caregiver has a particular susceptibility to viral infections—for example, those on cancer treatment, or prolonged steroid use, and those with immunodeficiency disorders. This can't happen with the inactivated vaccine. Some doctors are now giving IPV for the first two doses, followed by OPV for the next two. Others give only the OPV, and still others only use the IPV. At the time of this writing there is no general agreement about which vaccine to use. Your doctor or nurse practitioner will give you the latest information on the schedule of polio vaccine administration.

631. MMR: Measles, mumps, rubella. (Rubella is also called German measles or three-day measles.) Children are protected against these three viral diseases by a single combined shot, usually given at age twelve or fifteen months. This triple vaccine contains live weakened viruses. Reactions to the measles vaccine occur one to two weeks after the shot and resemble a mild case of measles. One child in ten will develop a fever as high as 103°F, beginning about a week after the immunization and lasting one or two days, and one child in twenty will have a mild rash.

A measles booster shot will be given when your child enters school (at age four to six years), along with the DTP and OPV boosters. The measles booster is given in the MMR combination. If your child does not receive the measles booster shot when she starts school, she should receive an MMR combination by age ten or twelve.

632. HIB: *Haemophilus influenzae B.* This disease, which is caused by the *Haemophilus* bacterium, is not related to the flu, which is caused by the influenza virus. The word "influenzae" in the name of this disease is one of those quirks of medical language. Most of the time, *Haemophilus influenzae* B causes a mild illness very similar to a common cold. Before the mid-1980s, when the vaccine was first administered, this mild condition often turned into one of the most common causes in children of serious, life-threatening illness. Since the HIB vaccine began to be administered, such illnesses have largely disappeared. Most of the vaccines against this disease are given in a series of three shots, two months apart, starting at age two months. A booster is given at age twelve to fifteen months.

633. Varicella. Recently introduced in the U.S., varicella is a live virus vaccine that prevents chicken pox or at least lessens its severity. It is now recommended that children between the ages of one and thirteen years who have not already had chicken pox receive this immunization—except those with a special immunity problem, those on high doses of steroids, or those who are pregnant.

634. Hepatitis B vaccine is a series of three shots that is recommended for all children. It provides immunity against the hepatitis B virus, which can cause serious liver damage and is highly contagious, especially at the time of birth. Older children, adolescents, and adults may also be given the vaccine in certain circumstances.

Recommended Immunization Schedule

Vaccines	*Age of administration*
DTP	#1 at 2 months
	#2 at 4 months
	#3 at 6 months
	#4 at 12 to 18 months
	#5 at 4 to 6 years
	#6 (Td only) at 11 to 12 years
Polio (OPV or IPV)	#1 at 2 months
	#2 at 4 months
	#3 at 6 to 18 months
	#4 at 4 to 6 years
MMR	#1 at 12 to 15 months
	#2 at 4 to 6 years

HIB	#1 at 2 months
	#2 at 4 months
	#3 at 6 months
	#4 at 12 to 15 months
Varicella	#1 at 1 to 13 years
Hepatitis B	#1 at birth to 2 months
	#2 at 1 to 4 months
	#3 at 6 to 18 months

Please note: *these recommended schedules change frequently!* New immunizations are being created all the time and ideas about when and how often to give them also vary. Your doctor or nurse practitioner will be up to date about the latest recommendations and side effects.

Children and Tobacco

Lately, professionals have been referring to tobacco use as a "pediatric disease." Although tobacco rarely causes illness in youths (its bad effects can take decades to show up), it is a pediatric disease in that the vast majority of confirmed smokers—those who just can't seem to quit—began smoking before their eighteenth birthday. If we can prevent teens from smoking in the first place, we will have gone a long way toward wiping out this tragic epidemic. How can we do so?

Your personal war on tobacco should begin when your child is very young. The message given about smoking needs to fit with your child's developmental level. For example, no child worries about the prospect of lung cancer in forty years; that is unimaginably far away. Children and teens care about specific, concrete outcomes. The younger child should learn that smoking will make him a worse athlete, less popular, and look like a dork. Teens need to hear that smoking makes them smell bad and causes bad breath (which the opposite sex *hates*), and that it is the opposite of cool. Instead of looking older, teens who smoke actually look *younger*, like children playing dress-up in their parents' clothes—in other words, like kids trying to look like adults.

Media images of robust, attractive people kayaking the

rapids with a butt in their mouth should be discussed and labeled as what they are: pure hype motivated by greed for profits. It should be an unequivocal family value that "smoking stinks." Also be sure to keep the lines of communication open. If your child is being tempted to smoke or has experimented with tobacco, she needs to feel free to discuss it with you, not worry that you will go ballistic. You will get a lot further by talking about it than by just forbidding that which you can't really stop from happening anyway.

After you've had honest conversations about smoking, avoid any further lectures, sharp questions, or snooping. That could only provoke a child to rebel. Don't be a scold. You're just going to have to count on your child's good sense. But you should set the example. Most important of all, you need to have established, from infancy, a relationship of mutual friendliness, respect, and trust.

Parental Smoking

Smoking is a dangerous habit. Each year smoking is linked to about 400,000 deaths. If you smoke, perhaps you'd like to quit, but it's just been too hard.

Now there is an even more compelling reason to kick the habit: your children. While we've known for a long time about smoking causing cancer and other lung diseases in adults, the harmful effects of passive smoking on children have just been discovered. Tobacco smoke in the air weakens your child's respiratory system, making her more susceptible to coughs, colds, asthma, and ear infections. Studies have implicated parental smoking in some (though certainly not all) cases of sudden infant death syndrome (SIDS). Smoke should be viewed as an environmental toxin—which, of course, it is. At the very least a "no smoking in the house or car" rule is vital. Smoking during pregnancy may cause miscarriage, premature birth, decrease in birth weight and serious complications during labor. While these problems occur more frequently when a pregnant mother smokes over a pack of cigarettes each day, any amount of smoking is hazardous to a growing fetus. However, I have a larger concern: children whose parents smoke are themselves more likely to smoke when they are teenagers and adults, so this dangerous habit tends to be passed along.

The short-term and long-term welfare of your children will serve as an added inducement to try again (and again) to quit, as millions have done successfully after several tries. Set an iron-clad quit date within the next two weeks. Obtain help with this difficult endeavor. Consult with your doctor. Find a smoking cessation program in your town that feels right for you. Some smokers benefit from nicotine replacement therapy (patch or gum), others find it preferable to quit cold turkey.

Don't be discouraged. You can do it, as countless others have. Keep in mind the years you may be adding to your life and the lives of your children and grandchildren.

Sun Care

635. Most of us were raised to believe that sun exposure is a healthy thing. The healthy glow of a sun tan makes us look great and feel terrific. The sun helps to create vitamin D. Sometimes we can even feel the sun's energy increasing (or draining) our own. In fact, in the days before all babies automatically got sufficient vitamin D from their formula or vitamin drops, and before the harmful effects of ultraviolet rays were fully understood, I recommended sunbaths for babies.

Now we know better. We lament our own wrinkles, sun spots, and freckles, which we now know were caused by too much sun exposure in our youth. We have learned that many adult skin cancers are caused by sunburns during childhood. Even the cataracts of the eye that many of us will develop later in life are partially related to exposure to the ultraviolet rays of the sun.

So it has to be your job to protect your child from too much sun exposure to prevent later trouble. This is not that hard to do but it takes constant mindfulness.

636. The fairer the skin, the greater the danger. African-Americans and others with darker skin have more natural protection from the sun because of the melanin—the dark pigment in their skin—but they should still exercise caution.

637. First, protect your child's skin from direct exposure to sunlight, especially between 10:00 A.M. and 2:00 P.M., when sunlight is the strongest and most harmful. Make sure your child wears protective clothing and a hat. A good general rule is that if your shadow is shorter than you are, the sun is strong enough to burn you. Remember that significant amounts of ultraviolet rays can damage the skin and eyes even on hazy or cloudy days. Use umbrellas at the beach. Look for a shady tree at a barbecue. Use long-sleeved shirts and pants, bonnets and caps, anything that will come between the skin and direct sunlight. Remember that not all clothing blocks the sun well and that it is still possible to get a sunburn through a shirt. Water does not block the sun at all, so be especially cautious during swimming.

Sunscreen, hats and sunglasses protect us from many of the harmful effects of sun exposure.

421

638. Sunscreen is a must. There are three effective chemicals in sunblocks or sunscreens: PABA esters, cinnamates, and benzophenones. Be sure that one or more of these are listed on the container. I don't recommend sunscreen for children under six months because it can irritate; for those under six months, it's best to avoid sun exposure altogether. But after six months, use *at least* 15 sun protection factor (SPF). This means that only one-fifteenth of the harmful rays get through, so that fifteen minutes of sun exposure with sunscreen is like one minute in the sun without sunscreen. Use a sunscreen that is waterproof. Slather it on liberally at least a half hour before sun exposure, and be sure not to miss any spots. Avoid the eyes, however; sunscreen stings! Reapply it frequently.

639. Next, use sunglasses, even with infants. The harmful effects (like cataracts) of ultraviolet light on eyes don't show up until much later in life, but the eyes should be protected at all times. You don't need to buy expensive sunglasses, as long as the label states that they block UV rays. The darkness of the lens has nothing to do with UV protection, the lenses must be coated with a special compound that specifically blocks out UV light. You should even use them with your infant. Baby shades are well tolerated by most infants, and they get the child used to wearing sunglasses as they get older.

If you have a fair-skinned child and live in a sunny climate, putting on sunblock cream or lotion should be part of his daily routine before leaving the house in the morning. And a second application should be done before he goes out to play after school.

RAISING MENTALLY HEALTHY CHILDREN

Introduction

In this section, I have separated out some of the characteristics that make for mentally healthy children. Of course, in some ways they are all interrelated: good self-esteem, for example, is part of being a cooperative, tolerant child (and vice versa). Additionally, I'm sure there are other characteristics you want to cultivate in your children that aren't listed here. This list is certainly not complete, it just represents some of the areas I think are important.

I would also not like anyone to misread this chapter. Remember that very little special effort is required to achieve the goals mentioned here. You don't have to send your child to fancy schools, buy expensive toys, or relentlessly bombard your child with special lessons. Positive traits in children emerge naturally when a child is given much love and nurturing. Then, when she is exposed to a variety of experiences, she has the confidence and motivation to learn them and to attempt to master those that match her inborn talents.

I'm certainly not talking about making superkids here. Of course, when a child is neglected or consistently ignored ("How many times have I told you to stop bothering me with your questions?"), his spirit and mind will fail to develop fully. However, even though it has been discovered that if you try hard enough, you can teach a two-year-old to read or even teach your one-year-old to recognize flash cards, this is not a particularly wise thing to do. Some parents—armed with the hope that all it takes is the right playthings from infancy and the right mental stimulation at home and in school—try to fashion a precocious, brilliant child.

I think that this particular kind of parental ambition, though understandable in a country where intelligence is so highly prized and at a time when computer experts seem to hold the key to the future, is mistaken and apt to backfire. Mental capacity is only one aspect of a person and may well fail to make him or her a success in life unless it is balanced with warmth, common sense, and a respect for others. There are always costs to pushing a child hard to succeed too early: the relationship between parent and child can become strained and overfocused on intellectual success rather than emotional closeness, and the child may neglect some areas of her development in an attempt to achieve mastery in one targeted area.

640. Special drills and special equipment are not necessary. In fact, I think that trying to create a superkid is a big, if understandable, mistake that many parents make. Of course, we all want our children to make the best use of their talents and to learn as much as they can, but early attempts to artificially try to inflate those talents are misguided and sometimes detrimental to the child. It's misguided because there is no real evidence that pushing a child—for example, to read—early on confers any later advantage. Being the first kid on the block to do almost anything doesn't mean that a child will end up any more competent than later bloomers. And it's detrimental because artificial precocity always comes with a cost. Attempts to jump ahead one area—for example, learning to read at an early age—almost always come at the expense of another important area of functioning, like getting along with other children. You may just succeed in making your child too one-sided and eventually rebellious. Children develop best when their inborn talents and nature are allowed to blossom at their own pace.

641. What stimulates normal, well-rounded development— emotional, social and intellectual? Babies and children, by their inborn nature, keep reaching out to people and to things. Fond parents, watching and coaxing, respond enthusiastically to their baby's first smiles with smiles of their own, head noddings and declarations of love. Repetitions of this scene, every waking hour for months, along with hugs, comforting during misery, and the offering of food at times of hunger keep reinforcing feelings of being well cared for. These first feelings form the foundation of a sense of basic trust upon which the child's future relationships with all the other people in her life will be built. Even her interest in things, and her later capacity to deal with ideas and concepts, in school and at work, will flow from this foundation of love and trust.

As the young child gets older, the natural interplay between the children reaching out to embrace the world and the parents' sensitive loving responses has been sufficient through the ages to produce bright, capable, sociable, loving young people.

There's only one real trick to raising a mentally healthy child: a loving, nurturing, and mutually respectful relationship between you and your child.

Self-Esteem

I agree that everybody, beginning in childhood, is entitled to a comfortable assumption that she is likable, that she is loved, and that she is doing her best in whatever her job is.

But I dislike using the word "self-esteem" because it sounds to me—and I suspect that it will sound to some parents—as if I'm advocating an overly self-satisfied attitude in their children, or as if I'm urging them to be constantly complimenting their children, whether they really deserve it or not, in order to be sure that their children are not being deprived of self-esteem.

642. Part of self-esteem is self-confidence. Praising a child can build self-confidence, but if the praise isn't genuine, children will see straight through it. One way of helping your child build self-esteem is to help him cope with a range of emotions and be reassured his parents can also deal with a range of emotions. The child who is showered with compliments only to be insulted when a parent is angry will not develop self-esteem. Rather he will be anxious and insecure. Consistency and firm limits do as much or more to build self-esteem than do hollow compliments.

I think the reason some highly conscientious parents might overdo it is because some of the most conscientious parents, feeling bad about the frequent disagreeableness and physical abuse dealt out to children in past centuries, have reacted by being excessively respectful of their children; but they have failed to ask their children to respect them. This partly accounts, I think, for the bad manners and demandingness of some children today.

I find it easier to emphasize and clarify aspects of *low self-esteem* and its causes, perhaps because my mother was particularly eager to ward off conceit in her children, which she thought of as obnoxious in itself and likely to lead to more serious faults. I still recall today how, when one of her friends complimented me on my looks in adolescence, she hastened to say, after the friend left, "Benny, you are not good looking. You just have a pleasant smile." All six of her children grew up feeling somewhat unattractive and under-achieving.

As a child I was so often reprimanded for "naughty" acts that every time I came home from playing or from school I felt a cloud of guilt around my shoulders. "What have I done wrong?" I would wonder, when actually I had rarely done anything wrong; I was a goody-goody. This was because my mother was so critical, so much on the lookout for misdemeanors that my five siblings and I felt chronically guilty. When I had occasionally done something slightly wrong, my mother would immediately detect it from my hangdog manner and demand to know what it was. I never tried to deny it; I thought there was no use. I believed she had a magical ability to detect wrongdoing and that the sooner I confessed the sooner the trial, sentencing, and punishment would be over!

I am describing how it worked in our family only to make

the point that in the matter of self-esteem the first and most important step, I feel, is not so much to build it up with a succession of compliments but to avoid tearing down the natural self-assurance with which children are born. Then you don't have to run the risks of conceit, and excessive self-satisfaction that can result from too much praise.

Most children, even during my childhood, were not given the sense of unworthiness that my stern mother instilled in my siblings and me; and many fewer children today are given even a moderate sense of guilt. Nevertheless, I believe, from noticing what goes on in many families, that the parents still depend for their discipline on scolding or at least on a tone of voice that says, "I expect you to do the wrong thing."

643. Now let's turn to the positive promotion of self esteem. I still wouldn't want to depend most of all on *frequent* compliments to my child, for every act of good behavior or for every small achievement. I'm thinking of the example of the child whose parents have been encouraging him to learn to swim by praising him to the skies every time he momentarily ducks his head underwater. After an hour of this he is still demanding "Watch me swim" every minute, though he has made no real progress; he has only developed a greater appetite for praise and attention. (If it sounds as if I am as scared of compliments as my mother was, at least you know I'm vigorously opposed to belittling and constant scolding.)

I think that, next to avoiding chronic scolding and belittling, the soundest way to foster self-esteem in your child is to show her an *enjoying* love. By that I mean not just a devoted love that proves your readiness to make sacrifices for her but an enjoyment of being with her, of hearing *some* of her stories and jokes, a spontaneous appreciation of *some* of her artwork and *some* of her athletic feats. You also show an enjoying love by occasionally suggesting an unanticipated treat, an excursion, or even a walk together.

I will add to "an enjoying love," showing an attitude of parental respect for the child, such as one might show to a valued friend. This means not being rude, not being disagreeable, not being indifferent to her but instead being polite and gracious. There is no reason for us to feel free to be rude, gruff, or indifferent to our children just because they are younger.

The one mistake most often made by parents who *do* show respect for their children is a failure to ask for respect *from* their children. It seems as though, in turning away from the typical oppression of children in past centuries, some superconscientious parents feel—at the unconscious level anyway—that they should make up for it by allowing their children to be rude and demanding. Children, like adults, feel more comfortable and happier when dealing with people who are self-respecting and who naturally, as a result, show they expect respect from others. But they don't have to be disagreeable about it. Ideally, respect is a two-way street.

Discipline

644. Discipline does not mean punishment. When most people use the word "discipline" what they really mean is "punishment." While punishment is a part of discipline (hopefully a small part), it is by no means the whole story. Discipline comes from the word "disciple." It really means "to teach."

That is the true goal of discipline: to teach children the rules of behavior, what society and other people expect of their behavior, so that they grow up to be socially productive and personally fulfilled individuals. Achieving that delicate balance is the art of disciplining children. Of course you could create a harsh system of rewards and punishments so that, like good little robots, your children would behave perfectly most of the time, but what would be the effect on the child's spirit, on his sense of self-worth, on his personal happiness, on his feelings toward others?

On the other hand, you can imagine a child whose every whim is slavishly indulged and whose every action, good or bad, is lavishly praised. Such a child might have a certain measure of happiness, but most people wouldn't want to get within ten feet of him. Your delicate task is to teach your child the *how* and the *why* of acceptable behavior, but never at the expense of his sense of self-worth and optimism.

645. Strict or casual discipline? This looms as a big question for many new parents, although most find their own balance in a little while. For a few parents it remains a worrisome question, no matter how much experience they've had.

Another word used for a casual discipline is "permissiveness," but I hesitate to use it because it means different things to different people. To some it implies merely an easygoing, casual style of management. But to others it means foolishly overindulging a child, letting him do or have anything he wants, and this is apt to produce an obnoxious, spoiled, rude child.

I don't believe that strictness or casualness is the real issue. Good-hearted parents who aren't afraid to be firm when it is necessary can get good results with either moderate strictness or moderate casualness. On the other hand, a strictness that comes from harsh feelings or an excessive permissiveness that is timid or vacillating can lead to poor results. The real issue is what spirit the parent puts into managing the child and what attitude is instilled in the child as a result.

646. Stick to your convictions. I think that good parents who naturally lean toward strictness should raise their children that way. Moderate strictness—in the sense of requiring good manners, prompt obedience, orderliness—is not harmful to children so long as the parents are basically kind and so long as the children are growing up happy and friendly. But strictness is harmful when parents are overbearing, harsh, and chronically disapproving or when they make no allowances for a child's age and individuality. This kind of severity produces children who are either meek and colorless or mean-spirited.

Parents who incline to an easygoing style of management, who are satisfied with casual manners as long as the child's attitude is friendly, or who happen not to be particularly strict—for instance, about promptness or neatness—can also raise children who are considerate and cooperative, as long as the parents are not afraid to be firm about those matters that do seem important to them.

When parents get unhappy results from too much permissiveness, it is not so much because they demand too little, though this is part of it, as it is because they are timid or guilty about what they ask or because they are unconsciously encouraging the child to rule the roost.

If parents are too hesitant in asking for reasonable behavior—because they have misunderstood theories of self-expression, because they are self-sacrificing by nature, or because they are afraid of making their children dislike them—they can't help resenting the bad behavior that comes instead. They keep getting angry underneath, without really knowing what to do about it. This bothers their children, too. It is apt to make them feel guilty and scared, but it also makes them meaner and all the more demanding. If, for example, babies acquire a taste for staying up in the evening and the parents are afraid to deny them this pleasure, they may turn into disagreeable tyrants who keep their mothers and fathers awake for hours. Parents are bound to dislike them for their tyranny. If parents can learn to be firm and consistent in their expectations, it's amazing how fast the children will sweeten up and the parents will, too.

In other words, parents can't feel right toward their children in the long run unless they can make them behave reasonably, and children can't be happy unless they are behaving reasonably.

647. The parent who shies away from discipline. Quite a few parents shy away from guiding and controlling their children (though they may play often with them), leaving most of this work to their spouse. I think of fathers who hide behind the paper or remain glued to the television set when a crisis occurs. Mothers who aren't entirely sure of themselves may get into the habit of saying, "Just wait until your father gets home!"

Some of the nonparticipating fathers explain, when their wives reproach them, that they don't want their children to resent them the way they often resented their fathers.

Instead they want to be pals with their children. It's good for children to have friendly parents who will play with them but children need parents to act like parents. They will have many friends in their lifetime, but only one set of parents.

When a parent is timid or reluctant to give leadership, the children feel let down, like vines without a pole to grow on. When parents are afraid to be definite and firm, their children keep testing the limits, making life difficult for the parents and also for themselves, until the parents are finally provoked into cracking down. Then the parents are apt to feel ashamed, and back off again.

The father who avoids the disciplinary role simply forces his wife to discipline for two. In many such cases, the father does not end up with the friendly relationship he seeks. Children know that adults get irritated when they keep misbehaving. When they are dealing with a father who pretends not to notice, they feel uneasy. Some children may fear this kind of father more than the one who participates freely in their management and expresses his irritation, so that they have opportunities to learn just what his displeasure means and how to deal with it. They find out that they can survive it, and this gives them a kind of self-assurance, just as they gain confidence when they overcome their fears and learn to swim or ride a bike or walk home in the dark. Whereas, with the father who dodges child management and hides his displeasure, the children may imagine that he is concealing an anger that is much more dangerous than it really is.

A great deal of study has been given to the psychology of children in the past half-century by educators, psychoanalysts, child psychiatrists, psychologists, and pediatricians. Parents have been eager to read the results; newspapers and magazines have obliged by publishing them. We have learned a great deal, bit by bit: that children need the love of good parents more than anything else; that they work hard, all by themselves, to be more grown-up and responsible; that many of the ones who get into the most trouble are suffering from a lack of affection rather than from a lack of punishment; that children are eager to learn if they are instructed in ways that are right for their age and if they are taught by understanding teachers; that some jealous feelings toward brothers and sisters and occasional angry feelings toward parents are natural; that a childish interest in the facts of life and in some aspects of sex is quite normal; that too harsh a repression of aggressive feelings and sexual interest may lead to neurosis; that unconscious thoughts are as influential as conscious ones; that each child is an individual and should be allowed to be so.

All these ideas sound commonplace today, but when they were first expressed they were very startling. Many of them ran counter to beliefs that had been held for centuries. It is not possible to change so many ideas about the nature and needs of children without mixing up a lot of parents. Parents who had a comfortable childhood and who are stable people have been least confused. They may have been interested in hearing about these new ideas, and they may have agreed. But when it came to actually managing their children, they did it in much the same way they were brought up themselves. And it has been successful with their children, as it was with them. This is the natural way to learn child care—from having been a child in a reasonably happy family.

648. Some common misunderstandings about discipline. The parents who have trouble with the new ideas are usually those who aren't too happy about their own upbringing. Many of them feel both resentful and guilty about the strained relations that existed at times between themselves and their parents. They don't want their own children to feel that way about them. So they welcome new theories. But they often read meanings into them that are not what the scientists intended. They may assume, for instance, that all children need is love; that they shouldn't be made to conform; that they should be allowed to express their aggressive feelings against parents and others; that whenever anything goes wrong it's the parents' fault; that when children misbehave the parents shouldn't get angry or punish them but should try to show more love.

All of these misconceptions are unworkable if carried very far. They encourage children to become demanding and disagreeable. They make children feel guilty about their excessive misbehavior. They make parents strive to be superhuman. When children behave badly, the parents try to suppress their anger for a while. But eventually they have to explode. Then they feel guilty and bewildered. This leads to more misbehavior on the child's part.

Some parents—who are very polite people themselves—allow their children to be surprisingly obnoxious, not only to themselves but to outsiders as well. They don't seem to see what is going on. Some of these situations, when studied carefully, reveal that the parents were always compelled to be much too good in their own childhood and to suppress all their natural resentment. Now they get a subtle glee from letting their own flesh and blood act out all the disagreeableness they themselves had to bottle up, pretending all the time that this is all according to the best modern theories of child rearing.

649. How feelings of guilt in the parents lead to discipline problems. There are many situations in which parents may always feel a bit guilty toward one child or another. There are obvious cases: the mother who goes to work without first settling in her own mind whether she will be neglecting her child; parents who have a child with a physical or mental handicap; parents who have adopted a baby and can't get over the feeling that they have to do a superhuman job; parents who have been brought up with so much disapproval that they always feel guilty until they are proved innocent; parents who studied child psychology in college, who know about all the pitfalls, and who feel they have to do a superior job.

Whatever the cause of the guilt, it tends to get in the way of easy management of a child. The parents are inclined to expect too little from the child and too much from themselves. They are often still trying to be patient and sweet-tempered when their overworked patience is really exhausted and the child is, in fact, getting out of hand and needs some definite correction. Or they vacillate when the child needs firmness.

A child, like an adult, knows when she is getting away with too much naughtiness or rudeness, even when her parents are trying to close their eyes to it. She feels guilty inside. She would like to be stopped. But if she isn't corrected, she's likely to behave worse and worse. It's as if she were saying, "How bad do I have to be before somebody stops me?"

Eventually her behavior becomes so provoking that the parents' patience snaps. They scold or punish her. Peace is restored. But the trouble with parents who feel guilty is that they are too ashamed of losing their temper. So instead of letting well enough alone, they try to undo the correction, or they let the child punish them in return. Perhaps they permit the child to be rude to them right in the middle of the punishment. Or they take back the penalty before it has been half paid. Or they pretend not to notice when the child begins misbehaving again. In some situations if the child does not retaliate at all, a parent begins to subtly provoke her to do so—without realizing, of course, what she or he is up to.

All of this may sound too complicated or unnatural to you. If you can't imagine a parent letting a child get away with murder or, worse still, encouraging it, it only shows that you don't have a problem with guilt feelings. Actually, however, guilt isn't a rare problem. A majority of conscientious parents let a child get out of hand occasionally when they feel they have been unfair or neglectful, but most soon recover their balance. However, when a parent says, "Everything this child does or says rubs me the wrong way," it's a pretty good sign that the parent feels overly guilty and is chronically submissive and permissive, and that the child is reacting to this with constant provocation. No child can be that irritating by accident.

If parents can determine in which respects they may be too permissive and can firm up their discipline, they may, if they are on the right track, be delighted to find that their child becomes not only better behaved but much happier. Then they can really love their child better, and the child in turn responds to this.

650. Is punishment necessary? Many good parents feel that they have to punish their children once in a while. But other parents find that they can successfully manage without ever having to punish. A lot depends on how the parents were brought up. If they were punished occasionally for good cause, they naturally expect to have to punish in similar situations. And if they were kept in line by positive guidance alone, they are apt to find that they can do the same with their children.

On the other hand, there are also a fair number of poorly behaved children. The parents of some of them punish a lot, and the parents of others never do. So we can't say either that punishment always works or that lack of it always works. It all depends on the nature of the parents' discipline in general.

Before we go further with the subject of punishment, we ought to realize that it is never the main element in discipline—it's only a vigorous reminder that the parents feel strongly about what they say. We have all seen children who were slapped and spanked and deprived plenty, and yet remained ill-behaved.

The main source of good discipline is growing up in a loving family—being loved and learning to love in return. We want to be kind and cooperative (most of the time) because we like people and want them to like us. (Habitual criminals are people who in childhood were never loved enough to make much difference to them. Many of them were also abused or were witnesses to significant violence and turmoil.) Children gradually lessen their grabbing and begin to share, somewhere around the age of three, not primarily because they are reminded by their parents (though that may help some) but because their feelings toward other children—of enjoyment and affection—have developed sufficiently.

Another vital element is children's intense desire to be as much like their parents as possible. They work particularly hard at being polite and civilized and responsible in the three- to six-year-old period. They pretend very seriously to take care of their doll children, keep house, go out to work, as they see their parents do.

651. The everyday job of the parent is to keep the child on the right track by means of firmness and consistency. Though children do the major share in civilizing themselves, through love and imitation, there still is plenty of work left for parents to do. In automobile terms, the child supplies the power but the parents have to do the steering. Some children are more challenging than others—they may be more active, impulsive, and stubborn than most—and it takes more energy to keep them on the right track.

Children's motives are good (most of the time), but they don't have the experience or the stability to stay on the road. The parents have to be saying, "We hold hands when we cross the street," "You can't play with that, it may hurt someone," "Say thank you to Mrs. Griffin," "Let's go in now, because there is a surprise for lunch," "We have to leave the wagon here because it belongs to Harry and he wants it," "It's time to go to bed so you'll grow big and strong," and so on and on.

652. How well the guidance works depends on whether the parents are reasonably consistent (nobody can be completely consistent), whether they mean what they say (and are not just sounding off), and whether they are directing or prohibiting the child for a good reason (not just because they're feeling mean or bossy).
You don't sit by and watch a small child destroy something and then punish him afterward. You resort to punishment (if you use it at all) once in a while when your system of firmness breaks down and you lose your self-control. Maybe your son, sorely tempted, wonders whether you still mean the prohibition that you laid down a couple of months ago. Or maybe he is angry and misbehaves on purpose. Perhaps he breaks something that's precious to you, by foolish carelessness. Or he's slightly rude to you at a moment when you are tense about another matter. Maybe he narrowly escapes being run over because he didn't look both ways. Indignation or righteous anger wells up in you. At such a moment you punish, or at least you feel like punishing.

The best test of a punishment is whether it accomplishes what you are after, without having other serious effects. If it makes a child furious, defiant, and worse behaved than before, then it certainly isn't working. If it seems to break the child's heart, then it's probably too strong for him. Every child reacts somewhat differently.

There are times when a child breaks a plate or rips his clothes because of accident or carelessness. If he gets along well with his parents, he feels just as unhappy as they do, and no punishment is needed. In fact, you may have to comfort him. Jumping on a child who feels sorry already sometimes banishes his remorse and makes him argue.

If you're dealing with an older child who is always fooling with the dishes and breaking them, it may be fair to make him buy replacements from his allowance. A child beyond the age of six is developing a sense of justice and will see the fairness of a reasonable penalty. However, I'd go light on the legalistic take-the-consequences kind of punishment before six, and I wouldn't try to use it at all before three. You don't want a small child to develop a heavy sense of guilt. The job of a parent is to keep the child from getting into trouble rather than to act as a severe judge after it's happened.

Some parents find that putting a child in his room and telling him that he can come out when he feels ready to cooperate works well. But a theoretical disadvantage of this technique is that it may make his room seem like a prison.

653. Avoid threats as much as possible. They tend to weaken discipline. It may sound reasonable to say, "If you don't keep out of the street with your bicycle, I'll take it away." But in a sense a threat is a dare—it admits that the child may disobey. It should impress him more to be firmly told he must keep out of the street, if he knows from experience that his parents mean what they say. On the other hand, if you see that you may have to impose a drastic penalty, like taking away his beloved bike for a few days, it's better to give fair warning. It certainly is silly, and quickly destroys all a parent's authority, to make threats that aren't ever carried out or that can't be carried out. Scary threats, such as of monsters and cops, are 100 percent wrong in all cases.

654. There are several reasons to avoid physical punishment. It teaches children that the larger, stronger person has the power to get his way, whether or not he is in the right. Some spanked children then feel quite justified in beating up on smaller ones. The American tradition of spanking may be one reason that there is much more violence in our country than in any other comparable nation.

When an executive in an office or a foreman in a shop is dissatisfied with the work of an employee, he doesn't rush in shouting and whack him on the seat of his pants. He explains in a respectful manner what he would like, and in most cases this is enough. Children are not that different in their wish to be responsible and to please. They react well to praise and high expectations.

In the olden days, most children were spanked, on the assumption that this was necessary to make them behave. In the twentieth century, as parents and professionals have studied children here and in other countries, they have come to realize that children can be well behaved, cooperative, and polite without ever having been punished physically or in any other way. I have known hundreds of such children myself, and there are countries in the world where physical punishment is unknown.

655. Parents who can't control their children or who have to punish frequently need help. A few parents have extreme difficulty controlling their children. They say their child "won't obey" or that he's "just bad." The first thing you see when you watch such a parent—let's say it's a mother—is that she doesn't appear to be really trying, even though she wants to and thinks she is. She threatens or scolds or punishes frequently. But one such mother almost never carries out a threat. Another, though she punishes, never in the end makes the child do what she said he had to do. And another makes him obey once, but five minutes later and again ten minutes later she lets him get away with it. Another laughs in the middle of a scolding or punishment. Another just keeps shouting at the child that he's bad or asks a neighbor, right in front of the child, whether she has ever seen a worse one.

Parents like these unconsciously expect the child's bad behavior to go right on and can do nothing effective to stop it. They are inviting misbehavior, without realizing it. Their scolding and punishing are only an expression of frustration. In their complaints to neighbors they are only hoping to get some comforting agreement that the child is truly impossible. Frustrated parents like these have often had an unsatisfactory childhood during which they never received sufficient assurance that they were basically good and well behaved. As a result they don't have enough confidence in themselves or in their children. These parents need a lot of help from an understanding professional.

656. You can be both firm and friendly. A child needs to feel that her mother and father, however agreeable, have their own rights, know how to be firm, and won't let her be unreasonable or rude. She likes them better that way. Their firmness trains her from the beginning to get along reasonably with other people.

Spoiled children are not happy creatures even in their own homes. And when they get out into the world, whether it's at age two or four or six, they are in for a rude shock. They find that nobody is willing to kowtow to them; they learn, in fact, that everybody dislikes them for their selfishness. Either they must go through life being unpopular, or they must learn the hard way how to be agreeable.

Conscientious parents often let a child take advantage of them for a while—until their patience is exhausted—and then turn on the child crossly. But neither of these stages is really necessary. If parents have a healthy self-respect, they can stand up for themselves while they are still feeling friendly. For instance, if your daughter insists that you continue to play a game after you are exhausted, don't be afraid to say cheerfully but definitely, "I'm all tired out. I'm going to read a book now, and you can read your book, too."

Or maybe she is being very balky about getting out of the wagon of another child who has to take it home now. Try to interest her in something else, but don't feel that you must go on being sweetly reasonable forever. Lift her out of the wagon even if she yells for a minute.

657. Let children know that their angry feelings are normal. When a child is rude to her parent—perhaps because she has had to be corrected or because she's jealous of her brother or sister—the parent should promptly stop her and insist on politeness. But at the same time the parent can say that he knows she is cross at him sometimes—all children get mad at their parents sometimes. This may sound contradictory to you; it sounds like undoing the correction. Child guidance work teaches us in case after case that a child is happier as well as better behaved if her parents insist on reasonably good behavior. But at the same time it helps a child to realize that her parents know she has angry feelings and that her parents are not enraged at her or alienated from her on account of them. This realization helps her get over her anger and keeps her from feeling too guilty or frightened because of it. Making this distinction between hostile feelings and hostile actions works out well in actual practice.

658. Don't say, "Do you want to . . ." Just do what's necessary. It's easy to fall into the habit of saying to a small child, "Do you want to sit down and have your lunch?" "Shall we get dressed now?" "Do you want to do wee-wee?" Another common approach is, "It's time to go out now, okay?" The trouble is that the natural response of the child, particularly between one and three, is "No." Then the poor parent has to persuade the child to give in to something that was necessary anyway.

These arguments use up thousands of words. It is better not to offer a choice. When it's time for lunch, lead him or carry him to the table, still chatting with him about the thing that was on his mind before. When you see signs that he needs to go to the bathroom, lead him there or bring the potty chair to him. Start undoing him without even mentioning what you're up to.

You might get the idea that I am advising you to swoop down on him and give him the bum's rush. I don't mean exactly that. In fact, every time you take a child away from something he's absorbed in, it helps to be tactful. If your fifteen-month-old is busy fitting one hollow block inside another at suppertime, you can carry him to the table still holding his blocks and take them away when you hand him his spoon. If your two-year-old is playing with a toy dog at bedtime, you can say, "Let's put doggie to bed now." If your three-year-old is chugging a toy automobile along the floor when it's time for the bath, you can suggest that the car make a long, long trip to the bathroom. When you show interest in what he's doing, it puts him in a cooperative mood.

As your child grows older, he'll be less distractible and have more concentration. Then it works better to give him a little friendly warning. If a four-year-old has spent half an hour building a garage of blocks, you can say, "Put the cars in soon now; I want to see them inside before you go to bed." This works better than pouncing on him without warning when the most exciting part of the play is still to come, or giving him a cross warning as if you never did see anything in garages except the mess they make on the floor.

All this takes patience, though, and naturally you won't always have it. No parent ever has.

659. Don't give the small child too many reasons. You sometimes see a child between the ages of one and three who becomes worried by too many warnings. The mother of a certain two-year-old boy always tries to control him with ideas: "Jackie, you mustn't touch the doctor's lamp, because you will break it, and then the doctor won't be able to see." Jackie regards the lamp with a worried expression and mutters, "Doctor can't see." A minute later he is trying to open the door to the street. His mother warns him, "Don't go out the door. Jackie might get lost, and Mommy couldn't find him." Poor Jackie turns this new danger over in his mind and repeats, "Mommy can't find him." It's bad for him to hear about so many bad endings. It fosters a morbid imagination. A two-year-old baby shouldn't be worrying much about the consequences of his actions. This is the period when he is meant to learn by doing and having things happen. I'm not advising you never to warn your child in words, but only that you shouldn't always lead him out beyond his depth with ideas.

I think of an overconscientious father who feels he should give his three-year-old daughter a reasonable explanation of everything. When it's time to get ready to go outdoors, it never occurs to him to put the child's coat on in a matter-of-fact way and get out. He begins, "Shall we put your coat on now?" "No," says the child. "Oh, but we want to go out and get some nice fresh air." She is used to the fact that her father feels obliged to give a reason for everything and this encourages her to make him argue for every point. So she says, "Why?" but not because she really wants to know. "Fresh air makes you strong and healthy so that you won't get sick." "Why?" says she. And so on and so forth, all day long. This kind of meaningless argument and explanation will not make her a more cooperative child or give her respect for her father as a reasonable person. She would be happier and get more security from him if he had an air of self-confidence and steered her in a friendly, automatic way through the routines of the day.

When your child is young, rely most heavily on physically removing her from dangerous or forbidden situations by distracting her to something interesting but harmless. As she grows a little older and learns the lesson, remind her with a matter-of-fact "No, no" and more distraction. If she wants an explanation or a reason, give it to her in simple terms. But don't assume that she wants an explanation for every direction you give. She knows that she is inexperienced. She counts on you to keep her out of danger. It makes her feel safe to have you guiding her, provided you do it tactfully and not too much.

660. Parents are bound to get cross. I think that idealistic young people approaching parenthood assume that if they are the right sort they will have unlimited patience and love for their innocent baby. But this is not humanly possible.

When your baby has been crying angrily for hours, despite all your patient efforts to comfort her, you can't go on feeling sympathetic. She seems like a disagreeable, obstinate, unappreciative creature, and you can't help feeling angry—really angry. Or perhaps your older son has done something that he knows very well he shouldn't have done. Maybe he was so fascinated with a breakable object of yours or so eager to join some children on the other side of the street that he couldn't resist the temptation to disobey. Or maybe he was cross at you for having denied him

442

something or angry at the baby for receiving so much attention. So he misbehaved from simple spite.

When a child disobeys a well-understood and reasonable rule, you can't simply be a cool statue of justice. Any good parent feels strongly about right and wrong. You were taught to feel that way back in your own childhood. It's your rule that has been broken. It's probably your possession that has been damaged. It's your child, about whose character you care a great deal, who has done wrong. It's inevitable that you feel indignant. The child naturally expects this and is not hurt by it if your reaction is fair.

Sometimes it takes you a long time to realize that you are losing your temper. The boy may have been putting on a series of irritating acts from the time he appeared at breakfast—making disagreeable remarks about the food, half deliberately knocking over a glass of milk, playing with something forbidden and breaking it, picking on a younger child—all of which you have tried to ignore in a supreme effort to be patient. Then at the final act, which perhaps isn't so bad, your resentment suddenly boils over, and it shocks you a little with its vehemence. Often when you look back over such a series of exasperating actions, you can see that the child has really been asking for firmness all morning and that it was your well-intentioned effort at patience that made him go from one provocation to another, looking for a check.

We also get cross with our children because of the pressures and frustrations we are feeling from other directions. A father, for example, comes home on edge from troubles that he's having in his work. He criticizes his wife, who then snaps at the older boy for something that ordinarily brings no disapproval, and he in turn picks on his younger sister.

661. Better to admit crossness. So far we have been discussing the inevitability of parental impatience and resentment from time to time. But it's just as important to consider a related question: can parents comfortably accept their cross feelings? Parents who aren't excessively strict with themselves are usually able to admire their irritation. A natural, outspoken good mother whose little boy has been bedeviling her is able to say to a friend, half jokingly, "I don't think I can stand being in the house with him for another minute," or "I'd enjoy giving him a thorough walloping." She may not carry out any of these thoughts, but she isn't ashamed to admit them to a sympathetic friend or to herself. It relieves her feelings to recognize them so clearly and to blow them off in talk. It also helps her to see what she has been putting up with and to be firmer in putting a stop to it.

It's the parents who set impossibly high standards for themselves, who have angry feelings at times but can't believe that good parents should, who really suffer. When they detect such emotions stirring in themselves, they either feel unbearably guilty or try strenuously to deny them. But if a person tries to bury such feelings they only pop up somewhere else—as tension, for example, or tiredness or a headache.

Another indirect expression of anger is overprotectiveness. A mother who can't admit that she feels antagonism toward her children may imagine instead all the awful things that could beset them from other directions; she worries excessively about germs, or about traffic. She tries to ward off these dangers by hovering over her children, and this tends to make them too dependent.

I'm not pointing out the problems created by denying crossness in order merely to relieve the uncomfortable feelings of the parent. In general, what makes a parent miserable makes the child miserable, too. When a parent believes that antagonistic feelings are too horrible to admit, the child absorbs the same dread of them. In child guidance clinics, we see children who develop fears of imaginary dangers—fear of insects, of going to school, of being separated from their parents—that prove on investigation to be a disguise for ordinary anger feeling toward their parents, which these perfectionistic children dare not recognize.

To put it the other way around, children are happier around parents who aren't afraid to admit their anger, because then they can be more comfortable about their own. And justified anger that's expressed tends to clear the air and leave everyone feeling better. I am talking not about being rough on children but about admitting your feelings. And I don't mean that all the antagonism expressed toward children is justified. Here and there you see a harsh, unloving parent who abuses a child at all hours of the day, verbally or physically, with little reason and no shame. What I have been discussing is the irritation of parents whose conscientiousness and devotion to their children is plain to see.

A loving parent who feels angry most of the time, whether it's expressed openly or not, is suffering from a real emotional strain and deserves help from a mental health professional. The anger may be coming from some entirely different direction.

662. Impatience and approval are part of child rearing. The very human tendency to react intensely to our children's behavior works positively for us as we strongly foster in our children the good traits that our parents fostered in us. We do this automatically, without having to think about it, because we learned our ideals so thoroughly in childhood. Otherwise, rearing our children would be ten times as hard as it is.

It's the feeling of particular irritation toward one child that makes parents feel most guilty, especially if there is no clear reason for it. A mother says, "This one always rubs me the wrong way. Yet I'm constantly trying to be sweeter to her and to overlook her bad behavior."

But feeling too guilty about our chronic impatience with one child or another may produce increasing complications in our relations with her. Our guilt then gets to be harder on her than our irritation.

The Facts of Life

663. Sex education starts early whether you plan it or not. It is common to think that sex education means a lecture at school or a solemn talk by a parent at home. This is taking too narrow a view of the subject. A child is learning about

445

the facts of life all through childhood, if not in a good way then in an unwholesome way. The subject of sex is a lot broader than just how babies are made. It includes the whole matter of how men and women get along with each other and what their respective places are in the world.

Let me give you a couple of bad examples. Suppose a boy has a father who is disagreeable and abusive to the mother. You can't educate the boy with a lecture at school telling him that marriage is a relationship of mutual love and respect. His experience tells him differently. When he learns about the physical side of sex, whether from a teacher or from other children, he will fit that information into the picture he has of a man being disagreeable to a woman. Or take the example of a girl who grows up feeling unwanted because she thinks her parents prefer her younger brother. She is going to resent men because she believes that they get all the breaks and that women are always the victims, and that this situation cannot be changed. It won't matter how many books or talks you give her about sex and marriage. Whatever she hears or experiences she will fit into the pattern she has fixed in her mind: the man takes advantage of the woman who is helpless to alter the pattern.

So children begin their sex education as soon as they can sense how their mother and father get along with each other, how they feel about their sons and daughters, and as soon as they become aware of differences between their bodies, their parents' bodies, and those of opposite-sexed brothers, sisters, and playmates.

664. I believe that sex is as much spiritual as it is physical and that children need to know that their parents feel this way. This is what makes falling in love such an intense emotional experience. The lovers want to care for each other, please each other, comfort each other. They eventually want to have fine children together. If they are religious people, they want God to be part of their marriage. These aspirations are part of what makes for a firm and idealistic marriage. This can't be explained to a one-year-old, of course, though the intense dependent love between him and his parents is laying the groundwork. But by the age of three, four, and five, when a child's generous love goes out to the parents, it is good for children to hear and see that their parents not only want to hug and kiss each other but that they also yearn to be kind, helpful, and respectful to each other. When parents answer children's questions at this age period and older, about where babies come from and what is the father's role, it's important for children to hear the parents speak feelingly about the part played by their devotion to each other, how they want to do things for each other, give things to each other, have children together, take care of them together, and how this goes along with the physical affection and wanting to put the seed from the penis into the vagina. In other words, parents shouldn't ever let the anatomical and physiological explanation of sex stand alone but always connect it with the idealistic, spiritual aspects.

Parents should set a good example for their children by showing helpfulness, thoughtfulness, kindness, and mutual respect, even when they disagree. They should occasionally point out the need of such qualities in marriage (without patting themselves on the back) when discussing some other couple.

665. Children ask questions around age three. Children begin to get more exact ideas about the things that are connected with sex around the ages of two and a half to three and a half. This is the "why" stage, when their curiosity branches out in all directions. They probably want to know why boys are made differently from girls. They don't think of it as a sex question. It's just another in a series of important questions. But if they gain the wrong impression, it will become mixed up with sex later and give them distorted ideas.

666. Where do babies come from? This question is also pretty sure to come up in the period around three. It's easier and better to begin with the truth rather than tell a fairy story and have to change it later. Try to answer the question as simply as they ask it. Young children are easily confused by too much information at one time. They understand more when information is given in small simple explanations. For instance, you can say, "A baby grows in a special place inside the mother, called the uterus." You don't have to tell them more than that for the time being.

But maybe in a few minutes, maybe in a few months, they want to know a couple of other things: How does the baby get inside the mother? How does it get out? The first question is apt to be embarrassing to the parent, who may jump to the conclusion that the child is now demanding to know about conception and sex relations. Of course, they are making no such demand. They think of things getting into the stomach by being eaten, and perhaps wonder if the baby gets in that way, too. A simple answer is that the baby grows from a tiny seed that was in the mother all the time. It will be months before they want to know or will be able to understand what part the father plays.

Some people feel that children should be told at the time of their first questions that the father contributes by putting his seed into the mother. Perhaps this is right, especially in the case of the little boy who feels that the man is left out of the picture. But most experts agree that it is not necessary to try to give a three- or four-year-old an exact picture of the physical and emotional sides of intercourse. It's more than children bargained for, you might say, when they asked their question. All that's necessary is to satisfy their curiosity at the level of their understanding and, more important, to give them the feeling that it is all right to ask anything.

To the question of how babies get out, a good answer is something to the effect that when they are big enough they come out through a special opening that's just for that purpose, called the vagina. It's important to make it clear that it is not the opening for bowel movements or for urine.

A young child is very apt to stumble on some evidence of menstruation and to interpret this as a sign of injury. A mother should be ready to explain that all women have this discharge every month and that it doesn't come from a hurt. Something about the purpose of menstruation can be explained to a child of three or older.

667. Why not the stork? You may say, "Isn't it easier and less embarrassing to tell them about the stork?" There are several reasons. We know that a child as young as three, who has a pregnant mother or aunt may have a suspicion of where the baby is growing from observing the woman's figure and from bits of overheard conversation. It's apt to mystify and worry him to have his parent nervously telling him something different from what he suspects is the truth. Even if he doesn't suspect anything at three, he is surely going to find out the truth or the half-truth when he's five or seven or nine. It's better not to start him off wrong and have him later decide that you're something of a liar. And if he finds that for some reason you didn't dare tell him the truth, it puts a barrier between you, makes him uneasy. He's less likely to ask you other questions later, no matter how troubled he is. Another reason for telling the truth at three is that children at this age are satisfied with simple answers. You get practice for and build a foundation for the harder questions that come later.

Sometimes small children who have been told where the baby is growing confuse parents by talking as if they also believe the stork theory. Or they may mix up two or three theories at the same time. This is natural. Small children believe part of everything they hear because they have such vivid imaginations. They don't try, as grown-ups do, to find the one right answer and get rid of the wrong ones. You must also remember that children can't learn anything from one telling. They learn a little at a time, and come back with the same question until they feel sure that they've got it straight. Then at every new stage of development they're ready for a new slant.

668. A step at a time usually satisfies. Realize ahead of time that your child's questions will never come in exactly the form or at the moment you expect. A parent is apt to visualize a scene at bedtime when the child is in a confidential mood. Actually, the question is more apt to be popped in the middle of the grocery store or while you are talking on the street with a pregnant neighbor. If it does, try to curb that impulse to shush the child. Answer on the spot if you can. If that is impossible, say casually, "I'll tell you later. These are things we like to talk about when other people aren't around."

Don't make too solemn an occasion of it. When children ask you why the grass is green or why dogs have tails, you answer in an offhand way that gives them the feeling that it is the most natural thing in the world. Try to get the same spirit of naturalness into your answers about the facts of life. Remember that even if this subject is charged with feeling and embarrassment for you, it is a matter of simple curiosity to them. Even if you feel embarrassed, chances are the child will not be bothered if your response is straightforward.

Other questions—"Why don't babies come until you are married?" or "What does the father do about it?"—may not come until children are four or five or older unless they observe animals or have friends with baby brothers or sisters. Then you can explain that the seed comes out of the father's penis and goes into the uterus, a special place different from the stomach, where the baby will grow. It may be some time before they try to visualize this situation. When they are ready for that, you can mention something in your own words about loving and embracing.

669. The child who hasn't asked. What about the child who has reached the age of four or five or more and hasn't asked any questions at all? Parents sometimes assume that this means the child is very innocent and has never thought of these questions. But most people who have worked closely with children would be inclined to doubt this. It is more likely that the child has gotten the feeling, whether the parents meant to give it or not, that these matters are embarrassing. You can be on the lookout for indirect questions and hints and little jokes that a child uses to test out parents' reactions.

I can think of several examples. A child of seven who was not supposed to know anything about pregnancy kept calling attention to his mother's large abdomen in a half-embarrassed, half-joking way. Here was a good chance—better late than never—for the parents to explain. A little girl who is at the stage of wondering why she isn't made like a boy sometimes makes valiant efforts to urinate standing up. There are occasions almost every day, in a child's conversation about humans and animals and birds, when a parent on the lookout for indirect questions can help the child ask what she wants to know. The parents then have an opportunity to give her a reassuring explanation, even though she hasn't asked a direct question.

670. How the school can help. If the mother and father have answered earlier questions with a minimum of discomfort, children will keep on turning to parents as they grow older and want more exact knowledge. But the school has a chance to help out, too. Many schools make a point of letting children in kindergarten or first grade take care of animals, such as rabbits, guinea pigs, or white mice. This gives them an opportunity to become familiar with all sides of animal life—feeding, fighting, mating, birth, and suckling of the young. It is easier in some ways to learn these facts in an impersonal situation, and it supplements what children have learned from their parents. But what they find out in school they probably want to discuss and clear up further at home.

By the fifth grade, it is good to have biology taught in a simple way, including a discussion of reproduction. At least some of the girls in the class are entering puberty and need some accurate knowledge of what is happening. The discussion from a somewhat scientific point of view in school should help the child to bring it up more personally at home.

I think that sex education, including its spiritual aspects, should be part of a broad health and moral education from kindergarten through grade twelve, ideally carried out harmoniously by parents and teachers.

671. Talking about sex. You might get the idea from articles that it should be easy for parents to talk about sex with their adolescent children. This is simply not so. Adolescents' acute awareness of their sexuality makes such a discussion embarrassing in many cases, especially between son and father. Many fathers and sons can't get to it at all, nor can quite a few mothers and daughters. Then the information— or misinformation—comes from friends, older brothers or sisters, books. A sound book made available by a parent can be helpful, either used alone or, better still, backed up by the parents' answers to questions.

It's preferable, just as in earlier childhood, for talk about sex to come up easily from time to time rather than to be one big solemn lecture. The parent has to be willing to bring it up early in puberty, though, because the child often doesn't do so.

672. Keep the tone wholesome. One mistake that is easy to make, especially if the parents themselves were brought up in fear of sex, is to concentrate on the dangerous aspects of sex. A nervous mother may make her daughter so scared of becoming pregnant that the poor girl has a terror of boys under all circumstances. Or the father may overfill his son with dread of venereal disease. Of course, the child who is moving into adolescence should know how pregnancy takes place and that there is a danger of disease in being promiscuous, but these disturbing aspects of sex shouldn't come first. The adolescent should think of it as primarily wholesome and natural and beautiful.

These discussions should include talking about contraception, with specifics about both the boy's and girl's responsibilities.

If you just can't find a way to get comfortable enough to talk about sex with your teenager, it's important to find another adult, trusted by both of you, who can do it.

Worried parents find it hard to believe, but what people who have studied young people well know, is that happy, sensible, successful adolescents rarely get into trouble with sex. All the common sense, self-respect, and kindly feeling toward people that they have built up through the years keep them on an even keel even when they are sailing through an entirely new phase of development. To turn it around the other way, the adolescents who get into trouble with the wrong kind of companions are usually children who for years have been mixed up within themselves and with others.

The danger of scaring a child about sex is partly that you make a sensitive child tense and apprehensive at the time and partly that you may impair that child's ability to adjust to marriage later.

673. Girls need to be told about sex by the beginning of puberty development (around age ten). They need to know that during the next two years their breasts will develop, hair will grow in the genital region and under the arms, that they will grow rapidly in height and weight, that their skin will change its texture and may become prone to pimples, and that in about two years they will probably have their first menstrual period. (These changes are discussed in Sections 459–463.) How you tell them about their menstrual periods makes a difference. Some mothers emphasize what a curse they can be, but it is a mistake to stress that part to a child who is still immature and impressionable. Other mothers emphasize how delicate a girl becomes at such times and how careful she must be. This kind of talk makes a bad impression, particularly on those girls who have grown up feeling that their brothers got all the advantages or who have been inclined to worry about their health. Girls and women can live perfectly healthy, normal, vigorous lives right through their menstrual periods. It is only the occasional girl who has cramps severe enough to keep her out of activities, and there are good treatments for cramps.

When a girl is on the threshold of womanhood, it's good for her to be looking forward to it happily, not feeling scared or resentful. The best thing to emphasize about menstruation is that the uterus is being prepared for the growing of a baby.

It helps put the child in the right mood during the months she is waiting for her first period to give her a box of menstrual pads. This makes her feel that she is grown up and ready to deal with life rather than waiting for life to do something to her.

674. Boys need to be told about sex by the beginning of puberty development (around age twelve). You should explain about the naturalness of erections and nocturnal emissions. Nocturnal emissions, which are often called wet dreams, are an ejaculation of semen (the fluid stored in the prostate gland) during sleep, often in the course of a dream of a sexual nature. Parents who know that nocturnal emissions are certain to occur and also that boys will at times feel a strong urge to masturbate, sometimes tell the boy that these things are not harmful if they don't happen too often. I think it's a mistake for a parent to set a limit. The trouble is that adolescents easily become worried about their sexuality, easily imagine they are "different" or abnormal. Being told, "This much is normal, that much is abnormal," is apt to make them more preoccupied with sex. Boys need to be told that it's equally normal to have many or few nocturnal emissions and that occasionally a perfectly normal boy will have none at all.

The Development of Sexuality

675. We are sexual beings to our very core from the day we're born until the day we die. Sexuality is inborn, part of our nature, but exactly how that nature is expressed depends largely on familial, cultural, and social values. Some cultures embrace human sexuality as a fundamental and natural part of day-to-day life. Our culture, on the other hand, has been strongly influenced by our puritanical forebears, leaving us disquieted about our sexuality and how to express it. If you look around at how sexuality is used in our culture—for advertisements, for titillation, to make a profit—it may seem as if we are getting less puritanical. But I think this is an illusion. In fact our society's obsession with sex is based on its very repression. It is the denial of our human sexuality that fuels its exploitation in all areas of life.

676. The expression of sexuality—your own as well as your child's—cuts to the very heart of your personal value system. What is the meaning of human sexuality? How should it be expressed? What values about sexuality do you want to imbue in your children? These are questions you will have to answer, first for yourself and then for your children.

I would like to help you do that by briefly reviewing human sexuality over the life span. I come to this discussion, like everyone else, with my own perspective, based on the following premises: (1) sexuality is a biological, pleasurable, sensual manifestation of the life force, an integral part of our human nature; (2) at its best, sexuality is a creative expression of love between two people; and (3) responsible sexual decision-making and a strong sense of values should be our goals for our children.

677. Infantile sensuality. Note that I'm referring to *sensuality,* which refers to taking pleasure in the physical senses, and not *sexuality,* which narrows the field to the reproductive organs. All babies take great, uninhibited pleasure in their bodies, especially in certain areas like the mouth and genitals. They eat with gusto, smacking their lips when sated, raising a ruckus when hungry. It is with unabashed pleasure that they delight in the pleasures of their body—being held, stroked, kissed, tickled, massaged. The pleasure principle reigns unapologetically supreme.

Over time—and depending on how the world responds to her sensuality—the infant begins to associate certain emotions and ideas with pleasurable sensations. If an infant who is rubbing her genitals is told "No! Don't do that! That's nasty!" she begins to associate that sensation with disapproval.

Of course, while she may stop that behavior, the desire for pleasure does not vanish, nor does the infant understand why this pleasurable activity is prohibited. A conflict is set up, often one of the infant's first, between the urgencies of the body and the prohibitions of society. Freud believed that the way in which this conflict gets resolved determines much of our character as adults.

678. Infants. By the second half of the first year, infants discover their genitals the same way they discover their fingers and toes, by randomly exploring all their body parts. They feel pleasure when they stroke their genitals, and as they get older, they remember these pleasurable sensations. So from time to time, they will stroke their genitals intentionally.

679. Toddlers. By eighteen to thirty months, children are becoming aware of gender differences, specifically focusing on the boy's penis and the girl's lack of one. This is how children see it, until they learn that girls have a vagina and a uterus in which to grow babies, which boys lack. This natural interest in the genitals at this time leads to an increase in masturbation.

680. Masturbation. By age three, children who haven't been forbidden and prevented from masturbating will do it from time to time. In addition to stroking their genitals with their hands, they may rub their thighs together, or rhythmically rock back and forth, or make pelvic thrusting motions while sitting on the arm of a couch or chair or lying on a favorite stuffed animal.

At this age, boys and girls will be openly interested in each other's bodies and, if permitted, will spontaneously engage in show-and-touch. Playing house and doctor helps to satisfy sexual curiosity, while also allowing children to practice being grown-up in more general ways.

Children at this age will also stroke their genitals to comfort themselves when they're tense or frightened or fear that something bad will happen to the genitals.

681. School-age children. Freudian psychologists believe there is a "latency period" of reduced sexual interest and activity between six or seven and the beginning of adolescence. But researchers in child development have observed that most of these children do continue to masturbate, although less openly and less frequently, for pleasure, and they continue to use the calming, comforting effects of masturbation to help deal with anxieties of all kinds.

Comparing penis size among boys, and appearance and size of clitoris among girls, is normal in this age group. It's part of the general process of seeing how you measure up to your peers.

682. Adolescents. Sexuality and romance are strained for the adolescent for several reasons. (I use the word "sexual" when I put the emphasis on biological instinct, and the word "romantic" when I mean the tender, highly personal, idealistic aspects of love between the sexes, which are mainly learned during a childhood spent with parents whose love is of this kind. I realize that this usage has various inaccuracies; I am also aware that to call anything romantic nowadays makes it seem to some people insipid or bogus.)

Adolescent sexuality emerges from two earlier, contradictory phases. Between three and six years children grew spiritually by idealizing their parents and became interested in romance, sex, and babies. Between six and twelve, through a complex interaction of emotions, they repressed much of their interest in romance and sex, turned away from their parents, and became absorbed in the impersonal outside world of school, social adaptation, laws, and legends.

In adolescence the biological pressures compel children to be preoccupied with sexual and romantic interests again. But their revived sexual drive will continue to be in conflict with earlier taboos for several more years, causing embarrassment, guilt, and awkwardness. The simplest example is the young adolescent's shyness in dealing with the opposite sex.

These conflicting emotions also cause trouble in children's relations with their parents. When the rush of strong romantic feeling wells up in early adolescence, it first starts—like a spring flood running down a dry riverbed—toward the parent of the opposite sex. Yet adolescents realize subconsciously that this is not right at all. So their initial job at this age is to steer the feelings away from the parent and toward someone outside the family. Children actually cover up their positive feelings toward a parent with negative ones. This is at least a partial explanation of why a boy so often picks fights with his mother and why a daughter may be surprisingly antagonistic toward her father at times.

At first the adolescent girl—and this is equally true of the adolescent boy—doesn't know at all clearly where her feelings belong. She becomes generally intense and romantic in her attitudes toward different kinds of people. Yet she may be nowhere near the age where she can show these feelings toward an individual of the same age and opposite sex, especially if she is shy and idealistic. She may develop a great admiration for a teacher of the same sex or for a heroine of fiction. It's only gradually that the barriers between the sexes are broken down. Perhaps the adolescent first dares to think romantically of someone in Hollywood. Then boys and girls in the same school begin to dream about each other; but it may take some more time before the shy ones can show their interest face-to-face.

Even after an adolescent's instincts have broken through the inhibitions of the earlier period and involved her in dating, a portion of her energy will still be held in reserve and invested in idealistic yearnings. Some part of this will ensure that her attitude toward the opposite sex is romantic and idealized. But another part, even at this relatively late stage of development, will still be sublimated into aspirations—which, on the surface, seem unrelated to sex or even romance—to create things of beauty or to make a great contribution to humanity.

In the very beginning of their interest in members of the opposite sex, some adolescents may be unable to recognize any sexual feeling toward a person for whom they feel respect and tenderness, only for those who seem debased in some way. For a few individuals this pattern unfortunately lasts for life. This is a sign of serious conflict, and parents who see this pattern should seek help from a child guidance clinic, psychiatrist, or psychologist.

Before children have become secure about their sexuality and integrated it into their personality, it remains a rather awkward, compelling, separate instinct. They feel a nagging curiosity about sex and a compulsion to find out by experimentation. These feelings run counter, of course, to their idealistic emotions. In fact, they may be tenderly in love with one person and still find themselves impelled to make advances—hesitant or bold—to others in a rather impersonal, promiscuous spirit.

Children in their early teens are apt to experience a series of intense infatuations, in each of which the sense of being in love is intense. But they can fall out of love as quickly as they fall in. They discover that they and their beloved really have little in common. Sometimes the reason is that one or both have changed. More often it's because they had originally fallen in love with an ideal they saw in each other, that had little to do with reality. As the years pass, they become more cautious and more realistic about the kind of person they need and can get along with. As they gradually mature, they also have more to give to each other—a vital ingredient of true love.

683. Teenage pregnancy. In earlier times a young girl who became pregnant was thought of as at least mildly delinquent because she had disobeyed her parents and her own principles. Now the greatly relaxed sexual standards and, to a lesser extent, the knowledge of how pregnancy can be prevented, have brought about a great increase in the frequency of sexual intercourse at earlier ages, and pregnancy among unmarried teenagers. To adults the most surprising, almost incomprehensible aspect of this is that only a minority of the teenagers who are sexually active practice birth control, even when they have been well instructed by their parents and physicians.

Why won't they take responsibility for their sexual activity? There are various overlapping explanations. To be prepared means to some of them that they expect to have intercourse, which many of them are not quite ready to admit. They prefer to think of each episode as an unexpected outburst of passion that won't be repeated. Some say that since they (or friends) have had intercourse a number of times without pregnancy, they assume that they are somehow immune to pregnancy. Others think that withdrawal is a reliable prevention. Some who are having conflicts with parents think of themselves as unloved, and they picture themselves as loving and being loved intensely by a baby. Some teenagers become sexually involved with a person whom they have come to love more or less tenderly and idealistically. Others are responding primarily to a physical urge and to an intense curiosity about the experience of intercourse. Fairly often these latter youths instinctively avoid experimenting with the person they love and respect—they select instead someone with merely physical appeal.

I used to fear that if parents took the initiative in arranging for their teenage children to have specific instruction in the prevention of pregnancy, it would be taken as encouragement for early sexual experimentation and for casual, non-loving affairs. Now I'm convinced that the greater danger is of pregnancy caused by ignorance and irresponsibility. I believe that the parents must take the initiative. They must not only instruct their children, or arrange for instruction, but also reemphasize from time to time, especially if they expect their teens to engage in sexual activity, that *people who have intercourse must take serious responsibility for birth control on every single occasion,* out of consideration for the baby, for their parents, and for their present and future lives. At the same time, parents can speak about their own ideals, explaining that sex is as much spiritual as physical, that they, as do many young people, think it is better for young people to wait until they are confident that their love is deep and long-lasting before having sexual relations, and that delaying does not mean any lack of sexual power or normality.

684. How much modesty in the home? In less than a century Americans have made a full swing from the excessive modesty of the Victorian period to the partial nudity of bathing suits and to complete nudity in quite a few homes today. Most people agree (and I certainly do) that today's casual attitude is a lot healthier. Preschool teachers, children's psychiatrists and psychologists generally agree that it's wholesome for young children of both sexes to see each other undressed at times in the home, at the beach, and in the bathroom of a preschool.

However, there's also evidence that young children get upset by regularly seeing their parents naked, although they may not show it and may even keep their feelings hidden until they are adults. The main reason is that young children's feelings for their parents are so intense. A boy loves his mother much more than he loves any little girl. He feels much more rivalrous with his father and more in awe of him than he feels toward any boy. So the sight of his mother naked may be a little too stimulating, and the chance to compare himself unfavorably with his father every day may make him feel inadequate. This sense of inadequacy might stay with him long after he too has mature genitals. Sometimes a boy can be so envious he may feel like doing something violent to his dad. (Nudist fathers have told me about their three- and four-year-old sons making snatching gestures at the father's penis during morning shaving.) Then the boy feels guilty and fearful. A little girl who regularly sees her father nude also may be too stimulated.

I don't want to claim that all children are upset by parental nudity. Many may not be, especially if the parents are doing it out of a wholesome naturalness and not in a lascivious or showy way. Yet we don't always know the effect on the child, so I think it's a little wise for parents to keep reasonably covered and to keep children out of the bathroom while a parent is bathing or using the toilet. If you are uncomfortable, your children will sense it. This increases the emotional charge of the situation.

A parent is caught off guard occasionally when a curious child tries to come into the bathroom. The parent shouldn't then act shocked or angry. It's only necessary to say, "Will you wait outside until I get dressed?" After the age of six or seven, most children begin to want a little more privacy for themselves, at least at times, and I think it's good to respect this.

Music

685. Music is a part of everyone's life from the beginning. Lullabies are sung to infants everywhere, and it's clear that all cultures have their own native music. Making music seems to be a part of being human.

But there's more than meets the ear when it comes to the importance of music for children. In the 1990s scientists made a startling discovery: preschoolers who were given piano or singing lessons were better able to complete mazes, draw geometric figures, copy patterns, and these children may even have superior mathematical and reasoning abilities compared to children who had no musical training.

How is this possible? For one thing we know that music is processed primarily by the right side of the brain, which happens to be where spatial, mathematical, and reasoning ability also reside. Early in life, music may provide exercise for the right side of the brain, which later pays off in its better general functioning. This is another example of how brain growth and development are affected by early experiences.

The practical implications of these findings are as clear as they are fun: infants and children hear music from their earliest months. In infancy this can take the form of the parent singing lullabies at bedtime, singing songs while holding the baby, or playing audiotapes while she is in her crib. As your infant gets older you can engage in musical games, like "Itsy Bitsy Spider" or "Ring around the Rosie." Give her a toy piano or xylophone to bang on. Make sure that your day care or baby-sitter routinely includes singing and dancing as a regular part of the day.

Once your child is school age, you can consider school-based or private music lessons. I think this is always worth a try, but remember that ability to play music is a gift, and some children are naturally better musicians than others. Encourage your child to play whatever instrument she chooses, but if she decides she doesn't like it or doesn't want to practice, I wouldn't push too hard. Rather than turn music lessons into one more power struggle, I'd try dancing or singing experiences.

A good example of how young children learn to enjoy music at an early age is Suzuki violin lessons, where children learn to play in a group. The group spirit keeps their enthusiasm alive, whereas individual lessons require an inner determination to master a difficult challenge, which many young children lack.

The best way to have your child learn to appreciate music is to make it a part of your everyday life. Go to concerts together. Sing along with the car radio together. Dance at home whenever the spirit moves you. An appreciation of music is a gift you can give your child that will pay off, in more ways than one, for the rest of her life and offer her a lifetime of rewards.

Manners

Some call ours an uncivil society and if you look around you, you may agree. It seems to be increasingly acceptable for adults and children to use swearwords, to yell at each other for the slightest reason, to cut in front of others in line. The rule seems to be: "Every man for himself. Get ahead while you can."

I remember when people were more courteous, when the pace was slower, and when getting ahead was not the prime ambition. There are many reasons for this breakdown in civility, and now many parents seem to feel that it's old fashioned to care about manners and that children should be allowed to develop naturally. Some people have even accused me of being responsible for such "over-permissive" practices—an accusation I find ironic because I think I'm just the opposite. I think that teaching good manners should be part and parcel of all child rearing. Good manners give the right message to children, that there are certain acceptable ways to do things in our society, that showing courtesy toward others makes everyone happier and more loving.

686. Good manners come naturally. Teaching children to say "please" or "thank you" is really not the first step. The most important thing is to have them like people and feel good about their own worth as a person. If they don't, it will be hard to teach them even surface manners.

It is also important to avoid making them self-conscious with strangers. We're apt, especially with our first child, to introduce him right away to a new grown-up and make him say something. But when you do that to a two-year-old, you get him all embarrassed. He learns to feel uncomfortable as soon as he sees you greeting somebody, because he knows he's about to be put on the spot. It's much better in the first three or four years, when a child needs time to size a stranger up, to draw the newcomer's conversation away from him, not toward him. A child of three or four is likely to watch a stranger talking to his parent for a few minutes and then suddenly break into the conversation with a remark like "The water came out of the toilet all over the floor." This isn't Lord Chesterfield's kind of manners, but it's real manners because he feels like sharing a fascinating experience. If that spirit toward strangers keeps up, he'll learn how to be friendly in a more conventional way soon enough.

It is also important for children to grow up in a family whose members are always considerate of each other. Then they absorb kindness. They want to say thank you because the rest of the family say it and mean it. They enjoy shaking hands and saying please. The example of parents' politeness toward each other and toward the children is crucial.

I think it's critical to teach children how to be polite and considerate—it doesn't always come easily, especially with younger children. It's a useful exercise to think about what is important in your family. Just what kind of courtesy and manners would you like to see in your children? Then be sure to set the right example. If this is done in a friendly spirit, they will be proud to learn. More important, everybody likes children with sensibly good manners and resents those who are rude or thoughtless. So parents owe it to their children to make them likable. The appreciation the children receive then makes them friendlier in turn.

Duties and Chores

687. Let them enjoy their duties. How do children learn to perform various duties? By their very nature, they start out feeling that dressing themselves, brushing their teeth, sweeping, and putting things away are exciting and grown-up things to do. If their parents succeed in keeping on good terms with them as they grow older, they will enjoy going on errands, carrying packages, and raking the lawn, because they still want to have a part in important jobs and to please their mother and father. By age two they can be expected to go through the motions of picking up their playthings. By three they should have such small chores as helping to set the table or empty the wastebaskets, even though they don't save parents much work. By seven or eight they should be carrying out genuinely useful jobs each day. No one is able to bring up our children so that they will be cooperative all the time, but if we realize that children want to be helpful, we are less likely to make household tasks sound like unpleasant duties or to assign them when we're irritable.

Children can't be expected always to be responsible about their duties—even at fifteen years old. (Most adults lapse into irresponsibility at times, too.) They have to be reminded. If you can find the patience, try to make the reminder matter-of-fact and polite, as if you were speaking to an adult. It's the nagging, belittling tone that kills all pride in a job. It also helps a lot to assign children tasks that they can do in the company of other members of the family, whether it's dish-drying or lawn-mowing. Then the grown-upness of the task and the fun of helping will spur them on.

688. Dressing themselves. Between age of one and eighteen months, children begin to try to undress themselves. (They pull the toe of the sock directly toward their stomachs, which makes it stick.) By about two, they can do a pretty good job of stripping themselves. Now they try hard to put their clothes on, but they get all tangled up. It probably takes them another year to learn to put the easier garments on right, and another year still—until about four or five—to handle the trickier jobs, like laces and buttons.

This period from eighteen months to four years requires a lot of tact. If you don't let your child do the task he is able to, or if you interfere too much, it's apt to make him angry. If he never has a chance to learn at the age when it appeals to him, he may lose the desire. Yet if you don't help him at all, he'll never be dressed and may get frustrated at his own failure. You can help him tactfully in the jobs that are possible. Pull his socks part way off so that the rest is easy. Lay out the garment that he's going to want to put on. Interest him in the easier jobs while you do the hard ones. When he gets tangled up, don't insist on taking over but straighten his clothes out so that he can carry on. If he feels that you are with him and not against him, he is much more cooperative. It takes patience, though.

Another source of conflict concerns who is going to choose the child's outfit. Some parents never allow a child to choose. For some it is a daily struggle. One solution is to agree on certain activities when the child chooses, within reason (no party shoes at the beach), and certain special events (holidays, weddings) when the parent will have the final choice. I think one reason parents get so upset about clothes is that they feel they'll be judged by their child's appearance.

689. Putting things away. When your child is very young and you still expect her to pick up and put things away after she is through playing, you can do it as part of the play, with enthusiasm: "The square blocks go here, in big piles, and the long blocks go there. Over here let's pretend there's a garage, and all the cars go here to sleep at night." By the time she is four or five, she has fallen into the habit of putting things away and enjoying it. Many times she does it without any reminder. But if she still needs help at times, join in sociably.

If you say to a three-year-old, "Now put your things away," it sounds unpleasant. Even if she enjoys doing it, you are handing her a job that practically no three-year-old has the perseverance to carry through. Furthermore, she's still at a very balky stage. Cheerfully helping a child to put things away not only develops a good attitude in her but is easier for you than long arguments.

Having duties and chores at home is often a child's first introduction to responsible behavior. These tasks help set the stage for her understanding that there is more to life than just caring for herself, that part of life involves taking care of others. They also teach that tasks sometimes must be finished even if she's not in the mood to do so. And they teach her that she is a valued member of a larger group— the family in this case, society as a whole later. No matter how much she complains and balks, chores are a means of fostering her identification with the family and learning essential lessons for later life.

Reading

690. Promoting a love of reading. The world is flying by at a dizzying pace. Television hypnotizes children and sets expectations for a thirty-second attention span. Images emerge, only to be replaced by others. Our amusements are largely passive: we sit back and watch them unfold on a television, a computer screen, and the silver screen. Is there a price to be paid for this frenetic passivity? I believe there is.

One study showed that when television was introduced to a Canadian town, the children's reading levels declined. Unlike most amusements, reading is an activity requiring *active* participation. We must do the reading ourselves—

actively scan the letters, make sense of the words, and follow the thread of the story. Reading requires, above all, imagination—filling in the blanks of the story, inventing what the villain looks like, putting yourselves in the shoes of the heroine. It is this sort of active involvement that is lost through our mass media. Our children seem to be in peril of requiring ever more sensory stimulation. Does this stunt the development of an active inner life?

691. There are more reasons to foster reading in children. The ability to read is a prerequisite for school success. After all, even computer nerds must first learn to read the textbooks. Studies have shown that avid readers are better students. Using books to help children with their problems *(bibliotherapy)* seems to work better than using videos because it requires the child's participation in the process. In short, reading is one of the few lifelong pleasurable and educational activities that doesn't require electricity.

I suggest you begin to foster in your children a love of reading and the printed word from the start. By four to six months you can begin to read to your child. Get thick cardboard books so he can suck on them and drool all over them. Of course he isn't interested in the pictures or story at this time. But you are laying the groundwork, as he learns to enjoy sitting in your lap, being close to you and sharing this strange picture book in front of you.

As he gets older, say nine to twelve months, the content becomes more important. Book sharing is a wonderful way to promote language development. Bright and colorful pictures become the inspiration for new words. They help the child understand that pictures are representations of real objects. Use a lot of enthusiasm and expression as you point out the pictures!

Once your child is eighteen months old or so, the stories themselves will begin to have meaning. He may begin to see that there is a difference between words and pictures, and begin to wonder what these letters are all about. While he is not yet reading, he is learning to look at books and to enjoy the experience—the prerequisites for successful reading.

I'd suggest you read to your child as often as possible, once or twice a day at least. Additionally, reading a bedtime story or, for older children, a chapter a night of a long book is a wonderful bedtime ritual that involves closeness, warmth, and imagination.

As your child gets older, you can encourage his own reading—of quality comic books, children's magazines, and books. What is important is that a child be an avid reader. Of course you should encourage good books and fine children's literature, but it's important that he read something he likes. Children enjoy subscribing to magazines and receiving mail with their name on it.

692. A family reading hour is another way to promote reading. Your children then witness sustained reading by the adults and learn that such reading is a strong family value. Ask friends to give books as presents for birthdays. Keep magazines and books around the house. I'm concerned that reading not become a lost art, made obsolescent by the electronic media. The gift of reading is the gift of imagination, access to new worlds, and school success. Make sure it is a gift your child comes to appreciate and love.

Play and Outgoingness

693. Play is the work of children. When we see children building with blocks, pretending to be airplanes, learning to skip rope, we're apt to think, in our mixed-up adult way, that these are just amusements, quite different from serious occupations such as doing homework and holding a job. We are mixed up because most of us were taught in our own childhood that play was fun, that schoolwork was a duty, and that a job was a grind.

The baby passing a rattle from one hand to the other or learning to crawl downstairs, and the small child pushing a block along a crack on the floor, pretending it's a car, are both hard at work learning about the world. They are training themselves for useful work later, just as much as the high school student studying geometry. Children love their play not because it's easy but because it's hard. They are striving every hour of every day to graduate to more difficult achievements and to do what older children and grown-ups do.

The parents of a one-year-old boy complain that he gets bored with hollow blocks and wants only to fit pots and pans together. One reason is that he knows his parents "play with" pots and pans and not with blocks. That makes pots and pans more fun.

694. Simple toys are best. Children usually love simple toys best and play with them longest. This isn't because children are simple; it's because they have so much imagination. There are, for example, two very different kinds of toy trains: one is made of metal, painted to look real, and meant to run on a track; the other is made of plain, flat wooden blocks that link together easily. All that young children can do with the realistic train is push one car along the floor; it's too hard for them to put the cars on the track or hitch them together. They can't even put anything in the passenger coach until the top breaks off. After a while they get bored. The wooden block cars are different. Children can link a string of blocks together and admire the long train. Two make a trailer truck. They can pile small blocks on top, call it a freight train, and make deliveries. When they are bored with dry land, the blocks become separate boats or a string of barges with a tug. Children can go on like this forever.

Sometimes parents with little money to spend feel sad that they can't buy a shiny automobile for their children to pedal or a playhouse. But think what children can do with a large cardboard carton. By turns it can be a bed, a house, a truck, a tank, a fort, a dollhouse, and a garage.

Don't take this idea so seriously that you never get your children a really fine plaything. The time will come when she wants a tricycle or an express cart with all her heart, and you will want to buy one for her if you can. I only mean that simple things come first. Add the fancier toys as you can afford them and as you find out what your children really enjoy.

The baby, before he can use his hands, loves to watch bright-colored or black and white objects that hang on a string tied across the sides of his crib and that move slightly in the draft. In the last half of the first year, he loves objects that he can handle and rattle and chew, such as plastic toys (small rings on a big ring, for example). There's no paint to come off, and there's no danger from chips, as there is with thin celluloid toys.

From around age one to a year and a half, the child is fascinated with putting one thing into another and pushing or pulling it around. The block that runs on wheels and has holes for pegs is a favorite, but a plain box with a string is as good. As a matter of fact, pushing comes before pulling, and that's why the bell on wheels, pushed with a stick, is so popular. Hollow blocks won't interest a child for as long as pots, pans, strainers, and spoons will.

Soft dolls and woolly animals are loved by most children throughout the early years. Others see no sense in them.

As children get toward the age of two, they become more interested in copying. First, it's the immediate things that mother and father do, like sweeping, washing dishes, and shaving. As they grow beyond two, their imaginations become more creative. This is the period for dolls and doll furniture, trucks and cars, and above all, blocks. Blocks piled on top of each other are the Empire State Building; end to end they make a train. They can be laid out on the floor in the outline of a house or a boat to sit in, and so on indefinitely. A good-size bag of wooden blocks of different shapes is worth ten toys to any six-year-old.

695. Let children play at their own level. A grown-up playing with a child often is tempted to make the play too complicated. Parents who have bought their small child a doll with a whole wardrobe of clothes would like to dress the doll just right, beginning with the underclothes. But the little child may want to start with the red overcoat. A mother buys her small, sick daughter a box of crayons and a coloring book. The child picks up an orange crayon and rubs it back and forth across the page, not trying to keep within the lines, not worrying that she's using orange for sky and grass. It's hard for a parent not to say, "Oh, no, not like that. See, you do it this way." Or a father who has never had enough chance to play with trains produces a whole set for his three-year-old at Christmas. The father can't wait to get started. He fits the tracks together. But the child has grabbed one of the cars and has shot it across the room, smack into the wall. "No, no!" says Father. "You put the car on the track like this." The child gives the car a push along the track, and it falls off at the curve. "No, no," says Father. "You have to wind up the engine and let the engine pull the car." But the poor child hasn't the strength to wind up the engine or the skill to put the cars on the track, and he doesn't care about realism yet anyway. After the father has been impatient for fifteen minutes, the child develops a strong dislike for tin trains and an uncomfortable feeling of not being able to measure up to his father's expectations, and he wanders off to do something else.

Children become interested in dressing dolls properly, coloring carefully, and playing trains realistically at certain stages of development. You can't hurry them. When you try, you only make them feel incompetent. This does more harm than good. Your children love to have you play with them if you are willing to play at their level. Let them show you how. Help them if they ask you to. If you've bought them a toy that is too complicated, either let them misuse it in their own way or tactfully hide it until they're older.

696. Generosity can't be forced. When children first begin to play around each other, they are apt to grab things from each other without much ceremony. Small children who have a possession never give it up to be nice. They either hang on like grim death, perhaps whacking at the attacker, or they give it up in bewilderment. Parents, seeing these goings-on, are sometimes horrified. If your two-year-old always seems to be the grabber, it doesn't mean that she's going to be a bully. She's too young to have much feeling for others. Let her grab sometimes. If she's doing it constantly, it may help to let her play part of the time with slightly older children who stand up for their rights. If she always intimidates a certain child, better keep them separated for a while. If your child is hurting another or looks as if she were planning murder, pull her away in a matter-of-fact manner and get her interested in something else. It's better not to heap shame on her—that will only make her feel abandoned, and more aggressive. If the child goes on being unusually aggressive when she's three or older and doesn't seem to be learning anything about cooperative play, it's time to look into her adjustment at home. It's in these early, less serious problems that a family social agency or a child guidance clinic can help a parent and child most easily and most thoroughly.

If your child at two doesn't share her possessions, she is behaving normally for this age. She will come around to generosity very gradually, as her spirit grows up and as she learns to enjoy and love other children. If you make her give up her treasured cart whenever another child wants it, you only give her the feeling that the whole world is out to get her things away from her—not just the children but the grown-ups, too—and this makes her even more possessive. When a child is reaching the stage when she's beginning to enjoy playing with others, somewhere around three, you can help to make a game of sharing. "First Johnny has a turn pulling the cart and Catherine rides in it. Then Catherine pulls the cart and Johnny has a turn to ride in it." This makes sharing fun instead of an unpleasant duty.

COMMON BEHAVIOR PROBLEMS

Sibling Rivalry

697. There is bound to be some jealousy between siblings. If it is not severe, it probably helps children to grow up more tolerant, independent, and generous. In a general way, the more agreeably parents get along with each other, the less jealousy there is. When all the children are satisfied with the warm affection they receive, they have less reason to begrudge the attention their parents give to their brothers and sisters.

Basically, the thing that makes each child secure in the family is the feeling that his parents love him and accept him for who he is. If they constantly compare him unfavorably to another sibling, either openly or in their thoughts, he senses it, and feels unhappy and resentful toward the other children and the parent.

A harassed mother who is trying hard to treat her jealous children with perfect justice may say, "Now, Susie, here's a little red fire engine for you. And, Tommie, here is one exactly like it for you." Each child then, instead of being satisfied, suspiciously examines both toys to see if there is any difference between the two. It's as if the mother said, "I bought this for you so you wouldn't complain that I was favoring your brother," instead of implying "I bought this for you because I knew you'd like it."

The fewer comparisons, complimentary or uncomplimentary, between siblings the better. Saying to a child, "Why can't you be polite like your sister?" makes him resent his sister and the very idea of politeness. If you say to an adolescent girl, "Never mind if you don't have dates like your sister. You're much smarter than she is, and that's what counts" it belittles her unhappiness at not having dates and implies she should not be feeling what, in fact, she is feeling—a setup for further rivalry.

It generally works better if parents keep out of most of the fights between children who can stand up for themselves. When parents concentrate on pinning the blame, it leaves one warrior feeling more jealous. To a greater or lesser degree, children squabble because of jealousy because each would like to be favored by the parents. When parents are quick to take sides, in the sense of trying to decide who is right and who is wrong, it encourages the children to fight again soon. The fight then becomes a tournament to see who can win Mom's allegiance, at least this time. Each wants to win the parents' favor and see the other scolded.

If you do feel you have to break up a fight, to protect life and limb or to prevent rank injustice or to simply restore quiet, it's better simply to demand an end to the hostilities, refuse to listen to arguments, act disinterested in who is right and who is wrong (unless a flagrant foul has been committed), concentrate on what's to be done next, and let bygones be bygones. Sometimes you might suggest a compromise, other times distraction might save the day, and other times the children may need to be separated and sent to neutral, somewhat boring but very separate locations.

I feel that parents should not ignore very frequent quarrels. I would suggest that parents say to their children "Think how unhappy it makes everyone feel when you argue like that. It certainly makes me unhappy too."

698. Jealousy of a new baby. Imagine this scenario: your partner comes home one day with another woman and says to you: "Dear, I love you as much as I always have, but now this person is going to live with us too. By the way, she is also going to take up a lot of my time and attention because I'm crazy about her and she is more helpless and needy than you are anyway. Isn't that wonderful? Aren't you delighted?" How nice do you think *you* would be?

I heard of a child who ran to the door when the visiting nurse was leaving and called out, "You forgot to take your baby."

Rivalrous feelings are often more intense in a firstborn child, because he has been used to the spotlight and has had no competition. A later child has already learned to share his parents' attention since his birth. He can see that he's still just one of the children. This doesn't mean that second and third children don't have deep feelings of rivalry toward the next child. They do. More depends on how the parents handle the situation than whether the child is firstborn or not.

699. Jealousy can be helpful as well as hurtful. Jealousy and rivalry invoke strong emotions, even in grown-ups. They can be more disturbing to the very young child because he doesn't know how to deal with them. Though it can't be completely prevented, you can do a great deal to minimize it or even to convert it into positive feelings. If your child comes to realize that there is no reason to be so fearful of a rival, it strengthens his character so that he will be better able to cope with rivalry situations later in life, at work, and at home. What is important is not that the child feels jealous, which is normal, but just how he resolves the feeling. Putting his feelings into words helps him master them. You can say "I know you are angry and jealous but hurting the baby won't help." You can add, "And I love you too. I love you *and* the baby." If a two-year-old has slapped the baby, for example, you can guide his hand into a caress and say, "He loves you." The older child's feelings are a mixture; you can help the love to come out on top.

700. Preparing the way for the baby. It is good for a child to know ahead of time that he is going to have a baby brother or sister, if he is old enough to understand such an idea at all (around a year and a half), so that he can get used to the idea gradually, though that is still far from the reality. Of course, you have to gear your explanations to your child's developmental level. And no amount of explanation can really prepare him for the feeling of having a real live, demanding baby in the house. Your job is just to begin the dialogue about having a new brother or sister, where the baby will sleep, and what the sibling's role will be in his care, and to provide constant reassurance that you love him as much as ever. Don't overdo your enthusiasm or expect him to be enthusiastic about the baby.

The arrival of the baby should change an older child's life as little as possible, especially if he has been the only child up to that time. Emphasize the concrete things that will stay the same: you'll still have your same favorite toys; we'll still go to the same park to play; we'll still have our special treats, we'll still have our special time together.

It is better to make all possible changes several months ahead of time. If the older child isn't yet weaned, it will be easier for him if you do it now and not when he is feeling displaced by the new baby. If his room is to be given over to the baby, move him to his new room several months ahead, so that he feels that he is graduating because he is a big boy, not because the baby is pushing him out of his own place. The same applies to advancing to a big bed. If he is to go to preschool, he should start a couple of months before the baby arrives. Nothing sets a child's mind against preschool so much as the feeling that he is being banished to it by an interloper. But if he is already well established in preschool, he has a social life outside the home, which will tend to lessen his feelings of rivalry at home.

701. During labor and delivery. Some parents hope to decrease sibling rivalry by including the young child in the delivery itself. I disapprove because this may be much too disturbing for a young child and too hard for them to understand.

702. After the delivery, when the baby is cleaned up and everyone is nice and calm, the sibling should be shown the child. He should be encouraged to touch the baby, talk to her and help out in some simple task, like going to get a diaper and bringing it over. He should get the feeling that he is an integral part of this family unit and that his presence is welcomed. He should visit as much as he wants, but not be forced to if he doesn't.

703. When the mother brings the baby home. It's usually a hectic moment when the mother comes back from the hospital. She is tired and preoccupied. The father scurries about, being helpful. If the older child is there, he stands around feeling left out, thinking warily, "So this is the new baby!"

It may be better for the older child to be away on an excursion, if this can be arranged. An hour later, when the baby and the luggage are in their place and the mother is at last relaxing on the bed, is time enough for the child to come in. His mother can hug him and talk to him and give him her undivided attention. Since children appreciate concrete rewards, it's nice to bring a present home for the sibling. A baby doll of his own or a wonderful new toy help him not to feel abandoned. You don't have to keep asking him "So how do you like your new sister?" Let *him* bring up the subject of the baby when he is ready to; and don't be surprised if his comments are unenthusiastic or hostile.

It's tactful to play down the new baby in the early weeks. Don't act too excited about her. Don't gloat over her. Don't talk a lot about her. As far as is convenient, take care of her while the older one is not around. Fit in her bath and some of her feedings when he is outdoors or taking his nap. Many young children feel the greatest jealousy when they see the mother feeding the baby, especially at the breast. Give him a bottle or a turn at the breast, if he wishes. It's a little sad to see an older child trying a bottle out of envy of the baby. He thinks it's going to be heaven. But when he gets up his courage to take a suck, disappointment spreads over his face. It's just milk, after all, coming slowly, with a rubber taste. He may want a bottle off and on for a few weeks, but there's not much risk that he'll want to go on with it forever if the parents give it to him willingly and if they do other things to help him learn to deal with his jealousy. If he's around when you feed the baby, he should be allowed in freely. But if he is downstairs playing happily, don't attract his attention to what's going on. The goal is not to avoid rivalrous feelings altogether—that is impossible—but rather to minimize them in the first weeks, when the awful reality of the situation for the older sibling is beginning to sink in.

704. Other people play a part in jealousy, too. When a family member walks into the house, he should suppress the impulse to ask the child, "How's the baby today?" Better to act as if he has forgotten there is a baby, sit down, and pass the time of day. Later he can drift on to have a look at her when the older one is interested in something else. Grandparents who make a big fuss over the baby can be a problem, too. If the grandfather meets the older sibling in the front hall with a big package tied up in satin ribbon, and says, "Where's that darling baby sister of yours? I've brought her a present," the brother's joy at seeing his granddad turns to bitterness. If parents don't know a visitor well enough to coach her in how to act, they can keep a box of inexpensive presents on the shelf and produce one for the older child every time a visitor comes with a gift for the baby.

705. Playing with dolls may be a great solace to the older child, whether girl or boy, while the mother is caring for the baby. He wants to warm his doll's bottle just the way his mother does, and have reasonable facsimiles of the clothing and equipment that his mother uses. But doll play shouldn't take the place of having the child help care for the real baby; it should only supplement it.

706. Helping the child to feel more grown up at this time. A great majority of young children react to a baby's arrival by yearning to be a baby again, at least part of the time. This developmental regression is quite normal. They may, for example, lose ground in toilet training and begin to wet or soil themselves. They may lapse into baby talk and act helpless about doing things for themselves. I think parents are wise to humor the craving to be a baby at those moments when it is very strong. They can even good-naturedly carry the child up to his room and undress him, as a friendly game. Then he can see that he is not being denied these experiences, which he imagines are delightful but which may prove disappointing.

The drive to continue to grow and develop usually soon overtakes the desire to regress, as long as the temporary regressions are handled sympathetically and good-naturedly. For your part, you can help by not paying so much attention to these episodes of regression and by appealing, most of the time, to the side of him that wants to grow up. You can remind him of how big, strong, smart, or skillful he is, how much more he is able to do than the baby. I don't mean that you should be constantly giving him over-enthusiastic sales pitches, but that you should remember to hand him a sincere compliment whenever it is appropriate. And I'd avoid pushing him too hard to be a grown-up. After all, if you are constantly calling all the things that the child temporarily yearns to do "babyish" and all the things that he's temporarily reluctant to do "grown up," he can only conclude that he wants to be a baby for sure.

You'll notice that I'm not suggesting direct comparisons that imply that the parents definitely prefer the older child to the baby. To feel that he is favored may gratify a child temporarily, but in the long run he will feel insecure with parents who are partial because he feels that they might change their preference. The parents should, of course, let their love for the baby be evident. I'm only emphasizing the importance of giving the older child chances to feel proud of his maturity and to remember that there are lots of disadvantages to being a baby.

707. Turning rivalry into helpfulness. One of the ways in which a young child tries to get over the pain of having a younger rival is to act as if he himself is no longer competing in the same league as the baby. Instead, he becomes a third parent. Of course, when he's feeling very angry with the baby, he may happily act the role of the disapproving parent. But when he's feeling more secure, he can be the kind of parent you are, one who teaches the baby how to do things, gives him toys, wants to assist in feeding and bathing and clothing him, comforts him when he's miserable, and protects him from dangers. You can assist his role-playing by suggesting how he can help you at times when it wouldn't occur to him, and by showing real appreciation for his efforts. Sometimes it's not even pretend help: parents of twins, who are often desperate for assistance in caregiving, have told me they were amazed to find how much help they received from a child as young as three years with tasks like fetching a bath towel, a diaper, or a bottle from the refrigerator.

A small child almost always wants to hold the baby, and parents are apt to hesitate for fear he may drop her. But if the child sits on the floor (on a carpet or blanket) or in a large stuffed chair or in the middle of a bed, there's little risk, even if the baby is dropped.

In such ways the parents can help a child to actually transform resentful feelings into cooperativeness and genuine altruism. The stresses and strains of coping with a new sibling can be transformed into new skills in conflict resolution, cooperation and sharing. These are lessons that are hard won, that only children may have to learn much later in life. Perhaps learning to cope with the challenges of not being the only show in town is a lesson that is most valuable of all to later success.

708. Jealousy takes many forms. If a child picks up a large block and swats the baby with it, the mother knows well enough that it's jealousy. But another child is more polite. He simply observes the baby without much enthusiasm or comment. One child focuses all his resentment against his mother and grimly digs the ashes out of the fireplace and sprinkles them over the living room rug in a quiet business-like way. Another with a different makeup becomes mopey and dependent, loses his joy in the sandpile and his blocks, and follows his mother around, holding on to the hem of her skirt and sucking his thumb.

Occasionally you see a small child whose jealousy is turned inside out. He becomes preoccupied with the baby. When he sees a dog, all he can think of to say is, "Baby likes the dog." When he sees his friends riding trikes, he says,

"Baby has a tricycle, too." In this circumstance, some parents might say, "We found that we didn't have to worry about jealousy at all. Johnny is so fond of the new baby." It is fine when a child shows love for the baby, but this doesn't mean that jealousy isn't there. It may show up in indirect ways or only in special circumstances. He may hug the baby just a little too tight. Perhaps he's fond of her indoors but is rude when strangers admire her on the street. A child may show no rivalry for months until one day the baby creeps over to one of his toys and grabs it. Sometimes this change of feeling comes on the day the baby begins to walk.

A child usually feels a mixture of
love and jealousy of the baby.

Being overly solicitous of the baby is just another way of coping with the stresses, but at its root is the same cauldron of mixed feelings—both love *and* jealousy—that drive other children to regress or indulge in wrathful fits. It's wise to go on the assumption that there is always some jealousy and some affection, whether they both show on the surface or not. The job is not to ignore the jealousy or to try to forcibly suppress it or to make the child feel deeply ashamed about it, but to help the feelings of affection to come out on top.

709. How to handle different kinds of jealousy. When the child attacks the baby, a parent's natural impulse is to act shocked and to shame him. This doesn't work out well for two reasons. He dislikes the baby because he's afraid that his parents are going to love her instead of him. When they threaten not to love him any more, it makes him feel more worried and cruel inside. Shaming also may make him bottle up his feelings of jealousy. Jealousy does more harm to his spirit and lasts longer if it is suppressed than if it is allowed to stay out in the open.

As a parent in this situation, you have three jobs: to protect the baby, to show the older child that he is not permitted to put his mean feelings into action, and to reassure him that you still love him and that he is really a good boy. When you see him advancing on the baby with a grim look on his face and a weapon in his hand, obviously you must jump and grab him, tell him firmly that he can't hurt the baby. (Whenever he succeeds in being cruel, it makes him feel guilty and more upset inside.) But within this situation lies the opportunity to teach the child that his feelings are understandable and acceptable—it is the acting on those feelings that is not permitted. You can turn your grab into a hug and say, "I know how you feel sometimes, Johnny. You wish there weren't any baby around here for Mommy and Daddy to take care of. But don't you worry, we love you just the same." If he can realize at a moment like this that his parents accept his angry feelings (but not his angry actions) and still love him, it is the best proof that he doesn't need to worry.

As for the child who spreads the ashes around the living room, it's natural for you to feel exasperated and angry, and you will probably reprove him. But if you realize that he did it from a deep sense of despair and anxiety, you may later feel like reassuring him. Try to remember what might have happened that sent him over the edge.

710. The child who turns mopey in his jealousy, being of a more sensitive and introspective nature, needs affection, reassurance, and drawing out even more than the child who

*The jealous one must be restrained,
but he also needs reassurance.*

eases his feelings by being aggressive. With the child who doesn't dare show directly what's bothering him, it may actually help him to feel better if you can say understandingly, "I know that sometimes you can feel mad at the baby, and angry with me because I take care of her," and so on. If he doesn't respond after a while, consider hiring a temporary helper for the baby if you can afford one, and see if he can recover his old zest for life through more individual attention for a short while.

It is worthwhile consulting a children's psychiatrist or psychologist about the child who cannot seem to get over his jealousy, whether it takes the form of constantly misbehaving or moping or being obsessed with the baby. The therapist may be able to draw the jealousy to the surface so that the child can realize what's worrying him and get it off his chest.

If the jealousy comes out strongly only after the baby is old enough to begin grabbing the older child's toys, it may help a great deal to give him a room of his own, where he can feel that he and his toys and his buildings are safe from interference. If a separate room is out of the question, find a big chest or cupboard for his things, with a latch that the baby can't work. Not only does this protect his toys, but having a latch that only he can operate gives him a great sense of being important and in control.

711. Should he be urged or compelled to share his toys with the baby? I would never compel a young child to share with the new baby, much as I'd like him to *want* to. Try suggesting that he give the baby a plaything that he has outgrown. This may appeal to his pride in his relative maturity so he can demonstrate a generosity of spirit toward the baby that is not really there. But for generosity to have any meaning, it must come from inside—the person must feel secure, loving, and loved first. Forcing a child to share his possessions when he is feeling insecure and selfish only makes him feel more put upon and undervalued.

Generally speaking, jealousy of the baby is strongest in the child under five, because he is much more dependent on his parents and has fewer interests outside the family circle. The child of six or more is drawing away a little from his parents and building a position for himself among his friends and teachers. Being pushed out of the limelight at home doesn't hurt so much. It would be a mistake, though, to think that jealousy doesn't exist in the older child. He, too, needs consideration and visible reminders of love from parents, particularly in the beginning. The child who is unusually sensitive or who has not found his place in the outside world may need just as much protection as the average small child. Stepchildren whose relationships in the family might be shaky anyway may need extra help and reassurance. Even the adolescent girl, with her growing desire to be a woman, may be unconsciously envious of her mother's new parenthood or pregnancy. I heard one bitterly remark: "I thought my parents were beyond that sort of thing."

There's one caution that I'd like to add here that may sound contradictory. Conscientious parents sometimes worry so much about jealousy and try so hard to prevent it that they make the older child less secure rather than more so. They may reach the point where they feel positively guilty about having a new baby, feel ashamed to be caught paying any attention to her, and fall all over themselves trying to appease the older child. If a child finds that his parents are uneasy and apologetic toward him, it makes him uneasy, too. His parents' guilty behavior reinforces his own suspicion that there is dirty work afoot and inclines him to be more mean to both baby and parents. In other words, the parents should be as tactful as possible to the older child but should not be worried, apologetic, submissive, or lacking in self-respect.

712. Doesn't the new baby need some attention, too? We have certainly been thinking exclusively about the older child's jealousy of the baby and even talking about ignoring the baby at times for the sake of the older sibling. I've emphasized how much attention and affection new babies require. But in their early days and months, they mercifully sleep a good deal; the minutes of the day when they require attention are relatively few. This fits in well with the needs of the older child. It's in the early days and months that he will most need extra attention and demonstrations of affection. If this can be done early on, he gradually accustoms himself to the baby and loses his alarm by the time the baby needs a full share of the family's attention.

If the new baby has colic, or for some other reason needs lots of extra attention, the older child will need extra reassurance that his parents love him just as much as before. It may be helpful for the parents to divide their chores up to be sure that one parent is always available to the older child. He'll also need to be reassured that nothing he thought or did is responsible for the baby being sick. Remember that young children are very egocentric—that is, they think that everything that happens in the world is because of them.

Stranger Anxiety

713. Early stranger anxiety may be seen by five months in the doctor's office if the doctor gets too close too soon. The baby, lying on the examining table, stops looking around or playing with his hands, freezes, and watches the stranger intently, anxiously. Then his abdomen rises and falls with increasing rapidity, his chin begins to pucker, and he wails loudly and frantically. He may continue to cry inconsolably for fifteen minutes, still lying on his back. He is too young for evasive action.

By a year, stranger anxiety has a different picture compared to five to eight months. As the pediatrician approaches, the baby struggles to her feet on the examining table, trying to push herself off the table and into her mother's arms. Her mother pushes her back. The baby is yelling as loud as she can. Every once in a while she looks back over her shoulder, sees that the doctor is still there and resumes pushing and shrieking. Five minutes later she is acting as cheerful as if nothing had been bothering her, and in another ten minutes she may be playing with the doctor's equipment or even offering some of it to the doctor.

Separation Anxiety

714. If a mother goes away for a number of weeks, to care for *her* ailing mother for instance, her baby of six to eight months is likely to go into a depression, especially if the mother has been the only caretaker up to that time. The baby is visibly depressed, loses her appetite, is unresponsive to known and unknown people, is more often found to lie on her back just rolling her head from side to side, no longer tries to sit up or explore her environment.

At two to two and a half years of age, separation from the mother no longer produces depression. Instead, it results in dramatic, severe anxiety. If a mother or father is called out of town by an emergency or decides to take an all-day job without preparing the child for the transition to care by a sitter or at a day care center, the child may show no marked distress while the parent is away; she seems to like the sitter. In retrospect the child was too well behaved to be normal. But when the parent returns, all the pent-up anxiety breaks out into the open. The child rushes to cling to them. She cries out in alarm whenever her mother goes into the next room. She won't let the sitter do anything for her, won't let her come near, in fact is rude in repulsing her. At bedtime she clings to her mother or father with a grip of steel so that she can't be put in her crib. If her parent finally gets free and heads for the door, the child unhesitatingly scrambles over the side of the crib, though she has never dared do this before, and rushes after her mother or father. It's a truly heartrending picture of panic. If the parent succeeds in getting the child to stay in her crib, the baby may sit up all night.

In cases in which the mother has to be away for a number of days or the child is put in the hospital for several days, the child may "punish" her mother by refusing to recognize her when they are reunited. When she decides to recognize her mother again, she may scream at her in a rage or begin hitting her.

715. By the age of three years there is much less chance of panic because you can explain the new situation to the child with a fair chance that she will understand well enough to be reassured. But you can't be sure how she will react. There are insecure children, overly sensitive children, and children who have known only their parents may continue to resist being left at a day care center or with an unfamiliar sitter.

716. Even at five and six a few children will resist being left at kindergarten or first grade at the beginning of the term. There is less chance of this if there are older children in the family, for the youngest will have been talking for months about her desire to go to school like her siblings.

How much pressure should you put on the child of three to six years who resists going to school? I feel that a parent should be willing to stay in the classroom—in the background—for a few days while the child gets used to the teacher, the other children and the fascinating activities. But there should be no more than a week of this familiarizing— less if the child is willing. The experienced teacher has learned that the combination of a determined child and a very tenderhearted parent changes the situation: no longer is it a matter of separation anxiety; it is instead a power struggle which the child can always win by acting panicky.

It sometimes helps to have the father escort the reluctant child to school. In any case the child should not be deceived. She should be told that she has become friends with the teacher and the other children, so tomorrow mother will not be staying at school. The parent should say good bye once, cheerfully, and then leave.

Temper Tantrums

717. Almost all children have temper tantrums between one and three years. They've gotten a sense of their own desires and individuality. When they're thwarted they know it and feel angry. Yet they don't usually attack the parent who has interfered with them. Perhaps the grown-up is too important and too big. Also, their fighting instinct isn't very well developed yet.

When the feeling of fury boils up in them, they can't think of anything better to do than take it out on the floor and themselves. They flop down, yelling, and pound with their hands and feet and maybe the head.

A temper tantrum once in a while doesn't mean anything; a child is bound to be frustrated sometimes. A surprising number of tantrums are a result of fatigue or hunger, or of putting a child into a situation that exceeds his capabilities. (Most shopping mall tantrums fall into this category.) If the tantrum is of this sort, a parent can ignore the apparent cause and deal with the underlying problem: "You're tired and hungry, aren't you? Let's get you home and fed and to bed, and you'll feel a lot better."

Frequent tantrums are most often due to the fact that the parents haven't learned the knack of handling this behavior tactfully. (The child's stage of development is also a factor in temper tantrums. See Section 782.) If your child is having frequent temper tantrums ask yourself the following questions: Does she have plenty of chance to play freely outdoors? Are there things for her to push and pull and climb on there? Indoors, has she enough toys and household objects to play with, and is the house childproofed? Do you, without realizing it, arouse balkiness by telling her to come and get her shirt on instead of slipping it on without comment, or asking her if she wants to go to the bathroom instead of leading her there or bringing the potty to her? When you have to interrupt her play to get her indoors or to meals, do you frustrate her directly, or get her mind on something pleasant? When you see a storm brewing, do you meet it head-on, grimly, or do you distract her to something else?

718. You can't dodge all temper tantrums. Parents would be unnatural if they had that much patience and tact. When the storm breaks, try to take it casually and help to get it over. You certainly don't give in and meekly let the child have her way; otherwise she'd be throwing tantrums all the time on purpose. You don't argue with her, because she's in no mood to see the error of her ways. Getting angry yourself only forces her to keep up her end of the row. Give her a graceful way out. One child cools off quickest if the parents fade away and go about their own business matter-of-factly, as if they can't be bothered. Another with more determination and pride sticks to her yelling and thrashing for an hour unless her parents make a friendly gesture. They might pop in with a suggestion of something fun to do, and a hug to show they want to make up, as soon as the worst of the storm has passed.

It's embarrassing to have a child put on a tantrum on a busy sidewalk. Pick her up, with a grin if you can force it, and lug her off to a quiet spot where you can both cool off in private.

Swearing and Naughty Words

719. In three- and four-year-old children. Around four years of age, children may go through a phase of reveling in bathroom words. They cheerfully insult each other with expressions like "You great big poop," and "I'll flush you down the toilet," and think they are very witty and bold. You should consider this a normal development that usually soon passes. In my experience the young children who continue to delight in using naughty words are those whose parents are openly shocked and dismayed and who threaten dire consequences for continued use of bathroom language.

This often has the opposite of the intended effect. The child thinks to herself: "Hey, this is a pretty good way to stir things up. This is *fun!* This gives me power over my parents!" Her parents, in turn, become increasingly upset with her.

The easiest way to stop a young child from using naughty words is to simply ignore them. If the words float out into space and nothing comes back, the child is apt to lose interest.

720. In elementary school children. As they grow older, all children learn swearwords and "dirty" words from their friends. Long before they know what the words mean, they know that they are naughty. Being human, they repeat them to show that they are worldly-wise and not afraid to be a little bad. It's usually quite a shock to conscientious parents to hear these words coming from the mouths of their supposedly sweet innocents.

What's a good parent to do? As with the three- or four-year-old, it's better not to act horribly shocked. For timid children this has too strong an effect; it worries them, makes them afraid to be around children who use bad words. But most children who find they have shocked their parents are delighted, at least secretly. Some of them go on cussing endlessly at home, hoping to get the same rise. Others, stopped at home by threats, use their bad language elsewhere. The point is that when you show children that they have the power to scandalize the whole world, it's like handing them a full-size cannon and telling them, "'For goodness' sake, don't set it off." On the other hand, I don't think that you have to sit mute and just take it. You can just tell your child firmly that you and most people don't like to hear those words and you don't want them to use them. End of discussion.

721. Teenagers. Lastly, comes the cursing of some teenagers, who liberally interject curse words into many of their conversations. These expletives serve multiple purposes: to express disgust or contempt (a common feeling in many teens), to underline the importance of the topic, to discharge emotion, to show frank disregard for arbitrary and old-fashioned societal taboos. But cursing at this age primarily serves as a mark of belonging to one's peer group. It is reasonable for you to assert your wishes about them—no swearing at school, for example, no swearing in my presence, and no swearing in front of your little brother. You will lose any debate about whether swearing is good or bad, but your child already knows that some behaviors make you unhappy.

Messiness

722. Let them get dirty sometimes. Small children want to do a lot of things that get them dirty, and those things are good for children, too. They love to dig in earth and sand, wade in mud puddles, splash in water in the sink. They want to roll in the grass, and squeeze mud in their hands. When they have chances to do these delightful things, it enriches their spirit, makes them warmer people, just the way beautiful music or falling in love improves adults.

Small children who are always sternly warned against getting their clothes dirty or making a mess, and who take these warnings to heart, will become inhibited and mistrustful of the things they enjoy. If they become really timid about dirt, it makes them too cautious in other ways also, and keeps them from developing into the free, warm, life-loving people they were meant to be.

I don't mean to give the impression that you must always let your children make any kind of mess that strikes their fancy. But when you do have to stop them, don't try to scare them or disgust them; just substitute something else a little more practical. If they want to make mud pies when they have their Sunday clothes on, have them change into old clothes first. If they get hold of an old brush and want to paint the house, set them to work (with a pail of water for "paint") on the woodshed or the tiled floor of the bathroom.

Dawdling

If you ever have seen a parent trying to jump-start a dawdling child in the morning, you will vow that you will never get in that fix. The parent urges him, warns him, scolds him to get out of bed, to get washed, to get dressed, to eat his breakfast, to start for school.

723. The dawdling child wasn't born that way. He was made that way gradually, in most cases, by constant pushing:

"Hurry up and finish your lunch." "How many times do I have to tell you to get ready for bed?" It's easy to fall into the habit of prodding children, and this can build up an absentminded balkiness in them. Parents say they have to nag or the child won't get anywhere. It becomes a vicious circle, but the parent usually starts it, especially an impatient parent or one who doesn't leave enough time to allow for children's naturally slow pace.

In the early years, before a child is capable of carrying out directions, lead him through his various routines. As he gets old enough to want to take over responsibilities, step out of the picture as fast as you can. When he slips back and forgets, lead again. When he goes to school, let him think of it as *his* job to get there on time. It may be better to quietly allow him to be late to school once or twice, or to miss the bus and school altogether and find out for himself how sorry he feels. A child hates to miss things even more than his parent hates to have him miss them. That's the best spring to move him along.

You may have the impression that I think children should not be held to any obligation. On the contrary. I think they should sit down at the table when the meal is ready and get up in the morning at the proper time. I'm only making the point that if they are allowed to use their own initiative most of the time, are reminded in a matter-of-fact way when they've clearly failed to do something on their own, are not prodded unnecessarily in advance, and are not hurried all the time, they usually find strategies to overcome their slow-starting nature.

Whining

724. It's in the preschool and early school years that whining is most common. I want to talk about the special problem of the chronic, continual whiners who make themselves and their parents miserable. This is a pattern of excessive demandingness that takes weeks and months to become fully established and quite a while to overcome. (I'm speaking only of the habitual whining of the child who is physically well. There are other, less common cases where children whine because of chronic physical illness or acute

492

unhappiness following such events as their parents' divorce.)

The whiner's words may vary—"There's nothing to do," she keeps complaining on a rainy day, or "Why can't I stay up for this program?"—but the wheedling, whining, nagging tone is unmistakable. And it's the same request repeated again and again. Most of the requests are quite natural, in the sense that they are for things or activities that all children enjoy, but they are made repeatedly and in an unreasonable way.

Many children whine at only one parent, not both, although some are equal opportunity whiners. In this case, whining often expresses not simply a habit or a mood in a child but also an attitude toward, or a slightly disturbed relationship with, that parent. Often, too, a parent who has two or more children will tolerate whining in only one. I remember spending a day with a family in which the mother was a no-nonsense person with three of her four children. They were polite, cooperative, independent, cheerful individuals, but the five-year-old girl bugged her mother endlessly. She complained of boredom, hunger, thirst, and cold, when she herself could easily have found remedies for these small needs.

The mother would ignore her for a while. Then she'd suggest that the girl get what she wanted. But she'd say it in an indecisive or apologetic tone. She never got masterful, even after an hour of steady whining. Sometimes she would even begin to whine back to "quit the whining." The end result: a nonproductive, mewling duet.

In one sense, such whining is not a serious disturbance. But it's certainly a pain in the neck to the other members of the family and to their friends, and it can lead to a mountain of frustration in the parent who hears it most often.

725. Why do some parents tolerate whining? I believe that, unconsciously at least, some parents feel that the child has the right to keep making excessive demands, that the parents have to be submissive because they may be guilty of something—not giving the child what she needs, perhaps, or of not loving her enough. Extremely conscientious parents who were brought up with a lot of criticism from their own parents, and who as a result are easily made to feel inadequate, often begin child care with at least a mild sense of guilt about their lack of knowledge on the subject and with a fear that they'll do the wrong thing.

There are various reasons for parents to feel unconsciously guilty toward only one of their children. The parent may not have been fully ready for the pregnancy, may have resented the unborn child, may have gotten off on the wrong foot with a baby who, for example, was very fretful or demanding, or may be reminded of a family member who made the parent's life miserable in the past and aroused a great deal of both hostility and guilt, emotions which now determine that parent's behavior toward the child.

So it's often submissiveness or guilt that makes parents unable to draw the line and resist promptly, firmly, and matter-of-factly. That would stop the whining, because children always know when parents *really* mean no. But the parents of whiners usually can't be that definite. Instead of saying, "No, you cannot have a snack now, it's almost time for lunch," they say, "Well, maybe just a little snack." So the child makes a new demand: "Can I have a cookie for my snack?" The parent says, "Well, maybe, just one cookie," but the child has caught on by now, and with a gleam in her eye she grabs a big handful of cookies. Ever the opportunists, children are experts in perceiving and capitalizing on parental indecision.

726. There are definite, practical steps you can take, if your child is an habitual whiner. First you have to decide whether your attitude feeds the whining. You may be using some expression of evasiveness or hesitation or submissiveness or guilt, mixed with the inevitable irritability that comes from feeling victimized. This is the most difficult step, because parents are usually quite unaware of anything except their impatience and the child's constant demands. If you can't see any uncertainty in your behavior, try to think of other reasons your child feels it necessary to whine, and then ask yourself how you may be unwittingly reinforcing the whining—for example, by paying too much attention to it or by finally giving in to stop the onslaught.

When parents have a natural self-confidence about managing their children and are doing it effectively, they usually can show a friendly manner combined with clearness and firmness. The child is kept in a cooperative mood by the friendliness and the parent's certainty gives the child the explicit guidance she needs and wants. Confident parents don't engage in endless arguments with their child about the limits they've set. If allowed, children will keep this conversation going forever and probably outnegotiate the parent at every turn. State your case, set your limits, and end the conversation pleasantly but decisively.

727. Parents should make as many rules as necessary to cover all the usual pleas and then stick to them with determination and consistency. Bedtime is always to be at a certain hour; only certain television programs may be viewed; friends may be invited for a meal or an overnight only at a certain frequency. These are the family rules, etched in stone by benevolent dictators. There are just no arguments about them.

If your child whines that he has nothing to do, it's smarter not to be drawn into suggesting a variety of possible activities, which a child in this mood will scornfully and with relish shoot down, one by one. You can toss the responsibility back to the child, without getting bogged down in futile arguments, by saying, "Well, I've got a ton of work to do, but then I'm going to do some fun stuff afterward." In other words, "Follow my example: find things to do for yourself. Don't expect me to amuse you or argue with you."

It's right for children to be allowed to ask for something special occasionally. And it's right to give freely what they ask for, as long as you feel it is their due and is what you want to give. But learn to prevent their whining and your frustration by setting limits confidently and promptly, before their demands become incessant and petulant.

Biting

728. It's natural for babies around one year to take a bite out of their parent's cheek. Their teething makes them want to bite anyway, and when they feel tired they're even more in the mood for it.

I don't think it means much, either, when a child between one and two bites another child, whether it's in a friendly or angry spirit. Children at that age can't express their frustrations or desires in words, so their frustration or desire to dominate comes out in primitive ways, like biting. Additionally, they can't really put themselves in their victim's shoes; usually they don't even realize how much it hurts the other child.

A parent or other caregiver can say firmly, "That hurts! Be gentle," putting the child down briefly or removing him from the play group for a moment. The idea is simply to give him the message that this behavior makes you unhappy, even if he is too young to understand exactly why.

729. If biting is a problem between ages two and three, you have to decide if this is an isolated problem or not. Consider how often the biting occurs and how he is getting along otherwise. If he is tense or unhappy much of the time and keeps biting other children for no good reason, it's a sign that something is wrong. Perhaps he is being disciplined or restricted too much at home and is frantic and high-strung. Perhaps he has had too little chance to get used to other children and imagines them to be dangerous and threatening. Perhaps he is jealous of a baby at home and carries over the fear and resentment to all other small children, as if they were competitors, too. If biting is but one of many aggressive and worrisome behaviors, then it is only a symptom of a larger problem and it is that larger problem, rather than the biting, that should draw your attention.

Usually, however, biting comes out of the blue like a thunderbolt in an otherwise model citizen. In this case it is a normal developmental challenge and not a mark of some sort of psychological problem. Still, most parents of biters worry a lot, imagining that their sweet child may grow up to be a cruel adult. But biting is usually a temporary developmental challenge that even the gentlest of children go through.

730. If your child is a biter, there are a number of strategies that can help it to diminish. First, as always, you need to attempt to prevent the biting before it starts. Are there predictable times it occurs? If so, a little more adult supervision during those times is often useful. Is the child often frustrated because he is the least competent member of his play group or because your limit-setting is inconsistent? You may need to consider changing his daily routine. Also be sure to give him lots of positive attention when he is behaving well. (For some children, biting another child is the only time they receive a lot of attention!) If the child's frustration is obviously escalating, try redirecting his attention to another activity. If the child is old enough, you can discuss the problem at another time and ask him to help you think about how it hurts and what else he could do when he has the urge to bite.

If the biting has already occurred, you need to give him the firm message that it makes you unhappy and that you do not want him to do it again. Tell him not to do it again. Then sit with him for a few minutes while the message sinks in. Hold his hand or hug him firmly if he tries to go away. Avoid long lectures.

Some parents who have been bitten by an infant or a one-year-old ask if they should bite back. Parents should be able to control their child better by staying in charge as a friendly boss than by descending to the child's age level to battle with bites, slaps, or shouts. Besides, when you bite or slap a very young child, he's apt to keep it up, either as a fight or as a game or because he believes that if you are capable of such behavior, why shouldn't he be? The only thing you need to do is to keep from being bitten again by drawing back when he gets that gleam in his eye, showing him clearly that you don't like it and won't let it happen.

731. Biting usually abates and disappears by the age of three. At that time the child has learned to use words to express his desires or vent his frustrations. He also has a better ability to restrain his impulses. I'd be concerned if children this age continue to bite. Consult with your doctor, nurse practitioner, counselor, friend, or other parents with similar concerns.

Aggression

732. The development of aggression. Aggression is a part of the human condition. Anger as a discrete emotion emerges in the second six months of life. Our job as parents is to help our children find acceptable ways to express and deal with their aggression. The child's love of his parents and wish to be loved by them normally provides a strong motivation for the child to learn to cope with aggression. In the course of growing up, children are able to bring their aggressiveness more and more under control, provided their parents encourage this. One- to two-year-olds, when they're angry with another child, may bite the child's arm without hesitation. But by three or four they have already learned that physical aggression is not acceptable. However, they like to pretend to shoot a pretend bad guy. They may even pretend to shoot their mother or father, while grinning to assure them that the gun and the hostility aren't to be taken seriously. Also by this time they have words and can be encouraged to express their anger in words rather than actions.

In the six- to twelve-year-old period, children will play an earnest game of war, but it will have lots of rules. There may be arguments and roughhousing, but real fights are relatively infrequent. At this age children usually don't shoot at their mother or father, even in fun. It's not that the parents have become stricter; the children's own conscience has. They say, "Step on a crack, break your mother's back," which means that even the thought of wishing harm to their parents now makes them uncomfortable.

In adolescence, aggressive feelings become much stronger, but by then most children are able to channel them into athletics and other competitions or into kidding their pals.

733. What about playing with guns and war toys? Is gun play good or bad for children? For many years I emphasized its harmlessness. When thoughtful parents expressed doubt about letting their children have pistols and other warlike toys, because they didn't want to encourage them in the slightest degree to become delinquents or militarists, I would explain how little connection there was. I'd explain that playing at war is a natural step in the disciplining of the aggression of young children; that most clergymen and pacifists probably did the same thing; that an idealistic parent doesn't really need to worry about producing a scoundrel. I explained that the aggressive delinquent was not distorted in personality by being allowed to play bandit at five or ten but was neglected and abused in his first couple of years and lacked a loving relationship when his character was beginning to take shape; that as a result he was doomed before he had any toys worthy of the name.

But nowadays I'd give parents much more encouragement in their inclination to guide their child away from violence. A number of occurrences convinced me of the importance of this.

734. Aggression in our society. One of the first things that made me change my mind was an observation of an experienced nursery school teacher. Her children were crudely bopping each other much more than previously, without provocation. When she remonstrated with them, they would protest, "But that's what the Three Stooges do." (This was a children's TV program made from old movie "shorts," full of violence and buffoonery, which had recently been introduced and which immediately became very popular.) This attitude of the children showed me that watching violence can lower a child's standards of behavior. Recent psychological experiments have shown that watching brutality on film stimulates cruelty in adults, too.

What further shocked me into reconsidering my point of view was the assassination of President Kennedy and the fact that some schoolchildren cheered when they heard about this. I didn't blame the children so much as I blamed the kind of parents who will say about a president they dislike, "I'd shoot him if I got the chance!"

These incidents made me think of other evidence that Americans have often been tolerant of harshness, lawlessness, and violence. We were ruthless in dealing with the Indians. In some frontier areas we slipped into the tradition of vigilante justice. We were hard on the later waves of immigrants. At times we've denied justice to groups with certain religious or political views. We have crime rates way above those of other, comparable nations. A great many of our adults and children have been endlessly fascinated with dramas of western violence and with brutal crime stories in movies and on television. We have had a shameful history of racist lynchings and murders, as well as regular abuse and humiliation. Infants and small children are brought to hospitals with severe injuries caused by gross parental brutality.

Of course, some of these phenomena are characteristic of only a small percentage of the population. Even those that apply to a majority of people don't necessarily mean that we Americans on the average have more aggressiveness inside us than do the people of other nations. I think rather that the aggressiveness we have is less controlled, from childhood on.

In order to have a more stable and civilized national life, we should bring up the next generation of Americans with a greater respect for law and for other people's rights and sensibilities.

735. There are many ways in which we could and should teach these attitudes of respect. One simple opportunity we could utilize in the first half of childhood is to show our disapproval of lawlessness and violence in television programs and in children's gun play.

I also believe that the survival of the world now depends on a much greater awareness of the need to avoid war and to actively seek peaceful agreements. We owe it to our children to prepare them very deliberately for this awesome responsibility. But I see little evidence that this is being done now.

When we let people grow up feeling that cruelty is all right provided they know it is make-believe, provided they sufficiently disapprove of certain individuals or groups, or provided the cruelty is in the service of their country (whether the country is right or wrong), we make it easier for them to go berserk when the provocation comes.

But can we actually deprive American children of their toy guns or of watching their favorite western or crime programs? I think we should. I believe that parents should firmly stop children's war play and any other kind of play that degenerates into deliberate cruelty or meanness. I don't mean the parents should interfere in every little quarrel or tussle, but if I had a three- or four-year-old son who asked me to buy him a gun, I'd tell him, with a friendly smile, not a scowl, "I don't want to give you a gun for even pretend shooting because there is too much meanness and killing in the world, and we must all learn how to get along in a friendly way together." Then I'd ask him if he didn't want some other present instead.

If I saw him soon afterward using a stick for a pistol in order to join a gang of children who were merrily going "bang-bang" at each other, I wouldn't rush out to remind him of my views. I'd let him have the fun of participating, as long as there was no cruelty. If his uncle gave him a pistol or a soldier's helmet for his birthday, I myself wouldn't have the nerve to take it away from him. If when he was seven or eight he decided he wanted to spend his own money for battle equipment, I wouldn't forbid him. I'd remind him that I myself would not buy war toys or give them as presents but that from now on he would be playing more and more away from home and making more of his own decisions; he can make this decision for himself. I wouldn't give this talk in such a disapproving manner that he wouldn't dare decide against my policy. I would feel I'd made my point and that he had been inwardly influenced by my viewpoint as much as I could influence him. Even if he should buy weapons then, he would be likely to end up—in adolescence and adulthood—as thoughtful about the problems of peace as if I'd prohibited his buying them, perhaps more so.

One reason I keep backing away from a flat prohibition is that it would have its heaviest effect on the individuals who need it least. If all the parents of America became convinced and agreed on a toy-weapons ban on the first of next month, this would be ideal from my point of view. But this isn't going to happen for a long time, unless perhaps terrorists set off a nuclear bomb and shock the world into banning all weapons, real and pretend.

A small percentage of parents—those who are most thoughtful and conscientious—will want to dissuade their children from playing with war toys, but their children are most apt to be sensitive and responsible. So I think it's carrying the issue unnecessarily far for those of us who are particularly concerned about peace and kindliness to insist that our young children demonstrate a total commitment to our cause while all their friends are gun toters. (It might be practical in a neighborhood where a majority of parents had the same conviction.) The main ideal is for children to grow up with a fond attitude toward all humanity. That will come about basically from the general atmosphere of our families. It will be strengthened by the attitude that we teach specifically toward other nations and groups. The elimination of war play would have some additional influence, but not as much as the two factors above.

Hyperactivity

736. What is hyperactivity? If you ask ten different professionals, you will probably get ten different answers. There are two good reasons for that. First, we don't really know what causes ADHD (attention deficit hyperactivity disorder), although there are lots of theories. Most believe that children with true ADHD have a subtle difference in the chemistry or "wiring" of their brain that makes it hard for them to pay attention or restrain their impulses. (By the way, the theory that sugar causes overactivity has been pretty well discredited. There is also very little evidence to blame ADHD on anything in the child's diet.) Second, there is no special test for ADHD. The diagnosis is based solely on the child's behavior, and opinions about that behavior can differ.

We do think that most children with ADHD are born with it, and we feel that if it hasn't shown up by age seven, the child doesn't have it.

737. What do we know about ADHD? First, about one elementary school child in twenty-five is believed to have ADHD. Second, many more boys than girls are affected. Third, a child with true ADHD is impulsive, very active and fidgety, and has a shorter attention span than most other children his age. He may also have a hot temper, be emotionally immature, and have a difficult time making friends. And fourth, it is estimated that about 40 percent of children with ADHD also have a learning disability (see Sections 871–874). All of these traits conspire to make it difficult for a child with ADHD to do well in school and at home and to make friends.

Probably you know at least one child who fits this description, maybe even your own. How can you tell if your child has ADHD? Probably, you can't for sure. The best thing to do is to talk to your child's doctor or nurse practitioner about your concerns. She may be able to sort out the reasons for the behaviors, or she may refer the child for an evaluation by an experienced professional, such as a child psychiatrist, psychologist, or developmental pediatrician. Typically, the professional will spend at least a few hours with the child. She will also talk to or send questionnaires to all of the important adults in the child's life (including his parents and teachers). This is especially important because children with "true" ADHD show behavioral problems almost everywhere, especially in school and other places where they are expected to pay attention, follow the rules and generally behave themselves. Even with the most careful evaluation, however, it can be very difficult to tell if a child is just very active but normal, if he is overactive due to anxiety or stress, or if he indeed has ADHD.

738. There are many kinds of treatment available to children with ADHD. Most children benefit by more than one of them. It's a mistake, for example, just to treat the child with drugs without trying to change the way parents and teachers deal with his challenging behavior.

Medications—for example, methylphenidate (Ritalin), dextroamphetamine (Dexedrine) and pemoline (Cylert)—are generally used if a child truly has ADHD. These medications are *not* tranquilizers; they are, in fact, stimulants and seem to work by stimulating the parts of the brain that control attention and the child's ability to restrain his impulses. Medications have been found to be effective in about three out of four children. Experience has also shown that, when used correctly, they are relatively safe with few bad side effects.

There has, however, been an alarming increase in the use of these medications by children in the past ten years. Professionals argue whether there are more children than ever with ADHD or whether we are just too quick to throw drugs at any child with behavior problems. My own view is that medications for ADHD are both overused *and* under-used. It is true that some professionals try to solve *all* behavior problems with medications: if a child is too active, well, then give him drugs. On the one hand, this is clearly simplistic and wrong-headed. On the other hand, there is no question that medications have been of enormous benefit to many children with ADHD. An unwarranted fear of medications for ADHD is as bad as an overreliance on them.

If you have a child with ADHD (or one who at least sometimes acts as if he does), you might want to join an ADHD parent group in your community (see the Guide to Child and Family Resources, page 859). Many parents find it helpful to share their experiences and feelings with others who are in the same boat. Children with ADHD are difficult to raise for anyone. Often it is other parents who offer the best advice and support on how to handle a child with ADHD. You might also check out some of the excellent books for parents on ADHD at your local bookstore.

In the long run, children with ADHD can do very well. As they mature, most learn to cope with their attention problems and impulsiveness. Although we think that a person has ADHD for their entire life, its manifestations change over time. The overactivity tends to subside, for example, leaving feelings of restlessness in its place. Most adults with ADHD find the kind of job that plays to their strengths and minimizes their shortcomings. I'd hate to think of someone with ADHD working as an air traffic controller! The adults who seem not to do so well with their ADHD tend to be those who were aggressive as children and those who lack self-esteem.

I'd especially like to advise you to keep a close eye on your child's self-esteem (see Sections 642–643). A child with ADHD has a hard time of it through no fault of his

504

own and through no fault of his parents: he was born with this difference in his nature. He may well have a hard time making friends, he gets into trouble all the time, adults are always angry at him for one thing or another—it's easy to see why he might grow up thinking that he's not a very good or competent person.

Sometimes parents feed into a negative self-image by focusing on the bad behavior and ignoring the good behavior. Find something that your child is good at, especially if it takes advantage of his naturally high energy level. Be sure he understands that it is his behavior that you object to, not who he is as a person.

With early diagnosis, the use of different treatments such as medications, behavior modification techniques, counseling around issues of low self-esteem, close attention to academic success, recognition of coexistent learning disabilities or other behavioral disorders, and special therapies for any and all of these, children with ADHD can do very well.

COMMON DEVELOPMENTAL CHALLENGES

Toilet Training

739. Parental readiness. Everyone talks about the child's readiness to be trained, but parents have to be ready too. Many feel anxious about the whole business. I think the anxiety is partly based on the fact that we live in a society that teaches us to be ashamed of and disgusted by our bowel and bladder functions.

Anxiety can also come from an internal pressure to have your child succeed with toilet training the "right" way at the "right" time. And for working parents, there's often an external pressure to get toilet training done as early as possible so as to ease the burden on a full-time baby-sitter or to get a toddler into a day-care center that doesn't accept children in diapers.

Some parents have misinterpreted "don't push" and "don't force" as "don't train." That is *not* what I am saying here. Don't be intimidated by the child's first resistance. There is a delicate balance between training and not pushing. To train without pushing is the ideal way.

As the first step toward toilet training your child, you should sort out your own mixed feelings. If you have negative feelings, try to find a way to use at least a neutral, interested tone of voice when, for example, you're changing your two-year-old's diaper and she's really made a big mess. Instead of comments about how dirty and smelly it is, you need to say something like "Oh, my, what a big poop you made today! If you made it in your potty seat, you wouldn't have to lie still all this time while I clean you up and change you. Next time you have to go, you can tell me, and I'll help you use your special potty seat."

Once you are familiar with your own feelings, you'll be more ready for your child's toilet training. As you begin to recognize your child's signs of readiness, you'll be in the best position to help her accomplish this important task.

740. Learning to use the toilet is an important step. The start of toilet training normally overlaps with young children's newly found sense of themselves as separate, independent beings. At this age they want more independence and control over everything they do. They are just learning what's theirs and that they can decide whether to keep it or give it away. They are naturally fascinated by what comes out of them and pleased by their own growing mastery over when it comes out and where it goes.

They gain control of two orifices of the body that previously functioned automatically, and this gives them a lot of pride. In fact, they're so proud at first that they try to perform every few minutes. They are accepting the first serious responsibility assigned to them by their parents. Successful cooperation on this project will give parents and child a new confidence in each other. And the child who was previously a lighthearted messer with food and BM now begins to take satisfaction in cleanliness.

You may think of this shift as primarily meaning no more soiled diapers. That's important, all right. But the preference for cleanliness that a child gains at around two years means a lot more than that. It's actually the foundation for a lifelong preference for unsticky hands, for clean clothes, for a neat home, for an orderly way of doing business. It's from their toilet training that children get some of their feeling that one way of doing things is right and another way is not. This helps them to develop a sense of responsibility and to become systematic people. This is how toilet training plays a part in the formation of a child's character and in building the basic trust between child and parents. So if you take advantage of your child's natural desire to become more grown-up and self-sufficient, toilet training will be a lot easier for both of you.

Bowel Control

741. The first year. In the first year a baby shows very little awareness of bowel function and doesn't participate voluntarily in moving her bowels. When her rectum becomes sufficiently full, and particularly after a meal when the muscular activity of the stomach stimulates the entire intestinal tract, the movement presses against the inner valve of the anus and causes it to open somewhat. This stimulates a squeezing, pushing-down action of the abdominal muscles. The baby, in other words, does not decide to push the way an older child or adult does, but she pushes automatically.

During the first year there is a small amount of readiness for partial training in some babies in the sense that they always have their first movement of the day within five or ten minutes after breakfast. If parents wish to do so, they can sit such babies on the potty seat every day just in time to "catch" the movement. After a few weeks of this, the baby's nervous system becomes conditioned to push as soon as she feels the toilet seat under her. This is a small degree of *training,* but it's not *learning* because the baby is not really conscious of the bowel movement or of what she herself is doing. She's not cooperating knowingly. And some babies who have been "caught" early in this way are more apt to rebel later through prolonged soiling or bed-wetting. I don't recommend any training efforts in the first year.

742. Between twelve and eighteen months. At this age children gradually become conscious of when a bowel movement occurs. They may pause in what they are doing or change facial expression momentarily, though they are nowhere near ready to notify a parent.

They are likely, as they gaze fondly at their BM in their diaper or lying on the floor or accidentally caught in the potty, to develop distinctly possessive feelings for it. They are proud of it as a fascinating personal creation. They may sniff the smell appreciatively, as they have been taught to

508

sniff a flower. Such positive pride in the movement, including its smell, and the enjoyment of messing in it if the opportunity arises are characteristic reactions of this period and can, in the latter half of the second year, be changed relatively easily into a preference for being clean. I don't think it's wise or necessary to give a child a strong disgust for his bowel movements or for any other body function. But the readiness for a preference for cleanliness is part of what helps a child to become trained and stay trained.

One aspect of this possessiveness, as those parents have discovered who have succeeded in "catching" movements early in the second year, is a reluctance about giving up the BM to the pot and to the parent. Another aspect is anxiety about seeing the BM flushed away in the toilet; to some small children this is as disturbing as if they saw their arm being sucked down the toilet.

743. Indirect signs of readiness. Beginning in the second year other aspects of readiness appear that we don't ordinarily associate with toilet training. Children now feel an impulse to give presents, and take great satisfaction from this—though they usually want them right back again. Their contradictory feelings may show in the way they hold out one of their toys to a visitor but refuse to let go of it.

It's at this age that children become fascinated with putting things in containers and watching them disappear and reappear.

Gradually they want to imitate more and more of the activities of their parents and older brothers and sisters. This drive can play an important part in training.

They take great pride in learning any skill that they can carry out independently, and they enjoy being praised for their accomplishment.

744. Balking. Children who have taken to the idea of using the potty seat early in the second year often suddenly change their pattern. They sit down willingly but never have a movement as long as they sit there. Right after getting up, they move their bowels in a corner of the room or in their pants. Parents sometimes say, "I think my child has forgot-

ten what it's all about." I don't believe children forget that
easily. I think that their possessive feeling about the movement has become temporarily stronger and that they are
simply unwilling to give it up. Early in the second year they
have an increasing urge to do everything for themselves, in
their own way, and toileting may seem too much like the
parents' scheme. So they hold the movement in, at least
until they can get away from the seat, which symbolizes
giving it up and giving in.

If this resistance persists for many weeks children may
hold back not only when on the seat but for the rest of the
day if they can manage it. This is a psychological type of
constipation.

Balking is more apt to occur in the first half of the second
year than in the second half. This is a signal for you to wait
at least until about the middle of the year to start training,
and to let the child feel that it is he who has decided to
control his bowel and bladder, rather than that he is giving
in to parental demands.

745. Between eighteen and twenty-four months. Around
eighteen to twenty-four months, a majority of children
show more definite signs of readiness.

They are learning about where objects go when they are
out of sight—do they disappear forever or do they stay
where you put them even if they are not directly visible?
This more sophisticated way of viewing the world (before it
was out of sight, out of mind!) is another element in
readiness to understand toilet training. When they get
interested in putting away their toys and clothes, they've
gained the further idea that certain things belong in certain
places.

They are now recognizing that their parents are different
from them, and this growing separation fuels a desire to
please the parents and fulfill their expectations. At the same
time they take great pride in learning any skill that they can
carry out independently, and they enjoy being praised for
their accomplishments.

Body awareness is increasing so that they have a greater
sense of when a movement is coming or being passed. They

may stop playing for a few seconds, or they may act a bit uncomfortable afterward. They may make some kind of sign or sound to the parent to indicate that the diaper is soiled, as if they'd like to be cleaned up. This notification is more likely to appear if the parent gently reminds the child to tell her if he has had a BM. Usually it takes a little longer, with some encouragement from the parent, before children will become sufficiently aware of an impending BM to be able to notify in time to be helped. This bodily awareness is another prerequisite for independent toilet learning and the ability to control these orifices.

In addition, children's ability to move around is now much improved. They can walk and climb almost anywhere, and certainly can independently get onto the potty chair. They are able to pull their diaper or pants down by themselves.

Last, but not least, they have developed the intellectual ability to understand what their parents expect of them and a desire to cooperate so they can be "big" like their older brother or sister and their mother and father.

Taken together, a child who has arrived at these developmental milestones is probably ready to begin the fine art of bowel and bladder control.

746. A philosophy of training. Dr. T. Berry Brazelton, a pediatrician who has long been interested in toilet training, has worked out the following philosophy and method, which I'll summarize. He has advised this method for thousands of children in his practice, and 80 percent of them achieved success at bowel and bladder training— abruptly and simultaneously—at an average age of twenty-eight months. They gained night control at an average age of three years. These are excellent results by any standards.

Dr. Brazelton's basic principle is that children should become trained of their own free will—without force, coercion, or criticism. In this way, he believes, they can be trained most easily, and there will also be the least likelihood of later soiling and bed-wetting problems. (Of his cases, only $1\frac{1}{2}$ percent were still bed-wetting at five years of age. This contrasts with 15 percent of adults in one Europe-

an country noted for its vigorous toilet-training philosophy.) He advises parents to use tactful suggestions and
flattery but no disapproval for failure. No pressure to sit
down on the seat if the child has any disinclination. No
detention on the seat—even for a second—when the child
wants to get up. The children decide of their own free will to
gain control when they feel able, because they want to be
grown-up. This method requires that the parents trust in
their children's desire to mature and that they be willing to
wait without impatience.

But remember, this does not imply an absence of expectation on the parents' part. Once a decision to train the child
is made, at about age two, the parents' attitude is always the
same—a consistent, kind expectation that the child will use
the toilet as older children and adults do. This is expressed
as mild praise when the child is successful and encouragement, not anger or criticism, when he chooses not to
comply.

747. The adult toilet or a potty seat? A few babies become
accustomed from the start to a baby toilet seat attached to
the adult toilet seat. If such an arrangement is used, it's
preferable to use one that has an attached footrest so that
the child can feel more steady. The parents should also get a
steady footstool, or build a sturdy box to serve as a step, so
that the child can learn to climb up on the seat alone.

I myself think it's preferable to use a child's small seat
over a potty, close to the floor, up to two and a half years.
Children feel friendlier toward a small piece of furniture
that is their own and on which they can sit down by
themselves. Their feet can stay on the floor, and there is no
height to make them feel insecure.

For boys, don't use the urine guard that comes with the
seat. It too often hurts a boy when he is getting on or off.
Then he won't use the seat again.

748. The first stage. The first step in training should *not* be
to take the child's diaper off and sit him on the seat. That's
too strange and sudden. It's much better to let him get used
to the seat for at least a few weeks, as an interesting piece of

furniture to sit on with all clothes on, rather than as a contraption parents will use to take his BMs away.

749. The second stage. When your child has accepted the seat, you can suggest casually that he use it with the lid up for BMs, the way his parents use the toilet seat. (Children at this age are easily alarmed by being hurried or pushed into an unfamiliar situation.) You can show how you sit on the grown-up toilet seat.

Let the child get up and leave the seat immediately if desired. The experience will be helpful, no matter how brief it is. The child should think of sitting on the seat not in any sense as an imprisonment but as a voluntary ritual carried out with pride.

You can use the same approach with a baby's toilet seat that attaches to the adult toilet, though it is not as appealing as a small seat on the floor.

If the child has not been willing to sit down without diapers, allow a week or so before suggesting it again.

You can explain again how Mommy and Daddy use their toilet that way, and perhaps one or two of the child's older acquaintances. It often helps to have your child watch a friend perform. (If he has an older brother or sister he will probably have watched and learned already.)

After the idea of depositing the BM or urine in the potty has been discussed a couple of times, you can take off the child's diaper at a time when a movement is most likely, lead him to the seat, and suggest that he try it. Don't push him if he doesn't want to. Try another time or another day. Some day, when the movement does go into the potty, this will help him to understand and cooperate.

In addition, right after a movement in the diaper, take it off, lead the child to the seat, and show him the movement while you put it in the potty. Explain again that Mommy and Daddy sit on their seat to have their BMs, that he has his own seat, and that someday he will do his BM in it—just like them.

If you have had no success in catching a movement or a urination, drop the business again for a few weeks and then try gently again—no urging, no reproaching.

750. Flushing. At this stage don't flush the BM from the diaper down the toilet until the child has lost interest and gone on to something else. Most one- to two-year-olds are fascinated with the flushing at first and want to do it themselves. But later some of them become frightened by the violent way the water flushes the movement away, and then they are afraid to sit on the seat. They probably fear that they might fall in and be swirled away in a watery rush. Until two and a half years, I'd empty the potty and flush the toilet after the child has left the room.

751. When the child takes an interest. If the child begins to be interested and cooperative, take him to the seat two or three times a day, especially if he gives the slightest signal of readiness to urinate or have a BM. If he allows himself to be "caught," for example, after a meal, or when he has been dry for a couple of hours, praise him for being so grown-up—"just like Daddy" or Mommy, brother, sister, or admired friend—but don't overdo it. At this age a child doesn't like to be too compliant.

752. Going by themselves. When you're sure your child is ready for the next step—going by himself—let him play for periods without any clothes on from the waist down. Put the potty seat nearby, indoors or out, explaining that this is so that he can go all by himself. If he is not resistant, you can remind him every hour or so that he may want to go all by himself. If he gets bored or resistant or has an accident, put him back in diapers and wait.

753. Fear of painfully hard movements. Sometimes a child gradually or suddenly gets into a spell of unusually hard movements that are painful to pass. Collections of small, hard pellets—the result of what is sometimes called spastic constipation—are rarely painful. It's usually the hard movement in one large piece, with a wide diameter, that is to blame.

As it is passed, this movement may tear a tiny slit, or fissure, in the edge of the stretched anus, which may bleed a little. When a fissure has occurred, it is likely to be stretched open again each time another movement is passed. This is quite painful, and the fissure may thus be kept from healing for many weeks. You can easily see how a child who has once been hurt may dread a repetition and fight against toileting again. It may become a vicious circle, because if the child succeeds in holding back the movement for several days, it is more likely to be hard.

It's important to notify the doctor promptly if a child begins to have hard movements, particularly in this sensitive second year, so that the doctor can consider a change in the diet or a medication to keep them soft. Adding prunes or prune juice to the diet every day, if the child likes them, usually works. I've had success with a slurry of bran, applesauce, and prune juice. Children love it, and it moves things along very nicely. More whole grain wheat and oats in cereal, bread, and crackers may help some. It may also help to have the child sit cross-legged in warm water in the bathtub a couple of times a day for ten to fifteen minutes. An ointment containing a mixture of petroleum jelly and lanolin can be gently dabbed onto the anal area as often as necessary.

It helps to keep reassuring the child for a while that you know he is worried for fear another movement will hurt the way the previous one did, but that he doesn't need to worry anymore because the movements are now kept soft by the medicine or diet changes. A child who remains frightened and resistant or seems to continue to have pain should be examined by the doctor for the possibility that a fissure has been created and is not healing.

Bladder Control

754. Simultaneous bowel and bladder control. The appropriateness of Dr. Brazelton's method is shown by the fact that when children feel ready to control themselves, they usually achieve bowel and bladder control almost simultaneously. In other words, by the first part of the third year, there is sufficient readiness—in terms of awareness and of physical competence—for both bowel and bladder control. All that is then necessary is the child's wish to be grown-up in these respects; very little special effort is required on the parents' part to achieve bladder control.

755. Attitudes toward BMs and urine. There are interesting differences in children's attitudes toward their BMs and their urine that may help you to understand their behavior.

Bladder control tends to come slightly later than bowel control because it's easier for the anal sphincter (valve) to hold on to a solid than for the urethral sphincter to hold on to urine. (The anal sphincter becomes much less effective during diarrhea, as you know.)

Children rarely make an issue of daytime urination. It seems that urine doesn't matter to them as a possession the way BMs do.

Bladder function tends to mature by itself, irrespective of training efforts. The bladder empties itself frequently in the first year. But by fifteen to eighteen months it begins to retain urine for a couple of hours, even though no training has been started. In fact, an occasional baby becomes spontaneously dry at night by a year of age.

The bladder retains urine for longer periods during sleep than during wakefulness, and dryness may be discovered after a two-hour nap months before daytime control is achieved.

There may continue to be occasional accidental wettings in the daytime for several months after children have gained general control of urine. This happens when they are preoccupied with play and don't want to interrupt it.

756. Training pants. When your child can successfully control his BMs and bladder, put him in training pants that he can pull down by himself. This further step toward independence will lessen the chance of backsliding. But don't use pants before the child is generally succeeding; they won't do any good for a child who is not succeeding, and you will have wasted their reinforcing value.

757. Inability to urinate away from home. It sometimes happens that a child around two has become so well trained to his own potty chair or toilet seat that he can't perform anywhere else. You can't urge him or scold him into it. He will probably wet his pants eventually, for which he shouldn't be scolded. If he is painfully full, can't let go, and you can't get home, put him in a hot bath for half an hour.

Tell him it's okay to urinate in the bathtub. This will probably work. Keep this possibility in mind when you take him traveling, and bring along his own seat if necessary. It's better to get a child used to urinating in different places early, including outdoors. There are portable urinals for boys and for girls to which they can become accustomed at home and which can then be taken along when they visit. Some children are more comfortable in diapers when they're away from home or can be reassured that they can have the choice of diapers when leaving home.

758. Standing up to urinate. Parents are sometimes worried because a two-year-old boy won't urinate standing up. It isn't necessary to make an issue of this. He'll get the idea sooner or later, when he sees older boys or his father standing. Some boys will urinate in a can or urinal as a step toward urinating in the toilet.

759. Staying dry at night. Many parents assume that children learn to stay dry through the night only because the parent takes him to the toilet late in the evening. They ask, "Now that he is reasonably dry in the daytime, when should I begin to toilet-train him at night?" This is a mistaken idea, and it makes night dryness sound like too much of a job. It's closer to the facts to say that a child just naturally becomes dry at night when his bladder becomes mature enough, provided he isn't nervous or rebellious. This is shown clearly by the fact that one baby in a hundred regularly stays dry at night from the age of twelve months, although the parents have made no training effort at all and although the child wets throughout the day. And a few children, late in the second year or early in the third, stay dry at night before they have much control in the daytime. The bladder can retain urine for longer periods during sleep because the kidneys automatically produce less urine and make the urine more concentrated when a person is quiet and asleep.

Most children become dry at night around three years of age. Boys tend to be later than girls, high-strung children later than relaxed ones. Slowness in becoming dry at night is often a family trait (see Sections 814–818 on bed-wetting).

I don't think it is necessary for parents to do anything

special about night training beyond expressing the consistent expectation that the child will make an effort to be dry at night. The natural maturing of the bladder plus the idea that urine belongs in the toilet will take care of most cases. Of course, it helps a little if the parents share in children's pride when they begin to have dry nights. If, six or eight months after daytime control is achieved, your child expresses a wish to leave his diaper off at night, you can act pleased that he wants to try, and let him.

760. Teach proper wiping. When your daughter shows an interest in wiping, you'll have to negotiate letting her wipe first, with you finishing up, until she can do a complete job by herself. This is the time to start teaching little girls to wipe from *front to back,* to prevent urinary tract infections.

761. Expect setbacks. Mastery of bowel and bladder functions occurs in little steps for most children. You can expect plateaus and setbacks to be scattered among the gains. Emotional upsets, illness, traveling, a new baby—these can cause setbacks even in a child who seemed fully trained. Avoid scolding and punishing when this happens. When the inevitable accidents occur, your child will need reassurance that he'll regain control soon and that you know he still wants to be grown-up in this respect.

762. Backsliding on bowel control after bladder control is achieved. Many children, more often boys, when they train themselves for urine, stop giving up their BMs on the potty. They apparently can't give in to all of their parents' requests at once. If you push or cajole at this point you may make the child retain his BM inside, which may lead to painful, hard BMs, adding a potent new reason for holding back. Tell the child he can wait to do his BM until he has a diaper on.

Sleep

763. How sleep works. Scientists have been carefully studying how sleep works for the past twenty years and have learned how very complicated a process it is. Going to sleep is not like simply turning off a switch. On the contrary, it's a very active process whereby a certain part of the brain changes the chemistry of another part to produce sleep. These chemical changes cause us to lose our usual consciousness and fall asleep.

The purpose of sleep is not entirely understood. Some believe that it is the time we turn short-term memories into long-term memories. We have also learned that sleep seems to enhance the functioning of the immune system; perhaps that is why we feel like sleeping a lot during illness. In babies, sleep is believed to help to maintain and organize within the brain the newly learned skills, and it may even play a role in how the brain is wired (see Sections 147–149). Children also seem to do the majority of their growing while asleep. Whatever sleep's purpose, it must be very important in children, since the younger they are, the more they sleep.

764. Sleep occurs in cycles. Sleep is a very orderly process. Every hour and a half (only an hour in newborns), sleep predictably goes from light (REM) sleep to deep sleep (which has four distinct stages of its own). This is why some infants cry out or partially awaken every hour or two—that is when they are cycling into active, light sleep. (An esteemed colleague used to explain how the stresses of his life made him "sleep like a baby. I wake up every hour and cry!").

765. How much sleep does a child need anyway? The average newborn sleeps sixteen hours a day. (Sleep issues in the first months are discussed in Sections 147–152.) Six-month-olds sleep about fourteen hours and twelve-month-olds about thirteen hours. The average two-year-old needs ten to twelve hours of sleep at night plus a nap. The nap or rest usually shortens as he grows from two to six, and bedtime at night stays the same. Between the ages of six and nine, the average child can usually give up an hour of his night's sleep, half an hour at a time and, for instance, go to bed at 8:00 P.M., if he gets up at 7:00 A.M. By age twelve, he will probably be able to clip off another hour and go to bed at 9:00 P.M.

These are average figures. There is a lot of variation. Some babies and children require a lot of sleep, others very little. You don't need to worry that a baby isn't getting enough sleep to meet his needs, although he may not be getting enough sleep to meet your needs. That brings up an important feature of sleep problems: the sleep problem is almost never the baby's; it is the family's. Every baby will get as much sleep as he needs. If he decides to get that sleep in the middle of the day and stays happily awake at night, however, that can be a problem for his sleep-deprived parents. If he needs to sleep only ten hours a day, his parents may not have time to take care of the rest of the family, to complete the chores that can be done only when he sleeps, and to get enough sleep themselves.

As babies get older, they gradually sleep less and less. You're apt to notice this first in the late afternoon. In time they become wakeful at other periods during the day. Each baby develops a personal pattern of wakefulness and tends to be awake at the same time every day. Toward the end of the first year, most babies are down to two naps a day; and between one and one and a half years, they will probably give up one of these.

766. It is only during infancy that you can leave the amount of sleep entirely up to the baby. A child by the age of two is a much more complicated being. He may need more sleep, but be kept from getting it by loneliness, fear of being left alone, fear of the dark, fear of nightmares, fear of wetting his bed, or excitement from stimulating experiences. He may be all keyed up from competing with an older brother, or burning up with jealousy of a younger sister. He may be on edge each evening because there is always a tug of war with his parents about when he is to go to bed or because he is worrying about his schoolwork or the TV thriller he has been watching. You can't say that an older child doesn't need more sleep just because he won't take it.

767. Naps. Many children stop going to sleep at naptime around the age of three or four, but most of them still need a rest or at least a quiet play period indoors after lunch. Many wise schools provide a rest period through the sixth grade. It all depends on the individual child's temperament and activity. I think it's a good idea for you to continue a nap or quiet time for as long as your child seems to benefit. The rule for the child should be: you don't have to sleep during the quiet time, but you do have to slow down and rest for a while.

This brings up another sleep issue: you can't make a child go to sleep, and you shouldn't try. What you can do is make him go to bed and rest. He may choose to read quietly, or you may decide to meditate with him—it's up to him.

768. Which room? Whether children should sleep in a room by themselves or with another child is largely a practical matter. If it's possible, it's fine for children to have a room of their own, especially as they grow older, where they can keep their own possessions under control and have privacy when they want it. The main disadvantage of two young children in the same room is that they are apt to wake each other up at the wrong times. However, sharing a room also has its advantages. Siblings must then learn to negotiate for space, and learn consideration by being quiet and letting the other one sleep, rather than engaging in long conversations into the night. Sharing a bedroom can foster a certain closeness between siblings, but it can also induce chronic battles over turf.

769. The parents' bed. Some small children go through a period of waking up frightened at night. They may repeatedly come into the parents' room, perhaps crying persistently, and the parents may take them into their bed with them so that they can all get some sleep. This seems like the most practical thing to do at the time, but it can turn out to be a mistake. Even if the child's anxiety lessens during the following weeks, he is apt to cling to the security of his parents' bed, and there is the devil to pay getting him out again. A good rule is to take him promptly and matter-of-factly back to his own bed. Of course, there are exceptions, such as illness or true fear, when it would seem cruel to cast the child out into his lonely room. But even then it is best to take him to his own room rather than give him confusing messages.

But I would let the exceptions prove the rule and cheerfully bring them back to their own beds most of the time.

Then comfort the child in his own room. Sit down beside his crib or bed in the dark and reassure him that you are there and that there is nothing to fear. Stay with him until he goes to sleep. You may have to do this for a few nights, if that's what he needs.

Sometimes a parent will lie down on the bed with the child, to comfort him. This can lead to other problems. The child is soothed for that night, but enjoys the special cuddle time so much that he easily comes to demand the same service every night. After a night or two, he also begins waking up when the parent gets up to leave the room. So it's best, in the long run, to sit in a comfortable chair next to the bed.

770. Letting your child come into your bed for a cuddle in the morning is a different story. This is a fine way for parents and children to have a special warm and loving time together, so long as it doesn't make either parent uneasy, for example, by stirring up sexual feelings.

771. Going to bed. Three or four factors can make the difference between the child who goes to bed willingly and the one who stalls and argues.

First of all, *Keep bedtime agreeable and happy.* Remember that sleep is delicious and inviting to tired children if you don't turn it into an unpleasant duty. Have an air of cheerful certainty about it. Second, *Expect children to turn in at the hour you decide* as surely as you expect them to breathe. It's good for children to be able to persuade parents to change their minds once in a while about bedtime—on New Year's Eve, for instance—but bedtime comes too often for regular arguments. Until children are at least three or four, and in any case until they are responsible enough to like to get themselves to bed, lead them rather than push them with words. Carry the very small child affectionately. Lead the three- or four-year-old by the hand, both of you still chatting about what you were talking about before.

Third, remember that *Small children are comforted by bedtime rituals.* For example, the dolly is put in her bed and tucked in. Then the teddy bear is put in the child's bed. Then the child is tucked in and kissed. Then the parent pulls down the shade or puts out the light. Try not to rush going to bed, no matter how much of a hurry you are in. (On the other hand, it isn't wise to let the child keep lengthening the rituals.) Keep it peaceful. Tell or read a story regularly if you have time. It shouldn't be scary. Most children are helped in going to bed by having a cozy toy animal or doll for company in bed.

772. How long in the crib? I think it's sensible to keep two-year-olds in the crib as long as they have not learned to climb out of it. I've heard too many stories of two-year-olds who became evening wanderers just as soon as they were graduated to youth beds. Do not force a two-year-old to give up her crib to a younger sibling; this may foster sibling rivalry. Buy or borrow another one for the new baby.

Common Sleep Problems

773. Chronic resistance to going to bed. This sleep problem develops insidiously. In most cases it grows out of colic or irritable crying. It can be thought of as a problem with sleep-onset associations. If a baby has been miserable with colic most evenings for her first two or three months, her parents may have found that she is more comfortable when they carry her around. This also makes the parents feel better. By the time she is three or four months old, it gradually dawns on the parents that she doesn't seem to be in so much pain or misery anymore—her cry is now angry and demanding. She wants her walking time because she's used to it and thinks she's entitled to it. She almost glares when her mother sits down for a well-needed rest, as if to say, "Woman, get going!"

A baby who becomes engaged in a nightly struggle to keep her parents walking has to really train herself to stay awake, and she succeeds step-by-step as the months go by—first staying awake until 9:00 P.M., then to 10:00, 11:00, and even midnight. Her parents say her lids often close and her head droops while they're carrying her, but that as soon as they start to lay her down she wakes up with an indignant yell.

Such a sleep problem is exhausting to both baby and parent. The baby is apt to become irritable in the daytime, too, and may eat less well. The parents can't help getting more and more irritated and resentful. A baby just shouldn't be able to put adults through a performance like this every night. The parents know it, but don't know what to do about it. Even the baby senses, I think, that she shouldn't be able to get away with such tyranny.

The habit is usually easy to break once the parents realize that it is as bad for the baby as it is for them. The cure is simple: put the baby to bed at a reasonable hour, say good night affectionately but firmly, walk out of the room, and don't go back.

Most babies who have developed this pattern will cry furiously for twenty or thirty minutes the first night, and then when nothing happens, they suddenly fall asleep! The second night the crying is apt to last only ten minutes. The third night there usually isn't any at all.

It's important not to tiptoe in to be sure the baby is safe or to reassure her that you are nearby. This only enrages her and keeps her crying much longer. Some parents find it very helpful to set a kitchen timer for twenty or thirty minutes, so they can look at the timer when they are convinced the baby has been crying for hours.

It's hard on the kindhearted parents while the crying

lasts. They imagine the worst: that the baby's head is caught in the slats of the crib, that she has vomited and is lying in a mess, that she is in a panic about being deserted. From the rapidity with which these sleep problems can be cured in the first year, and from the way babies immediately become much happier as soon as this is accomplished, I'm convinced that they are only crying from anger at this age.

If several nights of crying will wake other children or anger the neighbors, you can muffle the sound by putting a rug or blanket on the floor of the baby's room and a blanket over the window. Soft surfaces of this kind absorb a surprising amount of the sound. It is sometimes worthwhile to explain the problem to touchy neighbors in order to reassure them that it will take only a few nights and to ask for their indulgence.

774. Waking in the night. Some babies go to sleep like angels, but develop the habit of waking in the middle of the night, usually in the second half of the first year or early in the second year. Sometimes this starts with an ear infection that wakes them with pain. When the doctor makes the diagnosis the parents may feel guilty that they hadn't suspected a physical disease. Then, when the baby stirs and whimpers on succeeding nights, they hurry in apprehensively, to comfort him, though it's actually very unlikely that the pain has recurred.

I suspect the baby catches some of their anxiety and, in addition, enjoys all this partying in the middle of the night. Sometimes the wakefulness seems to start during a painful stage of teething. All babies, like older people, half wake a number of times each night, when they are in the light sleep stage, and shift position. When they have been picked up and treated to company and a snack for several nights, I imagine they learn to rouse themselves from half awake to wide awake, to have more fun.

In a few cases a baby may come to wake not just once but several times, to stay awake longer and longer each time, to demand not just company but to be walked, and to resist being put back to bed by crying furiously.

Most cases can be cured easily: the baby has to learn that

there is nothing to be gained by waking and crying. This can usually be accomplished in two or three nights by letting her cry and not going to her at all. She is apt to cry for twenty or thirty minutes the first night (it may seem like much longer), ten minutes the second night, not at all the third.

One additional requirement is necessary, in my experience. The baby must not see the parents when she wakes up. If she sees them, even if they pretend to be asleep, this angers her and stimulates her to keep up the crying indefinitely. It is essential to put her to bed in a different room from theirs. If this is absolutely impossible, a screen or curtain can be rigged to prevent her from seeing the parents.

Some believe that these waking-in-the-night problems between six and eighteen months are primarily due to separation anxiety and that the best treatment is for the parents to go into the baby's room, sit down beside the crib without turning on the light, and keep murmuring something reassuring such as "Don't worry, Mommy is right here. Go back to sleep now," until the baby does so. The key is to do less and less every night to comfort the baby. If the first night you lightly stroke the baby, then continue the soothing voice on the second night, but don't stroke the child. This method usually takes a lot longer than the first one because it takes the child longer to realize she has to get herself to sleep. Certainly if it works it will be easier on parent and child than letting the child cry for two or three nights. If the baby simply won't go back to sleep this way, or if the waking continues for weeks, you can use the less tenderhearted method.

775. The baby who vomits. Some babies and young children vomit easily when enraged. The parent is apt to be upset and may show it by anxious looks, by rushing to clean up, by being more sympathetic afterward, by being quicker to come to the baby at the next scream. This lesson is not lost on children, and they are likely to vomit more deliberately the next time they're in a temper. And they also come to be frightened by the vomiting they induce, because their parents are frightened by it. I think parents should try to harden their hearts to the vomiting if the baby is using it to bully them. If they are trying to get the baby over a refusal to go to bed, they should stick to the program and not go in. They can clean up later, after the baby has gone to sleep.

776. Mild separation anxiety. I don't want to leave the impression that every two-year-old who objects to being put to bed should be sat with. Far from it. Severe separation anxiety is rare, but mild reluctance to being separated is very common. There are two varieties. The first consists of trying to keep the parent in the room. A child will urgently say, "Wee-wee!" though he went to the bathroom just a few minutes ago. This puts the parent in a quandary. On the one hand she knows it's an excuse, but on the other hand she wants to encourage cooperation from the child by being cooperative herself. So she says, "Once more." As soon as the child is back in bed and she starts to leave, he cries, "Drink of water!" looking as pathetic as a person dying of thirst. If his parent complies, he keeps alternating these two requests all evening.

I think that such a child is feeling just *slightly* worried about being left alone. Usually the best and most practical way for the parent to reassure him is to remind him in a friendly, firm, and breezy tone that he just had a drink and went to the bathroom, and then to say good night and leave the room without hesitation. If parents allow themselves to be detained or to look troubled and uncertain, it's as if they're saying, "Well, maybe there is something to be nervous about." Even if a child whimpers and cries for a few minutes, I think it is wiser not to go back. It's much easier on the child to learn the lesson right away with a little unhappiness than to have the struggle drag on for weeks.

As I said earlier, I have never had a general philosophy of "Let them cry." In this instance I have been discussing a relatively rare problem of chronic resistance to sleep which takes weeks and months to develop (see Section 773).

777. Climbing out of the crib. Another type of mild bedtime anxiety is when a two-year-old learns to climb out of his crib soon after being put to bed and appears at the parents' side. He's smart enough to be very charming at such a time. He's happy to chat or to be cuddled—things he has no time for during the day. This makes it very hard for the parents to be firm. But firm they have to be, and promptly take him back to bed. Otherwise, repeated climbing out of bed may develop into an unpleasant battle lasting an hour or more every night.

When a climbing-out-of-bed problem in a two-year-old has gotten completely out of hand, parents sometimes ask if it is all right to lock the child's door. I don't like the idea of a child crying himself to sleep behind a locked door. Usually if you are firm and consistent in returning him promptly to his bed, he will learn the situation is hopeless and give up the quest.

One exception to this, however, occurs when a child roams the house, unbeknownst to his parents, in the middle of the night. This is a potentially extremely dangerous situation. In that case, if the problem persists despite your firm admonitions, I would consider putting a gate on the door or even a chain lock. In my experience the threat and the wherewithal to confine a child to his room at night are usually sufficient to stop the dangerous nighttime roaming. You rarely, if ever, actually have to lock the child in his bedroom.

778. When a child is afraid to go to bed, some people try to solve the problem by having either an older or younger brother or sister sleep in the same room, but it can cause a problem for an older sibling. Surprisingly, having a baby in the room may do the trick.

779. Nightmares. All children begin to have bad dreams between the ages of three and six. We're not sure why. Even in adults, two-thirds of all dreams have a disturbing emotional tone. Dreaming seems to trigger our deepest fears more easily than our deepest joys. While recurring nightmares may indicate significant stress in the child's waking life, usually they are just another part of growing up.

When your child awakens from a nightmare, perhaps crying or even screaming, you should comfort her by telling her that everything is all right, that she was just having a dream, and that dreams aren't real. Then you can ask her to tell you about the nightmare, so you'll know what issues to deal with. Continue to reassure her that it was only a dream, like make-believe, and that you won't let anything bad happen to her in real life. Remember, dreams have magical powers, but so too do parents. Stay with her until she falls back to sleep. In the comforting light of day you can discuss further what dreams are, why they don't hurt you, and how everybody has them. As with fears, you cannot banish monsters from your child's dream life, but you can help her in a reassuring way to cope with them.

780. Night terrors. These also occur normally, though far less frequently than nightmares, in three- to six-year-olds. Night terrors are very different from nightmares. They seem to be caused by some temporary disturbance in the nervous system during deep sleep. Night terrors tend to run in families and all children who have them grow out of them within a few years at most. When a child has a night terror, he starts screaming. Even though his eyes are wide open with a glassy-eyed stare, he doesn't respond when you talk to him. In fact, he seems unaware of your presence. That is for a good reason: he is actually still fast asleep. You might have a hard time waking him. If you succeed, he will have no memory of why he appeared to be so terrified, and he'll also have no memory of it in the morning. A night terror may last as long as thirty minutes, although it's usually much briefer, before the child goes back into quiet sleep.

You can't really comfort a child who's having a night terror since he's asleep while it is happening. You can hold him firmly (he may struggle), rock him, and reassure him that he's all right, that he's just having a bad dream, and that you'll stay with him until he goes back to sleep.

An occasional child will have frequent night terrors, and in that case the doctor may prescribe a special medicine to be given at bedtime for several days or weeks, until the night terrors stop.

781. Sleepwalking. This also seems to be due to a temporary disturbance in the nervous system during deep sleep.

Sleepwalking tends to run in families and in the great majority of cases disappears within a few months or years without any special treatment. A child who sleepwalks has a glassy stare and garbled speech, but she can usually clumsily complete some purposeful activities. For example, I knew a child who had a predilection for urinating into a waste-basket.

If you catch your child sleepwalking, firmly lead her back to bed, reassuring her that she'll go right back to sleep and that you'll stay with her until she does. If she is a real wanderer—some walk out-of-doors and even get into dangerous situations—you need some way to tell when she is sleepwalking. A bell or buzzer on her bedroom door can help. Occasionally, some parents need to lock the door from the outside to protect their child from danger.

Children never remember sleepwalking. Your doctor or nurse practitioner can prescribe the same bedtime medicine that's used for night terrors for the occasional child who sleepwalks often or gets into physical danger while sleep-walking. The medicine is effective and is usually needed for only several days or weeks.

Temper Tantrums

Almost all two-year-olds have temper tantrums and almost all four-year-olds don't. This suggests that tantrums are a normal phenomenon at certain stages of early development and not at others. Let's look at what it is about a two-year-old that makes having tantrums so common.

782. Tantrums occur when a child is frustrated. Frustration plays a significant role in *every* young child's daily life. Just think about their circumstances. The world is a very bewildering place. Try as they might, at their developmental level it is impossible for them to make sense of why most things happen, what is going to happen next, and how to solve problems. At the same time, their budding independence urges them to venture out from the safety and control of their parents. These explorations of the world are always hair-raising for the parents as the young experimenter struggles to learn his limits. But he doesn't really know his limits, and his reach exceeds his grasp. He wants to do certain things but lacks the requisite motor control and intellectual understanding to succeed. Additionally, his ability to delay gratification is minuscule. When he wants something, he wants it *now!* There is no "later" to his way of thinking.

So it is that the two-year-old invariably experiences lightning-quick reversals of fortune, unfulfilled longings, and unachievable ambitions and he becomes overwhelmed. His life is, in short, an often frustrating existence. (Of course, it is also exhilarating when successes are won.)

In addition to feelings of frustration, the young child lacks the language skills needed to fulfill his goals and soothe his disappointments. Just think how important using words is in coping with frustration in your own life and you'll understand why limited expressive language skills are related to tantrums. The young child understands a lot more language than he can express. He may have some notion of a solution to his dilemma but just can't communicate it very well (if at all). Frustration then begets more frustration as his feelings heat up.

Finally, young children lack the ability to inhibit their feelings. As we mature, we learn how to dampen and not act upon strong feelings, but a young child has no such skills. When the intense emotions of frustration finally come to a boil and need relief, he requires an outlet for them. His options, however, are limited. He can't talk about them. He can't suppress them. He can't deny them. What *can* he do? He can have a temper tantrum. He flops down, screams, pounds his hands and feet, bangs his head against the floor. He is like a volcano that has to blow its top before serenity and peace can again reign.

So tantrums can be understood as a developmental inevitability. Some children have very mild, occasional tantrums; others have more frequent, intense tantrums. Certainly temperament plays a role. Children who are very intense in all of their emotions will also have intense tantrums. Children who have a hard time adapting to unfamiliar experiences may have a lower frustration tolerance. Children who are generally distractible can often have their tantrums averted by diverting their attention away from the frustrating trigger. Many tantrums are a result of fatigue or hunger.

These are the usual reasons for tantrums. Of course if a child is very stressed for some reason, he is likely to have tantrums more often. In these cases, there are usually clues other than just the tantrums (like sleep problems, unhappiness) that tell you something is amiss. Finally, a child with a medical problem may have more tantrums. You should think about these possibilities if the tantrums seem excessive in number (for example, more than three times every day) or duration (more than fifteen minutes) or if they persist beyond the age when the child can express himself fluently—typically by age four.

783. How to handle tantrums. There are three possible ways to deal with tantrums: (1) try to avoid frustration in your child's life (possible to only a small extent); (2) distract him when a tantrum is brewing (successful in some children some of the time); (3) simply ride out the storm.

Fashioning a frustration-free world for your child sounds like a worthy goal, but it simply can't be done beyond a certain point, and it would probably be a bad idea anyway; a child who grows up without learning to deal with frustration will be completely unprepared for the real world. You can, however, ensure that your home is childproof in a way that makes saying no less necessary. Make sure your child has adequate time for very active, physically tiring play to help to dissipate some of his boundless energy. And allow him to gain some control over his world by allowing him to make frequent small choices. Say, for instance, "Do you want to take your nap in your red or your green pajamas?" and not "Do you want to take a nap now?" A child who feels he has at least some control over at least part of his world is likely to have fewer tantrums.

Most children build up to a tantrum. If you can tell that one is in the offing, try distraction: "Oh. Look at that birdie. He's flying. Let's go see." If you're very lucky, the child's attention will be deflected from the frustrating circumstance at hand and will move on to something else. Distraction is always worth a try—but don't get your hopes up that it will always work.

Once a tantrum begins, there is little to do but ride it out. Make sure the child is in a safe place and can't hurt himself as he thrashes about. Then simply ignore the tantrum as you matter-of-factly go about your business. It is the *child's* responsibility to gain control over his emotions. He should know that you don't bear a grudge against him for having the tantrum, but neither are you thrilled about it. I think it's generally a mistake to pay too much attention to the child during a tantrum. This may unintentionally reward the child for having a tantrum, as he (quite unconsciously) associates having a tantrum with parental attention. While I don't think such reinforcement causes tantrums to begin with, I think it takes away the motivation to learn to overcome them.

So when the storm breaks, try to take it casually and help him to get it over. When he gains control, you can cheerfully say, "Do you feel better now? I'm sorry you lost control"— *not,* "You're bad for having a tantrum"—and suggest an activity to do. Don't dwell on the tantrum. It happened, it's over, and it's time to move on.

You certainly don't give in and meekly let the child have his way; otherwise he'll be throwing tantrums all the time on purpose. You don't argue with him, because he's in no mood to see the error of his ways. Getting angry yourself only forces him to keep up his end of the row. Give him a graceful way out. One child cools off quickest if the parent fades away and matter-of-factly goes about her own business. Another with more determination and pride will stick to yelling and thrashing for an hour unless his parent makes a friendly gesture. The mother might pop in with a suggestion of something fun to do, and a hug to show she wants to make up, as soon as the worst of the storm has passed.

It's embarrassing to have a child throw a tantrum on a busy sidewalk. Pick him up, with a grin if you can force it, and lug him off to a quiet spot where you can both cool off in private. If it happens in the supermarket, you can whisk him off to the car, wait for the storm to subside, and then go back into the store.

Tantrums are no fun, but neither are they the end of the world. Eventually time will effect a lasting cure. Most temper tantrums arise from anxiety, but they can also lead to manipulation. Therefore a balance between helping the child to feel safe and loved and yet reassured that limits are firm is what is needed.

Death

784. Helping children to cope with death. Death is a fact of life that every child must grapple with. For some, the death of a goldfish is their first exposure; for others, it is the death of a grandparent. In many cultures, death is viewed as a natural occurrence, and no attempt is made to isolate it from everyday life. Our culture, on the other hand, remains very uneasy about the whole thing. People tend to die in institutions, not at home with family present. We use euphemisms to talk about death: "He kicked the bucket . . . went to sleep . . . bought the farm"—anything to distance us from the reality that, in fact, he *died*. And we wonder whether young children would be too stressed by attending the funeral.

If adults are uncomfortable with the notion of death, it is no wonder that many are even more perplexed about how to help children deal with it. Some would just as soon deny the whole thing. That dog lying motionless at the side of the road? "He's just resting. He's fine. What did you learn in school today?" Others choose to avoid the concrete and focus solely on the ethereal: "The angels came and took Grandpa and now he's up in heaven with Grandma." Still others duck the question altogether: "Don't you worry about what death is. No one is going to die soon. Where do you get such ideas?"

Like most things in life, children can best learn to deal with death when their parents answer their questions at their level and treat it as a natural subject to talk about. Obviously the impact and meaning of a child's first exposure to death depend on a number of circumstances: how old the child is and her developmental level of understanding, what and who died and how close he was to the child, the cause of death and whether it was expected or sudden.

785. In the preschool years, children's ideas and misconceptions about death are influenced by the magical tendencies of their thinking in general. Children this age may believe, for example, that death is reversible and that the dead person will come back someday. They are too young to understand death's immutable finality. They also tend to feel responsible for everything that happens in their world, including death, and may fear punishment for unkind thoughts they had about the dead person or animal. They may also view death as "catching," like a cold, and worry that someone else will soon die. They tend to think in very concrete terms: "How will Uncle Bob breathe if he's in the ground?" Parents can help a child by being equally concrete: "Uncle Bob won't breathe anymore. He also won't eat with us anymore or brush his teeth."

It should be emphasized to children at this age that they in no way caused the death and that death is a part of the life cycle. Parents should also help their child deal with grief by acknowledging that losing a friend or grandparent is very sad and that it is sad to think that person won't be coming back. By dealing with their own feelings, parents can help the child deal with her feelings.

Comforters

Babies and small children use a wide variety of things and methods to comfort themselves when they are tired or unhappy: a stuffed animal or a piece of fabric to stroke (some call these transitional objects); their thumb or fingers, a pacifier or bottle to suck; a habit like rocking or head-rolling. From the age of six months onward, babies are able to use these sucking, stroking, or rocking habits at tired or unhappy moments to bring back the complete, enveloping security that their parents formerly provided.

786. The first sense of separateness. At about six months of age babies begin to realize dimly that they are separate persons. Perhaps it would be more accurate to say that their unfolding instincts make them begin to insist on a slight physical separateness from their parents and on their right to do some things for themselves, and that they then become aware of the importance of this separateness. I am thinking of the way many six-month-olds show impatience with being cuddled in their parent's arms during feedings; they try to sit up straight instead. They want to hold on to their own bottle. They may even try to get the parent's hand off it by jerking it sideways. From now on, until they are fully mature adults, children will continue to insist on a gradually increasing independence, emotional as well as physical.

787. Comforters to recapture the security of early infancy. But the young child over six months old, when she is very tired or frustrated, craves to slip back to early infancy, when being fed in her parent's arms was all there was to paradise. (Psychologists call this tendency to retreat under stress regression; even a competent adult may become childishly helpless or demanding when ill.)

On the other hand, children are unwilling to give up the precious bit of independence they have achieved. This is where various comforters come in. By means of them, the infant attains pleasure and security without giving up independence. Thumb-sucking or pacifier-sucking reminds them of the pleasure of being fed from breast or bottle in their parent's arms. Stroking a cuddly toy animal or a cherished blanket or diaper recalls the good sensation when they gently stroked their mother's clothing or the blanket they were wrapped in during feeding. (Puppies and kittens have an instinct to stroke their mother's breasts when nursing, which helps to make the milk flow. The human infant's impulse to stroke while nursing is perhaps a remnant of the same instinct in our prehuman ancestors.) When babies rock themselves against the back of a stuffed chair or roll their heads from side to side in bed, they are creating again the rhythmic soothing they experienced as fretful young infants when their parent rocked or walked them.

As a young child learns to re-create comforting aspects of her parents out of, for example, a cuddly toy and her thumb, there is a subtle but monumental shift in power. During these times, it's no longer the parent who envelops her or controls her; the infant assumes some measure of control over her own comfort. (It's interesting to see how a young child will sometimes abuse the object that is so precious to her; she will slap it crossly or slam it heartlessly against the furniture.)

Why do I make such an issue of comforters? Partly because their use gives us an understanding of the great psychological importance to children of establishing independence, which they begin to do by six months, and of the meaning of regression. But also, in a very practical way, it explains a number of perplexing things about early childhood. For instance, I think that thumb-sucking in the first half year of infancy is simply an expression of babies' need to suck, especially when they're hungry. But after six months thumb-sucking becomes something else: a reminder of early infantile comfort, which children now need only when they're sleepy or upset. That is to say, the thumb becomes a comforter, such a precious comforter that most children won't give it up willingly until many years later.

788. The pacifier, too, changes its meaning after the age of six months. It goes from satisfying the need to suck to being a comforter at regressed times of day. But the pacifier is not usually as precious as the thumb; most children will give it up at one or two years of age if the parent does not continue to encourage its use. (A child is apt to suck either her thumb or pacifier, not both.)

789. The meaning of the bottle changes, too. I think that the reason that many babies become more and more attached to the bottle after six months is that their parents have fallen into the habit of handing them their bottle to drink by themselves in bed. In this way the bottle becomes a precious comforter. If children become intensely attached to it in this way, they are apt to remain very attached to it until one or two years of age, whereas the bottle given while the child is sitting in the parent's lap cannot become a precious comforter in place of the parent—because the parent is right there.

790. Some children do not adopt any comforter such as a cuddly toy or piece of cloth, a precious bottle, pacifier, or thumb. I don't know why. I haven't been able to see any psychological differences between those who do and those who don't. I don't know of any important reason to encourage children to adopt a precious comforter or to discourage them, except for certain practical considerations in regard to the bottle in bed (Sections 237 and 262) and the pacifier (Sections 808–811).

791. The strokable comforter. In my experience the children who are thumb-suckers are more likely than the non-thumb-suckers to become attached to a strokable comforter also. It's as if they slip back to early infancy through the thumb-sucking pleasure and then want to add the pleasure of stroking something, too. Let's face it, some of us adults do the same thing (I, for example, am twiddling my hair as I think of the right words to write), although we tend to call them nervous habits.

Some children develop an intense attachment to an object which lasts for several years; others develop only a mild attachment which weakens after a while; still others shift from one object to another.

792. When the attachment to a cuddly toy or piece of cloth is intense, it is apt to raise practical problems. The child may want to carry the comforter at all times, everywhere. It is going to become increasingly dirty and eventually tattered. Usually the child objects vigorously to a washing or cleaning of the object and rejects a substitute out of hand. If the object gets lost, the child will be in real despair and will probably be unable to go to sleep for hours.

I think it is unfair—and it's usually impossible—to try to break a child's attachment to a comforter after it has been well formed. However, I've known parents who were ingenious and firm enough to keep the problem within bounds because they felt very strongly about this: they insisted from the beginning that the object stay in the child's room, or at least in the house.

It is better to sneak a blanket or diaper away from the child at night, at regular intervals, for washing and drying before it ever gets gray, so that it won't change so drastically in color and smell; the smell of a comforter is important to some children. Better still would be to acquire a duplicate, an identical toy or piece of cloth, and to keep substituting the clean one from time to time, without the child knowing. It is impossible to wash and dry most stuffed animals overnight, but you can do a fair job of washing the surface with soap and water and a washcloth or brush. Dry the toy with a hair dryer or an electric fan. (Don't use cleaning fluid; you won't be able to get it all out by morning.) Some stuffed animals, depending on what they're stuffed with, can be put into an old nylon stocking (to hold them together) and put through the washer and dryer.

793. Is there any harm in letting a child become dependent on a cuddly comforter and take it to bed? None that I know of except the parents' distress at its dinginess and at its symbolic meaning that the child still has dependency needs. There is no way to prevent its happening anyway. Almost all children will receive soft toys during their first year, and it's usually not until they're fifteen to eighteen months old and begin to insist on carrying one object with them that their parents realize what has happened.

Most babies outgrow the dependence sometime between two and five years of age. (A few will cling longer.) It's wise for the parent to remind them in an encouraging tone—a couple of times a month, not every week—that someday they'll be a big girl or boy and won't need it anymore. This kind of hint and confidence will help them to outgrow the comforter as soon as they are able.

Thumb-Sucking

794. The meaning of thumb-sucking. The main reason that young babies suck their thumbs seems to be that they haven't had enough sucking at the breast or bottle to satisfy their sucking need. Sucking also helps babies relieve physical and emotional tension. Dr. David Levy pointed out that babies who are fed every three hours don't suck their thumbs as much as babies fed every four hours and that babies who have cut down on bottle-feeding time from twenty minutes to ten minutes because the nipples have become old and soft are more likely to suck their thumbs than babies who still have to work for twenty minutes. Dr. Levy fed a litter of puppies with a medicine dropper so that they had no chance to suck during their feedings. They acted just the same as babies who don't get enough chance to suck at feeding time. They sucked their own and each other's paws and skin so hard that the fur came off.

795. All babies aren't born with the same urge to suck. One baby never nurses more than fifteen minutes at a time and yet never puts a thumb in her mouth, and another whose bottles have always taken twenty minutes or more thumb-sucks excessively. A few begin to thumb-suck in the delivery room, and they keep at it. I suspect that a strong sucking instinct runs in some families. We now know that some babies suck their thumbs while they're still in the uterus and some are even born with sucking blisters on their hands or arms.

796. You don't need to be concerned when babies suck their thumbs for only a few minutes just before their feeding time. They are probably doing this only because they're hungry. It's when babies try to suck their thumbs as soon as their feeding is over, or when they suck a lot between feedings, that you have to think of ways to satisfy the sucking craving. Most babies who thumb-suck start before they are three months old.

I might add here that the thumb, finger, and hand chewing that almost all babies do from the time they begin to teethe (commonly at around three or four months) should not be confused with thumb-sucking. Naturally, the baby who is a thumb-sucker is sucking at one minute, chewing at another, during his teething periods.

If your baby girl begins to try to suck her thumb or finger or hand, I think it's preferable not to stop her directly but to try to give her more opportunity to suck at the breast or the bottle or the pacifier. If your baby hasn't been a confirmed thumb-sucker from birth, the most effective method by far to prevent the habit is the ample use of the pacifier in the first three months. In addition there are two other matters to consider: the number of feedings, and how long each feeding takes.

797. When to pay attention to thumb-sucking. The time to pay attention to thumb-sucking is when babies first try to do it, not when they finally succeed. I make this point because lots of babies haven't much control over their arms for the first few months of their lives. You see such babies struggling to get their hands up and searching around with their mouths. If by good luck they get their fists to their mouths, they suck them vigorously as long as their hands happen to stay there. These babies, just as much as the skillful thumb-suckers, are showing a need to suck longer at the breast or bottle.

The very young baby needs help most, because the sucking need is strongest in the first three months. From then on it tapers off. In most babies I think it's about gone by six or seven months. The thumb-sucking that persists after six months is a comforting device, not an expression of sucking need.

798. Thumb-sucking in breast-fed babies. I have the impression that breast-fed babies are less apt to be thumb-suckers. This is probably true because mothers are inclined to let them go on nursing as long as they want to. The breast is never completely empty, so the mother leaves it up to the baby. When a baby finishes a bottle, it's done. He stops because he doesn't like to suck air or because his parent takes away the bottle. The first question, then, about a breast-fed baby who is trying to suck his thumb is this: Would he nurse longer if allowed to? If so, let him nurse for thirty or even forty minutes at times if this is convenient for you. (To go beyond forty minutes is too time-consuming.) A baby gets most of the milk from a breast in the first ten to fifteen minutes; the rest of the time he's satisfying his craving to suck, lured on by a small trickle of milk. In other words, if he nurses for thirty-five minutes, he gets only slightly more milk than if he had nursed for twenty. A breast-fed baby, allowed to nurse as long as he wants, may vary surprisingly. He may be satisfied with ten minutes at one feeding and want as much as forty minutes at another. This is an example of how breast-feeding is adaptable to a baby's individual needs.

If a baby being nursed on one breast at each feeding

doesn't want to nurse any longer, there's nothing that you can do to make him. But if he is getting both breasts at each feeding and begins to suck his thumb, you can try two methods to make him nurse longer. See if he can be satisfied with one breast at each feeding, nursing as long as he will. If his hunger can't be satisfied that way, then at least let him nurse longer at the first breast. Instead of taking him off in ten minutes, let him stay on for twenty, if he will. Then put him to the second breast for as long as he wants.

799. Thumb-sucking in bottle-fed babies. With the average bottle-fed baby, thumb-sucking is most likely to begin at about the time he learns to finish his bottle in ten minutes instead of in twenty. This happens because babies get stronger as they get older, but the rubber nipples get weaker. Bottles with plastic screw-on rings have nipples with a special opening near the edge for air intake. You can slow down this kind of bottle by screwing the ring on tighter. This partly blocks the air intake and keeps more of a vacuum in the bottle. The next thing to do is to get new nipples, leave the holes as they are, and see if that lengthens the bottle time. Of course, if the nipple holes are too small, some babies stop trying altogether. Try to keep the nipple holes small enough so that a bottle takes twenty minutes, at least during the first six months. I am talking now about the actual number of minutes that the baby is sucking. Naturally, it wouldn't help to lengthen the feeding time by pausing in the middle of the feeding.

800. With a thumb-sucker, it's better to go slowly in omitting feedings. It's not just the length of each feeding but also the number or frequency of feedings in the twenty-four hours that determines whether a baby satisfies the sucking instinct. So if a baby is still thumb-sucking even though you have made each breast- or bottle-feeding last as long as possible, it is sensible to go slowly in dropping other feedings. For example, if a three-month-old baby seems willing to sleep through the late evening feeding at the parents' bedtime but is doing a good deal of thumb-sucking, I would suggest waiting a while longer before dropping the late evening feeding—perhaps a couple of months, provided the baby is still willing to drink when awakened.

801. The effect on the teeth. You may be worried about the effect of thumb-sucking on the baby's jaws and teeth. It is true that thumb-sucking often pushes the upper front baby teeth forward and the lower teeth back. How much the teeth are displaced will depend on how much the child sucks her thumb and, even more, on what position she holds her thumbs in. But dentists point out that this tilting of the baby teeth has no effect on the permanent teeth that begin coming in at about six years of age. In other words, if the baby gives up thumb-sucking by six years of age, as happens in a great majority of cases, there is very little chance of its displacing the permanent teeth.

But whether thumb-sucking displaces the teeth or not, many parents prefer to have their child give it up as soon as possible. The suggestions I have been making are the ones that I think will end thumb-sucking soonest.

802. Why not use restraints? Why not tie babies' arms down to keep them from thumb-sucking? This would cause them a great deal of frustration, which could produce new problems. Furthermore, it usually doesn't cure the baby who is thumb-sucking a lot, because it doesn't respond to the baby's need for more sucking. We have all heard of despairing parents who use elbow splints or put bad-tasting liquid on the baby's thumbs, not just for days but for months. And the day they take off the restraint or stop the liquid on the thumb, the thumb pops back in the mouth.

To be sure, some parents say they have had good results from using such methods. But in most of these cases, the thumb-sucking was very mild. Many babies do a little thumb-sucking off and on. They get over it quickly, whether you do anything or not. I think that restraints and bad-tasting liquid only make the confirmed thumb-sucker do it more in the long run.

803. Thumb-sucking in the older baby and child. Up to now we have been talking about thumb-sucking in the early months. But by the time a baby is six months old, thumb-sucking is turning into something different. It is a comforter that she needs at special times. She sucks when she is tired or bored or frustrated, or to put herself to sleep. When she can't make a go of things at the more grown-up level, she retreats to early infancy when sucking was her chief joy.

Even though thumb-sucking satisfies a different need after the age of six months, of course it is the baby who first sucked her thumb to satisfy her sucking need who goes on doing it, but she now does it for comfort. It's very rare for a child beyond the age of a few months or one year to begin to thumb-suck for the first time. There is no point in worrying about lengthening the sucking time of the six-month-old or twelve-month-old. Is there anything that the parents need to do? I don't think so, if the child is generally outgoing, happy, and busy and if she sucks mainly at bedtime and occasionally during the day. In other words, *thumb-sucking by itself is not a sign of unhappiness or maladjustment or lack of love.* In fact, most thumb-suckers are very happy children, and children who are severely deprived of affection don't thumb-suck. If a child is sucking a great deal of the time instead of playing, parents should ask themselves whether there is anything they ought to do so that she won't need to comfort herself so much. Another child may be bored from not seeing enough of other children or from not having enough things to play with. Or perhaps she's having to sit in her playpen for hours. A boy of a year and a half may be at loggerheads with his mother all day if she is always stopping him from doing the things that fascinate him instead of diverting him to playthings that are permissible. Another boy has children to play with and freedom to do things at home, but he's too timid to throw himself into these activities. He thumb-sucks while he watches. I give the examples only to make it clear that if anything needs to be done for excessive thumb-sucking, it is to make the child's life more satisfying.

804. Elbow splints, mitts, and bad-tasting stuff on the thumb only make the child miserable. They won't stop the habit any more often in older children than they do in small babies. I think that they tend to prolong the habit. The same applies to scolding a child or pulling his thumb out of his mouth. You often hear the recommendation that you give children a toy when you see them thumb-sucking. It certainly is sound to have enough interesting things around for them to play with so that they won't be bored. But if every time their thumb goes in the mouth you jump toward them and poke an old toy into their hands, they'll soon catch on.

805. What about bribing? If your child is one of the rare ones who is still thumb-sucking at the age of five, and you are beginning to worry about what it will do to the permanent teeth when they come in, you will have a fair chance of succeeding if the bribe is a good one. A girl of four or five who wants to get over her thumb-sucking may be helped by having her fingernails painted like a woman's. But practically no child of two or three has the willpower to deny an instinct for the sake of reward. You're apt to make a fuss and get nowhere.

So if your child is thumb-sucking, see to it that his life is good. In the long run it will help him if you remind him that someday he will be grown-up enough to stop. This friendly encouragement makes him want to stop as soon as he is able. But don't nag him.

806. Most important of all, try to stop thinking about it. If you keep on worrying, even though you resolve to say nothing, the child will feel your tension and react against it. Remember that thumb-sucking goes away all by itself in time. In the overwhelming majority of cases, it is over before the second teeth appear. It doesn't go away steadily, though. It decreases rapidly for a while, and then comes back partway during an illness or when the child has a difficult adjustment to make. Eventually it disappears for good. It rarely stops before three years. It usually peters out between three and six.

Most of the babies who go on thumb-sucking until they are one or more years old do some kind of stroking at the same time. One little boy rubs or plucks a piece of blanket, or diaper, or silk, or a woolly toy. Another strokes his earlobe or twists a lock of his hair. Still another wants to hold a piece of cloth right up close to his face and perhaps stroke his nose or lip with a free finger. These motions remind you of how younger babies used to gently feel their mother's skin or clothing when they were suckling at the breast or bottle. And when they press something against their faces, they seem to be remembering how they felt at the breast.

807. Ruminating. Sometimes babies and young children get into the habit of sucking and chewing on their tongue until their last meal comes up, somewhat the way a cow does, a practice known as ruminating. This is a rare condition. Some cases begin when thumb-sucking babies have their arms restrained. They turn to sucking their tongues instead. I would certainly advise letting such babies have the thumb back immediately, before the ruminating becomes a habit. Be sure also that the baby has enough companionship, play, and affection. Other cases of rumination occur when there is marked disturbance in the parent-child relationship.

The Pacifier

808. A pacifier is helpful for fretfulness. A pacifier is a blind nipple (without a hole in it) attached to a disk that rests against the baby's lips to keep the nipple from being pulled entirely into the mouth. On the back of the disk is a ring by which the pacifier can be held by the baby.

One satisfactory model is made of one piece of soft rubber, which means it won't bother the baby's face if she goes to sleep on it, and, more importantly, the baby won't be able to pull the nipple off the disk and choke on it. The only problem with this model is that the long nipple may reach to the back of the throat and gag the baby. Other pacifiers have a short nipple with a ball-shaped end. Some babies take this better, probably because it's shorter and softer. Another type has the nipple flattened on one side. Despite claims made by the manufacturer, there is no scientific evidence that this design is any better.

809. A baby who has periods of mild irritability can often be entirely quieted by having a pacifier to suck. We don't know whether this is true because the sucking soothes some vague discomfort or whether it simply keeps the baby occupied with a deep-seated reflex to suck.

810. The pacifier, when used correctly, is an efficient way to prevent thumb-sucking. Most babies who freely use a pacifier for the first months of life never become thumb-suckers, even if they give up the pacifier at three to four months.

Some would then ask, What's the use of a pacifier to avoid thumb-sucking, when pacifier-sucking is just as unattractive? The answer is that babies who become regular thumb-suckers in their first three months may continue to be thumb-suckers for years. By contrast, most pacifier-suckers are ready to give it up within a few months. Most of the rest give it up by one or two years of age. Finally, a pacifier is less likely to push the teeth out of position.

811. How can you use the pacifier to prevent thumb-sucking? In the first place, many babies—perhaps 50 percent—never try to thumb-suck at all or do it only casually and for brief periods. For them there is nothing to prevent and no need to get involved with a pacifier (unless there is colic).

If the baby becomes used to the thumb over a period of weeks or months, the chances are that he will refuse the pacifier. He has learned to enjoy not only the sensations in his mouth but also the sensations on his thumb. So if you plan to use a pacifier, start it in the first few days or weeks of life.

The best time to offer a pacifier is whenever the baby is searching around with his mouth and trying to suck on anything that is handy. In the early months a baby is seldom awake except before and after feedings, so these are the logical times. The idea is to give the pacifier to him not as little as possible, but as much as he can use it in the first three months, so that he will be satisfied and able to readily give it up later on.

Two problems can interfere with the efficient use of the pacifier. In some cases where its use would be helpful parents are reluctant to use it at all or come around to trying it so late that the baby, who would have taken it in the first weeks, won't take to it now.

The second problem is that parents who have used the

pacifier successfully for fretfulness are apt to develop such a dependence on it—for comforting the baby any time he so much as whimpers—that they can't get over the habit of popping it into the baby's mouth many times a day, even after he is ready to give it up (usually between two and four months).

If a baby isn't willing to give up the pacifier—at any age—I don't think it's right to take it away. But I think there are very good reasons to stop offering it at three or four months to babies who are showing, by spitting it out soon after it is put in their mouths, that they really don't need or want it anymore. In any case, I wouldn't try to get him off the pacifier in a single day. Take a week or two to cut down and don't be afraid to increase its use again for a day or two if he seems to have a special need for comfort. But decrease again when he's willing.

If your baby is still on the pacifier after five or six months and wakes several times a night because he's lost it, put several in his bed at bedtime so that there's a better chance of his finding one by himself. Or pin one to his nightie sleeve. (Don't put a long cord on a pacifier to hang it around the baby's neck or tie it to the crib bar. This can be dangerous, as the cord can become wrapped around the baby's finger, wrist, or neck.)

When a baby has a few teeth, he can pull the nipple of an old, tired pacifier off the disk or chew pieces out of the nipple. These pieces may cause serious choking if swallowed the wrong way. So buy new pacifiers when the old ones become at all weak or crumbly.

Nail-Biting

812. Nail-biting is a sign of tenseness. It is more common in relatively high-strung children who are inclined to worry a lot, and it tends to run in families. They start to bite when they are anxious—for instance, while waiting to be called on in school, while watching a scary episode in a movie. It isn't necessarily a serious sign in a generally happy, successful child, but it is always worth thinking over.

Nagging or punishing nail-biters usually doesn't stop them for longer than half a minute, because they seldom realize they are doing it. In the long run, it may increase their tension. Bitter medicine on the nails will be seen by the child as a punishment. That only gives him something more to feel tense about and may prolong the habit.

The better course is to find out what some of the pressures on the child are and try to relieve them. Is she being urged or corrected or warned or scolded too much? Are you expecting too much in the way of lessons? Consult the teacher about her school adjustment. If movie, radio, and TV violence makes her much more jittery than the average child, simply forbid her to watch such programs.

If your child is otherwise well adjusted, I wouldn't make too much of nail-biting, but if it is one of a host of worrisome behaviors, then counseling with a school psychologist or a social worker at a family agency could prove helpful. It is the cause of the child's anxiety, not the nail-biting itself, that should be of most concern.

Nail-biters for whom it is just an isolated nervous habit generally want to stop if they sense ridicule by schoolmates and friends. Such disapproval from peers often provides the fuel to try to kick the habit. A manicure set for a girl may give her additional motivation. Sticker charts for bite-free days or small stickers on the fingers can serve as a visual reminder not to bite. Some children who are old enough to understand that it's not meant as a punishment find bitter-tasting nail solution a reminder not to chew on their nails. But parental nagging may prove counterproductive. Remember that isolated nail-biting isn't pretty, but neither is it the end of the world. Most children will eventually stop of their own accord. Don't put so much emphasis on this small habit that it hurts your relationship and focuses on an inconsequential part of your child's personality.

Soiling

813. Soiling of the clothing with feces (encopresis) is a symptom of poor bowel control, which can occur any time after four years old. In the typical case a school-age child (it's almost always a boy) begins to stain his underpants with stool, long after being toilet-trained. What is bewildering to the family is that he barely seems to notice it has happened and claims to have had no sensation of passing the stool; even more incomprehensibly, he denies even smelling it. This tendency to deny something that is extremely obvious and distasteful to everyone else is characteristic of this problem. Of course, his friends and family do not deny the odor or avoid the child. Other children may unmercifully tease him, call him Stinky, and shun him, so this is a very distressing and humiliating problem that causes the parents justifiable concern.

Soiling is usually the result of persistent retention of the stool that leads to constipation and leaking of feces around the large retained stool. Constipation occurs in many children as a result of decreased fluid intake, a painful bowel movement, forced toilet training, or certain medicines. Often it happens after some stressful situation in the family, especially if there has been a sudden separation from an important family member. In some instances, stool retention may be brought on by the birth of a baby, a divorce, or a death in the family. Other changes, such as going to a new school or camp, may make some children uncomfortable if the bathroom does not allow for privacy.

Most children who retain stool and develop constipation do not soil. In the susceptible child, excessive and chronic constipation causes poor functioning of the muscles that control bowel movements. Staining of underwear or, in some cases, a formed stool results. Less often, soiling occurs in a child without constipation.

In very mild cases or in those instances when the child was never completely toilet trained and never gained complete control of his bowel functions, a kind, consistent effort to toilet-train the child may be of help. In most cases, your doctor or nurse practitioner will recommend nutritional changes (a high-fiber diet with lots of fluids and limited dairy products) to treat and prevent constipation; occasionally medications to soften the stool are used. It is also helpful to acknowledge the child's embarrassment and to let him know it's not his fault. Perhaps the doctor or nurse practitioner will use a drawing of the intestine to provide the child with a visual image of the stool retention–soiling process. A structured toilet-training program can be planned with your child's doctor. In cases that have gone on for a long time, with much family stress and a poor response to medical treatment, it's often necessary for the child and parents to be seen by a child psychiatrist, psychologist, or social worker.

Parents can help by recognizing the importance of soiling, which can seriously interfere with peer relationships and self-esteem, by seeking professional help promptly, and by never shaming, embarrassing, or criticizing the child.

Bed-Wetting

814. The medical term for bed-wetting is "enuresis." It refers to those children who wet their beds after the time when most children are dry at night. One child may stop wetting the bed earlier or later than another child. It's like the development of walking—some children walk at nine months, others not until fifteen or sixteen months. The range of onset of a skill like walking is guided by family history and individual maturity of the nerves and muscles that control balance and movement.

It is not surprising that the bladder acts the same way. The bladder is a hollow cavity made from a muscle wall. For a child to be dry at night, the bladder muscle must relax to allow more urine to accumulate while a tiny muscle (called the bladder sphincter) at the end of the bladder tightens. This process of muscle relaxation and tightening keeps urine in the bladder at night until the child awakens, goes to the bathroom, and urinates.

815. The bladder and sphincter muscles mature at different times. By age three and a half, about two-thirds of all children are dry at night; by age four, about three-quarters of all children are dry. Over the next six years, the 25 percent of children who wet the bed at age four gradually achieve nighttime control. At eight years old 90 to 95 percent are dry, and by twelve years old only 2 to 3 percent of children continue to wet their bed, some throughout adolescence (bed-wetting after puberty may, in fact, be a wet dream). Parents, sibling, and other relatives of children who wet the bed beyond five years old often had the same experience during their childhood. It once seemed that most bed-wetters were deep sleepers. Parents told me that their child could sleep through a telephone ringing, music, and other loud sounds. Research, however, that compared bed-wetters with those children who stay dry showed no differences in the pattern of sleep. For some unknown reason, girls have less nighttime bed-wetting than boys. On a rare occasion, persistent bed-wetting may be associated with delayed or difficult toilet training.

816. Some children who have been fully trained and have been dry for an extended period may begin to wet again. The usual causes of this behavior are stress, illness (in particular, a urinary tract infection), and the onset of psychological problems. Common events that may be associated with bed-wetting are the arrival of a new baby in the family, a move to a new home or apartment, a transfer to a new school, or exposure to scary movies or videos. If the symptoms continue after the stress or illness has been removed, I suggest a consultation with your doctor or nurse practitioner. She may refer your child for an evaluation with a child psychologist or psychiatrist.

817. For most bed-wetting children, the approach is different. Bladder control at night comes about gradually after four years of age in about 25 percent of all children. Most children are not psychologically damaged if parents convey a neutral or a positive attitude by either ignoring the wet bed or explaining to their child that many kids wet the bed and that he will be able to stay dry as he grows and matures. Bed-wetting may undermine the self-esteem of some children, and interfere with their social development and peer relationships. For instance, school-age children who continue to wet are understandably reluctant to accept invitations from their friends to sleep over.

Since avoiding or lessening shame and self-doubt is an important part of any treatment program, I want to add that both mother and father should look for opportunities to build lasting self-esteem in the child. A mother should carefully avoid nagging, scolding, or belittling the child and instead express confidence that he will succeed sooner or later in gaining control. The father should make an effort to spend some time with his son or daughter on a daily basis, to recognize the child's achievements, no matter how small, listen to his stories, and laugh at his jokes. Both parents should maintain an interest in their child's attempts to remain dry, expressing pleasure when success occurs and encouragement when he fails.

818. Bed-wetting that has persisted without a long period of dryness in a child who is growing well physically and psychologically without other symptoms is usually not significant. When it is associated with daytime wetting, difficult or painful urination, unexplained recurrent fever, increased consumption of water and other fluids, or belly-aches, you should bring it to the attention of your child's doctor or nurse practitioner. In the absence of any of these symptoms, and after a normal physical examination, most doctors will be comfortable with watching a five-year-old child without any intervention. Some doctors and nurse practitioners may check the urine for an infection or other problems.

Since most children will gain nighttime control of the bladder by age eight, the only treatment usually necessary is for the parents to help the child avoid shame, self-doubt, and embarrassment. For those school-age children and adolescents whose bed-wetting has led to poor self-esteem or who are inhibited from accepting sleep-over invitations or going to summer camp, measures can be taken that will help until the child develops his own control. Buzzer alarms are available that ring when the bed first gets wet (awakening the child and reminding him to urinate in the toilet), as are pills that increase the amount of urine the bladder will hold and a nose spray that decreases the amount of urine made during sleep.

In summary, it seems clear that there are different causes of enuresis including family disposition, sex of the child, stress and illness, a precipitating event such as the arrival of a new baby in the family, and less commonly, a lack of adequate toilet training. However, regardless of the cause, both parents and child should understand that the problem is common and that a great majority of bed-wetters gain control sooner or later through a combination of understanding and a consistently positive parental attitude.

Stuttering

819. Stuttering is common between ages two and three. We don't entirely understand stuttering, but we know several things about it. It often runs in families, and it's much more common in boys than girls. Trying to change a left-handed child to right-handed sometimes appears to start it. The part of the brain that controls speech is closely connected to the part that controls the hand that a person naturally prefers. If you force a left-handed child to use his right hand, it seems to confuse the nervous machinery for talking.

We also know that a child's emotional state has a lot to do with stuttering. Most cases occur in somewhat tense children. Some stutter only when they are excited or when they are talking to one particular person. One little boy began to stutter when a new baby sister was brought home from the hospital. He didn't show his jealousy outwardly. He never tried to hit or pinch her. He just became uneasy. A girl of two and a half began to stutter after the departure of a fond relative who had been with the family a long time. In two weeks her stuttering stopped for the time being. When the family moved to a new house, she was quite homesick and stuttered again for a period. Two months later her father was called into the army. The family was upset, and the little girl started stuttering again. Parents report that their children's stuttering is definitely worse when they themselves are tense. I think children who, during too much of the day, are talked to and told stories, urged to talk and recite, and shown off are especially likely to stutter. Stuttering may also start when a parent decides to be stricter in discipline.

Why is stuttering so common between two and three? There are two possible explanations. This is the age when a child is working very hard at talking. When he was younger, he used short sentences that he didn't need to think out: "See the car," "Wanna go out." But when he gets past two, he tries to make up longer sentences to express new ideas. He may start a sentence three or four times, only to break off in the middle because he can't find the right words. His parents, worn out by his constant talking, don't pay too much attention. They say "Uh-huh" in an absentminded way while they go about their business. So the child is further frustrated by not being able to hold his audience. It is also possible that the balkiness that is a part of this rather tense stage of development affects his speech, too.

820. What to do about stuttering. You may be especially distressed if you yourself or some relative has had a lifelong struggle to overcome stuttering. But there is no cause for alarm. I think nine out of ten children who start to stutter between two and three outgrow it in a few months' time if given half a chance. It's only the exceptional case that becomes chronic. Don't try to correct the child's speech or worry about speech training at two and a half. Look around to see what might be making the child tense. If he was upset by being separated from you for a number of days, try to avoid further separations for a couple of months (Section 421). If you think you have been talking to him or urging him to talk too much, try to train yourself out of it. Play with him by doing things instead of by always talking things. Does he have plenty of chances to play with other children with whom he gets along easily? Does he have toys and equipment enough, indoors and out, so that he can invent his own games without too much bossing? I don't mean that you should ignore or isolate him, but when you're with him be relaxed and let him take the lead. When he talks to you, give him your full attention so that he doesn't get frantic. If jealousy is upsetting him, see what you can do to prevent it. Stuttering in most cases lasts a number of months, with ups and downs. Don't expect it to go right away; be content with gradual progress. If you can't figure out what is wrong, talk the situation over with a child mental health professional. A "tongue tie" (when the frenulum, the fold of skin that runs from the middle of the underside of the tongue to the floor of the mouth, appears to be too short to allow free movement of the tongue) has nothing to do with stuttering and should not be cut.

There are specially trained speech therapists who work with very young children. Some schools and hospitals have special speech classes or clinics in which older children can receive special training. This is often helpful, but it is by no means always successful. It is most valuable for the school-age child who wants assistance. For the child who is of a distinctly nervous type, it might be better to consult a child mental health professional first to see if it's possible to discover and remove the causes of the tension. The Consumer Information Division of the American Speech, Language and Hearing Association has a list of qualified speech therapists throughout the country. Call (800) 638-8255 or write to 10801 Rockville Pike, Rockville, MD 20852.

Rhythmic Habits

821. Rocking, jouncing, head-rolling, and head-banging are reported in 5 to 15 percent of normal children. This usually occurs between six and eight months of age and generally stops by four years. Teething or an ear infection may cause a sudden onset of symptoms. In rocking, a baby sitting in a chair or couch will rock hard against the back and let it bounce her forward again. Jouncing is when a baby gets on all fours and jounces back and forth against her heels. A baby may roll her head from side to side while lying in the crib. Head-banging occurs when a baby bangs her head repeatedly against a hard surface like the head of the crib. This is the most distressing of rhythmic motions to parents because of an understandable fear that the child may injure herself. But she won't.

Rhythmic habits are common, but they're rarely severe enough to injure a child. Since they usually reflect developmentally appropriate self-stimulation, parents can be quickly reassured. Children who have been abused or neglected may body-rock or head-bang excessively and constantly. In these children, a thorough medical and psychosocial history will reveal the larger problem.

822. What's the meaning of these rhythmic movements? They usually appear during the second half of the first year, when babies naturally acquire a sense of rhythm. The movements are usually carried out—as are thumb-sucking or the stroking of a soft toy—when the child is tired, sleepy, or frustrated (see Sections 786 and 803). So I think they come under the heading of comforters and represent a desire to reproduce the experience of being rocked and carried by a parent in very early infancy.

Rhythmic behaviors are infrequent in most children and occur at specific moments—when sleepy, bored or upset. The same movements, especially head-banging, occur frequently and intensely in some children who are emotionally neglected or physically abused. If you see such behavior occurring with great regularity in your child, discuss it with your child's doctor or nurse practitioner.

The Premature Baby

A baby weighing much under five pounds will probably need to remain in a hospital where an incubator and expert care are available.

823. It's hard to get over your anxiety. Most premature babies develop quite normally, allowing for their prematurity. Though they gain weight slowly at first, they usually gain and grow more rapidly for a while later to make up for this. Naturally, they cannot make up for their youngness. The baby who was born two months early and has become "one year old" should be thought of as really a ten-month-old.

824. By the time a premature baby weighs six pounds, he needs no more coddling or worrying than any baby. This can be very hard for the parents to believe. In the beginning the doctor may have cautioned them against being too optimistic and then only gradually become more reassuring. The baby probably had to be in an incubator, watched constantly by nurses and doctors, and fed by tube at first. The parents might not have been able to get near him most of that time, though most hospitals are now encouraging parents to touch and, where possible, hold and feed their premature babies from the very beginning. The mother may have had to go home from the hospital without him, and both parents then lived a strange kind of parental life for a number of weeks, knowing in a theoretical way that they had a baby but not completely feeling as if they did. As such parents say, "Sometimes it felt like he was the hospital's baby, not ours."

It's no wonder that when the doctor finally says, "Now you can take him home," the parents may feel quite frightened and unready. They may find all kinds of reasons why they can't take him home yet. The nurses and doctors understand these feelings of uncertainty and can help you with them. Make sure that you have practiced, under the nurses' supervision, providing all of the care the baby will need at home, so you'll know you've got it right. It helps to spend as much time as possible at the hospital with the baby in the last few days before he comes home.

When the baby at last comes home, all the worries that all new parents experience—about room temperature, baby temperature, breathing, hiccups, burps, bowel movements, breast-feeding, formula-making, schedule, crying, colic, spoiling—hit the parents of a premature baby with triple force. It may take weeks before they gain self-confidence and months before they are convinced that their baby is as healthy, husky, and advanced as any other child conceived at the same time.

825. Worrisome relatives and neighbors. Meanwhile, other troubles may come from the outside. Neighbors and relatives often act more anxious, more awestruck, more preoccupied than do the parents. They question, they exclaim, they fuss until the parents can hardly stand it any longer. A few of the visitors insist on telling the parents all the wild stories they have heard about how frail and susceptible premature babies remain. This kind of talk would be bad enough for the parents to hear if it were true. It's particularly unfortunate for them to be subjected to untruths of this sort at a time when they are trying to overcome their own anxiety.

826. Feeding. Premature babies are often discharged from the hospital when they weigh about four pounds. You can find out how much and how often your baby is being fed at the hospital and go on from there. If the baby is bottle-fed, you can expect to be able to gradually increase the feeding size and the time between feedings when the baby seems ready, just as if he were full term.

The main thing to be on guard against in the beginning is attempting to get the baby to take more milk, and later more solids, than he wants. This is a great temptation because he looks so thin. You feel that if you could squeeze a little more milk into him he would fatten up faster and thus be better able to throw off any germs. But resistance to disease has nothing to do with fatness. Your baby, like every other, has his individual pattern of growth and an appetite to take care of it. If you push food beyond what he is eager for, you only take away his appetite and slow up his weight gaining.

Like full-term babies, premature babies are not begun on solids until age four to six months nowadays. Because of the parents' anxiety about growth, it's important here, too, to be tactful, to give him plenty of time to get to like solids, and to increase the amount only as he shows his enthusiasm. In other words, avoid feeding problems.

827. Breast-feeding a premature baby. A mother who wants to breast-feed will have been regularly pumping her breasts and providing her milk for her baby during his hospital stay. As the baby becomes larger and stronger, the nurses can help the mother start breast-feeding, usually before the baby comes home. Getting the baby on breast-feeding is a gradual process. He is used to bottle-feedings, tends to tire easily, and has a small mouth. You can get help from someone who is experienced and comfortable with breast-feeding a premature baby. Often the hospital nurses can refer you to a nurse who is a lactation specialist in your community, or you can call the local La Leche League (see Guide to Child and Family Resources, page 859).

828. No other precautions. He can have a tub bath as soon as he comes home (make sure you keep him warm). Once he is gaining weight well, he can go on outings like any normal newborn baby.

The parents certainly don't need to wear masks even

when he first comes home. He has to get used to the ordinary family germs. He shouldn't be exposed to outsiders with colds or other infections any more than any baby or child should, but otherwise no special precautions are necessary or wise.

829. Vulnerability. Parents should be aware that some of these babies have a lower threshold for stimulation, and parents should not feel guilty or frantic when they find their baby is more easily overstimulated and less easily soothed.

830. Immunizations are started at two months after birth, as with full-term infants. This is because, if anything, premature babies have fewer reactions to shots, and they especially need protection from illnesses such as whooping cough.

An organization of parents and professionals that can help you and your doctor is: Parent Care, Inc., $101\frac{1}{2}$ South Union Street, Alexandria, VA 22314. You can call them at (703) 836-4678.

DEVELOPMENTAL DISABILITIES

Children with Disabilities

Having a child with a disability or chronic problem sets a family on an unexpected journey. This is not the journey that anyone expected or prepared for. It can be an arduous journey: uncertainties are heightened, the road is steeper, and the destination is uncertain. Parents are suddenly thrust into an unfamiliar world of medical subspecialists, of high-tech medical equipment and imposing medical facilities, of new jargon, of interaction with a host of habilitative specialists, of a world that seems very far from the one they grew up in and had in mind for their child.

Conditions such as impaired hearing, impaired vision, mental retardation, emotional disabilities, cerebral palsy, and learning disabilities will require a variety of special services.

831. A delicate balance. There is the potential for sorrow on this road, to be sure, but many parents also tell us of the joy. Having a child with a disability presents opportunities for growth to many parents and their other children which they might have missed otherwise—opportunities to learn compassion, empathy, and an expanded definition of love. Many relationships between spouses are strengthened by sharing this journey—though some others are shattered by the stress. Many learn to appreciate the beauty and wonder of loving a child with a disability.

You need to achieve a delicate balance and it's a hard one. It's a balance between meeting the needs of your disabled child and caring for the rest of your family and for yourself. It requires making priorities and a wise investment of your limited energy and time. There is no perfect way to be a parent of a child with disabilities. There are *always* trade-offs: sometimes you just need to get away for your own peace of mind; sometimes you feel that you're neglecting one family member while you attend to the needs of another; sometimes you feel as if you're just not up to the task.

This is all par for the course; you can't do it all. The good news is that you don't *need* to do it all—after all, no one ever has. You and your family have hidden strengths and enough resilience to withstand almost anything except the lack of love. Perhaps achieving a balance is not a good metaphor after all. Perhaps it's more like being on a seesaw: sometimes you're way up, other times you're way down, but most of the time you find that you're balanced in the middle.

Here are some tips to help you find that balance.

832. Cope with your grief. *All* parents who have a child with a disability grieve. This is entirely normal and understandable. You first have to mourn the loss of the perfect child you didn't get before you can learn to accept the one you did. You must work through the stages of grieving: shock, denial, sadness, anger, and finally accommodation. You'll notice that I don't use the word "acceptance" because I'm not certain that most parents ever really accept this blow from fate. Rather, I believe the goal is an accommodation to this new reality that allows you to integrate it into your life in such a way that your capacity for love, joy, and personal growth is largely retained.

Another misconception about the stages of grieving is that you go through them, resolve them one at a time, and then move on to the next and then the next. Most parents say that all of these stages of grieving are always there, that these feelings become much less intense, but are always lurking below the surface. So you find yourself feeling angry or depressed for no apparent reason—at the supermarket, perhaps—until you realize that your grief has for some reason emerged at this time. Grief reactions become worrisome only when a father or mother seems to be locked into one of them with no room to move on—the parent who is angry at everybody, or who is so depressed as to be unable to get out of bed in the morning, or who persistently refuses to acknowledge the reality of the child's circumstances. Although such responses are not uncommon early on, I'd be concerned only if they rendered the parent unable to function or if they persisted without progression for many months.

833. Do something about your guilt. The other almost universal reaction by a parent to a child with a disability is guilt. I have been struck and saddened by the seemingly limitless capacity of parents to feel guilty about their child's condition. The parent thinks, "It *must* be something I did wrong," and is endlessly preoccupied with what that might have been, despite reassurances from professionals that the condition was an unfortunate accident. One parent told me that, deep down inside, she was convinced her child's malformed hand was caused by the aspirin she took during her pregnancy (although it had nothing to do with it). Others recurrently relive the scene of an accident and berate themselves: "If only I had not let him ride his bicycle on that street, this never would have happened."

834. Don't go it alone. Sometimes the isolation of having a child with a disability seems overwhelming; but there are millions of parents contending with similar issues. Almost every imaginable condition has a national group. (I have listed many of these in the Guide to Child and Family Resources, page 859.) Their home branches offer information; but more importantly, they welcome parents who are in similar straits and who want to discuss common issues and feelings. Others just want one or two parents to call for advice and support. However it feels right for you, seek support. I also recommend subscribing to *Exceptional Parent* magazine (555 Kinderkamack Road, Oradell, NJ 07649,

800-372-7368), which is full of wonderful information and articles about the problems and joys of parenting a child with a disability.

835. Learning disability specialist. Find a learning disability specialist at your school or a special education teacher, or tutor, or child guidance person who specializes in your child's particular disability. Ask for referrals for therapy and help that is available in the classroom and at home. The reference list in the back of this book might be useful. Some cities have listings in the Yellow Pages that might help you meet your child's particular need.

It's important to have one primary adviser who can refer you to specialists in your child's particular disability. The medical, educational, and economic aspects must be coped with. One of the most helpful developments in recent years is the formation of parent groups for each disability to help you find facilities to help you cope with feelings of depression, guilt, frustration, and grief, and to give you emotional support.

836. Learn all you can about your child's condition. Chances are that you knew little about your child's condition at the beginning. The more you understand about it, the less mysterious it will be, the better you will be able to understand the doctors, and the more you will be able to help the therapists. Write to the national organizations that deal with this problem. Check out books from the library. And talk to your child's doctor, nurse practitioner or social worker.

837. Organize. The demands on parents of a child with disabilities can seem overwhelming—doctor's appointments, therapy sessions, diagnostic tests, school visits, and so on. You will need to become efficient if these responsibilities are not to take over your life. Many parents keep a loose-leaf binder filled with information about what has been done and what has gone on. They then bring this notebook with them to all appointments. Try to schedule as many visits on the same day as possible and look for places that offer one-stop shopping.

838. Become an advocate for your child. You may find you have to negotiate between large bureaucracies and multiple professionals. Sometimes the school system doesn't offer what you believe would be the optimal program, tailored to your child's special needs. Insurance companies may balk at paying for certain tests or therapies. Some communities are insensitive to the needs of people with disabilities and don't provide appropriate support. In such cases an insistent, knowledgeable parental voice can make all the difference. But you will need to learn exactly what services your child is legally entitled to receive, how your health insurance handles children with disabilities, what accommodations the school will make, etc.

839. The good news is that there is no voice so powerful as that of a persistent parent. Don't be easily discouraged when your efforts meet resistance. Your lone voice can move many systems in a way that others may be powerless to do. Join up with a national coalition of parents to make your single voice part of a chorus to influence legislators and the courts. We as a society are often more apt to pay lip service to a cause, but are reluctant to actually provide the necessary resources. Like everything else, you'll get better and better at advocating for your child and eventually your efforts will often succeed.

840. Don't let your child's label obscure the real person underneath. There is a tendency by all of us to define a child by his disability. That's the reason we have changed our terminology. You'll notice I don't write about "disabled children," but about "children with disabilities." It is, I think, a subtle but important distinction. The former implies that the disability is the most important and defining factor about the child, the latter implies that he is a child first, with a disability but also with many other traits.

It's your job to really see the child underneath the labels, to get to know him in all his human complexity—his strengths, his way of thinking, his responses to the world, and his joys as well as his problems. It can be a difficult assignment; sometimes the demands of the disability obscure everything else. But over time you'll find that you achieve a more complete understanding of your child, one that includes all aspects of who he is, one that accords him the status that is his birthright—to be viewed as a human being, not a label, with all the complexity, problems and joys that *that* label implies.

841. Don't neglect the child's siblings. Children with disabilities require extra effort, physically and emotionally. Given your limited and already stretched energy, it's easy to pour all of your thought and energy into this one child. After all, he needs it the most, doesn't he? And all of his healthy siblings are doing fine anyway, aren't they?

This attitude is a common trap. When this happens, the healthy siblings may come to resent the focal point of family life—their sibling's disability. They wonder why it takes a problem to engage their parents' attention. Some start to cause trouble themselves, as if to say, "Hey, I'm your child also. What about me?"

Parents need to show the healthy siblings the love and attention they need also. It's a difficult balance to achieve. There is no perfect solution and you shouldn't feel guilty because you can't do everything for everybody. But your healthy children will appreciate your frequently telling them how much you love them, how you'd like to spend more time with them, even if you can't right now. They need to see you make an extra effort to spend some special time with them, even if it's only once a week. It's also helpful to offer to include them, if they wish, in some of their sibling's evaluation or therapy sessions. This takes the mystery out of some of the attentions he is receiving, and they get to see the boredom and tedium involved in these processes.

Having a sibling with a disability can be an enriching experience for your healthy children. Many such children learn the meaning of compassion, of tolerance for differences among people, of empathy with the suffering of others, and the ability to handle peer gibes for having a "weird" sibling.

842. Don't neglect your other relationships. Your relationship with your spouse will require care and attention. The statistics are thought-provoking: about a third of marriages seem to crumble under the stress of this situation, a third remain the same, and a third are strengthened and enriched by meeting the challenges together. This last group does not happen by accident. It takes open communication and mutual trust and support. Most of all, it takes work and a commitment to invest energy in the relationship itself.

Your relationships with friends and your community are likely to change also. Having a child with a disability can be a profoundly isolating experience, if you let it. Or it can enrich your relationships with your circle of friends. Many parents learn who their real friends are—those who offer love and support, not those who shy away. You can be the best possible parent only when you don't neglect the other important things in your life. You need and deserve to have friends, to go out with them and have a good time, to get away from your daily responsibilities.

In one study parents of a child with a disability were asked what was the biggest area of need in their lives. It was respite—someone to take care of their child for a time so that they could attend to these other aspects of their lives, so they could go to a movie or the shopping mall or just visit friends or family.

843. Respite equals freedom. It can come from professional agencies, friends, church or synagogue, and family. Don't feel that you should never leave your child. She needs to learn to separate from you, just as any child does, just as you need to feel comfortable when she is in the care of others.

844. Don't neglect your community. Many communities and religious groups rally in support of their members with disabilities, but they can't do so if they are not involved in their care. Introduce your child to your neighbors, to your place of worship, to the community as a whole. Help them to understand the needs of children with disabilities. I think you will be gratified at the outpouring of support from your community when they learn about and get to know your child as a person.

845. Don't neglect yourself. To be the best parent you can be means to be the best person you can be. That means taking the time to meet your own needs. Most martyrs eventually come to resent their martyrdom and the cause of it. You can provide the best care for your child when you feel happy and fulfilled as a person. No one can tell what that will take. For some parents it means finding excellent services for their child and going back to work. Others choose to devote more of their time to their children. There is no right or wrong decision here, just whatever will work best for you. Being aware of the support, relationships, and goals you need in your own life will help you make the right decisions for you and your family.

846. Regular school when possible. Many children have conditions that do not interfere with attending the regular neighborhood school and learning in a regular class. Most orthopedic disabilities, heart disease that does not seriously limit a child's activity, and peculiarities of appearance such as birthmarks fall into this category. It's best for such children to go to a regular neighborhood school. They will be living the rest of their lives among average people, and it's best for them to start thinking of themselves as average in almost all respects.

In previous times, it was believed that children with disabilities that interfere with ordinary classroom learning—such as impaired hearing or vision, for instance—should be sent from the start to special day schools in their own community or, if none was available, to specialized boarding schools. In more recent years it has been realized that though the education of children with disabilities is extremely important, their adjustment and their happiness are even more important. This means keeping in mind the sociability they will acquire from being with children without disabilities as well as with other children with disabilities, and the wholesome view they will take of the world and themselves if they grow up thinking of themselves as normal people in most respects, as well as the security they will gain from living at home with their family.

The younger children are, the more they need the close, loving, understanding kind of care, the sense of really belonging, that they are more likely to get at home than in even the best of boarding schools. So there has been an increasing effort to provide for children with disabilities in regular day schools and, when appropriate, to keep them in regular classes as much of each day as is possible. This means increasing school budgets and training more specialized teachers so that local schools can have such facilities. It means in one case that the child with disabilities may spend part of each day in a special class and other periods in a regular classroom. It is good for other children to know and understand about various disabilities. In some cases a special teacher can coach the regular classroom teacher in how to teach a subject so that the child with a disability can comprehend and participate, or she may teach the child directly.

Mental Retardation

847. First, let's be clear about what mental retardation is. A child is said to have mental retardation when, before the age of eighteen, she is functioning very much below the average for her age in at least two of the following areas: intellectual capacity, language skills, ability to take care of herself, social skills, ability to plan ahead, schoolwork, recreational interests, and vocational abilities.

Professionals used to divide children with mental retardation into those who were mildly, moderately, severely, and profoundly retarded, depending on the degree of the disabilities. But it is often difficult to apply such a category to a child who, for example, is able to function reasonably well in one setting, such as a special group home, but not in another—say, a chaotic home. Rather than just judging what the child can and cannot do, many are now categorizing children with mental retardation according to the type and intensity of supplemental services the child needs to attain her highest potential. Some children, for example, require only occasional supplemental services, others require some extra help all the time, still others require major help all the time, and some are completely dependent on others to take care of all aspects of their lives.

We often don't use the label "mental retardation" until a

child has reached a certain level of development when it becomes clear that she will always function well below average. In most children who are less than six years of age or so, we say they have "developmental delays" instead. This label implies that the child is below average but it is still unclear how much catching up she will do in the next years, especially with supplemental educational services. Since young children often show unexpected progress in their developmental function, there is sometimes a gray area where no one can predict if a developmental delay will turn into mental retardation or normal function. So if your child has been called developmentally delayed remember that the key question is not only how your child is functioning now but where she is expected to be in another five years.

848. Causes of mental retardation. You can roughly divide cases of real mental slowness into three groups: organic, experiential (or environmental), and idiopathic. *Organic* cases are those in which the brain is abnormal, either because it was malformed during development in the womb (for example, due to a genetic defect) or because physical damage was done to the brain (a brain infection or an environmental toxin, for example).

Many cases of mild mental retardation are *experiential* in the sense that the child has had insufficient mental stimulation to foster normal development or has faced some other psychological problem. This type of mental retardation is largely preventable through special educational programs for young children, such as early intervention programs and Head Start. Unfortunately only about one in four children under age three with developmental delays are enrolled in such programs because there are just not enough to go around.

Of course the distinction between organic and experiential mental retardation is not always clear; many children experience both. Perhaps neither the organic damage nor the lack of environmental stimulation would have been enough to cause mental retardation, but the two in combination tip the scales.

Idiopathic mental retardation simply means that a cause cannot be determined with our present fund of knowledge.

849. Being accepted enables slow children to make the most of their abilities. The behavior problems that a few slow children develop are sometimes due not to low intelligence but to mistaken methods of handling. If the parents feel that the child is queer or shameful, for instance, their love may not go out to him in sufficiently full measure to give him security and happiness. If they mistakenly believe that they are to blame for his condition, they may insist on "treatment" of all kinds without acknowledging measures that disturb him without benefitting him. If they jump to the conclusion that he is a hopeless case who will never be "normal," they may neglect to provide him with the playthings, the companions, the proper schooling that all children need to bring out their best abilities. One great danger is that the parents, trying to ignore the signs that a child is slow, trying to prove to themselves and the world that he is just as bright as the next child, will push him all along the line—try to teach him skills and manners before he is ready, get him into a class that he isn't up to, and coach him at home in his lessons. The constant pressure makes him balky and irritable, and being frequently in situations in which he can't succeed robs him of self-confidence.

The slow child whose parents have had only an average amount of schooling and are living happily on a modest scale often makes out better than the child who is born into a college-educated family or one that has high ambitions for worldly success. The latter are more likely to assume that it's vital to get good marks at school, to go to college, to get into a profession. Many useful and dignified jobs can be performed well by people who have less than average intelligence. It's the right of every individual to grow up well enough adjusted and well enough trained to be able to handle the best job that he has the intelligence for.

The slow child should be allowed to develop in his own pattern, to have behavior that is appropriate for his stage of mental growth rather than for his age. He needs opportunities to dig and climb and build and make believe when he is ready for these activities, and he needs playthings that appeal to him, chances to play with children he can enjoy and keep up with, even if they are a year or more younger in age. When he goes to school, he should be placed in a class where he can feel that he belongs and is accomplishing something.

850. A child's progress may be slowed down by a pessimistic attitude on the part of parents and teachers. Careful educational assessment and an individually designed program may accelerate his mental growth so that he can make up for some of his retardation. Like any child, he will benefit from feeling that he is loved warmly and enjoyed for his appealing qualities.

Anyone who has observed groups of slow children knows how natural and friendly and appealing most of them are, particularly the ones who have been accepted naturally at home. And when they are busy at play or schoolwork that is right for them, they have the same eager, interested attitude that average and superior children do. In other words, the "dumb" look comes more from feeling out of place than from having a low IQ. After all, most of us would have a dull look in an advanced lecture on relativity.

851. The care of a slow child at home. The child who is only mildly or moderately slow is, of course, usually cared for at home. This is the place where he, like the average child, gets the most security. It will be good for him to go to a preschool, if possible, where the teachers can decide whether he should be with his own age or younger children.

Parents, when they become convinced that a child is slow in his mental development, may ask the doctor or social worker what special playthings and educational material they should buy and what special instruction they should give the child at home. This is due to people's natural tendency to think, at first, that a handicapped child is different from other children. To be sure, a retarded child may have interests and capabilities that are not up to his chronological age; they correspond more to his mental age. He is apt to want to play with younger children and with toys suitable for that younger age. He might not begin to try to tie his shoelaces or to pick out letters at age five or six. He may also have difficulty in interpreting what he sees or hears.

Parents of a child of average intelligence don't have to ask a doctor or read a book to find out his interests. They simply watch him playing with his own possessions and with the possessions of neighbors and sense what else might appeal to him. They observe what he is trying to learn and help him tactfully.

It really should be just the same with a slow child. You watch to see what he enjoys. You get him the playthings that are sensible. You help him locate the children he has fun with, every day if possible. You teach him the skills he wants assistance with.

852. The right school placement is vital. It is wise to get the opinion and guidance of a psychologist or child psychiatrist, privately or through a child guidance clinic or through the school system, when it is suspected that a child is slow. He should not be placed in a class that is way beyond him. Every day that he is unable to keep up, his self-confidence will be reduced a little, and having to be left back a grade or demoted will discourage him a lot. If he is only slightly slow and the school program is one in which every child can contribute according to his ability, he may be able to move along with children his own age.

It is not ideal to delay his school attendance. If the school's policy is flexible, he should begin school even earlier than usual. Special preschool programs for slow children are being developed around the country. Special educational approaches are called for.

853. The more seriously retarded child. The child who at eighteen months or two years is still unable to sit up, who shows little interest in people or things, presents more complicated problems. She will have to be cared for like a baby for a long time. The solution depends on the degree of retardation, the temperament of the child, how she affects other children in the family, whether by the time she is active she can find playmates and activities to keep her happy, whether there is a special class in one of the local schools that will accept and suit her. Most of all, it depends on whether her parents find predominant satisfaction or strain in caring for her. Some of these questions can't be answered until the child is several years older.

854. Some parents can take a retarded child in stride. They can find ways to care for him that don't exhaust them. They are able to enjoy his agreeable qualities, not be upset by the difficulties he presents, and not become too wrapped up in his care. The other children in the family will take their cue mainly from the parents in these respects. The acceptance by the rest of the family brings out the best in the retarded child and gives him a good start in life. He may benefit most by living at home indefinitely.

Other parents who are equally devoted find themselves becoming increasingly tense and impatient in caring for a child with such special needs. This may impair their relationship with each other and their other children. These parents need a lot of help from a doctor who specializes in this field and who will usually be working with a team which includes a social worker and a children's psychologist or psychiatrist. With this help, the parents may acquire a more comfortable attitude, or they find a more satisfactory solution in a residence elsewhere than home, preferably in a small group or a foster home.

Still other parents find that they can throw themselves into the care of a seriously retarded child without a feeling of undue strain and even with an enjoyable devotion. But an outsider can see that their sense of obligation to the child is so intense that they are not thinking enough of each other, the other children or their own normal interests. In the long run, this is not healthy for the family as a whole or even for the retarded child. The parents need help in gaining a sense of proportion and in easing up in their preoccupation.

When the parents feel unable to cope with the care of the retarded child, they should consult at length with a family social agency or an agency specializing in the care of retarded children. Sometimes counseling provides the practical and emotional support that the parents need. Or it may lead to the search for a foster home or small group home for the care of the child. The tendency in recent years has been to avoid, if possible, placement in large institutions.

The Association for Retarded Citizens (ARC) of the United States, 500 East Border Street, Suite 300, Arlington, TX 76010, may be able to suggest local resources. Their phone number is (817) 261-6003.

855. Down syndrome (trisomy 21). This is a special type of genetic organic mental retardation but there is also a disturbance of bodily growth. (Down is the name of the doctor who first advanced knowledge of this condition in modern times.)

There are other distinctive characteristics. Physical growth is slow, and the child does not reach full size. Intelligence develops very slowly in most cases, but in a few it develops to a fair degree. Many of these children are characteristically sweet-natured.

856. Trisomy 21 refers to the underlying cause, an extra number 21 chromosome or an extra piece of genetic material on the 21 chromosome, present from the beginning of the life of the embryo. Sometimes there is a risk of recurrence in future pregnancies. Other times the condition occurs by chance, though it is more likely to occur toward the end of a woman's childbearing years. Chromosome studies of the fetus and parents can determine which situation is present and what the risk is for future pregnancies. Early in pregnancy an amniocentesis (a test of the fluid surrounding the fetus) or "CVS" (a test of the placenta) can determine whether or not there is a trisomy 21 condition. These tests are offered to a pregnant woman who is over thirty-five years old when the risk for Down syndrome is greater. Then the parents can decide whether or not they want to continue the pregnancy.

As in other forms of mental slowness, the best course for the future depends on how the child develops, the local opportunities for classes and playmates, how difficult or how comfortable it proves for the parents to carry out their other jobs and this special one, too. Some children with Down syndrome are reared at home enjoyably and without undue strain on parents and other children. In other cases, it turns out that as the child grows older, she and the rest of the family would be happier if she were cared for in another residence, preferably a small group home. Continued counseling is helpful to the parents in arriving at the best decision.

SCHOOL AND LEARNING PROBLEMS

School Difficulties

857. Capability in school is the first big responsibility we put on our children. That's why we should view school failure with the same urgency with which we view a high fever: it's an indication that something is wrong and that steps should be taken promptly to discover the cause. Of course, this is easier said than done; the possible causes of school failure are many.

For example, on the physical side there is hunger from inadequate nutrition, hearing or vision difficulties, chronic illness, learning disabilities (see Sections 871–874), and problems with attention (see Sections 636–638). On the psychological side are neglect, parental conflict, physical and sexual abuse, emotional conflicts, and wrong placement.

858. It's very rare for a child to fail purely on the basis of "laziness." Children who have given up their efforts to do their lessons aren't lazy at all. Children are born to be curious and enthusiastic. If they lose this, it's because there is some problem in the child's ability to learn or because of some deficiency in the school's ability to deal with the child's problem. Whether the cause of the school failure is environmental, physical, emotional, or some combination, parents should take the matter seriously.

859. Have a friendly, non-scolding discussion with your child about her learning problem. Do this in a gentle and supportive manner. What does she think is causing the problem? Ask for details about what happens in school and how she thinks and feels.

860. Meet with the teacher and principal. It's best to approach them as collaborators and not as the enemy. Many parents simply assume that the child's problems are the teacher's fault and hostilely challenge her. While the teacher or the school may contribute to the problem, it is not helpful to start out with that notion.

861. When feelings and emotional symptoms are a significant aspect of the problem an appointment should be scheduled with the child's doctor or nurse practitioner. When a psychological problem in the child or family conflicts are discovered, a referral to a psychiatrist, psychologist, or other mental health professional is recommended. Emotional causes, like physical ones, can be identified and treated successfully by competent professionals, thus removing this major hindrance to your child's development.

862. There are many approaches that educators and parents can take to minimize or eliminate school difficulties. I would suggest trying a nongraded class for a while to see if removing the pressure of grades will make the child feel less inadequate. I've taught in a medical school which did not have grades. The students were greatly relieved by the absence of this pressure. I feel that the same beneficial effect can be achieved with children who are not succeeding in elementary and secondary schools.

I want to emphasize strongly that repeating a grade is usually a painful disaster, particularly if it occurs beyond the first few grades. The social and emotional consequences and the blow to self-esteem often result in a child eventually dropping out of school, particularly when he reaches junior high school.

863. There is much that parents can do outside the school setting to help the child who is having serious academic

problems. The key to a rewarding learning experience is to find ways to encourage responsibility that is appropriate for your child's learning skills. Take advantage of the fact that most children are curious about the world around them. When you share and encourage that curiosity, the child's interest in learning grows. Explore with your child her special interests. Allow the child to guide you and listen for eagerness in certain subjects. Follow up such interest with field trips, reading materials and projects of the child's choice.

If possible, each child should have a quiet place in which to study. However, if the family uses its time together to watch television endlessly, it will be hard for the poor student to stay interested in schoolwork. Rather than restricting TV hours for the children, it's a matter of setting a good example yourself. If parents spend some of their time in the evening reading and writing, then the child soon realizes that learning is important. Studies show that children spend more hours watching television than they spend in school, but I know of families who refuse to have a TV at all in their homes, and they seem to survive quite well.

In summary, I have tried to demonstrate that the causes of school difficulties are varied and complex. When parents, educators, doctors and mental health professionals work together, the chances of identifying the problem and correcting it are greatly increased.

What a School Is For

864. The main lesson learned in school is how to get along in the world. Different subjects are merely means to this end. In the old days, it used to be thought that all a school had to do was teach children how to read, write, figure, and memorize a certain number of facts about the world. I heard a teacher tell how, in his own school days, he had to memorize a definition of a preposition that went something like this: "A preposition is a word, generally with some meaning of position, direction, time, or other abstract relation, used to connect a noun or pronoun, in an adjectival or adverbial sense, with some other word."

Of course, he didn't learn anything when he memorized

that. You learn only when things have meaning for you. One job of a school is to make subjects so interesting and real that children want to learn and remember information for the rest of their lives.

You can go only so far with books and talk. You learn better from actually living the things you are studying. Children pick up more arithmetic in a week from running a school store—making change and keeping the books—than they learn in a month out of a book of cold figures.

There's no use in knowing a lot if you can't be happy, get along with people, and hold the kind of job you want. The good teacher tries to understand each child in order to help each pupil overcome weak points and develop into a well-rounded person. The child who lacks self-confidence needs chances to succeed. The troublemaking show-off has to learn how to gain the recognition he craves through doing good work. The child who doesn't know how to make friends needs help in becoming sociable and appealing. The child who seems to be lazy has to have her enthusiasm discovered.

A school can go only so far with a cut-and-dried program in which everyone in the class reads from page 7 to page 23 in the textbook at the same time and then does the examples on page 128 of the arithmetic book. This works well enough for the average child who is well adjusted anyway. But it's too dull for the bright pupils, too speedy for the slow ones. It gives the boy who hates books a chance to stick paper clips in the pigtails of the girl in front of him. It does nothing to help the girl who is lonely or the boy who needs to learn cooperation.

865. How schoolwork is made real and interesting. If you start with a topic that is real and interesting you can use it to teach all manner of subjects. Take the case of a third-grade class in which the work of the term revolves around Indians. The more the children find out about Indians, the more they want to know. The textbook is a story about the Indians, and the children really want to know what it says. For arithmetic they study how the Indians counted and what they used for money. Then arithmetic isn't a separate subject at all, but a useful part of life. Geography isn't spots on a map; it's where the Indians lived and traveled, and how life on the plains is different from forest life. In science study the children make dye from berries and use it to dye cloth. They can make bows and arrows and Indian costumes.

People are sometimes uneasy about schoolwork's being too interesting, feeling that a child needs mostly to learn how to do what's unpleasant and difficult. But if you stop and think of the people you know who are unusually successful, you'll see that in most cases they are the ones who love their work. In any job there's plenty of drudgery, but you do the drudgery because you see its connection with the fascinating side of the work. Darwin was a wretched student in all his subjects in school. But in later life he became interested in natural history, performed one of the most painstaking jobs of research that the world has ever known, and worked out the theory of evolution. A boy in high school may see no sense in geometry, hate it, and do badly in it. But if he is studying to be a navigator of planes, sees what geometry is for, and realizes that it could save the lives of the crew and passengers, he works at it like a demon. The teachers in a good school know well that every child needs to develop self-discipline to be a useful adult. But they have learned that you can't snap discipline onto children from the outside, like handcuffs; it's something that children have to develop inside, like a backbone, by first understanding the purpose of their work and feeling a sense of responsibility to others in how they perform it.

866. How school helps a child with difficulties. A flexible, interesting program does more than just make schoolwork appealing. It can be adjusted for the individual pupil. Take the case of a girl who had spent her first two years in a school where teaching was done by separate subjects. She'd had great difficulty learning to read and write, had fallen behind the rest of the class, and felt ashamed about being a failure. Outwardly she wouldn't admit anything except that she hated school. She had never gotten along too easily with other kids anyway, even before her school troubles began.

Feeling that she was stupid in the eyes of the others made matters worse. She had a chip on her shoulder. Once in a while she would show off to the class in a smarty way. Her teacher used to think that she was just trying to be bad. Of course, she was really attempting, in this unfortunate way, to gain some kind of attention from the group. It was a healthy impulse to keep herself from being shut out.

She transferred to a school that was interested in helping her not only to read and write but also to find her place in the group. The teacher learned in a conference with her mother that she used tools well and loved to paint and draw. He saw ways to use her strong points in the class. The children were all painting together a large picture of Indian life to hang on the wall. They were also working cooperatively on a model of an Indian village. The teacher arranged for the girl to have a part in both these projects. Here were things she could do well without nervousness.

As the days went by, she became more and more fascinated with Indians. In order to paint her part of the picture well, in order to make her part of the model correctly, she needed to find out more from the books about Indians. She wanted to learn to read. She tried harder. Her new classmates didn't think of her as a dope because she couldn't read. They thought more about what a help she was in creating the painting and the model. They occasionally commented on how good her work was and asked her to help them. She began to warm up. After all, she had been aching for recognition and friendliness for a long while. As she felt more accepted, she became more friendly and outgoing.

867. Linking school with the world. A school wants its pupils to learn firsthand about the outside world, about the jobs of the local farmers and businesspeople and workers, so that they will see the connection between their schoolwork and real life. It arranges trips to nearby industries, asks people from the outside to come in and talk, encourages classroom discussion. A class that is studying food may have an opportunity, for example, to observe some of the steps in the growing, harvesting, transportation, and marketing of vegetables.

868. Democracy builds discipline. Another thing that a good school wants to teach is democracy, not just as a patriotic ideal but as a way of living and getting things done. A good teacher knows that she can't teach democracy out of a book if she's acting like a dictator in her classroom. She encourages her pupils to decide how to tackle certain projects as well as the difficulties they will later run into. She lets them figure out among themselves which one is to do this part of the job and which one that. That's how they learn to appreciate each other. That's how they learn to get things done, not just in school but in the outside world, too.

Studies have shown that children with a teacher who tells them what to do every step of the way will work while she is in the room, but when she goes out, a lot of them will start fooling around. They figure that lessons are the teacher's responsibility, not theirs, and that now they have a chance to be themselves. But these studies also showed that children who help to choose and plan their own work and cooperate with each other in carrying it out accomplish almost as much when the teacher is out of the room as when she is present.

Why? They know the purpose of their work and the steps to accomplish it. They feel that it is their work, not the teacher's. Each one wants to do a fair share because each is proud to be a respected member of the group, and each feels a sense of responsibility to the others.

This is the very highest kind of discipline. This training, this spirit, is what makes the best citizens, the most valuable workers, and even the finest soldiers.

869. Cooperating with other child specialists. Even the best of teachers can't solve all the problems of their pupils alone. They need the cooperation of the parents through PTA meetings and individual conferences. Then parent and teacher will understand what the other is doing and share what they know about the child. The teacher should even be able to get in touch with the child's scout master, minister, and doctor, and vice versa. Each can do a better job by working with the other.

It's particularly important in the case of a child with a chronic ailment that the teacher and school nurse know just what it is, how it's being treated, what he or she can do or watch for in school. It's just as important for the doctor to know how the disease is affecting the child during school hours, how the school can help, and how treatment can be prescribed so as not to work against what the school is trying to accomplish with the child.

Some children will have problems that the regular teacher and the parents, no matter how understanding, can solve better with the help of mental health professionals. Most schools have a guidance counselor, psychologist, or visiting teacher trained to help children, parents, and classroom teachers understand and overcome a child's school difficulties. When the problem is deep-rooted, it is wise to turn to a child psychiatrist or psychologist to assist the school personnel.

870. How to work for good schools. Parents sometimes say, "It's all very well to talk about ideal schools, but the school that my child goes to is pretty cut-and-dried and there's nothing I can do about it." That may or may not be true. When towns and cities do have superior schools, it is because the parents there know their value and have fought for them. But a neighborhood group in a larger city may find itself powerless against the bureaucracy of the central board of education and the indifference of municipal officials who serve special interests rather than the people generally. An important step would be to replace each central board of education with a number of neighborhood boards made up of representatives of local parents and teachers, the people who care most about children's education.

Parents can join their local PTA, go to meetings regularly, and show the teachers and principals and superintendents that they are interested and will back them up if they are using sound methods. They can also vote and campaign for the election of local officials who will work for constant improvement in the schools and actively support school bond issues.

Many people fail to realize how much fine schools can accomplish in developing useful, happy citizens. They object to increasing the school budget for smaller classes, better-paid teachers, teacher aides, computers, carpentry shops, laboratories, music, and after-school recreation programs. Not understanding the purpose or value of these proposals, they naturally think of them as unnecessary frills meant only to amuse children or to create jobs for more teachers.

Even from a strictly cash point of view, that's penny wise and dollar foolish. Money spent wisely for better child care pays back the community tenfold. First-rate schools that succeed in making each child feel that she really belongs, as a useful and respected member of the group, drastically reduce the number of individuals who grow up irresponsible or criminal. The value of such schools shows even more in all the other children (who would never be criminals anyway) who take their place in the community as better workers, more cooperative citizens, and happier individuals in their own lives. How better can a community spend its money?

Learning Disabilities

There was a time, not so long ago, when only two reasons were presented for why a child was having difficulty with reading, writing, and arithmetic. Either he "wasn't trying" or else he was just "not as bright as other children." Now we know that this is a simplistic and inaccurate view of learning disabilities.

871. The term "learning disability" refers to difficulties in acquiring and using language (including spoken language, reading, and spelling) and/or mathematics. A disability may exist in one or several areas. Although the precise cause of learning disabilities is still not known, most scientists and educators believe that alterations in the structure or chemistry of the brain are major factors. Learning disabilities tend to run in families, although this is not always the case. They also occur more frequently in boys than in girls.

It's helpful to remember that a learning disability—let's say in reading—can be caused by any one of a number of problems or by a combination of problems. Maybe he can't see the differences between letters, or he has a hard time understanding spoken words, or he cannot remember, or he can't pay attention, or he has difficulty keeping letters and words in their proper order. It's not enough to say that he has a learning disability in reading. We must question exactly what is interfering with his ability to learn a particular skill.

Let's consider an example. To you and me the word "dog" looks entirely different from the word "god." But most young children, when they are just beginning to read, think these words look much the same, because each spells the other backwards. They occasionally read "was" for "saw" and "on" for "no." In writing they sometimes reverse letters, especially those like small "b" and small "p," or confuse them with "d" or "q." This is normal when children are first learning to read; but as the months go by, most learn to perceive and remember letters and words more accurately and these mistakes become infrequent and disappear, usually by the end of second grade.

But about 10 percent of children, most of them boys, have much more than the average difficulty recognizing and remembering the appearance of letters and words. They continue to reverse words and letters for several more years. It takes them much longer to learn to read reasonably well, and some of them remain poor spellers for life, no matter how much they are drilled. (For example, George Washington was a terrible speller.)

872. Although learning disabilities appear to be primarily the result of brain immaturity or dysfunction, stress or some other emotional upheaval may make them more obvious or severe. Maybe the parents are going through a divorce or there is a new baby in the family, or possibly a death. Or, in addition to the learning disability, the child may be emotionally immature; he may have exaggerated fears or nightmares or significant problems getting along with peers. Any of these circumstances could intensify the existing problem in learning.

873. In addition, learning disabilities are often a cause, in and of themselves, of emotional problems. Learning disabilities have nothing to do with intelligence. A child can be as smart as a whip but still unable to learn. Many children with learning disabilities quickly get the idea that they are dumb and often come to hate school because they cannot keep up with the other students. They need to be reassured by parents and teachers that this is a special learning problem that can be solved with the help of tutors, learning disability specialists and mental health professionals.

In addition, classmates are quick to notice a child's learning problems. I remember one child who was never chosen to be on the spelling team because of her poor spelling skills. She was shamed and teased by some of her classmates. Teachers who are sensitive to this can avoid exposing the child's difficulties to the rest of the class.

874. The diagnosis of learning disabilities can be complex. I would recommend that any child who does not seem to be working up to his potential be evaluated. Work closely with the school, exploring whatever diagnostic services they offer. If you are not satisfied or if help is unavailable, learning disability specialists and mental health professionals are readily available in most cities. Do not wait, because time is precious. Children with learning disabilities who struggle through the early elementary grades without help often become discouraged and defeated and never regain their optimism and excitement about learning.

Diagnostic evaluations should include testing of speech, vision, and hearing, and a series of specialized tests that examine in detail the components of learning. Examination by a pediatrician, child neurologist, and/or child psychiatrist should be part of the evaluation to address any neurological or psychological aspects to the learning disorder. Make sure you sit down with the evaluator at the end of the examination and understand exactly what has been found. The more you understand, the better able you will be to find ways to overcome your child's problem. (For example, to use spoken language instead of written language to give instructions.)

Most children with learning disabilities benefit from certain changes in the classroom (for example, sitting closer to the teacher and blackboard) and in the curriculum, as well as specialized supplemental instruction in the problem areas both in school and at home, with the help of tutors.

Most good public and private schools recognize the existence of learning disabilities and have some services intended to diagnose and correct them. Since these problems, particularly the more severe ones, continue to interfere with learning throughout life, high schools, colleges and universities, and businesses also have special programs that help adults develop into successful and self-confident individuals and productive members of society.

And remember not to focus on the disability to the exclusion of the child's abilities. Parents need to make sure that a child's talents and strengths are recognized and appreciated.

The Gifted Child

In a class in which everyone is expected to work at exactly the same level, the child who is smarter than most others may become bored because the work seems too easy or repetitious. Should such a child be advanced to the next higher grade level or stay in a classroom with other children her age? What should a caring parent do in such a situation?

I believe that sensitive parents are aware of their child's skills as much as, and in some cases more than, the teacher. Therefore, if you think your child could benefit from placement in an advanced class, discuss this possibility with the teacher and the school counselor. Regardless of the decision, it is your responsibility to see that your child's skills are being dealt with in a way that will maximize her potential.

Skipping a grade is not always the answer, nor is such a decision without risks. If your daughter is large for her age and advanced socially, the move may be beneficial. But if she is too small to compete in games or be popular and if she has younger interests than the other members of the class, she may become isolated or lonely.

875. Very intelligent children demonstrate their abilities well before they enter school through their curiosity, language development, and interest in reading and writing. Educators have known for a long time that encouraging such curiosity and interests by talking and reading to young children on a daily basis and exposing them to the world around them is the best way to help children of all capabilities.

The education of gifted school-age children (and all others as well) can also be greatly enhanced by involvement in stimulating activities, which parents can provide and share with them. Visits to museums, the zoo, and the library will feed eager learning hunger. You may also want to include concerts, travel, and nature hikes. Such ventures can enrich your child's experience and help her bring back to the classroom a wider knowledge of the world at large.

In some instances parents are more ambitious for their children than they perhaps realize, and they push intellectual achievement at the expense of raising an emotionally secure, well-rounded human being. For instance, when the child is playing house at the age of four, the parents may show only casual interest. But when the child begins reading, the adults' eyes light up and their interest becomes intense. The child senses their delight and responds with greater ambition. The result may be a child who is weaned away from the natural occupations of her age and turned into a scholar before her time.

876. Parents wouldn't be good parents if they didn't delight in their children's fine qualities. But it is necessary to distinguish between the child's interests and the parents' eager hopes. If parents who are intensely ambitious can honestly admit this to themselves and are on guard against using their ambition to run their children's lives, the children will grow up to be happier, abler, and intellectually and emotionally more secure. This applies not only to early reading and writing but also to putting pressure on a child at any age, whether the issue is schoolwork, music lessons, athletics, or social life.

Caroline Zachry, the great progressive educator, always emphasized that you don't have to have special classes for gifted children or put all bright children in one class. A well-trained teacher can enrich the daily work of the extra-bright children so that they are adequately stimulated but not pulled out of their age group, where they probably belong socially.

The Unpopular Child

877. For the unpopular child, every day brings new trials. He's belittled and teased by his peers, victimized by bullies, the last to be picked for any sport. It's as hard a row as a child may have to hoe. The unhappy result in the worst cases is an increasing sense of isolation and alienation, meager self-esteem, depression, and a sense of hopelessness about the future.

Of course, all is not lost by any means for the unpopular child. Some studies have suggested that some unpopular children become the most successful adults. Having learned to cope with adversity and nonacceptance, they often emerge from childhood with less need to conform and more self-directed ambition. It is important for parents to understand that I am not talking now about the child who has some friends but who occasionally feels unpopular or excluded from the in-group; I am talking about the child who has few or no friends and is isolated, teased, and abused most of the time.

In most instances a child who is very unpopular is one who does not meet the expectations and patterns of behavior of his classmates and peers. Such children do not understand what is expected of all members of the peer group and do not anticipate how others will respond before they act or speak. Because they are often immature and self-centered, they do not know how to ask for something without causing offense, and they lack awareness of how their actions and words are being perceived by their peers. In other words, markedly unpopular children are isolated because they do not act in age-appropriate ways, because their behavior and words are not similar to those of the healthier members of the peer group. In short, the most isolated and unhappy children usually have significant emotional problems which explain their difficulties. Other children, of course, do not understand this. They simply know that the unpopular child does not know how to play as they do, that he won't follow the rules in games, or that he insists on having things his way all the time. They reject the unpopular child because he is different from them. This is not a difference based on race or religion or ethnicity. It is a difference based on deviation from the standards and expectation of the peer group. As cruel as his peers may be, their judgment is taken seriously by professionals as an indication that something may be significantly wrong with the unpopular child and that the problem needs to be investigated.

878. Helping the unpopular child. If your child is very unpopular, take the matter seriously. Do not shrug it off as unimportant. Observe his behavior with other children and try, as best you can, to determine how often he acts different or provokes or withdraws from the others. If your concerns remain, speak to other parents, teachers, and caring adults who will be honest with you about your child's behavior. As I mentioned previously, if the isolation and unpopularity are extreme, then evaluation by a child psychiatrist or psychologist is usually indicated. The best way to solve the problem is usually a combination of therapy and efforts on the part of caring parents and involved adults such as teachers and friends to minimize the harmful effects of the isolation and abuse until the child begins to change. Some of the following suggestions may help you and your child.

Invite one friend to your home to play, or take him with your child to the park, a movie, or some other place of mutual interest. Taking just one friend avoids your child being the odd man out. Watch your child's behavior during these excursions, and after the potential friend has left, gently point out ways in which your child's behavior was inappropriate, selfish, or cruel.

The unpopular child of any age always is treated better when adults are around to supervise play activities. For this reason, enroll your child in group activities such as sports, religious events, or dance classes. Explain your problem to the group leader and ask for her help. It will not be a new or unusual problem to anyone who has worked extensively with children. Many children, by adolescence, will have found one or two friends who have similar interests, and this is a great comfort and helps them to build other friendships.

When your child has had a difficult experience with other children, be available and listen empathetically. Do not scold or reprimand. Always make your home a safe refuge and your interactions with him an unshakable source of comfort, love, and self-esteem.

Remember that parental understanding and unequivocal love, the support of other adults, and in some instances professional evaluation and treatment can go a long way toward helping an unpopular child get along.

School Avoidance

879. "School avoidance" is a term used for a child's reluctance to go to school regardless of the cause. Some children throughout the elementary grades and even in high school can have severe difficulty with, even genuine fear of, going to school. The specific reason must be discovered in each case.

The most common cause of school avoidance in kindergarten is separation anxiety. Not all children by the time they reach kindergarten age have progressed far enough developmentally to be comfortable away from their mothers for long periods of time. And yet we in effect ask our five-year-olds to come to a strange, very big building in which they may feel lost at first. (I remember one bewildered child who got off the school bus on the first day of school and said to the principal who was standing nearby, "Hey, mister, is this school?") In addition, we expect them to give themselves up to strange adults and to share these grown-ups with a roomful of other children who are also strangers. Most children adjust readily, but some may not.

880. How should the situation be handled? If parents and teachers see that their basic aim is to help the child separate from home and adjust to school and the outside world, much can be done. If, on the other hand, their only interest is in formal learning, they may miss an opportunity to help the child grow emotionally.

First, as in all cases of problem behavior, an attempt should be made to understand the meaning of the child's behavior. It may range from simply being very young to a reaction to the anxiety of overly anxious parents. Or the child may be chronically ill. If we recognize that the behavior may be due to different factors, it follows that our response must vary accordingly. Some teachers insist that the boy or girl be left at school despite a flood of tears; others request that the child's mother or father spend several days in the classroom until their child becomes familiar with the new surroundings and people. (I hope that the policy of banning all mothers and fathers from the classroom on the first day of kindergarten or first grade will soon be replaced by a more flexible approach based on an understanding of the individual situation.)

881. During the early elementary school years and after, it is not unusual for children to have difficulty remaining in school because of fears and worries. Some children do not want to come to school because they have no friends or because they are being teased on the playground. If your child does not fit in because of marked racial or cultural differences, a consultation with the teacher or a change of classroom or school may be in order. But if the child is overly reluctant to join the group or her behavior is seen as odd by most of the other children, referral to a child psychiatrist, psychologist, or other mental health professional should be considered. A failure to be accepted by elementary school classmates is one of the most common indications of emotional problems.

Children may also avoid school because they are worried about what is happening at home. If parents are fighting or absent, or if caretakers are unkind, a child may cling to his parents. In other instances a child's worries about his parents' safety and well-being while the child is away at school may be based not on reality but on the child's guilt about hostile thoughts he is having about his parents. This does not sound likely but psychiatrists have found it to be a fairly common reason.

The changing body is a cause of constant preoccupation and concern to all adolescents and may result in school avoidance. For those who develop early or late, and for those who stand out because of some unusual physical characteristic, this preoccupation can overshadow everything else. One tall twelve-year-old girl was mortified when a male teacher casually mentioned that she was taller than he. This confirmed her own feelings that she was very unattractive and peculiar and made going to school each day a torture. Considerable support from her parents and counselors helped her to remain in school, but not without emotional pain. Her concern with her height continued through the high school years. She was sure that boys would find her unattractive, and later when she went away to college, she chose a large out-of-state college because she had heard that most of the boys were very tall there.

Gym day is often marked by high absenteeism among preadolescents. For the child who is going through puberty and also struggling with other emotional issues that undermine her confidence and self-esteem, the thought of dressing and undressing in front of others and of being forced to perform physical activities that will expose real or imagined inadequacies is more than she can bear. Trying to avoid school becomes, for her, the only solution.

882. Older adolescents may also avoid school. As with younger children, the reasons are multiple and must be explored. Some of the most common ones are obesity or other personally unacceptable physical characteristics, lack of friends, shame over severe academic difficulties, and fear of rejection by the opposite sex.

A child's persistent avoidance of school, regardless of age, should be considered as an emergency requiring prompt attention. Every effort should be made by parents, educators, and school counselors to determine the cause. Professional help may be required in many instances to determine the reasons. Once the cause of the problem is determined, specific corrective measures can be started. Meanwhile, you should insist that your child stay in school. If she is allowed to avoid school she will probably find it even more painful and difficult to go back later on.

The Child Who Can't Eat Breakfast Before Going to School

This problem comes up occasionally, especially with first and second graders, at the beginning of school in the fall.

Some conscientious children are so overawed by the big class and the sovereign teacher that they can't eat early in the morning. If parents force them to, they are likely to vomit on the way to school or after they arrive. This adds a feeling of disgrace to their troubles.

883. The best way to handle this is to leave the children alone at breakfast time. Let them take only fruit juice if that is all they can comfortably swallow. If they can't drink, let them go to school empty. It's not ideal for children to start the day hungry, but they'll become relaxed and able to eat breakfast sooner if you leave them alone. Such children usually eat fairly well at lunch, and then make up for all they've missed by eating a huge supper. When they get used to school and their new teacher, they will be able to eat breakfast provided they don't have to struggle against their parents, too.

Even more important for the child who is timid at the beginning of school is for the parent to talk things over with the teacher so that she can understand and work to overcome the difficulty at school. She can make a special effort to be friendly and to help the child in the projects he is working on, so that he can find a comfortable place in the group.

You can also make sure the child is not rushed through the breakfast time. Get up early enough that the morning meal is leisurely. And avoid repeating, "Hurry up and eat." Simply have the food ready and on the table and allow a good hour for the child to help himself to whatever he wants and leave the rest.

Helping Children with Their Lessons

884. Sometimes a teacher will advise parents that their child is falling behind and needs tutoring in a subject. Sometimes the parents have the idea themselves. This is something to be careful about. If the school can recommend a good tutor whom you can afford, go ahead and hire him. Too often parents make poor tutors, not because they don't know enough, not because they don't try hard enough, but because they care too much and become too upset when their child doesn't understand. I learned that as a seven-year-old. If a child is already mixed up in his lessons, an impatient parent may be the last straw. Another trouble is that the parents' method may be different from that being used in class. If the child is already baffled by the subject as presented in school, the chances are that he will be even more baffled when it's presented in a different way at home.

I don't want to go so far as to say that a parent should never tutor a child, because in some cases it works very well. I'd only advise a parent to talk it over thoroughly with the teacher first, and then quit right away if it isn't going well. Whoever is tutoring the child should keep in touch with the teacher, at regular intervals.

885. What should you do if children ask for help with their homework? If they are puzzled and turn to you for clarification, there's no harm in straightening them out. (Nothing pleases parents more than to have a chance occasionally to prove to a child that they really know something.) But if your children are asking you to do their work for them because they don't understand it, you'd better consult the teacher. A good teacher prefers to help children understand and then let them rely on themselves. If the teacher is too busy to give your child some extra time, you may have to lend a hand; but even then you should just help him to understand his work; you should not do it for him. Your child can have many teachers but only one mother and father. Your role as parent is more important.

Relations Between Parent and Teacher

886. It's easy to get along with a teacher if your son is the teacher's pride and joy and doing well in class. But if your child is having trouble, the situation is more delicate. The best parents and the best teachers are all very human. All take pride in the work they are doing and have possessive feelings toward the child. Each, no matter how reasonable, secretly feels that the child would be doing better if the other would only handle him a little differently. It's helpful to the parents to realize at the start that the teacher is just as sensitive as they are, and that they will get further in a conference by being friendly and cooperative.

Some parents are afraid of facing a teacher, but they forget that just as often the teacher is afraid of them. The parents' main job is to give a clear history of the child's past, what his interests are, and what he responds to well or badly and then to work with the teacher on how best to apply this information in school. Don't forget to compliment the teacher on those parts of the class program that are a great success with the child.

Occasionally a child and teacher just don't "fit" temperamentally, no matter how hard they both work at it. In these cases, the principal can be involved in the question of whether to move the child to another class.

Parents should avoid blaming the teacher if their child is unsuccessful in class. If the child hears the parents badmouthing his teacher, he will learn to blame others and to avoid taking responsibility for his contribution to his problems. You can still be sympathetic: "I know how hard you are trying," or "I know how unhappy it makes you when your teacher is dissatisfied."

DAY CARE, BABY-SITTERS, AND OUT-OF-HOME ISSUES

Children and Caregivers

887. A very particular need of young children is continuity in their caregivers. From the age of a few months they come to love, count on, and get their security from the one or two people who take the major part of their care. By four months of age babies will become seriously depressed, losing their smile, their appetite, and their interest in things and people if the parent who has cared for them disappears. There will be a depression, lesser in degree, if the person who assists the parent on a regular basis leaves. Small children who have been moved from one foster home to another several times may lose some of their capacity to love or trust deeply, as if they never really learned how to attach to just one or two people and as if it's too painful to be disappointed again and again.

So it's important that the parent or the other caretaker not give up during the first two or three years, or give up only after a substitute has very gradually taken over. And it's important to be as sure as possible that the substitute plans to stick with the job. It's important, in the group care of young children, that if there are two or more staff people assigned to one group of children, each child be assigned to one staff member so that there will be a relationship more like that of child and parent.

598

888. Various caretaking alternatives. Who will provide children with the affection, the firm guidance, and the responsiveness to their questions and achievements that good parents naturally give?

The best situation is one in which the mother's and father's work schedules can be arranged so that both can work a reasonably full shift and yet one or the other can be at home for most of the day. This can be done much more easily by industrial workers who can arrange to work different shifts, or by parents whose employers offer flexibility in working hours. An appropriate caregiver can fill in the hours not covered by the parents. Of course, it's critical for the parents to be together during sleeping times as well as for some of the children's waking hours.

Another solution is for one or both parents to cut down to part-time jobs for two to three years, until the child is mature enough to attend preschool or a day-care center. This is becoming more and more difficult, however, as families require two bread-winners to meet the family expenses.

A relative with whom the parents see eye to eye may be an ideal caregiver; but the relative who lives close by and is willing to take on such a heavy responsibility is hard to find these days.

Some working parents engage a housekeeper or sitter or caregiver ("caregiver" seems a more meaningful word than "sitter") to come to their home to care for a child for part of the day. If it's for most of the day this person may well become the second most formative influence on the young child's developing personality, after the parents. So the parents should try to find a person who shows much the same kind of love, interest, responsiveness, and control as they do.

889. Qualities in a parent substitute. Far and away the most important trait is the person's disposition. Most likely it will be a woman. Toward children she should be affectionate, understanding, comfortable, sensible, and self-confident. She should love and enjoy them without smothering them with attention. She should be able to control them without nagging or severity. In other words, she should get along with them happily. It is a help when interviewing a prospective caregiver to have your child with you. You can tell how she responds to a child better by her actions than by what she says. Avoid the person who is cross, reproving, fussy, humorless, or full of theories.

A common mistake that parents make is to look first of all for a person with a lot of experience. It's natural that they should feel more comfortable leaving a child with someone who knows what to do for the colic or the croup. But illnesses and injuries are a very small part of a child's life. It's the minutes and hours of every day that count. Experience is fine when it's combined with the right personality. With the wrong personality, it's worth very little.

Cleanliness and carefulness are more important than experience. You can't let someone make the baby's formula who refuses to do it correctly. Still, there are many rather untidy people who are careful when it's important. Better a person who is too casual than one who is too fussy.

Some parents focus on the education of a caregiver, but I think it's unimportant compared with other qualities, especially for young children. Others are concerned that the caregiver may speak little English. I think it is wonderful for children to grow up learning more than one language. In the vast majority of cases they will not be confused by the different languages of the caregiver and parents and, if the caregiver stays with the child for years, the child may reap the benefits of having learned two languages in his early years.

A common problem is that a grandmother or other caregiver may favor the youngest child in the family, especially one who was born after she joined the household. She may call that one Granny's baby. If she can't understand the harm in doing this, she should not stay. It does irreparable harm to leave children in the care of a person who does not give them security.

Sometimes, inexperienced young parents settle for a caregiver about whom they don't really feel right because they've decided they can't do any better or because the person talks a good line, for example, about giving security to the child. The parents should keep looking until they find someone they really like.

There's also the very common—and human—concern of *whose child it is.* Some caregivers have a great need to take over the child, to push the parents aside, and to show that they always know best. They may be quite unconscious of this need, and they can rarely be reformed. It's natural for parents to be unconsciously jealous when they see how dependent and affectionate their child has become toward a caregiver. This may make them excessively critical—even disrespectful—of the caregiver. Certainly if a caregiver is any good, a child will become attached to her, and parents will have twinges of jealousy. But if they can be conscious of this and face it honestly, they can adjust to it.

In a sense, then, the most important questions for caregivers and parents are whether they can be honest with themselves, listen to each other's ideas and criticisms, keep the lines of communication open, respect each other's good points and good intentions, and cooperate for the benefit of the child.

890. Care after the age of three for children whose parents work outside the home. Most children, somewhere between two and three years, gain enough independence and outgoingness to be able to profit from a good group situation—a preschool or day-care center—and to enjoy it.

After six years, and particularly after age eight, children seek and enjoy independence, turn more to outside adults, especially to good teachers, and to other children for their ideals and companionship. They can get along comfortably for hours at a time without having to turn to a close adult for support. After school they still ought to have a feeling that they belong somewhere. A motherly or fatherly neighbor may be able to substitute until one of the working parents comes home. After-school play centers are valuable for all children, but particularly for those whose parents work.

Because of the lack of affordable, good-quality after-school play centers or groups, there are millions of latchkey children in our country. After school, they let themselves into their apartments or houses with their own keys, and fend for themselves until a parent comes home from work. This is another example of the need for a change in our public policies about children.

Baby-Sitters

Baby-sitters are a boon to parents and can help a child to develop independence, but you and your child should know your sitter well. Let's assume that it's a woman, though there is no reason why it should not be a man. For night sitting with a baby who doesn't waken, it may only be necessary for the sitter to be sensible and dependable. But for babies who waken and for children about five months old who might waken, it's important for the sitter to be a person the child knows and likes. It is frightening to most children to waken and find a stranger.

If the sitter is to care for the children or even just put them to bed, you should be sure from seeing her in action with your children that she understands and loves children and can manage them with kindliness and firmness. So try to engage the sitter a few times while you and she will be there together for a while. Then the young children can get used to her before she has to do too much for them directly. As the children gradually accept her, she can do more for them.

It is certainly important that you stick to one or two sitters as much as possible. You can learn about capable sitters or about a reliable agency through a friend whose judgment you trust.

891. Young or old? It's a matter of maturity and spirit rather than years. I've occasionally seen a child as young as fourteen who was extremely capable and dependable, but it's unfair to expect such qualities in most children that age. And some adults may prove unreliable or harsh or ineffectual. One older person has a knack with children. Another is too inflexible or too anxious to adapt to a new child.

To keep things straight, it's sensible to have a permanent notebook for the sitter, listing the child's routine, some of the things she may ask for (in her words), the telephone numbers of the doctor and of a neighbor to call in an emergency if you can't be reached, bedtime hours, what the sitter may help herself to in the kitchen, the whereabouts of linen, nightclothes, and other things that may be needed, how to turn the furnace up or down.

But most of all, you should know your sitter and know that your child trusts her.

Managing Family and Career

892. Parents who know that they need a career or a certain kind of work for fulfillment should not simply give it up for the sake of their children. Their children would not benefit from such a sacrifice. Instead, I think such parents should work out some kind of compromise between their two jobs and the needs of their children, usually with the help of other caregivers, especially during the critical first three years of a child's development. Sometimes a suitable family member, such as a grandmother or aunt, is willing to take on the care of the young child. Other times the parents use professional caregivers.

893. When to return to work. Though parents can return to outside jobs at any stage after the baby's birth, a good rule is the later the better. Taking three to six months off is great if you can manage it. This gives the baby time to settle in to pretty regular feeding and sleeping routines and to get used to the rhythm of her family. It also gives the mother time to adjust to her own physiological and psychological changes and to establish nursing or switch from breast to bottle, if she wants to before returning to work.

The Family and Medical Leave Act of 1993 requires employers with more than fifty employees to allow up to twelve weeks of unpaid leave for a mother or father after the birth or adoption of a child. This United States law is a fine example of a progressive, family-centered policy that came about as a result of pressure from many child advocate groups.

When a new mother plans to go to work or return to

work, she should allow two to four weeks—the longer the better—for a period of overlap while she is still at home and the baby is getting used to the substitute. In other words she should not disappear from the baby's life until the baby feels familiar and secure with the substitute (see Section 713).

Day Care and Preschool

894. Many children benefit from group experience in the period between age two or three and kindergarten, but it certainly isn't necessary in every case. Group care is particularly valuable for the only child, for the child without much chance to play with others, for the child who lives in a small apartment, and for the child whose parents find her difficult to manage.

By the age of three, *every* child needs other children of the same age, not just to have fun with but also to learn how to get along with. This is the most important job in a child's life. Children need space to run and shout in, apparatuses to climb on, blocks and boxes and boards to build with, trains and dolls to play with. They need to learn how to get along with other grown-ups besides their parents. Few children nowadays enjoy all these advantages at home. Good group care is crucial to the parents as well as to the child in the growing number of families in which both parents work outside the home.

895. "Day-care center" is a term used to specify out-of-home group care of children during their parents' working hours, often 8:00 A.M. to 6:00 P.M. Some day-care centers are subsidized by government agencies or by private companies. At its best, day care offers the advantages of the preschool: an educational philosophy, trained teachers, and full educational equipment.

The concept of the day-care center in the United States originated during World War II when the federal government wanted to encourage mothers with young children to work in war industries. It is primarily for the care of children from age two to five, but it may also include the after-school care of kindergartners and first and second graders.

896. Preschool. The American preschool concept was developed not for just the custodial care of children of working mothers and not just to prepare children specifically for the three R's of elementary school. The aim is to give children of three and four a variety of valuable experiences that will help them grow up in all respects and make them more sensitive, capable, and creative people. These experiences often include dancing and making rhythm music, painting easel pictures from their own inspiration, finger painting, clay modeling, block building, vigorous outdoor play, and playing house, which is really playing family. Ideally, there are quiet corners for individual play and for those times when a child feels the need to rest. The aim is to nurture a broad variety of capabilities—academic, social, artistic, musical, and muscular. The emphasis is on initiative, independence, cooperation (discussing and sharing play equipment instead of fighting over it), and on incorporating the child's own ideas into play.

897. Is preschool good for young children? There is a raging debate in the U.S. about the value or harm of preschool for very young children.

Some claim that group experiences are inappropriate for children in the first few years of life. They argue that every child needs one or two significant caretakers who are crazy about him, who give him their undivided attention, and who have a strong attachment to him. It is this strong early bond, they argue, that allows them, when they are adults, to sustain an intimate relationship with one person. The opponents of day care worry that if children are raised at an early age by multiple caretakers, they will never attain this capacity for intense attachment. Finally, they contend that there is no better teacher for a child than an intensely involved parent.

Day-care advocates tell a different story. They assert that there are many proper ways to raise a young child. They point to other cultures where infants are raised by siblings and extended family without apparent ill effects. They remind us that there are no studies demonstrating high-quality day care to be in any way harmful to the emotional development of children. They worry that parents who work and send their infants to day care will feel needlessly guilty that they are somehow hurting their child.

Let me tell you where I stand on this contentious issue. I believe that infants are resilient creatures, up to a certain point, and that there is no reason why *high-quality* day care should harm their development. Children need adults who are devoted to them most of all, whether it's a single parent or a group of day-care teachers. They need consistency in their relationships, but this can be provided at home and in many day-care centers.

A few studies have looked at the differences between children who went to day care and those who didn't; those studies show that very high quality day care—of small groups of children by carefully selected, well-trained teachers—is not harmful and has beneficial effects. On the other hand, if large groups of children are cared for by poorly trained teachers, the experience may have the opposite effect. However, one finding is quite interesting. This study suggested that children who go to group day care for an extended period tend to be more oriented toward and responsive to their peers but less so to adults. Children who do not attend group care tend to be more oriented toward adults (often becoming the teacher's pet) and less responsive to their peers. Is one better than the other? I think not. It simply depends on what kind of adult you want your child to be.

Everyone does agree, though, that the *quality* of day care is critical for children's well-being. As more children are placed in group day cares at earlier ages, it is critical to ensure that their emotional and intellectual needs are being met. This is especially important given what we now know about the role of early experience on the child's brain development (see Section 22). Responsive, nurturing, stimulating, consistent care is vital and can be provided only by a stable, well-trained staff in a well-funded day-care setting.

Unfortunately, there are nowhere near enough day-care centers with such high standards. And what few there are are too expensive for the average family. The only solution is unending political pressure for local and federal substitutes.

898. Should you send your child to day care? I think this is a very personal decision that must be based on your family's needs. If you want to send your infant to a day care, I wouldn't feel at all guilty about it. He'll do just fine, so long as the quality of the care is high. In the long run, children do best when their parents are happy and fulfilled. It's much better for a child to attend a good day-care center than to be at home with a parent who is lonely and miserable and who resents staying at home all day with the baby. On the other hand, if you do choose to stay home full-time with your baby for as long as possible, then that's a wonderful choice also. I think the advocates on both sides do a disservice to parents when they imply that there is only one way to handle the situation. The best situation is the one that works best for your family.

Types of Day Care

899. There are four types of day care to choose from: care by relatives, in-home care, family day care, and group care. Each has its advantages and disadvantages:

Care by relatives works well when you have a good relationship with them and agree on child-rearing philosophy.

In-home care, where a baby-sitter or nanny takes care of your child and perhaps a few others, usually offers more flexible hours, a homelike environment without an abrupt transition to another setting, and perhaps more attention, depending on the number of children. In-home care can be quite expensive, however.

Family day care is when a caretaker cares for a number of children in her own home. This is less costly than in-home care and the caretaker is often licensed to ensure at least minimal quality standards. The group experience offers the child peer interactions on a regular basis. However, if the groups are too large, individual attention from the adults may be inadequate.

Center-based day care is becoming increasingly popular.

Day-care centers are licensed and are usually open year-round. They offer a stable, structured setting with an explicit child-care philosophy which you can evaluate. However, this type of care tends to be expensive. Also, sometimes the staff turnover is high, so your child won't be consistently cared for by the same person. The level of training of the staff and the child-to-staff ratio are quite variable. There are great differences in the quality of day-care centers, as there are with the other types.

My own preference for the care of children under the age of two or three is for family care. Ideally, the child's own mother and father between them would care for the children at least half of their waking hours by means of adjustments of the parents' work schedules. The rest of the day, whether this means two hours or eight hours, the child could be cared for by a live-in or live-out caregiver or in family day care with another family.

Choosing a Day-Care or Preschool

900. First you need to compile a list of the available day-cares or preschools in your community. Call them to find out if they offer the kind of care you want. Ask for the names and phone numbers of families served by the program. Call them and ask about the details of the care, including the use of physical punishment and other discipline techniques.

901. Visit potential sites. Stay for a few hours in each one and watch for warm, nurturing interactions between the caregivers and children, appropriate supervision and safety measures, and whether activities are appropriate to the children's developmental levels. Are the children relaxed? Do they trust the teachers and turn to them for help? Do they cooperate with other children and get involved in few fights? A friendly relationship between teachers and children will show in the relationships among the children.

902. Find out about the child-to-staff ratio. The recommended ratio for children under the age of two is 3:1; twenty-five to thirty months, 4:1; thirty-one to thirty-five months, 5:1; three-year-olds, 7:1; four- and five-year-olds,

8:1; six- to eight-year-olds, 10:1; and nine- to twelve-year-olds, 12:1. Ask about their policy for excluding sick children.

903. Visit the day-care center on a regular basis. Unannounced visits during the day will reassure you that all is well. Parents should feel welcome at the school and their visits should be allowed at any time.

904. The first days at preschool. The four-year-old who is outgoing takes to preschool like a duck to water and doesn't need any gentle introduction. It may be quite different with a sensitive three-year-old who still feels closely attached to his parents. If his mother leaves him at school the first day, he may not make a fuss right away, but after a while he may miss her. When he finds she isn't there, he may become frightened. The next day he may not want to leave home.

With a dependent child like this, it's better to introduce him to school gradually. For several days his mother might stay nearby while he plays and then take him home again after a time. Each day the mother and child stay for a longer period. Meanwhile, he is building up attachments to the teacher and other children that will give him a sense of security when his mother no longer stays.

Sometimes a child seems quite happy for several days, even after his mother has left him at school. Then he gets hurt and suddenly wants her. In that case, the teacher can help the mother decide if she should come back for a number of days. When a mother is staying around the school, she ought to remain in the background. The idea is to let the child develop his own desire to enter the group, so that he forgets his need for his mother.

Sometimes the mother's anxiety is greater than the child's. If she says good-bye three times over, with a worried expression, he may think, "She looks as if something awful might happen if I stay here without her. I'd better not let her go." It's natural for a tenderhearted mother to worry about how her small child will feel when she leaves him for the first time. Let the preschool teacher advise you. She's had a lot of experience.

A child who starts with some genuine anxiety about

separating from the parent may learn that this gives him control over a highly sympathetic parent. He may then progressively exploit this control.

When a child becomes reluctant or fearful about returning to a school with understanding teachers, I think it is usually better for the parents to act quite confident and firm and explain that everybody goes to school every day. In the long run, it's better for the child to outgrow his dependence than to give in to it. If the child's terror is extreme, the situation should be discussed with a child mental health professional.

905. Reactions at home. Some children make hard work of preschool in the early days and weeks. The large group, the new friends, and the new things to do get them keyed up and worn out. If your child is too tired at first, it doesn't mean that she can't adjust to school, but only that you have to compromise for a while until she is used to it. Discuss with her teacher whether it would be wise to cut down her school time temporarily. In one case, coming to school in the middle of the morning is the best answer. Taking the easily tired child home before the end of the school day works less well because she hates to leave in the middle of the fun. The problem of fatigue in the early weeks is further complicated in an all-day school by the fact that a certain number of children are too stimulated or nervous to go to sleep at nap time at first. Keeping the child at home one or two days a week may be the answer to this temporary problem. Some small children starting preschool preserve their self-control in school in spite of fatigue but let loose on the family when they come home. This calls for extra patience and a discussion with the teacher.

A well-trained preschool teacher ought to be, and usually is, a very understanding person. A parent shouldn't hesitate to talk over the child's problems with the teacher, whether or not those problems are connected with school. A teacher gets a different slant and has probably faced the same problems before in other cases.

906. How to get a day-care center or a preschool in your community. You may say, "I believe in the importance of my child's going to preschool or to a day-care center, but there is none in my community." Such schools aren't easy to start. Well-trained teachers, plenty of equipment, indoor and outdoor space are all necessary and all cost money. Good schools are never cheap, because a teacher can satisfactorily take care of only a small number of children. They have most commonly been formed on a private basis, with the parents paying the full expense; by churches, which provide the space; or by colleges, for the training of students in child care. In the long run, a sufficient number of preschools and day-care centers will be created and operated with government funds only if the citizens of the community convince the federal and local governments that they want them, and vote for local and federal candidates who make a pledge to work for them.

Traveling with Children

907. Traveling brings out the best and the worst in families. Time spent together in the pursuit of adventure, fun, and pleasure is all to the good. Assuming the role of expert guide for your wide-eyed children as you show them sights they've only read about in school is enjoyable for parents as well as children.

However, sibling squabbles may escalate, especially when the ride gets boring. Somebody *always* has to go to the bathroom, even if, despite your urging, he refused to do so at the last rest stop. Everybody in the family has a different agenda: one just wants to get to the next town; another insists on stopping right here this second; one enjoys camping under the stars; another prefers staying in a cozy, clean motel; one wants to get up at 6:00 A.M. for an early start; another wants to sleep late (after all *it's a vacation*). These squabbles and differences of opinion call for firm and clear parental leadership.

To ensure that your trip is successful, I offer some tips:

908. Food for an infant. The most convenient way to feed an infant while traveling is easily **breast-feeding.** The only potential problem is a little less milk supply if you don't remember to drink fluids and relax a little.

If you are **bottle-feeding** you need to consider the facilities you will have available and how long you will be away from a refrigerator. Buy prepared, ready-to-use formula in disposable bottles with disposable nipples. These bottles don't have to be refrigerated, and there is nothing to wash or sterilize. They are expensive, but you probably will not be traveling for long. Powdered formula is cheaper. The powder and water can be measured ahead of time, in separate containers, and mixed just before you feed your baby.

Most **solid foods** should be in jars. I'd try to keep them cool—for example, in a storage container with a block of artificial blue ice. Your baby can be fed directly from the jar. If you are not refrigerating the jars, discard all remaining food. If you are keeping it cool, you can save it safely for eight to twelve hours. Don't worry about providing every food that your baby usually gets. Just take enough of the foods he likes best and digests most easily. Many traveling babies do not want as much as they usually eat at home. Don't urge him to eat anything he doesn't want, even if he's taking much less food than usual. You might try feeding small amounts at more frequent intervals.

909. Food for a child. It's better to keep small children from eating unusual food. When buying food for them in public places, avoid particularly cakes and pastries with moist fillings, milk puddings, cold meats, cold fish, cold eggs, and creamy salad dressings, including sandwiches and salads that contain them. These foods are easily contaminated with poisonous bacteria if carelessly handled or not properly refrigerated. Better stick to hot foods, fruit that you peel yourself, crackers in plastic containers. Of course you can make your own peanut butter and jelly sandwiches. Even if you are expecting to feed your child at roadside restaurants, or if he will eat the meals provided on a plane, bring a bag of snacks in case meals are delayed or unappetizing. Sushi (vinegared rice), without the fish, makes a good traveling food. It does not need refrigeration.

910. Fluids. Mild dehydration is a common occurrence on trips, not just from overdoing it on hot days but also during long flights or drives. Everyone should be encouraged to drink fluids frequently (and make frequent rest stops).

911. Pack a traveling medicine chest. Be prepared for minor illnesses, cuts, and scrapes. I'd suggest you bring at least the following: bandages, antibiotic ointment, tweezers (for removing splinters), syrup of ipecac (to induce vomiting if your child eats something he shouldn't have), your usual decongestant, children's acetaminophen (for fever or pain), white vinegar and rubbing alcohol (a 50-50 mixture works great for swimmer's ear), steroid cream (for poison ivy and other itchy rashes), and lots of sunscreen. Of course, make sure you pack enough of any medicine that your child is already taking, and be sure that all immunizations are up to date (take the immunization record with you). Take all of your doctors' phone numbers with you, just in case.

912. Amusements. When you travel with a small child, don't forget to take along the cuddly toys and blankets that your child usually takes to bed. They will be an extra comfort in traveling. (Be sure to label them with your name and address.) In addition to the child's favorite toys, it is wise to take a few new playthings that will take up a lot of time: miniature cars or trains, a small doll with several articles of clothing or other equipment, a coloring or cutout book, a new picture book, cardboard houses or other objects to fold and assemble, a pad of paper, pencils, and crayons. There are wonderful books at your bookstore on amusements for children on the road. They contain a lot of creative ideas for games they can play without equipment. I'd have each child over the age of three pack her own backpack full of her favorite games.

913. Cleaning supplies. A large box of cleansing tissues is essential. A couple of large plastic tablecloths are valuable, to protect the mattress from bed-wetting, to cover the carpet if a small child is eating in a hotel room or a baby is sitting on the floor, or to cover a bed on which a baby is being changed. A wet facecloth, kept in a plastic bag to retain its moisture, can be very helpful, although most parents now buy prepared wipes that come in individual packets for traveling. (Avoid the ones that contain alcohol and perfumes. They can irritate the skin.) Disposable diapers, which you may otherwise avoid, are very convenient. Also take along the favored potty chair.

914. Car travel. In car travel, it is wise to stop not only at regular mealtimes but also in midmorning and midafternoon, for a snack and for a chance for children to run around for a few minutes in a place, perhaps a field or a playground in a city park, where they don't have to be constantly warned to stay out of the road.

It's vital that babies travel in cars in government-approved carriers. Children under 45 pounds will need government-approved car seats, and larger children, like adults, must wear seat belts and shoulder straps at all times (see Sections 554–564).

If your child has a tendency to develop motion sickness, it may help for her to sit high enough to see out of the car. Encourage her to look out the window rather than to read or color. Your doctor can tell you about some medicines that are helpful in preventing motion sickness.

A good rule for car travel is to plan to stop for the night by 4:00 P.M., so you'll have more chance of finding a motel room and avoid driving on for hours with tired children. Many drivers get the bit in their teeth about making a certain distance and refuse to stop even though it's getting late. But if they solemnly agree before the trip to a certain stopping hour, there's more chance they will be reasonable. And remember, the second leading cause of car accidents (after alcohol) is the driver falling asleep at the wheel.

915. Airplane tips. Some babies and children have trouble with ear pain when the airplane begins to take off and descend for a landing. Older children, who can understand the need to swallow to avoid the pain, can be given something to swallow (juice boxes work well) or to chew on. Babies should be awakened as soon as the plane starts to descend and offered the breast or bottle, to keep them swallowing. If a child has a cold, ask your doctor about long-acting decongestant medicine that can be given to keep the Eustachian tubes open during the trip.

At this time, the use of car seats in airplanes is controversial. The Federal Aviation Authority contends that because air travel is so safe, more children's lives would be lost if families had to buy an extra ticket for their infant, because their parents would then opt to drive, which is far more dangerous. Most airlines will allow you to use a car seat on board if there is space available. You should use a rear-facing seat until your baby weighs about 20 pounds, a front-facing seat when he weighs 20 to 40 pounds, and the airplane's seat belt when he weighs over 40 pounds.

916. Going to restaurants with children. Most children will get restless while waiting to be served in a restaurant, unless it is a fast-food place. In most cities, there are a few restaurants that cater to families with small children, and they provide special activities to keep children from becoming bored. But at most other restaurants, it's best to bring paper and pencils and perhaps a coloring book or two to keep the children occupied until the food is served. This also keeps them busy when they're finished eating and the adults feel like having a second cup of coffee. (A bored child running loose in a restaurant can be annoying to other diners and can easily become involved in an accident.) You can bring food from home for your baby.

Relations with Grandparents

917. Grandparents can be a great help to young parents in all kinds of ways. They can also derive great pleasure from their grandchildren. They often ask wistfully, "Why couldn't I have enjoyed my own children the way I enjoy my grandchild? I suppose I was trying too hard and feeling only the responsibility."

In many parts of the world grandmothers are considered experts, and a young mother takes it for granted that when she has a question about her baby or needs a little help, she'll ask her mother. When a mother has this kind of confidence in the grandmother, she can get not only advice but comfort. In our country, though, a new mother is often more inclined to turn to her doctor first, and some women don't ever think of consulting their mothers. This is partly because we are so used to consulting professional people about our personal problems—doctors, guidance counselors, marriage counselors, social workers, psychologists, clergy. Also, we take it for granted that knowledge advances rapidly, and so we often think that anyone who knew how to do a job twenty years ago will be behind the times today.

A more basic reason is that many young parents still feel too close to adolescence. They want to prove to the world and to themselves that they can manage their own lives. They may be afraid that the grandparents will want to tell them what to do, as if they were still dependent, and they don't want to put themselves back in that position.

918. Tensions are normal. In some families, all is harmony between parents and grandparents. In a few, disagreements are fierce. In others, there is a little tension, most commonly concerning the care of the first child, but it wears off with time and adjustment.

The fortunate young woman who has lots of natural self-confidence can turn easily to her mother for help when she needs it. And when the grandmother makes a suggestion on her own, the mother finds that she can accept it if it seems good, or she can tactfully let it pass and go her own way.

But most young parents don't have that amount of assurance at first. Like almost everybody else in a new job, they are sensitive about possible inadequacies, touchy about criticism.

Most grandparents remember this well from their earlier days and try hard not to interfere. On the other hand, they have had experience, they feel they've developed judgment, they love their grandchildren dearly, and they can't help having opinions. They see surprising changes from the time when they cared for babies—flexible feeding schedules, delayed feeding of solid foods, later toilet training. Even when they accept new methods, they may be bothered by what seems to them to be excessive zeal in carrying them out. (When you are a grandparent yourself, you'll probably understand better what I mean.)

I think that if young parents have the courage, they can keep relations most comfortable by permitting or even inviting the grandparents to speak up about their opinions. Frank discussions are usually, in the long run, more comfortable than veiled hints or uneasy silences. A mother who is pretty sure she is managing the baby properly can say, "I realize that this method doesn't seem quite right to you, and I'm going to discuss it again with the doctor to be sure that I've understood his directions." This doesn't mean the mother is giving in. She certainly reserves the right to make her own decision in the end. She is only recognizing the grandmother's good intentions and evident anxiety. The young mother who shows reasonableness will reassure the grandmother not only in regard to the present problem but also in regard to the future in general.

A grandmother can help the mother do a good job by showing her confidence in her and by accepting her methods as far as possible. This puts the mother in a mood to ask advice when she is in doubt.

When the children are left in the care of the grandparents, whether for half a day or for two weeks, there should be frank understanding and reasonable compromising. The parents must have confidence that the children will be cared for according to their beliefs in important matters—that, for instance, they won't be compelled to eat food they don't like, be shamed for bowel accidents, or be frightened about policemen. On the other hand, it's unfair to expect grandparents to carry out every step of management and discipline as if they were exact replicas of the parents. It won't hurt children to be a little more respectful to the grandparents, if that's what they want, to have their meals on a different schedule, or to be kept cleaner or dirtier. If the parents don't feel right about the way the grandparents care for the children, of course they shouldn't ask them to take care of them.

919. Some parents are sensitive about advice. More than average tension may arise if the young mother (or father) has felt a lot of parental criticism throughout her childhood. This inevitably leaves her inwardly unsure of herself, outwardly impatient with disapproval, and grimly determined to demonstrate her independence. She may take to new philosophies of child rearing with unusual enthusiasm and push them hard. They seem like a wholesome change from what she remembers. They are also a way to show the grandparents how old-fashioned they are and to bother them a bit. It's really fun to battle about theory when you're mad at the opponent. The only trouble is that it's the child's upbringing that provides the ammunition on both sides. All I'm suggesting is that parents who find that they are constantly upsetting the grandparents should at least ask themselves whether they might be doing some of it on purpose, without realizing it.

920. The managerial grandmother. Occasionally there is a grandmother so constituted that she has always been too managerial with her own child and she can't stop even though her child is now a parent. Such a young parent may have a tough time at first keeping a perspective. For instance, a daughter dreads advice. When it comes, it makes her angry, but she dare not express her feelings. If she accepts the advice, she feels dominated. If she turns it down, she feels guilty. How, then, can the beginning mother in this situation protect herself? It sounds as if she'd have to lift herself by her bootstraps. In a way she does have to, but it can be done gradually, with practice.

In the first place, she can keep reminding herself that she is the mother now and that the baby is hers to take care of as she thinks best. She should be able to get support from the doctor if she has been made to doubt her own method. She is surely entitled to the support of her husband, especially if it's his mother who is interfering. If he thinks that in a certain situation his mother is right, he should be able to say so to his wife, but at the same time he can show his mother that he stands with his wife against interference.

The young mother will come out better if she can learn gradually not to run away from the grandmother and not to be afraid to hear her out, because both these reactions reveal, in a way, that she feels too weak to stand up to her. Harder still, she can learn how not to get boiling mad inside or how not to explode outwardly in a temper. You might say she's entitled to get angry, which is true. But pent-up anger and explosions are both signs that she has already been feeling submissive for too long out of fear of making the grandmother mad. A dominating grandmother usually senses these indirect signs of timidity and takes advantage of them. A mother shouldn't feel guilty about making her mother mad, if it must come to that. Actually, it shouldn't be necessary to blow up at the grandmother—or at least not more than once or twice. The mother can learn to speak up for herself right away, in a matter-of-fact, confident tone, before she gets angry: "The doctor told me to feed her this way" or "You see, I like to keep him as cool as possible" or "I don't want her to cry for long." A calm, assured tone is usually the most effective way to convince the grandmother that the mother has the courage of her convictions.

In these occasional situations that contain a lot of continual tension, it is often helpful for the parents, and perhaps the grandparents also, to consult a professional person—a wise family doctor, a psychiatrist, a social worker, or a sensible minister—in separate interviews, so that each can present the picture as she or he sees it. Eventually they can all come together for a final discussion. In any case it should be understood that, in the end, the responsibility and the right to make decisions belong to the parents.

NEW ISSUES: PREPARING FOR THE TWENTY-FIRST CENTURY

Our Children Are Our Future

921. Why we need idealistic children. A child raised to have ideals will have no lack of opportunities to apply them in the twenty-first century. There are enormous, frightening problems in our country and in the world. Through our reliance on initiative and materialism we have accomplished technological miracles. But as our physical needs are met, it becomes embarrassingly evident that we in the United States have made little progress in human relations, in spiritual serenity, or in world security. Our rates of divorce, suicide, and crime are among the highest in the world. Our race relations are barbaric—a disgrace to a nation that pretends to believe in freedom, equality, and God. We have areas of poverty and demoralization in a country that could be well on the way to solution in a year if only we would face our responsibilities. Millions of dollars are spent persuading us to buy automobiles with five times the necessary horsepower, and to buy cigarettes, which cause cancer.

We know how to produce food with fantastic efficiency, but we have held production down in spite of the fact that there are more hungry people in the world than ever before in history.

We have an overwhelming supply of the most dangerous weapons the world has ever known. Even though the cold war has ended, we are in imminent danger of annihilation, particularly from accidental launching. Because of our power, we often interfere arrogantly in the affairs of other nations and arouse worldwide resentment.

Our only realistic hope, as I see it, is first to bring up our children with a feeling that they are in this world not for their own satisfaction but primarily to serve others. Children are proud to think that they can be truly useful, and they will rise to the challenge. This attitude can be instilled when they're very young. Even babies of nine months shouldn't be allowed to get the impression that it's all right to pull their mother's hair or to bite her cheek. They can learn that they owe her respect. Between one and two years children shouldn't be allowed deliberately to break their own possessions or to make a mess with them. By age two they can be expected to go through the motions of helping pick up their playthings. By three they should be given such small chores as helping to set the table or emptying the wastebaskets, even though they don't save parents much work. By seven or eight they should be carrying out genuinely useful jobs each day. As adolescents, they can volunteer in hospitals and other institutions or tutor younger children.

In family conversations children should hear their parents' concern about problems of the community, the nation, the world. They should see that their parents are contributing directly to the solutions by participating in the work of local groups and committees.

In school, children should study not only the great accomplishments of their nation but also its deficiencies and mistakes. Their schools should contain children from various races and backgrounds, not just out of fairness to minority groups but so that all kinds of children can learn to appreciate and get along with each other. High school and university students, while they are preparing for their eventual occupations, should spend time analyzing the unsolved problems in their own chosen field—the human as well as the technical problems. It's also important, I think, for youths while they are still in school to volunteer or work for pay in part-time jobs where they can serve people who have serious unmet needs, then to discuss these problems in class so that they won't acquire a critical or condescending attitude toward those who are different from them.

Superkids

922. Can you make superkids? When a child is neglected or consistently ignored—"How many times have I told you? Stop bothering me with your questions."—his spirit and mind will fail to develop fully.

At the other extreme, it has been discovered that if you try hard enough you can teach a two-year-old to read and you can even teach your one-year-old to recognize flashcards. Such discoveries have inspired some parents with the hope that with the right playthings from infancy, the right mental stimulation at home and in school, a child can be developed into a brilliant individual, on his way to a distinguished career. I think that this particular kind of parental ambition, though understandable in a country where intelligence is so highly prized and at a time when computer experts seem to hold the key to the future, is mistaken and apt to backfire.

Mental capacity is only one aspect of a person and may well fail to make him a success in life unless it is balanced with warmth and common sense. When parents concentrate on the intellect alone, they may make their child a somewhat lopsided person who won't fit into any job or won't get any joy out of life.

923. What stimulates normal, well-rounded development—emotional, social, and intellectual? Babies and children, by their inborn nature, keep reaching out to people and to things. Fond parents, watching and coaxing, respond enthusiastically to their baby's first smiles with smiles of their own and by nodding and declaring their love. Repetitions of this scene, every waking hour for months, along with hugs, comforting during misery, and offering food at times of hunger, keep reinforcing feelings of love and trust. These acts form the foundation on which the child's future relationships with all the other people in her life will be built. Even her interest in things, and her later capacity to deal with ideas and concepts, in school and at work, will depend on this foundation of love and trust.

At one and two years of age children mature by striving to copy their parents' actions, and parents foster this development by showing their pleasure at each tiny accomplishment. That's how vocabulary expands at age two, for example. By three years, children become intensely curious about everything they see or hear, and they turn to their parents for explanations and encouragement. Between three and six, children mature emotionally and intellectually by striving to pattern themselves after their beloved parents.

This natural interplay between the children reaching out and the parents responding has been sufficient through the ages to produce plenty of bright, capable, sociable, loving young people. Special drills and special equipment are not necessary, at least until the school years.

If you try to make children "super" through your interest and initiative, you may rub them the wrong way and create an aversion to your plan. Or you may succeed and make them one-sided robots.

The same risks apply, I think, in overemphasizing a little girl's prettiness or in trying too hard to make a boy into an athlete. Children should grow up feeling that they are appreciated and loved for their whole person and personality, not primarily for their brains or their looks or their muscle or their musical ability. It's all right to appreciate a child's special gift, as long as it is considered of secondary importance.

Computer Literacy

924. There's no doubt about it: your children should grow up feeling comfortable with computers. The advent of personal computers has changed the way we gain information, keep track of our finances and household duties, communicate with others, interact with media, and write papers and letters. And there is every reason to believe we have just begun to scratch the surface. In the twenty-first century, computers are likely to play an ever larger role in our lives, both at home and at work.

A child who is not comfortable and knowledgeable about computers will be like a tourist in a foreign land who can't speak the language. He'll have a hard time getting what he wants, and he'll always have to look to others for assistance. In fact, learning to use a computer is a little bit like learning a language. And just as in learning a language, the sooner the child begins the better. Then the rules for using it become second nature to the child and more sophisticated ways to use it are easily acquired.

Using a computer is also a lesson in rule-governed logic for the young child. Once he understands the rules of how to operate a computer, things always proceed in an exceedingly orderly way. Any error is invariably the child's error, which he soon learns. It is then up to him to follow the rules if he wants to play the game successfully. This kind of direct, logical cause and effect is an instructive lesson for young children, who are struggling to master this concept in a much messier and less logical real world.

If you can afford one, I'd suggest getting a home computer and learning to use it yourself. There are wonderful interactive programs you can buy that are appealing and simple enough for even very young children and which you will enjoy using with your child. This kind of fun and games on the computer will help your child to feel at ease and learn the basics, such as how to point and click the mouse, which can happen as early as three or four years of age.

If you can't afford a computer, I wouldn't worry too much about it. Starting at school age is still plenty early. But you should make sure that your child's school does teach the use of computers as part of its curriculum.

925. There are many ways for children to use (and abuse) a computer, so its use will require some supervision and guidance on your part (see Sections 928–930 on the Internet). Certainly it is a marvelous means of getting at information. Encyclopedias, maps, and dictionaries are all available at the click of the mouse. It's also great for writing reports for school and for other word processing. Some children's software is very educational and makes learning fun by incorporating clever, interactive games. The ambitious child may even learn how to program the computer and come to terms with its mysterious inner workings. All of this is wonderful preparation for the business and pleasure of the new age. But I wouldn't let my child become so absorbed and obsessed that he has no time for friendships, games, or reading. Limit the hours.

Computer Games

926. There is a darker side to the world of computers. I'm speaking about the majority of computer games. Most of these are variations on the theme of kill (shoot, laser, karate kick, maim, beat up) the bad guys. These games are unimaginative carryovers of violent Saturday morning cartoons. The best that can be said of them is that they may help promote eye-hand coordination in children. The worst that can be said is that they sanction, and even promote, aggression and violent responses to conflict. But what can be said with much greater certainty is this: most computer games are a colossal waste of time.

For some children these mindless shoot-'em-up computer games have an almost addictive quality. The good news is that the computer game addicted child typically cuts down on watching violent television shows. The bad news is that passively watching violent cartoons is supplanted by interactively *participating* in violent cartoons. This may represent a subtle improvement, but it is still an unwholesome pastime for children.

Your job with regard to video games is much the same as it is with television viewing: to help pick the right video games and to set limits on how much time is to be spent playing them. Which video games are acceptable? Generally these are ones that are intended to teach, that convey information in an interactive and fun fashion. Others, while not primarily educational in intent, rely on intellectual skills (like deciphering clues) to achieve the goal. I'd suggest consulting one of the many wonderful guidebooks for parents that describe and rate software for children. These change often, so be certain to use an up-to-date guide.

927. How much time should a child be allowed to spend perched before a computer? This, of course, will depend on the individual child, his age, why he is using the computer, and whether his use of it allows him to neglect other important parts of his life, like family relationships, friendships, and self-invented games.

In general, with young children it's best if most of the time is spent using the computer with another person present. As they get older, they can assume more independence, but it is still your job to supervise, limit the time, and make sure the computer is being used for constructive purposes. There is a lot more to life than computer games. I would want my child also to learn how to play outdoor games, make friends, and have noisy fun. You can't force your child to engage in such activities, but you can strictly limit his time at the computer and see whether it leads to a better balance of occupations. If not, you've done your best and will have to be satisfied with producing a computer whiz.

The computer can be restricting, yes, but it also represents an opportunity to learn and to communicate at a high level. Help your child to make the most of that opportunity and minimize the potential pitfalls.

Cruising the Internet

Suppose your child said to you this evening: "See you later. I'm going off on my own to a strange and wonderful city. I'll be back in an hour or two." You learn that this city is known to have it all: new people to meet, unlimited places to go, museums on every topic you can imagine and some you can't.

928. How should you respond? After your initial panic subsided, you'd first take into account your child's level of maturity. Can she really negotiate a big city on her own? If she can, do you trust her not to go into dangerous places where she could be harmed? What museums are appropriate for someone her age? How soon should she come back?

The Internet is just such a city. As a responsible parent, like it or not, you are going to have to come to terms with it. For children, the Internet provides an exciting opportunity for independence and freedom, like a dress rehearsal for that real visit to a real new city, but with fewer of the dangers and a lot of friends along for the ride.

Your children know that the Internet allows for accessing information on a computer in a way that is easily accessible and almost infinite in scope. Its potential for teaching is immense. So-called chat rooms, where people can participate in roundtable discussions, can offer support from like-minded peers. There are even chat rooms where children with disabilities can talk to children around the world who have the same disabilities. It is a resource for breaking through isolation and creating a sort of global village. Some children find this aspect alone remarkably helpful and enjoyable.

But along with these very real advantages comes danger, especially for children. Unfortunately, as in the real world, in the virtual world of the Internet there are individuals who prey on children's innocence and immaturity to serve their own selfish needs. A children's chat room, for example, can turn into a lewd monologue by an adult posing as a child. The anonymity afforded by the Internet can be used for unsavory ends by exploiters of children. Additionally, many Website programs devoted to violence or pornography are easily accessible to the clever, ambitious child.

Some parents are so anxious about the potential dangers of the Internet that they forbid access to it altogether. I think that's a mistake. Children will have to learn to deal with the information superhighway one way or another. If they are well prepared and responsible, a treasure trove of wonderful experiences awaits them. If they are not comfortable with using the computer to communicate and to acquire information, they may be at a disadvantage later— in the workplace and socially.

I'd look at preparation for the Internet as just like preparing your child to read a book, to drive a car, or to say no to drugs or premature sexual relations. It's another opportunity for you to protect them from dangers of which they are not aware and to discuss what's important to your family when it comes to utilizing this amazing new resource. In other words, it's another opportunity to teach responsible decision-making.

929. Learn about the Internet yourself. To ensure that the Internet is a constructive, safe, enlightening tool for your children, you should let your child teach you about it, if he already knows, or learn about it together. That way, at least for a time, you can surf the Net together, talking about what and where you want to go, discussing what to do and not to do, and stating your expectation of good manners. By sharing this experience, you will have the opportunity to talk things over in a way you'll miss if you never learn the first thing about the Internet. You'll get to know what kind of chat rooms and information sites are out there and how they operate. This familiarity will allow you to better judge what sites pose a threat to your child and when you are being unjustifiably old-fashioned and insecure.

930. Set rules for accessing the Internet. To set rules that are fair, here are some questions you can ask yourself:

- **At what age should I allow my child to browse the Internet unsupervised?** I think there always needs to be *some* level of supervision, even if that only means an occasional glance at the screen while your teenager is on-line. Preteens require more direct contact and discussion of what they are doing on the Internet. When younger children use the Internet you should be at their side for much of the session. Chat rooms, unless well supervised, should be avoided by young children. Discuss your child's experiences with him and use it as an opportunity to express your confidence in his ability to use the Internet responsibly.

- **What are fair time limits?** Like television, you should set a time limit on how long the Internet can be accessed each day. It's unhealthy for a child to be lost in the virtual world of his computer to the neglect of real-life conversations, experiences, and friends.

Here are some useful rules to teach your children:

- **Never give personal information to anyone on-line.** This means never to give your address, your phone number, or the name of your school to someone you don't know.

Don't send photographs of yourself to anyone you haven't met in person. *Never tell anyone else your password.* Remind your child that, although chat room correspondents may seem like your friends, they are really strangers. You need to be as discreet with these strangers as with those you meet on the street.

- **Discuss how to deal with inappropriate or offensive information.** This is an opportunity to discuss what is accepted in your family and what is not. If a message appears that makes the child feel uncomfortable, he should be advised to turn off the machine *immediately* or move to another site on the Internet. He should then tell you about it so you can discuss what it does and doesn't mean.
- **Discuss "Netiquette."** Remind your child that, as in all situations, you expect him to behave considerately toward others and with good manners. That means no inappropriate or rude communication while under the cloak of anonymity. If there is a breach, the privilege may be withdrawn.
- **Consider using parental control features on commercial on-line services or purchasing "blocking program" software.** Many on-line services offer a way for parents to limit the child's access to carefully screened and supervised children's information sites and chat rooms. Similarly, you can buy software that essentially limits what can be accessed and makes it difficult to inadvertently or purposely access adult chat rooms or information sites. Some software keeps logs that allow you to see exactly where your child has been.

These programs allow for technological baby-sitting and supervision. They can be quite reassuring, especially with a younger child. However, for older children they may represent an easily overcome obstacle that they can dismantle at will. Additionally, the control feature may make the taboo sites even more tantalizing, like forbidden fruit. The bottom line is that there is no substitute for instilling a sense of responsibility and values in your child so that he will make the right choices on his own. For such a child, the world of the Internet can be a magic carpet to wonderful new worlds of information and experience.

Alcohol and Other Drugs

931. The importance of good relationships. Parents who have had a good relationship with their children from the beginning don't have to worry about their children suddenly going off the deep end with drugs. What do I mean by good relationship?

Friendliness rather than predominantly scolding. Mutual trust. Expecting the best. Openness in conversations, whether they are about day-by-day happenings or serious matters of morality. Mutual respect, politeness, and visible love. When I say "from the beginning," I mean from the age of two or three. It is difficult to make up for lost time during adolescence.

One important family value that helps a child navigate these difficult times is open and clear channels of communication. In some families certain topics—such as fooling around with drugs—are either taboo or else will elicit such a firestorm of anger and anxiety from the parents that the children never dare to bring those subjects up. Don't be fooled; not discussing drugs has little to do with not using them. In fact, silence probably increases the likelihood of drug use. What happens is that the child goes to others to talk about this issue, usually friends who may have a very different perspective on the advisability and potential consequences of drug use from yours. When there is an open climate for discussion in the home, parents give their children increasing freedom and decision-making opportunities, expect their children to behave in increasingly responsible ways, and discuss what is happening in their children's lives as they continue to mature as individuals. Therefore, if you want your kids to make wise choices, you must really look at your means of communication.

So, on the one hand, the relationship should be easygoing; on the other hand, neither parent nor child should be reluctant to bring up "embarrassing" subjects. I'm not saying the parent should treat the child exactly like an adult friend. This would be carrying it too far during the preschool and elementary school years, but parents should encourage and respect their children's increasing maturity during the high school years. They should also expect their adolescent children to respond to increased respect and freedom with increasingly responsible behavior.

To be a parent means to be concerned about your children—and there are many things to be concerned about. A 1996 survey indicated that 24 percent of eighth graders and 40 percent of high school seniors had used an illicit drug in the past year. Some 28 percent of high school seniors are regular cigarette smokers, 80 percent said they have tried alcohol, and 30 percent reported having been drunk (five or more drinks in a row) during the two weeks preceding the survey.

932. Drug culture. American children are being raised in a drug culture, plain and simple: if you have a problem, take a pill. We grow up with the implicit understanding that drugs are a legitimate solution to many problems.

In the younger years, children imitate their parents. Many parents have alcohol or drug problems, or too readily turn to drugs to solve problems of all sorts. If children see their parents using drugs such as alcohol and tranquilizers, they may find it easier to justify their own use of drugs.

As children get older, peer influence becomes increasingly important. Sadly, drugs are easily available to them at this vulnerable time. Adolescence is a time when children are making a tremendous effort to be independent. Drugs appear to give an immediate answer to some of the needs they have. The drugs can make them feel more comfortable and help them be accepted by their friends.

933. Drug increase. During the 1980s there was a gradual decline in the use of marijuana, alcohol, and tobacco. Recent studies show that there has been a significant rise in drug use in the 1990s. And children are becoming involved at younger ages.

There are many reasons why teens use drugs. One important influence leading to this increase might be the economy which offers many youths very little hope for the future. There are more unemployed adults today in some areas of some cities than employed ones, which discourages young people.

There are a number of other factors, as well: the decline of the importance of the family, increasing divorce rates, an increasing number of families with both parents working outside the home, the absence of a father in the home, unstable marriages, and lower incomes for single mothers— all have an effect on the amount of drug use. A feeling of hopelessness can lead many children to seek answers in drugs.

Teens are looking for a place in the world. There seems to be a lack of a stable place where they can gain strength and grow.

This is the background against which drug abuse occurs. It should be noted that, although many teens experiment with drugs, not all go on to become addicted.

934. Different types of drugs. A drug is a drug is a drug. First off, you should remember that alcohol is the drug most frequently and heavily abused by adolescents. Other drugs get more publicity, and the expression "drugs and alcohol" leads people to infer that alcohol isn't a drug. But alcohol does more damage to more teenagers than all other drugs combined. Many teenagers see drinking by parents and even by characters on television, where the negative effects are rarely shown. This makes it seem glamorous. Just because a drug is illegal (like marijuana) doesn't mean its potential for harm is greater than a drug that is legal (like alcohol). We have given a confusing, mixed message to our youth, who have to wonder at the inconsistency of allowing some drugs to be legalized while banning others that appear less harmful.

Youths also understand that all drugs are not the same. Parents tend to lump them all together; heroin is like cocaine is like LSD. But each drug is unique in its effects (some put you to sleep and make you passive while others wake you up and make you aggressive), in its addictive potential, and in its health impact (cocaine can cause sudden death but a glass of wine a day may actually be good for the heart).

As adults, we only undermine our credibility by lumping all drugs together or by implying that all drugs have an equal potential for harm. Experimenting with marijuana is simply not the same as experimenting with heroin or cocaine. If you treat it as such, you are likely to be seen as hopelessly out of it and naive by the very person you'd like to help—your child.

935. Marijuana. Our attitude toward marijuana has changed over the last twenty years. At one time we said it was harmless because there was no physical dependency. Now that notion has changed, perhaps because the plant itself has become more powerful and more concentrated.

Younger children are using marijuana more because it is easier to buy and they think it is harmless. They have a powerful desire to find out all there is to know about life— especially the possibly dangerous aspects.

Many children also have an impulse to run risks—taking wild chances, accepting dangerous dares, being proud of burning the candle at both ends, proving their courage. This is one reason why so many boldly take up smoking tobacco while older people are striving to give it up.

At the same time they may be secretly afraid of facing new and difficult situations. A drug like alcohol may hold the promise of numbing inhibitions, erasing apprehensions, and increasing courage sufficiently to get a youth over the threshold of taking a chance—of lovemaking, for example.

The use of marijuana is in a somewhat different category from that of alcohol and other more dangerous drugs. A large percentage of young people—even of junior high and high school age—have tried it at least a few times. Though it does not necessarily lead to the use of other drugs, it is viewed as a "gateway" drug, one that may lead users to try other drugs.

Most of the young people who have used marijuana use it much less often than daily. The less common individual who regularly smokes several times a day and remains in a state of mild intoxication should not be thought of as having been ruined by marijuana but as a person who has lost his sense of purpose and seeks comfort in marijuana, just as other individuals have chronically abused alcohol and more dangerous drugs. In these heavy, regular users there is loss of ambition and energy that can interfere, during the time of this heavy use, with the teenager's moving forward in life: in his education, work, and relationships. As of this writing the other damage that has been proved is a lowering of sex hormone and sperm count in males who use it amply and regularly, interference with short-term memory and concentration, and harm to the lungs. Young people keep up with the news about marijuana and lose confidence in adults who make exaggerated or discredited claims.

As a life-and-death issue marijuana is much less of a health risk over the life span than tobacco, which causes 400,000 deaths a year, and alcohol, which claims 100,000 lives, ruins families, and incapacitates tens of thousands of people each year. Nevertheless, we should not be lulled into overlooking marijuana's risks and dangers.

936. Experimentation versus abuse versus dependence. There is a big difference between light use, or experimentation with drugs, and drug abuse. Most teenagers are curious and want to take risks. And in a stressful and drug-filled society, they will experiment with drugs both out of curiosity and as a way of getting their needs met. A majority of teens will smoke marijuana at a party on the weekend or drink alcohol at parties with their friends. (About 80 percent of teenagers say they drink at least occasionally.)

If you find some marijuana in your child's room, this does not necessarily mean that he is a heavy drug abuser. It is quite possible that he is experimenting out of curiosity or has smoked only infrequently.

On the one hand, all drug abusers probably began by experimenting. On the other hand, most teens who dabble in drugs eventually give it up and don't go on to become chronic abusers. Since at least half of all teenagers in the United States have tried an illicit drug at some point, it's not helpful for you to respond to a one-time experiment or infrequent use in the same way as you would to frequent or chronic use. In fact, a hysterical overreaction to a brief flirtation with drugs may do more harm than good. I'm not saying that experimentation is okay, but I think you should recognize that even the best teens in this day and age are curious and flirt with drugs. If that happens, it's your job to have a dialogue.

Bear in mind that very few teens who experiment with drugs go on to have a long-term problem. If discussions about drug use are handled right, with open dialogue, often this challenge helps the child to refine her decision-making skills and alerts her to the dangers of risk-taking. These are hard-won lessons, indeed, but very useful ones.

Most children outgrow their drug use sooner or later. They begin to see that the cost outweighs the satisfactions. But if they are using drugs, parents will need to focus attention on the potential problems to prevent serious drug abuse or dependence.

Serious drug abuse. Dependence and abuse occur most often in youths who are somewhat immature, self-centered, and passive, and who have little sense of direction in life.

Dependency on dangerous drugs is an extreme situation and is largely confined to the period from mid-adolescence to about age thirty, during which many individuals are groping for their identity—for a place and an active function in the world.

Before speaking to a young teenager about drugs, parents need to get comfortable enough about the subject (with professional help, if necessary) so they don't just lecture and threaten. An excellent book on this subject is Dr. Robert Schwebel's *Saying No Is Not Enough* (New York: Newmarket Press, 1998).

937. Preventing adolescent drug abuse. A very important question to consider is how you can try to protect your children from harmful frequent use of drugs. Even occasional use of drugs should be cause for concern. We know, for example, that drugs and alcohol are responsible for at least half of all motor vehicle fatalities, the leading cause of death in fifteen- to nineteen-year-olds.

If you look at the personal problems that increase the risk of serious drug abuse by teenagers—parents who use drugs; depression and other psychiatric problems; low self-esteem, anxiety, and a sense of powerlessness; and the feeling of being unable to control the world—then one means of prevention is to raise happy, healthy children. Of course, that's exactly what you are trying to do now.

If I were to choose one basic skill to instill in your young child so that he has the strength to avoid drug abuse, it would be good decision-making skills based on a core set of values.

Children who make good decisions are generally those whose values tell them what is right and what is wrong and whose strength of character allows them to resist the urging of their friends to be cool like everyone else. To experiment with drugs or not to experiment with drugs involves, above all, a choice.

938. Delaying initiation. Research has shown that delaying initiation of drug use to a later age will reduce the amount of harm from drugs—that is, the later the person begins using drugs, the less harm is likely to occur.

This is common sense: the older a person is, the more developmental tasks he will have mastered and the better able he will be to handle various substances. Therefore, consider these three recommendations:

1. Discourage drug use from a health standpoint.
2. Accept that some drug use may occur, especially considering the drug culture and what we know from child development.
3. At least try to delay the onset of the drug use that will occur.

939. Symptoms of drug abuse. There are no obvious signs of early drug use, unless you happen to see it happening. The only way to know if your child is just beginning to use drugs is through open communication.

Once drug use reaches abusive levels, certain types of behavior may tip you off. However, even this behavior is not proof of drug abuse; it may have other causes. Either way, you should still give it your attention.

- Inexplicable and frequent mood swings
- Apparent lying about what he has been doing when out of the house
- An unaccountable decline in school performance including increased tardiness and truancy

- Appearing listless and "hung-over"
- Repeated injuries
- Significant weight loss or weight gain
- Shortened attention span
- Depression
- School failure or suspension
- Jumpiness or anxiety
- Deteriorating health
- Personality changes, such as paranoia or increased forgetfulness

It's a frightening list for any parent. Just remember these types of behavior are a serious concern no matter what the cause. You shouldn't jump to any rash conclusions, but keep alcohol and other drug abuse in mind as you try to make sense of seemingly unexplainable changes in your child.

940. If your child is using drugs. If you suspect that your child is using drugs, you don't have to panic, but you should be concerned, and you do want to do something, because there is potential for harm.

There are different approaches depending on the amount of drug use and age of the child. With younger children you will want to set firm, nonnegotiable rules about drugs.

With older adolescents you want to help your child make his own wise decisions about drugs, rather than clamp down with rules that he will have a strong impulse to break. First, on a one-to-one basis you need to discuss the problem openly. If you don't know what you're up against, it will be harder to fashion a response. You need to gather some information such as: What are you using? How much are you using? How often? Why do you think you are using this drug? What do you get from it? What do your friends say? What are your concerns about your drug use?

Don't try to get answers to all of your questions in one meeting. If for some reason you cannot establish a dialogue with your child, then you need to consider having another adult attempt it.

Young people need an adult to talk to, professional or not, a person who has a natural understanding of child development and who will not think first of punitive approaches.

941. The younger child and the older child. In general, if the child is under fourteen, then your advice should be clear and firm: "You are not to use drugs. You are not ready to make such dangerous decisions." A child at this age has not had enough experience with life to be able to handle decisions about drugs.

As parents you have more control at this age than you'll have later on, so use it.

Also, early signs of drug use should alert you that there is something going on with your child that you need to pay attention to. You can set firm boundaries that are more effective than with the older child. Continue to discuss with your child why he is using drugs and what it means for him.

If your child is 15 or older, the situation is very different. This is the stage in his life when you want to give him more freedom, not less, and you should. More restrictions usually don't work for a child who is ready to rebel anyway.

You will get further if you focus on discussions that invite the child to talk about his feelings. Listen to and accept him rather than trying to change him. Be ready to hear what is really going on with your child, not just ready to punish him for his behavior.

942. Drug testing. If your child denies drug use but you are very suspicious, you might consider arranging a medical checkup. If your child has a good relationship with her doctor or nurse practitioner, she may be willing to divulge her secrets and obtain help from a professional.

I'm not a big fan of urine tests for teens who deny drug use, but in a few special situations—certainly not in all cases—drug testing may be appropriate.

Parents should not be in a panic. If the child shows all the signs of drug use, if he seems to be lying, and if there is no other explanation of these signs, then the testing may bring the child to the table and force him to confront his drug use. Sometimes drug testing and even regular drug monitoring will actually help children gain control of their lives. It may also give the child and parents a common ground for discussion.

However, the test may cause further negative feelings if not done tactfully and it may do more harm to the relationship than the parent wants to risk.

943. Talking with children about drugs. Regardless of the age of your children, I think it's important always to let them know that they can discuss anything with you and that you will respond in an honest and constructive way. You may not like the subject, but burying your head in the sand about it will prevent you from offering guidance and support to your child when she may need it the most.

And instead of passively waiting for your child to bring up the subject of drugs, you should ask her about it in a nonjudgmental, nonanxious, nonhysterical tone of voice. This will let her know that you understand that drugs are an issue for all children, that you take the issue seriously, and that you are available to talk about it at any time. Keeping your own fears and feelings contained while you talk about this volatile subject can be quite difficult, but it's simply not helpful to your child if your response isn't calm, collected, and constructive.

First, you need to elicit her feelings and ideas about drugs. You can ask, "Why do you think so many kids try drugs?" "What do they like about drugs?" "Do you think anything is wrong with trying drugs?" "What harm might come of experimenting with drugs?" "Have you thought about using drugs?" "Do you think that some of your friends might be using drugs?" "Have you tried drugs?" No matter what the answer, you should show respect and thoughtfulness, not horror and panic, toward your child's viewpoint. Remember that the child's answers to such questions will indicate the strength of her defenses against (or vulnerabilities to) drug use. You need to understand what your child's views are with regard to drug use before you can consider strategies to prevent use or abuse.

It is essential you have accurate information about alcohol and drug use. Adolescents have their antennae attuned to inaccuracies, especially from their parents. If a parent rants hysterically about how marijuana makes you crazy, and the child knows full well that his marijuana-using friends are not crazy, then parental credibility is seriously undermined and anything the parent says thereafter is greeted with a disbelieving, wary eye.

I think it's helpful to have objective pamphlets or books that discuss the effects and consequences of various drugs, including alcohol. You and your child can read these together and discuss what you have read. Your child needs to view you as a repository of factual information to whom she can go when she has questions, and not as an antidrug propagandist. (Don't worry, the real effects of alcohol and other abuse are bad enough. You won't need to exaggerate them.)

Your discussions can also serve to remind your child about the importance of making good decisions and resisting peer pressure. Rather than delivering a sermon or stern lecture, it's best to engage in a conversation. A good general rule is: if you're doing all the talking, you're probably not going to get very far. Your goal should be to help your child see the downside of experimenting with drugs and then allow her to come to her own conclusions about avoiding drug abuse, which may entail resisting peer pressure to use drugs and not indulging her curiosity about her effects.

During these conversations about drugs, it's your job to reflect back what your child has said. Label her feelings ("It sounds as if you're a little nervous and a little excited about using drugs"); inject potential consequences to her contemplated actions ("So do you think that if you drink alcohol you might get out of control like your friend or have an accident?"); clarify the child's motivations ("It sounds as if you're worried that you'll lose your friends if you don't smoke a joint with them. Do you think that's true?").

At this point you can make your own views about drug and alcohol use clear. You may believe, for example, that any use of drugs is a mistake, and then give your reasons for feeling that way. It is also wise to emphasize that you know you don't really have the power to prevent your older teenage child from doing whatever she wants to do, but that you trust her to make the right decisions and to do her best. It is often the parents' confidence and faith in their child to do the right thing that is the key to providing the strength to resist peer pressure.

At this point, if your child is committed to not using drugs, you could role-play with him or her to show how to resist the urgings of friends: "Let's say your friend says to you, 'Come on. Don't be chicken. It's fun. Don't be a wuss!' What might you say to him?" If your child can't come up with a good face-saving reply to this pressure, you can offer suggestions: "What about saying, 'You can do what you want, but I think it's a mistake to mess around with drugs. Too many bad things can happen. I'd rather be with you when you don't feel like getting stoned.'"

Here are some facts that you may want to call attention to: Even a mild drug like marijuana makes it easier for some heavy users to get off the track. The stage of life you are going through now is the most difficult of all, with many changes and tensions; some people who use drugs lose their drive and their sense of direction. I wish that you would wait until you are eighteen or twenty when things will have settled down and you'll know more about what you want out of life, before you decide whether or not to drink, smoke tobacco, or smoke marijuana. But of course it is you who will have to make the decision.

This advice will be a lot more persuasive, of course, if the parents are not abusing alcohol, tobacco, tranquilizers, or stimulants themselves.

After these discussions, I would count on my child's good sense. She might well use these various drugs at times. (Most of us parents in our youth went against our parents' requests on tobacco or alcohol, or other drugs at least occasionally.) Teenagers, like adults, usually are not aware that their judgment and skills are impaired when they are under the influence of alcohol or marijuana or other "recreational" drugs. You can encourage them to use a designated driver—someone who won't use alcohol or other drugs that evening—whenever they go to a party. And you can reassure them that they can telephone you for a ride home with no questions asked, whenever they feel they don't have a safe ride or can't drive safely themselves.

But you should know that further lectures—or sharp questions or snooping—will do no good and might actually provoke and tempt your child to rebel.

Heroin is, of course, extremely dangerous from every point of view. LSD (acid) often causes serious emotional disturbance. The abuse of amphetamine (speed) may lead to physical collapse and serious emotional disturbance. Cocaine and its smokable form, crack, are extremely dangerous and addictive.

But young people do not suddenly go off the deep end with these dangerous drugs. Those who do abuse drugs will usually have given signs of gradually slipping off the track: deterioration of school performance; loss of interest in hobbies, friendships, athletics; and lethargy. When such changes in behavior and attitude occur, it is time to confront the youth with your observations and with your loving concern, not with reproaches or anger. You need to make it very clear to your older teen that this is a serious problem and that you will help and support her 100 percent, but that, in the end, it must be her decision to take control and overcome this problem.

At this point, you will also need to decide if this problem warrants professional intervention or if it can be handled within the family. I'd suggest a meeting with your doctor or nurse practitioner to discuss the situation and review your options. In my experience, parents often wait too long to seek professional help. A drug counselor, a mental health professional, family therapy, therapeutic groups for substance-abusing teens—all can be of enormous benefit. You don't have to wait until the problems are totally out of hand to seek help. The sooner you act, the better.

You will also need to decide how to deal with this issue with the family. There are many books on the market—some good, some bad—dealing with drug use in children. However you choose to handle the situation, you should remember that using open communication to help your child make the right decisions on her own is the best long-term solution.

944. Treatment for drug abuse. What to do if your child is abusing alcohol or other drugs? There is no way around it: drug use that causes any of the behavior patterns discussed above is a serious problem and you can't just ignore it. Your child needs help and he needs it now. You do too.

945. Heavier users. In treatment, as much as we wish the drug use would instantly cease, there should not be heavy pressure to stop immediately. The drug has obviously been meeting some need for the child. Don't force the child to lie about his probable continual use. You will get further if you find out what needs are being met by the drug and address those needs. One of those may be to feel more popular. Drugs are also used to forget problems, reduce depression, reduce anger, and feel comfortable in social situations.

Children under pressure to change usually fight it or fake it. A good treatment program is one that understands this. We have to stop the rush to get the child to quit immediately if we are going to be successful. The child needs the space to figure out who he is. A rush by the therapist to achieve quick success, though reassuring to parents, generally leads to bad treatment, rebelling, and lying on the part of the child.

A quick but weak and insincere "commitment" may make the adults feel better, but doesn't really address the issues that led the child to drugs in the first place. A good treatment program is one that helps the child understand that he needs to change, not one that demands he change instantly. He needs to figure out the harmfulness of drugs. Professionals who understand child development, and who understand that the drugs meet some needs for the child, are usually more permanently successful in the long run. Before the child will give up drugs, he has to understand that he can get these needs met elsewhere without the health risks associated with the use of alcohol, tobacco or other drugs. A good professional must understand this and help the child identify his needs and find other options that will meet those needs.

Raising Nonviolent Children

946. Look no further than today's headlines: the rate of violence by teens has risen sharply, even as the overall prevalence of violent acts by adults in the United States has declined. This state of affairs has changed the way we view youths. Whereas we used to think of children as in need of adult protection, now we often think that adults need protection from youths. Many teens are already labeled "predators" and regarded as beyond redemption. The age at which a teen can be prosecuted as an adult has been lowered in many states. And the United States appears to have the highest rate of teenage violence in the world. Our society seems somehow to promote violence and aggression in at least some youths.

I think it's too easy to blame all these woes on media violence or an overpermissive society, although these don't help. The roots of teen violence can often be traced to certain components of early upbringing combined with a peer group that encourages susceptible youths to commit violent acts.

What are the backgrounds of teens who tend to become violent? First, they are often themselves the victims of or witnesses to parental violence. Early on, such experiences are very traumatic to the child, who may cry and express fear and anxiety. Such a child learns to be ever vigilant, constantly on guard, waiting for the next trauma.

With time, however, these stressful emotions undergo a change. They are simply too intense to bear. The child slowly becomes numb to the trauma and then becomes an aggressor himself. Aggressiveness is an understandable defense against overwhelmingly painful emotions.

Some children begin to identify with the perpetrator of the trauma, who is, after all, the powerful one—often a parent or an older child. And it seems morally permissible to imitate the parent.

Paradoxically, violent individuals almost always think of themselves as victims—victims of the government, of other bullies, of prejudice—and believe that their violent acts are therefore totally justified. In this way, the intergenerational cycle of violence is perpetuated.

There are other precursors to becoming a violent teen. These include being raised in a cold and loveless way and being punished excessively, often physically. Children with low self-esteem are more likely to become violent, especially in combination with some other risk factors. Impulsive, hotheaded children are more likely to use violence when frustrated or angry.

So, for whatever reason, children who later become violent learn to see the world as a cold and hostile place.

They develop a habit of thought that always attributes hostile intentions to others. Their view seems to be "The world is out to get me." Say, for example, that a little boy accidentally bumps into another little boy. Most would shrug it off as an accident. The aggressive child, however, believes the boy ran into him on purpose with the intention of hurting him, so he hauls off and slugs the other little boy. Things only deteriorate from there. The aggressive child sees the world as an unsafe place in which there are only victims and victimizers, so he (unconsciously) chooses the latter and becomes a bully. This power and the delight he takes in hurting others, in combination with his already numbed emotions, can make for a lethal mixture. Violent children tend to have little empathy; that is, they don't even recognize (much less feel) the suffering of others. They also come to believe that overpowering another person is a mark of strength and worth, that violence is a legitimate way to resolve conflict. And the brutalization of other children may be their only source of self-esteem, the only confirmation of their human worth.

All of these early developments conspire to promote violent behavior as the child gets older, but of course the story does not end there. Add to the proclivity for aggression one final ingredient: the availability of firearms. A violent youth even without a weapon is a threat to do bodily harm. A violent youth with a handgun is capable of murder. Perhaps more than any other factor, the rise in teen deaths due to violence can be attributed to the easy availability of handguns and other firearms.

947. Prevention and education are the keys. No one reading this book has purposely set out to raise a violent child and, of course, most of you won't. But I've come to believe that raising nonviolent children and teens is of paramount importance to our society and that all of us must do what we can to prevent violence before it starts.

Based on what we know about the precursors of violence, there are some rules I recommend for all families. First, the message at home should be clear and unequivocal: *No hurting!* That applies to the entire family. Physical punishments, like spanking, should not be used. When a young child is violent toward another, close attention and tender consideration are first given to the victim, not the aggressor. Then the aggressor should be made aware (to the best of his developmental capability) of how the violence felt to the victim: "That really hurt him. You wouldn't like it if someone did that to you." This is an attempt to begin to teach empathy, the ability to put yourself in another's shoes. Young children, being naturally self-centered, have only a limited ability to feel empathy. A two-year-old biter, for example, really doesn't understand what she's doing to the one she bites. But she certainly can understand that you seem to be paying a lot more attention to the other child than to her. As she gets older—say, around four, when children begin to get less egocentric and have superior language skills—she can begin to understand how it hurts others when she is aggressive.

With older children it's quite helpful to routinely talk about violence. You can ask what is happening at school. Are there fights? Why do you think kids fight? What do you do when someone wants to fight with you? Based on the answers, you can role-play how one could respond to various confrontations without using violence. For example, you can explore the motivation of the aggressor: "Why do you think he's picking a fight. Do you think it's because fighting makes him feel better? Do you think it's cool to fight a lot?"

Then you can go through how your child might respond to a situation that could escalate into violence. For example, you can have your child try saying: "I know you want to fight but this isn't worth fighting about. I don't really have anything against you. If you want to talk about things, then let's do that. But if you want to fight, I'm walking away. If you continue to bother me, I'll tell the teacher (or parent)."

Your goal is to devise nonviolent ways to defuse potentially violent situations. You are also trying to teach a calm, reasonable response to an ambiguous or volatile situation. Rather than just lashing out at the slightest invitation to fight, you'd like your child to think to himself: "Why is this guy doing this? Is he upset? Is he drunk? How can I calm him down? What possible good could come from fighting?"

Raising nonviolent teens is as easy, and as hard, as all the rest of parenting. On the one hand, child rearing that has been loving, reasonably consistent, and fair is the best immunization against the epidemic of teen violence. But, given the pervasiveness of violence among teens, this problem requires special attention and care, even in the gentlest of families. It is quite clear that violent people are made, not born. The creation of a nonviolent society, then, begins in the home, in the family, with you.

Media Exposure

Television, movies, and rock and roll have been blamed for the decline of everything, including western civilization as we know it. But are they really a cause of the decline in morality that many lament in our culture, or do they merely represent what people want to watch and hear? Perhaps both are true. There can be no doubt that popular culture has undergone a dramatic change during the past twenty years. From my vantage point that change looks like a coarsening of content and a decline of civility.

Consider these statistics: Young people spend more time (an average of twenty-three hours a week) watching television than in any other activity except sleeping. Children view an average of 10,000 murders, assaults and rapes, 20,000 commercials, and 15,000 sexual situations (of which only 175 include the use of birth control) on television per year.

So here's the situation: we are leaving our children in the care of an electronic baby-sitter for twenty-three hours of every week. This "sitter" tells our children that violence is an acceptable way to solve problems; that sex is especially exciting when it occurs without love and, besides, there are no real negative consequences anyway; and that owning the latest products is a measure of success and happiness. There seems to be very little similarity between the world the electronic baby-sitter is selling to our children and the world we would like to see. Why would parents entrust their children to such a caretaker?

The answer is complicated. Certainly many parents worry about the effects of the media on their children, but few make their feelings known to the networks and advertisers.

But television is so hypnotic that it's hard to resist, and censoring it would require a great deal of time and effort. Music is a wonderful pleasure, but how can you realistically try to prevent your child from hearing offensive lyrics? Movies can be a wonderful recreation and an enriching experience, but how can parents restrict their children from seeing excessively violent or crudely sexual films, short of throwing the television set out or being more vigilant?

Researchers agree that the media teach children (and adults) to view the world in a distorted way. For example, children who watch a lot of violent television believe the chance of being robbed or killed in real life is much higher than it really is. And TV also needlessly exposes children to an alternative universe where the values of everyday life are distorted in order to keep their attention.

That attention is exactly what the television networks are seeking. Many people incorrectly believe that the product line of the television industry is the commercials. In fact, the product sold by the television companies is the viewer's attention. The more of this product they accumulate, the more money they make from their commercials. Since television is a means to catch your attention (and not to educate, edify, or entertain, unless that catches your attention), it becomes clear why most programs try to appeal to the broadest base of viewers, which usually translates into sensationalism.

So instead of trying to limit your children's exposure to the media, I think the most important thing you can do as a parent is to help your children understand and make proper sense of what they see, read, and hear in the media, and help them learn to discriminate between what's real and truly important and what is media fantasy and hype.

Television

948. Of all the media, television has the most pervasive influence on children. There is no question that some programs, usually on the public broadcasting stations, provide wonderful learning experiences for children. These are the programs that educate in a fun way, that teach values of caring and kindness, and that appeal to the child's higher instincts. Unfortunately these shows are in the minority. Most children's television is meant to sell products and engage the child's attention through fast-paced, often violent buffoonery.

Another subtle but worrisome effect TV has on its viewers is its tendency to promote passivity and a lack of creativity. Watching TV requires zero mental activity on the viewer's part. You simply sit and let the images flow by. This is very different from reading, which forces you to use your imagination, or even listening to the radio. The viewer becomes a passive receptacle for whatever images the TV chooses to display. Watching TV is incompatible with creativity. Some believe that this sort of nonparticipatory viewing impairs children's ability to learn to read and fosters a short attention span.

So what's a parent to do? In my opinion, not having a TV at all seems to be a logical solution. That way children and the family cannot rely on passive entertainment and, as mankind did for thousands of years, learn to creatively and actively broaden their interests by reading, writing, or conversing with one another.

Since I recognize that this solution is far too extreme for most of you, there are some sound rules for making the best of television and minimizing its destructive effects on children.

949. The hours for watching television should be limited. Some children are glued to the set from the minute they come home in the afternoon until they are forced to go to bed at night. They don't want to take time out for supper or for homework or even to say hello to the family. There's also the temptation for parents to let their children watch endlessly because it keeps them quiet. It's better for the parents and child to come to a reasonable but definite understanding about which hours are for outdoors and friends, which are for homework, and which are for TV viewing. A maximum of one or two hours after homework or chores or other responsibilities is a reasonable limit for most families.

Of course, then everyone has to stick to the bargain. Otherwise the parents are apt to be nagging children about their duties whenever they catch them watching TV, and the children are apt to be turning the set on whenever they think the parents aren't paying attention.

For very young children the solution is easy because your control is close to absolute. Pick wonderful videotapes for them to view over and over again. They won't even realize that the TV can be used in any other way! When they do watch commercial TV, make sure you approve of the programs. As they get older, the V-chip should allow you to limit what stations they can access on cable TV—that is, if they are not clever enough to disable the mechanism themselves. If you use television at all as a baby-sitter, then it is entirely proper for you to make sure that it meets with your approval, as you would make sure with any baby-sitter.

I believe, for example, that parents should flatly forbid their children to watch violent programs. Young children can only partly distinguish between drama and reality. You can explain, "It isn't right for people to hurt each other and kill each other, and I don't want you to watch them do it." Even if your child cheats and watches such a program in secret, she'll know very well that you disapprove, and this will protect her to a degree from the coarsening effect of violent scenes.

As your child gets older, she'll certainly begin to bristle at your attempts at censorship: "Everybody else watches these cartoons, why can't I?" When this happens, you should stick to your guns. While it's true that children will undoubtedly watch the forbidden programs at friends' houses, you are still giving the message that this program does not conform with your family's values and that's why you don't want them to watch it.

950. Watch TV with your child. The best way to handle the unwholesome messages on TV is to watch it with your child and help her to become a discriminating, critical viewer. You can make comments on whether what you've just seen together bears any resemblance to the real world. If you've just seen a fight where someone gets punched and just shrugs it off, you can say, "That punch in the nose must really have hurt. Don't you think it did? Television isn't at all like real life, is it?" This also teaches empathy with the victim of violence rather than identification with the aggressor. When viewing a commercial, you can say, "Do you think what they are saying is true? I think they just want you to buy their product so they can get rich." You want your child to view commercials for what they are and begin to understand their manipulative intent. When viewing a scene with sexual content, you can comment how "that's not what it's like in real life at all. Usually that happens after people have known each other for a long time and really love each other."

You can use TV viewing to help your child learn to make sense of the world in a more realistic and wholesome way and to see TV for the fantasy it is. As these lessons are learned, your child can become immunized against wholesale acceptance of the media's messages.

951. Call and write letters to the television networks about what you like and don't like in children's programming. When the networks receive one letter, they assume that there are 10,000 people out there who feel the same way. So you can have an impact. I'd also suggest joining Action for Children's Television, 20 University Road, Cambridge, MA 02138, a national consumer organization that can provide you with many practical suggestions and general guidance in sensibly managing the way your family watches and uses television. You can call them at (617) 876-6620.

Movies

952. Fearfulness about movies and television. Movie-viewing is a risky business for children under the age of seven. You hear, for example, about a program like an animated feature that sounds like perfect entertainment for your small child. But when you get to the theater, you find that there is some episode in the story that scares the wits out of him. You have to remember that a child of four or five doesn't distinguish clearly between make-believe and real life. A witch on the screen is just as alive and terrifying to a child as a flesh-and-blood burglar would be to you. The only safe rule that I know is not to take a child under seven to a movie unless you, or someone else who knows small children well, has seen it and is positive that it contains nothing upsetting. Even then, young children should always go with a sympathetic adult who can explain any disturbing scenes and comfort the child when necessary.

953. What movies are appropriate for children? There are obviously no hard and fast rules here. The answer depends on your child's developmental level and maturity, her response to scary stories, her desire to see movies, and your family's values. Do you want to avoid violence altogether or just certain kinds, like very graphic violence? When do you think a child is mature enough to be exposed to sexual scenes, and what is acceptable in those scenes? I think that, if you err, it should be on the side of being overly restrictive about which movies you allow your children to see. It is much more harmful for a child to be exposed to an upsetting or inappropriate scene that she is not ready for than to be denied access to a movie she is actually mature enough to watch. When used as a point for discussion, conflicts about which movies are appropriate allow you to hear your child's side of the argument and why she feels she is totally ready and absolutely must see this movie. You can then discuss your view that loveless or brutal sex is not good at any age. Your child still won't like it, but you'll be teaching her your values in a very direct way and learning more about your child's world.

Rock and Roll

I remember well that in the early days of rock and roll parents worried about Elvis Presley's dancing on television. He was shown only from the waist up, lest his gyrating hips corrupt the multitudes of youthful viewers. A decade later the records of the Beatles were burned because of their allegedly depraved effects on the minds of adoring teens. More recently, the raw and violent lyrics of some songs have been blamed for the surge in violence among teenagers. The more things change, the more they stay the same.

If there is one common thread to the music of teenagers over the decades, it is to turn society's staid old music on its head and to rebel against the status quo. If the music of teenagers isn't found offensive by adults, it probably won't be very successful. Music, among other things, is a means by which each new generation differentiates itself from the old and provides itself with a bond of shared musical culture and identity.

This is not to say that offensive music is only in the ear of the beholder. It is distressing to hear lyrics that glorify aggression and disrespect toward women and aggrandize drug use. But is there a way to prevent your children from hearing such songs? I'd sit down with them and ask them questions about the songs: "Why does this song call women disparaging names? Why do the lyrics show such disrespect for the police? What do you think these sexy lyrics actually mean?" During such discussions with your child you can also clarify your view on the song's message: "I don't like songs that say drugs are good." You need to be thoughtful and respectful toward the music, even if you think it sounds like a band of screech owls, but you should also voice your views in a way that is not disrespectful of your child and his generation. If you appear to reject the music from the start, your child is likely to pigeonhole you as hopelessly out of it and discount anything you have to say.

Studies have shown that most offensive lyrics go in one ear and out the other for most children. Unlike movies and TV, I'm dubious that offensive lyrics really have much effect on most children's well-being. But the coarsening, offensive nature of some lyrics should not go unnoticed and undiscussed by you. It's yet another opportunity to enter into your children's culture and try to help them to clarify their ideas and thoughts about their most important art form.

The Changing Roles of Women and Men

Profound changes have occurred and are still occurring as a result of two trends: the progressive industrialization of our society, with men and women working away from home, and the efforts of women to secure equality for their sex.

954. Sex discrimination is still rampant. Women in our society had to fight for half a century to get the right to education, the vote, and to enter at least some of the professions. Yet in the 1990s they are still being grossly discriminated against—being ignored for the higher-paying jobs in most fields, receiving lower pay for doing the same work as men, and facing unjust laws and biased social customs. The women's movement has made some gains, but there is still a long way to go.

Of the women who stay at home to care for their children, many are proud of their occupation, and happy. Others feel sharply the lack of respect shown by a materialistic society to an occupation that pays no salary and in which there are no higher positions for which to compete. Many mothers, because of our pattern of relatively isolated homes, feel cut off during the day from the stimulation and fun of adult companionship. This is very different from the intimate communities of simpler societies.

Most hurtful to all women is the realization that they are considered—by many men and by many other women—a second-class sex as far as capabilities and influence are concerned.

955. The subordination of women is brought about by countless small acts beginning in early childhood. Some are consciously intended to be belittling. Most are thoughtless expressions of prejudice or of old tradition.

People are apt to show admiration for the accomplishments of little boys and for the cuteness of little girls. Girlish clothes are designed to make an adult say, "How pretty you look!" which is complimentary in one sense, but which also gives girls a sense that they are primarily appreciated for their appearance rather than for their achievements. Children's books show boys building things or going on adventures; girls watch the boys or play with dolls. Girls are commonly warned not to climb into trees or onto garage roofs because they are not strong enough or will get hurt more easily. Boys are given toy cars, construction sets, sporting equipment, or doctor kits. Girls are given dolls, sewing sets, nurse kits, or articles of adornment. There's nothing wrong with any of these gifts in themselves, especially if the child asks for them. The harm comes when adults consistently impose these distinctions, which imply that females (or males) are only good at a limited number of occupations.

Boys are assigned chores in the garage, in the basement, or on the lawn; girls work in the house. Of course, housework is important to the welfare of the whole family so it should be accorded dignity; but when it is done only by females, in a society that gives so much prestige to males, it will be considered menial by both sexes.

Many boys, because of their own sense of inferiority as individuals, taunt girls that they are not able to run fast or throw a ball, and so can't be on the team.

Some parents and teachers tell girls that, by their nature, they won't be able to study advanced mathematics or physics or to function as engineers. Many girls become convinced by adolescence that they will be inferior to men in such capabilities as abstract reasoning, executive ability, and emotional control. The acceptance of these aspersions in itself destroys self-confidence and thus brings about the very impairment of abilities that is alleged (by many men and some women) to be inborn in females.

956. Men need liberating, too. Perceptive women, in trying to liberate themselves, have realized that men, too, are victims of sexist assumptions—sexual stereotyping. Boys are taught that they mustn't show their feelings when they are hurt or frightened or unhappy. To the extent that they absorb this belief they lose some of their sensitivity to all feelings—other people's and their own—even positive feelings like tenderness and joy. (I've seen this in trying to help medical students understand the feelings of their patients.) They become emotionally restricted. They are less understanding—as husbands, as fathers, as friends, and as workers dealing with the public—and therefore more difficult to live with and deal with.

Boys learn early that men in our society are supposed to be tough, dauntless, aggressive, competitive, and successful. They must go into only the occupations that are traditional for men. Most of the males who can fit readily into this kind of pattern are at least slightly rigidified in personality as a result. They will hesitate to branch out beyond what's conventional—in their interests, in their friendships, and in their jobs.

The boys and men who don't enjoy toughness and competition are made to feel inferior or even peculiar. This may impair their effectiveness, whether they get traditional or unconventional work. It will lessen their sense of fulfillment.

When individuals feel obliged to conform to a conventional male or female sex stereotype, they are all cramped to a degree, depending on how much each has to deny and suppress their natural inclinations. Thus, valuable traits are lost to the society. And they are all made to feel inadequate to the degree that they fail to conform to the supposed ideal.

957. What is the meaning of work, for men and women? In simple nonindustrial societies—the kind for which our species was designed, through evolution—all adults and older children work in their own community at farming, fishing, weaving, cooking, the making of pots, and so on.

The work is carried on cooperatively and companionably by extended family groups or by the community-wide group. The purpose of work is to serve the group—not to make money or to get ahead of others. Children are always near their parents, but their care is incidental to the other work. A mother may carry a young infant in a sling while she works. Later she may entrust the baby to a four-year-old sister. Children begin to assist in serious adult work at an early age.

In preindustrial days in our own country, craftsmen and craftswomen got great creative satisfaction from the things they made for themselves and for others—household implements, decorations, woven fabrics, clothes, rugs, adornments, toys, and furniture. But in industrialized societies like ours the demands of industry have drastically artificialized and fragmented our home lives as well as our work lives. Many fathers and mothers go off to a job miles away. It may consist of dull, repetitive, impersonal work that gives no gratification in itself. Then the worker's satisfaction has to come solely from the money earned and the position held.

This has been true for so long that we assume these are

the normal satisfactions. Actually they are narrow, meager substitutes for the joy of creating something useful and beautiful, the way a craftsperson does. The focus on money and position tends to foster rivalry between workers, between neighbors, and at times between working husbands and wives in place of the warm glow that comes from working cooperatively for the benefit of family and community.

Couples who are ready to move in order to get the work or pay or advancement they want, or because regular moves for junior executives are a policy of the corporation, must leave behind the love and security of their extended family. They usually live in houses that are more or less isolated from each other, commonly without close ties to neighbors. They're often obliged to move so frequently that they have no time to put down roots in the community or to draw sustenance from it. This isolation and mobility may put particular strain on the parent who stays at home, as well as on the children.

958. In outside jobs for women and men, pay and prestige have traditionally been men's prime values in twentieth century America. From my point of view, this emphasis has played a major role in misleading many men into excessive competitiveness, excessive materialism, frequent neglect of relationships with wives and children (fathers have confessed this to me when their teenage sons or daughters got into trouble), neglect of friendships, neglect of community relationships and of cultural interests, and has led incidentally, to ulcers, heart attacks, and other stress-related health problems.

When the Women's Liberation Movement surfaced in the early 1970s, working women naturally focused on gaining equality in the workplace—equal pay for equal work and equal opportunity for advancement to the prestigious jobs. They are certainly entitled to these rights, though they remain largely out of reach.

So in demanding occupational equality with men, many women have, without realizing it, taken on what I think of as the narrow and often mistaken values of men. Women have, in a sense, joined the rat race. Some have acquired stress-related diseases such as ulcers and heart attacks. Others, who have succeeded in their careers, have felt deprived and guilty because of the all-day separation from their babies and young children. (Men would have felt this guilt, too, if they had been raised in a society that gave them equal responsibility for child rearing.) So the price of even partial equality based on pay and prestige has been high.

How much better it would have been (though it never would have happened) if men had had the good sense, in 1970, to raise their own consciousness and see that women have been wise in sensing through the centuries that family and feelings, participation in the community, and interest in the arts are the values that have given the deepest and longest-lasting gratification to most people and that the long-range satisfaction from many outside jobs—omitting perhaps the highly creative work of writers, composers, artists, inventors—is shallow by comparison.

I believe that it would greatly benefit American men, our families, and our society if men would elevate family and feelings to the highest priority. Then men and women could share a common aim, a common vision for their lives.

But why make such a fuss about minimizing the importance of the job? I'm not denying that a living income is absolutely essential—for the two-parent family and even more so for the single-parent family. But I'm concerned that our obsession with getting ahead at work is putting intolerable strain on family life, making women as well as men view the outside job as their central purpose in life, contributing to the breakup of marriages, and depriving thousands of young children of the security of a home where at least one parent is present for at least part of the day.

I believe that both boys and girls should be raised with a deep conviction that family is, for most people, the richest and longest-lasting satisfaction in life. Then women could feel less pressure to accept men's traditional values, and men, freed from their sex's narrow obsession of the past, could practice women's many skills and try to adopt their values.

DIFFERENT FAMILY CONSTELLATIONS

The Single Parent

959. Parenting is a tough job, no matter how you look at it, and being a single parent makes the job that much tougher. You don't have a supportive partner to ease the relentless day-to-day responsibilities of raising children. Everybody and everything depends on you. You don't get a real break or vacation. If you are the only bread-winner, financial worries add to your burden. It sometimes feels as if you just don't have enough physical and emotional energy to keep it all going.

How and why you became a single parent also make a big difference. Some of you chose to be one and have marshaled enough support from family and friends to feel confident about the road ahead. Some of you became single parents through some emotionally traumatic event—separation or divorce, abandonment, the death of a partner—and you feel that much more stress about your circumstances.

Being a single parent is no picnic, but it does have its rewards. You and your children may achieve a closeness that is not common in two-parent homes. You may discover strengths and talents that you never knew you possessed and come out of the experience a stronger, wiser person. And you should be reassured to know that the scientific literature shows that children who grow up in single-parent households usually do well, despite all the pitfalls and hardships along the way.

960. Pitfalls of single parenthood. I want to emphasize that single parents usually do a wonderful job of raising their children, but there are hazards. In my experience, one of the most common is to treat your children as best friends and confidants. It's especially easy, for example, to say to the oldest child, "You're the woman (or man) of the family now, and I'm really depending on you." This is entirely understandable. Without a consistent partner of your own, it is tempting to confide your feelings, hopes, and dreams to your children and make them your best friends. That may serve your needs, but what about theirs? By treating your children as peers, the line between parent and child is blurred. If you are upset about something, they will feel the responsibility of parenting you and attending to your needs.

Children have to go on with their own emotional growth and development, and this process will be interfered with if they have to act like substitute adults. While all normal children can take on extra chores and provide some emotional support to a distressed parent, no child can take on an adult role without serious consequences to her or his future emotional growth and development.

961. Children need their parents to maintain clear boundaries from them, especially with regard to privacy. Part of growing up is for children to find their way in the world that is different from their parent's, to have relationships and secrets that the parent never knows about, and not to be preoccupied with the parent's well-being. So I'd strongly suggest that you resist the temptation to make your child your best friend or, worse yet, your partner. Some single parents find it comforting to take their child after the first year of life into bed with them, rationalizing this one way or another. Again, this may suit mother's or father's needs, such as not to be lonely, but it may not be in the best interests of the child. He needs to remain a child and that means maintaining clear boundaries from his parent so he can find his own way.

962. Another potential pitfall for single parents is an unwillingness to set firm limits. This may occur for the best of reasons. Many single parents feel guilty because their children are not growing up with two parents. They worry that their children are missing something essential for their healthy development. They fret that they just aren't able to spend enough time with their children. As a result, the temptation is strong to slavishly indulge the child, giving in to her every whim and neglecting to set limits. One parent continued to give her very obese child daily hot fudge sundaes. After I talked with her a number of times, she finally began to cry and said, "I just feel so guilty that she doesn't see her father anymore and she loves the ice cream so much, I just can't say no."

It is not necessary or sensible for the parent to spoil the child with presents and kowtowing. In fact it's not wise for the parent to focus on the child for most of the time they are together, as if the child were a visiting princess. The child can be working on a hobby, doing homework, helping with the housework most of the time, while the parent does likewise. But this doesn't mean that they have to be out of touch. If they are in tune with each other they can chat and comment off and on, as the spirit moves.

963. The mother as single parent. Let's take the example of the child who has no father because of divorce or death, or because he was born to a single mother, or because a single woman adopted him. It would be foolish to say that the father's absence makes no difference to this child or that it's easy for the mother to make it up to him in other ways. But if the job is handled well, the child will grow up well adjusted.

The mother's spirit is most important. A single mother may feel lonely, imprisoned, or cross at times, and she will sometimes take her feelings out on the child. This is natural and won't hurt him too much. The important thing is for her to go on being a normal human being, keeping up her friendships, her recreations, her career, and her outside activities as far as she can and not have her life totally revolve around her child. This is hard if she has a baby or child to take care of and no one to help her. But she can ask people in, and take the baby to a friend's house for an evening if he can adjust to sleeping in strange places. It's more valuable to him to have his mother cheerful and outgoing than to have his routine perfect. It won't do him any good to have her wrap all her activity and thoughts and affection around him.

964. Children, young or old, boys or girls, need to be friendly with other men if the father is not there. With babies up to the age of a year or two, a good deal is accomplished if they can just be reminded frequently that there are such creatures as agreeable men, with lower voices, different clothes, and a different manner than women. A kindly grocer who just grins and says hello helps even if there are no closer friends. As children go on toward three and over, the kind of companionship they share with men is increasingly important. They need chances to be with and feel close to men and older boys. Grandfathers, uncles, cousins, scout masters, male teachers, a priest or minister or rabbi, and family friends can serve as substitute fathers if they enjoy the child's company and see him or her fairly regularly.

Children of three or over build up an image of their father that is their ideal and inspiration, whether they remember him or not. The other friendly men they see and play with give substance to the image, influence their conception of their father, make their father mean more to them. The mother can help by being extra hospitable to male relatives, sending her son or daughter to a camp that has some male counselors, picking a school, if she has a choice, that has some male teachers, encouraging a child to join clubs and other organizations that have male leaders.

The boy without a father particularly needs opportunities and encouragement to play with other boys, every day if possible, by the age of two, and to be mainly occupied with childish pursuits. The temptation of the mother who has no other equally strong ties is to make her son her closest spiritual companion, getting him interested in her preoccupations, hobbies, and tastes. If she succeeds in making her world more appealing to him and easier to get along in than the world of boys, where he would have to make his own way, he may grow up with predominantly adult interests. It's all to the good if a mother can spend time and have plenty of fun with her boy, provided she also lets him go his own way, provided she shares in his interests rather than having him share too many of hers. It helps to invite other boys to the house regularly and to take them along on treats and trips.

965. The father as single parent. Everything I've said about a mother raising a child alone applies to a father raising a child alone. But often there's an additional problem. Few fathers in our society feel completely comfortable in a nurturing role. Many men have been brought up believing that being a nurturing person is "soft" and therefore feminine. So many fathers will find it hard, at least at first, to provide the gentle comforting and cuddling that children need, especially young children. But, with time and experience, they can certainly rise to the task.

Divorce

It's been said that the family as an institution in America is dying. I don't think that's true. The family has certainly been changing. Since the mid-1980s fewer than 10 percent of American families have been made up of a father who goes out to work, a mother who stays at home, and two children. But the family, whomever it may include, is still the center of our daily lives. The family is where the great majority of us get our most important love and nurturance and support. I think that's what counts most, whether a family has two working parents, only one parent, children from previous marriages, or children only on weekends and holidays.

966. Separation and divorce have become common. In the United States, there are now about a million divorces a year. While you can read about "friendly divorce" in fiction and see examples of it in movies, in real life most separations and divorces involve two people who are angry with each other.

967. Marriage counseling. Divorce is disturbing to all members of the family in most cases, at least for a couple of years. Of course, it may be less upsetting than continued hostile conflict. But there is a third alternative—marriage counseling or family therapy or family guidance at a clinic, at a family social agency or with a private therapist. It's best, of course, if both husband and wife go into counseling on a regular basis, to get a clearer view of what has gone wrong and of the part that each partner is playing. It takes two to make a quarrel, but if one spouse refuses to acknowledge his or her role in the conflict, it may still be worthwhile for the other to get counseling on whether and how to save the marriage. After all, there were strong positive attractions in the beginning, and many divorced people say later that they wish they had tried harder to solve the problems and make a go of it.

It's usually true that when a couple disagree, each one feels that the other is mostly to blame. Yet an outsider can often see that the trouble is not that one or the other is a villain but that neither seems to realize how she or he is acting. In one case, each spouse may unconsciously want to be pampered like an adored child instead of contributing to the partnership. In another case, a bossy spouse has no idea how much she or he is trying to dominate the other, and the one who is being nagged may be asking for it. Very often an unfaithful partner is not really falling in love with someone else but is running away from a hidden fear or unconsciously trying to make their spouse jealous.

968. Telling the children. Children are always aware of and disturbed by conflicts between their parents, whether or not divorce is being considered. It is good for them to feel that they can discuss these situations with their parents, together or singly, in order to get a more sensible picture than their morbid imaginations may suggest. It is important for children to believe in both their parents, in order to grow up believing in themselves, so it is wise for the parents to avoid bitterly heaping blame, which is a natural temptation. Instead, they can explain their quarrels in general terms, without pinning the blame: "We get angry about every little thing"; "We quarrel about how to spend money"; "It upsets Mommy when Daddy takes several drinks."

It is wise to keep children from hearing the word "divorce" shouted in anger. When divorce is almost certain, it should be discussed, not just once but again and again. To young children the world consists of the family, which to them is mainly the father and mother. To suggest breaking up the family is like suggesting the end of the world. So the divorce has to be explained much more carefully to them than it would be to an adult: that the children will live most of the time with, let's say, their mother; that their father will live nearby (or far away); that he will still love them and will still be their father; that they will live with him according to some schedule; and that they can telephone him and write him letters anytime. It is also very important to tell the child over and over again that it wasn't anything she did that made her parents divorce. Young children are very egocentric and will imagine that it was their actions that caused the parents to separate.

Just as important as telling the children about the divorce is giving them ample opportunities to ask questions. You'll be amazed at some of their mistaken assumptions—for example, that they caused the divorce or that they may lose both parents. It is wise to get these misunderstandings straightened out as promptly as possible, but don't be surprised if young children slip back into weird misconceptions.

969. All children develop signs of tension. In one study children under six most often showed fears of abandonment, sleep problems, regression in bed-wetting and temper tantrums, and aggressive outbursts. Children of seven and eight expressed sorrow and feelings of aloneness. Nine- and ten-year-olds were more understanding about the realities of divorce, but they expressed hostility toward one or both parents and complained about stomachaches and headaches. Adolescents spoke of the painfulness of the divorce and of their sadness, anger, and shame. Some girls were handicapped in developing good relationships with boys.

The best way to help children is to give them regular opportunities to talk about their feelings and to reassure them that these feelings are normal, that they didn't cause the divorce, and that both parents still love them. Parents are often in too much emotional pain themselves to be able to do this with the children. Then it's important to find a professional counselor whom the children can see regularly.

970. Parents' reactions. Mothers who gain custody of the children usually find the first year or two after divorce very difficult. The children are more tense, demanding, and complaining; they are simply less attractive. The mother misses the part that the father played in making decisions, settling arguments, and sharing responsibility for plans. She is apt to feel tired out from working at a job and caring for the home and the children. She misses adult companionship, including the social and romantic attention of men. Worst of all, most mothers say, is the fear that they will not be able to earn a satisfactory living and to run the family. (They should have secured an adequate child support allowance in the separation agreement, but this doesn't guarantee that payments will arrive on time.) Many women say they receive great satisfaction and compensation in the end, when they prove to themselves that they can support and run a family without help. This gives them a sense of competence and confidence that they never had before in their lives.

One method that has proved practical and satisfying to some divorced women—for limiting expenses, sharing in the care of home and children, and having companionship—is to share a home or apartment with another divorced woman. Of course, they should know each other well before moving in together. Fathers who get custody of their children have the same problems as mothers, so there is no reason why they should not consider this alternative.

Some people imagine that divorced fathers without custody have a high old time and all the dates they can arrange, with no family responsibilities except child support payments and visitation. However, studies show that most fathers are miserable much of the time. If they get involved in casual affairs they soon find that these are shallow and meaningless. They are unhappy not to be consulted about important and unimportant plans for the children. They miss the company of their children. Even more, they miss having their children ask them for advice or for permission, which is part of what a father is for. Their children's weekend visits often settle into a series of fast-food emporiums and movies, which may satisfy the children's needs for pleasure but not their own or their father's need for a real relationship. Fathers and children may also find conversation difficult in this new situation.

Custody and Visitation

971. Custody. It was assumed in the first three-quarters of the twentieth century that children's needs would be best served, at least up to adolescence, by living mainly with and in the custody of the mother, unless she was clearly unfit. (It's interesting to learn that in the nineteenth century and earlier, when divorce was rare, custody was usually awarded to the father, because the children were property to which he was entitled.)

In recent years there has been increasing recognition that many fathers are just as capable of nurturing children as mothers, and now more judges take this into account in awarding custody. Naturally, but unfortunately, there is intense bitterness in many divorces. This creates a rivalry between the parents over custody and keeps them from focusing on what would be best for the children. Both of them assume that their custody would be best.

The factors to consider are these: Who has been providing most of the care, especially in the case of babies and small children who will badly miss their accustomed caregiver? What kind of relationship does each child have to each parent? What is each one's expressed preference, especially in later childhood and adolescence? How important is it for each child to live with a brother or sister (apt to be strong in the case of twins)?

In the past it has usually been assumed that the divorcing parents will be adversaries at court, in regard to custody, child support, alimony, and property settlement. The more this battling attitude can be avoided, especially in the case of custody, the better for the children. In recent years, there has been a movement for joint custody, to keep the noncustodial parent (more frequently the father) from getting the short end of the stick in visitation rights and, even more important, to keep that parent from feeling divorced from his children and feeling that he is no longer a real parent—a feeling that often leads to a gradual withdrawal from contact with the children.

When speaking of joint custody, some lawyers and parents mean an equal sharing of the children, such as four days with one, three with the other, or one week with one and then a week with the other. This may or may not be practical for the parents, or comfortable for the children. School-aged children have to keep going to the same school, and the same may be true for day care or preschool. Children like and benefit from routine schedules.

I myself prefer to think of joint custody as a spirit of cooperation between the divorced parents in regard to the children's welfare, which means first and foremost that they consult with each other about plans, decisions, and responses to the children's major requests, so that neither parent feels left out. (It may be very helpful to have a counselor, one who knows the children, to help the parents come to some decisions.) The second priority is to share the children's time in such a way that each parent keeps as closely in touch with them as possible, which will have to depend on such factors as the distance between the parents' dwellings, the capacity of the dwellings, the location of the school, the preferences of the children as they grow older. Obviously, if one parent moves across the continent, the visits will have to come at vacation times, though the parent can still keep in touch by letter and phone.

Joint custody is only practical when both parents believe that they can subordinate what bitterness they have toward each other for the benefit of their children. Otherwise the wrangling will be continuous. Then it's better to let one parent have custody and let the judge set the rules for visitation.

When a child, especially during adolescence, finds tensions building with the custodial parent, she may start thinking that the grass is greener on the other side. Sometimes it is better for this child to live with the other parent, at least for a while. But a child who moves back and forth several times may be trying to leave her problems behind rather than solve them. So it's important to try to get to the bottom of what's troubling her.

972. Joint custody. Parents can actually divide up the time that the child is with each parent. This is referred to as joint physical custody. It is also possible for a child to live primarily with either the mother or father when the parents share joint custody. This is often referred to as joint legal custody. In joint legal custody the parents consult one another about major decisions in the child's life—involving, for example, school, camp, health issues, and religious matters—and attempt to coordinate their decisions together. Joint custody is ideally approached in a spirit of cooperation between the parents.

At times after a divorce, some fathers will withdraw from their children (mothers may also withdraw when they are not the custodial parent). This can be very hard on their children who want and need to have both a father and a mother to be part of their lives. Fathers, when interviewed later, often describe that they felt disconnected, unimportant, and unneeded.

I think that joint custody lets both parents know that they are important in their child's life. Although it is a contract bound by the legal system, the most important thing here is the spirit of cooperation between the parents.

Joint custody can be a tricky business. Or it can work very well for the child, depending on the circumstances. More and more judges today are allowing joint custody because it seems fair to have both parents involved equally in the care of their children. The details need to be worked out smoothly for the child's best interests. In cases where there is unresolved anger between the recently separated parents, it may affect the child who feels caught in the middle. Counseling can be helpful in resolving these angry feelings.

If a parent has abandoned the family and then comes back into the family picture, then there may be increased concern as to whether this could happen again. And then, of course, the custodial parent worries about how the children will cope with the parent leaving once again. But if a parent shows interest in and concern for the children, it is important to support visits with the children.

The key in making joint custody work is for parents to put aside any anger and frustration in order to make the situation comfortable for the children. This will not be easy because many situations will require compromise and a willingness to adjust.

Apart from their legitimate complaints about each other, divorcing parents may feel guilty about their inability to hold their marriage together. This gives them a strong motive for putting all the blame on the other parent.

Clearly there is a danger when this kind of adversarial situation gets into the courts. It is for this reason that more family courts in many states are assigning impartial mediators to try to work with families, and this can be helpful for parents in setting up joint custody arrangements.

I think it is also helpful to have a more neutral person present when the child is going from one parent to the other on visits. Having a grandparent present can be very helpful in establishing a safe, neutral environment. This will be particularly important in the beginning after a separation or divorce when feelings are exposed and both parents may feel wounded and vulnerable. The neutral party will help both parents and the children to feel safe.

Joint custody can have significant positive ramifications for the children, if the parents can work together. Research on divorce has found that, in general, children have a better social, psychological, and academic adjustment when both parents remain part of their children's lives.

973. Scheduling visitation. Five days with the mother and weekends with the father has a practical sound and is a common schedule, but the mother may well want some weekend time with the children, when she can be more relaxed, and the father may want an occasional weekend without them. Much the same considerations may apply to school vacations. As the children get older, friends, sports, or other activities may draw them to one home or the other. So any schedule is apt to require flexibility.

It is vital that noncustodial parents not casually break

their appointments for visits. Children are hurt when they get the impression that other obligations are more important. They lose faith in the negligent parent and in their own worth. If appointments have to be canceled, this should be done ahead of time and substitutions made if possible. Most important of all is that the noncustodial parent should not break contact frequently or erratically.

974. Keeping visitation time comfortable. Some divorced fathers feel shy or awkward when visitation time comes, especially if their sons are visiting. Mothers may have the same problems, but much less often, because they commonly have custody. Besides, there is frequently greater tension between fathers and their sons than between fathers and daughters. Fathers often respond by simply providing treats—meals out, movies, sporting events, excursions. There is nothing wrong with these occasionally, but fathers shouldn't think of treats as essential on every visit; such behavior would signal that they are afraid of silences and will make these treats more obligatory every week.

The children's visits can generally be as relaxed and as humdrum as staying in their regular home. That means opportunities for activities such as reading, doing homework, bicycling, roller skating on the sidewalk, tossing baskets, playing ball, fishing, working on hobbies such as model building, stamp collecting, carpentry. Fathers can participate in those activities they enjoy, which provide ideal opportunities for casual conversation. The children can watch their regular TV programs, but I as a father would discourage a whole weekend of viewing. And part of the time the father can be following his own interests as he would in an unbroken family.

Parents often find that the children, especially younger children, are out of sorts when they make the transitions from one parent to the other. Especially on their return from a visit with the noncustodial parent, children may be irritable from tiredness. Sometimes it's simply that the child is having difficulty shifting gears out of one setting and into another. Each departure and return may remind the child, at least subconsciously, of the original departure of the noncustodial parent.

Parents can help by being patient during the transitions, by being absolutely reliable about time and place of pickup or drop-off, and by trying to keep these exchanges as free of conflict as possible.

975. Grandparents after a divorce. It's also important for the children to maintain as much contact with their grandparents as they had before the divorce. It can be very difficult to stay in touch with the parents of your ex-spouse, especially if you or they feel hurt or angry. Sometimes the custodial parent may say, "The children can see your parents during their visitation time with you. I won't have anything to do with your parents." But birthdays, holidays, and special occasions are never so conveniently arranged. Try to remember that grandparents can often be a great source of support and continuity for the children, so keeping in touch will be worth the extra effort. The grandparents' own emotional need to stay in touch with their grandchildren should also be respected.

976. Avoid trying to bias the children. It's vital that one parent not try to discredit or even criticize the other with the children, though this is a great temptation. Both parents feel a little guilty about the failure of the marriage, at least unconsciously. If they can get their friends, relatives, and children to agree that the ex-spouse is at fault, they can lessen the guilt. So they are tempted to tell the worst possible stories about their ex, leaving out any mention of their own contribution. The trouble is that children sense that they are made up of both parents and if they come to accept the idea that one was a scoundrel, they assume that they've inherited some of that. Besides, they naturally want to retain two parents and be loved by both. It makes them feel uncomfortably disloyal to listen to criticism. It's equally painful for children if one parent involves them in keeping secrets from the other parent.

By adolescence, children know that all people have imperfections, and they are not so deeply affected by the faults of their parents, though they can be plenty critical. Let them find the faults for themselves. Even at that age it's better policy for one parent not to try to win the children's allegiance by criticizing the other. Teenagers are prone to turn hot and cold on slight provocation. When they become angry at the parent they've favored they may do an about-face and decide that all the unfavorable things they've heard in the past about the other parent were unfair and untrue. Both parents will have the best chance of retaining their children's love for the long haul if they let them love both, believe in both, spend time with both.

It's a mistake for either parent to pump the children about what happened while they were visiting the other parent. This only makes children uneasy, and in the end it may backfire and make them resent the suspicious parent.

977. Dating for the parent. Children whose parents have been recently divorced consciously or unconsciously want them to get back together and think of them as still married.

They are apt to feel that dating represents faithlessness on the part of their parent and an unwelcome intrusion on the part of the date. So it is best for parents to go slowly and be tactful in introducing their dates to their children. Let the fact that the divorce is permanent sink in for a number of months. Be alert to the children's remarks. After a while you can bring up the topic of your loneliness and drop the idea that you may want to have a friend to date. It's not that you are allowing your children to control your life forever, you are simply letting them know that dating is a possibility and doing so in a way that is more comfortable for them than being presented with a person in the flesh.

If you are a mother who has been living with young children who rarely or never see their father they may beg you to marry and give them another "Daddy," which is good as far as it goes; but they may and probably will show evidence of jealousy as soon as you let them see the growing closeness between you and a man, and certainly by the time you marry again. The same thing happens to a father who's had custody of his young children, who want him to give them another "Mommy."

Stepfamilies

Years ago, with what I thought was great wisdom, I wrote a magazine article about stepparenting. Then in 1976 I became a stepfather and realized that I was quite incapable of following my own advice. I had advised stepparents to strictly avoid trying to be disciplinarians, but I kept reproaching my eleven-year-old stepdaughter for her consistent rudeness, and I kept trying to make her conform to a few rules of mine. This was one of the most painful relationships I ever experienced, and the one that taught me the most.

978. Perhaps the strongest reason that stepfamily relationships so often sour is that human beings at any age resent an intruder into an intimate family relationship. When I reproached my wife for not making her daughter treat me more civilly, she correctly pointed out that my two grown sons, approaching middle age, were barely civil to her at first. The resentment of my stepdaughter and of my two grown sons reminded me of a two-year-old first child's bitterness about the intrusion of a new baby.

My wife, stepdaughter, and I went for counseling, and the counselor told me that I was living in a fool's paradise if I thought that I could be quickly accepted by an eleven-year-old stepdaughter. It would take years, and it did.

It's no accident that so many fairy tales have an evil stepmother or stepfather as the villain. Stepfamily relationships lend themselves to mutual misunderstandings, jealousy, and resentment. A child has her mother all to herself after a parental divorce and forms an unusually close and possessive bond with the custodial parent. Then along comes a strange man who takes away the parent's heart, bed, and at least half of her attention. The child cannot help but resent this intruder, no matter how hard the stepparent tries to form a good relationship. The resentment often takes extreme forms. This gets under the stepparent's skin and he will feel the urge to respond with equal hostility. The new relationship between the adults quickly becomes strained because it feels like a no-win, either-or choice. The main thing for stepparents to realize is that this hostility, on both sides, is almost inevitable and not a reflection of their worth or of the eventual outcome of the relationship. The tension often persists for months or years and only gradually lessens. In rare other situations, the new parent may be much more easily accepted.

There are plenty of good reasons why life in a stepfamily is stressful, at least initially, for most children:

- **Loss:** By the time they enter a stepfamily, most children will have experienced significant loss—loss of one of the parents, or loss of friends because of a move. This sense of loss affects a child's early response to the new stepparent.
- **Loyalty issues:** The child may wonder, Who are my parents now? If I show affection to my stepparent, does it mean I can't or shouldn't love the parent who is no longer with me? How can I split my affections?
- **Loss of control:** No child has ever made the decision to have a stepfamily. The decision is made for him by adults. He feels a lack of control of events. The child feels buffeted by forces and people over whom he has no control.
- **Stepsiblings:** All of these stresses can be exacerbated by the presence of stepsiblings. The child wonders, What if my mother or father loves my stepbrother more than me? Why do I have to share my possessions, or my room, with this complete stranger?

979. Positive aspect of stepfamilies. These stresses are fairly universal, but by no means are they the whole picture. There are also a number of potential benefits. First, while difficulty is the rule in the beginning, most members eventually adapt to the new circumstance and accept their place in the new family constellation. But remember, this adaptation takes time. Often stepsiblings and stepparents establish close, long-lasting relationships. After all, each has the shared experience of a disrupted and reconstituted family. The "dual citizenship" of living in two separate families can enrich a child's understanding and acceptance of diversity and cultural difference.

980. General principles of stepparenting. There are some general principles that may or may not be helpful and that are certainly difficult to apply. The first step is for the parents to agree ahead of time on how they'll handle the children and to have realistic expectations of what the new family will be like.

It's important for the parents to understand, as I had to learn the hard way, that children need plenty of time to get used to the new arrangement. Be consistent with the children about family rules regarding bedtime, chores, and homework and allow time for them to accept these rules.

It is better for you, the stepparent, to avoid moving into the guiding and correcting role of a full parent until you have been accepted. If you immediately try to enforce such things as chores, bedtime, and curfews, you are sure to be judged as a harsh intruder even if you are laying down exactly the same rules as the natural parent.

On the other hand, it's not good for you to be submissive when the stepchild intrudes into your territory, for instance, abusing one of your possessions. Then you should say in a friendly but firm way that you don't like abuse, of yourself or your things. Yet you can't make an issue of every hostile angry look. You'd be grouchy all day. So ignore the small slights and save your comments for major infractions of the rules.

Last, but certainly not least, remember that many marriages and stepfamilies do not survive the stresses I have just described. If you are just a bit concerned about the relationships in your stepfamily, get professional help. An adult or child psychiatrist or psychologist has dealt with problems like yours many times and will be able to help. The help may take the form of guidance or direction for the parents on how to proceed, marital or family therapy, or individual counseling for one or more of the children. You may want to join a group of stepparents, or ask your child guidance center for information on such a group.

Your new family can be a source of love and happiness for all concerned if the difficult real and emotional issues involved are recognized and addressed. Good luck.

Multiple Births: Twins, Triplets, and More

Recent breakthroughs in infertility medicine have led to an increase of multiple births—twins, triplets, and more.

Coping with more than one infant takes patience, planning, and ingenuity. I once made an appeal to parents of twins to tell me what solutions they had found for their problems, so that I could pass them on. I got two hundred wonderfully helpful letters. As you might expect, they showed sharp differences of opinion in some respects, great unanimity in others.

981. Get help! All parents of twins agree that the work is overwhelming, especially at first, but that the rewards are great. You need all the help you can get, for as long as you can get it. If possible, hire somebody, even if you have to go into debt. Or beg your mother or another relative to come for a month or two. When there is no room and no privacy in the house, parents have even turned the garage into a bedroom for the helper, in suitable climates. Part-time assistance is a lot better than none at all: a high school student after school, a cleaning woman or a sitter once or twice a week. Encourage the neighbors to help regularly with certain feedings. It's surprising how much assistance can be gotten from even a three-year-old sister or brother of the twins.

This is a time, if there ever was one, for parents to show their thoughtfulness and generosity toward each other. They can work out schedules for sharing the endless work. They can give each other the extra, visible affection that parents need when they are called on to pour out unaccustomed amounts of loving care to their children.

The father may be able, in some jobs, to shorten his outside working day for several months. He may take his family leave when the babies first come home from the hospital. (There is apt to be a longer than average hospital stay for the infants, because they are often born prematurely.)

Even if the father has to continue to work an eight-hour day, he can do wonders between the time he comes home from work and the time he leaves the next morning. I once watched the father of quintuplets—and two older children—pitch in the minute he got home, feeding solids and bottles, giving baths, changing diapers, preparing the older children's and parents' supper and washing up after supper, and spending time with the older boys. On weekends he shopped, cleaned house, and did laundry.

982. Laundry. A diaper service is considerably cheaper than disposable diapers, which are convenient but very expensive. Now is the time, if at all possible, to get an automatic washer and dryer. They save hours of work and produce clean sheets, pads, shirts, and nighties even in rainy weather.

The babies' wash can be done daily or every other day, depending on what suits the parents' wishes. Frequency of change of sheets and pads can be decreased by placing a small additional waterproof sheet under the baby's hips. The diaper load can be reduced by changing diapers only once at each feeding, either before or after.

Laundry service, complete or partial, for the rest of the family is also an important saver of time and energy.

983. Shortcuts. Parents of more than one baby simply have to find shortcuts in housework. They can go through the house room by room, stripping it of unessential furnishings and other items that prolong housecleaning. Perhaps they should consider cleaning only half as often as before. They can select clothes for the family that don't wrinkle and soil quickly, that launder easily and that, as far as possible, don't need ironing. They can select foods that require a minimum of preparation and attention, let dishes soak clean in suds, and let them drain dry.

984. The right equipment can be enormously helpful. In the case of twins many parents find a single crib with a partition across the middle designed by themselves very practical for the first couple of months until the twins become too large and active. Cribs with springs that can be elevated save parents' backs and energy and can serve as diapering and dressing tables. An extra bassinet in which one fussing baby can be wheeled into another room helps to keep the other baby asleep. A great convenience in a two-story house is extra cribs and stores of clothing downstairs for the daytime, eliminating constant stair climbing. Much of the equipment can be borrowed or bought secondhand.

A hospital table on wheels or a tea table on wheels may be convenient for holding stacks of diapers, clothing, and sheets. It can be wheeled from crib to crib or from room to room.

A double baby carriage is too wide for most doors, and two babies sleeping that close together will begin to disturb each other within a few months. A double stroller, however, usually proves valuable for many months. A back-to-back stroller goes through doors more easily. Two car beds are useful, but remember that these are not the same as car seats. Each baby must have her own government-approved car seat. It's best to get the type that converts for larger babies rather than the one that has to be replaced when the baby weighs twenty pounds. Two inclined seats are really essential.

985. Bathing can be skimped on a great deal, if care is taken. The babies' faces can be kept clean with plain water on a washcloth. The diaper area can be washed daily with a soapy washcloth and the soap wiped off twice with a rinsed washcloth. As long as the babies' skin stays in good condition, the bath can be given every other day, twice a week, or even once a week. The complete bath can be given with a washcloth on a waterproof sheet (a sponge bath) if more convenient. It's hard to finish baths for two babies soon enough to avoid a lot of crying from one or both. There are several solutions: a helper to feed the baby who is bathed first; baths when both parents are available; different bath days or bath hours for different babies. If a tub bath is given (in sink, washstand, or tub) and if the babies can wait long enough, it's time-saving to bathe one right after the other in the same water. All bath equipment, clothing, crib, and bottles must be ready and close at hand before the bath is started.

986. Breast-feeding is practical and possible. From letters I received, I learned that twins are breast-fed for a number of months as often as single babies. (This proves again that there is no set limit to the amount of milk a mother can produce. The breasts supply whatever the baby or babies demand if the mother is going about it with the right method and attitude.) If the babies are too small to nurse well or if they stay in the hospital longer than the mother, then it is quite easy to establish the breast milk supply by means of a breast pump. As soon as the babies can nurse at the breast, they can both be put to breast together.

The mother must have a comfortable chair with good arm support. There are at least three possible positions. If the mother can half recline or recline, a twin can lie along each of her arms. If she sits up fairly straight, with pillows at each side, the babies can lie beside her, feet toward her back, heads held up to her breasts with her hands. It's also possible to lay the babies across the mother's lap, one more or less on top of the other, but with heads at opposite sides of the mother. The underdog doesn't object in these circumstances.

987. The making and storing of formula for two is cumbersome. Twins are usually small at birth and may need feedings on the average of every three hours, which adds up to sixteen bottles every twenty-four hours. Let's assume that you don't have to sterilize. If refrigerator space is a problem, the formula can be refrigerated in two quart-size jars. Then at each feeding, two nursing bottles are filled with the correct amount of formula. Using powdered formula saves money.

988. Feeding schedule. Most parents find that a modified demand schedule works best. They wait for the first baby to waken, feed him first, and then awaken the twin; or wake the twin once the first baby is positioned for feeding, so the babies can be fed together.

989. How to give bottles. How do you bottle-feed two babies at the same hours if only one parent is available? A few parents have trained one cooperative baby to wake half an hour after the other. But most parents find that both babies wake together and that there is nothing more nerve-racking than trying to feed one while the other howls. One solution in the early weeks is to lay the twins on a sofa or bed on either side of the parent, let's say the mother, their feet toward her back; in this position she can give two bottles at the same time. Another method is to use a bottle holder for one while she holds the other, alternating babies at each feeding.

But some parents find that a bottle holder, or propping a bottle on a folded diaper, doesn't work that well, at least in the early weeks. The baby may lose the nipple and cry, or he may choke. Then the parent has to hurriedly leave the other baby, who cries, in order to rescue the first. These parents find it more practical to use bottle holders or propping for both babies simultaneously, with the babies in inclined seats. The parent sits close by or between the babies, with both hands free to give whatever help is needed. As these parents correctly point out, they save enough time with bottle holders to be able to give the twins more and better cuddling at less hectic times.

If you find yourself confused about what you've done with which twin, you can record feedings, baths, and other tasks for a while. A notebook or a chalkboard will serve the purpose, or a cardboard clock face for each crib. It's not really necessary, though. A missed bath or an extra one won't hurt, and a baby will let you know about a missed feeding or refuse an extra one.

Many twins, like single babies, burp themselves if laid on their stomachs after feeding. Remember, too, that though some babies will be uncomfortable unless the bubble is gotten up, others don't seem to feel any difference and then there is no need to make the effort.

990. Feeding solid food. This has to be done efficiently, too. When it's all new to the twins, many parents spoon-feed one baby while the other takes the bottle, and then reverse the process. Additional time can be saved in another way: You can bunch the solids so that they are all given in two feedings a day instead of three. By the time the twins are skillful at taking solids, they can be propped up in infant seats or in the corners of bassinet, crib, or armchair, and spoon-fed together. Or there is an infant feeding table that comes in twin size, with seats that can be adjusted to a semi-reclining position for babies who can't sit up yet; parents find it extremely useful.

It is a great time-saver to spoon-feed twins simultaneously. One has just time enough to swallow a mouthful while the parent is loading the spoon and offering it to the other. It may not seem hygienic or polite to use one dish and one spoon, but it's so much more practical.

With twins, there's extra reason for an early start with finger foods (bread crusts, wholesome crackers, chopped cooked vegetables, chopped meats) and for relying on them heavily. There's also reason to encourage self-feeding by spoon at least by the age of twelve months.

991. A playpen is particularly valuable for twins (it's impossible to watch two crawling babies at once), and fortunately they are happy in it for longer hours and until a later age than single babies because of each other's company. (It can even be used as a double crib in traveling.) They should be put in it for play periods by two or three months, so that they won't become accustomed to freedom first. Heavy or sharp toys must be avoided because twin babies whack each other without realizing that it hurts. Later, if they begin to be bored in the pen together, one can be moved to a swinging chair, then the other. Such variations interest even the one in the playpen.

After the age of a year it's a great convenience to have a separate room for the twins to play in, with a gate at the door. It can be furnished so that the children can't easily hurt it or themselves (twins are ingenious, cooperative, and lightning fast in getting into mischief), and they will play happily in it much longer than a single child would.

992. Clothes and toys: similar or dissimilar? Some parents point out that since there is usually only one kind of play suit, for instance, in a store that appeals to the parents in terms of design, warmth, price, it is difficult if not impossible to dress twins differently. And their twins, they say, usually insist on wearing similar clothes at the same time. Other parents emphasize the opposite—about dresses, for instance—that it's usually impossible to buy two of a kind, so twins are compelled to dress differently. Still other parents say that since the twins have to wear mostly hand-me-down clothes, they dress differently from the start and enjoy having their own distinctly different clothes.

Some parents report that they have had to buy identical toys from the start, or their twins would be rivalrous and miserable. Others say that they usually buy different toys, except for particularly precious possessions like tricycles and dolls, and that twins learn to share happily from an early age.

I suspect that the attitude of the parents makes the biggest difference. If the parents take it for granted that twins must wear different clothes most of the time and share some of their playthings, either by necessity or on principle, the twins will generally accept this. But if the parents encourage the expectation of identical clothes and toys, and especially if they give in every time the twins insist, the children may well become more insistent with time. Of course, this same principle applies to single children: if parents are firm, children accept; if parents are hesitant, children argue.

It helps twins develop a sense of individuality about their own clothes and a liking for them if each has separate drawer and closet space and if similar garments are marked with names or other markings. Similar garments of different colors preserve some of the advantages of being both twins and individuals.

993. Individuality. This brings us finally to the philosophical question of how much to emphasize the twinness of twins and how much to encourage the individuality, especially with identical twins. The whole world is fascinated with twins, makes a fuss over them, likes them to look alike and be dressed alike, asks the parents silly questions about them ("Which is smarter?" "Which do you love best?"). It's hard for the parents not to play to the world's sentimental interest. Why not? The trouble is that this may give the twins the feeling that their only source of attraction is their cuteness as a look-alike, dress-alike pair. Looking exactly alike may seem appealing at three years of age. But if it ends up, as it occasionally does, in twins still trying to attract attention by dressing alike at thirty, so dependent on each other that they can't fall in love or marry, the result is not cute but sad.

Now, this doesn't mean that the parents should be afraid of ever dressing the twins alike or should be ashamed to enjoy the world's attention to their children. Twinness is fun for the twins and for the parents. Twins, in fact, develop special strength of personality from being twins: early independence of parental attention, an unusual capacity for cooperative play, and great loyalty and generosity toward each other.

But to avoid overemphasis on twinness, it's wise for parents, particularly with identical or very similar twins, to keep away from very similar names (it's hard enough to tell them apart even when the names are dissimilar), to refer to them by their names rather than as "the twins," to dress them alike only part of the time, to introduce them early and regularly to other children before they become used to each other's company exclusively, to let them make separate friends to the degree they wish, to encourage the neighbors to feel free to invite one of them over to play or to a party occasionally while the other twin has a chance to have his parents all to himself for a change.

In an occasional case, one twin becomes overly dependent on the other. Then it may be wise to separate them at times, placing them, for example, in separate play groups or in two different classrooms once they begin school. But it seems foolish and cruel to have an arbitrary rule about separation when there is no need.

994. Don't worry about favoritism. One further word of advice. Some conscientious parents become too worried at the start that they may give a bit more attention to one baby or always serve her first—because she's smaller, for instance, or more responsive. Strict impartiality is not necessary—in fact, it encourages a mechanical, forced kind of attention. Every child wants and needs to be loved naturally for her own lovable qualities. She is satisfied if she knows that she has a good niche of her own in her parents' hearts and does not worry then about what love her brother or sister is getting. But in the long run she will sense the hollowness of forced attention. A legalistically equal treatment will focus her attention on her rights and make her argue for them like a lawyer. Avoid systems like "Mother puts A's shirt on first, then B's pants on first," or "Today is A's chance to sit next to Daddy."

Gay and Lesbian Parents

As many as 10 million children currently live with 3 million gay or lesbian parents in the United States. These numbers are likely to increase. A growing number of gay and lesbian couples are choosing to become parents—through adoption, insemination, surrogate parenting, and foster care. Additionally, there are men and women who have had children in traditional marriages and subsequently discovered they were gay. While some of these parents remain married until their children are grown-up, others divorce and continue to share the job of rearing their children with their ex-spouse.

If you are not gay or lesbian, I'm sure you've asked yourself whether this kind of family is good for children. And if you are a gay or lesbian parent, you've learned firsthand some of the differences experienced in a nontraditional family.

995. What do we know about the children of gay and lesbian parents? There have been many studies looking at the development of children of gay and lesbian parents, and much has been learned.

Tests of psychological adjustment show no significant differences between the well-being of children raised by heterosexual parents and those raised by gay or lesbian parents. Like any family, what is most important for children is how loving and nurturing the parents are and whether or not the parents are aware of any special needs they may have. Since gay men and women can be as warm and caring (or as dysfunctional) as heterosexual parents, it is not surprising that the mental health of their children is comparable. These studies also show that the children of gay and lesbian parents are as likely to be heterosexual as are children growing up in more traditional families. At the same time, these children are often more tolerant of different sexual orientations and more sensitive to minority status. Most studies show that gay and lesbian parents make a special effort to expose their children to strong role models, both male and female, both heterosexual and gay. Furthermore, sexual abuse is statistically *less* likely to happen with gay and lesbian parents. Most intrafamily sexual abuse is committed by heterosexual males.

Children of gay and lesbian parents face challenges similar to those faced by other minorities. They may be teased and made to feel ashamed at school when classmates learn that their parents are gay. This torment can be especially cruel when the teacher, other school officials, and the parents of classmates make no effort to educate themselves and their families about gay and lesbian parents.

For children whose identity is in the process of formation, being viewed by peers as not normal and as a threat to the mainstream culture can create emotional conflict. Of course, such childhood trials can also build strength of character and empathy for others (and often do), but the process can be excruciating for parent and child alike. Many schools try to discourage teasing of *any* child by teaching respect for the values and lifestyles of other cultural groups. In these schools the teasing of children from alternative families is likely to be much less.

So the scientific data are quite clear: children usually do as well in gay and lesbian families as in traditional families. My feeling is that good parents are good parents. It is most productive to concern ourselves with whether parents are providing their children with love, consistency and thoughtful care, and not the nature of their intimate relationships.

996. For gay and lesbian parents. As you well know, being a parent is tough and it's harder still if you and your child are scorned by some of mainstream society. Certainly the experience of being a gay or lesbian parent is different depending on where you live. In some communities it is considered a totally acceptable type of family. This usually occurs in large cities where the state laws do not prosecute or condemn homosexual behavior. However, other communities so vilify nontraditional families that you might not feel comfortable even discussing the issue outside the family. That certainly makes your life tougher still.

Regardless of whether your community accepts or rejects your family, one of the issues you (as well as other cultural minorities) will have to face is that of the potential teasing of your child.

Like most parents, you'd like to protect your children from being hurt, even if it's not really possible. I'd suggest talking to them when they are young, explaining casually the nature of your family and how it is different from some other children's families. As your child gets older you can discuss how some people are afraid of that which is different and that which they do not understand. When these people are afraid they may show it by teasing or being mean. Then you might play out a few scenarios to help your child decide what to do if this occurs and to help your child explain the nature of your family to other children in a way that will help to win them over. Like every other issue, open and honest communication between you and your child is vital. Your attitude toward the opposite sex is also important. While you may choose a same-sex partner, it is important that you convey respect toward the opposite sex. Any mother who declares to her son that she hates men or sees all men in one way puts her boy in a situation where he risks losing her love if he chooses to be masculine and seeks male role models.

997. Legal issues are complicated. Since the United States does not recognize marriage between homosexuals, issues of decision-making for the child in the absence of the legal parent can be sticky. It's important to consult with a lawyer about potential legal issues in your state concerning the care of your child. Many states are now addressing this issue and some are legislating greater rights for gay and lesbian parents, but other states may not. You would do well to keep informed about local, state and federal rules as they evolve.

There are many books written for gay and lesbian parents that you might find useful. The Guide to Child and Family Resources at the back of this book includes the addresses and phone numbers of a few national gay and lesbian parent groups that can provide you with information and support. Many communities offer support groups for children (and parents) to share their experiences with others in similar circumstances. There are also some terrific books for children that address issues of gay and lesbian families. I'd also suggest that, assuming you're open about your lifestyle, you go to your child's school to discuss with the teacher how she feels about nontraditional families, if she has noticed any problems with the other children, and if such issues are ever discussed in class.

All parents and all children face special challenges. Your goal should not be to avoid all stress and travail—that's impossible, as you undoubtedly well know. Rather your goal should be to use those negative experiences to teach your child about tolerance, empathy, and consideration toward others.

For heterosexuals, the existence of gay and lesbian families offers you an opportunity to teach your child about different types of families and to value what is really important—not whether other families are different from yours, but whether they uphold those values your family respects: kindness, consideration, and warmth. Such lessons in tolerance and acceptance of diverse family structures will serve your child well in dealing with the exploding cultural diversity of the world of the twenty-first century.

Birth Order

998. Birth order and personality. Some scientists believe that birth order is an important determinant of personality development. These scientists cite studies showing that firstborn children as adults tend to be more conservative and staid. They seek ways to maintain the status quo. When new ideas are expressed, they tend to resist and cling to their old ways. Later-born children, on the other hand, tend to be more adventurous. They seek to upset the status quo. They embrace change in their thinking and lifestyle and seek new ways of looking at the world.

Why should this be so? Some speculate that this is all

because of the person's early family relations. The firstborn has his parents' undivided attention, at least for a time. His parents' energy and love are directed only at him for this period. Consequently, he strives to maintain parental approval and keep his status as king of the roost. He wants to maintain things as they are, because it's a pretty satisfying state of affairs as it is.

Later-born children, on the other hand, never have had their parents' undivided attention and have always had to compete with at least one other sibling to win their parents' favor. Consequently, they learn to upset the status quo, to engage in unique attention-getting behavior to be noticed in the crowd. They want to shake up the system since it's not working to their advantage anyway.

This is a somewhat simplistic way of looking at the effects of birth order on personality, but it probably contains a kernel of truth. Let's look more closely into some of the family dynamics with only, firstborn and later-born children.

999. The only child. Nowadays many parents, especially those who work outside the home, are having only one child. An only child can grow up as happily and comfortably as a child with brothers and sisters. But you have to be careful not to pin all your hopes and dreams on this one child, because that's too much of a burden for any girl or boy.

1000. Helping a first child to be outgoing. Most first children grow up happy and well adjusted, but a few of them have a harder time adjusting to the outside world.

Parents are apt to say, "The second baby is so easy. She doesn't cry. She is rarely a serious problem. She plays contentedly by herself, and yet she is so friendly if you go near her." When she's several years older, the parents say, "The second is such a friendly, outgoing child that everybody just naturally loves her. When we're walking down the street, strangers smile at her and stop us to ask how old she is. They only notice the older one afterward, to be polite. You can see that it hurts the older one's feelings. He craves attention much more than the second."

What makes the difference? One trouble is that the first baby in some families gets fussed over more than is good for him, especially after the age of six months, when he begins to be able to amuse himself. The parents may notice him, suggest things to him, and pick him up more than is necessary. This gives him too little chance to develop his own interests. He too seldom makes the first greeting because the parents always speak to him first. He may be shown off to other grown-ups too much. A little of this is harmless; a steady diet of it makes him self-conscious. When the first child is sick, the parents naturally hang over his bed with more concern and anxiety than they will show when they have had more experience. When he is naughty, they are more apt to take it seriously and to make a fuss about it.

A steady flow of fussy attention toward a child tends to lead him to assume that he is the hub of the universe and that everyone should automatically admire him whether he is being attractive or not. On the other hand, he hasn't been practicing how to make his own fun, to be independent of his parents, or how to be outgoing and appealing to people.

Of course, the answer is not to ignore a first child. He needs affection and responsiveness in good measure. But he also needs to learn to be independent. So let him play his own games as long as he is interested and happy, with the least possible interference, bossing, scolding, and anxious concern. Give him a chance to start the conversation sometimes. When visitors come, let him take the initiative himself. When he comes to you for play or for affection, be warm and friendly, but let him go when he turns back to his own pursuits.

Another factor that sometimes seems to make a first child unsociable is too serious an attitude on the parents' part. It isn't that the parents are grim people; they can be easygoing with their friends and their later children. They are just trying too hard with the first.

You know what I mean if you have ever seen tense people trying to ride a horse for the first time. They sit stiff as china dolls, don't know how to accommodate to the horse's movement, and are apt to be unnecessarily bossy. It's hard work for the horse and the rider. Experienced riders know how to relax, how to give in and conform to some of the horse's motions without losing their seat, how to direct the horse gently. Bringing up a child isn't much like riding a horse, but the same spirit works in both jobs.

A similar example is the young military officer who is put in charge of others for the first time. If he isn't too sure of himself, he may be unnecessarily solemn and strict in the beginning for fear he won't keep control. The more experienced person isn't afraid to be friendly and reasonable.

You may say, "The trouble is that I am inexperienced." But you don't have to have experience to do a wonderful job with a baby—all you need to start with is a friendly spirit. A child won't throw you the way a horse might (at least not until he's much older), and he won't laugh at you the way a squad of soldiers might. Don't be afraid to relax, and be agreeable. Better too easygoing than too stiff.

1001. The middle child. There's so much talk about middle children that sometimes you hear about "middle child syndrome," as if it were a disease. There's no such syndrome but it's true that sometimes a middle child feels that his older and younger siblings are thought of as special by their parents, and that makes him feel left out. (Feeling in the middle can happen with any child who isn't the oldest or youngest in a group of brothers and sisters.) I think the best thing you can do for a middle child is to avoid making comparisons with his siblings. If your middle child knows that you love him and appreciate him as an individual, that's what counts.

1002. The youngest child. This child may be thought of as special for several reasons. You often hear parents say of a youngest child, "He'll always be my baby." Of course there's nothing wrong with feeling that way, unless it interferes with parents letting the child grow up as he goes through each stage of development. Then there's the situation in which parents have been disappointed by their previous children. Maybe they didn't get the athlete or scholar they'd hoped for, and they put too much pressure on the youngest. Or they may have especially wanted a boy to carry on the family name, and when the youngest is another girl they let their disappointment show and make her feel there's something wrong with her. Just being aware of these possibilities will help you avoid them.

Adoption

1003. People have various reasons for wanting to adopt. A couple should decide to adopt only if both of them love children and want one very much. All children, biological or adopted, need to feel that they belong to and are loved by both father and mother deeply and forever if they are to grow up secure. An adopted child can easily sense a lack of love in one or both parents because she may not be as secure to begin with, having been through one or more previous separations. She knows that she was given up for some reason by her biological parents, and she may fear secretly that her adopted parents might someday give her up too.

You can see why it's a mistake to adopt when only one parent wants to, or when both parents are thinking of it only for practical reasons, such as to have someone to take care of them in their old age. Occasionally a woman who is afraid that she's losing her husband will want to adopt a child in the futile hope that this will hold his love. Adoptions for these reasons are unfair to the children and usually prove to be wrong from the parents' point of view too.

Parents with an only child who is not very happy or sociable sometimes consider adopting another to provide company. It is a good idea to talk this over with a mental health professional or the adoption agency before proceeding. The adopted child is apt to feel like an outsider compared to the other child. If the parents lean over backward to show affection for the newcomer, it may upset rather than help their biological child. This is a potentially risky business for all concerned.

There can be pitfalls, too, in adopting to "replace" a child who has died. Parents need time to work out their grief. They should adopt only because they want a child to love. There is no harm in adopting one who is similar in age or sex or appearance to the child who died, but the comparisons should stop there. It is unfair and unsound to want to make one individual play the part of another. She is bound to fail at the job of being a ghost, and she will disappoint the parents and become unhappy. She should not be reminded of what the other child did, or be compared with her out loud or in the parents' minds. Let her be herself. (Some of this applies also to the child who is born after an older one dies.)

1004. At what age should a child be adopted? For the child's sake, the younger the better. For a number of complex reasons this has not been possible for thousands of youngsters living in foster homes and institutions. Research has shown that these older children can also be successfully adopted. The age of children should not prevent their being placed. The agency will help older children and parents decide if this is right for them.

Some adoptive parents worry about heredity and how it will affect a child's future. The more we have learned about personality development, including intelligence, the clearer it becomes that although heredity plays a part, the environment in which the child grows up is critical. The love she receives and the feeling of belonging that she acquires are especially important. There is good evidence that specific social abnormalities, like violent behavior, immorality, delinquency, and irresponsibility, are not inherited.

A couple should not wait until they are too set in their ways to adopt. They've dreamed so long of a little girl with golden curls filling the house with song that even the best of children turns out to be a rude shock. It is not a matter of years alone, but of an individual's capacity to give a particular child what she needs. This is something to discuss with the agency.

1005. A great majority of the children waiting to be adopted are older. This means that most of the people who want to adopt babies or very young children will be unable to do so or will have to wait for a long time. These people may be tempted to adopt a baby through a lawyer or doctor. A lot of people think they won't have any trouble if they get a "gray market" baby this way, as opposed to a black market baby who is clearly being adopted without any legal procedures at all. Often these people discover that they too have difficulties, both legal and emotional, later on when, for example, the biological mother decides that she wants the baby back.

More unmarried parents are keeping and raising their children. Therefore, there are not as many very young children needing homes. However, there are other children waiting for parents. They are for the most part school-age. They may have a brother and sister from whom they don't want to be separated. They may have some physical, emotional, or intellectual handicap. They may be war orphans. They are as much in need of love and can be as rewarding to parents as any other child. These children do have some special needs, however. Since they are older, they may have had more than one foster care situation. Having lost parents (biological, then foster) already, they may be insecure and fearful of being rejected again. Children express this in a variety of ways, sometimes testing to see if once again they will be "sent back." These anxieties present adoptive parents with special challenges. As long as parents know about the challenges ahead of time and anticipate them (instead of expecting a child to be grateful) these children can be especially rewarding. It's the responsibility of adoption agencies to focus their attention on finding homes for these children, even more than on finding babies for adoptive parents.

If an older child has some special need, the agency staff and physicians will supply the adoptive parents with the information they will need. Most people have the capacity to be able to take good care of such children. It is the job of professionals to help inexperienced adopting parents to develop this capacity.

Nowadays many prospective adoptive parents already have children. They are not infertile and already have demonstrated parental ability. They wish to adopt out of humanitarian motives, wanting to do something for the child.

Single, gay, and lesbian parents are now given consideration as adoptive parents. Most waiting children need parents right away. Childhood passes quickly and a permanent parent now is of more value than the possibility of two parents some time in the future. So many agencies unable to find traditional couples have chosen to use single, gay, and lesbian parents. There are other good reasons for this in some cases: certain children have been emotionally bruised in such a way that it is better for them to have one parent of a particular sex; and other children have such a tremendous need for attention and care that the absence of a spouse allows a single parent or a nontraditional family to give the child what he needs.

1006. Adopt through a good agency. Probably the most important rule of all is to arrange the adoption through a first-rate agency. It is always risky for the adopting parents to deal directly with the biological parents or with an inexperienced third person. This leaves the way open for those parents to change their minds and to try to get their child back. Even when the law stands in the way of the biological parents, the unpleasantness can ruin the happiness of the adopting family and the security of the child.

A good agency will help the biological mother and relatives to make the right decision in the first place about whether or not to give the baby up. The agency will also use its judgment and experience in deciding which couples should be dissuaded from adopting. An agency worker can help the child and family during the adjustment period. The goal of all concerned is to help the child become a member of the adoptive family. Wise agencies and wise state laws require this adjustment before the adoption becomes final. One way to find out about the qualifications of an adoption agency is to call your state department of health. All state health departments have a section that licenses adoption agencies.

1007. Open adoption. In recent years, it has become increasingly common for the birth mother (sometimes the birth father also) and the adoptive parents to learn a lot more about each other than used to be the case. This varies from getting a general description of each other from the adoption agency to actually meeting each other at the agency. Sometimes the birth mother can choose which of several possible adoptive parents she prefers. And in some cases an arrangement is made for the birth mother to keep up with the child—for example, receiving a snapshot of the child and a letter from the adoptive parents once a year or more often.

We don't yet know how these open arrangements will work out in the long run, particularly the ones that provide continuing contact between the birth mother and the adoptive parents. I think it's good for the birth mother and adoptive parents to know more about each other at the start, because this can prevent a lot of anxious wondering on both sides. But I'm not sure how it will work out emotionally for the child and all the adults involved to have regular contact over the years. It seems to me that this could interfere with the birth mother letting go of her child emotionally, and it could also get in the way of the adoptive parents coming to feel that this is truly their child.

1008. When should an adopted child be told she is adopted? All of the experienced people in this field agree that the child should be told she is adopted. She's sure to find out sooner or later from someone, no matter how carefully the parents think they are keeping the secret. It is practically always a very disturbing experience for an older child, or even an adult, to discover suddenly that she is adopted. It may disturb her sense of security for years.

The news shouldn't be saved for any definite age. The parents should, from the beginning, let the fact that she's adopted come up naturally and casually, in their conversations with each other, with the child, and with their acquaintances. This will create an atmosphere in which the child can ask questions whenever the subject begins to interest her. She will find out what adoption means bit by bit, as she gains understanding.

Some adopting parents make the mistake of trying to keep the adoption secret; others err in the opposite direction by stressing it too much. Most adopting parents have, quite naturally, an exaggerated sense of responsibility at first, as if they have to be letter-perfect to justify the fact that someone else's child has been entrusted to their care. If they go too earnestly at the job of explaining to the child that she's adopted, she may begins to wonder, "What's wrong with being adopted, anyway?" But if they accept the adoption as naturally as they accept the color of the child's hair, they won't have to make a secret of it or keep reminding her of it. They should remind themselves that, having been selected by the agency, they're probably darned good parents and the child is lucky to have found them. They should not fear the missing biological parent. Adoptive parents need to resolve their fears and anxieties or they will communicate them to the child.

Let's say that a child around three hears her mother explaining to a new acquaintance that she is adopted, and asks, "What's 'adopted,' Mommy?" She might answer, "A long time ago I wanted very much to have a little baby girl to love and take care of. So I went to a place where there were a lot of babies, and I told the lady, 'I want a little girl with brown hair and blue eyes.' So she brought me a baby, and it was you. And I said, 'Oh, this is just exactly the baby that I want. I want to adopt her and take her home to keep forever.' And that's how I adopted you." This makes a good beginning because it emphasizes the positive side of the adoption, the fact that the mother received just what she wanted. The story will delight the child, and she'll want to hear it many times.

Children who have been adopted at an older age will need a different approach. They may have memories of their biological and foster parents. Agencies should help both the child and the new parents to handle this. It is important to realize that questions will surface repeatedly during different stages of this child's life. They should be answered as simply and honestly as possible. Parents should allow the child to freely express her feelings and fears.

Between the ages of three and four, like most children, she will want to know where babies come from. It is best to answer truthfully but simply enough so that the three-year-old can understand easily. But when her adopted mother explains that babies grow inside the mother's abdomen, it makes her wonder how this fits in with the story of picking her out at the agency. Maybe then, or months later, she asks, "Did I grow inside you?" Then the adopting mother can explain, simply and casually, that she grew inside another mother before she was adopted. This is apt to confuse her for a while, but she will get it clear later.

Eventually a child will raise the more difficult question of why her biological parents gave her up. To imply that they didn't want her would shake her confidence in all parents. Any sort of made-up reason may bother her later in some unexpected way. Perhaps the best answer and nearest to the truth might be, "I don't know why they couldn't take care of you, but I'm sure they wanted to." During this period when the child is digesting this idea, she needs to be reminded, along with a hug, that she's always going to be yours now.

All adopted people are naturally intensely curious about their biological parents, whether they express this curiosity or not. In former times, adoption agencies told adopting parents only the vaguest generalities about the physical and mental health of the biological parents. They completely concealed their identities. This was partly to make it easy for the adopting parents to answer, "I don't know" to the extremely difficult questions a child would ask about her origin and about why she was relinquished. And it was even more to protect the privacy of the biological parents who, in most cases, were unmarried and who, in their subsequent separate lives, may have kept the early pregnancy a secret. Today the courts, in recognition of the individual's right to know, have sometimes compelled an agency to reveal the identity of the biological parents to an adopted youth or adult who has demanded that information. In some cases, when this has led to a visit, it has had a beneficial effect on the turbulent feelings and obsessive curiosity of the adopted individual. In other cases, however, such a visit has been disturbing to the youth, to the adopting parents, and to the biological parents as well. Any such demand by an adopted youth or adult needs to be discussed at length with the agency people, with all its pros and cons, whether or not the case is ever brought to court.

1009. The adopted child must belong completely. The adopted child may have the secret fear that her adopting parents, if they change their minds or if she is bad, will someday give her up, just as her biological parents did.

Adopting parents should always remember this and vow that they will never, under any circumstances, say or hint that the idea of giving her up has ever crossed their minds. One threat uttered in a thoughtless or angry moment might be enough to destroy the child's confidence in them forever. They should be ready to let her know that she is theirs forever at any time the question seems to enter her mind— for instance, when she is talking about her adoption. I'd like to add, though, that it's a mistake for the adopting parents to worry so about the child's security that they overemphasize their talk of loving her. Basically, the thing that gives the adopted child the greatest security is being loved, wholeheartedly and naturally. It's not the words but the music that counts.

FAMILY STRESSES AND CRISES

Child Abuse and Neglect

1010. Most parents get angry enough at their children once in a great while to have the impulse to hurt them. You may feel angry at a baby who continues to cry for what seems like hours when you have done everything possible in the way of comforting her, or at a child who has broken your precious possession right after you have asked him to put it down. Your justified rage boils up, but in most cases you have enough control to avoid taking your frustration out on the child. (I remember when I was a medical student, picking up my own endlessly crying six-month-old baby in the middle of the night and yelling, "Shut up!" at him, barely able to control myself from physically hurting him. He hadn't slept through the night for weeks, and his mother and I were exhausted and at our wits' end.) You may feel ashamed and embarrassed after such an incident. If you remember that the majority of parents have the same experience, you'll be able to talk to your spouse or the baby's doctor about it and get the support and help you need.

There has been a lot of study and attention given to child abuse and neglect in recent years. Abuse may be emotional, physical, or sexual. Neglect may be emotional or physical. Child abuse and neglect occur among all economic classes, though somewhat more frequently among poor people whose poverty adds one more major pressure to their stressful lives. If a baby is premature or sick, requiring more than the usual amount of care, she may be more likely to be abused. Girls are more often sexually abused than boys, usually by heterosexual men.

Most of the adults who abuse or neglect a child in any way are not brutal or insane people, but they have had a momentary loss of physical and emotional control. Close contact with patients who have lost control repeatedly reveals that a majority of them were abused, neglected, or molested in their own childhood, that they have little physical or emotional support from family and friends, and that they tend to have unreasonably high expectations of the abused child. They profit greatly from counseling, but especially from joining a group of parents with similar problems. There they can learn that physically attacking a child only gives the child the message that physical violence is a way to solve problems. Children who are hit tend to hit others, which is why adults who were abused as children tend to abuse their own children.

The purpose of the laws regarding child abuse and neglect is not to punish the parents but to help them, through counseling, to understand and cope with the various pressures on them that they have taken out on the child, and to have more realistic expectations about the child's ability to live up to their expectations. The preference is almost always to keep the child in her home while the parents are supported and helped. But if the risk is temporarily too great, she is placed in a foster home until the family is ready to care for her again.

1011. Sexual abuse. It's important to realize that a great majority of sexual molestations of children are carried out not by depraved strangers but by family members, stepparents, friends of the family, baby-sitters, or other people already known to the children.

One recommendation that has been made is talks by police officers in schools, warning children of strangers who offer candy and rides. I fear that such talks, if carried out by authorities without special training, could give excessive morbid fears to millions of children and yet have very, very limited usefulness. I would suggest instead that parents themselves issue any warnings they think wise, depending on their evaluation of the risks. To make warnings less frightening, I would tell a young child (three to six years old)—preferably when she asks some question or when the mother has discovered sex play with another young child—that an older child may want to touch her private parts, her clitoris or vagina, but she shouldn't let him or her. She can be told to say, "I don't want you to," and to tell her mother about it right away. Then the mother can add, "Sometimes a grown-up may want to touch you, or want you to touch him, but you should not. Tell him you don't want him to. Then tell me. It won't be your fault." This last is mentioned because children characteristically don't report these incidents because they feel guilty, especially if the molester is a relative or family friend. Boys are also the victims of molestation, though much less often than girls are.

Sexual abuse is difficult for parents to suspect and for doctors to diagnose because shame, guilt or embarrassment leads to silence and because physical signs of abuse are usually absent. When, on occasion, there is genital or rectal pain, bleeding, trauma or signs of infection you should be concerned about the possibility of sexual abuse and request an evaluation from your child's doctor or nurse practitioner. (It's important to know that most mild vaginal infections in prepubertal girls are not a result of sexual abuse.)

Most children who have been abused sexually exhibit unusual behaviors not seen previously such as sexual behaviors inappropriate for the child's developmental age. I remember one abused child who seemed to enjoy imitating adult sex acts in front of other children. This kind of behavior is not consistent with normal sexual exploration among children such as "you show me yours, and I'll show you mine." Also, a child who masturbates compulsively and often in public places is expressing an interest in sexual activity more frequent and intense than seen in normal masturbation in children (see Section 680). Other behaviors found to be associated with sexual abuse in children and adolescents are less specific including withdrawal, excessive anger or aggression, running away from home, fears (especially of situations related to the abuse), changes in appetite, sleep disturbances, a recent onset of bed-wetting or soiling or a decline in school performance. Of course, these behavior changes occur in children and adolescents as a result of many other stresses. In fact, in most cases they are not indicative of sexual abuse. I want to emphasize the importance of interpreting these behaviors in context. I am concerned with parents who look for abuse in every behavior, and I hope that as a parent you will develop a cautious sensitivity to the behaviors in children that may suggest abuse. You child's doctor or nurse practitioner may be a helpful resource in interpreting unusual behavior your child may exhibit.

1012. How to get help. In many places, parents have organized branches of one of the several national organizations for the prevention of child abuse and neglect. They prepare informational pamphlets about prevention for both parents and children and put them into schools and libraries. And they have local celebrities, whom the children know well, make public service announcements about how children can protect themselves. These are played on local television and radio stations.

A national organization of parents and professionals that helps with this problem is the National Committee for Prevention of Child Abuse, 332 South Michigan Avenue, Suite 1600, Chicago, IL 60604. Their phone number is (312) 663-3520. They have free booklets on child abuse, child abuse prevention, and parenting. They can tell you how to get help in your area and whether they have a local chapter near you. Many large cities have child abuse hot lines that you can call if you feel that you're losing control. Then your local child welfare agency may also be able to help.

Missing Children

There has been a lot of publicity about missing children in recent years. All but a few of the children who disappear are kidnapped by divorced noncustodial parents who feel unfairly deprived.

Most of the other missing children are teenagers, most of them girls, who have run away because they feel unloved or unfairly treated. Of the runaways, the young ones soon reveal that they are runaways and give themselves up. The older ones may evade detection and use this path for leaving home for good.

Of course, all children should be taught never to go anywhere with a stranger, no matter what the stranger tells them, as soon as the children are old enough to leave their homes by themselves.

Using Child Mental Health Professionals

Frequently in this book I advise you to consult a child mental health professional. Parents are apt to be confused about what psychiatrists, psychologists, and social workers are for and what the differences between them are.

All of these professionals are trained to understand and treat all kinds of behavior and emotional problems of children. Back in the nineteenth century, psychiatrists were mainly concerned with taking care of the insane, and for that reason some people are still reluctant to consult with mental health professionals. But as we have learned how serious troubles usually develop out of mild ones, mental health professionals have turned more and more attention to everyday problems. In this way they can do the most good in the shortest time. There's no more reason to wait to see a child mental health professional until children are severely disturbed than there is to wait until they are in a desperate condition from pneumonia before calling the doctor or nurse practitioner.

1013. Psychiatrists are medical doctors who specialize in mental and emotional disorders. They can prescribe medications to alleviate emotional and psychological problems and they often also offer individual and group counseling. A child psychiatrist has additional training in handling the problems of children and adolescents.

1014. Psychologists are nonmedical professionals who specialize in one of the many branches of psychology. Psychologists who work with children are trained in such subjects as intelligence testing, aptitude testing, and the causes and treatment of learning and behavior problems as well as emotional problems. A psychologist may have a master's degree but will usually hold a Ph.D.

1015. A psychiatric social worker has had two years of classroom and clinic training after college, leading to a master's degree. Psychiatric social workers can evaluate a child, his family, and his school situation and can treat behavioral problems in the child and in the family.

1016. A psychoanalyst is a psychiatrist, psychologist, or other mental health professional who has had extra training and education in the causes and treatment of psychological and emotional problems. Psychoanalysts sometimes offer more in-depth treatment, by intensive psychotherapy. A child psychoanalyst, like a child psychiatrist, has even further training with children and adolescents.

1017. Whom should you pick? In cases where medication is the primary treatment, a child psychiatrist will usually be the best bet. In most circumstances, however, the professional title is not nearly so important as the individual behind the academic degree. Ask friends and family for a recommendation. Interview the prospective professional first and see if you have positive feelings about him or her.

In a city you can inquire about a child guidance clinic, a private children's psychiatrist, or a psychologist for testing. Direct your inquiry to your regular doctor, a large hospital, the school principal or superintendent, or a social service agency, or seek a referral from your health care provider, a psychiatric society, or a psychoanalytic society. Probably you will have limited choices from your insurance provider. Find out exactly what mental health benefits they allow before you begin treatment. If you have no luck or live in a smaller place, you can write to the National Mental Health Association, 1021 Prince Street, Alexandria, VA 22314-2971, or call (800) 969-6642. They will tell you the nearest place where you can get help.

Someday I hope there will be child guidance clinics connected with all school systems, so that children, parents, and teachers will be able to ask for advice on all kinds of minor problems as easily and as naturally as they can now inquire about immunizations, diet, and the prevention of physical disease.

1018. Family social agencies. Most cities have at least one family social agency, and some large cities have Catholic, Jewish, and Protestant agencies. These agencies are staffed by social workers trained to help parents with all of the usual family problems—child management, marital adjustment, budgeting, chronic illness, housing, finding jobs, finding medical care. They often have consultants—psychiatrists, psychoanalysts, or psychologists—who help with the most difficult cases.

Many parents have grown up with the idea that social agencies are for destitute people only and mainly provide charity. This is the opposite of the truth today. The modern family agency is just as glad to help solve small problems as large ones (they're easier), as glad to assist families who can afford to pay a fee as those who can't (that way they can expand their services).

MEDICAL ISSUES

Communicating with Your Doctor or Nurse Practitioner

In most cases the parents and the doctor or nurse practitioner soon come to know and trust each other and get along fine. But occasionally, since they are all human beings, there are misunderstandings and tensions. Most of these are avoidable or easily cleared up with frankness on both sides.

Unless expense is of no concern, it's a good idea to discuss charges when you first engage a physician. This is easier to do at the start than later on. Though the discussion of fees may embarrass you, remember that they're an old story with the doctor, who should be able to handle it with ease. Many physicians will lower their fees for people with below-average incomes and are glad to know of the need ahead of time.

1019. A health maintenance organization (HMO) or other managed care health system usually requires a co-payment at the time of an office or clinic visit. You can be informed about these charges when you sign up with a health care plan for your family. At that time, you will also be given a list of doctors or nurse practitioners who practice in the plan. If you are given an opportunity to choose a clinician for your child, ask other parents about their experience with a doctor or nurse practitioner. This may give you helpful information about the person's practice style and help with your decision.

707

Most new parents are bashful in the beginning about asking questions that they are afraid are too simple or silly. It's foolish to worry about this. If there's any kind of question on your mind, you're entitled to an answer—that's what doctors are for. Most doctors and nurse practitioners are pleased to answer any questions that they can, the easier the better. It is a good idea to write down your questions before each doctor's visit.

Even if you feel sure that your doctor will be grumpy about something that is probably not serious but that you are nonetheless concerned about, call anyway. Your child's health is more important than the doctor's feelings or your own.

It often happens that a parent asks about a problem and the doctor explains part of it but gets sidetracked before having answered the parent's most important question. If a mother is bashful, she may hesitate to come back to that point and simply go home unsatisfied. She should encourage herself to be bold, to make clear exactly what she wants to know, so that the doctor can give her the answer or, if necessary, refer her to some other professional.

Often, on getting home from an office visit, parents find that they forgot to bring up their most important question or questions, and are ashamed to call back so soon. Doctors are not bothered by this; they are quite used to it.

1020. You are partners. Your doctor or nurse practitioner is the medical expert, but *you* are the expert about your children. Their ability to give you advice and offer treatment will often depend on the quality of the information you give them. Communication is a two-way street and needs to be built on mutual trust and respect. Remember, both of you have the same goal: to allow your child to grow up to be a healthy, happy, and productive adult.

1021. Lay your feelings on the table. If you are upset or anxious or concerned, it's best to let your doctor or nurse practitioner know how you feel. Some parents are too intimidated to express their misgivings about the doctor's diagnosis or the way he handles their child during a physical examination. If you have something on your chest, unload it—in a respectful and open way. If these feelings are out in the open they can be addressed. If you keep them inside, your consternation will probably grow and you'll have missed an opportunity to improve the channels of communication. Most doctors and nurse practitioners aren't so insecure and thin-skinned that they require absolute obedience and compliance with everything they say or do.

Regular Checkups

1022. Regular visits. The way to be sure that your baby is doing well is to have her checked by a doctor or nurse practitioner regularly. Most practices suggest a visit within the first two weeks after delivery and then at two, four, six, nine, twelve, fifteen, eighteen, and twenty-four months, and yearly thereafter. If you'd like more visits, don't be too shy to ask for them.

During a regular checkup, the doctor or nurse practitioner will ask you questions about how the baby is doing. The baby will be weighed and measured to see how she's growing. She'll be given a full physical examination to be sure she's healthy. For the first eighteen months, she'll receive immunizations at almost every visit.

You should always come to a checkup armed with five or ten questions that you want to ask. It's a good idea to keep a little notebook (some parents use the baby's immunization and growth record) handy for writing down questions when they come to mind at home. You should also document important developments, such as a reaction to an immunization or a rash, that you may later need to know the date of.

Even if your baby is perfectly healthy, these visits serve to give the immunizations that will keep him healthy. They also allow you to form a relationship of trust and familiarity with the doctor or nurse practitioner. Then, if and when you have questions or concerns or significant medical issues to address, you will know how best to work together. At its best, your relationship with your doctor or nurse practitioner should be a collaborative one in which your ideas and wishes are considered and respected, and where you feel comfortable about bringing up *anything* that might affect your children's well-being.

Office Visits for Illness

Some parents remember that when they were sick as children the doctor made home visits. It seems wrong to them to take a sick child out to the doctor's office. Of course, the office visit is more convenient for the busy doctor. But doctors wouldn't advise it if it were not beneficial in many illnesses and entirely safe in these days of heated cars. With many throat infections, for example, it is now important to take a throat culture to discover whether a streptococcus bacteria is the cause. If it is, the use of antibiotic medication is essential. If not, it is better not to prescribe it. It is often helpful during an undiagnosed illness to get a urine specimen or a blood count. After an injury an X-ray may be desirable. In these situations and many others, doctors can do a better job in their offices or in a hospital emergency room.

1023. X-rays. X-rays were once used routinely for diagnosis—for example, to determine the normality of a pregnancy or for the intensive treatment of acne—until it was realized that they could be harmful. Since then, thoughtful people have become cautious, and some have resisted any X-rays, no matter how necessary. However, there is actually very little radiation in any single X-ray and no appreciable risk at all. It's all a matter of balancing risks. The risk from an undiagnosed infection of a tooth or the lungs is much greater than the risk from a single X-ray picture. If you have a particularly strong fear of radiation, you should say so to your doctor or dentist so that he can take this into account. But if he still urges the X-ray, I myself would go along as parent and patient.

1024. Asking for a second opinion. If your child has some illness or condition that worries you intensely and you would like another expert opinion, it is always your right to ask for a second opinion. Many parents are hesitant about doing so, fearing that this would express lack of confidence in, and hurt the feelings of, their doctor or nurse practitioner. But it is a regular procedure in the practice of medicine, and the doctor should be able to take it in stride. Actually, doctors, like any other human beings, sense uneasiness in the people they deal with, even when it is unspoken, and it makes their job harder. A second opinion usually clears the air for them as well as for the family.

Frankness works best. I think the main point to remember in all these situations is that if you are unsatisfied with your doctor or nurse practitioner's advice or care, you should bring the problem out into the open right away in the most matter-of-fact manner you can muster. An early meeting of minds is easier for both of you than allowing your tension and irritation to accumulate inside you.

Sometimes, though, a parent and doctor find that they can't get along together, no matter how frank and cooperative they try to be. In this case it's better all around to admit it openly and find a new doctor. All health professionals, including the most successful, have learned that they don't suit everybody, and they accept this fact philosophically.

Telephone Calls to Your Doctor or Nurse Practitioner

1025. The time for telephone calls. Find out the policy of your pediatric practice for taking calls about ill children. Most practices have a nurse during the workday who answers questions about illness and decides if the child needs to see a doctor. Find out if there is a preferred time to phone during the day, particularly about a new illness that may require a visit to the office. A majority of illnesses in children first show definite symptoms during the afternoon, and most doctors would like to know about them as early in the afternoon as possible so that they can plan accordingly.

At night or on weekends, however, it's a different story. All practices have a number to call if you are worried about your child. Usually you will reach an answering service, which will notify the doctor or nurse who is on call that night. The on-call professional could be your doctor or nurse practitioner (if you're lucky), but it is more likely to be someone who doesn't know you or your child at all. This can lead to trouble, especially if the severity of the child's illness is underestimated by the on-call doctor or nurse.

The practice of "phone medicine" is fraught with dangers. It's often hard for the doctor or nurse to tell if your child is really sick and should be seen right away or if the problem can wait until the office opens the next day. That's why the information you relate to the on-call doctor or nurse is so vital.

1026. What to tell the doctor or nurse. Before calling, make sure you have the following information handy (write it down if you need to):

1. What, exactly, are the troubling symptoms? When did they start? How often are they occurring? Are there any other symptoms?
2. What are your child's vital signs: temperature, trouble breathing, pallor. (You should take her temperature whenever your child is sick for no apparent reason.)
3. What have you tried to do for this problem? Has it worked?
4. How sick does your child appear to be? Is she alert or lethargic? Bright-eyed or dazed? Happy and playful or miserable and crying?
5. Does your child have any past medical problems that could relate to your current concern?
6. Is your child on any medications? If so, what are they?
7. How worried are you about the situation?

The quality of the phone diagnosis will depend on the quality of the information you give. Doctors and nurses, being human, sometimes forget to ask all of these important questions, especially late at night. It's up to you to make sure that all important information is related on the phone so an appropriate decision can be made.

1027. When to call the doctor. After you've raised a couple of babies, you'll have a good idea which symptoms or questions require prompt contact with the doctor and which can wait till tomorrow or the next visit. Until then you're going to have to use your judgment.

New parents often feel more comfortable with a list of symptoms that require a call to the doctor. No list, however, can be anywhere near complete. After all, there are thousands of different diseases and injuries. You always have to use your own common sense. A good general rule is that if you're really concerned, you should call, even if it's unnecessary. I'd rather you called a little too much in the beginning when it wasn't really necessary, than to not call when you should have because you didn't want to appear foolish or bother the doctor or nurse on call.

A few general guidelines. By far the most important rule is to consult the doctor promptly, at least by telephone, if a baby or child looks or acts sick. By this I mean such signs as unusual tiredness, drowsiness, or lack of interest; unusual irritability, anxiousness, or restlessness; or unusual paleness. This is particularly true in the first two or three months of life when a baby can be seriously ill without fever or other specific symptoms and signs of illness. If a child looks sick, you should contact your doctor or nurse practitioner, whether or not the child has specific symptoms. The converse is also usually true: if a child looks well, is playful and active and alert and bright, then serious illness is unlikely no matter what the symptoms.

Still there are other, more specific symptoms you should be aware of that should alert you to call your doctor or nurse practitioner.

1028. Fever. How high or low it is is less important than whether the child seems really sick. A young baby can be quite sick with little or no fever, while a high fever often accompanies a mild infection after the age of three or four years. As a general rule, consult the doctor if the baby has a temperature of 101°F or more. You don't have to call in the middle of the night if the baby has a 101°F fever with a mild cold, but otherwise seems happy (except in infants less than three months old, when you should call the doctor for *any* fever). In that case you can call in the morning. But if the baby does look sick, even without any fever, call promptly, especially in the first two or three months. (For more on fever, see Sections 1045–1051.)

1029. Difficulty breathing. You can tell if a baby or child is having breathing trouble in a number of ways. But first I'd suggest you familiarize yourself with your child's breathing pattern when she is well. Note how fast she breathes, how hard she works to breathe, if she makes any noises when breathing. If you are aware of how she breathes when she is healthy, you'll be better able to decide if her breathing has really changed when she's sick.

Here are some of the signs and symptoms of breathing difficulty:

- **Retractions.** You may notice an infant is working very hard to breathe, drawing in the muscles (retractions) in the stomach, chest and neck. Retractions are a sign that it requires extra effort for him to get air into his lungs. Something is wrong in that case. Some infants may also make grunting noises when they breathe out, or their breathing out may be prolonged with increased effort.
- **Tachypnea.** This is when the rapidity of breathing (respiratory rate) increases. Fever itself, without breathing trouble, causes faster breathing. Remember that children normally breathe faster than adults. The upper normal limit for newborns and infants is around forty breaths a minute; for a preschooler, about thirty breaths a minute; and for ten-year-olds and beyond, about twenty breaths a minute. The best way to tell respiratory rate is simply to count the breaths for a full minute. I'd suggest you measure your child's respiratory rate, asleep and awake, when she is well. That way you'll know how she normally breathes and be in a better position to decide if the rate is really different when she's sick. Sometimes a child will breathe a little fast for a short time and then revert back to normal. Children who are really ill—for example, with pneumonia—have respiratory rates that stay high. So unless your child looks sick, I wouldn't panic after one measurement. Wait a bit, try to bring her fever down, if she has one, and then recheck her breathing.

1030. Noisy breathing. Children with chest infections or asthma usually have noisier breathing than usual. It may be hard for you to tell exactly where the noise is coming from.

Sometimes it's just from mucus in the nose—not really a lung problem at all. Other times, it may come from the windpipe (stridor) and will be loudest when the child is breathing in. Croup begins with noisy breathing because the windpipe is infected, often accompanied by a barking cough and a hoarse voice or cry. Sometimes the noise comes from farther down in the lungs. If these are high-pitched, almost musical noises, usually louder when breathing out, they may be wheezes, as children with asthma are prone to. Noisy breathing is relatively good news in that it signifies that enough air is moving around the area to make noise. If a child continues to have retractions and tachypnea but begins to have less noisy breathing, there may be too little air moving around the obstructed area even to make noise. This is a true medical emergency.

1031. Pain. Pain is the body's internal alarm that something is wrong. Children who are born without the ability to feel pain (a very rare condition) suffer from frequent, sometimes life-threatening bone fractures, cuts and bruises. If a child is experiencing pain, you should try to figure out, as best you can, where it's coming from. Press on his skin all over to look for sore spots. See if you can move all his joints without his crying. Look for a rash or skin discoloration. If the pain is not severe and there are no other symptoms (such as fever), you can probably safely wait and watch. If the pain seems unduly severe, if the child cannot be consoled, or if he seems quite ill, then by all means call the doctor. When in doubt, call.

1032. Sudden decrease in appetite is sometimes a sign of illness. It doesn't need to be reported if it occurs only once and if the child is as comfortable and happy as ever. But if the child acts differently in other respects, especially if there is abdominal pain, the doctor should be called. There are periods in childhood when the rate of growth slows down and children seem to eat less.

1033. Colds. In general, you should call the doctor if the cold is more than mild, if it lasts longer than ten days, and if the child seems sicker or develops new symptoms.

1034. Hoarseness of voice accompanied by difficulty in breathing should always be reported immediately, especially if there is associated drooling.

1035. Vomiting of any unusual type should be reported promptly, especially if the child looks sick or different in any other way. This does not apply, of course, to the spitting up after meals that is so common at first.

1036. Diarrhea of the more serious sort, such as bloody diarrhea and significant diarrhea in infants, should be reported to the doctor immediately. The milder kinds can wait. Look for signs of dehydration, (decreased urine output, dry mouth and decreased tears) and report them to your doctor or nurse practitioner. *Blood in the bowel movements or blood in the vomitus or in the urine should be reported promptly.*

1037. Injury to the head should be reported if the baby loses consciousness or isn't happy and healthy looking within 15 minutes or begins to look more lethargic and dazed as time goes by or if he begins to vomit after the head injury. Inflammation of the eye or injury to the eye should be reported promptly. Bulging of the soft spot should be reported, as should a sunken soft spot, if the baby looks sick.

1038. Ingestion of poisons. If your child has eaten anything that might possibly be dangerous, you should reach your Poison Control Center, doctor or nurse practitioner immediately. It's a good idea to keep the phone numbers of your doctor and poison control center posted beside your telephone and your house well stocked with syrup of ipecac so you can give it *when instructed to do so* by Poison Control, your doctor, or your nurse practitioner (see Section 1085).

1039. Rashes. Consult the doctor about all persistent or unusual rashes. It's easy to be mistaken. If a child seems sick with a rash or if the rash is extensive, you should call the doctor right away.

Remember, this is only a partial list of situations when you should call your doctor or nurse practitioner. *When in doubt, call!*

Alternative Therapies

If you are like most people, you consult an *allopathic* doctor or nurse for your child's checkups and sick visits. These professionals practice modern Western medicine, just as I do. We use modern technology to diagnose and treat all manner of problems and we rely on scientific studies to confirm that what we are doing is actually beneficial. Allopathic medicine has allowed us to improve our life expectancy and perform medical miracles, from polio vaccine to antibiotic drugs, undreamed of by our grandparents.

1040. But there are limitations to the capacities of Western medicine. Sometimes what we do has unintended side effects, so that the cure becomes worse than the disease. Sometimes too much human interference seems to upset nature's plan. Often we take care of specific problems but lose sight of the whole child. And not infrequently we are frustrated by the limitations of modern medicine to cure certain ailments.

For these reasons, more than 50 percent of Americans now look to older or alternative systems of medical care to help themselves or their children. These systems include nutritional treatments, herbal remedies, meditation, acupuncture, yoga, chiropractic, homeopathy, naturopathy, and massage.

Western medicine has recently begun to give serious study to alternative medicines. Hypnosis, for example, has been proved very successful, with even very young children, in helping them cope with pain, reduce anxiety, or improve performance. Many allopathic doctors consider hypnosis (or self-hypnosis) a well-established therapy. Infant massage has been shown to improve the outcome of some prematurely born infants. Acupuncture can help with some painful disorders. Herbs are being used more and more. Many foods are being used to treat and prevent cancer.

Although my basic philosophy is that of a physician trained in allopathic medicine, with time and experience I have come to realize that other systems of medicine, many of which are centuries old, provide insights into healing that have eluded traditional medicine.

1041. How are you to evaluate the claims made by nontraditional (or traditional, for that matter) medical people about the cure and prevention of disease? This is not an easy question to answer.

If you are going to try an alternative medical treatment for your child, your doctor or nurse practitioner may or may not be sympathetic. You can, however, research this topic in your local library, a bookstore, or the book section of your health food store. I recommend a book written by Kathi Kemper, an allopathic pediatrician, called *The Holistic Pediatrician* (New York: HarperCollins, 1996), which tries to be objective in evaluating alternative therapies for the twenty-five most common childhood ailments. I also suggest *Perfect Health* by Deepak Chopra. Or you can attend any number of health conferences or workshops.

Part of what makes it difficult to know if a particular medical treatment actually works is the *placebo effect.* This is a therapeutic benefit that occurs because the person believes in the efficacy of a treatment. If we *believe* we are being cured, the chances are better that we really will be! Placebo effects occur in both allopathic and alternative treatments. The field of psychosomatic medicine is intensively studying the fascinating relationship between mind and body—another example of how yesterday's nontraditional medicine sometimes becomes today's mainstream medicine.

I think that so-called alternative therapies are going to increase in the coming years, so it will be up to you to become an informed health care consumer. Alternative therapies should not necessarily be thought of as substitutes for traditional Western medicine. More often they are utilized as additional therapies—to treat the emotional as well as the physical side of the illness, for example. I myself, over the years, have utilized, with apparent benefit, meditation, acupuncture, massage, hypnosis, and certain forms of yoga and homeopathy.

Handling a Child with an Illness

1042. Spoiling is easy. When children are really sick, you give them lots of special care and consideration, not only for practical medical reasons but also because you feel sorry for them. You don't mind preparing drinks and foods for them at frequent intervals or even putting aside a drink they refuse and making another kind right away. You are glad to get them new playthings to keep them happy and quiet. You ask them often how they feel, in a solicitous manner. Children quickly adjust to this new position in the household. If they have a disease that makes them cranky, they may be calling and bossing a parent like old tyrants.

Fortunately, at least 90 percent of children are on their way to recovery within a few days. As soon as the parents stop worrying, they stop kowtowing to the child who is unreasonable. After a couple of days of minor clashes, everyone is back to normal.

But if children develop a long illness or one that threatens to come back, and if a parent has a tendency to be a worrier, the continued overconcern may have a bad effect on the children's spirits as they absorb some of the anxiousness of those around them. They're apt to be demanding. If they're too polite for that, they may just become excitable and temperamental, like spoiled actors. It's easy for them to learn to enjoy being sick and receiving sympathy. Some of their ability to make their own way agreeably may grow weaker, like a muscle that isn't being used.

1043. Keep them busy and polite. It's wise for parents to get back into normal balance with the sick child as soon as possible. This means such little things as having a friendly, matter-of-fact expression when entering the room, rather than a worried one; asking them how they feel today in a tone of voice that expects good news rather than bad and perhaps asking only once a day. When you find out by experience what they want to drink and eat, serve it up casually. Don't ask timidly if they like it or act as if they were wonderful to take a little. Keep strictly away from urging unless the doctor feels it is necessary. A sick child's appetite is more quickly ruined by pushing and forcing.

If you are buying new playthings, look particularly for the types that make children do all the work and will give them a chance to use their imagination: blocks and building sets; sewing, weaving and bead-stringing kits; painting, modeling and stamp-collecting supplies. These make demands on children and occupy them for long periods, whereas toys that are merely beautiful possessions quickly pall and only whet the appetite for more presents. Deal out one new plaything at a time. There are lots of homemade occupations, like cutting pictures out of old magazines, making a scrapbook, sewing, building a farm or town or doll's house of cardboard and masking tape. Discourage excessive TV and video games.

During an illness, a child is allowed up when he or she feels well enough, with rare exceptions.

1044. If children are going to be laid up for a long time, but are well enough to study, get a teacher or a tutor or the best teacher in the family to start them on their schoolwork again for a regular period each day, just as soon as possible.

If they're human, they will want company part of the time, and you can join in some of their occupations or read to them. But if they want more and more attention, try to avoid arguments and bargaining. Have regular times when they can count on your being with them and other times when they know you are going to be busy elsewhere. If they have a disease that isn't catching and the doctor lets them have company, invite other children in regularly to play and to stay for meals.

The hardest part can be when the child is over her illness but not yet fully back to her old self. You have to use your best judgment about how much special consideration she still needs. It all adds up to letting children lead as normal a life as is possible under the circumstances, expecting reasonable behavior toward you and the rest of the family, and avoiding worried talk, looks, and thoughts.

Fever

WARNING: *Never give aspirin to a child or teenager for fever or for cold or flu symptoms unless the doctor prescribes it.* Only acetaminophen, ibuprofen, and other nonaspirin products should be used for these symptoms in children and teenagers. If it turns out to be a viral illness, especially influenza or chicken pox, aspirin can make the child more susceptible to Reye's syndrome, an uncommon but very dangerous condition (see Section 1193).

1045. What's fever and what isn't? The first thing to realize is that a healthy child's body temperature doesn't stay fixed at 98.6°F. It is always going up and down a little, depending on the time of day and what the child is doing. It's usually lowest in the early morning and highest in the late afternoon.

This change during the day is only a slight one, however. The change between rest and activity is greater. The temperature of perfectly healthy small children may be 99.6°F or even 100°F right after they have been running around, but temperature of 101°F probably means illness, whether the child has been exercising or not. The older child's temperature is less affected by activity. All this means that if you want to know whether your child has a slight fever due to illness, you must take his temperature after he has been really quiet for an hour or more.

1046. What causes fever with illness? Fever is part of the body's response to many infectious diseases and occasionally to other illnesses as well. Scientists believe that fever was originally a way to help the body fight off the infection, because some germs are more easily killed at higher temperatures.

When a person has a fever, the illness sets up a series of changes in the body that cause the "set point" for temperature in the brain to be raised. The temperature "set point" in the body is determined in the brain (in the *hypothalamus*). It works very much like the thermostat for the furnace in your house. Normally the body's thermostat mechanism adjusts (up or down) the heat generated by metabolism to maintain the usual body temperature. When the body is fighting off a germ, chemicals are produced that raise the set point and the body temperature is raised. That is one reason why we feel cold when we have a fever. We're not really cold—we're too warm—but the rising body temperature is below the newly raised set point, and this is experienced as feeling cold. Fever medicines work by chemically turning the set point back down.

Many parents assume that the fever itself is bad and want to give medicine to bring it way down, no matter how many degrees it is. But it's well to remember that the fever is not the disease. The fever is one of the methods the body uses to help overcome the infection. It is also a help in keeping track of how the illness is progressing. In one case the doctor wants to bring the fever down because it is interfering with the child's sleep or exhausting the patient. In another case the doctor is quite willing to leave the fever alone and concentrate on curing the infection.

In most feverish illnesses the temperature is apt to be highest in the late afternoon and lowest in the morning—but don't be surprised if a fever is high in the morning and low in the afternoon. There are a few diseases in which the fever, instead of climbing and falling, stays high steadily. The most common of these are pneumonia and roseola infantum. A below-normal temperature (as low as 97°F) sometimes occurs at the end of an illness, and also in healthy babies and small children in the morning. This is no cause for concern so long as the child is feeling well.

1047. The thermometer. The only difference between an oral (mouth) and a rectal thermometer is in the shape of the bulb. The bulb of the rectal thermometer is round so that it won't be so sharp. A mouth thermometer has a long slender bulb so that the mercury can be warmed more quickly by the mouth. The markings on the two thermometers are exactly the same and mean the same thing—in other words, they are not marked differently to allow for the difference of temperature between the mouth and rectum. One very popular thermometer has a bulb shape that is somewhere in between the round bulb of the rectal thermometer and the long bulb of the oral thermometer, making it convenient for using in either area. Any of these can be used for taking axillary (armpit) temperature.

Now about the difference between mouth, axillary, tympanic, and rectal temperatures. That of the rectum is highest because it is well inside the body. That of the mouth is lowest because the mouth is cooled by the air being breathed through the nose. There is usually less than one degree's difference in temperature between the rectum and the mouth. The temperature of the axilla is in between.

Most thermometers register well enough in a minute in the rectum. If you watch a thermometer sometime when it is in a baby's rectum, you can see that it goes up very rapidly at first. It gets within a degree of where it is going to stop in the first twenty seconds. After that it barely creeps up. This means that if you are nervous taking the temperature of a struggling baby, you can take the thermometer out in less than a minute and have a rough idea what the temperature is.

It takes longer to register the correct temperature in the mouth—one and a half to two minutes. This is because it takes the mouth a while to warm up after being open and because the bulb is partly surrounded by air. It takes four minutes to take an accurate axillary temperature but you can get a rough idea in a couple of minutes.

Some parents now prefer electronic digital readout thermometers. These take less time to provide an accurate reading of the temperature and the numbers are easy to read. Most are as accurate as a mercury thermometer, but they are more expensive. For especially uncooperative children, there are electronic digital readout thermometers that you hold on the outside of the ear canal. They sense the temperature of the eardrum. While these are usually accurate, the thermometer needs to be placed exactly right or inaccurate temperatures may appear. They are also costly. I wouldn't advise them unless there is no other practical way to take your feisty child's temperature.

1048. Reading the thermometer. Taking the temperature is a bugaboo to many parents. They find a mercury thermometer hard to read. If you just can't seem to get the hang of reading it, I'd suggest a digital readout thermometer. But 99 out of 100 parents can learn to read a mercury thermometer if they keep at it.

It might be easier for you to get someone else to show you how to read one, but here goes. Most thermometers are engraved the same way. They have a long mark for each degree and a short mark for each two-tenths of a degree— that is, 0.2, 0.4, 0.6, 0.8. Only the even degrees—94, 96, 98, 100, 102, 104—are numbered on the thermometer because of lack of space. There is an arrow pointing to the "normal" mark, 98.6. Many thermometers are marked in red above the normal point.

Reading the thermometer is very easy once you get the knack. Most thermometers are somewhat triangular in shape, with one edge sharper than the rest. This sharp edge

should point toward you. In this position the degree marks are above and the numbers are below. Between them is the space in which the mercury shows. Roll the thermometer very slightly until you see the band of mercury. Don't worry too much about the fractions of degrees.

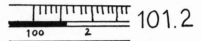

1049. Taking the temperature. Before taking your child's temperature, shake the thermometer down. Hold the upper end of the thermometer (the end opposite the bulb) firmly between your thumb and finger. Now shake the thermometer vigorously with a sharp, snapping motion. You want to drive the mercury down at least as far as 97°F. If it doesn't go down, you aren't snapping hard enough. Until you get the hang of it, shake the thermometer over a bed or couch. Then if it slips out of your hand, it won't break. The bathroom is the worst place of all to shake a thermometer because of the hard surfaces. If a thermometer does break, be sure to keep children away from any contact with the mercury, which can be absorbed through the skin.

If you are taking a rectal temperature, dip the bulb of the thermometer into petroleum jelly or cold cream. The best possible position for a baby is lying on his stomach across your knees. The child can't squirm out of this position very easily, and his legs will hang down out of the way. Insert the thermometer gently into the rectum, an inch or less. Push it in with a light touch, letting the thermometer find its own direction. If you hold it stiffly, it may poke the baby inside. Once the thermometer is in, it is better to shift your grip off the end of the thermometer, because if the baby struggles, the twist-

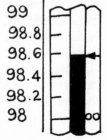

ing might hurt. Instead, lay the palm of your hand across the baby's buttocks, lightly holding the thermometer between two of your fingers, as shown in the illustration.

You can also take the rectal temperature with the child lying on her side on the bed with her knees up a little. It is harder to find the rectum when the child is lying flat on her stomach. The worst position is with the child lying on her back. It is hard to get to her rectum, and her feet are in position to kick your hand accidentally—or on purpose.

By the time the child is a year and older, it's psychologically preferable to take the temperature in the armpit (*axilla*). She is beginning to be aware of her body, her dignity, her security. She's apt to be bothered or even alarmed by having something poked into her rectum. You can get a satisfactory temperature by placing the bulb of the thermometer in her armpit and then holding her arm flat against her chest for four minutes (look at your watch). There should be no clothes between the arm and the chest,

of course, just the bulb of the thermometer. You can use a
rectal or mouth thermometer in the armpit.

After the age of five or six a child can usually cooperate in
keeping the thermometer bulb under his tongue with his lips
closed. Then you can take the temperature by mouth or
armpit, whichever is more convenient. It makes little difference if the temperature is 99.8° or 99.6°F. The doctor will
be interested in the *approximate* temperature. When you
report the temperature to the doctor, tell him what the
thermometer actually says, and then add "by mouth," "by
axilla," or "by rectum." I say this because sometimes a
parent who has the mistaken idea that the mouth temperature is the only correct one takes the child's temperature by
rectum, figures what the mouth temperature would be, and
then tells the doctor that figure. Usually the best times to
take the temperature are in the first part of the morning and
late in the afternoon.

You clean a thermometer by washing it with lukewarm water and soap. You can then wipe it off with rubbing alcohol, but be sure to rinse it with cold water to get rid of the alcohol taste before using it again.

1050. How many days should you go on taking the temperature? Here is what happens occasionally. A child has a bad cold with a fever. The doctor sees the child or gets reports regularly and has the parents take the temperature twice a day. Finally the fever is gone, and the child is convalescing well, with only a mild cough and running nose. The doctor tells the parents to let the child go outdoors as soon as the cold is gone completely. Two weeks later the parents telephone to say that they and the child are getting desperate staying indoors, that the running nose and cough have been completely gone for ten days, that the child looks wonderful and eats well, but that the fever is still going to 99.6°F each afternoon. As I explained earlier, this is not necessarily a fever in an active child. The ten days of staying indoors and worrying over the temperature have all been a waste and a mistake.

Under most circumstances, when the temperature has stayed under 101°F for a couple of days, it's a good general rule to forget about the thermometer unless the doctor asks you to continue or unless the child seems sicker in any way. *Children should be kept home from school until the temperature has been normal for twenty-four hours and they are definitely feeling better,* though all cold symptoms don't have to be gone. Don't get in the habit of taking the temperature when a child is well.

1051. Treatment of high fever until you reach the doctor. Between the ages of one and five years, children may develop a fever as high as 104°F, sometimes even higher, with the onset of a mild infection, such as a cold, a sore throat, or the flu, just as they would with a serious infection. On the other hand, a dangerous illness may never bring a temperature higher than 101°F. So don't be influenced too much, one way or the other, by the height of the fever. Get in touch with the doctor when your child looks sick or different, whatever the temperature.

Sometimes a child feels especially uncomfortable with a high fever. If on the first day of an illness a child's temperature is 104°F or higher, and if it will be an hour or more before you can speak to the doctor, even on the telephone, you can bring the fever down a little with an anti-fever medication such as acetaminophen or ibuprofen. These come in both solid and liquid forms. Follow the directions on the package for the correct dose. (Be sure to keep these medications out of your child's reach and in a childproof container.) Remember that doses change based on age and weight.

The medicine to bring the fever down should be given one time only, unless you still haven't reached the doctor after three to four hours, in which case you can give a second dose.

You may want to give your child a bath or to wipe their skin with a wet cloth or sponge. The purpose of the tepid bath or wet rub is to bring the blood to the surface by rubbing and to cool it by the evaporation of the water off the skin. (Alcohol has traditionally been used in a wet rub, but if it is applied very freely in a small room, too much may be inhaled. Anyway, water is just as good, even if it doesn't smell so important.) These methods provide only temporary relief, however, because the body's thermostat remains set at a higher temperature and will quickly cause the fever to return.

When a child's fever is very high and he is flushed, use only light covers at ordinary room temperature, perhaps as little as a sheet. Your child will be more comfortable that way, and it may help his temperature come down.

Parents often worry that prolonged high fever can cause a convulsion. This isn't true. Usually it's the abrupt increase in temperature at the onset of an illness that occasionally causes a convulsion in small children (Section 1189). The reason for trying to bring a high fever down is to help the child feel less miserable, not to prevent a convulsion.

Diet During Illness

1052. Diet during illness. Your doctor or nurse practitioner will tell you what diet to use in each of your child's illnesses, taking into account the nature of the disease and the child's taste. Diet during infant diarrhea is discussed in Sections 345–346. What follows are some general principles to guide you until you are able to get medical help.

1053. Diet for a cold without fever. The diet during a cold without fever can be entirely normal. However, children may lose some of their appetite with even a mild cold because they're indoors, because they're not taking the usual amount of exercise, because they're a little uncomfortable, and because they're swallowing mucus. Don't urge them to take more food than they want. If they're eating less than usual, offer them extra fluids between meals. People sometimes have the idea that the more fluid, the better the treatment. There is no harm in letting children drink all that they feel like drinking, but excessive amounts of fluid don't do any more good than reasonable amounts.

1054. Diet during fever until you can consult the doctor. When children have fever above 102°F with a cold, flu, sore throat, or one of the contagious diseases, they usually lose most of their appetite in the beginning, especially for solids. In the first day or two of such a fever, don't offer them solid food at all if they don't seem hungry, but do offer fluids frequently when they're awake.

Orange juice, pineapple juice, and water are the most popular fluids, but don't forget water. It has no nourishment, but that's unimportant for the time being. It's for this very reason that it often appeals to the sick child most. Other fluids depend on the child's taste and the illness. If a child has an infection that causes sores in his mouth, he may not want citrus drinks that are acidic and make the sores sting. Some children love grapefruit juice, lemonade, pear juice, grape juice, and weak tea. Popsicles are also a good source of fluid. Older children like carbonated drinks such as ginger ale and fruit-flavored sodas. Some cola drinks contain small amounts of caffeine, a stimulant, so it's preferable to avoid them.

Cow's milk is not recommended for a child when he is sick—or when he is well, for that matter. Dairy products may cause more mucus complications and cause more discomfort with upper respiratory infections.

1055. When a fever continues, a child is apt to have a little more appetite after the first day or two. If your child is hungry in spite of a high fever, she may be able to take simple solids like toast, crackers, soft creamy cereal, or applesauce.

Foods that children often do not want and that cannot be digested during fever are cooked or raw vegetables, meats, poultry, fish, and fats such as butter, margarine, cream, and other dairy products. However, Dr. Clara Davis in her experiments on diet found that children often crave vegetables during convalescence—after the fever is gone—and digest them well.

One rule is more important than any other: *Do not urge a sick child to eat anything that she doesn't want unless the doctor has a special reason for urging it.* It's only too likely to be vomited, to cause intestinal upset, or to start a feeding problem.

1056. Diet when there is vomiting. Of course, vomiting occurs in many different diseases, especially at the beginning when there is fever. It occurs because the stomach is upset by the disease and is not able to handle the food. The diet depends on many factors and should be prescribed by the doctor. However, if you cannot reach the doctor immediately, you can follow these suggestions.

It's a good idea to give the stomach a complete rest for at least a couple of hours after the vomiting begins. Then if the child is asking for it, give a sip of water, not more than half an ounce at first. If this stays down and she begs for more, let her have a little more, say 1 ounce about fifteen minutes later. Increase the amount gradually up to 4 ounces (half a glass) if she craves it. If she has gone this far without vomiting, you can try a little diluted apple juice or decaffeinated tea. It is better not to go beyond 4 ounces at a time the first day. Some children tolerate Popsicles well.

If several hours have gone by since the vomiting and the

child is begging for solid foods, give something simple, like a cracker, or a piece of toast, a little banana, or a tablespoon of applesauce. Do not give milk or milk products.

The vomiting that goes with a feverish illness is most apt to occur on the first day and may not continue even if the fever goes on.

Small specks or streaks of blood sometimes show in the vomited material when a child is retching violently. This is not usually serious in itself, but you should mention it to your doctor or nurse practitioner.

1057. Diet when there is diarrhea. By the time a child is two or more, there is much less chance of severe or prolonged diarrhea. Until the doctor can be reached, the best treatment is rest and as much of his normal diet as he seems hungry for. Research has shown that the traditional "diarrhea diet" of sugary fluids such as Jell-O water, soda drinks, or apple juice actually increases and prolongs diarrhea, so this approach is no longer recommended.

Some children like to drink oral rehydration solutions, which you can buy at the drug store or supermarket. They are simply lightly sugared water with added minerals that the body loses during diarrhea. Usually they are not necessary for a *mild* diarrhea—that is, occurring only a few times a day—but can be very helpful for significant diarrhea, when dehydration (see Section 346) is a concern. At that time your doctor may recommend an oral rehydration solution.

The key feature of diet during diarrhea is to make sure your child takes in sufficient fluids so as not to become dehydrated because the intake (the drinking) is less than the output (the diarrhea). The fluid should not be water, tea, or other liquids that do not replace mineral losses. Best is a rehydration solution.

1058. Avoiding feeding problems at the end of illness. If a child has a fever for several days and wants little to eat, he naturally loses weight. This worries parents the first time or two that it happens. When the fever is finally gone and the doctor says it's all right to begin working back to a regular diet, they are impatient to feed the child again. But it often happens that the child turns away from the foods that are first offered. If the parents urge him to eat, meal after meal and day after day, his appetite may never pick up.

Such a child has not forgotten how to eat, nor has he become too weak to eat. At the time the temperature went back to normal there was still enough infection in his body to affect his stomach and intestines. Just as soon as he saw those first foods, his digestive system warned him that it was not ready for them yet.

When food is pushed or forced onto a child who already feels nauseated because of illness, his disgust is built up more easily and rapidly than if he had a normal appetite to start with. He can acquire a long-lasting feeding problem in a few days' time.

As soon as the stomach and intestines recover from the effects of most illnesses and are able to digest food again, children's hunger comes back with a bang—and not just to what it used to be. Children are usually ravenous for a week or two in order to make up for losses. You sometimes see such children whimpering for more, two hours after a large meal. By age three, they may demand the specific foods that their starved system craves most.

The parents' course at the end of illness is to offer children only the drinks and solids they want, without any urging, and to wait patiently but confidently for signals that they are ready for more. If their appetite has not recovered in a week, the doctor should be consulted again.

Giving Medicine

1059. It's sometimes quite a trick getting a child to take medicine. The first rule is to slip it into her in a matter-of-fact way, as if it has never occurred to you that she won't take it. If you go at it apologetically, with a lot of explanation, you convince her that she's expected to dislike it. Talk about something else when you put the spoon into her mouth. Most young children open their mouths automatically, like birds in their nest.

Tablets that don't dissolve can be crushed to a fine

powder and mixed with a coarse, good-tasting food, like applesauce. Mix the medicine with only one teaspoon of the applesauce, in case she decides she doesn't want very much. Bitter pills can be mixed in a teaspoon of applesauce, rice syrup, or rice milk.

Eye ointments and drops can sometimes be applied during sleep. They can also be given to a small child by placing him on your lap with his legs around your waist and out of kicking range. Place his head gently but firmly between your knees and hold with one hand while applying the medicine with your other hand. (This position is also good for suctioning the nose or inserting nose drops.)

When giving medicine in a drink, it's safer to choose an unusual fluid that the child does not take regularly, such as grape juice or prune juice. If you give a strange taste to orange juice, you may make the child suspicious of it for months.

1060. Don't give medicine without a doctor's or nurse practitioner's advice. And don't continue to give it without keeping in touch with that doctor. Here are some examples of why not. A child has a cough with a cold and the doctor prescribes a certain cough medicine. Two months later the child develops a new cough, and the parents have the prescription renewed without consulting the doctor. It seems to help for a week, but then the cough becomes so bad they have to call the doctor anyway. The doctor or nurse practitioner realizes right away that the disease this time is not a cold but pneumonia; he would have suspected it a week earlier if the parents had called.

Parents who have treated colds or headaches or stomachaches a few times in the same way come to feel like experts—which they are, in a limited way. But they're not trained, as a doctor is, to first consider carefully what the diagnosis is. To them, two different headaches (or two stomachaches) seem about the same. To the doctor, one may have an entirely different meaning from the other and may call for different treatment.

People whose children have been treated by a doctor or nurse practitioner with one of the antibiotics (such as penicillin) are sometimes tempted to use it again for similar symptoms. They figure that it produces wonderful results, is easy to take, and they know the dosage from the last time—so why not? First, the medicine may not be effective any longer, or the child may need a different dosage or a completely different medication. Secondly, the antibiotics may interfere with diagnosis when the doctor is finally consulted. Finally, children occasionally develop serious reactions to the use of these drugs—fevers, rashes, anemia. These complications, fortunately, are rare, but they are more likely to occur if the drugs are used often, especially if they are used improperly. That is why they should be given only when a doctor or nurse practitioner has decided that the danger from the disease and the likelihood of benefit from the medicine outweigh the risks of treatment. Even the continued use of as common a drug as acetaminophen can occasionally cause serious trouble. For the same reasons, you should never give the neighbor's, friend's, or relative's medicine to a child.

Overuse of antibiotics may lead to resistance in the bacteria. "Antibiotic," by the way, really means "anti-life." I would prefer to see terms like "antibacterial," "antifungal," or "antiviral" used, which would be more accurate and be specifically for what they are treating.

1061. Cathartics and laxatives (drugs to make the bowels move) should not be used for any reason—especially stomachache—without consulting a doctor. Some people have the mistaken idea that stomachache is frequently caused by constipation, and they want to give a cathartic or laxative first of all. There are many causes of stomachache (see Sections 1127–1139) and some, such as appendicitis and obstruction of the intestines, are made worse by a cathartic or laxative. Therefore, since you don't know for sure what is causing your child's stomachache, it is dangerous to treat it with a strong medicine.

1062. Generic prescriptions. A generic prescription is one that doesn't use the trade name for a medicine but uses the chemical name instead. In most cases, medicines prescribed in this way are cheaper than those prescribed by the advertised trade name, even though it's exactly the same medicine. You should ask your doctor about using generic prescriptions. Most—but not all—of the time, it's a good idea.

Isolation for Contagious Diseases

1063. There are many ways for an infectious disease to be transferred from one person to another. Some are transmitted by coughing, some by touching the person. Either way, the germ has to get from one person to another. You won't catch something just by being in the room unless that germ has somehow made its way from the sick individual to your body. Some infectious diseases, like chicken pox or measles, are very contagious; others are relatively hard to transmit (like HIV or hepatitis B).

On general principles, I think it's a good idea to keep a child with a contagious disease in the house until he no longer has a fever and the doctor or nurse practitioner says that he no longer is contagious. I think it's sensible to keep the amount of intimate contact (kissing, hugging and cuddling) between a child with a contagious disease and other members of the household to a minimum, except for the one person who is taking care of the sick child. This precaution helps to prevent others from catching the disease unnecessarily. If your other children were exposed to the sick child before you knew what the disease was, they will most likely catch it anyway, but it is just as well for them not to be continually overexposed. Another reason for keeping sick children isolated is so that they will not be picking up new germs from others to complicate their illness.

In most places, grown-ups in the family—except those who are schoolteachers or food handlers—are not restricted from leaving the home or going to their jobs when a member of the household has a contagious disease. You have to use your own good sense, though, about visiting families who have susceptible children. The chances of your carrying the germs to other children are practically zero so long as you keep away from them.

Just the same, you're not going to be very welcome if the parents are fussy, especially if the disease is one that is dreaded, such as meningitis or whooping cough. They'll blame you if anyone in their family catches that disease any time in the next year. On the other hand, don't hesitate to visit if the disease your child has is one of the less feared ones, if you have had the disease, if your friend doesn't worry, and if her children are out of the way when you visit.

For the sake of other small children and your own conscience, keep your children away from other small children, particularly during the period when your children may come down with a disease.

Hand-washing is extremely important after handling a sick child.

Going to the Hospital

How to Help Your Child

1064. Between the ages of one and four years, the child is most worried about being separated from the parents. He feels as if he is losing them forever when they first leave him after each hospital visit. Between visits he may remain anxious and depressed. When the parents come to see him, he may silently reproach them by refusing to greet them at first. Parents should stay with the child, if possible.

After the age of four the child is apt to be more fearful about what's going to be done to him, the injury to his body, and the pain. It won't do for the parents to promise that the hospital will be a bed of roses. If unpleasant things happen, as they surely will, the child will lose confidence in his parents. On the other hand, if he is told *everything* bad that might happen, he is apt to suffer more in anticipation than he will when he is there.

The most important thing is for the parents to show all the calm, matter-of-fact confidence they are capable of, without forcing it so much that it sounds false. Unless the child has been a hospital patient before, he tries anxiously to imagine what it will be like, perhaps fearing the worst.

737

The parents can set his mind at rest better by describing hospital life in general rather than by arguing with him about whether it's going to hurt a lot or a little. You can tell him how the nurse will wake him in the morning and give him a bath right in bed, how the meals will come on trays and be eaten in his own bed, how there will be time to play, how he may use the bedpan or urinal instead of the bathroom, how he can tell the nurse if he needs something. You can also tell him about visiting times and about all the other children who will keep him company in the ward.

You can talk about what favorite toys and books he's going to take with him and about a TV set with a remote control, or perhaps there is a small radio that he can take from home or borrow. He'll be interested in the electric button for calling the nurse.

It's fair to dwell on these more pleasant everyday aspects of hospital life because even at the worst, the child will spend most of his time amusing himself. I wouldn't avoid discussing the medical program altogether, but let the child see that it's a small part of hospital life.

The Association for the Care of Children's Health, 7910 Woodmont Avenue, Suite 300, Bethesda, MD 20814, (800) 808-2224, is an international association of professionals who work with children in various health settings. There are also parent members. This group has a large number of books and pamphlets that are available to help parents help sick children (and their brothers and sisters) when it becomes necessary to go to the hospital. The books and booklets are low in cost, and the pamphlets are free. If you have a children's hospital near you, they can tell you whether or not there is an affiliate branch of the association in your area. Also, many children's hospitals now have Child Life professionals who are trained to make hospitalization easier for children.

Many children's hospitals also have hospital preview programs for children whose hospitalization is planned ahead of time. The child and parents can come to the hospital a few days before the actual admission and see various parts of the hospital and have their questions answered. In many hospital preview programs, slide shows and puppet shows are used to explain ahead of time what the hospital experience is going to be like.

1065. Let them tell you their worries. Most important of all is giving your child the opportunity and license to ask questions and tell you what he imagines. Young children view these things in ways that would never occur to adults. In the first place, they often think they have to be operated on or taken to the hospital because they have been bad— because they haven't worn their boots or haven't stayed in bed when sick or have been angry with other members of the family. A child may imagine that his neck has to be cut open to remove his tonsils or his nose removed to get to the adenoids. So make it easy for your child to raise questions. Be ready to hear about strange fears, and try to reassure him about them.

1066. Let them know ahead of time. If you know days or weeks ahead of time that your child will be hospitalized, you will want to decide when to tell him. If there is no chance of his finding out, I think it is kinder to wait to tell a small child until a few days before it's time to leave. It won't do him any good to worry for weeks. It may be fairer to tell a seven-year-old some weeks ahead if he's the kind who can face things reasonably, especially if he has some suspicions. Certainly don't lie to a child of any age if he asks questions, and never lure a child to a hospital pretending it's something else.

1067. Anesthesia. If your child is going to have an operation and you have a choice in the arrangements, you can discuss the matter of anesthetists and anesthesia with the doctor. How a child accepts the anesthesia is apt to make the biggest difference in whether he becomes emotionally upset by an operation or goes through it with flying colors. Often in a hospital there is one or another anesthetist who is particularly good at inspiring confidence in children and getting them under without scaring them. It is worth a great deal to obtain the services of such an anesthetist if you have a choice. In some cases, there is also a choice as to the kind of anesthetic that the doctor is considering and this also makes a difference to the child psychologically. Generally speaking it is less frightening to the child to start with gas. Naturally, the doctor is the one who knows the facts and has to make the decision, but when the doctor feels that there is an equal choice medically, the psychological factor should be considered carefully.

You shouldn't use the expression "put to sleep" when you explain the anesthesia to a child. That can lead to a child's developing sleep problems after surgery. Instead, explain that the anesthesia causes a special kind of sleep, from which the anesthetist will awaken the child as soon as the operation is over.

It's been shown that having a parent present when the anesthesia is given makes a child much less frightened and nervous about the surgery and cuts down on the need for drugs to calm the child.

1068. Visiting. The parent should stay in the hospital with a child between the ages of one and five years if at all possible, especially in the daytime. At the very least, a parent should visit daily. Most hospitals now have rooming-in facilities so that a parent or other adult well known to a child can stay overnight in the child's room.

If the parents are able to visit only intermittently, the visits can create temporary difficulties for the small child. The sight of the parents reminds him how much he has missed them and how much he has lost. He may cry heartbreakingly when they leave or even cry through the entire visiting period. The parents are apt to get the impression that he is miserable all the time. Actually, young children adjust surprisingly well to hospital life when the parents are out of sight, even though they are feeling sick or having uncomfortable treatments. I don't mean that the parents should stay away. The child gets security from realizing that his parents always do come back when they leave. The best the parents can do is to act as cheerful and unworried as possible. If the parents have an anguished expression, it makes the child more anxious. It is best for the parents to stay with the child with no separations, or very few.

First Aid and Emergencies

Cuts

1069. Soap and warm water for cuts and scratches. The best treatment for **scratches and small cuts** is to wash them with soap and warm water. *Careful washing is the key to preventing infection.* After drying the cut with a clean towel, it should be covered with a bandage to allow it to remain clean until the cut is healed. Washing should continue once a day until the cut has completely healed.

For **large cuts** that spread open, you should, of course, consult your doctor. Many of these larger cuts will require stitches to close the wound and lessen the chance of a disfiguring scar. It is important to keep the stitches clean and dry until they are removed. Inspect the wound each day for signs of infection such as increased pain, swelling, redness, or drainage from the wound.

Wounds that might be contaminated by dirt or soil or those caused by dirty objects such as knives should be reported to your doctor. The doctor may recommend **a tetanus booster shot,** especially for deep cuts or puncture wounds. If your child has completed the initial series of three shots and has received a tetanus booster in the last five years, he may not need a tetanus booster. It is always best to check with your physician if you are uncertain.

Occasionally, a wound occurs when someone falls on broken glass or wood. In these cases a **splinter or retained piece of foreign material** (glass, wood, or gravel) may remain in the wound. Unless the small fragment of material can easily be removed it is advisable to have a physician evaluate these cuts. An X-ray may be required to locate the foreign object and to decide if it should be removed. Any cut that does not heal properly or becomes infected (with redness, pain or drainage) may have a retained foreign object such as a splinter.

Splinters

1070. Removing splinters. Next to small cuts and bruises, splinters are probably the most common minor injury during childhood. I like to use what I call the soak-and-poke approach to removing splinters: Wash the area with soap and water, then soak it in fairly hot water for at least ten minutes. Use a hot compress if you can't cover the area with water. (You'll have to reheat your water or compress every couple of minutes.) If one end of the splinter is sticking out of the skin, you can now grasp it with a good pair of tweezers and gently pull it out. If the splinter is entirely under the skin, you'll need a sewing needle that's been wiped with rubbing alcohol. The soaking softens the skin so that you can gently prick it open with the tip of the needle, opening enough skin so that you can grasp the splinter with the tweezers. After the splinter is out, wash the area with soap and water and then cover the area with a clean bandage.

Don't poke at the skin too much. If you can't get the splinter out after the first soak, give it another ten minutes of hot soaking and then try again. If you still can't get it, let your doctor take over.

Bites

1071. Animal (or human) bites. The mouths of all animals, even humans, contain many bacteria that can cause infection. A bite injury usually results in a deep puncture wound which may be more difficult to clean than a simple laceration. A physician should be notified for all bites. Meanwhile, first aid is the same as for cuts, with emphasis on copious irrigation and cleansing with soap and water.

The most common complication of an animal or human bite is a **bacterial infection.** To prevent an infection from developing, your doctor or nurse practitioner may prescribe an antibiotic at the time of the initial treatment. Even if your child is receiving antibiotics, the wound should be carefully checked for any sign of infection, such as redness, swelling, tenderness, or drainage. If any of these develop, a repeat visit to your physician is indicated.

Rabies, which is a life-threatening infection, is an important consideration with animal bites. Wild animal bites from foxes, raccoons, and bats should be considered as potentially rabies-producing. Depending on where you live and the immunization status of the animal, domestic animals such as pet dogs and cats can also potentially transmit the rabies virus. You rarely need to worry about gerbils, hamsters, or guinea pigs carrying rabies. Although there is no treatment for rabies once the infection has developed, it can be prevented through special vaccines given as soon as possible after the bite.

Your doctor can advise you on the best course of treatment for all types of animal bites as well as the need for rabies vaccination. Another resource that may be of benefit concerning the risk of rabies infection is your local board of health or your state department of public health. They may also assist you in observing the animal after the bite to be certain it is not sick with symptoms of rabies.

Bleeding

1072. Bleeding. Most wounds bleed a little for a few minutes. This is helpful because it washes out some of the germs that were introduced. Only profuse or persistent bleeding (*hemorrhage*) requires special treatment. The key to stopping the bleeding in most cuts is to apply direct pressure while elevating the wound. Have the child lie down and put a pillow or two under the limb. If the wound continues to bleed freely, press on it with a sterile gauze square or any clean cloth, until the bleeding stops. Clean and bandage the wound while the limb is still elevated. When bandaging a cut that has bled a lot or is still bleeding use a number of gauze squares (or folded pieces of clean cloth) on top of each other so that you have a thick pad over the cut. Then, when you snugly apply the adhesive or gauze roll bandage, it will exert more pressure on the cut and make it less likely to bleed again.

Severe bleeding. If a wound is bleeding at an alarming rate you must stop the bleeding immediately. Apply direct pressure to the wound and elevate the limb if possible. Make a pad of the cleanest material you have handy, whether it's a gauze square, a clean handkerchief, or the cleanest piece of clothing on the child or yourself. Press the pad against the wound and keep pressing until help arrives or until the bleeding stops. *Don't remove your original pad.* As it becomes soaked through, add new material on top. If the bleeding is easing up and you have suitable material, apply a pressure bandage.

The pad over the wound should be thick enough so that when it is bandaged it presses on the wound. If the pressure bandage doesn't control the bleeding, continue hand pressure directly over the wound. If you have no cloth or material of any kind to press against a profusely bleeding wound, press your hands on the edges of the wound or even in the wound.

Most hemorrhages can be stopped by simple direct pressure. If you are dealing with one that can't stop, continue to apply direct pressure and have someone call an ambulance. While awaiting the ambulance, have the patient lie down, keep her warm, and elevate her legs and the injured body part.

Nosebleeds

1073. Nosebleeds. There are a number of simple remedies for stopping a nosebleed. Just having a child sit still for a few minutes is often sufficient. To avoid swallowing a lot of blood, have your child *sit up with his head bent forward* or, if he's lying down, turn his head to one side so that his nose points slightly down. Keep him from blowing his nose or pressing and squeezing it with his handkerchief.

Nosebleeds usually occur from the front part of the nose. You can sometimes stop a severe nosebleed, by gently pinching the whole lower part of the nose for five minutes. (Look at your watch; five minutes seems like an eternity in these circumstances.) Let go slowly and gently. If the nosebleed continues for ten minutes in spite of these measures, get in touch with the doctor. If you have a bottle of nose drops that relieve nasal congestion, wet a small, loose wad of cotton with the nose drops and tuck it into the front part of the nostril. Then squeeze the nose again. This will more than likely stop the bleeding.

Nosebleeds are most frequently caused by trauma to the nose, repeated nose-picking, allergies, and colds or other infections. If a child has repeated nosebleeds from no apparent cause, he needs to be examined by the doctor or nurse practitioner to make sure he does not have a problem with his ability to form blood clots. If a child has persistent nosebleeds it may be necessary to cauterize (seal) an exposed blood vessel that is always breaking. Your doctor can easily do this in his office, usually just after the nose has stopped bleeding.

Nosebleeds in infants are not common. They should be reported to your doctor or nurse practitioner.

Burns

1074. Burns. Burns usually result from accidental contact with hot water, although hot oil, grease, and other substances can also produce injuries to the skin. Even prolonged exposure to the sun can result in a significant burn. Burns are categorized into one of three types: first-degree burns involve only the most superficial layer of the skin and usually produce only redness to the area; second-degree burns have injured the deeper layers of the skin and they usually result in the formation of blisters; and third-degree burns involve the deepest layers of the skin, often damaging the nerves and blood vessels beneath the skin. Third-degree burns are serious injuries and often require a skin graft.

The initial treatment of a burn is to place the injured area under cold water (not ice water) as quickly as possible. *Never apply any ointment, grease, butter, cream or petroleum product.* Your doctor will need to remove these and this may make your child's pain worse. After rinsing the burn with water, cover the area with a bulky sterile dressing. This will decrease the pain associated with the burn.

If any blisters are forming, leave them intact. Never break one as the fluid inside them is sterile. When you open a blister you allow germs to enter the wound. If a blister does break, it is better to remove all the loose skin with a pair of nail scissors or a pair of tweezers that have been boiled for five minutes. Then cover with a sterile bandage. A doctor or nurse practitioner should see any blister that has broken as they will often prescribe a special antibiotic ointment to prevent infection. If the blister remains intact but shows signs of infection—pus in the blister, for example, and redness around the edge—you should certainly consult your doctor or nurse practitioner. Never put iodine or any similar antiseptic on a burn unless you are directed to so by your doctor or nurse practitioner.

Except for mild sunburn injuries *a physician or nurse practitioner should see all burn injuries.* This is especially important on the face, hands, feet, and genital area, where delays in treatment can lead to scars or functional impairments.

1075. Sunburn. The best treatment for sunburn is not to get it in the first place. Severe sunburn is painful, dangerous, and unnecessary. A half hour of direct sunshine at a beach in summer is enough to cause a burn on a fair-skinned person who is not prepared for the sun (see Sections 635–639).

For relief of sunburn, you can apply cool water and give a mild nonaspirin pain reliever such as ibuprofen or acetaminophen. If blisters develop, they should be treated as described in the previous section. With a moderately severe burn, a person may have chills and fever and feel ill. Then you should consult a doctor or nurse practitioner, because sunburn can be just as serious as a heat burn. Keep sunburned areas completely protected from sunshine until the redness is gone.

1076. Electrical injuries. Most electrical injuries in children occur in the home and are relatively minor. The degree of injury is directly proportional to the amount of current that passes through the child, and this in turn is dependent on how much the child is grounded. Water or moisture of any kind decreases grounding and creates the potential for significant injury. For this reason, no electrical device should ever be operated in a bathroom where a child is washing or bathing.

Most electrical injuries produce a shock that causes the child to withdraw reflexively from the painful stinging sensation. With a more significant injury, your child may develop a burn characterized by a blister or area of redness. You may also note an area of charred tissue, which represents a dead piece of skin. Most of these burns should be treated with wound care as described in Section 1074 on burns.

There a few special circumstances that require extra medical attention. An electrical current can travel through nerves and blood vessels. If your child has an entrance and exit wound, the current may have damaged nerves and blood vessels along the way. If your child has any neurologic symptoms such as numbness or tingling, or if she complains of pain, she should be examined by your doctor.

Occasionally children will develop an electrical burn after they bite into an electrical cord, perhaps a small burn near the corner of the mouth. All children with this type of burn need to be evaluated by a physician. Since all burns can leave scars, your child may need special care to avoid developing a scar that could interfere with his ability to smile and chew.

Skin Infections

1077. When your child develops a skin infection. If a child has a boil, an infection at the end of his finger, or an infected cut of any type, it should be examined by the doctor or nurse practitioner. If there is an unavoidable delay in reaching her, the best first aid treatment is to soak the infected area in warm water or apply warm, wet dressings. This softens the skin, hastens the time when it will break and allow the pus to escape. The warm water will then keep the opening from closing over again too soon. Place a fairly thick bandage over the infection and pour enough warm water into the bandage to make all of it thoroughly wet. Let it soak for twenty minutes, and then replace the wet bandage with a clean, dry one. Repeat this wet soak three or four times a day while you're trying to reach the doctor or nurse practitioner. If you have an antibiotic ointment, you can apply it over the affected area, although this should not replace the visit to the doctor.

If a child has fever with a skin infection, if there are red streaks starting from the site of infection, or if he has tender lymph glands in his armpit or groin, *the infection is spreading seriously* and should be considered a medical emergency. Get the child to a doctor, nurse practitioner, or hospital at once, because antibiotics are vitally important in combatting serious infections.

Foreign Objects

1078. Objects in the nose and ears. Small children often stuff things—beads, small pieces from toys or games, or wads of paper—into their noses or ears. Do not push the object any farther in, in your efforts to take it out. Don't try to go after a smooth, hard object; you are almost certain to push it in farther. Using a pair of tweezers you may be able to grasp a soft object that isn't too far in. If your child won't sit still, be careful with sharp tweezers, as they can cause more damage than the foreign object itself. Even if you can't see the object, it may still be there.

Sometimes an older child may be able to expel the object by blowing her nose, but don't try this if she's so young that she sniffs when told to blow. Other children often sneeze the object out in a little while. If you have a decongestant nose spray, squirt a little in the child's nose before having her blow her nose. If the object stays in, take the child to your doctor or nurse practitioner or to a nose specialist. Foreign objects that remain in the nose for several days usually cause a bad-smelling discharge tinged with blood. A discharge of this kind from one nostril should always make you think of this possibility.

Sprains

1079. "Sprain" and "strain" are the terms used to describe a stretched or torn ligament, tendon, or muscle. Muscles are attached to the bone by thick cordlike structures known as tendons. Ligaments are the strong tissues that provide support to a joint, the area where two or more bones join together. Falls, sports injuries, and unusual twists and turns can produce a sprain or a strain. A sprain can be serious and may require as much treatment as a broken bone.

If your child sprains an ankle, knee, or wrist, have him lie down for a half hour and elevate the sprained limb on a pillow. Put an ice pack over the area of the injury. This will help to prevent swelling and decrease the pain. If the pain resolves and your child can resume normal movement of the injured area without discomfort, there is no need to see a doctor or nurse practitioner. If swelling occurs or the area is very tender, you should consult your doctor or nurse practitioner, because a bone may have been cracked or broken. An X-ray will be required to determine if the bone is broken. Even if the X-ray is normal, your child may require a cast or a splint to immobilize the injury and allow the ligaments and tendons to heal properly. In the few days after the injury your doctor or nurse practitioner may prescribe exercises, heat treatment, and therapy to treat the sprain. It is important to follow these instructions because excessive movement of the sprained area may reinjure the ligaments, leading to more pain or even further susceptibility to chronic injuries, while complete immobility may cause residual stiffness and decreased range of motion.

Fractures

1080. Fractures. A fracture is a broken or splintened bone. Broken bones in children can be quite different from what occurs in adults. Children may fracture or break the growth center of the bone, typically found at the end of long bones. Only one side of a bone may break (greenstick fractures), or they may have the typical adult pattern, which is a crack through both surfaces of a bone.

When you look at an injured extremity, it may be difficult to distinguish between a sprain and a fracture, since a fracture, like a sprain, may not appear deformed. Most fractures usually are swollen and tender, like sprains, so only a doctor or nurse practitioner can distinguish them and she will often need an X-ray to tell the difference.

A fracture should be suspected when your child complains of persistent pain or where there is swelling or a bruise at the site of the injury. Avoid further injury to a suspected fracture by preventing further movement to that area. If possible apply a splint and ice to the area, and then take your child to see a doctor or nurse practitioner.

1081. Splinting. Splinting reduces pain by keeping the limb from moving and prevents further damage that could be caused by movement of the broken bones. To be most effective, a splint needs to be applied in such a way that it prevents movement at the joint above and below the injury. For an ankle injury, the splint should reach to the knee; for a break in the lower leg, it should go up to the hip; for a broken wrist, the splint should go from the fingertips to the elbow; for a broken lower or upper arm, it should go from the fingertips to the armpit.

You need a board to make a long splint. You can make a short splint for a small child by folding a piece of cardboard. Move the limb with extreme gentleness when you are applying the splint to it and avoid any movement near the area of the injury. Tie the limb to the splint snugly in four to six places, using handkerchiefs, strips of clothing, or bandages. Two of the ties should be close to the break, on either side of it, and there should be one at each end of the splint. After you apply the splint, place an ice bag over the area of the injury. Never apply ice (without a bag) directly to an injury, and as a general rule, apply ice for no more than twenty minutes at any one time. For a **broken collarbone** (at the top of the chest in front) make a sling out of a large triangle of cloth and tie it behind the child's neck so that it supports the lower arm across the chest.

Neck and Back Injuries

1082. Neck/back injuries. Our spinal column is the part of the nervous system that connects to the brain, controls the breathing muscles, allows movement of all extremities, and is responsible for normal bladder and bowel functioning—to name only a few of its functions. It is generally protected from injury by the bony column known as the vertebral column. Because of the seriousness of a neck or back injury, it is important not to move the patient so as not to risk further injury. *Only a specially trained health care professional should move a child whom you suspect has a neck or back injury.*

If the child must be moved and professional help has not arrived, one person should be assigned to hold the child's head and neck in a neutral position. When moving the child, keep her head and neck in this exact position at all times. Never turn the body separately from the head. These maneuvers will decrease the chance of further injury to the spinal cord.

Head Injuries

1083. Head injuries. A fall on the head is a common injury at any age. Even before a baby has begun to walk, she may suffer a head injury by rolling off a bed or a changing counter. *If a child loses consciousness after a fall, she should certainly be examined by a doctor immediately.* Any child who suffers a head injury should be carefully observed. If after a fall on the head, a baby cries immediately and then stops crying within fifteen minutes, keeps a good color, and doesn't vomit, there is little chance that she has suffered an injury to her brain. She can be allowed to resume her normal activities right away.

When a head injury is more severe, the child is apt to vomit, lose her appetite, be pale for a number of hours, show signs of headache and dizziness, alternate between agitation and lethargy, and seem sleepier than usual. If a child has any of these symptoms, you should get in touch with your doctor or nurse practitioner so she can examine the child.

A swelling that puffs out quickly on a child's skull after a fall doesn't mean anything serious in itself if there are no other symptoms. It is caused by a broken blood vessel just under the skin.

Even if the child does not exhibit any immediate symptoms, she should be observed closely for the next twenty-four to forty-eight hours.

In the event that your child has suffered a serious injury,

your doctor may schedule a special X-ray called a CAT scan to look at the brain and to diagnose any problems such as a skull fracture or blood clot on the brain.

Finally, keep an eye on your child's performance in school after a head injury. Children who have a concussion—that is, a head injury with loss of consciousness or memory loss for the incident—may develop difficulty with concentration or memory loss.

In the case of a dental injury, see Sections 622–624.

Swallowed Objects

1084. Swallowed objects. Babies and small children can swallow any small object that they place in their mouth. The real danger occurs if these items get caught in the windpipe or breathing tubes. The most common items that children aspirate (that is, inhale into the breathing tubes) include food items such as grapes, nuts, hot dogs, raisins, popcorn, and seeds. Other less common but potentially dangerous objects include bones, peanut shells, small toys, button batteries, and small parts of toys and games. A very dangerous food is peanut butter eaten directly off a spoon or knife. If it is aspirated into the lungs it cannot be removed, and can result in a fatality. Peanut butter should only be eaten spread on a piece of bread.

Items that get stuck in the breathing tubes can prevent adequate oxygen from reaching the child's lungs. *The sudden onset of breathing difficulties, coughing, harsh barking sound, or inability to speak or cry are all symptoms of a foreign-body aspiration and require immediate first aid (see Sections 1089–1091). There is not time to call a physician.*

The foreign object can completely obstruct the breathing tubes leading to a life-threatening situation. This usually means the object has gotten caught near the vocal cords and a life-saving maneuver, such as the Heimlich maneuver, may be needed to remove the obstruction. Should an otherwise healthy child suddenly fall unconscious without any obvious reason, the most common cause is that she is choking on a foreign object. Therefore, all parents should be familiar with emergency treatment of choking. (See Sections 1089–1091.) Most choking episodes can be prevented.

These objects can take another path and enter the digestive system. Usually they pass directly through the stomach and intestines without difficulty. However, they can also become stuck somewhere in the digestive tract, usually the esophagus (the tube between the throat and stomach). The objects that are most likely to do so are needles, straight pins, coins, and button batteries. These can cause coughing or choking, the sensation of having something caught in the throat, pain or difficulty with swallowing, refusal to eat, drooling, or persistent vomiting.

If your child has swallowed a smooth object, like a prune pit or a button, without discomfort, the object is likely to pass without difficulty (although you should still notify your physician or nurse practitioner). Obviously, if the child develops vomiting pain or any of the symptoms listed above, you should consult your doctor right away.

If your child has swallowed a button battery, let your doctor know, because a battery can cause erosion of the lining of the intestines.

When your child has swallowed an object, an X-ray is typically required to locate it. Your physician can then tell you if it will pass through the intestines or if a special procedure is required to remove it.

Finally, *never give ipecac or a cathartic to a child who has swallowed an object.* These will not help and they can possibly make the situation worse.

Poisons

1085. There are over 2 million calls each year to poison control centers about children who have ingested potential poisons. When childproofing your home, place *the phone number of the nearest poison control center* right next to your phone. Always keep on hand a one-ounce bottle of **syrup of ipecac** for each child in the family.

Every medicine, prescription item, vitamin, and household product should be considered poisonous to your child. Even medicines that your child may take on a regular basis can be dangerous if they are taken in large enough quantities. Some substances are dangerous though they may not seem so, like tobacco (one ingested cigarette is dangerous for a one-year-old), boric acid, aspirin, vitamin pills containing a combination of iron, plant and insect sprays, some plants, nail polish remover, perfume, and dishwasher detergent. Even medications that your child takes on a regular basis can be harmful if ingested in large quantities. It is always best to be certain by calling the poison control center or your doctor or nurse practitioner for advice.

If you suspect your child has ingested a potentially toxic or unknown substance you should do the following:

1. Stay with your child and make sure she is breathing and alert. Remove any remaining substances or solutions to prevent her from ingesting any more. *Do not delay seeking help because your child seems well.* The effects of many poisons—aspirin, for instance—may take hours to show but can be prevented by early treatment.

2. Do not induce vomiting in a child who is unconscious or having a convulsion or who seems to be getting very sleepy after having taken the foreign substance. Call 911 or your local emergency unit for immediate help.

3. Place a call to your local poison control center. Tell them the name of the medication or product, as well as the amount of the substance your child swallowed, if known.

4. Be prepared to administer syrup of ipecac, but do not administer syrup of ipecac unless you are instructed to do so by the poison control center, your doctor, or your nurse practioner.

   The dose of syrup of ipecac is as follows: 6–12 months, give 10cc (2 teaspoons); 1–12 years, give 15cc (1 tablespoon); more than 12 years, give 30cc (2 tablespoons). You will be asked to give some liquids with the syrup of ipecac (milk or water will suffice). Approximately twenty minutes after taking the syrup of ipecac your child will begin to vomit.

   If your child swallows a harmful substance and you can't reach a poison control center, emergency room, or doctor, read the label on the ingested substance. Often it will tell you if you should induce vomiting.

Substances for which *you should not induce vomiting* include kerosene, turpentine, ammonia, gasoline, liquid auto polish, lye, drain cleaner, benzene, caustic lime, liquid furniture polish, bleach, insect sprays, cleaning fluids, and strong acids (sulfuric, nitric, hydrochloric, carbolic).

5. The poison control center can then tell you whether to take your child to the hospital for further treatment. Take with you any remaining pills or poison for identification at the hospital.

1086. Poisons on the skin. Although we often think of the skin as a protective barrier, it is important to realize that medications and poisons can be absorbed through the skin and can reach toxic levels within the body. If your child's clothes or skin should come in contact with a potential poison, remove the contaminated clothing and steadily flush the skin with plenty of plain water for ten minutes. Then gently wash the area with soap and water and rinse well. Place the contaminated clothing in a plastic bag, keeping it away from other children. Call the poison control center or your doctor. If they refer you to a hospital, take the contaminated clothes with you in case they wish to test the clothes to identify the poison.

1087. Harmful fluids in the eye. If a child is accidentally squirted or splashed in the eye with a possibly harmful fluid, *flush the eye promptly.* Have the child lie on his back and blink as much as possible while you flood the eye with lukewarm (not hot) water poured from a large glass held 2 or 3 inches above his face. Don't force the eyelid open. Keep this up for fifteen minutes and then call the poison control center, your doctor or nurse practitioner. Some liquids, especially caustics, can cause serious damage to the eye and require a medical evaluation by your doctor or an eye specialist. Try to keep the child from rubbing his eyes.

Allergies

1088. An allergic reaction occurs when our body responds to something it recognizes as foreign (different from itself). The stimulus can be a food, a pet, a medication, or an insect bite. It is helpful to think of allergies as producing mild, moderate, or severe symptoms.

Children who have mild allergies may complain of watery, itchy eyes. Often there is associated sneezing or a stuffy nose. On occasion they may develop **hives,** a very itchy localized swelling of the skin that looks like a large mosquito bite. More moderate allergic symptoms occur when, in addition to hives, the child develops respiratory symptoms such as wheezing and coughing. Finally, a small number of children have **very severe reactions** which can occur within minutes after contact with an allergic stimulus. These children may develop hives or breathing problems, including complete blockage of the airway and low blood pressure. This type of severe reaction is known as *anaphylaxis* and represents a medical emergency.

Mild allergic symptoms are usually treated with medications known as *antihistamines* such as Benadryl. More serious reactions may require treatment with a shot of adrenaline. Any child who has moderate or severe allergic reactions needs to be evaluated by a physician, who may recommend that you carry an *Epi-Pen* with you for your child. This is a spring-loaded device which can deliver adrenaline to your child if he is having a serious allergic reaction. Finally, your child's physician may evaluate the child using allergy testing to determine the offending stimulus and counsel you and your child on how to avoid it in the future. She may also recommend desensitization treatments (allergy shots).

Choking and Artificial Respiration

A child may stop breathing because of choking, smothering, drowning, smoke exposure (inhalation), a serious lung infection, or electric shock. If the child's breathing is not restarted quickly, he will suffer oxygen deprivation and this may lead to brain damage. If the loss of oxygen continues for several minutes, his heart will stop beating and he will require emergency CPR (cardiopulmonary resuscitation).

1089. Every adult should be trained in life-saving techniques and CPR. Courses are offered by fire departments, the Red Cross, and many hospitals and clinics. These courses will teach you how to try to start the heart beating if it has stopped, and how to administer artificial respiration.

The first step, whenever a person stops breathing, is to start artificial respiration promptly. Keep it up until he can breathe by himself or until help comes. *Never give artificial respiration to a person who is breathing on his own.*

1090. When a child has swallowed something and is coughing hard, trying to get it up, give her a chance. Coughing is a protective mechanism intended to remove the foreign object from the lungs. Coughing is the best way to clear an object from the air passages. If the person is able to breathe, speak, or cry, stay close by and ask someone to call for help. Do not make any attempt to remove the object. Do not slap her on the back, turn her upside down, or reach into her mouth and try to pull the object out; each of those actions can drive the object tighter into the airway, causing choking with complete obstruction of breathing.

1091. When a child is choking and unable to breathe, cry, or speak, the object is completely blocking the airway, and air is not entering the breathing tubes. If the child is conscious, follow the emergency steps outlined below. If the child is unconscious and not breathing, have someone call an ambulance while you begin emergency treatment for an unconscious child. Remember to look for signs that the airway is completely obstructed (no crying, speaking, or coughing).

For a Choking Infant up to One Year Old

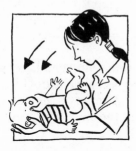

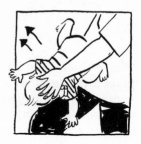

1. **If the baby is conscious,** slide one hand under her back to support her head and neck. With your other hand, hold her jaw between your thumb and fingers, and let your forearm lie along her abdomen.

2. Place the child so she is lying face down with her head lower than her trunk. Support her abdomen with your forearm that is resting on your thigh.

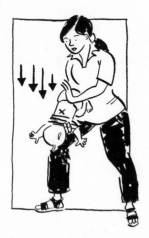

3. With the heel of one hand, give the baby up to five rapid blows in the middle of the back, high between the shoulder blades.

4. If the object was not dislodged by the back blows, turn the infant face up while supporting her back with your forearm. Remember that the child's head should be lower than her feet. Place your middle and index fingers on her breastbone, in the center of her chest just below the nipple line. Give four rapid compressions, pressing the breastbone down about a half inch to an inch each time.

5. If the baby doesn't start to breathe or has become unconscious, have someone call for help while you attempt to begin artificial respiration. First, look for the object in the back of the baby's throat by *grabbing the tongue and the lower jaw* between your thumb and fingers and lifting upward. If you see something, slide your little finger down along the inside of her cheek to the base of her tongue and use a hooking motion to sweep the object out. (Don't poke your finger in her mouth if you can't see anything; this could make the blockage worse.)

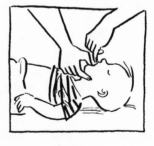

6. Next, reposition the baby to begin artificial breathing by opening her mouth by *lifting the baby's chin* as you press back on the forehead. (See figure.)

7. If the baby still hasn't started to breathe, tilt her head back, lift up her chin, and completely cover both her mouth and nose with your lips. Breathe into her two times, each time for about one and a half seconds and with just enough pressure to make her chest rise.

8. If the air does not enter the baby's lungs, her air passage is still blocked. Start with the back blows again, and repeat steps 3 through 7. Continue repeating the sequence until the baby starts to cough, breathe, or cry, or until help arrives.

For a Choking Child over One Year Old

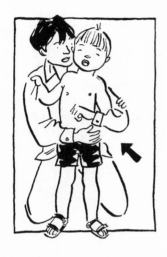

1. **If the child is conscious,** start with the Heimlich maneuver. Kneel or stand behind the child and wrap your arms around his waist. Make a fist with one hand and put the thumb of your fist just above the child's navel, staying well below his breastbone.

2. Cover your fist with your other hand and press your fist into the child's abdomen with a quick upward thrust. Be very gentle with younger or smaller children. Repeat the Heimlich maneuver until the object is expelled. This should get the child to breathe or cough. (If this treatment stops the choking episode, call the doctor even if the child seems fully recovered.)

3. If the child still isn't breathing after a Heimlich, open his mouth by grasping both the tongue and the lower jaw between your thumb and fingers, and lift the jaw. Look in his throat for the object. If you see something, slide  your little finger along the inside of his cheek to the base of his tongue, and use a hooking motion to sweep the object out. (Don't poke your finger around in his mouth if you can't see anything, or can't hook the object; this could make the blockage worse.) Repeat the Heimlich maneuver until the foreign body is removed or the patient becomes unconscious.

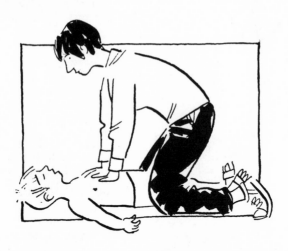

4. If the child becomes unconscious, use the Heimlich maneuver with the child lying on his back. Kneel at his feet (or straddle the legs of an older or bigger child). Put the heel of one hand above his navel, staying well below his breastbone. Put your other hand over your fist with the fingers of both hands pointing toward his head. Press into his abdomen with a quick upward thrust. Be gentle with smaller or younger children. Repeat until the object is expelled.

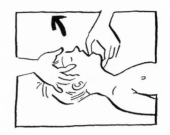

5. **If the child remains unconscious** or if you can't remove the object, have someone call for help immediately. With the child on his back, open his air passage by tilting his head back and lifting his chin with your fingers. Pinch his nose, cover his mouth completely with yours, and breathe into him two times. Use just enough breath to make his chest rise. If you can't make his chest move, reposition the airway and attempt to give him two more breaths.

6. If the air does not enter the child's lungs, repeat steps 4 and 5. Continue to alternate mouth-to-mouth breathing and the Heimlich maneuver until the child resumes breathing or until help arrives.

How to Give Artificial Respiration

Each of your breaths goes into the victim. With an adult, breathe at your natural speed. With a child, use slightly quicker, shorter breaths. **Never give artificial respiration to a person who is breathing.**

1. First open the air passages by properly positioning the child's head. Do this by tilting the forehead back while lifting up on the chin with your fingers. Maintain this position every time you provide a rescue breath.

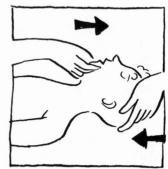

2. With a child's small face, you can breathe into the nose and mouth together. (With an adult, breathe into the mouth while pinching the nose shut.)

3. Breathe into victim, using only minimal force. (A small child's lungs cannot contain your entire exhalation.) Remove your lips, allowing the child's chest to contract while you take in your next breath. Breathe into the child again.

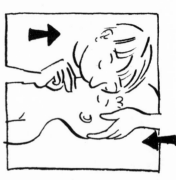

Home First Aid Kit

1092. When an emergency situation develops, it is human nature to become upset and anxious. This is not the time to locate bandages, phone numbers, and other first aid equipment which may have been placed in various closets throughout the house. I am a strong advocate of advanced preparation and would suggest that you keep a small first aid kit in your house to be used in an emergency.

A small box that you can purchase at your local hardware store would suffice. The following should be included in the kit.

A list of emergency telephone numbers including:

1. How to reach an ambulance or emergency response team in your community (Most communities use 911 for emergencies.)
2. Poison control center
3. Your child's physician or nurse practitioner
4. A neighbor to call should you need an adult to assist you

The following first aid equipment:

Sterile bandages
Sterile Band-Aids
An Ace bandage or a similar elastic wrap
Eye patch
Adhesive tape
Ice pack
Bottle of syrup of ipecac *(to be used only after consultation with your local poison control center, physician, or nurse practitioner)*
Any emergency medications your child may require
A thermometer
Petroleum jelly
Small scissors
Tweezers
Antiseptic solution
Antibiotic ointment
Anti-fever medications
A bulb syringe
1 percent hydrocortisone cream

Common Illnesses of Infancy and Childhood

Colds

1093. Your child will probably be sick with colds (*upper respiratory infections or URIs*) ten times as often as with all other illnesses combined. We only partly understand colds at the present time. Most colds are started by a filterable virus. This is a germ so small that it can pass (filter) through unglazed porcelain, so small that it cannot be seen through an ordinary microscope. It is believed that more than two hundred different viruses can cause the common cold. If nothing else happens, the virus cold goes away in about three to ten days.

Cold viruses can lower the resistance of the nose and throat to more troublesome bacteria, such as the streptococcus, the pneumococcus, and the *Haemophilus influenzae* bacteria. In these circumstances they are called secondary invaders; in other situations, they may start infections all by themselves. These germs often live in healthy people's noses and throats during the winter and spring months, but do no harm because they are held at bay by the body's resistance. It's only after the cold virus has lowered the resistance that these other germs get their chance to multiply and spread, potentially causing pneumonia, ear infections, and sinusitis.

The best thing you can do to avoid a cold is to avoid close physical contact with anyone who has one.

1094. Colds in the infant. If your baby has a cold during his first year, the chances are that it will be mild. He may sneeze in the beginning; his nose will be runny or bubbly or stuffy. He may cough a little. He is not likely to have any fever. When his nose is bubbly, you wish you could blow it for him, but it doesn't seem to bother him. On the other hand, if his nose is obstructed with thick mucus, it may make him frantic. He keeps trying to close his mouth and is angry when he can't breathe. The stuffiness may bother him most when he tries to nurse at the breast or bottle, so much so that he refuses altogether at times.

Bubbling and obstruction can often be relieved by sucking the mucus out with a **nasal syringe.** Compress the bulb, insert the tip into the nose, and release the bulb. A drop or two of salt water can be put into the nostril before suctioning. Remember that the inside lining of the baby's nose is very sensitive, so don't push too hard, and try to limit suctioning to times when it's really needed, such as before eating or sleeping.

Extra moisture in the room sometimes helps to prevent the nasal secretions from drying out, and it may make the mucus thinner. If the obstruction is severe, the doctor may prescribe nose drops or a medication by mouth for use just before nursing. In other respects the baby may not lose much of her appetite. Usually the cold is gone in a week. Sometimes, though, a small baby's cold can last an unbelievably long time, even though it stays mild. When a cold lasts longer than two weeks, check with the doctor or nurse practitioner.

Of course, babies' colds can become severe. They can develop into ear infections, sinusitis, and other complications. The baby may develop a fever a few days into the illness, possibly indicating a secondary bacterial infection. If she has a frequent, deep, or wheezy cough, she should be examined by a doctor or nurse practitioner, even if she has no fever. The same rule applies if she looks sick with a cold. Remember that a baby can be quite sick and not have a fever, especially in the first two or three months of life. In those first two or three months, resistance to infection is diminished. Fever during that period should also be checked by a doctor or nurse practitioner.

1095. Colds and fever after infancy. Some children go on having the same mild colds, without fever or complications, that they had during infancy. It's more common, though, when children are over six months old for their colds and throat infections to act differently. Here is a common story. A little girl of two is well during the morning. At lunchtime she seems a little tired and has less appetite than usual. When she wakes up from her nap she is cranky and her parents notice that she is hot. They take her temperature, and it's 102°F. By the time the doctor examines her, the temperature is 104°F. Her cheeks are flushed and her eyes are dull, but otherwise she doesn't seem particularly sick. She may want no supper at all, or she may want a fair amount. She has no cold symptoms, and the doctor hasn't found anything definite except that her throat is perhaps a little red. The next day she may have a little fever, but now her nose may begin to run. Perhaps she coughs occasionally. From this point on, it's just a regular mild cold that lasts anywhere from two days to two weeks.

There are several variations to this typical story. Sometimes the child vomits at the time her fever is shooting up. This is particularly apt to happen if her parents have unwisely tried to get her to eat more of her lunch than she wanted. (Always take a child's word for it when she loses her appetite.) Sometimes the fever lasts several days in the beginning before the cold symptoms appear. Sometimes the fever lasts for a day or two and then goes away without any running nose or cough taking its place. In this case, the doctor may call it grippe, or flu. These terms are commonly used for infections that have no local symptoms (like running nose or diarrhea), only generalized symptoms (such as fever or a sick-all-over feeling). You suspect that this kind of one-day fever is sometimes a cold that was stopped in its tracks: the child seems perfectly well for a day or two after her fever is gone, but then she promptly develops a running nose or cough.

I am making the point that children over the age of six months may start their colds with a sudden fever, so that you won't be too alarmed if this happens. You should, of course, always consult the doctor or nurse practitioner when your child falls ill with a fever, because occasionally it may mean a more serious infection.

When children are five or six years old, they're more apt to be starting their colds without much fever again.

Fever that begins after a cold is well under way has a different meaning entirely from the fever that comes on the first day. It usually indicates that the cold has spread or become worse. This isn't necessarily serious or alarming. It only means that the doctor should see the child again to make sure that her ears, bronchial tubes, and urinary system are still healthy.

1096. Calling the doctor. You don't need to call the doctor when your child has only a running nose or a slight cough. But you should call if new symptoms develop such as **ear pain, frequent coughing,** or **fever occurring several days after the cold began,** which suggests some complication. **Rapid breathing, irritability,** or **excessive tiredness** with a cold should also prompt you to call the doctor or nurse practitioner.

1097. Treatment. Most doctors and parents don't keep a child indoors or prescribe any special treatment for a: simple cold. Remember, colds are caused by viruses. Antibiotics are used only if there is a secondary *bacterial* infection. The overuse of antibiotics for simple colds is causing strains of bacteria to become resistant to those antibiotics. As a result, when the child is truly ill with the bacterial infection, the usual antibiotics may not work.

If your child is particularly susceptible to frequent and prolonged colds or to complications such as bronchitis and ear infections, you may want to be fussier. I have the impression from observing children's and my own colds that chilling may make a cold worse. (Experiments have proved that chilling does not cause a cold to start.) So I think it's sensible to keep such a young child indoors for a day or two, except in warm weather.

1098. Keeping the air moist in an overheated room. The doctor sometimes recommends humidifying the air of the child's room when she has a cold. This counteracts dryness and soothes her inflamed nose and throat. It is particularly valuable in the treatment of a tight, dry cough or very thick mucus. Extra moisture is less necessary in warm weather when the heat is off. An ultrasonic humidifier, which produces a cool mist, can cost as little as $40 or as much as $400. But a regular cool-mist humidifier costing $30 or less does an adequate job. With either type of cold-mist humidifier, it's important to clean the water reservoir at least once a week with a mixture of a cup of chlorine bleach in a gallon of water. This will prevent the growth of molds and bacteria in the reservoir, which then could be blown into the room.

An electric steam vaporizer gets moisture in the air by boiling water, using an electric heating element that fits into a large glass jar of water. It is much less expensive, may be less comfortable because it heats up the room, and is also less safe because a small child may touch it or knock it over. If you buy one of these steam vaporizers, get a large size that holds a quart or more and turns itself off when the water boils away.

1099. Nose drops. The doctor may prescribe nose drops. Generally speaking, they fall into two groups. The first is salt water (saline) nose drops. You can make these at home by dissolving a quarter teaspoon of table salt in 4 ounces of warm water, or you can buy them at the drugstore. These are good for loosening up thick mucus so a child can blow it out more easily. The thinned mucus can be sucked out with a suction bulb for a baby. Suction the nose about one minute after one or two saline drops are placed in the baby's nose.

The other general class of nose drops is made up of solutions that shrink the tissues in the nose. This opens up more space for breathing and gives the mucus and pus a better chance to drain. The main drawback is that after the tissues have been shrunk for a time, they will expand again, sometimes more than before. This may leave the nose stuffier than ever and may be irritating to the delicate membranes if it's done too often.

There are two situations in which the shrinking kind of nose drops is useful. The first is when a baby is so stuffed up that she is frantic. She can't nurse without becoming irritable or gagging, and her sleep is interrupted. (This condition may be relieved by suction with a nasal syringe alone.) Older children with colds who cannot sleep comfortably may also benefit from these nose drops. The second situation is in the late stages of a bad cold or sinusitis, when the nose is filled with a thick secretion that does not discharge by itself.

Nose drops should be used only on a doctor's recommendation and no more often than every six hours. Don't use them for more than five days unless the doctor says to go on. One disadvantage of nose drops is that many small children fight them. There are only a few conditions in which nose drops do enough good to be worth getting the child all upset.

In some cases, the doctor may prescribe a medicine to take by mouth to shrink the nose tissues. Many doctors use the liquid medicine rather than nose drops because it decreases secretions in the sinuses and bronchial tubes (airways) as well as in the nose.

1100. How to instill nose drops. Nose drops do a lot more good if they get back into the inner and upper passages of the nose. Suck out the mucus in the front of the child's nose with a nasal syringe. Then have her lie on her back across a bed with her head hanging well down over the side. Insert the drops and try to keep her in this position for half a minute while the drops work back and up.

1101. Cough medicines. No cough medicine can cure a cold, in the sense of killing the germs. It can only make the windpipe a little less ticklish or loosen up the mucus. A person who has an infection in the windpipe or bronchial tubes needs to cough once in a while to bring up the mucus and pus. It is particularly important that a baby's cough not be suppressed too much. The doctor prescribes a cough medicine to keep the cough from being so frequent that it tires the person out or interferes with sleep and feeding or irritates the throat. Any child or grown-up who has a cough that is that frequent should be under the care of a doctor. Your doctor may recommend a safe cough medicine. Never give a child adult cough medicine.

1102. Resistance to colds. Many people believe that they are more susceptible to colds when they're tired or chilled, but this has never been proved. Common sense tells us that adequate rest and appropriate outdoor clothing in cold climates is reasonable for children and adults.

Houses and apartments that are kept too hot and dry during the winter season parch the nose and throat, and this may cause difficulty breathing when the nose is filled with mucus. The air in a room that's 75°F is excessively dry. Many people try to moisten the air by putting pans of water on the radiators, but this method is almost completely worthless (and dangerous for small children). The right way to keep enough moisture in the air in winter is to keep the room temperature down to 70°F or below (68°F is a good figure to aim at); then you won't need to worry about the humidity. If you can't control the heat, you can use a cold-mist humidifier to keep the air moist.

1103. What is the effect of diet on resistance to colds? Naturally, every child should be offered a well-balanced diet. But there is no proof that a child who is already receiving a reasonable variety of foods will have fewer colds if given a little more of one kind of food or less of another.

Also, there is no proof that larger than normal doses of vitamin C will prevent colds.

1104. Age is a factor in resistance to colds. With more children in day care and preschool, children between four months and two years get more colds, have them longer, and experience more complications. (The average is seven colds a year in northern cities in the United States—more if there are children in the family attending school.) After the age of two or three years, the frequency and the severity grow less. Nine-year-olds are apt to be laid up only half as much as they were at six, and twelve-year-olds only half as much as at nine. This should comfort the parents of a small child who seems to be forever sick.

1105. The psychological factor in colds. There is evidence that certain children and grown-ups are more susceptible to colds when they are tense or unhappy. I think of a boy six years old who was nervous about school because he couldn't keep up with the class in reading. Every Monday morning for several months he had a cough. You may think he was putting it on. It wasn't so simple as that. It wasn't a dry, forced cough. It was a real, thick one. The cough would improve as the week went by, and by Friday it would be all gone, only to reappear again on Sunday night or Monday morning. There's nothing too mysterious about this. Scientists have learned that emotions and the immune system are closely linked. Stress appears to lower the body's immunity to infection by its effect on the white blood cells and other chemicals that ward off infections

1106. Exposure to other children. Another factor that influences the number of colds a child has is the number of children he plays with, especially indoors. The child living isolated on a farm has few colds because he is exposed to few cold viruses. The average child in preschool, day care, or elementary school, however, has plenty. People can give their infection to others for at least twenty-four hours before they begin to show signs of it themselves. At times they can carry the virus and pass it on to others without ever showing symptoms themselves.

1107. Can the spread of colds in a family be checked? Most colds that are brought into the home are caught by the younger children, at least in mild form, especially if the house is small and everyone has to use the same rooms. The viruses of colds and other infections get passed from one person to another in the spray of sneezes and coughs, so it's worthwhile for parents—especially those with a sore throat—to avoid sneezing, coughing, or breathing directly into their baby's or child's face. They should wash their hands with soap before handling things that will go into the baby's mouth to prevent the transfer of a large number of germs.

If an outsider has any hint of a cold or any other illness, be very firm about not letting the person in the same house as the baby or within a couple of yards of the carriage outside.

Ear Infections

1108. Ear infections are common in young children. Some children get ear infections with most of their colds; others never do. The ears are much more apt to be infected in the first three or four years of life. In fact, there is a slight inflammation of the middle ear in a majority of colds at this age, but it usually comes to nothing, and the child has no symptoms.

1109. What is an ear infection? An ear infection (*otitis media*) is an infection of the middle ear, caused by a bacteria or a virus. The middle ear is a small chamber, behind the eardrum, that connects to the back of the throat via a small channel called the Eustachian tube. When this tube is blocked for any reason—such as mucus from a cold or swelling from an allergy or enlarged adenoids—the fluid in the middle ear cannot drain into the back of the throat. Bacteria or viruses that are in the back of the throat then travel up the Eustachian tube and infect the stagnant fluid in the middle ear. Pus is formed, and the middle ear becomes inflamed and painful.

Usually the ear doesn't become inflamed enough to cause pain until after a cold has been going for several days. The child over two can tell you what is the matter. A baby may keep rubbing his ear, or he may just cry piercingly for several hours. He may or may not have fever.

Any time your child has an earache, you should get in touch with the doctor or nurse practitioner that same day, particularly if there is any fever. The antibiotics that are used when necessary work much better in the early stages of ear infections.

Suppose it will be several hours before you can reach the doctor. What can you do to relieve the pain? Lying down aggravates ear pain, so keep the child's head propped up. A hot-water bottle or an electric heating pad may help, but small children are often impatient with them. (Don't let a child fall asleep on a heating pad; this could result in a burn.) Acetaminophen or ibuprofen will relieve a certain amount of pain. Instilling warm (not hot) mineral oil into the ear may provide some relief. What will help even more, if you happen to have it on hand, is a dose of a cough medicine containing codeine that the doctor has prescribed for that particular child. (A medicine prescribed for an older child or adult might contain too much of the drug.) Codeine is an efficient painkiller as well as cough remedy. If the earache is severe, you can use all these remedies together, but never use more than one dose of the codeine cough medicine without talking to your doctor.

Once in a while an eardrum breaks very early in an infection and discharges a thin pus. You may find the discharge on the pillow in the morning without the child ever having complained of pain or fever. Usually, however, the drum breaks only after an abscess has been developing for several days, with fever and pain. Since the ear infection causes pressure on the eardrum, when it bursts the pain is much improved. The pus now has a way to drain and sometimes this in itself cures the infection. So a discharge of pus from the ear almost certainly means an ear infection, but it can also mean that the infection is on the road to recovery or will be easier to manage with antibiotics. The eardrum usually heals over nicely in just a few days and will not cause further problems.

In any case, if you find your child's ear discharging, the most that you should do is to tuck a loose plug of absorbent cotton into the opening to collect the pus, wash the pus off the outside of the ear with soap and water (don't put water into the ear canal), and get in touch with the doctor. If the discharge leaks out anyway and irritates the child's skin, gently wash the pus off the skin around the ear. Never insert a cotton swab into the ear canal.

1110. Chronic ear infections. Some children have repeated ear infections in the first years of life, with a resistant fluid accumulation behind the eardrum. Your doctor or nurse practitioner, especially if the ear infections are interfering with the child's hearing, may deal with this in one of three ways. First, she may prescribe an antibiotic to be taken on a daily basis, often for months. The purpose of the antibiotic is to prevent the fluid in the middle ear from becoming infected, even when it cannot drain out the Eustachian tube. This works quite well for some children, less well for others. Second, she may look for allergies that may cause fluid to remain in the ear and encourage infections. Finally, she may refer the child to an ear specialist who will consider inserting tiny plastic tubes through the eardrums. This allows the air pressure to be the same in the middle ear as in the outer canal, which may reduce the chances of further infection or accumulation of fluid, and return the child's hearing to normal.

Tonsils and Adenoids

The tonsils and adenoids are meant to be there unless they are causing trouble. Tonsils and adenoids have been blamed for so many things in the twentieth century that many people think of them as villains that have to be removed eventually, and the sooner the better. This is the wrong way to look at them. They are there for the purpose of helping to overcome infection and build up the body's resistance to germs.

The tonsils and adenoids are made of *lymphoid tissue,* and are similar to the glands in the sides of the neck, the armpits, and the groin. Any of these glands, including the tonsils and adenoids, become swollen when there is infection nearby, as they labor to kill germs and build resistance.

1111. The tonsils. In normal, healthy children, the tonsils gradually become larger until the age of eight and then gradually decrease in size. In former times it was believed that all very enlarged tonsils were diseased and should be removed. Nowadays it is understood that the size is unimportant. It is extremely rare that tonsils (or adenoids) need to be removed.

Frequent colds, sore throats, ear infections, and rheumatic fever are not reasons for tonsillectomy. There is no need to remove the tonsils, even when they are large, in a child who is perfectly healthy and has few nose and throat infections. There is no reason to operate because of feeding problems, stuttering, or nervousness; in fact, the operation may make the child worse. There are, however, three acceptable reasons for a tonsillectomy: severe recurrent streptococcal tonsillitis, severe obstruction from unusually enlarged tonsils and adenoids, and an abscess in the tonsils.

1112. The adenoids. The adenoids are clusters of lymphoid tissue up behind the soft palate, where the nose passages join the throat. When they become greatly enlarged they may block this passageway from the nose and cause mouth breathing and snoring. They may also prevent the free discharge of mucus and pus from the nose, and thus help to keep bad colds and sinus infections going. Or they may block the Eustachian tubes and lead to chronic ear infections. In previous times these conditions were usually considered reasons for immediate removal of the adenoids. Nowadays, however, they can often be successfully treated with antibiotics and do not require removal.

There is also a condition, called **obstructive sleep apnea,** in which the adenoids are so large that they obstruct the breathing passages when the child sleeps. Not only does he snore loudly, which is not dangerous, but there are periods when he cannot breathe through the passages at all. The parents hear a long pause (more than five seconds) in the child's snoring, during which he cannot move air past his throat. This condition often requires removal of the adenoids to ensure open breathing passages at night.

Removing the adenoids does not necessarily make a child breathe through his nose. Some children become mouth breathers out of habit (they seem to be born that way) and not because of obstruction. And some children's noses are obstructed not by adenoids but by swollen tissues in the front of the nose—for instance, by hay fever or other forms of allergy. Occasionally an ear specialist will remove the adenoids in a child with chronic or recurrent ear infections as a way to drain the ear through the Eustachian tube.

If the tonsils are removed, the adenoids are sometimes cut out, too, but there may be reason to take out the adenoids alone if they are causing persistent obstruction, and to leave the tonsils.

The adenoids always grow back to some extent, and the body always tries to grow new lumps of lymphoid tissue where the tonsils used to be. This isn't a sign that the operation was done incompletely or that it has to be done again. It shows only that the body means to have lymphoid tissue in that region and tries hard to replace it.

Sore Throat, Tonsillitis, and Swollen Glands

1113. A sore throat without inflamed tonsils is called *pharyngitis.* A sore throat with inflamed tonsils is called *tonsillitis.* The main concern with sore throats is to detect and treat promptly with antibiotic drugs those caused by the streptococcus bacteria. It's wise to call the doctor in *all* cases of sore throat, especially if there is a fever of greater than 101°F. The doctor will do a throat culture or a rapid test for streptococcus if there is any suspicion. When a streptococcal infection occurs, an antibiotic will be prescribed by your doctor.

If the doctor does a strep throat test and finds that the sore throat is caused not by streptococcus but by a virus, he won't have to use antibiotics. Instead, the child can be given acetaminophen, rest, and plenty of fluids.

1114. Strep throat. This is the common name for a throat infection caused by the streptococcus bacteria. The child usually has high fever for a number of days and feels sick. Headache and stomach pain are common. The tonsils often become fiery red and swollen. The glands in the neck are swollen and sometimes tender. After a day or two, white spots or white patches may appear on the tonsils. Older children may complain of such a sore throat that they can hardly swallow; others complain of a stomachache or headache. Young children may be bothered surprisingly little by the sore throat. Usually in strep throat there are no signs of an upper respiratory infection or a cough.

1115. Scarlet fever. This is a throat infection with a particular type of streptococcus that causes a rash. The rash typically appears a day or two after the child gets sick. It begins on the warm, moist parts of the body, such as the sides of the chest, the groin, and the back. From a distance, it looks like a uniform red flush, but if you look at it closely, you can see that it is made up of tiny repetitive red spots, which are prominent on a red background. If you run your hand over this rash, it feels like fine sandpaper. It may spread over the whole body and the sides of the face, but the region around the mouth stays pale. The throat is red, sometimes fiery red, and after a while the tongue usually gets red, first around the edge. While it looks more dramatic than an ordinary strep throat, scarlet fever is not any more dangerous. The treatment is the same as for any sore throat caused by streptococcus. In rare cases, a toxin producing scarlet fever may produce a rash called toxic shock.

An individual whose tonsils have been removed can still have streptococcal throat infections.

1116. Other kinds of sore throat. There are all kinds and degrees of throat infections, caused by a variety of germs, primarily viruses. Many people feel a slight sore throat at the beginning of every cold. Often the doctor, in examining a child with a fever, finds a slightly red throat as the only sign of disease. The child may or may not notice any soreness.

Most of these sore throats are soon over. The child should stay indoors if he feels sick or has a fever. The doctor should be called if there is any fever, if the child looks sick, or if the throat is more than slightly sore (even if there is no fever).

Some children awaken many winter mornings with sore throats. They otherwise act well, and the sore throat goes away shortly. This kind of sore throat is due to dry winter air, not illness, and is of no significance.

Runny, stuffy nose colds can also cause sore throats,

especially in the early morning, because the mucus can run down the back of the throat during the night, causing irritation.

1117. Swollen glands. The lymph glands, or nodes, that are scattered up and down the sides of the neck sometimes become sore and swollen as a result of any disease in the throat, mild or severe. Nodes aren't usually infected, as described here, but react to a nearby infection. Truly, infected nodes (*adenitis*) is not what I am describing here. The commonest cause of swollen glands is tonsillitis. The condition may develop in the middle of the tonsillitis or a week or two later. If the glands are swollen enough to be visible, or if there is fever of 101°F or more, the doctor should certainly be called. Treatment with antibiotics may be called for in certain cases and is most valuable if begun early.

Neck glands may remain slightly enlarged for weeks or even months after some throat infections. They can come from other causes, too, such as infected teeth, scalp infections, and general diseases, like rubella (German measles). You should consult your doctor about them. But if the doctor finds the child generally healthy, don't worry about slightly swollen glands.

Croup and Epiglottitis

1118. "Croup" is the word commonly used to denote various kinds of laryngitis in children. There is usually a hoarse, ringing, barking cough (croupy cough) and some tightness in the breathing, especially when the child breathes in. Croup is caused by a virus that inflames and swells the tissues below the vocal cords.

1119. Spasmodic croup without fever. This is usually a mild form of croup that comes on suddenly during the evening. The child may have been perfectly healthy during the day, or she may have had the mildest kind of cold without a cough, but suddenly she wakes up with a violent fit of croupy coughing, she's quite hoarse, and she has difficulty breathing. The child struggles and heaves to get breath in. *She has no fever.* Croup is quite a scary picture when you see it for the first time, but usually it's not so serious as it looks. It may recur several times in early childhood. You should call the doctor promptly for any kind of croup.

1120. Croup (*laryngotracheobronchitis*). This form of croup is usually accompanied by a viral cold and fever. It is characterized by a croupy cough, tight breathing, and a loud sound as the child breathes air in. This may come on gradually or suddenly at any time of the day or night. The cough sounds like a dog or seal barking. Steaming may help or only partly relieve it. A child who has a hoarse, croupy cough with fever, especially with tightness of breathing and rapid breathing, must be put under the close, continuous supervision of a doctor without delay. If you cannot reach your doctor right away, find another doctor. If you can't reach any doctor, take your child to a hospital.

The emergency treatment of croup, until the doctor can be reached, is moist air. Use a cold-mist humidifier if you have one. (See Section 1098 for other ways to humidify.) A small room is preferable because you can humidify it faster. You can also take the child into the bathroom and run very hot water into the tub—to make steam, *not* to put the child in. If there is a shower, that will work best of all. A twenty-minute steam in the bathroom with the child sitting upright in your lap and the door shut is the best first treatment.

Humidifier or vaporizer steam works much better if it's concentrated in a makeshift tent. You can make a tent by draping sheets over a crib or over a small table placed on the bed, or you can tack them on the wall. When the child breathes the moist air, the croup will usually begin to improve rapidly. However, croup is made worse by an anxious child. If the makeshift tent is frightening to the child, it's better not to use it. You or another adult should stay awake as long as there are any symptoms of croup, and wake up two or three hours after the croup is over to make sure the child is breathing comfortably.

Spasmodic croup and viral croup sometimes come back the next night or two. To avoid this, have the child sleep in a room in which the air has been moistened, for three nights.

1121. Epiglottitis. This is an infection that sometimes looks like a severe croup with fever. The inflammation of the epiglottis (the trapdoor that covers the windpipe when you swallow food) is caused by the *Haemophilus influenzae* bacteria (and is often called H flu). A child with H flu epiglottitis usually becomes ill very quickly, appears very sick, leans forward, and is very unwilling to turn his head in any direction. He drools, refuses to take any food or liquids, and will usually make no sounds at all for fear of provoking a typical croupy cough. The reason for his refusal to turn his head is that he's keeping his neck in the position that gives him the most room for air to pass between the swollen epiglottis and the windpipe. Epiglottitis is a true medical emergency, and everything must be done to get the child to a doctor or hospital as quickly as possible. Fortunately, this life-threatening problem is rarely seen in children who have been immunized against the H flu bacteria.

Influenza, Bronchitis, and Pneumonia

1122. Influenza. The flu can be a miserable illness, with headache, sore throat, fever, muscle aches, cough, and running nose, and sometimes there is vomiting or diarrhea. Occasionally there is such severe pain in the calf muscles that the child is reluctant to walk. Fever can last a week or so, the cough even longer.

A person can come down with the flu just a few days after being exposed to it; usually symptoms start five to seven days after exposure. She will be contagious even before she begins to feel sick and will remain contagious until the fever is gone. This is why the illness spreads so rapidly.

Flu vaccines are available, but because of the way the virus changes, new vaccines must be made each year to keep up. Ask your doctor if you or your child would benefit from a flu shot. Children with asthma and other chronic lung conditions, heart disease, diabetes, and some neurological disorders should have the flu vaccine each year.

The treatment for influenza is to keep the child comfortable: have her rest at home until her temperature remains normal for twenty-four hours; offer fluids that appeal to the child every hour or even half hour, but do not force them;

and give her acetaminophen or ibuprofen for the fever and aches. (Don't give aspirin to children or teenagers with the flu; it increases their susceptibility to Reye's syndrome.)

The doctor should be called at the onset and again if the child seems unusually ill, has an earache or trouble breathing, or isn't getting better after several days. Ear infections, sinusitis, or pneumonia can follow influenza as secondary infections, and need treatment with antibiotics.

1123. Bronchitis. There are all degrees of bronchitis, from very mild with no fever to severe. Bronchitis simply means that a cold has spread down to the bronchial tubes. There is usually plenty of coughing. Sometimes a child seems short of breath. At times you can hear faraway squeaky noises as the child breathes. Parents worry when they think they hear mucus vibrating in the chest. Actually, the mucus is in the throat, and the noise it makes is transmitted to the chest, so this is no cause for concern.

A very mild bronchitis, without fever, without much cough, without loss of appetite, is only a little more serious than a nose cold. However, if the child acts sick, coughs frequently, is short of breath, or has a fever of more than 101°F, the doctor or nurse practitioner should be reached that same day, because medications are of great benefit in cases that require them.

1124. Pneumonia. Pneumonia is an infection, bacterial or viral, in the lungs themselves. Bacterial pneumonia usually comes on after a child has had a cold for several days, but it may start without any previous warning. You suspect it when the temperature climbs above 102°F, the breathing becomes rapid, and there is a frequent cough. Antibiotics bring about a prompt cure of the bacterial types of pneumonia if treatment is started early. Naturally, you should call the doctor if your child develops a fever and frequent cough.

More common are viral pneumonias, which many people call walking pneumonias. These pneumonias, though they are unresponsive to antibiotics, are often treated with them anyway, because a couple of them are hard to distinguish from bacterial pneumonia. Generally, the child is less sick, though the disease may last a long time. The usual picture is a slow but continuous improvement over a two- to four-week period.

1125. Bronchiolitis. Bronchiolitis is an inflammation by a virus of the small respiratory passages near the lungs (bronchioles). It is a wheezing respiratory illness that affects infants and toddlers, usually two to twenty-four months of age. Usually the baby has a cold in addition to a cough and wheezing. The infant usually breathes fast and works harder than normal to breathe out. Bronchiolitis can be mild or severe. Some babies become very short of breath and have to work very hard to breathe. They cannot comfortably eat or rest and become exhausted from the physical exertion. Although most babies with bronchiolitis do well and can be treated at home, about one in twenty will require hospitalization to carefully monitor the breathing status. There is a new antiviral medication that can sometimes help in cases of serious infection, but it can only be given in the hospital. There is also a serum to prevent this illness in high-risk babies; it needs to be given once a month.

Because bronchiolitis can occasionally lead to significant respiratory problems, it is important to contact your doctor or nurse practitioner so she can help you monitor your baby's symptoms. Most babies are better within seven to ten days, but a few babies may then wheeze with later colds.

Headaches

1126. Headaches are common among children and teenagers. Though a headache can be an early sign of a wide variety of illnesses ranging from the common cold to more serious infections, the most frequent cause by far is stress. Think of the child who's been memorizing for days a part for the school play, or the child who's been practicing extra hours after school for the gymnastics team. Often fatigue and tension and anticipation combine to produce real changes in the blood flow to the muscles of the head and neck, causing a headache.

When a small child complains of a headache, it's best to

call the doctor promptly, because it's more likely at this age that the headache is an early symptom of an oncoming illness. Older children and adolescents who have a headache can be given the appropriate dose of acetaminophen or ibuprofen, followed by a rest period—lying down, playing quietly, or engaging in another restful activity—until the medicine starts to work. Sometimes an ice pack helps. If a headache lasts as long as four hours after the child has taken a medication, or if other symptoms of illness (such as fever) develop, the doctor or nurse practitioner should be called.

A child who has frequent headaches should have a thorough physical examination, including a check of his vision. In such cases, it's worth considering whether something in the child's home life, school, or social activities may be causing undue stress. Headaches that are one-sided, or associated with visual lights or weakness of an extremity may be migraine.

If a headache comes on after a fall or a blow to the head, get in touch with the doctor promptly. Headaches in the morning or on rising, or that awaken a child at night, are usually serious.

Discuss with your doctor any recurrent early-morning headaches and any headaches associated with dizziness, blurred or double vision, nausea and vomiting.

Stomachaches and Upsets

1127. You certainly should get in touch with the doctor for any stomachache that lasts as long as an hour, whether it is severe or not. There are dozens of causes. A few of them are serious; most are not. A doctor or nurse practitioner is trained to distinguish among them and prescribe the right treatment. People are apt to jump to the conclusion that a stomachache is due either to appendicitis or to something that the child ate. Actually, neither of these is a common cause. Children can usually eat strange foods or an unusual amount of a regular food without any indigestion.

Before you call the doctor, take the child's temperature so that you can report what it is. The treatment, until you reach the doctor, should consist of putting the child to bed and giving him nothing to eat. If the child is thirsty, give him small sips of water.

1128. Common causes of stomachache. In the early weeks of life, stomachache is common in colic and indigestion (see Sections 321 and 337). When an infant appears to have a stomachache and is irritable or vomiting, your doctor should be called immediately.

After the age of a year, one of the commonest causes of stomachache is the onset of a simple cold, or sore throat, or flu, especially when there is fever. The stomachache is just a sign that the infection is disturbing the intestines as well as other parts of the body. In the same way, almost any infection may cause vomiting and constipation, especially in the beginning. A small child is apt to complain that her tummy hurts when she really means that she feels nauseated. She often vomits soon after this complaint.

1129. Constipation is a common cause of abdominal pain. It may be dull and may recur or it may be sudden and very painful (though it may go away just as suddenly). The pain is often worse after a meal. It may occur when a toddler is withholding stool during potty training (see Section 753). Constipation is also seen in older children when fluid intake is decreased or when activities allow the child to "forget" to go to the bathroom.

Many different stomach and intestinal infections can cause stomachache, sometimes with vomiting, sometimes with diarrhea, sometimes with both. The medical term for these is *acute gastroenteritis.* They are often called "stomach flu" or "intestinal flu," meaning a contagious disease caused by an unknown virus or bacteria. These infections often pass through several members of a family, one after the other. There may or may not be fever with any of them.

1130. Food poisoning is caused by eating food that contains toxins manufactured by certain bacteria. The food may or may not taste unusual. Food poisoning seldom occurs from food that has been thoroughly and recently cooked, because the cooking kills these germs. It's caused most often by pastries filled with custard or whipped cream, creamy salads, and poultry stuffing. Bacteria multiply readily in these substances if they remain out of the refrigerator for many hours. Another cause is improperly home-canned foods.

The symptoms of food poisoning are usually vomiting, diarrhea, and stomachache. Sometimes there are chills and sometimes fever. Everyone who eats the contaminated food is apt to be affected by it to some degree at about the same time, in contrast to an intestinal flu, which usually spreads through a family over a number of days. The doctor should always be called when you suspect food poisoning.

1131. Children with feeding problems often complain of stomachaches when they sit down to a meal or after they have eaten a little. The parents are apt to think the child has made up the stomachache as an excuse not to eat. I think that it's more likely that the poor stomach is all tightened up by the child's tense feeling at mealtimes, and that the stomachache is real. The treatment here is for the parents to handle mealtimes in such a way that the child enjoys the food. (See Sections 560 and 563.)

Other infrequent causes of stomachache are chronic indigestion with gas, intestinal allergies, inflamed lymph glands in the abdomen, and kidney disturbances. As you can well see, a child who has stomach pains—whether they are acute and severe or mild and chronic—needs a thorough checkup by the doctor.

1132. Dehydration can follow vomiting or diarrhea. Dehydration (excessive loss of body water) can be a result of either vomiting or diarrhea, or especially when the two problems occur together. It is most often seen in babies or very young children, because they don't have as much reserve body water as older children and adults, and because they can't understand the need to make themselves drink extra fluids when they're sick.

These are some signs of dehydration that you can watch for: urination less than every six to eight hours; his eyes look dry, and there may be no tears when he cries; his eyes may look sunken and shadowed; his lips and mouth look parched and dry; and in a baby, the soft spot on the top of the head appears sunken. If your child begins to show any signs of dehydration, get him to a doctor or to a hospital as soon as possible.

1133. Mood disturbances can cause stomachaches. Children who have never had feeding problems but who have other worries can have stomachaches, too, especially around mealtime. Think of the child who is nervous about starting school in the fall and has a stomachache instead of an appetite for breakfast, or the child who feels guilty about something that hasn't been found out yet. All kinds of emotions, from fear to pleasant excitement, can affect the stomach and intestines. They can cause not only pains and lack of appetite but also vomiting and diarrhea or constipation. Pain in such cases tends to be in the center of the abdomen. Since there's no infection, the child won't have fever.

This type of stomachache is common among children and teenagers and often follows a pattern of recurring two or three times a week or more. The pain is almost always in the midline, either around or just above the belly button. It is often hard for the child to describe.

Treatment involves identifying the stresses at home, at school, in sports, and in the child's social life, and then doing whatever is necessary to reduce them. Doctors have studied this condition, which they call recurrent abdominal pain syndrome. It's very important to realize that the pain experienced by these children is real pain and is not "all in the child's head" or "just to get attention."

1134. Appendicitis. Let me at the start contradict some common notions about appendicitis: There isn't necessarily any fever. The pain isn't necessarily severe. The pain doesn't usually settle in the lower right side of the abdomen until the attack has been going on for some time. Vomiting doesn't always occur, though loss of appetite is quite characteristic. A blood count doesn't prove that a stomachache is or isn't due to appendicitis.

The appendix is a little offshoot from the large intestine, about the size of a short earthworm. It usually lies in the central part of the right lower quarter of the abdomen. But it can be lower down, over toward the middle of the abdomen, or as far up as the ribs. When it becomes inflamed, it's a gradual process, like the formation of a boil. That's how you know that a sudden severe pain in the abdomen that lasts a few minutes and then goes away for good isn't appendicitis. The worst danger is that the inflamed appendix will burst, very much as a boil bursts, and spread the infection all through the abdomen. The condition that ensues is called peritonitis. Appendicitis that is developing very rapidly can reach the point of bursting in less than twenty-four hours. That's why any stomachache that persists for as long as an hour should be discussed with the doctor, even though nine out of ten cases will prove to be something else.

In the most typical cases of appendicitis, there is pain around the navel for several hours. Only later does it shift to the lower right side. There is apt to be vomiting once or twice, but it doesn't always occur. The appetite is usually diminished, but not always. The bowels may be normal or constipated, but they are rarely loose. After this has gone on for a few hours, the child's temperature is apt to be mildly elevated, but it's possible to have appendicitis without any fever at all. The child may feel pain when he pulls his right knee up, when he stretches it way back, or when he walks around.

You can see that the symptoms of appendicitis vary a lot in different cases and that you need a doctor to make the diagnosis. When doctors find a tender spot in the right side of the abdomen, they are suspicious of appendicitis, but sometimes they like to have a blood count to help them decide. An ultrasound may aid in the diagnosis.

It's sometimes impossible for even the most expert doctors to be absolutely certain that a child has appendicitis. When there is enough suspicion, however, an operation is usually performed. That is because if it *is* appendicitis, it is dangerous to delay surgery because the appendix could burst and cause an infection in the abdomen. If it is not appendicitis, it is unlikely that any harm will have been done.

1135. Intussusception. In this uncommon condition the intestine telescopes into itself and becomes obstructed. The two most prominent symptoms are vomiting and intermittent abdominal cramps in a baby who has seemed otherwise healthy. In one case the vomiting is more prominent; in another the pain is. The vomiting is more copious and repetitious than the usual spitting up of a baby. The cramps are sudden and usually severe. They come minutes apart, and between them the baby may be fairly comfortable or sleepy. After a number of hours (during which there may be normal or loose movements) the baby may pass a movement containing mucus and blood—the classic "currant jelly" or "prune juice" stool; but more often than not, this does not occur. This condition occurs most commonly between four and twenty-four months of age, though it may occur outside this age period. Though uncommon, intussusception requires emergency medical treatment without delay.

Also rare but serious are other types of **intestinal obstructions.** A part of the intestine gets kinked and stuck in a pocket in the abdomen, most frequently in an inguinal hernia (Section 1180). There is usually vomiting as well as sharp cramps.

1136. Chronic diarrheas. The most common type of chronic diarrhea occurs in a young child who is obviously thriving and not complaining of feeling sick. The diarrhea may begin spontaneously or with a stomach flu. The child may have three to five soft or runny and smelly bowel movements a day, though he may begin the day with a normal bowel movement. There may be mucus or undigested food in the bowel movements. His appetite remains good and he is playful and active. It is important to check with the doctor, but in this situation the child continues to gain weight normally and laboratory tests of the bowel movement reveal nothing abnormal. Usually the condition gradually gets better by itself. Often the diarrhea can be much improved by cutting down on juice in the child's diet. The single most likely culprit is apple juice. That's why this condition is sometimes called apple juice diarrhea or toddler diarrhea. In general, juice should be limited to 8 to 10 ounces a day.

There are several uncommon but more serious digestive diseases that cause chronic diarrhea in infants and young children:

1137. Cystic fibrosis. The two most common symptoms of this disease are foul-smelling diarrhea and a cough—but there is great variation in the other symptoms. In early infancy there may be frequent bowel movements that look normal but become mushy, greasy, and foul-smelling after solid foods are introduced. The rectum may protrude. The intestines may be obstructed right after birth by dry meconium and off and on again in later years by hard, dry bowel movements. Most infants have a good or even ravenous appetite in this disease. Nevertheless, malnutrition with poor growth sets in because of the inability to digest food properly. Persistent bronchitis develops, but this may not happen until later in childhood in a mild case.

This is a progressive, hereditary disease of certain glands, inherited from both sides of the family. The pancreas secretes insufficient digestive juices. The glands along the bronchial tubes secrete only dry mucus, in insufficient amounts, so infections can't be adequately prevented or coped with. The sweat glands put out too much salt. (A salt test is used in diagnosis.) In severe cases, without treatment, the greatest danger in infancy and early childhood comes from respiratory infections.

The primary aim of treatment is to keep the bronchial tubes cleared out with postural drainage (a type of firm, rhythmic massage for the chest) and antibiotic drugs as needed. The digestive symptoms are treated with a high protein, moderate-fat diet, by providing additional vitamins, and by adding pancreatic enzymes to the meals.

The child should be evaluated and have his treatment supervised at a special center for cystic fibrosis if at all possible. The national organization is Cystic Fibrosis Foundation, 6931 Arlington Road, Bethesda, MD 20814. Call 800-FIGHT CF.

1138. Other malabsorption conditions exist, the most common being the inability to digest certain sugars or the gluten in wheat. With this condition there is always diarrhea, sometimes foul-smelling, sometimes burning, often with cramps. Usually the child gains weight poorly and seems unwell. The condition resolves when the offending food is removed from the diet. It is important for you to work with your doctor to make sure the child's diet is still adequate nutritionally.

Following any prolonged diarrhea, a child may have a problem in digesting lactose, the sugar in milk. In the past these children were said to be allergic to milk. The problem is usually temporary. It is felt that the irritated lining of the intestines simply needs time to heal before normal digestion returns. A problem with the digestion of lactose in cow's milk may be inherited. Cramps or diarrhea usually start in school-age children. Elimination of cow's-milk products is the treatment.

1139. Worms are no disgrace, but need treatment. It horrifies parents to find worms in their child's movement, but there is no reason to be distressed or to decide that the child has not been properly cared for.

Pinworms, or **threadworms,** are the commonest variety. They look like white threads a third of an inch long. They live in the lower intestine but come out between the buttocks at night to lay their eggs. They can be found there at night or in the bowel movement. They cause itching around the anus, which may disturb the child's sleep. (In earlier times worms were thought to be the chief cause of children's grinding their teeth at night, but this is not so.) A clear description of the worm helps your doctor make the diagnosis. There is an efficient and simple treatment for pinworms, which a doctor or nurse practitioner should supervise.

Roundworms look very much like earthworms. The first suspicion comes when one is discovered in the bowel movement. They usually don't cause symptoms unless the child has a great number of them.

Hookworms are common in some parts of the southern United States. They may cause malnutrition and anemia. The disease is contracted by going barefoot in soil that is infested.

Constipation

Generally speaking, constipation refers to hard, dry stools, which are difficult to pass. It's not the number of bowel movements each day that determines whether or not a baby or child (or adult) has constipation.

1140. Temporary constipation is common during illness, especially if there is fever. In former days parents and doctors often felt that the fever was the most important symptom to treat and that children couldn't begin to recover until they were "cleaned out." Some people even believed that the constipation was the main cause of the illness. It's more sensible to realize that any disease that can make a person feel sick all over is apt to affect the entire stomach and intestinal system, slowing down the bowels, taking away the appetite, perhaps causing vomiting. These symptoms may appear several hours before any others. If you are delayed in reaching a doctor, you needn't feel that valuable time is being lost.

If you have to treat a sick child without a doctor, don't worry too much about the bowels. It's better to do too little than too much. If a child isn't eating anything, there isn't much for the bowels to move. Fluids can be offered frequently.

1141. Chronic constipation is not common in the older baby or child, especially those who eat a varied diet including whole grain cereals, vegetables, and fruits. If your child becomes constipated, talk about it with the doctor—don't try to treat the condition yourself, because you aren't sure what it is due to. It's very important, whatever treatment you use, that you do not get children concerned about their bowel function. Don't get into serious conversations about it with them, and don't connect their bowel function with germs or their health or how they feel. Don't encourage them to keep track of their movements or pay too much obvious attention to them yourself. Avoid giving enemas. Do what the doctor or nurse practitioner recommends as matter-of-factly, cheerfully, and briefly as possible, whether it's diet, medication, or exercise, and don't discuss the details with the child. You don't want to turn him into a hypochondriac.

But suppose you are unable to consult a doctor, and your little boy, otherwise healthy, gradually gets into a spell of constipation. (Naturally, if there is any symptom of illness, you must get your baby to the doctor or hospital somehow.) Give him more fruits or vegetables, if he likes either, two or three times a day. If he likes prunes or figs, serve them every day. Fruit and vegetable juices help, too. I've had good success with a slurry of applesauce, bran, and prune juice. Most children love the sweet taste and it works well. See that he has plenty of exercise. If he is four or five or older and, in spite of your efforts with diet, continues to have rather constipated and irregular movements that don't hurt him, relax until you can get a doctor's help.

Mineral oil is not considered safe for a child under three. If he chokes on it, he may inhale some into his lungs and possibly cause a chronic kind of pneumonia.

1142. Psychological constipation. There are two varieties of constipation that are largely psychological in origin and that start most frequently between age one and age two. If children at this age have one or two painfully hard movements, they may tend to hold back for weeks or even months afterward for fear of being hurt again. If they hold the movement in for a day or two, it's apt to be hard again, and this keeps the problem going. Occasionally when a parent goes at toilet training in too overbearing a manner, small children, being at an independent stage in their development, automatically resist and hold the movement back, which leads to constipation. (For a discussion of soiling due to constipation, see Section 813.)

1143. Painful movements and BM softeners. Painfully hard movements should be treated promptly in a child of one, two, or three years, to avoid the vicious circle of withholding and further constipation. Your doctor can recommend one of several preparations that will keep the movements soft. Treatment usually lasts for at least a month, to allow the child to become confident that the painful hardness will not recur. None of these preparations will act as a cathartic to soften and hurry an already hard movement. (A cathartic is a medicine that makes the intestinal muscles contract and cause a bowel movement. It should be used only when your doctor prescribes it.)

Genital and Urinary Disturbances

1144. Frequent urinating. Frequent urinating has several possible causes. When it develops in a child who was not frequent before, it may indicate some disease, such as an infection of the urinary system or diabetes. The child and a urine specimen should be examined promptly by the doctor.

A few individuals, even calm ones, seem to have bladders that never hold as much as the average, and this may be the way they were made. But some of the children (and adults, too) who regularly have to urinate frequently are somewhat high-strung or worried. In one case it's due to a temporary strain; in another it's a chronic tendency. Even the healthy, normal athlete is apt to have to go to the toilet every fifteen minutes just before a race.

The parents' job, then, is to find out what, if anything, is making the child tense. In one case it's the handling at home, in another it's relations with other children, in still another it's the child's school situation. Most often it's a combination of these. A common story involves the timid child and the teacher who seems severe. To begin with, the child's apprehensiveness keeps his bladder from relaxing sufficiently to hold much urine. Then he worries about asking permission to be excused. If the teacher makes a fuss about his leaving the room, it's worse still. It's wise to get a note from the doctor, not simply requesting that the child be excused but also explaining the child's nature and why his bladder works that way. If the teacher is approachable and the parent is tactful, a personal visit will help, too.

Occasionally in hot weather, when a child is perspiring a great deal and not drinking enough, he may pass his urine infrequently, perhaps not for eight hours or more. What does come is scanty and dark. The same thing may happen during a fever. A child in hot weather or when feverish needs plenty of chances and occasional reminders to drink between meals, especially when he is too small to tell his parents what he wants.

A fairly frequent cause of painful urination in girls is an inflammation of the area around the urinary opening, perhaps from some contamination with BM or irritation by bubble bath in the tub. This may make her feel as if she has to urinate frequently, though she may be unable or too scared to do anything, or she passes only a few drops. The doctor should be consulted and a urine specimen examined, to make sure the child has no bladder infection. Until then, she can be relieved by sitting several times a day in a shallow warm bath to which you have added a half cup of bicarbonate of soda. After the bath, gently blot dry the urinary region.

1145. Sore on the end of the penis. Sometimes a small raw area appears around the opening, or meatus, of the penis. There may be enough swelling of the tissues here to close up part of the meatus and make it difficult for the boy to pass his urine. This little sore is a localized diaper rash. The best treatment is to expose the sore to the air as much as is practical. Bathing daily with a mild soap will encourage healing. If the child is in pain from being unable to urinate for many hours, he can sit in a warm bath for half an hour and be encouraged to urinate while in the tub. If this doesn't make him urinate, the doctor should be called.

1146. Infections of the urinary tract. Infections in the kidneys or the bladder (cystitis) may cause a stormy illness with a high, irregular fever. On the other hand, most urinary tract infections are mild without a high fever. An older child may complain of frequent, burning urination, but most often there are no signs pointing to the urinary tract. These infections are more common in girls and in the first two years of life. Prompt medical treatment is necessary.

If there is a lot of pus, the urine may be hazy or cloudy, but a little may not show to the naked eye. Infected urine also smells somewhat like a bowel movement. On the other hand, a normal child's urine may be cloudy, especially when it cools, due to ordinary minerals in it. So you can't tell definitely from looking at the urine whether it is infected or not; your sense of smell is more reliable. Regardless of the color or odor of the urine, if your child complains of burning or pain when urinating, you should take her to the doctor. A urine culture is essential to make the diagnosis and to select the antibiotic.

In all cases of infection, the child's whole urinary system should be investigated thoroughly with special examinations. An ultrasound is not invasive and does not call for X-rays. Many doctors now recommend these studies after the first urinary tract infection. Urinary infections are more common in children who have abnormally formed urinary passages, although most children with urinary tract infections have perfectly normal urinary systems. If there is anything pointing to such an abnormality, it should be corrected before permanent harm is done to the kidneys. For this reason it is wise, after a child has had a urinary infection, for the doctor to check her urine again one or two months later to make sure the infection has not come back, even though she appears well. Infections are usually treated carefully for ten to fourteen days. Then there are several follow-up examinations over a period of time to see whether pus or bacteria has reappeared in the urine.

It's very important to teach girls to wipe themselves from front to back, after they urinate or have a bowel movement. This prevents the transfer of germs from the anal region into the opening of the urethra (the tube between the bladder and the outside world). Wiping from back to front ("wiping up") is considered a frequent cause of repeated urinary tract infections in girls.

1147. Pus in a girl's urine may not mean urinary infection. Pus can also come from a vaginal infection, even one so mild that there is no visible inflammation or discharge. For this reason it should never be assumed, without further investigation, that pus in an ordinary specimen means an infection of her urinary system. The first step is to secure a "clean" urine specimen. That means to separate the labia, sponge the genital region briefly and gently with a piece of wet absorbent cotton, and blot dry with a soft towel or a piece of dry absorbent cotton, before letting her pass urine for the specimen. The important test is the culture of the specimen to see whether there are bacteria and which type they are. A urine culture needs to be performed in a sterile manner.

Vaginal Discharge

1148. Treat the child considerately. It is fairly common for young girls to develop a slight vaginal discharge. A majority of these are caused by unimportant germs and clear up in a short time. However, a thick, profuse discharge that is irritating may be caused by a more serious infection and needs prompt medical treatment. A mild discharge that persists for days should be examined, too. A discharge that is partly pus and partly blood is sometimes caused by a small girl's having pushed some object into her vagina. If the object remains there, it can cause irritation and infection. If this is found to be the case, it is natural and sensible for her parents to ask her to please not do this again; but it's better not to make the girl feel really guilty or to imply that she might have hurt herself seriously. The exploring and experimenting she has done are not too different from what most children do at this age.

If there is delay in reaching the doctor, the burning sensation from a slight discharge can often be relieved without fuss by sitting the child twice a day in a shallow bath to which half a cup of bicarbonate of soda has been added.

Wearing white cotton panties, using unperfumed white toilet paper, and wearing clothes that provide adequate air ventilation to the vaginal area may help in the prevention and treatment of vaginal irritation. Proper wiping (from front to back) and avoiding bubble baths may also help.

A recurrent chronic or severe vaginal discharge in a child

may be a sign of sexual abuse. Your doctor may ask you questions about your child's caretakers and the possibility of abuse. A careful examination of the vagina and a culture of the discharge will be performed. Most young girls with a vaginal discharge have not been sexually abused. Your doctor may raise this issue as part of a complete examination.

Allergies

1149. Milk allergy and special formulas. Milk allergy is a lot less common than most people think it is. Young babies have many stomach complaints, but most are due to their immaturity rather than to allergy. Truly allergic babies tend to have classic allergic symptoms (see Sections 1150–1154) and to come from allergic families. Breast-feeding is ideal for babies from allergic families, but for babies already on formula who are having intestinal troubles, you and your doctor or nurse practitioner may want to consider switching formulas. Your doctor is most likely to recommend a more specialized formula based on your baby's special problems. To establish presence of allergy, after it subsides, the child should be challenged with small amounts of milk to see if it recurs. By one or two years of age, almost all babies should avoid any dairy products (see Section 547).

1150. Allergic nose troubles, including hay fever. You probably know some people who have ragweed hay fever. When ragweed pollen (found in the eastern part of the United States) gets in the wind in mid-August, these people start to sneeze and their noses begin to be stuffed up and itch and run. This means that the nose is allergic, or oversensitive, to the pollen, which doesn't bother other people at all. Some people have hay fever in spring because they are allergic to certain tree pollens. If your child develops a running itching nose that lasts for weeks, at the same time every year, you should consult your doctor or nurse practitioner. From the appearance of the inside of the nose, the type of symptoms after specific exposures in the environment, and your family history, he can tell what the child is allergic to. Liquid medicines or tablets, and nasal sprays are effective in eliminating the sneezing and congestion. Your doctor will prescribe these medicines for your child. In the most severe cases of hay fever, allergy injections may be recommended.

Other nose allergies may be less dramatic but more troublesome than hay fever. There are noses that are sensitive to the feathers in pillows or to dog hair, house dust, or any number of other substances. Such year-round allergies may keep a child stuffy or running at the nose, breathing through the mouth, month in and month out. The chronic obstruction may make an allergic child more susceptible to sinus infections. If your child is much bothered this way, your doctor or an allergy specialist may be able to find the cause.

The treatment is different in each case and depends on the causes. If the cause is goose feathers, you can change the pillow. If it's dog hair, you may have to give away the dog and substitute some other pet. If it's something hard to avoid, like house dust, the doctor may give your child injections of the offending substance over a long period. Stripping the room—especially the bedroom—may be recommended to lessen exposure to the dust and mites, especially if the symptoms occur mainly at night or first thing in the morning. You remove the rugs and curtains for good and give the room a wet-mopping every day. You eliminate all wool from the room and also the stuffed toys. You may buy dust-proof coverings for the mattress and pillow, use a mattress and pillows of foam rubber, or use a canvas cot with no pillow at all.

Allergy symptoms usually can't be eliminated completely. You have to be satisfied with partial improvement.

1151. Asthma. Asthma is responsible for a tremendous number of missed school days and hospitalizations of children. Instead of the sensitive organ being the nose, as in hay fever, it is the small bronchial tubes in the lungs. When the irritating substance reaches the small airways, they swell, thick mucus is secreted, and the passageways for air narrow. Breathing becomes difficult, labored, and noisy, especially expiration. When air is forced through the narrowed breathing passages, it makes a whistling sound, known as wheezing. Coughing occurs, and sometimes may even occur in the absence of wheezing (most commonly as a nighttime cough).

In those children whose airways are susceptible, an asthma attack is usually an overreaction to a variety of conditions and substances, including cigarette smoke, colds and respiratory infections, allergies, exercise, changes in the weather, stress, and specific foods. Some children have many triggers, while others react only to a single trigger. It is very important for you as a parent to try to identify your child's triggers. However, that is often impossible.

When an older child has chronic asthma, it's apt to be due to substances that float in the air, such as house dust and mites, horse dander, dog hair, or molds. Allergists call these inhalants. Foods can also play a part, especially in very young children. The child who has chronic asthma of more than slight degree is usually tested in an attempt to discover the offending substances. If the disease is neglected, the repeated attacks may harm the child's lungs; however, asthma can be very well managed with medicines and avoiding known triggers.

The treatment of asthma depends on the cause and is different in each case. Foods to which the child is sensitive are simply eliminated from his diet. When inhalants are the cause, the treatment is much the same as in year-round allergies of the nose. Episodes of asthma may be precipitated by an upper respiratory infection. Once an attack starts, additional asthma-specific medicines or inhalers are used.

If your child develops asthma, you need for her to see a doctor or nurse practioner. Although asthma is usually not dangerous, prompt diagnosis and treatment are essential. It is impossible to make predictions about asthma. Cases that start early in childhood are more apt to clear up in a few years than those that start later. Some cases go away after puberty; others continue through adolescence into adulthood.

The treatment of an individual attack of asthma depends a lot on how severe it is and on what the doctor finds helpful for that case. The best treatments are generally those that are inhaled in a mist form (*nebulized*) and recommended for prevention of attacks. Others are given by mouth or by injection for temporary relief when the child is having real difficulty breathing. Additionally, there is an inhaled medicine designed to prevent attacks that is given daily to children with asthma.

No children should be exposed to secondhand smoke, but it is especially important that children with asthma not be exposed, because the smoke irritates their sensitive bronchi.

A child who has recurring frequent episodes of asthma should be on a continuous preventive medication program. This consists of an inhaled drug to prevent the inflammation of the bronchial tube lining and, in some cases, another inhaled drug to prevent bronchospasm.

In the first two or three years of life, a child may have spells of wheezing and difficult breathing, not in response to an allergic or irritating trigger, but only when he has a real cold. Although this tendency is the most common in the first three years of life, it may remain a factor as the child grows older. It's discouraging to have a baby who regularly has this much trouble with colds, but there is a brighter side to the picture. The tendency to wheezing with colds, also known as reactive airway disease, is usually well on its way to disappearing. The doctor or nurse practitioner should be called, of course. Most of the infections that cause a cold are due to a virus; less common are bacterial infections that may require treatment. If the house is heated, it may help to get extra moisture in the air. There is a specific virus (RSV) that produces in infants acute infection of smaller bronchi causing wheezing (see Section 1125).

1152. Hives. Hives are considered, at least in most cases, to be due to an allergy, often to a medicine or a food. The most common kind of hive looks like a mosquito bite with raised red welts and a pale spot in the middle, where the blood has been pressed out by the swelling. They come and go and they itch, sometimes unbearably. A few individuals get hives repeatedly. But many people have them only once or twice in a lifetime. They are occasionally found to be caused by sensitivity to certain food. They can also come from some medicines, and they may appear at the end of certain infections. In many cases the cause cannot be discovered. The doctor can usually relieve an attack of hives with pills or an injection.

On very rare occasions, hives are accompanied by swelling of the inside of the mouth and throat, and difficulty breathing (*anaphylaxis*). If this happens, you should call an ambulance immediately. This can be a medical emergency.

1153. Eczema. Eczema is a rough, red rash that comes in patches. It's always associated with very dry skin. The resultant itching and scratching cause many of the problems of eczema. Like hay fever and asthma it is caused by allergy. In hay fever the nose is allergic (sensitive) to a pollen, like ragweed; in eczema the skin may be allergic to some food in the diet. When that food gets into the blood and reaches the skin, the skin becomes inflamed. In another case the skin may be allergic to a material, like wool, silk, or rabbit's hair, that comes in direct contact with the skin. A baby who has relatives with asthma, hay fever, hives, or eczema is more likely to have eczema.

Even when eczema is primarily due to a food allergy irritation of the skin from the outside may play a secondary part. One baby has eczema only when the skin is irritated by cold weather, another only in hot weather from the irritation of perspiration, and still another only in the diaper region from the irritation of the urine. If a baby has eczema only where wool comes in contact with his skin, he may be allergic to wool directly, or perhaps he is allergic to some food and the wool merely acts as an irritant.

In older children with a family history, emotional factors may play a role in producing eczema, and emotional stress may make the rash worse from time to time.

You need a doctor or nurse practitioner to diagnose and treat the condition. The easiest eczema to describe is the kind that comes in patches of rough, red, thick, scaly skin. When eczema is mild or just starting, the color is apt to be a light red or tannish pink, but if the condition becomes severe, it turns a deeper red, usually itches, and the child scratches and rubs it. This causes scratch marks and weeping (oozing). When the oozing serum dries, it forms crusts.

When a patch of eczema is healing even after the redness has all faded away, you can still feel the roughness and thickness of the skin.

The most common place for eczema to begin in a young baby is on the cheeks or the forehead. From there it may spread back to the ears and neck. The scaliness looks from a distance as if salt has dried there, especially on the ears. Near a year of age, eczema may start almost anywhere—the shoulders, the diaper region, the arms, the chest. Between one and three years, the most typical spots are the creases in the elbows and behind the knees.

Severe eczema can be a very trying disease to take care of. The baby is wild with the itching. The parents are wild trying to keep the child from scratching. The rash can last for months. It's important to keep the baby's fingernails clipped short. The less the baby can scratch her skin, the less chance there is of a secondary infection getting started in the scratched areas, from the bacteria that are always present on the skin. For babies who will tolerate it, making up a pair of white cotton mittens to cover the hands at night is helpful, since a lot of scratching can go on while the baby is asleep.

1154. There are several angles to the treatment of eczema. What a doctor does in studying and treating a case depends on many factors, including the baby's age, the location and character of the rash, the history of what new foods were introduced before the rash began, and how he responds to different treatments. The single most important thing the parent can do is to keep the skin well moisturized, using a plain moisturizing cream (no dyes or fragrance) several times a day. Ask your pharmacist to suggest one. Many cases are much improved by lotions and ointments alone. Use soap as infrequently as possible, since it robs the skin of oils. When you do use soap, use one with a lot of moisturizers, or use a non-detergent cleanser. Also, when drying skin after a bath, dab it dry, don't rub.

In the more persistent cases, an effort must be made to find out what food or foods the child is allergic to. Cow's milk is occasionally found to be the cause. A few babies can be cured only by giving up cow's milk altogether and shifting to artificial milk made from soy beans, rice, grains, or other special formulas.

In severe eczema in older babies and children who are eating a number of foods, the doctor experiments carefully by eliminating various foods from the diet. In severe and persistent cases, skin testing may be done by injecting samples of different foods. Hives will develop around the injections of foods to which the child is sensitive.

When an external irritant seems to be playing a part, that needs attention, too. Wool is very commonly irritating to eczema, and it is usually eliminated from the clothing. If the eczema is all in the diaper region, it is worthwhile to take all the precautions discussed in Sections 347–351 on diaper rashes. If cold, windy weather brings out the eczema, find a sheltered place for outings.

If for the time being you are out of reach of a doctor and your young child develops a severe itching eczema, you can rub 1 percent hydrocortisone cream on the itchy areas twice a day and give diphenhydramine (Benadryl) by mouth. If you are in the same situation with an older child who, for instance, develops a severe eczema after starting on egg, leave out the egg until you can get medical advice. It may take two weeks or more for the skin to clear up. Wheat is another common offender.

Keep in mind that in darker-skinned children, areas that have healed may look lighter than the rest of the skin. This tends to even out over time, but may take weeks. Nothing needs to be done in the meantime.

It is a mistake, though, for a parent to begin eliminating many foods from the diet without consulting a doctor or nurse practitioner. The reason is this: A case of eczema varies from week to week even with the same diet. When you change the diet around yourself you are apt to think that first one food, then another, is the cause. Every time the eczema becomes worse again, you become more confused. The danger is that you will make the diet so lopsided that the child's nutrition will suffer. If the eczema is not bothering the baby much, don't try any changes in the diet until you can get help.

The thing to remember about eczema is that it's a

tendency inside the child. It's not an infection, like impetigo, that you can get rid of completely. In most cases you have to be satisfied if you can just keep the rash mild. A majority of the eczemas that start early in infancy clear up completely, or at least become much milder, in the following year or two.

1155. Behavioral problems and allergies. In recent years all kinds of behavioral problems in children have been blamed on "allergies"—to vague substances in the air, to food additives, to food colorings, and so on. None of these claims has yet been proven scientifically, and many have been disproven. Many parents have brought their children to nonmedical practitioners who have performed very expensive tests and prescribed extremely complicated diets and other treatments. None of the results claimed for these approaches has been tested by the usual, accepted scientific methods. There have been reports of children becoming very ill after some of these treatments. I think it's best to have a frank talk with your doctor or nurse practitioner if you think that your child has a behavior problem due to an allergy and you want to try a treatment carried out by a nonmedical practitioner.

Skin Conditions

1156. Distinguishing among the common rashes. This section isn't meant to make you a diagnostician. If your child has a rash, you need your doctor's or nurse practitioner's help. Rashes vary so greatly among different individuals that even a skin specialist sometimes has difficulty diagnosing them. They confuse less expert people very easily. The purpose of this section is only to give you a few general pointers about the commoner rashes of children so as to relieve your mind until you can reach your doctor or nurse practitioner.

Scarlet fever. The child is sick for a day before the rash comes out, usually with headache, fever, vomiting and sore throat. The rash, which is a red blush that feels like sandpaper, starts in the warm, moist parts of the body, armpits, groin, and back (see Glossary, page 855).

Prickly heat may affect babies in the beginning of hot weather. It starts around the shoulders and neck and is made up of patches of many small tan-pink pimples, some of which develop tiny blisters (Section 357).

Diaper rash occurs in the area that is wet with urine. It shows up as pink or red pimples of various sizes or as patches of rough red skin (Sections 347–351).

1157. Insect bites. There are many different kinds of insect bites, from big puffy swellings the size of a half-dollar down to a simple blood-crusted spot without any swelling. But most bites have two common characteristics; there is a tiny hole or bump in the center where the stinger went in, and the bites are usually located on the exposed parts of the skin.

Any insect bite that is itching (a mosquito bite, for instance) or stinging may be partly relieved by applying a paste made by running a few drops of water into a teaspoonful of bicarbonate of soda (baking soda). For a bee sting remove the stinger, if visible, with tweezers and apply bicarbonate of soda. More effective for a wasp or hornet sting is to rub a drop of vinegar into the spot.

1158. Ticks can carry a number of diseases, such as Rocky Mountain spotted fever and Lyme disease, which have characteristic rashes. If you live in an area where ticks are present, check with your doctor about what precautions to take during tick season. You should remove a tick with a fine tweezer. Grasp the tick close to the skin and gently pull it straight out without a twisting movement. If you do not have tweezers, protect your fingers with a tissue and wash your hands thoroughly after you remove the tick.

1159. Scabies. Caused by a burrowing mite, this condition itches like crazy. It looks like groups of pimples topped with scabs, with a lot of scratch marks from the incessant itching. Scabies usually appears on parts of the body that are frequently handled: backs of hands, wrists, pubic area, and abdomen (but not on the back). Although scabies is not dangerous, it is very contagious and needs immediate treatment.

1160. Ringworm. This skin condition is not caused by a worm. It is a superficial fungal infection that causes circular patches of heaped up, rough, slightly reddened borders with clear centers, most commonly about nickel size. The outer rim is made up of little bumps. Ringworm does not appear suddenly but enlarges slowly over time. Often it appears around the time of a haircut. In ringworm of the scalp, there are round patches of scaly skin in which the hair is broken off short. The condition is mildly contagious. Treatment usually involves applying a cream to the rash for more than a month. When ringworm occurs on the scalp, a medicine to be taken by mouth will be prescribed by your doctor.

1161. Impetigo in a child past infancy will consist of scabs or crusts, partly brown, partly honey-colored. In fact, any scabs on the face should first be suspected of being impetigo. The infection is apt to start as a pimple with a yellowish or white blister on top, most often on the face, but this blister soon gets rubbed off and the scab takes its place. Other spots develop on the face and on any part of the body to which the child's hands can carry the infection. You should have the doctor or nurse practitioner see your child promptly for diagnosis and treatment. Impetigo is usually not a serious medical problem, but it spreads easily if neglected, and it is contagious. When impetigo is not treated, this "strep" bacteria infection may cause acute kidney disease.

1162. Poison ivy appears as clusters of small blisters of various sizes on shiny reddened skin. It itches, and usually occurs on the exposed parts of the body in spring and summer. Use 1 percent hydrocortisone cream and oral diphenhydramine (Benadryl) for mild cases. Consult your doctor or nurse practitioner about treatment if the outbreak is extensive.

1163. Head lice. It's easier to find the eggs than the lice. The eggs are tiny, pearly white, and egg-shaped, and each one is firmly cemented to a hair near the root. There may be itching red pimples where the hair meets the back of the neck. Look in the part line and behind the child's ears, especially. Many people incorrectly believe that head lice only occur under conditions of very poor hygiene, but they can exist in any child attending school or day care. Although they're gross, they're not really harmful. They are very contagious, however, and need treatment.

1164. Warts. Warts are caused by a viral infection under the skin. There are different types of ordinary warts that develop on the hands, the soles of the feet, the genitals, and the face. They tend to spread and should be seen by a doctor. In addition, there is a special type known as contagious warts (*molloscum cantagiosum*). At first they are round, smooth, waxy, the size of a pinhead, and white or pink in color. They multiply, enlarge, and become concave in the center. When present in large numbers, they may be treated to avoid spreading.

1165. Herpes. Herpes is a virus which is found worldwide. There are two main types of herpes. Type I is found in or around the mouth and usually is not sexually transmitted. During the initial infection, it commonly causes an illness in toddlers characterized by high fever, swollen glands, and the appearance of canker sores in the mouth—a miserable illness. Older children sometimes develop recurrent fever blisters along the edges of their lips, just as adults do. These too may be due to the Type I herpesvirus. In some children they recur in times of increased stress, fatigue, or illness, while in other children they never recur. An adult or child with Type I herpes shouldn't kiss anyone until the sores are gone.

Type II herpesvirus usually occurs on or around the genitals and is almost invariably a sexually transmitted disease. Small blisters develop and may break and form painful ulcers. It's the genital type that has received so much publicity and made people so worried. In a newborn it may cause an infection in the brain.

Washing with soap and water kills the herpesvirus. Specific treatment is available in some cases. So if parents and caregivers with either type of herpes wash their hands with soap and water after touching the areas where they have sores or ulcers, they won't pass the virus to a child they're caring for.

Infectious Diseases

Measles, Rubella, Roseola, Chicken Pox

1166. Measles ("*rubeola*"). For the first three or four days, measles has no rash. It looks like a bad cold that is becoming worse. Your child's eyes are red and watery. If you pull the lower lid down, you see that it is fiery red. The child has a hard, dry cough that becomes frequent. The fever usually goes higher each day. The rash comes out about the fourth day, when the fever is high, as indefinite pink spots behind the ears. They spread gradually over the face and body, becoming bigger and darker. The fever stays high, the cough remains frequent in spite of medicine, and the child feels pretty sick while the rash comes out fully, which takes one to two days. After that, your child should improve rapidly.

You may suspect a complication if the fever stays high for more than two days from the time the rash begins, or if the fever goes down for a day or more and then comes back. The most common complications are ear infections, bronchitis, and pneumonia. There is no current treatment for measles, other than prevention. The complications can be serious, and unlike measles itself, some can be successfully treated by modern drugs.

If your child has been fully immunized, measles is unlikely but not impossible. You should contact the doctor or nurse practitioner, whether you suspect the disease or not, when your child has a cough and a fever with a rash.

The first symptoms of measles begin anywhere from nine to sixteen days after exposure. The disease is contagious from the very beginning of the cold symptoms. It is unusual for a person to catch real measles twice.

Measles can and should be prevented by immunization at twelve months of age, and the child should get a booster shot at five years old. But if a child who has not been protected is exposed, the attack can still be prevented or made milder if an immunization is given within three days of exposure or if gamma globulin is given within six days of exposure. A couple of months later, when the gamma globulin effect has worn off, it is very important to have the child immunized against measles.

1167. Rubella ("German measles"). The rash of rubella looks much like the rash of real measles, but the two diseases are entirely separate. In rubella there are no cold symptoms (running nose or cough), but the child's throat may be a little sore. His fever is usually low (under 102°F), and he may hardly feel sick at all. The rash consists of flat pink spots, which usually cover the body the first day. The second day they are apt to fade and run together so that the body looks flushed instead of spotty. The most characteristic sign is swollen, tender glands on the back of the skull, behind the ears, and on the sides of the neck toward the back. These glands may swell before the rash comes out, and the swelling is apt to last some time after the disease is over. In some cases the rash is so slight that it is not noticed. There may be arthritis especially in the older patients.

Rubella usually develops from twelve to twenty-one days after exposure. The child usually doesn't need to stay in bed. A doctor or nurse practitioner should make the diagnosis, because rubella is easily confused with rubeola, scarlet fever, and certain virus infections. There is no specific treatment for rubella.

It can be bad for a woman to have rubella during the first three months of pregnancy because of the chance of her baby acquiring defects from the disease. If she is exposed at this time, she should promptly discuss the situation with her doctor.

Rubella immunization should be given to all children at age twelve months and repeated at five years old.

1168. Roseola. The proper name for this disease is *exanthem subitum,* but it's easier to call it roseola, short for roseola infantum. It is a less well known but common contagious disease. It usually occurs between the ages of one and three years, rarely afterward. The child has a steady high fever for three or four days without any cold symptoms and usually without seeming to be very sick. (Occasionally there is a convulsion on the first day because of the fever.) Suddenly the fever falls to normal and a flat pinkish rash, something like the rash in measles, comes out on the body. By this time the child no longer looks ill but may be cranky. The rash is gone in a day or two, and there are no complications to worry about.

Roseola can be hard to diagnose until the rash erupts. By then, however, the child's fever is down and she is feeling well. Roseola is caused by a herpesvirus VI or VII.

1169. Chicken pox (*"varicella"*). The first sign of chicken pox is usually a few characteristic pimples on the body, face, and scalp. These pox are raised up like ordinary small pimples, but some of them have tiny yellow water blisters on top ("like a dew drop on a rose petal"). The base of the pimple and the skin around it are reddened. The delicate blister head breaks within a few hours and dries into a crust. The eruptions usually itch. When trying to make the diagnosis, a doctor or nurse practitioner searches among all the crusted pimples to find a fresh one that still has the blister. New pox continue to appear for three or four days.

An older child or adult may feel sick and have headache or fever the day before the pox appear, but a small child doesn't notice these symptoms. The fever is usually slight at the beginning but may rise during the next day or two. Some children never feel sick and never have a temperature of more than 100°F. Others feel quite sick and have high fever.

A medication is sometimes used to shorten the duration or severity of chicken pox. You can discuss whether it is advisable for your child with your doctor or nurse practitioner. Chicken pox can be confused with other diseases, such as impetigo, so you should call your doctor or nurse practitioner for any rash, especially if there is a fever or the child feels sick.

The doctor may prescribe a mild antihistamine to help relieve the itching. Acetaminophen may help the child feel better, especially if he has fever. (Don't give aspirin to children or teenagers with chicken pox; it increases their susceptibility to Reye's syndrome.) The itching can also be relieved by soaking in a lukewarm corn starch, baking soda, or oatmeal powder for ten minutes, two or three times a day. Use 1 cupful for a small tub, 2 cups for a large one. The dry cornstarch should be placed in a 2–4-cup container. Then add cold water slowly, stirring constantly, until the cornstarch is completely dissolved. (This prevents the formation of lumps.) Then add the cornstarch solution to the bathwater.

Try to prevent your child from rubbing the scabs off, which can lead to a secondary bacterial infection or scarring. Wash the child's hands three times a day with soap, and cotton gloves worn at bedtime will help prevent the damage caused by scratching during sleep.

Chicken pox usually develops between eleven and nineteen days after exposure. The usual rule is to let a child go out and back to school on the sixth day after the onset of the rash. In mild cases, a child may return sooner if the rash is crusted with scabs. The dried scabs are not contagious and should not be a reason to keep the child quarantined.

There is now an immunization against chicken pox which will either lessen the severity of the disease or prevent it altogether (Section 633). Complications due to "strep" may be serious and can be treated.

1170. Other infectious diseases with rashes. Other common cold or intestinal viruses (with names like adenovirus, ECHO, Coxsackie virus) can come with rashes. Often they are faint polka-dot rashes on the body, sometimes spreading to the face, arms, and legs. They fade in a couple of days.

Whooping Cough, Mumps, and Diphtheria

1171. Whooping cough ("*pertussis*"). There's nothing about whooping cough in the first week to make you suspect that disease. It's just like an ordinary cold with a little runny nose and a little dry cough. It is during the second week that the first suspicion arises. Now you notice that the child is beginning to have long spells of coughing at night. She coughs eight or ten times on one breath. One night, after several of these long spells, she gags and vomits. Or maybe she whoops. The whoop is the crowing noise she makes trying to get her breath back after a spell of coughs.

It's possible, although quite uncommon, for a child to get whooping cough even after being immunized with the vaccine. But these cases usually aren't bad enough to reach the whooping stage, and in some there isn't even vomiting. The diagnosis is then based on the character of the cough in the second week (cough, cough, cough, cough, cough, cough, cough, cough—a string of coughs in rapid succession without a breath in between) and on the fact that there are other cases in your neighborhood.

You should never jump to the conclusion that your child has whooping cough simply because she develops a bad cough in the first few days of a cold. In fact, a bad cough in the beginning of a cold argues against the diagnosis of whooping cough.

Whooping cough lasts for weeks and weeks. In an average case, the whooping stage lasts four weeks, in a severe case two or three months. A doctor thinks of whooping cough whenever a dry cough lasts a month in a child under a year of age, and in an older child if there's been an outbreak of the illness in the area.

When there is a doubtful case and it is important to make the diagnosis, laboratory tests can sometimes help.

Your doctor will prescribe treatment, based on the age of the child and the severity of the case. Antibiotics are useful in that they prevent the disease from spreading. Cough medicines are often used but usually have only a small effect. Most cases do better when in cold air, day and night, but naturally the child must be protected against chilling. Children are sometimes allowed to play outdoors throughout the disease, as long as they have no fever. They should not play with other children until after they have received treatment with erythromycin, an antibiotic. Some children have many fewer coughing spells when they are kept in bed. When vomiting is a problem, frequent small meals stay down better than the regular three full meals. The safest time of all to feed children is right after they have vomited since they usually won't have another bad spell for some time.

Since whooping cough is sometimes a serious disease, especially in babies and young children, it is important to call a doctor promptly when there is a suspicion. There are two main reasons for this: to make sure of the diagnosis and to prescribe the right treatment. Special treatment is called for and is valuable in infants. It's a disease to avoid like the plague if you have a baby in your household. The main danger at this age is exhaustion and pneumonia. (See Section 629 about pertussis immunization.)

Whooping cough takes five to fourteen days to develop after exposure.

1172. Mumps. Mumps is principally a viral disease of the saliva glands, most commonly the parotid glands, which lie in the hollow just under the ear lobe. First the gland fills in the hollow; then it causes the whole side of the face to swell. It pushes the lobe of the ear upward. If you run your fingers up and down the back part of the jawbone, you can feel that the hard swelling runs forward, covering part of the jawbone.

When a child has a swelling in the side of his neck, a question always comes up: is it mumps, or is it one of the other, rarer diseases of the parotid gland (which may recur repeatedly), or is it an ordinary swollen gland (one of the lymph glands in the side of the neck)? The ordinary lymph glands that sometimes swell after a sore throat are lower down on the neck, not tucked up under the earlobe. The hard swelling does not cross the jawbone.

When a small child develops mumps, the swelling under the ear is usually the first thing you notice. An older child may complain of pain around his ear or in the side of his throat, especially on swallowing or chewing, for a day before the swelling begins. He may feel generally sick. There is often little fever in the beginning but it may go higher on the second or third day. Most commonly the swelling begins on one side, but spreads to the other side in a day or two. Sometimes it takes a week or more to spread to the other side, and in some cases the second side never swells.

There are other saliva glands beside the parotids, and mumps sometimes spreads to these, too. The submaxillary glands are tucked up under the lower part of the jawbone.

The sublinguals are just behind the point of the chin. Occasionally a person gets one of the complications of mumps without having had a swelling in any of the saliva glands.

A very mild mumps swelling may go away in three or four days; the average swelling lasts seven to ten days.

Mumps can spread to the testicles in men and boys who have reached puberty. This usually involves only one testicle. But even when both are inflamed, this does not usually cause sterility (inability to have children). Adolescent boys and men should avoid exposure. The ovaries in the female may also be affected, but that rarely affects childbearing ability in later life.

Sometimes a person who believes he had mumps previously will again get a swelling of a parotid gland. Most doctors believe that one attack or the other was caused by some germ other than the mumps virus or by a tiny stone obstructing the salivary duct. Generally a person can't have mumps twice because one attack confers immunity for life, but he can certainly catch real mumps if he mistakenly believes he had it before. Therefore I'd advise unimmunized men and boys who have reached puberty not to expose themselves unnecessarily when there is mumps in the family.

All children should receive mumps vaccine at twelve months of age and again at five years old. It is given in a combined shot with the measles and rubella vaccines.

You should call the doctor for a suspected case of mumps. It is important to be certain of the diagnosis. If it turns out to be a swollen lymph gland, the treatment is quite different.

Mumps takes two to three weeks to develop after exposure.

1173. Diphtheria. Diphtheria is a serious but completely preventable disease. If your child is given three injections in infancy and booster shots at eighteen months, four to six years, and every ten years thereafter, there's practically no chance of his catching it. It begins with a sick feeling, sore throat, and fever. Dirty-white patches develop on the tonsils and may spread to the rest of the throat. Occasionally the disease begins in the larynx with hoarseness and a barking cough; the breathing becomes tight and difficult.

In any case, you should call a doctor promptly when your child has sore throat and fever or when he has any croupy symptoms. The treatment of any case of suspected diphtheria is the immediate use of special drugs.

The disease develops within a week after exposure.

Poliomyelitis and Tuberculosis

1174. Poliomyelitis. This viral disease has been almost eliminated wherever polio vaccine has been systematically used. Every child should be protected in early infancy against the three types of polio, with the Sabin oral vaccine or the Salk vaccine injections (see Section 630).

The disease begins, like so many other infections, with a general sick feeling (malaise), fever, and headache. There may be vomiting, constipation, or a little diarrhea. Most cases do not go on to paralysis, and of those that do, a fair number recover completely. If there is any paralysis remaining after the acute stage of the infection is over, it is vitally important that the child continue to have regular, expert medical attention.

1175. Tuberculosis. Tuberculosis is different in infants, children, and adults. Most people think of tuberculosis as it occurs typically in adults. A spot, or cavity, develops in the lung and produces such symptoms as fatigue, loss of appetite, loss of weight, fever, cough, and sputum.

Tuberculosis in childhood usually takes other forms. In the first two years of life, resistance is not as strong as in later years, and there is more chance of the infection spreading to other parts of the body. That is why you never take the slightest chance of exposing a baby to a known case of tuberculosis unless the doctor and the X-ray guarantee that the person has been completely cured. This is also a reason for anyone in a household who has a chronic cough to be examined and given a tuberculin test. Also it's wise to have a new housekeeper, caregiver, or any other new member of the household tuberculin-tested. If the test results are positive, an X-ray of the chest should be made.

In later childhood, tuberculosis is more common and less likely to cause serious trouble. This is not a reason to treat it lightly or take any chances. Tuberculin tests show that in some cities as many as 10 percent of all children have had a slight infection with tuberculosis by the time they are ten years old. Most of these cases have been so mild that no one suspected that anything was wrong at the time. An X-ray may show, at most, a little scar where the infection healed in the lung or in the lymph glands at the roots of the lungs.

Sometimes, however, a childhood type of tuberculosis is active enough to cause symptoms such as fever, poor appetite, poor color, irritability, fatigue, and perhaps a cough. There isn't much sputum, and what there is, is swallowed, of course. The infection may be in other parts of the body, such as the bones, kidneys, the neck glands, or the lining around the brain, but most commonly it's in the lungs and in the lymph glands at the roots of the lungs.

In most of these active cases, healing gradually takes place over a period of one to two years if the child is well cared for and only a scar is left. Proper treatment with special drugs will foster healing and prevent a serious spread of infection. Children with tuberculosis are usually not contagious and frequently do not need to be separated from their families for treatment.

As children reach adolescence, they become more susceptible to the serious, adult type of tuberculosis. This should be kept in mind whenever an adolescent or young adult is run-down, tired, loses appetite or weight, whether or not there is any cough.

1176. The tuberculin test. A few weeks after tubercle bacilli (the germs that cause tuberculosis) have gotten into the body, a person becomes "sensitized" by actively making antibodies to the bacilli. After that, if tuberculin (material from dead tuberculosis germs) is injected into the skin, a raised spot develops. This is called a PPD skin test. Redness alone at the site of a TB shot does not mean a positive test. Only the presence of a raised area of a certain size determines a positive test. Lots of parents worry unnecessarily about the redness, only to find out that the test is actually negative because there is no raised area. A health care professional should evaluate the test site to determine the significance of any response to the TB test. While the area may react by turning red, a positive diagnosis is only based on the development of a raised spot of a certain size. Generally speaking, if a person has ever had a tuberculosis infection, he will react with a positive test result for the rest of his life, even though the infection was healed long ago.

Tuberculin skin tests are given periodically throughout childhood in routine examinations in communities where tuberculosis is seen frequently. The test is also done when a child isn't doing well or has a chronic cough, or when tuberculosis is discovered in another member of the household.

If your child is ever found to have a positive tuberculin test, which is not impossible when you consider how many children are positive, you have to keep a sense of balance. There's no need to be alarmed, since a great majority of the cases discovered throughout middle childhood have either healed already or will heal gradually with care. On the other hand, you don't want to neglect any precautions, and it is very important to follow up with your doctor.

The first step is the doctor's investigation of the child's case. An X-ray of the lungs is essential in all cases to see if there are any signs of active infection or of healed scars. Sometimes the doctor orders other tests.

All children who have developed a positive tuberculin test, even those without evidence of active disease, should receive specific antituberculosis drugs for at least nine months. During that time, if the disease is inactive, they can live normal, active lives. The doctor may ask for further X-rays at intervals. Modern drug therapy is generally effective and free from serious side effects.

Aside from the affected child, every other member of the household (and any other adult the child regularly comes in contact with) must be tested to discover, if possible, where the tuberculosis germs came from and to find out if other children in the household have been infected. In many cases no disease is found in any adult in the household, and it has to be assumed that the child picked up the germs from some source outside the home. In the other cases, an active case of tuberculosis is sometimes found in the least suspected adult in the house. It's a lucky thing for the person to have the disease discovered at an early stage, and it's lucky for the rest of the family to have the danger removed. No person with active tuberculosis should stay in a house with children, but should go somewhere else for drug therapy until the doctor says there is no chance of contagion.

Other Health Concerns

Joint Problems

1177. Rheumatic fever is another so-called autoimmune problem. Following an infection with the streptococcus bacteria (like a strep throat), the body makes antibodies to fight off the infection. For some reason these antibodies also fight against some of the person's own internal organs. Rheumatic fever, therefore, takes many forms. It can affect the joints, the heart, the skin, and other parts of the body. When not treated promptly and adequately, an attack is apt to last for weeks or months. Furthermore, this disease tends to recur again and again throughout childhood whenever the child has another strep throat.

Sometimes rheumatic fever takes a very acute form with high fever. In other cases, it smolders for weeks with only a little fever. When there is severe arthritis, it travels around from joint to joint, causing the affected areas to become swollen, red, and exquisitely tender. In other cases, the arthritis may be mild—just an ache off and on in one joint or another. If the heart is being affected severely, the child is visibly prostrated, pale, and breathless. In some cases, it is discovered that the heart has been damaged by some past attack that was so mild it was not noticed at the time.

In other words, rheumatic fever is an exceedingly variable disease. Naturally, you consult your doctor or nurse practitioner if your child develops any of the symptoms in a severe form. But it's just as important to have a child examined who has vague symptoms, like paleness, tiredness, slight fever, mild joint pains or unexplained rash.

Nowadays we have several drugs that are effective in clearing up streptococcal infection in the throat and in hastening the end of the rheumatic inflammation in the joints or the heart. As a result, heart valves are no longer so likely to be damaged in the first attack. More important still, children who have had one attack of rheumatic fever can usually be kept from having further attacks and further heart damage. They must continue indefinitely, under the doctor's continuing supervision, to take an antibiotic by mouth or by injection (to prevent new streptococcal infections) absolutely regularly, right into adulthood. Rheumatic fever can be prevented if the strep throat is treated within seven days of onset.

1178. Joint pains and growing pains. In the olden days, it was thought natural for children to complain of growing pains in their legs and arms, and nobody worried about them.

A child between the ages of two and five may wake up crying complaining of pain around his thigh, knee, or calf. This happens only during the evening but may recur each night for weeks on end. Some people believe this pain is caused by cramps in the muscles or by the aching of the rapidly growing bones.

Generally, if the pains move from place to place, if there is no swelling, redness, local tenderness, or limp, and if the child is entirely well otherwise, it is unlikely that a serious cause for growing pains will be found. If the pain is always in the same spot on the same limb, or if other symptoms are present, the problem should definitely be brought to medical attention.

There are many other causes for pains in the arms and legs, and you can see that you need a health care professional to examine, test, and decide in every case.

Heart Problems

1179. Heart murmurs. A heart murmur is simply a whooshing sound made by blood as it is pumped through the heart. Although the term "heart murmur" has an alarming sound to parents, it's important to realize that a great majority of heart murmurs don't mean anything serious. Generally speaking there are three kinds: *functional* (or innocent), *acquired,* and *congenital.*

A **functional or innocent murmur** is just a murmur that doesn't come from a congenital malformation or from rheumatic fever. In fact, the heart is perfectly normal. These innocent murmurs are very common in early childhood. They tend to fade out as the child reaches adolescence. Your doctor tells you about an innocent murmur in your child so that if it is discovered later in childhood by a new doctor, you can explain that it has been there all along.

An **acquired murmur** in childhood comes from rheumatic fever, which inflames the valves and may leave scars on them afterward. This causes them either to leak or to obstruct the proper flow of blood. When a doctor hears a murmur in a child's heart that wasn't there before, it may mean that active rheumatic inflammation is going on. In this case, there will be other signs of infection, such as fever, rapid pulse, and elevated blood count. The doctor will treat such a child with drugs until all signs of inflammation go away, even if it takes months. If there have been no signs of active infection for some time, the murmur may be due to old scars left over from a previous attack.

In former years, the child with an old murmur was sometimes treated as a semi-invalid for years, forbidden to play active games or sports, even though there were no signs of active infection. A doctor's tendency nowadays is to let the child who is completely over the active stage of inflammation go back gradually to as normal a life as possible, including the games and sports that he can do easily, if the healed scars do not noticeably interfere with the efficient working of the heart. There are two reasons for this. The muscles of the heart, as long as they are not inflamed, are strengthened by ordinary activity. Even more important is keeping these children's spirits healthy—preventing them from feeling sorry for themselves, from feeling that they are a hopeless case, that they're different from everyone else. Such children should receive absolutely regular medication, however, to prevent further streptococcus infection.

A murmur caused by **congenital heart disease** is usually discovered at birth or within a few months afterward (occasionally not till several years later). Such a murmur is usually not caused by inflammation. Instead, the heart was improperly formed in the first place. The important thing is not so much the murmur itself but whether the malformation interferes with the efficiency of the heart. If it does, the baby may have blue spells, or breathe too hard, or grow too slowly. A baby or child with a congenital heart murmur needs a careful investigation by specialists. Many of these murmurs can now be cured by surgery.

If a child with a congenital murmur can exercise without turning blue and without becoming abnormally out of breath, and if she grows at the normal rate, it is important for her emotional development that she not be thought of or treated as an invalid but that she be allowed to lead a normal life. She does need to avoid infections, especially influenza, for which she can be given a vaccine each year.

Children with congenital or acquired heart disease should receive antibiotic therapy before having any dental work done and prior to surgery, to prevent germs from traveling from the mouth wound to the heart.

Hernias and Hydrocele

1180. Hernias. A hernia is simply the protrusion of an organ or tissue through an abnormal opening in the muscles or skin of the body. The most common hernia of all, protruding navel, is discussed in Section 369.

The next most common is in the groin (*inguinal* hernia). There is meant to be a small passage from inside the abdomen, down along the groin (the groove between the abdomen and the thigh) into the scrotum (in the case of a boy), to carry the blood vessels and nerves that go to the testicles. This passageway has to pass through the layers of muscle that make up the wall of the abdomen. If these openings in the muscles are larger than average, a piece of intestine may be squeezed out of the abdomen and down the passageway when the child strains or cries. If the intestine goes only partway down, it makes a bulging in the groin. If it goes all the way down into the scrotum, the scrotum looks very enlarged for the time being. Inguinal hernia does occur, though less commonly, in girls. It appears as a protrusion in the groin.

In most hernias the intestine slips back up into the abdomen when the baby or child is lying down quietly. It may push down every time he stands up, or it may go down only once in a great while when he strains hard.

Occasionally an inguinal hernia becomes strangulated. This means that the intestine has become stuck in the passage and that the blood vessels have been kinked and shut off. It is a form of intestinal obstruction. This causes abdominal pain and vomiting and calls for emergency surgery.

Strangulation of an inguinal hernia occurs most often in the first six months of life. Usually it is a hernia that has not been noticed before. The parent changes the baby because he is crying so hard and notices the lump in his groin for the first time. It is not wise to try to push the lump down with the fingers. However, while waiting to see the doctor or nurse practitioner, you can elevate the baby's hips on a pillow and apply an ice bag (or crushed ice in a sock with a plastic bag around it) to the area. These procedures together may make the intestine slip back into the abdomen. You shouldn't feed the baby by breast or bottle until you have discussed the situation with the doctor, because it's better for the stomach to be empty if anesthesia and surgery are needed.

If you suspect a hernia in your child, you should, of course, report it to the doctor or nurse practitioner right away. Nowadays inguinal hernias are usually repaired promptly by surgery. It is not a serious operation, it is almost always successful, and the child is often out of the hospital on the same day.

1181. Hydrocele, or swelling around a testicle. Hydrocele is often confused with hernia because it also causes a swelling in the scrotum. Each testicle in the scrotum is surrounded by a delicate sac that contains a few drops of fluid. This helps to protect the testicle. Quite often in newborn babies there is extra fluid in the sac that surrounds a testicle, and this makes it appear to be several times its normal size. Sometimes this swelling takes place at a later period. A hydrocele is usually nothing to worry about. The fluid diminishes as the baby gets older in most cases, and then nothing needs to be done for it. Occasionally an older boy has a chronic hydrocele, which should be operated on if it is uncomfortably large. You should not try to make the diagnosis yourself. Let the doctor decide whether it's hernia or hydrocele.

Eye Problems

1182. Reasons for seeing the eye doctor. Children need to go to an eye doctor if their eyes turn in (cross-eyes) or out (walleyes) at any age; if they are having any trouble with schoolwork; if they complain of aching, smarting, or tired eyes; if their eyes are inflamed; if they are having headaches; if they hold their books too close when they read; if they cock the head to one side when looking at something carefully; or if their vision is found to be defective by the chart test. Chart testing should be performed by your child's regular doctor or nurse practitioner between three and four years of age, and at each well-child visit thereafter. However, just because your child can read a chart satisfactorily in school does not guarantee that her eyes are all right. If she is having symptoms of eyestrain, she should be examined anyway.

1183. Nearsightedness (myopia) means that close objects appear sharp, but distant objects are blurred. This is the most common eye trouble that interferes with schoolwork. Nearsightedness develops most between six and ten years. It can come on quite rapidly, so don't ignore the signs of it (holding the book closer, having trouble seeing the blackboard at school) just because the child's vision was all right a few months before.

1184. Inflammation of the eye (*"conjunctivitis"*) can be caused by many different viruses, bacteria, or allergy. Most of the mild cases, where the eye is only slightly pink and the discharge from the eye is scant and clear, are caused by ordinary cold viruses and accompany colds in the nose. You should be more suspicious of inflammation when there is no nose cold. It is a good idea to get in touch with your doctor or nurse practitioner anyway, but particularly when the white of the eye becomes reddened, when there is pain or when the discharge is yellow and thick. Bacterial conjunctivitis can be treated with antibiotic ointments or drops as prescribed by your doctor. In all cases of conjunctivitis, the infection is quite contagious. Spread can be decreased significantly by frequent hand-washing after any contact with the infected eye or with the discharge.

1185. Styes. A stye is an infected eyelash follicle. In that way it is similar to a pimple anywhere else. A stye is caused by ordinary bacteria that happen to be rubbed onto the eyelid. The stye usually comes to a head and breaks. Your doctor or nurse practitioner may prescribe an ointment to promote healing and prevent spreading. A stye feels more comfortable after applying warm compresses and this also hastens its coming to a head and breaking. (Eyelids are very temperature sensitive, so only use warm—not hot—water.) The main trouble with a stye is that one often leads to another, probably because when the first one breaks the germs are spread to other hair follicles. This is a reason to try to keep a child from rubbing or fingering her eyelid when a stye is coming to a head or discharging.

Just as with conjunctivitis, an adult with a stye should wash his hands thoroughly before doing things for a baby or small child, especially if the stye has been touched, because the germs are easily passed from person to person.

1186. Things that don't harm children's eyes: watching television, sitting too close to the set, reading an excessive amount, reading in poor light, or holding the book close.

Neurological Problems

1187. Seizures and convulsions. A seizure is caused by abnormal electrical discharges in the brain. The result of these discharges will depend on where in the brain they occur. When most people think of a seizure, they picture the generalized type, where the entire brain is involved. In this case, the person loses consciousness and has convulsive twitches of the arms and legs. But seizures can also involve just a very small part of the brain. In such cases, the person may remain awake and experience twitching in only part of his body or he may momentarily lose concentration and stare blankly.

A full-blown convulsion is a frightening thing to see, especially in a child, but most seizures are not dangerous in themselves. Most convulsions stop in a short time, whether or not any treatment is given.

In most generalized convulsions, the child loses consciousness, his eyes roll up, his teeth are clenched, and his entire body or parts of his body shake with twitching movements. His breathing is heavy, and there may be a little frothing at his lips. Sometimes he will urinate and pass a bowel movement.

1188. What to do during a generalized convulsion. Telephone for the doctor right away. If you cannot reach one immediately, don't worry. The convulsion will usually be over anyway and the child will be asleep by the time you actually talk to the doctor. Actually there is very little you need to do for a child during a convulsion except keep her from hurting herself. Try to have her on the floor or some other place where she can't fall and injure herself. Turn her on her side to allow saliva to run out of the corner of her mouth. Make sure that her flailing arms and legs do not strike something sharp. Look at your watch to time the duration of the seizure. Try to keep cool and remember that most seizures end within a few minutes (although it *seems* like hours) and do no harm. If the seizure lasts more than five minutes, it is advisable to call 911 or your local emergency response team in case it continues for more than ten minutes. After a seizure, there is usually a period of sleepiness where the child may seem minimally responsive and disoriented. When the seizure is over and the child is fully awake, and a fever accompanies the seizure, give acetaminophen for fever, followed by a tepid bath or wet rub.

1189. Seizures with fever. By far the most common cause of convulsions in young children is fever. These febrile seizures occur in 4 percent of children under age five. The seizure usually occurs at the beginning of an illness with fever, such as a cold, a sore throat, or the flu. (Seizures with fever are much more rare after the first day or two of fever.) When the fever comes on quickly, it seems to make the nervous system excitable. Some children at this age are trembly at the start of a fever, even though they don't have convulsions. Others even hallucinate (they may see tiny insects, other animals, or bright colors) and become temporarily disoriented. If the irritability leads to abnormal electrical discharges in the brain, a seizure ensues.

Therefore, if your young child has a convulsion at the onset of a fever, it doesn't necessarily mean that there is a serious disease, nor does it mean that the child is going to have more convulsions in later life. The odds are that it is a simple seizure with fever. If the seizure occurs in the first year of life, there is about a 50 percent chance that the child will have at least one more seizure with fever in the future. If the first episode occurs after a year, there is about a 25 percent risk of recurrence. Most studies show that the vast majority of children who have seizures with fever outgrow them and do not suffer from any problems because of them.

Of course, any child who has a seizure should see his doctor or nurse practitioner or be taken to an emergency room, especially after the first episode, to make sure that it indeed was a simple seizure with fever and not another kind of disease. There can be other causes at different age periods.

There is no agreed-upon treatment of seizures with fever except to try to administer a fever medication at the beginning of any potential infectious illness. Unfortunately, it often happens that by the time the parent is aware of the possible illness, the fever has already gone up and the child has had a seizure.

For children with recurrent seizures with fever, the doctor may prescribe an antiseizure medication to prevent further seizures.

1190. Epilepsy is the name given to convulsions that occur repeatedly in an older child, without any fever or other disease. Nobody knows the real cause in the great majority of cases. The two most common forms of epilepsy are *grand mal* and *petit mal.* In generalized grand mal attacks, the person loses consciousness completely and has convulsions. In partial, petit mal attacks, the seizure is so brief that the person doesn't fall or lose control of herself but may just stare or stiffen momentarily.

Every case of epilepsy should be investigated by a neurologist. Though the condition is often chronic, several drugs are helpful in stopping or reducing the frequency of the spells.

For information on local services, you can write to the Epilepsy Foundation of America, 4351 Garden City Drive, Landover, MD 20785, phone (800) 332-1000.

Sudden Infant Death Syndrome (SIDS)

1191. About one in every thousand babies born in the United States dies of sudden infant death syndrome (or crib death). Most commonly a baby between three weeks and seven months of age (three months is the most common age) is found dead in his crib. There is never an adequate explanation, even when a postmortem examination (autopsy) is done.

The parents are shocked—a sudden death is much more shattering than one that follows a worsening illness. They are overwhelmed by guilt, assuming that they should have paid more attention to the cold if the baby had one, that they should have noticed something, or that they should have gone in to check on the child, even though there was no reason to do so. But no sensible parent would call a doctor for the very slight cold that some of these children have. And if the doctor had seen the baby, she would not have used any treatment because there would not have been any reason to do so. No one could have anticipated the tragedy.

All infants should be put to sleep on their backs, unless there is a medical reason not to do so. This simple change in sleep from front to back has reduced the number of SIDS deaths by 50 percent.

Though sudden infant death syndrome has been studied extensively, there is still no satisfactory scientific explanation for it. At this time we don't know if there is one cause of SIDS or many causes. There has been speculation about suffocation in the bedding, heart irregularities, allergy, low blood sugar, sudden overwhelming infections, and impaired arousal during sleep, but there is no solid proof for any of these. New theories about the cause of sudden infant death syndrome are brought out frequently. Check with your doctor or nurse practitioner.

The important thing to remember is that SIDS is not due to anything the parents have done or left undone. It is not preventable as far as anybody knows, although it does appear that the chances of avoiding SIDS improve for infants who sleep on their backs (Section 150).

There will usually be depression in the parents lasting for many weeks, with ups and downs. They may experience difficulty concentrating and sleeping, poor appetite, and heart or stomach symptoms. They may feel a strong urge to get away or a dread of being alone. If there are other children, the parents may fear to let them out of their sight, want to shun responsibility for caring for them, or treat them irritably. Some parents want to talk; others bottle up their feelings.

Other children in the family are sure to be upset, whether they show ordinary grief or not. Small children may just cling, or behave badly to get their parents' attention. Older children may appear remarkably unconcerned; but experience tells us that they are trying to protect themselves from the full force of grief and guilt. It is hard for adults to see why a child should feel guilty, but all children have resentful feelings at times toward their brothers and sisters, and their primitive unconscious thinking may tell them that their hostile feelings brought about the death.

If the parents avoid talking about the dead baby, their silence may add to the other children's guilt. So it is good for the parents to talk about the baby, to explain that a special sickness of babies caused the death and that it was not the fault of anyone. Euphemisms like "The baby went away," or "She never woke up," simply add new mysteries and anxieties. It's particularly helpful if the parents try to respond in a gentle way to every one of the children's questions and comments, so that they will feel that it is all right to bring up their deeper worries, too.

The parents should seek counseling from a family social agency, a guidance clinic, a psychiatrist, a psychologist, or a clergy member so that they can express and come to understand their overwhelming feelings.

The National Sudden Infant Death Syndrome Foundation, Inc., 10500 Little Patuxent Parkway, Suite 420, Columbia, MD 21044, phone (800) 221-SIDS, has chapters in many cities, where parents can get help and comfort from others who have gone through this tragedy. The foundation prepares literature, solicits funds, and supports research.

Hormonal Disturbances

1192. Several hormonal diseases and a few hormonal medicines have a definite effect on human beings. For example, when the thyroid gland is not secreting sufficiently, a child's physical growth and mental development will be slowed down. She will be sluggish, have dry skin, coarse hair, and a low voice. Her face may appear puffy. Insufficient thyroid secretion may also cause obesity. Her basal metabolism—the rate at which her body burns fuel when resting—will be below normal. The proper dose of thyroid medication will bring about remarkable improvement.

Some people who have read popular articles on hormonal glands assume that every short person, every slow pupil, every nervous girl, every fat boy with small genitals merely has a hormonal problem that can be cured by the proper tablet or injection. This assumption is not supported by what is known scientifically at the present time. It takes more than one symptom to make a hormonal disease. A child whose height is within the normal range, for example, is unlikely to have a hormonal problem.

In many cases when a boy is heavy during the years before puberty development, his penis appears smaller than it really is because his plump thighs are so large in comparison and because the layer of fat at the base of his penis may hide three-quarters of its length. Most of these boys have a normal sexual development in puberty, and many of them lose their excess weight at that time.

Certainly every child who is not growing at the usual rate or in the usual shape, or who appears dull or nervous or out of line in any other way, should be examined by a competent physician. If the doctor finds that the child's stature is only her inborn constitutional pattern or that her mental state is due to real troubles in her daily life, then what she needs is assistance in her adjustment to life, not a further search for magic.

Reye's Syndrome

1193. This uncommon but serious condition can cause permanent damage to the brain and other organs. It can also be fatal. Its cause is not completely understood, but it usually occurs during a viral illness. It is now known that children and adolescents who receive aspirin when they have a viral illness, especially influenza or chicken pox, are much more likely to get Reye's syndrome than those who are given acetaminophen or another nonaspirin product.

Acquired Immune Deficiency Syndrome (AIDS)

1194. AIDS (*"acquired immunodeficiency syndrome"*) is caused by the human immunodeficiency virus (HIV). Once HIV gets into the bloodstream, it impairs the body's ability to develop immunity to other infections. So a person with AIDS can die of an infection which, in a normal person, would soon be cured by the body's own protective mechanisms. It has been estimated that 20 million people in the world are infected by HIV.

HIV is most commonly transmitted from body fluids such as semen and vaginal secretions to blood during intercourse. It is also transmitted from blood to blood in drug users who share needles. The transmission of HIV is higher in homosexual men who practice anal intercourse, because the lining of the rectum is more easily injured than the lining of the vagina. HIV also may be transmitted by infected men and women, even when there are no symptoms, during intercourse. HIV can also be transmitted in a blood transfusion when the blood is not screened.

AIDS in children is almost always caused when mothers transmit HIV during pregnancy or at the time of birth. Not all pregnant women with HIV or AIDS transfer the infection to their child. Medications given during pregnancy can greatly reduce the chance that the baby will have the virus.

With proper treatment, the babies who are infected are surviving for longer and longer periods of time. At the time of this writing there is strong optimism that using a combination of anti-AIDS medications at the same time will change it into a manageable disease with a long life expectancy.

HIV is not spread by hand or body touch, or by kissing, or living in the same home, or sitting in the same classroom, swimming in the same pool, eating or drinking from the same utensils, or by sitting on the same toilet as someone with AIDS. Although AIDS is highly lethal and has spread throughout the world, it is not a highly contagious disease.

1195. How to talk to children and teens about AIDS. By mentioning the subject even in a casual way, you make it possible for your child to ask questions and get your reassurance and support. Most likely, your child will hear about AIDS from TV, videos, movies, or at school. Parents should be comfortable with talking to their children about AIDS in a way that is consistent with their child's developmental age.

The two greatest protections against contracting HIV, I feel, are education about safe sex techniques and a belief that the spiritual aspects of sexual love, including the desire of many adolescents raised with high ideals to postpone intercourse until there is a deep commitment, are as important and as worthy of respect as the purely physical. I've explained in Section 664 why I believe that the positive aspects of sex and love, including the spiritual side, should come first, over a considerable period of time. This is to prevent, if possible, a casual attitude that permits intercourse after brief acquaintance. The main reason for early education is that preteens are much more willing to listen to their parents. If preteens or teens have become anxious about AIDS, they need to know all the ways in which the disease is not transmitted, and they need to know how to keep their sexual contacts "safe."

Children should learn that the greatest risk of becoming infected with HIV comes from unprotected sex with multiple partners. The greater the number of sexual partners, the greater the chance that one of them has AIDS or is carrying

HIV without having developed the symptoms of AIDS. Ideally, they should also know, before intercourse, about the present health of previous sexual partners. The surest way, of course, is to delay intercourse until marriage or until the partners are very sure of a deep attachment to each other.

They should also know that condoms—latex, not lamb-skin—offer much, though not total, protection during intercourse and that the diaphragm and the pill do not. Preteens and teenagers should also understand the risks drug addicts take when sharing drug equipment with each other. The fact is that children are hearing about intravenous drug use and anal intercourse in relation to AIDS on television and in the media. That makes open communication and information-sharing with parents all the more important.

Scoliosis

1196. This is a curvature of the spine that usually appears between the ages of ten and fifteen. It is a problem of growth rather than posture. Schools in many states screen for this condition. About 4 percent of all children in this age group have a detectable curvature of the spine. It's twice as common in girls as in boys, and it tends to run in families. The cause is unknown. Any curvature warrants an evaluation by a physician. Many cases can simply be watched but never require intervention.

The treatments for scoliosis—bracing and surgery—are complex, expensive, and controversial. If treatment is recommended for your child, you or your child's doctor should get in touch with the Scoliosis Research Society of the American Academy of Orthopedic Surgeons for their most recent recommendations. You can write to them at 222 South Prospect Avenue, Park Ridge, IL 60068, or call (708) 698-1627.

AFTERWORD

A Better World for Our Children

There are unprecedented strains on American families today. I'll merely list them here, to remind you of how many and varied they are. With the responsibility of raising a child you may become much more sensitive to many of them. Some have been discussed in more detail elsewhere. I believe they can be remedied if we will only recognize them.

More than half of the mothers of preschool children now have to work outside the home. Yet there is not nearly enough high-quality day care, so thousands of children are being deprived and their parents are made to feel guilty.

Working women are still sharply discriminated against—in pay and prestige.

Divorce and the stepfamily, both highly stressful to all concerned, have doubled in frequency since 1975. Child-support judgments are cruelly low, and many fathers soon quit paying, laying a financial burden on the single mothers.

Assembly-line systems in factories and in offices deprive workers of any creative satisfaction.

The rich are getting richer, but the rest are getting poorer. Homelessness is widespread and is particularly devastating to children.

Alcohol and other drug abuse is both a result and a cause of family demoralization.

Teenage pregnancy has become common.

Violence is much greater in the United States than in any

835

other industrial nation—in terms of murder within the family, rape, and child abuse. Parallel with this is the despiritualization and the brutalization of sexuality.

Racial discrimination is still bitter.

Our most basic disturbance, I believe, is the intense competitiveness and materialism of our society, which has convinced many people that getting ahead in their work is the most important thing in life and that family happiness, friendship, and moral and cultural interests should be sacrificed if necessary. Fathers whose adolescents have gotten into trouble have confessed regretfully to me that they allowed no time to get to know their children. Parents transmit their excessive competitiveness to their children. An extreme example is the attempt to teach reading to two-year-olds and, in general, to create superkids.

Human beings normally crave spiritual beliefs, and in some other parts of the world, they balance their materialism with devotion to their religion. But for many Americans these other values have faded, and only their materialism remains strong. I think this is the main reason for the despair of some adolescents and the quadrupling of the teenage suicide rate. Another factor has been their concern about nuclear annihilation.

There are two broad and necessary paths we should take, I believe, to reduce these tensions and make our society more cooperative and happier. The first is to raise our children with different ideals. The second is to become much more politically active.

We should raise our children not primarily to get ahead of others, I believe, but to become kind, cooperative, feeling people who will give family life a high priority, who will participate in the community, who will enrich their spirits with cultural interests, and who will not let their jobs distort their lives. Children should be expected to be kind and helpful from the age of two and should volunteer for hospital, institutional, and tutoring work during adolescence. Schools should stop grading. Parents should refrain from punishing. They should forbid the viewing of violence and explicit sex in movies and on TV.

The other way to start improving our society is for citizens to become much more politically active, in order to take control of the government away from special interests such as arms makers, who exert enormous influence now and absorb trillions of dollars of government funds. These dollars should be devoted instead to people's needs—for day care, schools, health, homes, and to improve the opportunities for the poor and aged.

Political activity includes voting in primaries as well as in elections. (Only half of our citizens now bother to vote.) People should interrogate and listen to the candidates on the issues, rather than pay too much attention to their personalities. Citizens should write and telephone their senators, representatives, and the president, not just once, or once a year, but whenever an issue comes up that is important to them, to their children, and to their community.

GLOSSARY OF MEDICAL TERMS

Throughout this book I have tried to explain medical conditions without using medical jargon. Most doctors and nurse practitioners will do the same. Nevertheless, there may be words that you are unfamiliar with. This glossary is meant to help you understand medical terms with which you may not be familiar. If your doctor's office or the hospital seems like a strange, exotic foreign land to you, then learning its language is the first step in becoming a knowledgeable advocate for your child's medical care.

Abrasion: A superficial scrape of the skin.

Abscess: A collection of pus due to a walled-off infection, causing pain, fever, swelling, and redness at the site. To be cured, an abscess usually needs to be cut open and allowed to drain.

Adenoiditis: An infection and inflammation of the lymph glands above the tonsils.

ADHD: Attention deficit hyperactivity disorder, also known as ADD (attention deficit disorder); hyperactivity.

AIDS: Acquired immunodeficiency syndrome, caused by HIV, which damages the body's ability to ward off infection.

Allergic rhinitis: An allergy that causes a runny, stuffy nose.

Allergy: A condition in which the body is especially sensitive to certain substances that trigger a response by the immune system characterized by inflammation, sneezing, itching, and/or rash.

Alopecia: Baldness or bald spots.

Amblyopia: Poor, dim vision despite a normal eye; in

children often caused by a wandering eye that did not focus sharply during the early years of life.

Amenorrhea: The absence or abnormal cessation of menstrual periods.

Anemia: A reduction in the number of red blood cells in the circulatory system, or a reduction in hemoglobin, the pigment in red cells that carries oxygen.

Anorexia nervosa: A psychological eating disorder marked by an abnormal fear of obesity, deliberate significant weight loss by reducing food intake, and a distorted body image; typically seen in adolescent girls.

Antibiotic: A chemical substance (like penicillin) that inhibits the growth of or kills bacteria. (Antibiotics have no effect on viruses. There are other chemicals when given internally that will kill a few viruses.) "Antibiotic" really means "anti-life." I would prefer to see terms like "antibacterial," "antifungal," or "antiviral" used, which would be more accurate and specifically for what they are treating.

Apgar score: A score from 0 to 10 that rates the newborn infant's well-being at 1, 5, and 10 minutes after delivery by rating from 0 to 2 the heart rate, breathing effort, muscle tone, responsiveness, and skin color. A perfect score is 10; less than 6 is considered low.

Apnea: Temporary cessation of breathing efforts for at least ten seconds.

Arteriosclerosis: A condition marked by the hardening and thickening of the arteries.

Artery: A blood vessel that carries blood away from the heart and to the tissues.

Arthritis: Inflammation of the joints resulting in pain and swelling.

Artificial respiration: A part of cardiopulmonary resuscitation (CPR) where air is forced into the victim's breathing passages by another person or by a bag-and-mask apparatus.

Asphyxia: Suffocation; a state where there is not enough oxygen and too much carbon dioxide in the blood.

Aspiration: Breathing liquid or solid substances into the windpipe.

Asthma: A chronic respiratory disease marked by recurrent wheezing due to spasm, inflammation, and mucus build-up in the small breathing passages; may be caused by allergies or by nonallergic agents such as smoke.

Athlete's foot: A fungus infection of the feet marked by redness and scaling between the toes.

Autism: A neurological condition where the child has disordered language and disordered relationships to people; occurs on a spectrum ranging from mild to severe.

Autoimmune disease: An illness (like lupus or rheumatic fever) where the body's immune system turns against tissues in the person's own body, causing damage to those tissues.

Bacteremia: The presence of bacteria in the blood.

Bacteria: Very small round or rod-shaped organisms that can cause infections when introduced into the body. (Antibiotics combat *only* bacterial infections.)

Birthmark: A mole or blemish that is present from birth.

Blood poisoning: A bacterial infection or toxins from bacteria in the blood.

Boil: A painful pus-filled nodule under the skin, often starting in a hair follicle or a skin pore, caused by bacterial infection, usually staphylococcus.

Bronchiolitis: An inflammation of the small bronchial tubes due to a viral infection, causing wheezing and difficulty breathing.

Bronchitis: Inflammation of the larger bronchial tubes; can be caused by a viral or bacterial infection.

Bronchopulmonary dysplasia (BPD): A condition of some premature infants in which there is scarring and chronic swelling and inflammation of the lungs; typically improves as the infant grows and new lung tissue is formed.

Bulimia: A psychological eating disorder marked by periods of binge eating followed by self-induced vomiting or purging.

Cancer: Abnormal growth of cells that are malignant in that they invade the surrounding tissues and can travel and take root (metastasize) to other sites.

Candida: A yeastlike fungus that causes diaper rash and mouth infections in infants.

Canker sore: Recurrent ulcerations of the mouth or lips; the cause is usually unknown. May be due to herpesvirus Type I.

Cardiopulmonary resuscitation (CPR): An emergency measure taken to maintain blood flow to the brain following a cardiac arrest or absence of breathing, using artificial respiration and chest compressions.

Cellulitis: Infection and inflammation of the tissue just below the skin.

Cerebral palsy: A neurological condition due to brain damage or of no known cause, usually before birth, that causes impairment of the use of muscles, movement, and posture; not a progressive disease.

Chicken pox: A contagious disease caused by the varicella virus and marked by fever and an itchy vesicular rash. Can be treated if severe.

Chlamydia: An unusual bacterium that lives only inside the cells of the body's tissues; probably the most common sexually transmitted disease. Also can cause pneumonia and conjunctivitis in first year of life.

Circumcision: The removal of the foreskin of the penis.

Cleft lip, cleft palate: A congenital fissure in the lip and/or the roof of the mouth.

Clubfoot: A congenital deformity of the foot marked by twisting in of the ankle, heel, and toes.

Cold: A viral infection of the upper breathing passages, nose, and throat. Does not respond to antibiotics.

Cold sore: A small blister on the lips or next to the lips; caused by the herpesvirus; also called a fever blister.

Colitis: Inflammation of the colon; cause may be infectious, autoimmune, or unknown.

Colostrum: Thin, milky, yellowish fluid, full of protein, antibodies, and minerals but low in carbohydrates and fat, secreted by the glands in the breast before the true milk arrives.

Coma: A prolonged state of unconsciousness from which the person cannot be aroused; often caused by trauma, poisoning, infection, shock, or heart and lung disorders.

Concussion: A temporary impairment of consciousness with loss of responsiveness and awareness lasting for seconds, minutes, or hours after a head injury; may be accompanied by memory loss for the traumatic event.

Congenital: Existing at or before birth (not the same as genetic) and caused by hereditary or environmental influences.

Congestive heart failure: Inability of the heart to pump sufficient blood to meet the body's demands; causes a backing-up of the blood circulation leading to swelling in the body, weakness, and shortness of breath.

Conjunctivitis: An inflammation, with redness and with or without discharge, of the membrane over the white of the eye; typically caused by a viral or bacterial infection or an allergy.

Constipation: Infrequency or difficulty in passing bowel movements, often because of dry, hardened feces.

Convulsions: Violent involuntary twitching of the muscles due to an abnormal electrical discharge in the brain.

Cradle cap: Greasy yellowish crust on the scalp; due to excess production of oils; can cause rash and irritation of the face and groin; also called seborrhea.

Craniosynostosis: Premature closure of the different sections of the skull, leading to reduced growth perpendicular to the joined area.

Cyanosis: Reduced oxygen in the blood, leading to a bluish skin color.

Cyst: A small closed sac below the skin, usually containing fluid.

Cystic fibrosis: A hereditary disease of the secretory glands which is an inability to secrete chloride across all membranes, causing pulmonary and digestive problems.

Cystitis: Inflammation of the bladder, usually due to a viral or bacterial infection or chemical irritation.

Dehydration: A condition in which an excessive amount of water has been lost from the body, resulting in decreased fluids in the tissues and circulation; usually due to vomiting and/or diarrhea without adequate liquid intake to compensate for the loss of fluids. It may occur in hot weather because of sweat losses.

Dermatitis: Inflammation of the skin caused by allergies, infection, or irritation.

Diabetes mellitus: A disease in which the pancreas does not secrete sufficient insulin, resulting in very high levels of sugar (glucose) in the body; causing excessive urination leading to extreme thirst and hunger, weight loss, and weakness if untreated. Childhood-onset diabetes is usually more severe and insulin dependent than adult-onset diabetes. Treatment is typically with at least two shots of insulin a day and careful dietary control.

Diarrhea: Watery and frequent bowel movements, usually caused by a viral infection; also may be due to a bacterial infection or another intestinal disease.

Diphtheria: A severe bacterial disease, rarely seen now, marked by a severe sore throat, high fever, and weakness.

Doula: An experienced woman who provides continuous emotional and physical support for a couple (or a woman) during labor and delivery.

Dysentery: Inflammation of the intestines, especially the colon, with frequent, painful, bloody, mucusy bowel movements. Usually infectious in origin and caused by bacteria, parasite, or protozoan organisms.

Dysphagia: Difficulty in swallowing; typically due to cerebral palsy or some anatomical abnormality of the throat.

Eczema: Inflammation of the skin marked by blistery red bumps, itching, scaling, and crusting; usually due to allergies or direct irritation of the skin.

Edema: An excess of fluids accumulating in the tissues.

Encephalitis: Inflammation of the brain; typically caused by a virus infection.

Encephalopathy: A generalized disturbance of the brain causing changes in behavior, consciousness, and/or seizures; usually noninfectious. Lead poisoning is one example.

Encopresis: Soiling of the underpants with feces, usually secondary to constipation.

Endocarditis: An inflammation of the lining of the heart; usually due to a bacterial infection or rheumatic fever.

Endocrine system: The system of hormone-secreting glands such as the thyroid and adrenal glands.

Enuresis: Involuntary discharge of urine after the age of five.

Epilepsy: A disease with episodic, recurrent seizures caused by an underlying disorder that affects the electrical activity of the brain.

Epistaxis: A nosebleed.

Erythema: Redness of the skin caused by increased blood flow, usually due to inflammation or infection. Seen also in sunburn.

Esophagus: The muscular tube through which food passes from the throat to the stomach.

Failure to thrive: A syndrome in young children whose rate of weight gain and possibly growth are chronically and significantly below the average; may be due to illness and/or psychosocial disturbances.

Febrile: Feverish.

Febrile convulsions: Seizures that only occur with an elevated temperature; usually not dangerous and usually don't lead to epilepsy.

Fetal alcohol syndrome: A congenital syndrome of birth defects caused by exposure to excessive amounts of alcohol during pregnancy; can lead to poor growth, learning problems, and a characteristic facial appearance.

Food poisoning: Vomiting and diarrhea caused by eating food contaminated with bacteria.

Foreign body: An object that becomes lodged in a body cavity, such as the nose, ear, or vagina.

Fracture: A break or crack in a bone, usually diagnosed by X-ray study.

Fragile X syndrome: A genetic syndrome seen mainly but not exclusively in males, marked by a spectrum of developmental, learning, and behavioral problems as well as characteristic physical features. Caused by a mutation on the X chromosome; probably the most common inherited form of mental retardation.

Frostbite: Damage to tissues, usually in fingers, toes, nose, and ears, due to exposure to very cold temperatures.

Fungus: A class of low-level vegetable organisms including yeast, molds, and mushrooms. Can cause mild or serious infections requiring treatment with antifungal medications.

Gamma globulin: A blood product containing antibodies to various bacterial and viral diseases; used for prevention of certain diseases such as hepatitis and measles and for treatment of certain diseases, such as Kawasaki's syndrome and immune deficiency states.

Gangrene: An infection, usually bacterial, causing the death and decomposition of tissues, leading to poor blood supply to the area and further invasive infection.

Gastroenteritis: Inflammation of the lining of the stomach and intestines, usually leading to vomiting and/or diarrhea, typically caused by a viral infection, but also can be due to a bacterial or parasitic infection or other causes.

Gastroesophageal reflux: Regurgitation of stomach contents back into the esophagus; can lead to heartburn, vomiting, and aspiration.

Giardia: A protozoan organism that can infect the intestines and cause diarrhea and/or abdominal pain; usually comes from contaminated drinking water.

Glaucoma: Abnormally increased pressure of the fluids of the eyeball, leading to blindness if untreated.

Gynecomastia: Excessive development of the male breasts, often seen in twelve- to fifteen-year-old boys; typically resolves spontaneously.

Haemophilus influenzae: A bacteria that can cause significant infections in young children; now becoming rare because of early immunization against it; also called H flu.

Hay fever: An allergy with congestion, runny nose, sneezing, and watery eyes, which recurs the same time every year; often due to a sensitivity to pollen.

Health maintenance organization (HMO): A managed care health system where a primary care doctor (or nurse practitioner) coordinates medical care including prevention, diagnosis and treatment. A co-payment at the time of an office or clinic visit may be required.

Heart murmur: A whooshing sound made by blood as it is pumped by the heart. Can signify an abnormality of the structure of the heart, although most do not.

Heat stroke: Delirium, convulsions, or coma due to a rectal temperature above 106°F. Usually due to excessive exercise in hot weather, almost never due to infection.

Hemangioma: A benign tumor made up of blood vessels, usually found in the skin.

Hematocrit: The percentage of the blood occupied by red blood cells. A low hematocrit, often caused by iron deficiency in young children, means the same as anemia.

Hematuria: Blood in the urine; the blood can come from anywhere in the urinary tract, including the kidneys or bladder.

Hemoglobin: An iron-containing pigmented chain within the red blood cell that carries oxygen from the lungs to the tissues.

Hemophilia: A hereditary disease seen almost always in boys, marked by an inability to clot the blood following trauma, leading to bleeding into joints and other deep tissues.

Hemoptysis: Coughing up blood from the respiratory tract. In childhood, not caused by TB.

Hemorrhage: Profuse bleeding.

Hemorrhoids: Swollen enlarged veins in the rectum, causing pain, itching, and occasional bleeding.

Hepatitis: Inflammation of the liver, causing jaundice and discomfort, usually due to a viral infection or a chemical or drug that is toxic to the liver.

Hepatomegaly: An enlarged liver.

Hernia: The protrusion of tissue or an organ through an abnormal opening in the muscles below the skin; typically seen in the navel area (umbilical hernia) or in the groin (inguinal hernia).

Hip dislocation: Usually a congenital disorder where the thigh bone (femur) does not sit properly and securely in the hip joint; can lead to an abnormally formed hip joint if left untreated.

Hirsute: Excessively hairy.

HIV: Human immunodeficiency virus, the causative agent of AIDS.

Hives: An allergic reaction causing itchy red welts of the skin with a pale area in the middle.

Hydrocele: A collection of fluid around the testicles, causing swelling of the scrotum; usually resolves spontaneously.

Hydrocephalus: An abnormal accumulation of fluid in the brain. If left untreated, it can cause pressure and destruction of brain tissue; usually managed with a piece of tubing (a shunt) that drains the fluid from the brain to the abdomen or chest.

Hypertension: Abnormally high blood pressure.

Hyperthyroidism: Excessive secretion of thyroid hormone by the thyroid gland, causing a very fast heart and respiratory rate, weight loss, bulging of the eyeballs, irritability, and hyperactivity; usually treated with medications.

Hypospadias: A congenital abnormality of the penis in which the opening of the urinary tract (urethra) is found on the underside of the penis or even below the penis; requires surgical repair if significant.

Hypothyroidism: Abnormally low secretion of thyroid hormone by the thyroid gland, causing low muscle tone and activity, constipation, lethargy, and a weak, hoarse cry; can be easily treated with thyroid hormone given by mouth. Screening at birth allows this condition to be identified before damage occurs.

Hypotonia: Abnormally low muscle tension or activity when at rest; sometimes described as a floppy baby.

Hypoxia: Decreased amount of oxygen in the blood, usually due to a respiratory problem.

Impetigo: A bacterial (usually strep or staph) infection of the skin, very contagious, with a thick yellow crust.

Inflammation: The body's response to injury, irritation, or infection; a complicated process marked by pain, heat, redness, and swelling caused by a flood of blood elements, such as white blood cells and various chemicals, to the site.

Influenza: A Type A or B viral illness marked by fever, chills, lethargy, muscle aches, and respiratory symptoms, lasting three to fourteen days.

Ischemia: Insufficient blood flow to tissues.

Jaundice: A yellow tinge to the skin, mucous membranes, and whites of the eyes caused by excess bilirubin in the blood, usually due to temporary immaturity of the liver in a newborn or by bile duct obstruction or inflammation of the liver in older children.

Knock-knees: A deformity of the legs in which the knees are abnormally close together and the ankles are spread too far apart.

Laceration: A cut in the skin; may require stitches depending on location, depth, and severity of the wound.

Laryngitis: Inflammation of the voice box causing hoarseness or loss of voice, usually caused by a self-limited viral infection.

Lazy eye: When one of the eyes does not focus on the object, but turns either inward or outward (*strabismus*); often requires patching of the unaffected eye to promote focusing of the lazy eye.

Leukemia: Cancer of the white blood cells, marked by anemia, bleeding, infections, and swollen lymph glands. Some forms of leukemia are now curable with chemotherapy and radiation therapy.

Lice: Small, flat-bodied parasites that usually make their home in hairy areas of the body, where they lay small white eggs (nits) that stick to the bottom of the hair shafts; lice are a common childhood nuisance, quite contagious but essentially harmless.

Lockjaw: An early sign of tetanus in which the jaws are clenched shut due to the tetanus toxin, which is rare because of immunization.

Lupus (systemic lupus erythematosus): An autoimmune disorder in which the body's immune system attacks its own tissues, especially in the skin, joints, and kidneys.

Lyme disease: A newly described disease caused by a bacteria (*spirochete*) carried by the deer tick. Symptoms include a distinctive skin rash, followed by fever, fatigue, headaches, joint aches, and later on, sometimes various nervous system symptoms. Prevention involves avoiding the deer tick or prompt removal following a bite. Antibiotics are helpful, especially when given early in the disease.

Lymphadenopathy: Enlarged lymph glands; may be due to a variety of disease states and infections that stimulate the lymphoid tissue to fight the disease.

Lymph glands: Round pouches that make lymph and excrete it into the bloodstream. These tend to enlarge when warding off an infection.

Lymphocytes: White blood cells that fight off viral and bacterial infections.

Malaria: An infectious disease caused by a protozoan parasite that lives in red blood cells; marked by recurring cycles of fever, chills, and sweating; spread by the mosquito; can be treated with various antimalarial drugs.

Measles (*rubeola*): A viral infection marked by fever, chills, rash, conjunctivitis, and upper respiratory symptoms.

Melanoma: Cancer of the pigment-secreting cells of the skin; may occur in moles. Melanomas in adults are, in part, triggered by sunburns in early childhood.

Meningitis: Inflammation of the membranes that line the brain and spinal cord, usually due to a bacterial or viral infection; marked by headache, stiff neck, and vomiting. Bacterial meningitis is a medical emergency, while viral meningitis is largely self-limited and does not cause serious problems. An exception is herpesvirus, which produces brain inflammation.

Microcephaly: An abnormally small head, often associated with mental deficiency since an abnormally small head means that there is an abnormally small brain. However, sometimes it is simply a family trait with no mental problems at all.

Migraine: A specific kind of periodic headache, usually one-sided and accompanied by nausea, vomiting, and visual disturbances. Migraines often run in families.

Mittelschmerz: Abdominal pain occurring in the middle of the menstrual cycle, presumably due to ovulation.

Mole: A pigmented, slightly raised, sometimes hairy blemish in the skin. Most moles are benign but certain kinds are prone to turning into cancer in later life and must be removed.

Molluscum contagiosum: A contagious viral infection of the skin that causes pearly white bumps with a central depression. These are benign but may last months to years without treatment.

Mongolian spots: Bluish black superficial coloring of the skin, usually in dark-skinned infants. These typically occur on the buttocks and back but can be found anywhere. They fade in time and are not associated with any problems.

Mongolism: An old-fashioned, no longer acceptable term for Down syndrome (trisomy 21).

Mononucleosis: A viral infection (the Epstein-Barr virus, or EBV) marked by swelling of the lymph glands (especially those in the neck), sore throat, fatigue, fever, and rash. The illness can last several weeks; there is no specific treatment.

Mucus: A slippery, slimy, thick substance secreted by glands to provide protection to the lining of the breathing and other passages (mucous membranes). These cells are stimulated to produce more mucus by infectious agents.

Mumps: A viral illness that attacks and inflames the saliva-secreting glands of the face and neck, and occasionally the pancreas, testicles, ovaries, or brain. There is no specific treatment.

Muscular dystrophy: A group of inherited conditions marked by gradual and progressive muscle wasting. There are different forms of muscular dystrophy, some severe, some mild. There is no treatment.

Nephritis: Inflammation of the tissues of the kidney, usually causing blood in the urine; may be caused by an autoimmune disorder (as in nephritis following a streptococcal infection) or an infectious disorder.

Nephrotic syndrome: A kidney disorder in which the kidney excretes excessive amounts of protein into the urine, causing low protein levels in the blood and swelling (edema) of the body. Medications such as steroids are sometimes helpful.

Nevus: A mole.

Obstructive sleep apnea: A condition occurring when the child sleeps in which the breathing passages in the back of the throat become obstructed and the child cannot breathe despite active efforts to do so; sometimes caused by very large adenoids. Can cause significant problems if not treated promptly, usually by removing the adenoids and the tonsils.

Osteomyelitis: An infection, usually bacterial, of the bone. Can take many weeks or months to cure because the blood supply to the bone is weak and antibiotics do not penetrate well.

Otitis externa: Swimmer's ear; a bacterial infection of the ear canal.

Otitis media: A middle ear infection caused by a bacteria or a virus.

Pediculosis: *See* Lice.

Pelvic inflammatory disease (PID): Infection of the uterus, Fallopian tubes, and genital tract; usually occurs in adolescents fifteen to nineteen years of age; caused by the bacteria (typically chlamydia, gonorrhea, or a variety of other organisms) ascending from the vagina into the genital tract; can cause infertility if not treated promptly with antibiotics.

Peptic ulcer: An area of the stomach where the lining is raw, inflamed, and irritated by stomach acids. Now known to often be caused by a bacterial infection from *Heliobacter pylori,* which can be treated with antibiotics.

Peritonitis: Inflammation of the membrane lining the abdomen and pelvis, usually a bacterial infection from a rupture of the intestines (as in a ruptured appendix).

Pertussis: Whooping cough; a contagious respiratory disease caused by a bacterial infection, marked by paroxysms of forceful coughing. Treatment includes antibiotics and supportive care.

Petechiae: Small, pinpoint, non-raised, round, dark red spots just below the skin caused by a hemorrhage in the small blood vessels; can be due to a viral or serious bacterial infection. Do not blanch.

Pharyngitis: Inflammation of the throat caused by a virus or bacteria, sometimes streptococcus.

Phimosis: A very tight foreskin of the penis so that it cannot be retracted over the shaft. May require circumcision, although it is normal in the first year of life when not accompanied by symptoms.

Pinkeye: *See* conjunctivitis.

Pinworms: A common intestinal infection of small, thin white worms. Typically the only symptom is itching around the anus. Effective treatment is available with oral medications.

Platelet: A very small circular disk found in the blood, which helps to promote coagulation of the blood and stop bleeding when a small blood vessel ruptures.

Pneumococcus: A bacteria causing infections in the lungs, ears, or nervous system, marked by rapid onset and high fever. Usually responds well to antibiotics.

Pneumonia: A bacterial or viral infection of the lung causing cough, fast breathing, and sometimes fever.

Polio: A contagious virus that attacks the nerves of the spinal cord responsible for voluntary movement. Completely preventable by childhood immunizations.

Proteinuria: Protein in the urine, caused by "leaky kidney." Seen in nephrotic syndrome, chronic kidney infections, and other kidney disorders.

Psoriasis: A chronic skin disorder marked by recurrent red itchy patches covered with silvery scales and plaques. Cause is unknown; there is no cure, but symptomatic treatment is with lubricating lotions, steroid cream, and sunlight.

Purpura: Purplish spots in the skin due to hemorrhage. Can be due to a low platelet count, a viral infection, or trauma or, less commonly, an autoimmune disorder such as Henoch-Schöenlein purpura.

Pyelonephritis: A bacterial infection of the kidney, causing fever, fatigue, and flank pain; treated with large doses of antibiotics.

Pyloric stenosis: An obstruction of the stomach in infants (typical age is three to four weeks), due to an enlarged circular muscle (*pylorus*) at the stomach outlet to the intestines; often requires surgical repair.

Quadriplegia: Paralysis of the body from the neck down.

Reactive airway disease: Inflammation and destruction of small passages in the lungs caused by some infections, pollutants, toxins, cold air, and tobacco smoke, producing wheezing and cough. This condition can be treated with medications.

Respiratory syncytial virus (RSV): A virus that is the primary cause of bronchiolitis in infants. May be prevented in high-risk infants. Treatment is available for extremely ill infants with RSV disease.

Rheumatic fever: An autoimmune disorder following an upper respiratory infection with the streptococcus bacteria, marked by inflammation of the heart, blood vessels, joints, nervous system, and skin. Treatment is primarily prevention of further streptococcal infections by taking penicillin daily.

Rhinitis: Inflammation of the mucous membranes of the nose, causing nasal discharge and stuffiness. Usually caused by a viral upper respiratory infection.

Rickets: Vitamin D deficiency causing abnormalities of the bone, usually due to a lack of vitamin D intake and/or limited exposure to sunlight.

Ringworm: A fungal infection (not a worm at all) of the skin with ring-shaped, reddish, itchy patches. Mildly contagious.

Roseola: A viral infection of infants due to herpesvirus VI or VII, marked by a very high fever for three or four days, followed by the eruption of a generalized rose-colored rash after the fever subsides and the child is well. No treatment is needed.

Rotavirus: A virus that is a major cause of vomiting and watery diarrhea throughout the world, usually occurring in the winter months.

Rubella (German measles): A viral infection marked by upper respiratory symptoms and a rash that looks very much like measles. Can cause birth defects if contracted early in pregnancy; preventable by childhood immunizations.

Salmonella: A bacteria that can cause severe diarrhea, fever, or bacteremia, or the person may be a carrier with no symptoms. It is spread by undercooked chicken, raw eggs, and live pet turtles. Typically treated with antibiotics.

Scarlet fever: A streptococcal throat infection accompanied by a generalized salmon-colored rash. Scarlet fever is no longer considered any more dangerous than any other strep infection.

Scoliosis: An abnormal curvature of the spine, usually of unknown origin. Early detection is the key to treatment.

Seizures: A sudden attack of twitches of the arms or legs, usually with a loss of consciousness, due to abnormal electrical stimulation in the brain. Recurrent seizures are known as epilepsy.

Septicemia: *See* Blood poisoning.

Sexually transmitted disease (STD): Any infectious disease that is transmitted through sexual intercourse or other intimate sexual contact. May be caused by chlamydia, gonorrhea, or syphilis.

Shigella: A bacteria that causes dysentery and high fever. Treatment is often with antibiotics.

Shingles: Painful skin lesions caused by the varicella (chicken pox) virus, which lives dormant in the nerves of the skin and then travels down the nerve, causing intense pain. The pain of shingles is usually mild in children, though it may be severe in adults. Shingles can be treated.

Shock: Inadequate circulation due to loss of blood volume causing inadequate oxygen to be delivered to the tissues. Marked by pale and clammy skin, low blood pressure, rapid heart rate. Can lead to unconsciousness and death.

Sickle-cell anemia: A genetic disease, primarily of people from African or Mediterranean origins, causing deformation of the red blood cells so that they look like a sickle. This causes the cells to become wedged in the small blood vessels, causing pain and tissue damage. There is currently no cure, except bone marrow transplant.

Sinusitis: Inflammation of the sinuses, of bacterial or viral origin.

Smegma: A normal thick, cheesy secretion that collects around the head of the penis and clitoris.

Spasticity: Increased muscle tone due to brain damage, causing stiff and awkward movements.

Spina bifida: A congenital defect marked by incomplete closure of the bones that encase the spinal cord, often associated with hydrocephalus and neurological problems of the lower body.

Splenomegaly: An enlarged spleen, often due to an acute infection or a blood disorder in which the red blood cells are broken down at a rapid rate (hemolytic anemia).

Sprain: An injury to a joint caused by excessive stretching but not tearing of the ligaments, marked by pain and swelling.

Strep throat: An infection of the pharynx with the streptococcal bacteria. Treatment is with penicillin or another antibiotic.

Stridor: A harsh sound made when the child breathes in, often heard in croup, allergic reactions, foreign body aspiration, and other infections of the throat.

Sudden infant death syndrome (SIDS): The unexpected death of an infant, typically three to four months of age, from unknown causes. The most common reason for death in the first twelve months of life.

Syphilis: A bacterial (*spirochete*), contagious, sexually transmitted disease that can infect any and all organ systems.

Swollen glands: *See* Lymphadenopathy.

Syncope: A fainting episode, usually caused by temporarily diminished blood flow and oxygen to the brain.

Tendonitis: Inflammation of the tendons, the fibrous cords that attach muscles to bone.

Tetanus: A deep-rooted bacterial infection that secretes a toxin which causes spasm of the muscles of the mouth (lockjaw) and then other muscles of the body. Prevented by routine childhood immunizations and a booster shot every ten years.

Thalessemia: A hereditary blood disorder in which the body produces abnormal hemoglobin, causing significant anemia.

Thrush: *See* Candida.

Tonsillitis: Inflammation of the tonsils, the lymphoid tissues in the back of the throat, from a bacterial or viral infection.

Tourette's syndrome: A disorder marked by chronic motor

tics (eye blinking, facial grimacing, head jerking) and vocal tics (repetitive throat clearing, grunting, or words). Probably a genetic disorder.

Trench mouth: A painful bacterial infection of the gums with grayish ulcerations. Often requires antibiotic treatment.

Tuberculosis (TB): A contagious infectious disease caused by *Mycobacterium tuberculosis,* causing infection in the lungs, lymph nodes, and other organs. Treatment usually involves taking one or several anti-TB drugs for at least nine months.

Ulcer: A painful disintegration of the surface of the lining of many organs, such as the stomach, usually due to inflammation or inadequate blood flow to the area.

Urinary tract infection (UTI): A bacterial (rarely viral) infection of the bladder or kidneys.

Urticaria: *See* Hives.

Vaginitis: Inflammation of the vagina with pain and a discharge, usually due to bacterial infection or a foreign body.

Varicella: *See* Chicken pox.

Virus: A minute infectious agent that can live only in the cells of a living host, causing infection. Only a few medications kill viruses; the usual antibiotics have no effect.

Wart: A viral infection of the skin causing a rough, heaped-up lump on the skin. There is no good treatment, although chemicals that help dissolve the wart are often used. Most will disappear on their own within two years.

Wheezing: The high-pitched whistling sound made by air passing through a narrowed airway. Heard in asthma, bronchiolitis, foreign-body aspiration, and other conditions in which the small respiratory tubes are narrowed.

Whooping cough: *See* Pertussis.

Yeast infection: A mild fungal infection, usually of the mouth, diaper area, or vagina.

GUIDE TO CHILD AND FAMILY RESOURCES

Don't Go It Alone!

If you have a concern about your child, your family, or yourself, the best general advice I can give you is: Don't go it alone. There are resources available on *any* problem you might encounter. Go to your local library or bookstore and see what's available. Talk to other parents in similar circumstances and find out what has worked for them. Seek the support and advice of those professionals you trust—your doctor or nurse practitioner, a teacher, a member of the clergy.

This section offers you another option. It includes national organizations that deal with a wide variety of child and family issues. Call or write them to see what pamphlets, books, and support groups they can offer. Check your local Yellow Pages. There may a local group near you.

Don't despair. With a little diligence you will be able to find the information and support you are looking for. (Please note, however, that these addresses and phone numbers are subject to change.)

Adoption

National Adoption Information Clearinghouse
Box 1182
Washington, DC 20013-1182
703-246-9095
Fax: 703-385-3206

National Adoption Center
800-TO-ADOPT

Adoptive Families of America
2309 Como Avenue
Saint Paul, MN 55108
800-372-3300
612-645-9955
Fax: 612-645-0055

AIDS

CDC National HIV/AIDS Hotline
American Social Health Association
Box 13827
Research Triangle Park, NC 27709
800-342-2437

Alcohol Abuse

National Clearinghouse for Alcohol and Drug Information
(NCADI)
Box 2345
Rockville, MD 20857-2345
301-468-2600
800-729-6686
http://www.health.org

American Academy of Pediatrics

AAP Public Education
Box 927
Elk Grove Village, IL 60009-0927
800-433-9016
847-228-5005

Anorexia Nervosa and Bulimia

American Anorexia/Bulimia Association
293 Central Park West

Suite 1R
New York, NY 10024
212-501-8351
Fax: 212-501-0342
http://www.members.aol.com/amanbu

Anorexia Nervosa and Related Eating Disorders (ANRED)
Box 5102
Eugene, OR 97405
541-344-1144
http://www.anred.com

National Eating Disorders Organization
6655 South Yale Avenue
Tulsa, OK 74136
918-481-4044
http://laureate.com

National Association of Anorexia Nervosa and Associated
Disorders (ANAD)
Box 7
Highland Park, IL 60035
847-831-3438
Fax: 847-433-4632

Asthma and Allergy

Asthma and Allergy Foundation of America
1125 15th Street NW, Suite 502
Washington, DC 20005
800-727-8462

Allergy Information Referral Line
American Academy of Allergy and Immunology
611 East Wells Street
Milwaukee, WI 53202
800-822-2762
Fax: 414-272-6070
http://www.aaai.org

Asthma Information Center and Hotline
Box 790
Springhouse, PA 19477-1790
800-727-5400

Attention Deficit Disorder

AD-IN: Attention Deficit Information Network
475 Hillside Avenue
Needham, MA 02194
617-455-9895
Fax: 617-444-5466
E-mail: adin@gis.net

CHADD: Children and Adults with Attention Deficit
Disorders
499 NW 70th Avenue
Suite 109
Plantation, FL 33317
800-233-4050
954-587-3700
Fax: 954-587-4599
http://www.chad.org

ADD Warehouse
300 Northwest 70th Avenue
Suite 102
Plantation, FL 33317
800-233-9273
Fax: 954-792-8545

Autism

Autism Society of America
7910 Woodmont Avenue
Suite 650
Bethesda, MD 20814-3015
800-328-8476
Fax: 301-657-0869
http://www.autism-society.org

National Autism Hotline/Autism Services Center
605 Ninth Street
Prichard Building
Box 507
Huntington, WV 25710-0507
304-525-8014
Fax: 304-525-8026

Auto Safety

NHTSA Auto Safety Hotline
800-424-9393

Bed-Wetting

National Enuresis Society
Box 6351
Parsippany, NJ 07054

Birth Defects

Association of Birth Defect Children
827 Irma Avenue
Orlando, FL 32803
800-313-2232
407-245-7035
Fax: 407-245-7087
http://www.birthdefects.org

March of Dimes/Birth Defects Foundation
1275 Mamaroneck Avenue
White Plains, NY 10605
888-MODIMES
914-428-7100
Fax: 914-997-4763
http://www.modimes.org

Breast-Feeding

La Leche League International Headquarters
1400 Meacham Road

Schaumburg, IL 60173
800-LALECHE
847-519-7730
Fax: 847-519-0035
http://www.lalecheleague.org

Cancer

American Cancer Society
1599 Clifton Road NE
Atlanta, GA 30329-4251
800-227-2345
http://www.cancer.org

Candlelighters Childhood Cancer Foundation
7910 Woodmont Avenue
Suite 460
Bethesda, MD 20814
800-366-2223
http://www.candlelighters.org

Cerebral Palsy

United Cerebral Palsy Association
1660 L Street NW
Suite 700
Washington, DC 20036
800-872-5827
202-776-0406
Fax: 202-776-0414
http://www.ucpa.org

Exceptional Parent Magazine
555 Kinderkamack Road
Oradell, NJ 07649
800-372-7368
201-634-6550
Fax: 201-634-6599
http://www.familyeducation.com
E-mail: epmag12@aol.com

Child Abuse and Neglect

Parents Anonymous
Check local listing

National Clearinghouse on Child Abuse and Neglect and Family Violence Information
Box 1182
Washington, DC 20013-1182
800-394-3366
Fax: 703-385-3200
http://www.calib.com/nccanch

Child Advocacy

American Academy of Pediatrics
Box 927
141 NW Point Boulevard
Elk Grove Village, IL 60009-0927
800-433-9016
847-228-5005 (to order materials)
Fax: 847-228-5097
http://www.aap.org

Children's Defense Fund
25 E Street NW
Washington, DC 20001
202-628-8339
Fax: 202-662-3510
http://www.childrensdefense.org

Child Welfare League of America
440 1st Street NW
Washington, DC 20001
202-638-2952
Fax: 202-638-4004

Chronic Conditions

Federation for Children with Special Needs
95 Berkeley Street
Suite 104

Boston, MA 02116
617-482-2915
Fax: 617-695-2939
http://www.fcsn.org

Cleft Palate

Association for the Care of Children's Health (ACCH)
19 Mantua Road
Mount Royal, NJ 08061
609-222-1742

Sibling Information Network
991 Main Street
East Hartford, CT 06108
203-832-7050

Consumer Products Safety

Consumer Product Safety Commission (CPSC) Hotline
800-638-CPSC

Cystic Fibrosis

Cystic Fibrosis Foundation
6931 Arlington Road
Bethedsa, MD 20814
800-344-4823
301-951-4422
Fax: 301-951-6378
http://www.cff.org

Day Care

National Association for the Education of Young Children
1509 16th Street NW
Washington, DC 20036-1426
800-424-2460
202-232-8777
Fax: 202-328-1846
http://www.naeyc.org/naeyc

National Association of Child Care Resource and Referral Agencies
1319 F Street NW
Suite 810
Washington, DC 20004
202-393-5501
Fax: 202-393-1109
E-mail: hn5018@handsnet.org

Deaf-Blind

DB-LINK: National Information Clearinghouse on Children Who Are Deaf-Blind
345 N Monmouth Avenue
Monmouth, OR 97361
800-438-9376

National Family Association for the Deaf-Blind
111 Middle Neck Road
Sands Point, NY 11050
800-255-0411 (V/TTY)
516-944-8900 (voice)
516-944-8637 (TTY)
516-944-7302 (Fax)

Depression

Depression Information
800-421-4211

Diabetes Mellitus

American Diabetes Association
National Center
1660 Duke Street
Alexandria, VA 22314
800-232-3472
703-549-1500

Juvenile Diabetes Foundation International
120 Wall Street

New York, NY 10005
800-533-2873
212-889-7575
Fax: 212-785-9595

Domestic Violence

National Council on Child Abuse and Family Violence
800-222-2000

Down Syndrome

Association for Children with Down Syndrome
2616 Martin Avenue
Bellmore, NY 11710
516-221-4700
Fax: 516-221-5867

National Down Syndrome Congress
1605 Chantilly Drive
Suite 250
Atlanta, GA 30324
800-232-6372
404-633-1555
Fax: 404-633-2817

National Down Syndrome Society
666 Broadway
8th Floor
New York, NY 10012-2317
800-221-4602
212-460-9330
Fax: 212-979-2873
http://www.ndss.org

Drug Abuse

Alateen, Al-Anon
1600 Corporate Landing Parkway
Virginia Beach, VA 23454

800-344-2666
757-563-1600
Fax: 757-563-1655

National Clearinghouse for Alcohol and Drug
Information
Box 2345
Rockville, MD 20847-2345
800-729-6686
301-468-2600
Fax: 301-468-6433
http://www.health.org

Drug Abuse Information and Treatment Referral Line
National Institute on Drug Abuse
c/o Phoenix Health Foundation
164 West 74th Street
New York, NY 10023
800-662-4357
Fax: 212-496-6035

Dyslexia

Dyslexia Research Institute
4745 Centerville Road
Tallahassee, FL 32308
904-893-2216
Fax: 904-893-2440

Orton Dyslexia Society
Chester Building
Suite 382
8600 Lasalle Road
Baltimore, MD 21286-2044
800-222-3123
410-296-0232
Fax: 410-321-5069
http://www.ods.org

Eating Disorders

See Anorexia Nervosa and Bulimia listing

Epilepsy

Epilepsy Foundation of America
4351 Garden City Drive
Landover, MD 20785-2267
800-332-1000
301-459-3700
Fax: 301-577-2684
http://www.esa.org

Fetal Alcohol Syndrome/Effect

Family Empowerment Network:
Support for Families Affected by FAS/FAE
610 Langdon Street
Room 523
Madison, WI 53703
800-462-5254
608-262-6590
Fax: 608-265-2329

Fetal Alcohol Education Program
1975 Main Street
Concord, MA 01742
508-369-7713

National Organization on Fetal Alcohol Syndrome
1819 H Street NW
Suite 750
Washington, DC 20006
800-666-6327 (66NOFAS)
202-785-4585
Fax: 202-466-6456

First Aid

The Heimlich Institute
2368 Victory Parkway
Suite 410
Cincinnati, OH 45206
513-221-0002

Fax: 513-221-0003
E-mail: heimlich@iglou.net

Foster Parents

National Foster Care Resource Center
102 King Hall
Eastern Michigan University
Ypsilanti, MI 48197
313-487-0374
Fax: 313-487-0284
http://emich.edu/public/iscfc

National Foster Parent Association
9 Dartmoor Drive
Crystal Lake, IL 60014
800-557-5238
815-455-2527
Fax: 815-455-1527

Fragile X Syndrome

National Fragile X Foundation
1441 York Street
Suite 303
Denver, CO 80206
800-688-8765
303-333-6155
Fax: 303-333-4369

Gay and Lesbian Children

Parents, Families and Friends of Lesbian & Gays, Inc.
1101 14th Street NW
Suite 1030
Washington, DC 20005
202-638-4200
Fax: 202-638-0243
http://www.pflag.org

Gay and Lesbian Parents

National Gay and Lesbian Task Force
2320 17th Street NW
Washington, DC 20009
202-332-6483
Fax: 202-332-0207
http://www.ngltf.org
E-mail: ngltf@ngltf.org

Gay and Lesbian Parents' Coalition International
Box 50360
Washington, DC 20091
202-583-8029
Fax: 201-783-6204
http://abacus.oxy.edu/qrd/www/orgs/glpci

National Center for Lesbian Rights
870 Market Street
Suite 570
San Francisco, CA 94102
800-528-6257
415-392-6257
Fax: 415-392-8442

Genetic Disorders

Alliance of Genetic Support Groups
35 Wisconsin Circle
Suite 440
Chevy Chase, MD 20815-7015
800-336-GENE
Fax: 301-654-0171
http://medhelp.org/www/agsg.htm

Gifted Children

National Association for Gifted Children
1707 L Street NW
Suite 550
Washington, DC 20036

202-785-4268
http://www.nagc.org

Grandparenting

Grandparent Information Center
c/o American Association of Retired Persons
601 E Street NW
Washington, DC 20049
202-434-2296
Fax: 202-434-6466

Handicapped Children

Federation for Children with Special Needs
95 Berkeley Street
Suite 104
Boston, MA 02116
617-482-2915
Fax: 617-695-2939
http://www.fcsn.org

National Easter Seal Society
230 West Monroe Street
Suite 1800
Chicago, Il 60606
800-221-6827
312-726-1494
http://www.seals.com

National Organization for Rare Disorders
Box 8923
New Fairfield, CT 06812-8923
800-999-NORD
203-746-6518
Fax: 203-746-6481
http://www.nord-rdb.com/~orphan

Headache

National Headache Foundation
428 W. Saint James Place

2nd Floor
Chicago, IL 60614-2750
800-843-2256
Fax: 773-525-7357
http://www.headaches.org

Head Injuries

Brain Injury Association
1776 Massachusetts Avenue NW
Suite 100NW
Washington, DC 20036-1904
800-444-6443 (helpline)
202-296-6443
Fax: 202-296-8850

Hearing Impairments

Alexander Graham Bell Association for the Deaf
3417 Volta Place NW
Washington, DC 20007-2778
202-337-5220 (V/TTY)
Fax: 202-337-8314
http://www.agbell.org

American Society for Deaf Children
1820 Tribute Road
Suite A
Sacramento, CA 95815
800-942-2732 (V/TTY)
916-641-6084
Fax: 916-641-6085
E-mail:ASDC1@aol.com

National Information Center on Deafness
Gallaudet University
800 Florida Avenue, NE
Washington, DC 20002
202-651-5051 (voice)
202-651-5052 (TDD)
202-651-5054 (Fax)
http://www.gallaudet.edu/~nicd

National Institute on Deafness and Other Communication
Disorders
Information Clearinghouse
One Communication Avenue
Bethesda, MD 20892-3456
800-241-1044 (Voice/TDD)
800-241-1055 (TDD/TT)
301-907-8830 (Fax)
http://www.nih.gov/nidcd
E-mail: nidcd@aerie.com

Heart Disorders

American Heart Association
7272 Greenville Avenue
Dallas, TX 75231-4596
800-242-8721
214-373-6300

CHASER: Congenital Heart Anomalies
Support Education and Resources
2112 N. Wilkins Road
Swanton, OH 43558
419-825-5575
Fax: 419-825-2880
E-mail: myer106w@wonder.em.cdc.gov

Hospitalization

Association for the Care of Children's Health
7910 Woodmont Avenue
Suite 300
Bethesda, MD 20814
800-808-2224
301-654-6549
Fax: 301-986-4553
http://www.ach.org

Illness, Terminal

Children's Hospice International
2202 Mount Vernon Avenue

Suite 3C
Alexandria, VA 22301
800-242-4453
703-684-0330
Fax: 703-684-0226
http://www.chionline.org
E-mail: chiorg@aol.com

Kidney Disorders

National Kidney Foundation
30 E. 33rd Street
11th Floor
New York, NY 10016
800-622-9010
212-889-2210
Fax: 212-689-9261
http://www.kid.org

Learning Disabilities

National Center for Learning Disabilities
381 Park Avenue South
Suite 1420
New York, NY 10016
212-545-7510
Fax: 212-545-9665

Learning Disabilities Association of America
4156 Library Road
Pittsburgh, PA 15234
412-341-1515
Fax: 412-344-0224
http://www.ldanatl.org

Lupus

Lupus Foundation of America
1300 Piccard Drive
Suite 200
Rockville, MD 20850

800-558-0121
301-670-9292
Fax: 301-670-9486
http://www.lupus.org/lupus

Mental Health

Federation of Families for Children's Mental Health
1021 Prince Street
Alexandria, VA 22314-2971
703-684-7710
Fax: 703-836-1040
http://www.ffcmh.org

National Clearinghouse on Family Support and Children's
Mental Health
Portland State University
Box 751
Portland, OR 97207-0751
800-628-1696
503-725-4040 (TDD)
Fax: 503-725-4180

Mental Retardation

The Arc (formerly the Association for Retarded Citizens)
500 E Border Street
Suite 300
Arlington, TX 76010
800-433-5255
817-261-6003

NADD Association for Persons with Developmental Disabilities and Mental Health Needs
132 Fair Street
Kingston, NY 12401
800-331-5362
914-331-4336
Fax: 914-331-4569

American Association on Mental Retardation (AAMR)
444 North Capitol NW

Suite 846
Washington, DC 20001
800-424-3688
202-387-1968
Fax: 202-387-2193
http://www.aamr.org

Muscular Dystrophy

Muscular Dystrophy Association
3300 E. Sunrise Drive
Tucson, AZ 85718-3208
800-572-1717
520-529-2000
Fax: 520-529-5300

Nutrition and Preventive Medicine

Physicians Committee for Responsible Medicine
5100 Wisconsin Avenue
Suite 404
Washington, DC 20016
202-686-2210
Fax: 202-686-2216
http://www.pcrm.org

American Holistic Medical Association
4101 Lake Boone Trail, #201
Raleigh, NC 27607
919-787-5146
Fax: 919-787-4916

Psoriasis

National Psoriasis Foundation
6600 SW 92nd
Suite 300
Portland, OR 97223
800-723-9166
503-244-7404
Fax: 503-245-0626
http://www.psoriasis.org

Sickle Cell Disease

Sickle Cell Disease Association of America
200 Corporate Pointe
Suite 495
Culver City, CA 90203-7633
800-421-8453
310-216-6363

Sickle Cell Disease Association of the Piedmont
1102 East Market Street
Greensboro, NC 27420-0964
800-733-8297
910-274-1507
Fax: 910-275-7984

Single Parents

Parents Without Partners International
401 North Michigan
Chicago, IL 60611
800-637-7974

Spina Bifida

Spina Bifida Association of America
4590 MacArthur Boulevard NW, #250
Washington, DC 20007-4226
800-621-3141
202-944-3285
Fax: 202-944-3295
http://www.infohiway.com/spinabifida

Spinal Cord Injuries

National Spinal Cord Injury Hotline
2200 Kernan Drive
Baltimore, MD 21207
800-526-3456
Fax: 410-448-6627
http://users.aol.com/scihotline

National Spinal Cord Injury Association
8300 Colesville Road
Suite 551
Silver Spring, MD 20910
800-962-9629
301-588-6959
Fax: 301-588-9414
http://www.spinalcord.org
E-mail: nscia2@aol.com

Stepparenting

Stepfamily Association of America
215 Centennial Mall South
Suite 212
Lincoln, NE 68508
800-735-0329
Fax: 402-477-8317
http://www.flyingsolo.com
E-mail: stepfam@aol.com

Stuttering

National Center for Stuttering
200 East 33rd Street
New York, NY 10016
800-221-2483
Fax: 212-683-1372
http://www.stuttering.com

National Stuttering Project
5100 East La Palma
Suite 208
Anaheim Hills, CA 92807
800-364-1677
714-693-7480

Stuttering Foundation of America
Box 11749
Memphis, TN 38111-0749
800-992-9392

901-452-7343
Fax: 901-452-3931

Sudden Infant Death Syndrome (SIDS)

National Sudden Infant Death Syndrome Resource
Center
2070 Chain Bridge Road
Suite 450
Vienna, VA 22182
703-821-8955
Fax: 703-821-2098
http://www.circsol.com/sids

Sudden Infant Death Syndrome Alliance
1314 Bedford Avenue
Suite 210
Baltimore, MD 21208
800-221-7437
410-653-8226
Fax: 410-653-8709

Tourette's Syndrome

Tourette Syndrome Association
42-40 Bell Boulevard
Suite 205
Bayside, NY 11361-2820
800-237-0717
718-224-2999
Fax: 718-279-9596

Twins

National Organization of Mothers of Twins Clubs, Inc.
Box 23188
Albuquerque, NM 87192-1188
800-243-2276
505-275-0955

Visual Impairments

American Council of the Blind
1155 15th Street NW
Suite 720
Washington, DC 20005
800-424-8666 (3-5:30 EST, only)
202-467-5081
Fax: 202-467-5085
http://www.acb.org

American Foundation for the Blind
11 Penn Plaza
Suite 300
New York, NY 10001
800-232-5463
212-507-7600
Fax: 212-502-7771

National Association for Parents of the Visually Impaired
Box 317
Watertown, MA 02272-0317
800-562-6265
617-972-7441
Fax: 617-972-7444

National Organization of Parents of Blind Children
1800 Johnson Street
Baltimore, MD 21230
410-659-9314
Fax: 410-685-5653
http://www.nfb.org

INDEX

D

Dairy products, 195, 346, 730-31
Dark, fear of, 285
Dating:
  adolescent, 320
  single parent, 673
Davis, Dr. Clara, infant feeding experiments, 731
Dawdling, 491-92
Day care, 604-11, 866-67
  center-based, 604-05, 607-08
  child to staff ratio, 608-09
  family day care, 607
  finding and choosing, 608-11
  first days at, 609-10
  how to get in your community, 610-11
  illness in, 772
  in-home care, 607
  preschool: is it good for young children?, 605-07
  reactions to, at home, 610
  types of, 607-08
  when to start, 604
  see also Preschool
Deafness, 867, 874-75
  temporary, in ear infections, 775
  see also Handicapped child
Death:
  coping with, 534-35
  fear of, 285-86
  of a parent, 659

Deformities, *see* Disabilities
Dehydration, 233, 786-87, 843
"Demand" feeding, 158-59, 162
Dentist, 408-09, 412-13
Dependence, child's:
  on bottle, 162, 175
  on comforters, 535-39
  at 1 year, 258-59
  at 2 years, 268-69
  overcoming, 272-73
  on pacifier, 546-48
  sibling jealousy as cause of, 452
  on sleeping with parents, 521-22
  spoiling as cause, 218-21
Depression:
  in mother, after childbirth, 74-76
  information resource, 867
"Designated driver," 641
Desserts, 192
  craving for, 348
Development:
  of babies, 248-54
    crawling, 251-52
    cruising, 252-53
    hands, use of, 249
    head, use of, 248-49
    hips, feet, legs, 253-54
    peek-a-boo, 28
    physical development and motor skills, 248-54
    play, 223-25
    right- and left-handedness, 249-50

M